Lecture Notes in Artificial Intelligence   9561

Subseries of Lecture Notes in Computer Science

Zygmunt Vetulani · Hans Uszkoreit
Marek Kubis (Eds.)

Human Language Technology

Challenges for Computer Science and Linguistics

6th Language and Technology Conference, LTC 2013
Poznań, Poland, December 7–9, 2013
Revised Selected Papers

 Springer

Editors
Zygmunt Vetulani
Adam Mickiewicz University
Poznań
Poland

Hans Uszkoreit
Deutsches Forschungszentrum f. Künstl.
  Intelligenz (DFKI GmbH)
Saarbrücken, Saarland
Germany

Marek Kubis
Adam Mickiewicz University
Poznań
Poland

ISSN 0302-9743   ISSN 1611-3349   (electronic)
Lecture Notes in Artificial Intelligence
ISBN 978-3-319-43807-8   ISBN 978-3-319-43808-5   (eBook)
DOI 10.1007/978-3-319-43808-5

Library of Congress Control Number: 2016947193

LNCS Sublibrary: SL7 – Artificial Intelligence

Printed on acid-free paper

This Springer imprint is published by Springer Nature
The registered company is Springer International Publishing AG Switzerland

Preface

As predicted, the demand for language technology applications has kept growing. The explosion of valuable information and knowledge on the Web is accompanied by the evolution of hardware and software powerful enough to manage this flood of unstructured data. The spread of smart phones and tablets is accompanied by higher bandwidth and broader coverage of wireless Internet connectivity. We find language technology in software for search, user interaction, content production, data analytics, learning, and human communication.

Our world has changed and so have our needs and expectations. Whatever we call the new form of technology-supported life and work – information society, digital society, or knowledge society – it is not going to stay the same since it is just the transitional phase on the way to a reality in which all these contemporary mega-trends – ubiquitous computing, big data, Internet of Things, industry 4.0, artificial intelligence – have organically merged. There is only one vision in which this breathtaking universal transformation of our world will not eventually overwhelm the mental capacity and nature of the human individual and not crush the volatile cultural fabric of our civilization, a vision in which the machinery will neither dwarf nor replace their masters.

In this vision, the powerful technology will be a much appreciated extension of our limited capacities, augmenting our cognition and serving those parts of our nature that are not possessed by machines such as desires, creativity, curiosity, and passion. In such a set-up, every human individual will feel central – and actually be central. There is no way to realize this vision without human language technology. If the technology does not master the human medium for communication and thinking, the human masters will feel like aliens in their own universe.

Technology that can understand and produce human language cannot only improve our daily life and work, it can also help us to solve life-threatening problems, for example, through applications in medical research and practice that exploit research texts and patient records. Of similar importance are software systems for safety and security that help recognize and manage natural and manmade disasters and that guard technology against abuse. The instability of the political situation at the global level is evidence of the dangers and challenges connected with the new information technologies that may easily degenerate into redoubtable arms in the hands of international terrorists or totalitarian or fanatical administrations.

The challenges that lie between us and the benevolent vision of human-centered IT are the complexity and versatility of human language and thought, the range of languages, dialects, and jargons, and the different modes of using language such as speaking, writing, signing, listening, reading, and translating. But we do not only face problems. In the last few years, powerful new generic methods of machine learning have been developed that combine well with corpus work and dedicated techniques from computational linguistics. Together with the increased computing power and means for handling big data, we now have much better tools for tackling the complexity of language. Finding appropriate combination of methods, data, and tools for each task and language creates an additional layer of challenges.

The research reported in this volume cannot cover all these challenges but each of the selected papers addresses one or several major problems that need to be solved before the vision can be turned into reality.

In the volume the reader will find the revised and in many cases substantially extended versions of 31 selected papers presented at the 6th Language and Technology Conference. The selection was made among 103 conference contributions and basically represents the preferences of the reviewers. The reviewing process was made by the international jury composed of the Program Committee members or experts nominated by them. Finally, the 90 authors of selected contributions represent research institutions from the following countries: Austria, Croatia, Ethiopia France, Germany, Hungary, India, Italy, Japan, Nigeria, Poland, Portugal, Russia, Serbia, Slovakia, Tunisia, UK, USA.[1]

What the papers are about?

The papers selected for this volume belong to various fields of human language technologies and illustrate the large thematic coverage of the LTC conferences. The papers are "structured" into nine chapters. These are:

1. Speech Processing (6)
2. Morphology (2)
3. Parsing-Related Issues (4)
4. Computational Semantics (1)
5. Digital Language Resources (4)
6. Ontologies and Wordnets (3)
7. Written Text and Document Processing (7)
8. Information and Data Extraction (2)
9. Less-Resourced Languages (2)

Clustering the articles is approximate, as many addressed more than one thematic area. The ordering of the chapters does not have any "deep" significance, it approximates the order in which humans proceed in natural language production and processing: starting with (spoken) speech analysis, through morphology, (syntactic) parsing, etc. To follow this order, we start this volume with the Speech Processing chapter containing six contributions. In the paper "Boundary Markers in Spontaneous Hungarian Speech" (András Beke, Mária Gósy, and Viktória Horváth) an attempt is made at capturing objective temporal properties of boundary marking in spontaneous Hungarian, as well as at characterizing separable portions of spontaneous speech (thematic units and phrases). The second contribution concerning speech, "Adaptive Prosody Modelling for Improved Synthetic Speech Quality" (Moses E. Ekpenyong, Udoinyang G. Inyang, and EmemObong O. Udoh), is on an intelligent framework for modelling prosody in tone languages. The proposed framework is fuzzy logic based (FL-B) and is adopted to offer a flexible, human reasoning approach to the imprecise

---

[1] This list differs from the list of countries represented at the conference, as we identified a number of PhD students (e.g., from Iran and Mali) affiliated temporarily at foreign institutes.

and complex nature of prosody prediction. The authors of "Diacritics Restoration in the Slovak Texts Using Hidden Markov Model" (Daniel Hládek, Ján Staš, and Jozef Juhár) present a fast method for correcting diacritical markings and guessing original meaning of words from the context, based on a hidden Markov model and the Viterbi algorithm. The paper "Temporal and Lexical Context of Diachronic Text Documents for Automatic Out-Of-Vocabulary Proper Name Retrieval" (Irina Illina, Dominique Fohr, Georges Linarès, and Imane Nkairi) focuses on increasing the vocabulary coverage of a speech transcription system by automatically retrieving proper names from diachronic contemporary text documents.

In the paper "Advances in the Slovak Judicial Domain Dictation System" (Milan Rusko, Jozef Juhár, Marian Trnka, Ján Staš, Sakhia Darjaa, Daniel Hládek, Róbert Sabo, Matúš Pleva, Marian Ritomský, and Stanislav Ondáš), the authors discuss recent advances in the application of speech recognition technology in the judicial domain. The investigations on performance of Polish taggers in the context of automatic speech recognition (ASR) is the main issue of the last paper of the Speech section, "A Revised Comparison of Polish Taggers in the Application for Automatic Speech Recognition" (Aleksander Smywiński-Pohl and Bartosz Ziółko).

The Morphology section contains two papers. The first one, "Automatic Morpheme Slot Identification Using Genetic Algorithm" (Wondwossen Mulugeta, Michael Gasser, and Baye Yimam), introduces an approach to the grouping of morphemes into suffix slots in morphologically complex languages, such as Amharic, using a genetic algorithm. The second paper, "From Morphology to Lexical Hierarchies and Back" (Krešimir Šojat and Matea Srebačić), deals with language resources for Croatian – a Croatian WordNet and a large database of verbs with morphological and derivational data – and discusses the possibilities of their combination in order to improve their coverage and density of structure.

Parsing-Related Issues are presented in four papers. The chapter opens with the text "System for Generating Questions Automatically from Given Punjabi Text" (Vishal Goyal, Shikha Garg, and Umrinderpal Singh) that introduces a system for generating questions automatically for Punjabi and transforming declarative sentences into their interrogative counterparts. The next article, "Hierarchical Amharic Base Phrase Chunking Using HMM with Error Pruning" (Abeba Ibrahim and Yaregal Assabie), presents an Amharic base phrase chunker that groups syntactically correlated words at different levels (using HMM). The main goal of the authors of the paper "A Hybrid Approach to Parsing Natural Languages" (Sardar Jaf and Allan Ramsay) is to combine different parsing approaches and produce a more accurate, hybrid, grammatical rules guided parser. The last paper in the chapter is an attempt at creating a probabilistic constituency parser for Polish: "Experiments in PCFG-like Disambiguation of Constituency Parse Forests for Polish" (Marcin Woliński and Dominika Rogozińska).

The Computational Semantics chapter contains one paper, "A Method for Measuring Similarity of Books: A Step Towards an Objective Recommender System for Readers" (Adam Wojciechowski and Krzysztof Gorzynski), in which the authors propose a book comparison method based on descriptors and measures for particular properties of analyzed text.

The first of the four papers of the Digital Language Resources chapter, "MCBF: Multimodal Corpora Building Framework" (Maria Chiara Caschera, Arianna D'Ulizia,

Fernando Ferri, and Patrizia Grifoni), presents a method of dynamic generation of a multimodal corpora model as a support for human–computer dialogue. The paper "Syntactic Enrichment of LMF Normalized Dictionaries Based on the Context-Field Corpus" (Imen Elleuch, Bilel Gargouri, and Abdelmajid Ben Hamadou) describes Arabic corpora processing and proposes to the reader an approach for identifying the syntactic behavior of verbs in order to enrich the syntactic extension of the LMF-normalized Arabic dictionaries. A multilingual annotation toolkit is presented in the paper "An Example of a Compatible NLP Toolkit" (Krzysztof Jassem and Roman Grundkiewicz). The article "Polish Coreference Corpus" (Maciej Ogrodniczuk, Katarzyna Głowińska, Mateusz Kopeć, Agata Savary, and Magdalena Zawisławska) describes a composition, annotation process and availability of the Polish Coreference Corpus.

The Ontologies and Wordnets part comprises three papers. The contribution "GeoDomainWordNet: Linking the Geonames Ontology to WordNet" (Francesca Frontini, Riccardo Del Gratta, and Monica Monachini) demonstrates a wordnet generation procedure consisting in transformation of an ontology of geographical terms into a WordNet-like resource in English and its linking to the existing generic wordnets of English and Italian. The second article, "Building Wordnet Based Ontologies with Expert Knowledge" (Jacek Marciniak) presents the principles of creating wordnet-based ontologies that contain general knowledge about the world as well as specialist expert knowledge. In "Diagnostic Tools in plWordNet Development Process" (Maciej Piasecki, Łukasz Burdka, Marek Maziarz, and Michał Kaliński), the third of the contributions in this chapter, the authors describe formal, structural, and semantic rules for seeking errors within plWordNet, as well as a method of automated induction of the diagnostic rules.

The largest chapter, Written Text and Document Processing, presents seven contributions of which the first is "Simile or Not Simile?: Automatic Detection of Metonymic Relations in Japanese Literal Comparisons" (Pawel Dybala, Rafal Rzepka, Kenji Araki, and Kohichi Sayama). Its authors propose how to automatically distinguish between two types of formally identical expressions in Japanese: metaphorical similes and metonymical comparisons. The issues of diacritic error detection and restoration – tasks of identifying and correcting missing accents in text – are addressed in "Spanish Diacritic Error Detection and Restoration—A Survey" (Mans Hulden and Jerid Francom). The article "Identification of Event and Topic for Multi-document Summarization" (Fumiyo Fukumoto, Yoshimi Suzuki, Atsuhiro Takasu, and Suguru Matsuyoshi) is a contribution in which the authors investigate continuous news documents and conclude with a method for extractive multi-document summarization. The next paper, "Itemsets-Based Amharic Document Categorization Using an Extended *A Priori* Algorithm" (Abraham Hailu and Yaregal Assabie), presents a system that categorizes Amharic documents based on the frequency of itemsets obtained from analyzing the morphology of the language. In the paper "*NERosetta* for the Named Entity Multi-lingual Space" (Cvetana Krstev, Anđelka Zečević, Duško Vitas, and Tita Kyriacopoulou) the authors present a Web application, NERosetta, that can be used to compare various approaches to develop named entity recognition systems. In the study "A Hybrid Approach to Statistical Machine Translation Between Standard and Dialectal Varieties" (Friedrich Neubarth, Barry Haddow, Adolfo Hernández Huerta, and Harald Trost), the authors describe the problem of translation between the standard Austrian German and the Viennese dialect. From the last paper of the Text Processing chapter, "Evaluation of Uryupina's Coreference Resolution Features for Polish" (Bartłomiej Nitoń), the reader will get familiar with an evaluation of a set of surface, syntactic, and anaphoric features proposed for coreference resolution in Polish texts.

The Information and Data Extraction chapter contains two studies. In the first one, "Aspect-Based Restaurant Information Extraction for the Recommendation System" (Ekaterina Pronoza, Elena Yagunova, and Svetlana Volskaya), a method for Russian reviews corpus analysis aimed at future information extraction system development is proposed. In the second article, "A Study on Turkish Meronym Extraction Using a Variety of Lexico-Syntactic Patterns" (Tuğba Yıldız, Savaş Yıldırım, and Banu Diri), lexico-syntactic patterns to extract meronymy relation from a huge corpus of Turkish are presented.

The Less-Resourced Languages are considered of special interest for the LTC community and were presented at the LRL conference workshop. We decided to place the two selected LRL papers in a separate chapter, the last in this volume. The first paper, "A Phonetization Approach for the Forced-Alignment Task in SPPAS" (Brigitte Bigi), presents a generic approach for text phonetization, concentrates on the aspects of phonetizing unknown words, and is tested for less resourced languages, for example, Vietnamese, Khmer, and Pinyin for Taiwanese. The final paper in the volume, "POS Tagging and Less Resources Languages Individuated Features in CorpusWiki" (Maarten Janssen), explores the hot topic of the lack of corpora for LRL languages and proposes a Wikipedia-based solutions with particular attention paid to the POS annotation.

We wish you all interesting reading.

March 2016   Zygmunt Vetulani
                                                    Hans Uszkoreit

Organization

Organizing Committee

Zygmunt Vetulani (Chair)	Adam Mickiewicz University, Poznań, Poland
Bartłomiej Kochanowski	Adam Mickiewicz University, Poznań, Poland
Marek Kubis (Secretary)	Adam Mickiewicz University, Poznań, Poland
Jacek Marciniak	Adam Mickiewicz University, Poznań, Poland
Tomasz Obrębski	Adam Mickiewicz University, Poznań, Poland
Grzegorz Taberski	Adam Mickiewicz University, Poznań, Poland
Mateusz Witkowski	Adam Mickiewicz University, Poznań, Poland

LTC Program Committee

Co-chairs: Zygmunt Vetulani, Hans Uszkoreit

Victoria Arranz	Adam Kilgarriff (†)	Adam Przepiórkowski
Jolanta Bachan	Cvetana Krstev	Georg Rehm
Krzysztof Bogacki	Eric Laporte	Reinhard Rapp
Christian Boitet	Yves Lepage	Mohsen Rashwan
Leonard Bolc (†)	Gerard Ligozat	Mike Rosner
Gerhard Budin	Natalia Loukachevitch	Justus Roux
Nicoletta Calzolari	Bente Maegaard	Vasile Rus
Nick Campbell	Bernardo Magnini	Rafał Rzepka
Khalid Choukri	Alfred Majewicz	Kepa Sarasola Gabiola
Adam Dąbrowski	Joseph Mariani	Frédérique Segond
Elżbieta Dura	Jacek Martinek	Zhongzhi Shi
Katarzyna	Gayrat Matlatipov	Włodzimierz Sobkowiak
Dziubalska-Kołaczyk	Keith J. Miller	Ryszard Tadeusiewicz
Tomaz Erjavec	Roberto Navigli	Marko Tadić
Cedrick Fairon	Asunción Moreno	Dan Tufiş
Christiane Fellbaum	Jan Odijk	Tamás Váradi
Piotr Fuglewicz	Nicholas Ostler	Cristina Vertan
Maria Gavrilidou	Karel Pala	Dusko Vitas
Dafydd Gibbon	Pavel S. Pankov	Piek Vossen
Marko Grobelnik	Patrick Paroubek	Tom Wachtel
Eva Hajičová	Adam Pease	Jan Węglarz
Roland Hausser	Maciej Piasecki	Bartosz Ziółko
Krzysztof Jassem	Stelios Piperidis	Mariusz Ziółko
Girish Nath Jha	Gabor Proszeky	Richard Zuber

LRL Workshop Program Committee

Co-chairs: Claudia Soria, Khalid Choukri, Joseph Mariani, Zygmunt Vetulani

Delphine Bernhard	Joseph Mariani	Claudia Soria
Nicoletta Calzolari	Asunción Moreno	Virach Sornlertlamvanich
Khalid Choukri	Stellios Piperidis	Marko Tadić
Daffyd Gibbon	Gabor Proszeky	Marianne Vergez-Couret
Marko Grobelnik	Georg Rehm	Zygmunt Vetulani
Girish Nath Jha	Kepa Sarasola Gabiola	
Alfred Majewicz	Kevin Scannell	

SAIBS Workshop Committee

Co-chairs: Adam Wojciechowski, Alok Mishra

Wojciech Complak	Alok Mishra	Zygmunt Vetulani
Arianna D'Ulizia	Miroslaw Ochodek	Agnieszka Wegrzyn
Fernando Ferri	Rory O'Connor	Adam Wojciechowski
Patrick Hamilton	Robert Susmaga	

Reviewers

Szymon Acedański	Christiane Fellbaum	Maciej Lison
Victoria Arranz	Tiziano Flati	Natalia Loukachevitch
Olatz Arregi	Piotr Fuglewicz	Wieslaw Lubaszewski
Jolanta Bachan	Maria Gavrilidou	Bente Maegaard
Delphine Bernhard	Dafydd Gibbon	Bernardo Magnini
Krzysztof Bogacki	Filip Graliński	Jacek Marciniak
Noémi Boubel	Eva Hajicova	Joseph Mariani
Jean-Leon Bouraoui	Elżbieta Hajnicz	Jacek Martinek
Sandrine Brognaux	Inma Hernaez	Gayrat Matlatipov
Nicoletta Calzolari	Krzysztof Jassem	Michal Mazur
Nick Campbell	Rafał Jaworski	Márton Miháltz
Khalid Choukri	Keith J. Miller	Alok Mishra
Justus Christiaan Roux	Marcin Junczys-Dowmunt	Deepti Mishra
Wojciech Complak	Sotiris Karabetsos	Asuncion Moreno
Adam Dabrowski	Adam Kilgarriff (†)	Jedrzej Musial
Łukasz Dębowski	Denis Kiselev	Agnieszka Mykowiecka
Moreno De Vincenzi	Cvetana Krstev	Girish Nath Jha
Elzbieta Dura	Marek Kubis	Roberto Navigli
Katarzyna	Eric Laporte	Tomasz Obrębski
Dziubalska-Kolaczyk	Yves Lepage	Jan Odijk
Cedrick Fairon	Gérard Ligozat	Maciej Ogrodniczuk

The reviewing process was effected by the members of Program Committees and invited reviewers recommended by Program Committee members.

Contents

Computational Semantics

Digital Language Resources

Ontologies and Wordnets

Written Text and Document Processing

Information and Data Extraction

Less-Resourced Languages

Speech Processing

Boundary Markers in Spontaneous Hungarian Speech

András Beke[✉], Mária Gósy, and Viktória Horváth

Research Institute for Linguistics, Hungarian Academy of Sciences,
33 Benczúr Street, Budapest, Hungary
{beke.andras,gosy.maria,horvath.viktoria}@nytud.mta.hu

Abstract. The aim of this paper is an objective presentation of temporal features of spontaneous Hungarian narratives, as well as a characterization of separable portions of spontaneous speech. Ten speakers' spontaneous speech materials taken from the BEA Hungarian Spontaneous Speech Database were analyzed in terms of hierarchical units of narratives (durations, speakers' rates of articulation, number of words produced, and the interrelationships of all these). We conclude that (i) the majority of speakers organize their narratives in similar temporal structures, (ii) thematic units can be identified in terms of certain prosodic criteria, (iii) there are statistically valid correlations between factors like the duration of phrases, the word count of phrases, the rate of articulation of phrases, and pausing characteristics, and (iv) these parameters exhibit extensive variability both across and within speakers.

Keywords: Articulation tempo · Pauses · Durations · F0 · Thematic units · Phrases

1 Introduction

Temporal characteristics of spontaneous speech are affected by a number of factors. The aim of the present study is an objective presentation of temporal features of spontaneous narratives including a characterization of the phrases in the narratives. An attempt is made at defining various units of spontaneous narratives and capturing objective acoustic-phonetic properties of boundary marking. We try to identify the factors determining the articulation rate of portions of speech within and across speakers and to find out whether the acoustic-phonetic parameters we analyze make up a characteristic pattern, and if they do, how they can be described.

Klatt [1] listed seven factors that determine the temporal patterns of speech: extra-linguistic factors (the speaker's mental or physical state), discourse factors (position within discourse), semantic factors (emphasis and semantic novelty), syntactic factors (phrase-final lengthening), morphological factors (word-final lengthening), phonological and phonetic factors (stress, phonological length distinctions), and physiological factors (segment-internal temporal structure). Additional factors may also play a role, like topic of discourse, speech type, speech situation, speech partner [2]. An analysis of tempo in Dutch interviews confirmed the distinct role of phrase length [3]. Dialect also seems to be a crucial factor, as shown by an analysis of speech rate in 192 speakers of American English from Wisconsin and North Carolina [4]. Similar results emerged from

© Springer International Publishing Switzerland 2016
Z. Vetulani et al. (Eds.): LTC 2013, LNAI 9561, pp. 3–15, 2016.
DOI: 10.1007/978-3-319-43808-5_1

an analysis of 267 h of spontaneous dialogues produced by Dutch speakers living in the Netherlands and in Belgium [5]. Both of the last-mentioned papers claim, in addition, that men tend to speak faster than women do, and that young speakers' speech rate is faster than that of older speakers. Some data gathered from speakers of (American) English partly contradict this, however: in a spontaneous speech material of nearly two hundred speakers, the speech tempo of forty-year-olds turned out to be the fastest, as opposed to both younger and older groups of speakers [4]. Significant differences were found between the speech rates of neutral spoken texts vs. ones produced in various joyful or sorrowful states of mind [6]. An increase of the speech rate may be caused by the fact that the speaker considers the given portion of the message less important; but it can also be due to some external factor like the behavior of the interlocutor.

The transformation of the speaker's ideas into speech may become slower due to conceptual planning becoming hesitant, construction of the utterance becoming difficult, or lexical selection becoming riddled by competitive lexemes at the given point. In the phrases of spontaneous Italian narratives, the tempo of syllables has been measured, and compared between pre-stress and post-stress positions [7]. The results showed that after phrasal stress, the tempo increased (by some 65 %), while in pre-stress positions, such increase was only by 33 %. The decrease of speech rate, on the other hand, where it occurred, was 15 % in a post-stress position and 40 % before the stressed syllable. It can be concluded that the temporal properties of a longer stretch of spontaneous speech are not constant and not independent of other prosodic properties of speech like stress, or intonation [8].

Inter-speaker variation is significant; but large variability can also be found across utterances of one and the same speaker. In spontaneous English conversations, for instance, 33 % large changes were attested in speech rate with one of the speakers [9].

Data from perceptual experiments make it probable that speakers tend to employ general features as boundary markers of thematic units (TU) and of phrases, ones that can also be used in decoding. Thematic units are portions of discourse exhibiting coherence of content that are appropriately structured both syntactically and prosodically [10, 11]. In determining phrases within spontaneous narratives or dialogues, on the other hand, primarily rises and falls of speech melody, as well as stress relationships are taken into consideration [12]. So-called idea units (brief coherent spontaneous text segments) are taken to be 2 s long on average, corresponding to roughly 6 English words.

It has been claimed that the acoustic-phonetic marking of prosodic boundaries is not universal and that prosodic boundaries do not necessarily coincide with either syntactic or semantic boundaries in Danish spontaneous speech [13]. In addition, pauses do not inevitably occur at prosodic boundaries and pauses themselves should not be considered to be boundary markers. Perceivable changes of speech melody and rhythm at boundaries seem to provide cues for boundary identification.

Speech tempo also seems to be a factor influencing boundary patterns [14]. The quantification of speech tempo that provides a single value for a spontaneous utter-ance or for a longer spontaneous speech sample seems to be insufficient, irrespective of whether articulation rate is considered in itself or various types of pauses are also taken into account [15]. Speech tempo values are extremely rough indicators of the nature of spontaneous speech and are not suitable to characterize long narratives or to make comparisons across speakers, dialects, languages or even speech situations. An articulation rate value (without pauses) or a speech tempo value including pauses as contributing to the overall rate of spontaneous speech are not informative enough since they do not show the changes within various parts/units of the speech samples. Speakers continuously adjust their speech rate to cognitive and environmental changes. The underlying adaptive processes unfold in time and involve continual changes in speaking tempo. A timekeeper is hypothesized to reflect the temporal structure of articulation events, thereby establishing a frame of reference for the tim-ing of successive motor commands [16].

This paper intends to reveal the internal tempo changes based on segmentation into thematic units and phrases in spontaneous speech. Analysis focuses further on the interactions of the duration of phrases, the word count of phrases, the rate of articulation of phrases, and pausing characteristics. There are three main research questions: (i) how thematic units and phrases can be defined in spontaneous narratives, (ii) what the interrelations are among various acoustic-phonetic cues that define phrases, and (iii) whether there are universal temporal patterns in spontaneous speech or, on the contrary, individual characteristics show totally different temporal structures in the processing of spontaneous utterances.

The findings of the present research will throw new light on temporal properties of spontaneous narratives, on covert processes of speech planning and pinpoint universal and individual characteristics, features characterizing several speakers and single speakers, respectively. We hypothesize that (i) spontaneous narratives can be segmented into units defined by acoustic-phonetic parameters: these are thematic units that are further segmentable into phrases, (ii) phrases exhibit characteristic temporal patterns, and (iii) thematic units are mostly universal but can also be taken to be based on individual peculiarities to some extent.

2   Subjects, Material, Method

For this study, we used 10 interviews of the BEA Hungarian Spontaneous Speech Database [17] in which the participants talk about their job, family, and hobbies. Five of the speakers are female, and five are male; all of them native speakers of Hungarian from Budapest; aged between 22 and 35.

The total material is 57 min long (3–8 min per informants), and was annotated in Praat 5.1 [18] at several levels (thematic units and phrases encoded orthographically and in phonetic transcription, and sound-level annotation). In the case of voiced segments, the first period was taken to be the boundary. Using a Praat script, we automatically extracted fundamental frequency (F0) and intensity. (We sampled both at every 200 ms.) The initial criterion of the definition of thematic units (TU) was that the interviewer opened a new topic by each question, that is, the preceding portion of text was a unit semantically, syntactically, and prosodically, as well. The interviewer started a new topic only when the speaker indicated, verbally or in some other manner, that s/he did not want (or could not) say anything more. Within thematic units, we separated phrases by either or both of the following two criteria: (i) an utterance flanked by (silent or filled) pauses on both sides, and/or (ii) a radical change both in fundamental frequency and intensity.

We automatically determined the occurrence and duration of all labeled silent and filled pauses, and of all phrases, and calculated automatically the rate of articulation, defined as the number of segments per total articulation time. The corpus included a total of 7863 words. The informants uttered an average of 177 words per minute. For statistical analyses, we used the SPSS 13.0 program (analysis of variance, correlation analysis).

3   Results

Description of the results will be organized in five subsections of temporal analysis which concern silent and filled pauses, temporal properties of thematic units, and phrases as well as articulation tempo.

3.1   Silent and Filled Pauses

Our analyses have confirmed that phrases can be reliably defined in terms of pauses. The corpus included 1326 silent pauses, of a mean duration of 510 ms (SD: 405 ms). The shortest pause took 23 ms, and the longest took 3036 ms. The number and durations of pauses found with individual speakers exhibited extensive variability (Fig. 1).

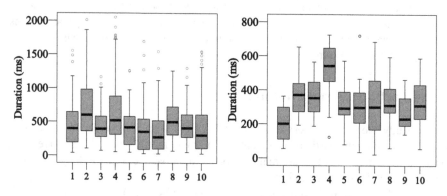

Fig. 1.   Duration of silent (left panel) and filled pauses (right panel) (1–5 = females, 6–10 = males)

The duration of silent pauses was significantly different across speakers ($F(9,1326) = 17.422$; $p < 0.001$). The number of filled pauses was 260 in the corpus. Their mean duration was 323 ms (SD: 153 ms). The shortest filled pause took 20 ms, and the longest one took 720 ms. Statistical analysis confirmed significant differences across speakers ($F(9,219) = 6.704$; $p < 0.001$), but a post-hoc test showed that the difference was only significant between a single speaker (speaker 4 in Fig. 1) and all the others. Correlation analysis showed that pausing exhibited individual differences across speakers; if the speech of a speaker was characterized by longer silent pauses, s/he also tended to produce longer filled pauses ($R^2 = 0.643$; $p = 0.045$).

3.2   Temporal Properties of Thematic Units

With 60 % of the speakers, the narrative could be segmented into three thematic units; the rest of the speakers produced 5 or 6 thematic units. Starting a new topic as the criterion for thematic unit boundaries was correlated with changes in fundamental frequency and intensity; thus, TU boundaries were predictable.

The mean duration of TUs was 56 s (SD: 48 s). The distribution of durations was lognormal (Fig. 2), meaning that most duration figures fell between zero and 100 s, and that the curve decreased in a protracted manner.

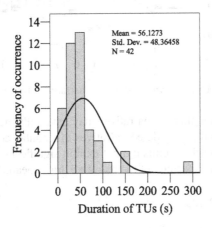

Fig. 2. The distribution of duration of TUs

In the duration of thematic units, with two exceptions, there were no significant differences across speakers (Fig. 3). TU durations of speakers 2 and 3 significantly differed, according to post-hoc tests, from the data of all the other speakers $(F(9,302) = 5.485; p < 0.001)$. These informants produced far longer thematic units than the others did (Table 1).

Table 1.   Duration of thematic units in individual speakers' narratives (f = female, m = male)

Speakers	Mean (s)	Standard deviation (s)	Minimum (s)	Maximum (s)
1f	44.95	10.40	33.15	52.75
2f	165.67	111.36	58.62	280.89
3f	115.34	32.87	86.71	151.23
4f	24.88	21.67	3.75	76.52
5f	43.35	6.95	36.21	50.11
6m	49.26	23.09	18.63	83.26
7m	43.35	22.03	21.92	70.04
8m	60.43	28.08	37.24	91.64
9m	39.32	15.06	24.55	54.65
10m	52.65	12.04	39.18	70.59

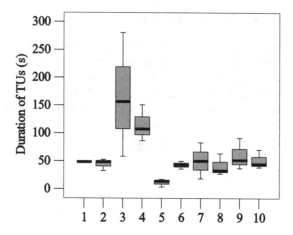

Fig. 3. The duration of TUs in individual speakers' narratives (1–5 = females, 6–10 = males)

The position of TUs within the narratives may have influenced their duration. For an analysis of this, we only considered narratives that contained three thematic units, given that the duration of these units did not exhibit significant differences. The trend was that TUs get shorter as the end of the narrative draws nearer (Fig. 4).

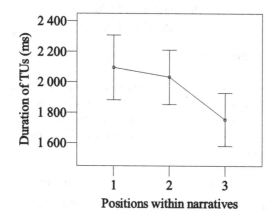

Fig. 4. Duration of TUs in various positions within narratives (1 = initial; 2 = medial; 3 = final)

Hungarian speakers produce almost 20 words less in a minute than English speakers do; the relevant figure for English is 196 words per minute [2]. This difference is obviously due to the fact that Hungarian, being an agglutinative language, has longer words (the average syllable count of Hungarian words in spontaneous speech is 3.5). The mean number of words per thematic unit was 245 (SD: 199), irrespective of whether they were content words or function words.

3.3 Fundamental Frequency and Intensity of Thematic Units

F0 changes seem to have a role in the separation of various phrases (and other units) in spontaneous speech. Findings confirmed this separation role using automatic methods [19, 20]. Results of the present study show that F0-values are higher at the beginning of a TU (in the case of about 70 % of all speakers) than at the end of a TU (the difference ranges between 6 Hz and 41 Hz), see Table 2. The intensity values revealed similar interrelations: 90 % of all speakers produced higher intensity at the beginning of TUs than at their end.

Table 2. Values of F0 at the beginning and end of TUs (f = female, m = male)

Speakers	Thematic units	Mean F0 (Hz)	F0-range (Hz)
1f	beginning	199.3	21.9
	end	159.7	46.5
2f	beginning	191.2	6.7
	end	150.8	55.3
3f	beginning	181.3	13.4
	end	157.4	15.7
4f	beginning	222.8	22.5
	end	186.2	14.8
5f	beginning	191.2	6.7
	end	150.8	55.3
6m	beginning	145.0	32.6
	end	101.7	0.8
7m	beginning	156.9	38.3
	end	138.2	33.0
8m	beginning	124.6	8.8
	end	131.3	48.5
9m	beginning	134.4	12.1
	end	128.5	11.1
10m	beginning	139.3	21.9
	end	114.7	46.5

3.4 Temporal Properties of Phrases

The number of phrases was 1394 in our material. Their number within TUs was not independent of whether the TU was initial, medial, or final in the narrative. Medial thematic units consisted of fewer phrases than the preceding or following ones (Fig. 5). The duration differences of phrases within thematic units were significant ($F(9,1394) = 11.175$; $p < 0.001$). Their variability was larger across speakers than that of the duration of thematic units. Speakers can be classified into two groups, one group produced relatively short phrases, while the other group produced relatively long ones.

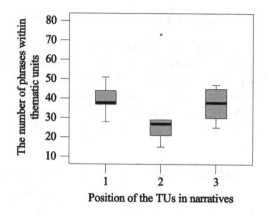

Fig. 5. The number of phrases within thematic units (in six speakers' material)

The position of thematic units within narratives also affected the length of phrases (Fig. 6). Narrative-final TUs were realized in shorter duration than the preceding ones ($F(2,750) = 3.277$; $p = 0.038$).

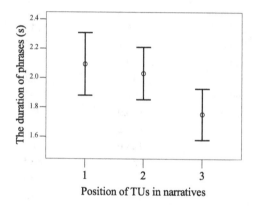

Fig. 6. The duration of phrases in terms of the position of TUs (1 = initial; 2 = medial; 3 = final)

3.5 Word Counts in TUs and in Phrases

We established the word count of each TU, irrespective of whether they were content words or function words. The mean number of words per TU was 245 (SD: 199). The smallest number was 147 words/min in a TU, and the largest was 206 words/min. The results show minor differences across TUs of the same speaker; but across speakers, the differences are larger.

The average word count in phrases within thematic units was 5.8 words (SD: 4.7, minimum: 3.4, maximum: 8.1). The average word count of phrases is lognormal, and exhibited significant differences depending on which TU the given phrase occurred in. The phrases of third thematic units contained fewer words on average than those of first and second ones (1st TU = 6.2 words; 2nd TU = 6.1 words; 3rd TU = 5.1 words;

$F(2,750) = 4.313; p = 0.014$). That is, towards the end of a narrative, it was not only the case that the thematic units got shorter, but also the phrases they contained were shorter and consisted of fewer words. We found strong linear correlation between the number of words in a phrase and its duration ($R^2 = 0.8603; p < 0.001$). This means that the longer the duration of a phrase the more words it consists of (Fig. 7).

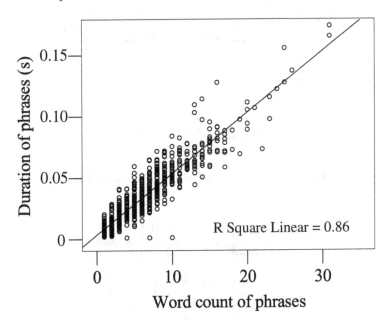

Fig. 7. The correlation between the duration and word count of phrases

3.6 Rate of Articulation

The slowest speaker exhibited a mean rate of articulation of 11.7 sounds/s (SD: 3.1), the fastest speaker exhibited 15.4 sounds/s (SD: 6.5). Statistical analyses confirmed significant differences of rate of articulation across speakers ($F(9,1387) = 13.168; p < 0.001$). However, a post-hoc test showed that three speakers differed from nearly all other speakers.

Among speakers producing three thematic units, we found two different tendencies in tempo changes across TUs. With three of them, the mean rate of articulation accelerated in the second TU compared to the first, and then got slower toward the end of the narrative. With the other three, on the contrary, the rate of articulation was slower in the second TU than in the first, and then a strong acceleration occurred toward the end of the narrative (Fig. 8).

Given that the rate of articulation changes continuously in the narratives, we performed continuous time analysis of the rate of articulation of phrases. As compared to the mean rate of articulation of the whole narrative, extremely fast and extremely slow values were both found in the individual phrases (Fig. 9).

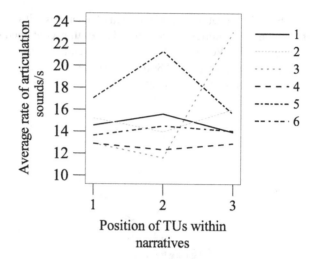

Fig. 8. Average rate of articulation in individual TUs

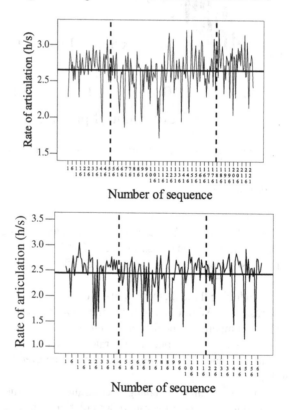

Fig. 9. Rate of articulation in two speakers' narratives (the horizontal line represents the average rate of articulation of the whole narrative; the vertical lines indicate the boundaries of TUs)

4   Conclusions

Spontaneous speech corpora make it possible to perform a thorough analysis of temporal properties of spontaneous speech. The mean tempo values can only be a point of departure, followed by detailed analyses of the complex temporal patterns of spontaneous utterances. In the present series of investigations, we determined thematic units and phrases, and gave objective values of the parameters measured. We found that (i) the majority of speakers (60 % in our case) organized their narratives in similar temporal structures, (ii) thematic units could be identified in terms of certain prosodic criteria, (iii) we found statistically valid correlations across factors like the duration of phrases, F0 changes, the word count of phrases, the rate of articulation of phrases, and pausing characteristics, and (iv) these parameters exhibited extensive variability both across and within speakers. The results of the present study speak in favor of the claim that changing temporal structures within spontaneous narratives indicate well segmentable units across speakers.

According to our data, speakers create TUs of roughly similar duration in their narratives, that is, we can assume the existence of a kind of "internal time control" as part of covert speech planning processes that determines how long speakers may dwell on a given topic in a non-conversational situation. This control function probably takes several factors into consideration, including the listener's assumed level of interest, the amount of information to be shared with the interlocutor, selection, avoidance of certain details, etc. While filled pauses did not differ in length in a statistically relevant manner, silent pauses did. This can be due to physiological factors like the regulation of breathing, but obviously a number of other factors play a role in how long silent pauses a speaker produces. Pauses, being generally accepted boundary markers, appear to be language specific in both their occurrence and phonetic properties [21, 22]. Narrative-medial TUs tend to consist of fewer phrases than the TUs before and after them. This can be due to the fact that the speaker tends to elaborate the first topic in relatively more detail, requiring more thought and speech planning, a fact that emerges in the production of a higher number of phrases. In the second topic, the speaker employs strategies of narrative construction more easily, speaks more concisely, and produces fewer phrases. In the case of the third topic, however, the speaker appears to lose interest, find solitary speech production inconvenient, or simply get tired, given that in everyday communication the construction of lengthier narratives is not typical.

All those factors may result in the fewer phrases that characterize the last TUs of narratives. The objective temporal data reflect the same pattern. Rate of articulation is expected to exhibit great variability both across and within speakers. The rate of articulation of individual speakers follows two clear tendencies, in which the second thematic unit has a crucial role. But the appearance of extreme values characterizes all phrases.

Our first hypothesis, according to which units defined by acoustic-phonetic parameters can be determined within spontaneous narratives, was confirmed. Thematic units were getting shorter towards the end of the narratives, whereas in terms of the number of words involved, there was no statistically confirmed difference across TUs.

Our second hypothesis was that the phrases making up the thematic units would exhibit particular temporal patterns. This was also confirmed. The duration of phrases showed a lot more variability across speakers than that of thematic units did. It appears, then, that phrases primarily exhibit speaker-dependent properties. Their duration is affected by where exactly they occur within a thematic unit. A strong correlation was found between the number of words in a phrase and its duration, confirming the claim that in longer phrases the speaker indeed produces more words than in shorter ones.

In our third hypothesis, we stated that the properties of thematic units are universal to a larger extent than they are speaker specific. On the basis of our results, this statement has to be qualified. Although the temporal organization of narratives exhibits a number of universal properties, individual properties may override these in interesting ways [23].

Narrative-internal tempo changes may depend on a number of further factors. The present paper demonstrated some objective characteristics of the ways narratives are organized, including properties that are true of speakers in general and those that characterize them individually.

Acknowledgements. This research was supported by the Hungarian National Scientific Research Fund (OTKA), project No. 108762.

References

1. Klatt, D.: Linguistic uses of segmental duration in English: acoustic and perceptual evidence. J. Acoust. Soc. Am. **59**, 1208–1221 (1976)
2. Yuan, J., Liberman, M., Cieri, C.: Towards an integrated understanding of speaking rate in conversation. In: Proceedings of the 9th International Conference on Spoken Language Processing, Pittsburgh, PA, pp. 541–544 (2006)
3. Quené, H.: Modeling of between-speaker and within-speaker variation in spontaneous speech tempo. In: Proceedings of Interspeech 2005, Lisbon, Portugal, pp. 2457–2460 (2005)
4. Jacewicz, E., Fox, R.A., Lai, W.: Between-speaker and within-speaker variation in speech tempo of American English. J. Acoust. Soc. Am. **128**, 839–850 (2010)
5. Verhoeven, J., De Pauw, G., Kloots, H.: Speech rate in a pluricentric language: a comparison between Dutch in Belgium and the Netherlands. Lang. Speech **47**, 297–308 (2004)
6. Schnoebelen, T.: Variation in speech tempo: Capt. Kirk, Mr. Spock, and all of us in between. In: Proceedings of 36th Conference on New Ways of Analyzing Variation: Diversity, Interdisciplinarity, Intersectionality, San Antonio, Texas (2010)
7. Cutugno, F., Savy, R.: Correlation between segmental reduction and prosodic features in spontaneous speech: the role of tempo. In: Proceedings of the XIVth International Conference of the Phonetic Sciences, San Francisco, pp. 471–474 (1999)
8. Keller, E., Port, R. Speech timing: approaches to speech rhythm. In: Proceedings of the XVIth International Conference of the Phonetic Sciences, Saarbrücken, pp. 327–329 (2007)
9. Chafe, W.: Prosody and emotion in a sample of real speech. In: Fries, P.H., Cummings, M., Lockwood, D., Spruiell, D. (eds.) Relations and Functions Within and Around Language, pp. 277–315. Continuum, London (2002)
10. Swerts, M., Geluykens, R., Terken, J.: Prosodic correlates of discourse units in spontaneous speech. In: Proceedings of the International Conference on Spoken Language Processing, Banff, pp. 421–424 (1992)
11. Georgakopolou, A., Goutsos, D.: Discourse analysis: an introduction. Edinburgh University Press, Edinburgh (2004)

12. Botinis, A., Gawronska, B., Katsika, A., Panagopoulou, D.: Prosodic speech production and thematic segmentation. PHONUM **9**, 113–116 (2003)
13. Grønnum, N.: A Danish phonetically annotated spontaneous speech corpus (DanPASS). Speech Commun. **51**, 594–603 (2009)
14. Laver, J.: Principles of phonetics. Cambridge University Press, Cambridge (1994)
15. Jessen, M.: Forensic reference data on articulation rate in German. Sci. Justice **47**, 50–67 (2007)
16. Schwartze, M., Keller, P.E., Patel, A.D., Kotz, S.A.: The impact of basal ganglia lesions on sensorimotor synchronization, spontaneous motor tempo, and the detection of tempo changes. Behav. Brain Res. **216**, 685–691 (2011)
17. Gósy, M.: BEA - a multifunctional Hungarian spoken language database. The Phonetician, 51–62 (2012)
18. Boersma, P., Weenink, D.: Praat: doing phonetics by computer (2010). http://www.fon.hum.uva.nl/praat/download_win.html
19. Künzel, H.J., Masthoff, H.R., Köster, J.P.: The relation between speech tempo, loudness, and fundamental frequency: an important issue in forensic speaker recognition. Sci. Justice **35**, 291–295 (1995)
20. Sztahó, D., Imre, V., Vicsi, K.: Érzelmek automatikus osztályozása spontán beszédben. In: Tanács A., Vincze, V. (eds.) VII. Magyar Számítógépes Konferencia, pp. 61–274. Szegedi Tudományegyetem, Szeged (2010)
21. Zellner, B.: Pauses and the temporal structure of speech. In: Keller, E. (ed.) Fundamentals of speech synthesis and speech recognition, pp. 41–62. John Wiley, Chichester (1994)
22. Tseng, S.-C.: Linguistic markings of units in spontaneous Mandarin. In: Huo, Qiang, Ma, Bin, Chng, E.-S., Li, H. (eds.) ISCSLP 2006. LNCS (LNAI), vol. 4274, pp. 43–54. Springer, Heidelberg (2006)
23. Russo, M., Barry, W.J.: Isochrony reconsidered. Objectifying relations between rhythm measures and speech tempo. In: Proceedings of Fourth Conference on Speech Prosody, 6–9 May 2008, Campinas, Brazil, pp. 419–422 (2008)

Adaptive Prosody Modelling for Improved Synthetic Speech Quality

Moses E. Ekpenyong[1](✉), Udoinyang G. Inyang[1], and EmemObong O. Udoh[2]

[1] Department of Computer Science, University of Uyo, Uyo, Nigeria
mosesekpenyong@uniuyo.edu.ng, mosesekpenyong@gmail.com,
udoiinyang@yahoo.com
[2] Department of Linguistics and Nigerian Languages, University of Uyo, Uyo, Nigeria
ememobongudoh@uniuyo.edu.ng, ememobongudoh@gmail.com

Abstract. Neural networks and fuzzy logic have proven to be efficient when applied individually to a variety of domain-specific problems, but their precision is enhanced when hybridized. This contribution presents a combined framework for improving the accuracy of prosodic models. It adopts the Adaptive Neuro-fuzzy Inference System (ANFIS), to offer self-tuned cognitive-learning capabilities, suitable for predicting the imprecise nature of speech prosody. After initializing the Fuzzy Inference System (FIS) structure, an Ibibio (ISO 693–3: nic; Ethnologue: IBB) speech dataset was trained using the gradient descent and non-negative least squares estimator (LSE) to demonstrate the feasibility of the proposed model. The model was then validated using synthesized speech corpus dataset of fundamental frequency (F0) values of ibibio tones, captured at various contour positions (initial, mid, final) within the courpus. Results obtained showed an insignificant difference between the predicted output and the check dataset with a checking error of 0.0412, and validates our claim that the proposed model is satisfactory and suitable for improving prosody prediction of synthetic speech.

Keywords: ANFIS · Prosody · Speech synthesis · Under-resourced language

1 Introduction

The formulation of prosodic structures (phrase breaks, pitch accents, phrase accents and boundary tones) of utterances remains a major challenge in Text-To-Speech (TTS) synthesis. Hence, the prediction of these elements largely depends on the accuracy and quality of error-prone linguistic procedures such as part of speech tagging, syntax and morphology analysis [1]. In tone languages, tones

---

M. Ekpenyong—Please note that the LNCS Editorial assumes that all authors have used the western naming convention, with given names preceding surnames. This determines the structure of the names in the running heads and the author index.

© Springer International Publishing Switzerland 2016
Z. Vetulani et al. (Eds.): LTC 2013, LNAI 9561, pp. 16–28, 2016.
DOI: 10.1007/978-3-319-43808-5_2

(characterized by the variation of speech within syllable) are lexically important as key determinants to speech fluency and therefore constitute the most significant prosodic features in speech synthesis of tone languages [2, 3].

The quality and acceptability of synthetic speech is determined by the prosodic well-formedness of the utterances [4]. Well-formedness is a product of various constraints and is classified into four categories namely, metrical, morpho-syntactic, semantic-pragmatic, and alignment. An utterance is prosodically well-formed if the rules that associates the segmental and prosodic tiers are consistent with those governing the formation of prosodic patterns in that language. Thus, a more comprehensive approach is required to account for the constraint hierarchy and effect at the various levels where linguistic and paralinguistic units are processed. This explains why some of the basic principles are violated. Optimality Theory [5] appears to offer some promising solutions in this area, but it is not clear how such a theory is applied in today's TTS synthesis.

The emergence of soft computing (SC) has offered attractive solutions for modelling highly nonlinear or partially defined complex systems and processes. SC techniques are known to cover two major optimization concepts: approximate reasoning and function approximation. Prominent SC techniques include evolutionary computing, fuzzy logic, neural networks and Bayesian statistics. To further improve the quality of synthesized speech, the fuzzy Logic (FL) technique in [6] is combined with the neural network (NN) technique, to obtain an Adaptive Neuro-fuzzy Inference System (ANFIS). The resulting system is then used to train and predict the accuracy of the prosodic features data - mainly the fundamental frequency (F0) of Ibibio tones (i.e., High - H, Low - L, Downstepped -D, Rising - LH, and Falling - HL), extracted at various contour positions (high, mid and low) from original (recorded) and synthesized speech corpora.

2   Tone and Prosody Prediction

One major aspect in TTS synthesis is the successful prediction of tonal events [7], and most predictive models require data labeled with intermediate representations such as Tone Boundary Index (TOBI) symbols. However, this approach is difficult, expensive and error prone [2]. In [8], sentence logarithmic F0 contour is represented as a superposition of tone features on phrase components as in the case of a generation process model - F0 model. The tone components were realized by concatenating their fragments at the tone nuclei predicted by a corpus-based method, while the phrase components were generated by rules under the F0 model framework. Beyond differences in F0 height and contours, tonal contrasts are often accompanied by systematic variations in duration and phonation [9]. A variety of techniques have been explored to improve prosody in tone language synthesis. Hence, with a larger speech corpus from a target speaker, a concatenative approach with unit selection of the F0 contour offers good performance [10, 11]. But, this approach greatly suffers for under-resourced languages, given the limited amount of available speech corpus. HMM-based approaches have provided solution to the data sparseness problem experienced by unit selection systems, and can be exploited to efficiently estimate relatively shallow features close to the text itself. In [2], these features are applied directly as contexts without attempting explicit prediction of intermediate representations. In [4], we arrived at a generic HMM sequence that describes the contextual dependency of the features with prosodic factors defined for tone language synthesis, as,

$$
\begin{aligned}
T_{Label} = \; & \overrightarrow{\theta}^{f}_{0,tone(i,1)} + \overrightarrow{\theta}_{tone(i,1)} + \ldots + \overrightarrow{\theta}_{0,tone(i,n-1)} + \overrightarrow{\theta}^{f}_{c(i,n-1),tonepat(i,n-1)} \\
& + \overrightarrow{\theta}_{tone(i,n)} + \overrightarrow{\theta}_{0,tone(i,n)} + \overrightarrow{\theta}^{f}_{c(i,n),tonepat(i,n)} + \overrightarrow{\theta}^{f}_{0,tone(i,n+1)} + \ldots \\
& + \overrightarrow{\theta}_{0,tone(i,N)} + \overleftarrow{\theta}^{b}_{C+1,tone(i,N)} + \overleftarrow{\theta}_{tpros(i,N)} + \ldots + \overleftarrow{\theta}_{tpros(i,n+1)} \\
& + \overleftarrow{\theta}^{b}_{c(i,n),tonepat(i,n)} + \overleftarrow{\theta}_{pros(i,n)} + \overleftarrow{\theta}^{b}_{c(i,n-1),tonepat(i,n-1)} \\
& + \overleftarrow{\theta}_{pros(i,n-1)} + \ldots + \overleftarrow{\theta}_{pros(i,1)}
\end{aligned}
\tag{1}
$$

where, $\overrightarrow{\theta}_{0,tone(i,n)\in\{1,2,\ldots,n\}}$, represents a vector of current tones of the intended language; $\overleftarrow{\theta}_{pros(i,n)}$, is a vector of current prosody of the language; $tonepat(i,n) \in \{(1,1),(1,2),\ldots,(i,n)\}$, describes the tone patterns defined by the tone pair iteration; $t(i,n), t(i,n+1); C(i,n) \in \{0,1,2,\ldots,C,C+1\}$, describes the co-articulation (effect of sound interaction) at inter-syllable locations between the current syllable, n, and the next syllable, $n+1$; $\overrightarrow{\theta}^{f}_{c(i,n),tonepat(i,n)}$ and $\overleftarrow{\theta}^{b}_{c(i,n),tonepat(i,n)}$, are the forward and backward transitions of the tone patterns, respectively, with its implied co-articulation. Eq. 1 is most suitable for modelling the state features of a HMM-based tone language synthesis system and is currently being investigated for completeness.

2.1   Predicting and Evaluating Prosodic Features

Once a prosodic model has been obtained for a system, the prosodic variation with its accompanying prediction scheme from input text can be determined. Early TTS systems relied on hand-crafted rules that predict prosody assignment based on simple part-of-speech (PoS) features or more elaborate syntactic parsing. The major drawback of this approach is extension and maintenance difficulties. Mostly, new rules for prosodic assignments are trailed by unforeseen and undesirable consequences. Corpus-based techniques - the use of relatively huge speech database have since rescued hand-crafted rule systems. They represent annotations of prosodic features and are used as training materials for machine learning algorithms, where decision procedures are derived from automated textual analysis. The automatically derived decisions appear to be limited by the amount of hand-labelled data available for training; but the provision of correct examples in the training corpus must sufficiently outweigh the data that could yield undesirable prediction, else, errors may easily go unnoticed. The challenges here extend beyond those involved in the derivation of prosodic patterning from grammatical information, since general text additionally requires semantic/pragmatic background information on emphasis and contrast, for instance.

But, with some degree of explicit control over prosodic variation, the naturalness of TTS systems could be improved. This control may be accomplished by providing precise user-specific markup capabilities. Evaluating TTS systems in general is extremely challenging. Today, most synthesis systems are of very high quality. Although subjective judgment ratings are mostly used to evaluate prosodic assignments, this subject (prosody assignment) remains a major research question.

3 Our Approach

3.1 The ANFIS Architecture

A block diagram showing the ANFIS process flow is presented in Fig. 1, with the fuzzifier, defuzzifier, rule base and fuzzy inference system as components. Fuzzifier converts the crisp inputs into linguistic variables (low, mid and high) using membership functions while, defuzzfier performs a scale mapping, and converts the range of values of output variables into the corresponding universes of discourse (UoD), thus finally producing a crisp output from an inferred fuzzy control action. The rule base consists of a number of fuzzy IF-THEN rules that guides the inference engine in its reasoning. The fuzzy inference engine forms the kernel of ANFIS. It has the capability of simulating human decision-making processes based on fuzzy concepts, and inferring fuzzy control actions by employing fuzzy implication with the rules of inference in the fuzzy rule base. The most common types of fuzzy inference methods are Mamdani and Sugeno methods [12]. The difference between these two methods lies in the consequent parameter of the fuzzy rules. This paper adopts the Mamdani inference mechanism for the evaluation and extraction of rules and production of the fuzzy output. The reason for using Mamdani is that it is intuitive and has widespread acceptance. In addition, it is well suited to human input. The ANFIS inference engine is a five layered architecture [13], and the rule base consists of rules of the form:

$$\text{IF } (x_j \text{ is } A_i^r) \text{ and } (y_j \text{ is } A_i^r) \text{ THEN } z \text{ is } C_i^r \tag{2}$$

where, r is the rule-number, x and y are input variables, z is the output variable. A_i^r, are the linguistic terms, characterized by the appropriate membership

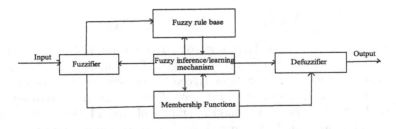

Fig. 1. A generic ANFIS Block diagram

function, μ_{A_n}. ANFIS uses a combination of gradient descent and least square estimator (LSE) depending on the application, with two sets of parameters: a set of premise and a set of consequent parameters. The process of parameter update is achieved using a forward and backward pass learning algorithm. The forward pass (FP) learning computes the neuron outputs, layer after layer, and identifies the consequent parameters by the LSE, leading to the final (single) output. The backward pass (BP) propagates error signals and updates the antecedent parameters according to a chain rule. Each layer of ANFIS consists of nodes described by the node function.

Layer 1 is the input fuzzification layer, where each node in this layer generates fuzzy membership grades for the inputs, and is given by:

$$\begin{aligned} O_i^1 &= \mu_{A_i}(x_i) & i &= 1, 2, \ldots, n \\ O_j^1 &= \mu_{A_j}(y_j) & j &= 1, 2, \ldots, n \\ O_k^1 &= \mu_{A_k}(L_k) & k &= 1, 2, \ldots, n \end{aligned} \tag{3}$$

The general form of the triangular MF is defined as [13]:

$$\mu(x) = \begin{cases} 1 & \text{if } x = b \\ \frac{x-a}{b-a} & \text{if } a \leq x < b \\ \frac{c-x}{c-b} & \text{if } b \leq x < c \\ 0 & \text{if } c = x \end{cases} \tag{4}$$

or

$$\mu_A = \max\left(\min\left(\frac{x-a}{b-a}, \frac{c-x}{c-b}\right), 0\right) \tag{5}$$

where, a and c, are parameters governing triangular MF; b is the value for which $\mu(x) = 1$, and is given as, $b = \frac{a+c}{2}$.

Layer 2, is the rule evaluation node, and uses either the disjunction or conjunction operator (AND or OR) to determine the firing strengths. This is evaluated using the max (Eq. (6)) or min (Eq. (7)) operator, respectively:

$$\mu_A B(x) = \max \mu_A(x), \mu_B(x) \tag{6}$$

$$\mu_A B(x) = \min \mu_A(x), \mu_B(x) \tag{7}$$

The firing strengths, O_i^2, are the products of the corresponding membership degrees obtained from layer 1, and is given as:

$$O_i^2 = w_i = \mu_{A_n}(x_i)\mu_{B_n}(y_j)\mu_{D_n}(L_k) \tag{8}$$

Layer 3 is the normalization layer and computes the ratio of each rule firing strength to the sum of all rules firing strength. The output, $\overline{w}_i$, is defined in Eq. (9). The defuzzification layer (layer 4), consists of consequent nodes for calculating the contribution of each rule to the overall output and is given in Eq. (10). The overall output of the ANFIS model is finally obtained by summing (aggregating) all incoming signals, by layer 5. In this paper, the centroid method as depicted in Eq. (11) is used for this purpose.

$$O_i^3 = w_i = \frac{w_i}{\sum_i w_i} \tag{9}$$

$$O_i^4 = w_i f_i \tag{10}$$

$$O_i^5 = M = \sum_i \overline{w}_i f_i = \frac{\sum_i w_i f_i}{\sum_i w_i} \tag{11}$$

3.2 Neuro-fuzzy System Model

A hybridized approach (a fusion of least-square and back propagation gradient descent methods) [14], is adopted in this paper for training and validating the input dataset. This approach consists of forward and backward passes. In the forward pass, each node's output proceeds until the fourth layer when the consequent parameters are identified by the least squares method. During the backward pass, the premise parameters are updated by gradient descent as the error signal re-propagates backwards. In Fig. 2, the proposed ANFIS-based model architecture is presented, illustrating the contribution of inputs to the various rules. The inputs are crisp (non-fuzzy) numbers limited to a specific range.

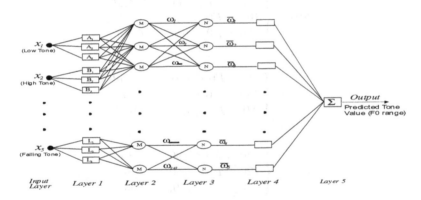

Fig. 2. Proposed ANFIS model

All the rules (a set of IF-THEN statements) are evaluated in parallel - from a set of decomposed linguistic terms (or membership functions) describing the various tones of the language, using fuzzy reasoning. The results of the rules are finally merged and distilled (defuzzified) using the membership functions. The membership functions are used to map the non-fuzzy input values to fuzzy linguistic terms and vice versa. They are used to quantify the membership terms, which mappings finally yield a crisp (non-fuzzy) output (number). Five linguistic variables were identified as input to the fuzzy inference system (FIS). These variables enumerate the tones (including the phonemic variations) of Ibibio,

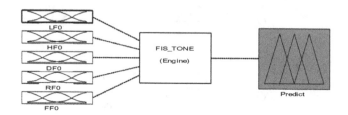

Fig. 3. FIS tone system

i.e., L, H, D, R, F tones. Figure 3 shows a MatLab interface implementing the FIS component of the ANFIS model.

Input Membership Functions: Three linguistic terms were defined over the Universe of Discourse (UoD) for each input variable. The linguistic terms are F0 values extracted from the speech contour described by: $F0(t) = \{initial, mid, final\}$, where, t denotes the linguistic variables.

Eqs. (12), (13), (14), (15) and (16) describe the membership functions of the respective linguistic variables. They represent experimental values annotated using the Praat annotation software:

$$\mu_L(F0) = \begin{cases} 80 \leq F0 \leq 150, & initial \\ 100 \leq F0 \leq 140, & mid \\ 55 \leq F0 \leq 90, & final \end{cases} \tag{12}$$

$$\mu_H(F0) = \begin{cases} 90 \leq F0 \leq 170, & initial \\ 145 \leq F0 \leq 190, & mid \\ 80 \leq F0 \leq 120, & final \end{cases} \tag{13}$$

$$\mu_D(F0) = \begin{cases} 140 \leq F0 \leq 190, & initial \\ 120 \leq F0 \leq 150, & mid \\ 80 \leq F0 \leq 130, & final \end{cases} \tag{14}$$

$$\mu_R(F0) = \begin{cases} 135 \leq F0 \leq 180, & initial \\ 120 \leq F0 \leq 170, & mid \\ 80 \leq F0 \leq 130, & final \end{cases} \tag{15}$$

$$\mu_F(F0) = \begin{cases} 100 \leq F0 \leq 150, & initial \\ 115 \leq F0 \leq 160, & mid \\ 80 \leq F0 \leq 130, & final \end{cases} \tag{16}$$

Output Membership Function: The output membership function was defined by assignment, following a careful analysis and observation of the speech data by domain experts. The output membership function is viewed as a continuum with each output element spreading across a spectrum area (selection) of the continuum.

ANFIS Engine: As earlier mentioned, the Mamdani-type fuzzy inference mechanism is used to formulate the mapping from a given input to an output using fuzzy logic. This mapping provides the basis on which decisions could be made or patterns discerned. The inference process includes the following: block building, structuring, firing, implication and aggregation of rules. The number of rules is determined by the complexity of the associated fuzzy system. Though we have established 3^5=243 rules for evaluating the tone contour patterns of the speech corpus, not all the rules fired. Snippets of the extracted F0 data used for training the ANFIS system and coded representations (1-initial, 2-mid,3-final) for building the respective rules, are shown in Tables 1 and 2, respectively.

Table 1. F0s of Ibibio tones, randomly selected for training

S/no	F0 (L)	F0 (H)	F0 (DH)	F0 (LH)	F0 (HL)	Predict
1	104	124	154	146	127	1
2	128	81	115	169	108	2
3	103	141	98	165	101	2
4	136	175	128	168	112	2
5	140	180	172	174	83	1
6	130	156	80	151	127	2
7	112	160	117	179	138	2
8	105	146	156	146	144	1
9	122	94	147	175	119	2
:	:	:	:	:	:	:
241	101	119	120	122	141	2
242	95	160	129	137	123	2
243	110	117	121	127	113	2

Details of the interface implementation of the fuzzy membership functions, rules and consequences can be found in [6].

Different implication operators fit different aggregation operators (e.g. union and intersection). Whereas the union operator uses the Mamdani and Larsen operators, the intersection uses the Lukasiewicz operator [15]. The Mamdani operator is applied in this paper. After inference, the overall result is a fuzzy value and should be defuzzified to obtain a final crisp output. There are different algorithms for defuzzification namely, Centre of Gravity (CoG) or Centroid Average (CA), Maximum Centre Average (MCA), Mean of Maximum (MoM), Smallest of Maximum (SoM) and Largest of Maximum (LoM). As earlier mentioned, the CoG algorithm (Centroid) as defined in Eq. (11) is used in this paper.

Table 2. Coded representation of Table 1 used for building the rules

Rule	F0 (L)	F0 (H)	F0 (DH)	F0 (LH)	F0 (HL)	Predict
1	1	1	1	1	1	1
2	2	3	3	1	3	2
3	2	1	3	1	3	2
4	2	2	2	1	3	2
5	2	2	1	1	3	1
6	2	2	3	1	2	2
7	2	2	3	1	1	2
8	2	1	1	1	1	1
9	2	3	2	1	2	2
:	:	:	:	:	:	:
241	1	3	2	2	1	2
242	1	2	2	2	2	2
243	1	3	2	2	3	2

4   Experiment and Results

4.1   FL Model Validation

To validate the feasibility of the proposed ANFIS model, we annotated and extracted, using Praat - a speech processing and annotation software, F0 values of Ibibio tones at various contour positions (initial, mid and final) from both recorded and synthesised speech corpus. Figure 4 shows a sample annotation of a synthesised Ibibio speech. The sample size used for this experiment were long utterances containing the various tones of the language selected from a set of 1140 sentences used for HMM-based Ibibio synthesis experiment [16]. An objective evaluation of the annotations revealed that falling (F) tones were wrongly perceived as either downstepped (D) or high (H) tones, mostly on the ọ (O – SAMPA equivalent) sound, which indicated a possibility of phoneme/tone confusion. The evaluation of phoneme and tone confusions for synthesised voices used for this experiment has been investigated in [17]. Using the extracted parameters, the degree of certainty (crisp output) of the FIS was simulated for the purpose of comparing the original and synthesised annotations. Tables 3 and 4 present the input (average F0) values at different contour positions for the various tones of Ibibio, and the simulated crisp output for original and synthesized voices, respectively. We observed from these tables that the degree of certainty of the original speech was higher, compared to the synthesised speech. This result implies that tone patterns of the original voices are well predicted by the FL system.

Generally, predictions at the final positions in both cases were poor. The reason for this may not be unconnected with the fact that rising (R) and falling (F)

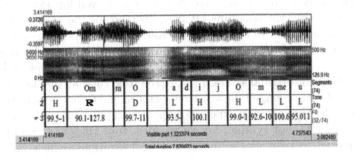

Fig. 4. Sample annotation of a synthesised male speaker

Table 3. Input F0s and crisp output for original male speaker

S/N	Position	Input (average F0)					Crisp output
		L	H	D	R	F	
1	Initial	98	130	165	158	125	0.693
2	Mid	120	168	135	145	138	0.664
3	Final	78	100	105	100	105	0.301

Table 4. Input F0s and crisp output for synthesised male speaker

S/N	Position	Input (average F0)					Crisp output
		L	H	D	R	F	
1	Initial	186	192	144	115	150	0.500
2	Mid	112	146	139	121	126	0.647
3	Final	85	98	87	88	97	0.250

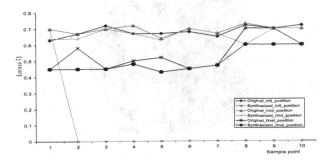

Fig. 5. Graph showing implication and aggregation of prosody rules

tones most rarely occur at the final positions in a well-formed Ibibio utter-
ance/sentence. Also, the resultant F0 averages used for the prediction at these
positions were gathered from a range of (tone) values appearing few distances
away from the end of the sentence(s). Figure 5 shows plots of rules predictions
at the various contour positions for the original and synthesized voices. In Fig. 5,
we observe that for original voices, most of the tone rules at the initial and mid
positions fired with average F0 predictions of 0.683 and 0.693, respectively; while
tone rules at the final position experienced poor firing - i.e. gave a low average F0
prediction of 0.542. For synthesized voices, most tone rules at the mid position
fired, compared to rules at the initial and final positions, which yielded poor
predictions of 0.07 and 0.498, respectively. The FIS results therefore call for an
investigation into the poor synthesis of tones at the initial and final positions in
a given utterance. In the next section, we re-train the synthesis data using our
ANFIS model to improve on the current results.

4.2   Model Training and Checking

A simulated structure of the proposed ANFIS model, generated in MatLab is
presented in Fig. 6.

As shown in Fig. 6, the proposed model is five layered, with five inputs,
each with 3 input membership terms. The rule base comprises 243 rules. The
properties of the ANFIS model are as listed in Table 5.

ANFIS model training was concluded at the 2nd epoch with training and
testing errors of 0.0545 and 2.276, respectively. The graph of the testing and
checking of the ANFIS model is presented in Fig. 7. In Fig. 7, the ANFIS output
is mapped against the checking dataset. We observed that there is an insignificant
difference between the predicted output (*) and the check dataset (+) with a
checking error of 0.0412. Hence the proposed solution is satisfactory and suitable
for improving prosody prediction of synthetic speech.

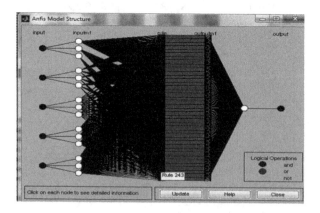

Fig. 6. Simulated ANFIS structure

Table 5. Properties of ANFIS model for prosody prediction

S/No	Parameter	Number
1	Nodes	524
2	Linear Parameters	1458
3	Nonlinear parameters	45
4	Training data pairs	170
6	Checking data pairs	37
7	Testing data pairs	37
8	Fuzzy rules	243

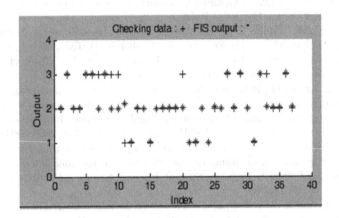

Fig. 7. Plots for checking and training data set

5 Conclusion and Future Work

The production of quality (natural and intelligible) synthetic speech depends, in part, on the correctness of the language's prosody. Prosody modelling is useful for associating the variations of prosodic features with changes in structure, meaning and context of spoken languages. These features to a great extent, contribute to enhancing the perceived quality of speech. This paper has presented an adaptive fuzzy Inference system for modelling the prosody of synthetic speech. The proposed model is suitable for the precise prediction of F0 contour patterns in human and synthetic speech. In the future, we shall explore the use of genetic algorithm in determining optimal parameters of the weights and structure of the current approaches and investigate the effectiveness of the design, in a bid to provide a more efficient solution to the prosody problem presented by tone language systems.

References

1. Xydas, G., Spiliotopoulos, D., Kouroupetroglou, G.: Modeling prosodic structures in linguistically enriched environments. In: Sojka, P., Kopeček, I., Pala, K. (eds.) TSD 2004. LNCS (LNAI), vol. 3206, pp. 521–528. Springer, Heidelberg (2004)
2. Ekpenyong, M., Urua, E.-A., Watts, O., King, S., Yamagishi, J.: Statistical parametric speech synthesis for Ibibio. Speech Commun. **56**, 243–251 (2014)
3. Ekpenyong, M., Udoh, E.O., Udosen, E., Urua, E.-A.: Improved syllable-based text to speech synthesis for tone language systems. In: Vetulani, Z., Mariani, J. (eds.) LTC 2011. LNCS, vol. 8387, pp. 3–15. Springer, Heidelberg (2014)
4. Di Cristo, A., Di Cristo, P., Campione, E., Veronis, J.: A prosodic model for text-to-speech synthesis in French. In: Botinis, A. (ed.) Intonation: Analysis Modelling and Technology, pp. 321–355. Kluwer, Amsterdam (2000)
5. Prince, A., Smolensky, P.: Optimality Theory: Constraints Interaction in Generative Grammar. Wiley-Blackwell Publishers, New Jersey (2004)
6. Ekpenyong, M., Udoh, E.O.: Intelligent prosody modelling: a framework for tone language synthesis. In: Vetulani, Z., Uszkoreit, H. (eds.) 6th Language and Technology Conference (LTC), Poznan, Poland, Fundacja Uniwersytetu im. A. Mickiewicza, pp. 279–283 (2013)
7. Zervas, P., Xydas, G., Fakotakis, N., Kokkinakis, G., Kouroupetroglou, G.: Evaluation of corpus based tone prediction in mismatched environments for Greek TtS synthesis. In: Proceedings of 8th International Conference on Spoken Language Processing (INTERSPEECH - ICSLP), Jeju, Korea, pp. 761–764 (2004)
8. Sun, Q., Hirose, K., Minematsu, N. Improved prediction of tone components for F0 contour generation of Mandarin speech based on the tone nucleus model. In: Proceedings of Speech Prosody Special Interest Group (SProSIG) Conference, Campinas, pp. 1–4 (2008)
9. Faytak, M., Yu, A.C.L.: A typological study of the interaction between level tones, duration. In: Proceedings of 17th ICPhS Conference, Hong Kong, pp. 659–662 (2011)
10. Raux, A., Black, A.W.A.: A unit selection approach to F0 modeling and its application to emphasis. In: Workshop on Automatic Speech Recognition and Understanding (ASRU), pp. 700–705 (2003)
11. Li, Y., Lee, T., Qian, Y.: F0 Analysis and modeling for cantonese text-to-speech. In: Speech Prosody Conference, Nara, Japan, pp. 169–180 (2004)
12. Nayak, P.C., Sudheerb, K.P., Rangan, D.M., Ramasastri, K.S.: A neuro-fuzzy computing technique for modelling hydrological time series. J. Hydrol. **291**(2004), 52–66 (2004)
13. Inyang, U.G., Akinyokun, O.C.: A hybrid knowledge discovery system for oil spillage risks pattern classification. Artif. Intell. Res. **3**(4), 77–86 (2014)
14. Mayilvaganan, M.K., Naidu, K.B.: Comparison of membership functions in adaptive network-based fuzzy inference system (ANFIS) for the prediction of groundwater level of a watershed. J. Comput. Appl. Res. Dev. **1**(1), 35–42 (2011)
15. Iancu, I.: A Mamdani type fuzzy logic controller. In: Dadios, E.P. (ed.) Fuzzy Logic - Controls Concepts, Theories and Application, pp. 325–350. InTech Publishers, Vienna (2012)
16. Ekpenyong, M.E.: Speech Synthesis for Tone Language Systems. Ph.D. thesis, Uyo, in Supervision Collaboration with CSTR, Edinburgh (2013)
17. Ekpenyong, M., Udoh, E.O.: Tone modelling in Ibibio speech synthesis. Int. J. Speech Technol. **17**(2), 145–159 (2014)

Diacritics Restoration in the Slovak Texts Using Hidden Markov Model

Daniel Hládek[✉], Ján Staš, and Jozef Juhár

Department of Electronics and Multimedia Communications, FEI,
Technical University of Košice, Park Komenského 13, 042 00 Košice, Slovakia
{daniel.hladek,jan.stas,jozef.juhar}@tuke.sk

Abstract. This paper presents fast and accurate method for recovering diacritical markings and guessing original meaning of the word from the context based on a hidden Markov model and the Viterbi algorithm. The proposed algorithm might find usage in any area where erroneous text might appear, such as a web search engine, e-mail messages, office suite, optical character recognition or helping to type on small mobile device keyboards.

1 Introduction

Character markings can often change the meaning of the word. It is common that diacritics are removed in the written communication and true meaning of the word is guessed from the context. This is caused by a very fast typing, small cell phone keyboards, insufficient international support for some devices and fact that many common e-mail services in recent past did not correctly understand non-English encodings and mangle special letters.

Restoration of diacritic marking is important because a proper natural language processing of web discussions or e-mails require understand the text as it was originally meant. Advertisement systems that statistically analyze content of emails in the free mail services are one of the main sources of financial income for the providers. Social networks and web discussions are also a target of extensive analysis for better focus of the displayed commercials. In this case the corrected data will be used to enhance a web-based training corpus [5] for a large-vocabulary automatic speech recognition system for the Slovak language [17].

Important part of the natural language processing, statistical language modeling and information retrieval is a preparation of text data. The problem is that the text data often contain typographical and grammatical errors that decrease its information value. This paper will focus on the problem of correcting possibly incorrectly typed sentence. Spell-checking refers to the task of identifying and marking incorrectly spelled words in a document written in a natural language [8].

As it is known from the world of word processors, the spell-checker containing a dictionary of correct words is probably able to find incorrect word form and

© Springer International Publishing Switzerland 2016
Z. Vetulani et al. (Eds.): LTC 2013, LNAI 9561, pp. 29–40, 2016.
DOI: 10.1007/978-3-319-43808-5_3

propose a list of corrections. Choosing the best matching correct word depends on the surrounding context. The user then can manually check the selected word, choose one of the proposed word forms, correct the word manually or proclaim that the correction is not necessary, because the word is truly correct.

The algorithm for correction of the text using an incorporated spell-checker then can be described as:

- check if the highlighted word is really incorrect;
- if it is, check if the correction is in the list of the proposed corrections;
- if a correction is in the list, choose the best possible one;
- if a correction is not available, then manually rewrite the word to its correct form.

In the case of a very large textual data, such as training corpora or web search indices it is simply not possible to use this method that requires human intervention. In order to improve the data it is necessary to reduce human work and do it as much as it is possible in an unsupervised way. One part of the work can be done using a rule based system that can solve the simplest correction by replacing by its usual correction. In the case when there are more corrections possible, a statistical approach is necessary in order to choose the best correction from the list according to the surrounding context.

2   The State of the Art

The problem of restoration of diacritics appears only in the languages whose writing system use such markings extensively, such as Turkish, Arabian, Romanian, Vietnamese, Czech, Polish and Slovak. Research on the available papers shows that the problem of automatic correction has already gained some attention, although not as big as it deserves.

The technique of finding misspelled word and providing a list of possible corrections is known for a long time in common word processing software, such as Microsoft Word or OpenOffice Writer. It is common that these applications also provide other tools, checking not only spelling, but also the grammar using a rule-based system. However, proposing a correction autonomously is still not common in the office area.

Grobbelaar and Kinyua [3] proposed a system capable of providing corrections for the South African language. Sirts [18] deals with spelling errors, caused by learners of Estonian. This approach utilizes hidden Markov model (HMM) and part-of-speech (POS) tagging in order to choose the best correction of a word. In [11], Li, Duan and Zhai focused on the correction of web search queries and used HMMs with discriminative training. Lund and Ringer [12] used a decision lists in order to improve OCR recognition accuracy. Rodphon et al. [16] used bigram and trigram probability to select the best word in the OCR recognition result in the Thai language. In [22], Zhou et al. used a tribayes method to propose the best correction.

The paper [10] gives a basic theoretical foundation for automatic corrections in the text and common types of errors. [14] proposes a diacritics restoration system for Vietnamese based on C.4.5 regression tree and Adaboost algorithm. [4,21] suggest approach for Romanian language using Viterbi algorithm. [13] proposes a rule-based approach focusing on letters in the Romanian language. [15] declares solution for Arabic language using an n-gram language model, [1] provides an evaluation of several Arabic diacritization systems. [2] provides a comprehensive study for multiple resource-sparse languages using TiMBL classifier. [23] uses maximum entropy classifier for the task. There are papers [12,16,22] focused on the more general problem of automatic correction of erroneous text, as it is in the optical character recognition (OCR) process in the office systems.

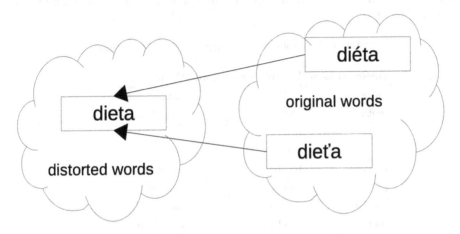

Fig. 1. Ambiguous mapping from priginal to distorted set of words

3   The Problem Description

This paper is focused on the Slovak language, but similar approach can be used for other Latin-based Slavic languages, or non-Slavic ones that use diacritics, such as Romanian or Arabic. The Slovak language is characterized by rich morphological forms and large vocabulary. It contains special markings such as acutes or carons that can be used together with the standard latin letters.

Diacritic mark means a different pronunciation of a letter and thus a different meaning of the word. The most common marking in the Slovak language is acute that can be added to any wovel (aeiou become áéíóú) and prolongs the pronunciation of a vowel. The second common type is caron which softens the pronunciation and can be added to the most of the consonants (tzcnlds become ť’žčňl’ď’š).

3.1 Correct Word Disambiguation

Removal of diacritics creates a mapping from the original word to its distorted form as it is shown in Fig. 1 (translations are in Table 1). Some examples of ambiguous words are shown in the Table 1. The problem is that there are more possible correct forms for one distorted form and recovering diacritic marking (reverse mapping from distorted form to the correct form) is ambiguous. This problem can be formalized as a classification problem, where a class (original word form) is assigned to a certain, possibly previously unknown input – the context of the word. In order to restore the original word form, it is necessary to propose a system that can decide the correct form from the context.

As it was shown in the literature overview, there are more possible solutions and it is possible to choose from a number of established text classification algorithms, such as maximum entropy classifier or Viterbi algorithm with hidden Markov Model.

Table 1. Examples of words with removed diacritics

Distorted form	Possible corect word	Meaning
dieta	diet'a	child
dieta	diéta	way of alimentation
pec	pec	owen
pec	peč	to bake
presne	presné	accurate
presne	presne	exactly
macka	mačka	cat
macka	macka	little bear

3.2 Error Types

According to [8,10], errors related to the misspelled words can be categorized into two basic classes:

- **non-word errors** - where the misspelled word is not a valid word in a language;
- **real-word errors** - where the word in question is valid yet inappropriate in the context, and hence not giving the intended meaning.

Paper [8] states that human typing leads to non-word errors that can arise due to three major factors:

- **typographic errors** - a result of motor coordination slips and are related to keyboard mis-punches (e.g. *"the"* - *"teh"*, *"spell"* - *"speel"*);
- **cognitive errors** - caused by the writer's misconceptions (e.g. *"receive"* - *"recieve"*, *"conspiracy"* - *"conspiricy"*);
- **phonetic errors** - a result of substituting a phonetically equivalent sequence of letters (e.g. *"seperate"* - *"separate"*).

4   The Spelling Correction System

Based on our previous work presented in [7] and overview of the available literature presented in the preceding section, the hidden Markov model representation
and the Viterbi algorithm is found to be the most suitable for the task.

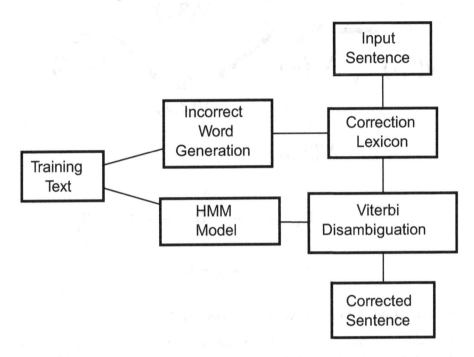

Fig. 2. The Proposed System

In the training step, some unlabeled training text is taken. The incorrect
word generation component simulates errors that can be made by users. Possible
incorrect words are stored in a lexicon together with correct forms. The correction lexicon and the training text are used to construcs a hidden Markov model.
Language model of the training text is used a transition probability matrix, the
correction lexicon is used to estimate observation probability matrix. Estimated
HMM can be used to find out the best sequence of corrections for given sentence
using Viterbi algorithm. The proposed system is depicted in Fig. 2.

To summarize, the automatic correction algorithm, processes a given
sentence:

1. applies rule based corrections in order to deal with the most simple errors;
2. identifies possibly incorrect words;
3. for every incorrect word proposes a list of corrections;
4. constructs a Viterbi trellis, evaluating all possible transitions between correct
   states;
5. using backtracking proposes the best sequence of correct states.

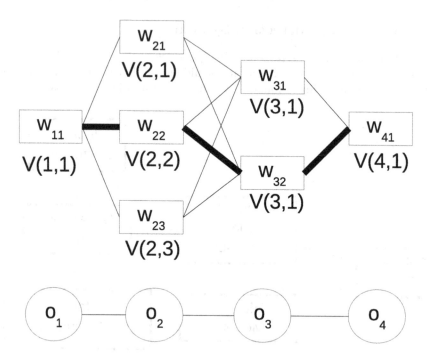

Fig. 3. The viterbi trelis

4.1   The Hidden Markov Model Representation

In the hidden Markov model (HMM) approach words that are distorted by errors in the sentence can be described as a sequence of observations o (the bottom part of Figure 3). Possible corrections w_{ti} for words o are hidden states of the HMM [11]. The Viterbi algorithm can assign the most probable sequence of the corrected words to the given list of possibly incorrect words.

The HMM is suited to model time-dependent properties of words. The Viterbi condition assumes that the next state (a word) depends only on preceding states. This condition is not entirely met for natural language because the order of words in a sentence is not mandatory. On the other hand, there are so many common expressions and sequences of words present that it can be assumed that this condition is met. To make a correct representation of this problem using the HMM framework in a way similar to [7]. It is necessary to correctly express basics components of the HMM: the observation matrix $P(o|w)$, and the state transition matrix $P(w|h)$.

4.2   Observation Probability Matrix

Observation matrix $P(o|w)$ is a probability of the occurrence of an incorrect form o (observation) in the case of presence of its correct form w (state). This probability can be estimated using a basic maximum likelihood method calculated as a ratio of the count of occurrence of the observed event (distorted word with original word, marked $C(o, w)$) and count of all occurrences of event (count of the distorted word $C(o)$) as it is shown in the Eq. 1:

$$P(o|w) = \frac{C(o, w)}{C(o)} \tag{1}$$

The counts C can be calculated from the training corpus. The other option is to use some heuristics to estimate it, or assume that every possible incorrect form has the same probability. The most important function of the observation probability matrix is to restrict the search space to those states that are possible for the given observation. Number of words in one observation column of the Viterbi trellis (boxes in Fig. 3) in time t is much smaller and it is not necessary to search for all words in the dictionary. Possible correct word forms for an incorrect observation can be calculated from the dictionary in advance.

4.3 Language Model as a State Transition Matrix

Statistical language model is a common tool for erroneous word corrections, as it is in [8] or [15]. The state set of a HMM is a list of all correct forms of words, given by the manually checked dictionary. The state-transition matrix is a language model of the target language [20] and expresses probability of occurrence of a word w according to it history h (that is again a sequence of words). In the case of n-gram language model, the maximum likelihood estimation $P(w|h)$ of the word w according to the context is given by:

$$P(w|h) = \frac{C(w, h)}{C(h)} \tag{2}$$

where $C(w, h)$ is count of the sequence (w, h) of word and its history and $C(h)$ is count of the context h in the training corpus. However, this formula cannot be used in practice, because in the case of insufficient training data counts of n-grams are often zero. This type of language model then incorrectly gives zero probability also for those situations that are perfectly valid in the given language.

As it was mentioned above, the Slovak language is characterized by many possible morphological word forms. As a consequence, each operation that considers statistical information about sequences of words, such as word spelling correction needs to have a proper method of training to improve performance of the system [20]. A method of adjusting resulting probability (smoothing) presented in [19] have to be chosen to estimate probability of events that had not been observed in the training corpus.

4.4 The Viterbi Algorithm

After state and observation probabilities are estimated, the most probable sequence of the corrections can be calculated using the Viterbi algorithm.

The Viterbi trellis is constructed from each possible correction w_{ti} for observed distorted form o and each node has assigned a certain value $V(t,i)$ that is used to find the best possible sequence as a path in this trellis, as it is shown in the Fig. 3. The Viterbi value of a node can be calculated using a recursive formula:

$$V(t,i) = P(o_t|w_{ti}) + \max_{j \in S_{t-1}} V(t-1,j)P(w_{ti}|w_{t-1,j}) \qquad (3)$$

where $V(t,i)$ is a Viterbi value for word w_i in time t, $P(o|w_{it})$ is observation probability similar to the Eq. 3. $V(t-1,j)$ is Viterbi value of word w_j in time $t-1$ and is a transition probability given by the language model, similar to the Eq. 2. The second part of the equation takes the history into the account. All possible states w_{t-1} for the last observation are taken and maximum of the product of the transition probability and last Viterbi value is found. The value us used for the calculation of the Viterbi value and the transition is remembered as the best for the given state.

In the beginning of the recursive calculation the starting state $V(0,0)$ can have assigned some constant value. When all Viterbi values $V(t,i)$ are calculated, the best preceding word is found for each possible correction. The whole process is depicted in the Fig. 3 where each observed word ot in a given sentence has assigned some possible correction w_{it} on the path marked with the bold line.

Table 2. Training Corpus

	Tokens	Sentences
Training part	49 592 554	2 910 180
Testing part	13 088 832	727 549

5   Experiments

The first step in the training process is a preparation of a training corpus. For this purpose, a collection of Slovak electronic books has been collected and automatically processed using a set of tools described in [5]. The collected corpus is characterized in the Table 2.

In order to evaluate the proposed system, the testing part of the corpus has diacritics artificially removed. A very large Slovak dictionary [9] has been used to check the training corpus and remove non-Slovak words. This testing set is used in the following experiments.

The training corpus preparation step includes word tokenization, sentence boundary identification, sentence and token filtering, transcription and training sentences correction as it is noted in [6]. The list of words have been constrained to the biggest manually checked the dictionary of the Slovak words (6.5 mil. of unique words) [9].

After the training data were prepared, a language model was constructed. For this purpose our language model training tool has been used to train a tri-gram language model using Knesser-Ney smoothing from the remaining part of the fiction corpus. The resulting language model contains 345 913 unigrams, 3 284 555 bigrams and 6 924 208 trigrams. This language model was used as a state-transition matrix for the HMM. The training set has been used to construct a list of possible corrections for each word and this list has been used for all following experiments. The experiments should evaluate the proposed approach and shown advantages of the Viterbi algorithm when compared to less sophisticated algorithms.

Table 3. Results of the baseline experiment

	Correct tokens	Incorrect tokens	% Incorrect from all
Words with markings	5 034 572	4 238	0,084
Words without markings	8 047 199	2 822	0,035
Words	13 081 771	7 060	0,054
Sentences	720 642	6 907	0,949

5.1 The Baseline Experiment

In the first experiment, the proposed system has been used to recover removed diacritics from the testing set. The recovered testing set then has been compared with the original testing set and errors have been counted. The words with and without markings were counted separately. Result of the first experiment is summarized in the Table 3.

5.2 The Naïve Bayes Classifier Experiment

The second experiment has been performed to compare the proposed approach and show usefulness of the HMM representation. For this purpose the Viterbi search has been omitted and pure Bayesian approach has been used. In this case the probability of each possible correct word is calculated using only result of previous two decisions, only language model is used in the classification process. This algorithm can be described as a recursive sequence, where input is language model and inspected sentence containing words without markings and output is a corrected sentence:

1. Take the first word with unknown history and for each possible correction find the most probable one according to the language model.
2. Take the second word and previous decision as history and for each possible correction find the most probable one.
3. Continue the process for each other word in the sentence.

The same training and testing set has been used. Results are summarized in the Table 4.

Table 4. The naïve bayes classifier experiment results

	Correct tokens	Incorrect tokens	% Incorrect from all
Words with markings	5 023 539	15 271	0,304
Words without markings	8 038 123	11 898	1,48
Words	13 061 662	27 169	2,08
Sentences	701 910	25 639	3.52

5.3 The Random Classification Experiment

The third experiment should compare previous methods of classification to random classification. In this case only list of possible corrections has been used and the correction has been selected randomly from the list of possible corrections for each word. The results in the Table 5 can be used for comparison the previous results.

Table 5. The random classifier experiment

	Correct tokens	Incorrect tokens	% Incorect from all
Words with markings	4 162 876	875 934	17,38
Words without markings	6 440 298	1 609 723	19,99
Words	10 603 174	2 485 657	18,99
Sentences	63 386	664 163	91,28

This experiment of random classification shows difficulty of the task of the automatic diacritics recovery for the Slovak language and importance of using statistical classification techniques. The comparison with the previous experiments tells us that even very simple method that selects the most probable correction according to the last decisions can bring significant improvement.

The experiments above show that the presented system is very accurate and can be used in real-world tasks. The next challenge is to extend the system to correct more types of errors – missing or exchanged letters. More possible errors will extend number of possible observations very much – the classification problem will be more difficult and the system will require more memory. The future research also should be focused on the utilization of the proposed system in our web-based training corpus preparation or in the processing of web discussions.

6 Conclusion

This approach can utilize human effort as much as possible and large amounts of text can be corrected in an unsupervised way. Alternatively, this approach can be used in a semi-automatic way, where the system autonomously proposes a correction and human operator can approve it. Decision then can be remembered and used in latter cases. As a result, probability of occurrence of OOV word is reduced and the well corrected training corpus should produce a better results.

This contribution is the first for the Slovak language and thus it can not be directly compared to other approaches. Still it can be used as a starting point for future research and it seems to be valuable for other languages. The presented results can be improved by better detection of the incorrect word and by improving the vocabulary. It also might be useful to try other classification techniques.

Acknowledgement. The research presented in this paper was supported by the Ministry of Education, Science, Research and Sport of the Slovak Republic under the research project VEGA 1/0386/12 (50 %) and Research and Development Operational Program funded by the ERDF under the project ITMS-26220220141 (50 %).

References

1. Bahanshal, A., Al-Khalifa, H.: A first approach to the evaluation of arabic diacritization systems, pp. 155–158 (2012)
2. De Pauw, G., Wagacha, P.W., de Schryver, G.-M.: Automatic diacritic restoration for resource-scarce languages. In: Matoušek, V., Mautner, P. (eds.) TSD 2007. LNCS(LNAI), vol. 4629, pp. 170–179. Springer, Heidelberg (2007)
3. Grobbelaar, L., Kinyua, J.: A spell checker and corrector for the native South African language, South Sotho. In: Proceedings of 2009 Annual Conference of the Southern African Computer Lecturers' Association, SACLA 2009, Mpekweni Beach Resort, South Africa, pp. 50–59 (2009)
4. Grozea, C.: Experiments and results with diacritics restoration in Romanian. In: Sojka, P., Horák, A., Kopeček, I., Pala, K. (eds.) TSD 2012. LNCS, vol. 7499, pp. 199–206. Springer, Heidelberg (2012)
5. Hládek, D., Staš, J.: Text gathering and processing agent for language modeling corpus. In: Proceedings of the 12th International Conference on Research in Telecommunication Technologies, RTT, pp. 200–203 (2010)
6. Hládek, D., Staš, J.: Text gathering and processing agent for language modeling corpus. In: Proceedings of 12th International Conference on Research in Telecommunication Technologies, RTT 2010, Veľké Losiny, Czech Republic, pp. 137–140 (2010)
7. Hládek, D., Staš, J., Juhár, J.: Dagger: the Slovak morphological classifier, pp. 195–198 (2012)
8. Jayalatharachchi, E., Wasala, A., Weerasinghe, R.: Data-driven spell checking: the synergy of two algorithms for spelling error detection and correction. In: 2012 International Conference on Advances in ICT for Emerging Regions (ICTer), pp. 7–13. IEEE (2012)
9. Krajči, S., Mati, M., Novotný, R.: Morphonary: a Slovak language dictionary, tools for acquisition, organisation and presenting of information and knowledge. Návrat, P., et al. (eds.) Informatics and Information Technologies, pp. 162–165 (2006)
10. Kukich, K.: Techniques for automatically correcting words in text. ACM Comput. Surv. **24**(4), 377–439 (1992)
11. Li, Y., Duan, H., Zhai, C.: A generalized hidden Markov model with discriminative training for query spelling correction, pp. 611–620 (2012)

12. Lund, W., Ringger, E.: Error correction with in-domain training across multiple OCR system outputs, pp. 658–662 (2011)
13. Mihalcea, R.F.: Diacritics restoration: learning from letters versus learning from words. In: Gelbukh, A. (ed.) CICLing 2002. LNCS, vol. 2276, pp. 339–348. Springer, Heidelberg (2002)
14. Nguyen, K.-H., Ock, C.-Y.: Diacritics restoration in Vietnamese: letter based vs. syllable based model. In: Zhang, B.-T., Orgun, M.A. (eds.) PRICAI 2010. LNCS(LNAI), vol. 6230, pp. 631–636. Springer, Heidelberg (2010)
15. Rashwan, M., Al-Badrashiny, M., Attia, M., Abdou, S., Rafea, A.: A stochastic arabic diacritizer based on a hybrid of factorized and unfactorized textual features. IEEE Trans. Audio Speech Lang. Process. **19**(1), 166–175 (2011)
16. Rodphon, M., Siriboon, K., Kruatrachue, B.: Thai OCR error correction using token passing algorithm. In: 2001 IEEE Pacific Rim Conference on Communications, Computers and Signal Processing, 2001, PACRIM, vol. 2, pp. 599–602. IEEE (2001)
17. Rusko, M., et al.: Slovak automatic dictation system for judicial domain. In: Vetulani, Z., Mariani, J. (eds.) LTC 2011. LNCS(LNAI), vol. 8387, pp. 16–27. Springer, Heidelberg (2014)
18. Sirts, K.: Noisy-channel spelling correction models for Estonian learner language corpus lemmatisation. In: Proceedings of the 5th International Conference Human Language Technologies - The Baltic Perspective, HLT 2012, Tartu, Estonia, pp. 213–220 (2012)
19. Staš, J., Hládek, D., Juhár, J.: Language model adaptation for Slovak LVCSR. In: Proceedings of the International Conference on AEI, pp. 101–106 (2010)
20. Staš, J., Hládek, D., Pleva, M., Juhár, J.: Slovak language model from internet text data. In: Esposito, A., Esposito, A.M., Martone, R., Müller, V.C., Scarpetta, G. (eds.) COST 2010. LNCS, vol. 6456, pp. 340–346. Springer, Heidelberg (2011)
21. Tufiş, D., Ceauşu, A.: Diacritics restoration in Romanian texts. In: A Common Natural Language Processing Paradigm for Balkan Languages, pp. 49–55 (2007)
22. Zhou, Y., Jing, S., Huang, G., Liu, S., Zhang, Y.: A correcting model based on tribayes for real-word errors in English essays. In: 2012 Fifth International Symposium on Computational Intelligence and Design (ISCID), vol. 1, pp. 407–410. IEEE (2012)
23. Zitouni, I., Sarikaya, R.: Arabic diacritic restoration approach based on maximum entropy models. Comput. Speech Lang. **23**(3), 257–276 (2009)

Temporal and Lexical Context of Diachronic Text Documents for Automatic Out-Of-Vocabulary Proper Name Retrieval

Irina Illina[1](✉), Dominique Fohr[1], Georges Linarès[2],
and Imane Nkairi[1]

[1] MultiSpeech Team, LORIA-INRIA, 54602 Villers-les-Nancy, France
illina@loria.fr
[2] LIA – University of Avignon, 84911 Avignon, France

Abstract. Proper name recognition is a challenging task in information retrieval from large audio/video databases. Proper names are semantically rich and are usually key to understanding the information contained in a document. Our work focuses on increasing the vocabulary coverage of a speech transcription system by automatically retrieving proper names from contemporary diachronic text documents. We proposed methods that dynamically augment the automatic speech recognition system vocabulary using lexical and temporal features in diachronic documents. We also studied different metrics for proper name selection in order to limit the vocabulary augmentation and therefore the impact on the ASR performances. Recognition results show a significant reduction of the proper name error rate using an augmented vocabulary.

Keywords: Speech recognition · Out-of-vocabulary words · Proper names · Vocabulary augmentation

1 Introduction

The technologies involved in information retrieval from large audio/video databases are often based on the analysis of large, but closed corpora. The effectiveness of these approaches is now acknowledged, but they nevertheless have major flaws, particularly for those which concern new words and proper names. In our work, we are particularly interested in *Automatic Speech Recognition* (ASR) applications.

Large vocabulary ASR systems are faced with the problem of *out-of-vocabulary* (OOV) words. This is especially true in new domains where named entities are frequently unexpected. OOV words are words which are in the input speech signal but not in the ASR system vocabulary. In this case, the ASR system fails to transcribe the OOV words and replaces them with one or several in-vocabulary words, impacting the transcript intelligibility and introducing the recognition errors.

Proper Name (PN) recognition is a complex task, because PNs are constantly evolving and no vocabulary will ever contain all existing PNs: for example, PNs represent about 10 % of words of English and French newspaper articles and they are more important than other words in a text to characterize its content [7]. Bechet and

© Springer International Publishing Switzerland 2016
Z. Vetulani et al. (Eds.): LTC 2013, LNAI 9561, pp. 41–54, 2016.
DOI: 10.1007/978-3-319-43808-5_4

Yvon [2] showed that 72 % of OOV words in a 265K-words lexicon are potentially PNs.

Increasing the size of ASR vocabulary is a strategy to overcome the problems of OOV words. For this purpose, the Internet is a good source of information. Bertoldi and Federico [3] proposed a methodology for dynamically extending the ASR vocabulary by selecting new words daily from contemporary news available on the Internet: the most recently used new words and the most frequently used new words were added to the vocabulary. Access to large archives, as recently proposed by some institutions, can also be used for new word selection [1].

Different strategies for new word selection and vocabulary increasing were proposed recently. Oger *et al.* [13] proposed and compared local approaches: using the local context of the OOV words, they build efficient requests for submitting it to a web search engine. The retrieved documents are used to find the targeted OOV words. Bigot *et al.* [4] assumed that a person name is a latent variable produced by the lexical context it appears in, i.e. the sequence of words around the person name and that a spoken name could be derived from ASR outputs even if it has not been proposed by the speech recognition system.

Our work uses context modeling to capture the lexical information surrounding PNs so as to retrieve OOV proper names and increase the ASR vocabulary size. We focus on exploiting the lexical context based on *temporal* information from *diachronic documents* (documents that evolve through time): we assume that the time is an important feature for capturing name-to-context dependencies. Compared to approaches of Bigot *et al.* [4] and Oger *et al.* [13], we also use the proper name context notion. However, our approaches focus on exploiting the documents' temporality using diachronic documents. Our assumption is that PNs are often related to an event that emerges in a specific time period in diachronic documents and evolve through time. For a given date, the same PNs would occur in documents that belong to the same period. Temporal context has been proposed before by Federico and Bertoldi [3] to cope with language and topic changes, typical to new domains, and by Parada *et al.* [14] for predict OOV in recognition outputs. Compared to these works, our work extends vocabulary using shorter and more precise time periods to reduce the excessive vocabulary growth. We are seeking a good trade-off between the lexical coverage and the increase of vocabulary size that can lead to dramatically increasing the resources required by an ASR system.

Moreover, the approaches presented in [3, 14] are a priori approaches that increase the lexicon before the speech recognition of test documents and are based on the dates of documents. This type of techniques has the disadvantage of a very large increase of the lexicon, which ignores the context of appearance of missing words in the documents to recognize. Our proposal uses a first pass of decoding to extract information relating to the lexical context of OOV words, which should lead to more accurate model of the context of OOV words and avoid excessive increase of vocabulary size.

This paper is organized as follows. The next section of this paper provides the proposed methodology for new PN retrieval from diachronic documents. Sect. 3 describes preliminary experiments and results. The discussion and conclusion are presented in the last section.

2 Methodology

Our general idea consists in using lexical and temporal context of diachronic documents to derive OOV proper names automatically from diachronic documents. We assume that missing proper names can be automatically found in contemporary documents, that is to say corresponding to the same time period as the document we want to transcribe. We hypothesize that proper names evolve through time, and that for a given date, the same proper names would occur in documents that belong to the same period. Our assumption is that the linguistic context might contain relevant OOV proper names or to allow to add some specific information about the missing proper names.

We propose to use text documents from the diachronic corpus that are contemporaneous with each *test* document. We want to build a locally augmented vocabulary. So, we have a test audio document (to be transcribed) which contains OOV words, and we have a diachronic text corpus, used to retrieve OOV proper names. An augmented vocabulary is built for each test document.

We assume that, for a certain date, if proper names co-occur in diachronic documents, it is very likely that they co-occur in the test document corresponding to the same time period. These co-occurring PNs might contain the targeted OOV words. The idea is to exploit the relationship between PNs for a better lexical enrichment.

To reduce the OOV proper name rate, we suggest building a PN vocabulary that will be added to the large vocabulary of our ASR system. In this article, different PN selection strategies will be proposed to build this proper name vocabulary:

- **Baseline method:** Selecting the diachronic documents only using a time period corresponding to the test document.
- **Local-window-based method** same strategy as the baseline method but a co-occurrence criterion is added to exploit the relationship between proper names for a given period of time.
- **Mutual-information-based method** same strategy as the baseline method but mutual information metric is used to better choose OOV proper names.
- **Cosine-similarity-based method** same strategy as the baseline method but the documents are represented by word vector models.

In all proposed methods, documents of the diachronic corpus have been processed by removing punctuation marks and by turning texts to lower case, like in ASR outputs.

2.1 Baseline Method

This method consists in extracting a list (collection) of all the OOV proper names occurring in a diachronic corpus, using a time period corresponding to the test document. Proper names are extracted from diachronic corpus using *Treetagger*, a tool for annotating text with part-of-speech and lemma information [15]. Only the new proper names (compared to standard vocabulary of our recognition system) are kept. Then, our vocabulary is augmented with the collection of extracted OOV proper names.

Augmented lexicon is built for each test file and for each time period. This period can be, for example, a day, a week or a month. The OOV PN pronunciations are generated using a phonetic dictionary or a grapheme-to-phoneme tool [10].

This method will result in recalling a large number of OOV proper names from the diachronic corpus. Therefore, we consider this method as our baseline. The problem of this approach is if the diachronic corpus is large, we can have a bad tradeoff between the lexical coverage and the increase of lexicon size. Moreover, only temporal information about document to transcribe is used. In the methods, presented in the following, the lexical context of PN will be taken into account to better select OOV proper names.

2.2   Local-Window-Based Method

To have a better tradeoff between the lexical coverage and the increase of lexicon size, we will use a local lexical context to filter the selected PNs.

We assume that a context is a sequence of $(2N+1)$ words centered on one proper name. Each PN can have as many contexts as occurrences.

In this method, the goal is to use the in-vocabulary proper names of the test document as an anchor to collect linked new proper names from the diachronic corpus. The OOV proper names that we need to find might be among the collected names. This method consists of several steps:

(A) In-vocabulary PN Extraction from Each Test Document: For each test document from the test corpus, we perform an automatic speech recognition with our standard vocabulary. From obtained test file transcription (that can contain some recognition errors) and we extract all PNs (in-vocabulary PNs).

(B) Context Extraction from Diachronic Documents: After extracting the list of the in-vocabulary proper names from the test document transcription, we can start extracting their "contexts" in the diachronic set. Only documents that correspond to the same time period as the test document are considered. In this method, a context refers to a window of $(2N+1)$ words centred on one proper name. We tag all diachronic documents that belong to the same time period as our test document. Words that have been tagged as proper names by *Treetagger* are kept, and all the others are replaced by "X". In this step, the substitution with "X" aims to save the absolute positions of the words composing the context. We go through all tagged contemporary documents from the diachronic corpus and we extract all contexts corresponding to all occurrences of in-vocabulary PNs of the test document: in the $(2N+1)$ window centred on in-vocabulary proper name, we select all words that are not labelled as "X" and that are new proper names (that are not already in our vocabulary). The idea behind using a centered window is that the short-term local context may contain missing proper names.

(C) Vocabulary Augmentation: From the extracted new PNs obtained in step B, we keep only the new PNs whose number of occurrences is greater than a given threshold.

Then we add them to our vocabulary. Their pronunciations are generated using a phonetic dictionary or an automatic phonetic transcription tool.

Using this methodology, we expect to extract a reduced list (compared to the baseline) of all the potentially missing PNs.

2.3 Mutual-Information-Based Method

In order to reduce the vocabulary growth, we propose to add a metric to our methodology: the *mutual information* (MI) [5]. The MI-based method consists in computing the mutual information between the in-vocabulary PNs found in the test document and other PNs that have appeared in contemporary documents from the diachronic set. If two PNs have high mutual information, it would increase the probability that they occur together in the test document.

In probability theory and information theory, the mutual information of two random variables is a quantity that measures the mutual dependence of the two random variables. Formally, the mutual information of two discrete random variables X and Y can be defined as:

$$I(X;Y) = \sum \sum p(x,y)\log\left(\frac{p(x,y)}{p(x)p(y)}\right) \tag{1}$$

In our case, X and Y represent proper names and $x = 1$ if it is present in the document and $x = 0$ otherwise. For example:

$$P(x=1, y=1) = \frac{number\ of\ documents\ containing\ x\ and\ y}{total\ number\ of\ documents} \tag{2}$$

The higher the probability of the co-occurrence of two proper names in the diachronic corpus, the higher the probability of their co-occurrence in a test document.

Finally we compute the mutual information between all the combinations of the variable X (X is the in-vocabulary PN extracted from the test document) and the variable Y (Y is the OOV proper name extracted from the contemporary documents from the diachronic corpus).

Compared to local-window-based method, only the step B is modified.

(B) Context Extraction from Diachronic Documents: After extracting the list of the in-vocabulary proper names from the test document transcription, we can start extracting their "contexts" in the diachronic set. Only documents that correspond to the same time period as the test document are considered. The list of in-vocabulary words from test document transcriptions is extracted like in local-window-based method. As previously, we tag all diachronic documents that belong to the same time period as our test document. Words that have been tagged as proper names by *Treetagger* are kept. Finally, the mutual information between each word from in-vocabulary PN list and each extracted new PNs from diachronic document is calculated. If two PNs have high mutual information, this increases the probability that they both appear in the document to transcribe.

Using this methodology, we expect to extract a shortlist (compared to the reference method) potentially missing PNs.

2.4   Cosine-Similarity-Based Method

In this method we want to consider additional lexical information to model the context: we will use not only proper names (as in the previous methods) but also verbs, adjectives and nouns. These words are extracted using *Treetagger*. They are lemmatized because we are interested in the semantic information. The other words are removed.

In this method we propose to use the term vector model [16]. This model is an algebraic representation of the content of a text document in which the documents are generally represented by the word vectors. The proximity between the documents is often calculated using the cosine similarity. So we will represent diachronic documents and documents to transcribe as a word vectors and use the cosine similarity between vector models of these documents to extract relevant PNs.

We use the same steps as in the previous methods, with the following modifications:

(A) In-vocabulary PN Extraction from Each *Test* Document: As in the previous methods, each test document is transcribed using the speech recognition system and the standard vocabulary. Then, each document to be transcribed is shown by the histogram of occurrences of component words: vector of words (*bag of words*, BOW). As stated above, only the verbs, adjectives, proper names and common names are lemmatized and considered.

(B) Context Extraction from Diachronic Documents: Each selected (according to the time period) diachronic document is also represented by the BOW in the same way as above. Then, we build the list of new PNs by choosing from selected diachronic documents the words that have been labeled as "proper name" and which are not in the standard vocabulary. This list is built in the same manner as in the previous methods. For each PN of this list, we calculate a *PNvector*. For this, first of all, a common lexicon is built: it contains the list of words (verbs, adjectives, nouns and proper names) that appear at least once in the selected diachronic document or in the document to transcribe. Then, every BOW are projected on the common lexicon. Finally, the *PNvector* is calculated as the sum of the BOW of the selected diachronic documents in which these new PNs appear.

For each PN from this list, we calculate the cosine similarity between the BOW and its *PNvector* of the document to transcribe. The new OOV PNs whose cosine similarity is greater than a threshold are selected.

(C) Vocabulary Augmentation: This step is the same as step C of the local-window-based method.

Compared with previous methods, cosine method takes into account broader contextual information using not only proper names but also verbs, adjectives and nouns present in the selected diachronic documents and in the test document.

3 Experiments

3.1 Test Corpus

To validate the proposed methodology, we used as test corpus five audio documents extracted from the ESTER2 corpora [8] (see Table 1). The objective of the ESTER2 campaign was to assess the automatic transcription of broadcast news in French. The campaign targeted a wide variety of programs: news, debates, interviews, etc.

Table 1. Date of test documents.

Doc1	Doc2	Doc3	Doc4	Doc5
2007/12/20	2007/12/21	2008/01/17	2008/01/18	2008/01/24

Table 2 presents the occurrences of all PNs (in-vocabulary and out-of-vocabulary) in each test document with respect to our 97k ASR vocabulary. To artificially increase OOV rate, we have randomly removed 75 proper names occurring in the test set from our 97k ASR vocabulary. We call this vocabulary a *standard vocabulary*. Finally, the OOV proper name rate is about 1 % (404/38525).

Table 2. Proper name coverage in test documents.

	Number of diff. words	Number of occur.	In-vocab PNs	OOV PNs	OOV PN occur.
Doc1	1350	4099	86	44	93
Doc2	1446	4604	89	39	70
Doc3	1958	11803	43	25	63
Doc4	2107	10152	90	39	71
Doc5	1432	7867	48	27	107
All	–	38525	–	–	404

In this preliminary experiment (Table 2), in-vocabulary PN extraction is performed from manual transcription of test documents instead of automatic speech transcription. The goal of this preliminary study is to validate our proposed approaches.

3.2 Diachronic Corpus

As diachronic corpus, we have used the *Gigaword* corpora: *Agence France Presse* (AFP) and *Associated Press Worldstream* (APW). French Gigaword is an archive of newswire text data and the timespans of collections covered for each are as follows: for AFP May 1994 - Dec 2008, for APW Nov 1994 - Dec 2008. The choice of Gigaword and ESTER corpora was driven by the fact that one is contemporary to the other, their temporal granularity is the day and they have the same textual genre (journalistic) and domain (politics, sports, etc.).

Using *Treetagger*, we have extracted 45981 OOV PNs from 6 months of the diachronic corpus. From these OOV PNs, only 103 are present in the test corpus, which corresponds to 71 % of recall. It shows that it is necessary to filter this list of PNs to have a better tradeoff between the PN lexical coverage and the increase of lexicon size.

3.3   Transcription System

ANTS (Automatic News Transcription System) [9] used for these experiments is based on Context Dependent HMM phone models trained on 200 h broadcast news audio files. The recognition engine is Julius [12]. Using SRILM toolkit [17], the language model is estimated on text corpora of about 1800 million words. The corpus of texts comes from newspaper articles (*Le Monde*), broadcast transcriptions and data collected on the Internet. The language model is re-estimated for each augmented vocabulary.

The baseline phonetic lexicon contains 218k pronunciations for the 97k words.

4   Experimental Results

4.1   Baseline Results

We call **selected PNs** the new proper names that we were able to retrieve from diachronic documents using our methods. We call **retrieved OOV PNs** the OOV PNs that belong to the *selected PN* list and that are present in the test documents.

We build a specific augmented vocabulary for each test document, each chosen period and each method. The augmented vocabulary contains all words of standard vocabulary and the *selected PNs* given by the chosen method and corresponding to the chosen period. So, we need to estimate the language model (n-gram probabilities) for these retrieved OOV PNs. For this we have chosen to completely re-estimate the language model for each augmented vocabulary using the entire text corpus (see Sect. 3.3). The best way to incorporate the new PNs in the language model is beyond the scope of this paper.

Our results are presented in terms of *Recall* (%): number of retrieved OOV PN versus the number of OOV PNs contained in the document to transcribe. We place ourselves in the context of speech recognition. In this context, the fact that PN present in the document to recognize is not in the vocabulary of the recognition system will produce a significant error because the PN cannot be recognized. However, adding to the vocabulary of the recognition system a PN that is not present (pronounced) in the test file, will have little influence on the recognized sentence (if we add too many words, there may increase the confusion between words and thus cause errors). So, in our case, the recall is more important than precision. Thus, we will present the results in term of recall.

For the recognition experiments, *Word Error Rate* (WER) is given.

In order to investigate whether time is a significant feature, we studied 3 time intervals in the diachronic documents:

- 1 day: using the same day as the test document;
- 1 week: using 3 days before until 3 days after the test document date;
- 1 month: using the current month of the test document.

As we build an augmented vocabulary for each test file, the results presented in Table 3 are averaged over all test files. Table 3 shows that the use of diachronic documents whose date is closest to that of the test document (document to transcribe) allows greatly reduce the number of added new proper names while maintaining an attractive recall. For example, limiting the time interval to 1 month reduces the set of PN candidates to 13069 (Table 3) while still retrieving 67.6 % of the missing OOVs, compared to 45 981 candidates (6 months) for almost the same recall (67.6 %, cf. Sect. 3.2). Moving from a one month time period to one day, we reduced the number of selected PNs by a factor of 14 (13069/925) while the recall is reduced by a factor of 1.5. This result confirms the idea that the use of the temporal information reduces the list of selected new PN for augmented vocabulary while maintaining a good recall. In the rest of this article, we will study three time periods (one day, one week and one month).

Table 3. Coverage in test documents of retrieved OOV PNs. Average over all test files.

Time period	Selected PNs	Retrieved OOV PNs	Recall (%)
1 day	925	16	44.0
1 week	4305	21	58.6
1 month	13069	24	**67.6**

Table 4. Local-window-based results according to window size and time period.

Time period	Window size	Selected PNs	Retrieved OOV PNs	Recall (%)
1 day (occ > 0)	50	164.6	11.8	33.9
	100	253.4	13.2	37.9
1 week (occ > 1)	50	344.0	16.4	47.1
	100	596.4	17.4	50.0
1 month (occ > 2)	50	589.8	19.0	54.6
	100	1137.2	20.4	**58.6**

4.2 Local-Window-Based Results

Table 4 presents the results for the local-window-based method on the test corpus for the three studied time periods and for different window sizes. The threshold *occ* is used to keep only the selected PNs whose number of occurrences are greater than occ.

Compared to the baseline method, the local-window-based method reduces significantly the number of selected proper names and only slightly decreases the recall. For example, for a period of one day and window size of 100, the number of selected PNs is divided by 3.6 compared to baseline method, while the recall drops to 6 % (253.4 versus 925 and 37.9 % versus 44.0 %). For the period of one month, the filter allows to divide the number of selected PNs by 11, losing only 9 % of recall compared to the baseline method. This shows the effectiveness of the proposed local-window-based method.

We notice that we were not able to recall 68 % of the missing PNs as we did using the baseline. 58.6 % of recall is the maximal value that we obtain using this methodology.

4.3 Mutual-Information-Based Results

Table 5 shows the results for the method based on mutual information using different time periods and thresholds. Two PNs having a mutual information greater than this threshold will be added to selected PN list. The best recall is obtained using a time period of one week.

Table 5. Mutual-information-based results according to threshold and time period.

Time period	Threshold	Selected PNs	Retrieved OOV PNs	Recall (%)
1 day (occ > 0)	0.05	10.6	5.0	14.4
	0.01	295.0	12.8	36.8
	0.005	421.2	14.2	40.8
	0.001	531.2	15.4	44.25
1 week (occ > 1)	0.05	3.8	3.0	8.6
	0.01	50.8	8.8	25.3
	0.005	228.6	12.0	34.5
	0.001	947.8	18.4	**52.9**
1 month (occ > 2)	0.05	2.6	1.6	4.6
	0.01	21.2	7.2	20.7
	0.005	56.4	9.4	27.0
	0.001	806.4	17.2	49.4

As for local-window-based method, the use of the diachronic documents from one day period is sufficient to obtain a recall of over 30 %. For the recognition experiments (see Sect. 4.4) we will set the threshold to 0.001 for all time periods.

4.4 Cosine-Similarity-Based Results

The results for the method based on cosine similarity are shown in Table 6. In order to further reduce the number of selected PNs, we keep only the PNs whose number of occurrences is greater than a threshold depending on the time period.

Table 6. Cosine-similarity-based results according to threshold and time period.

Time period	Threshold	Selected PNs	Retrieved OOV PNs	Recall (%)
1 day (occ > 0)	0.025	813.4	15.4	44.3
	0.05	437.6	14.4	41.4
	0.075	131.4	11.2	32.2
	0.1	51.8	8.4	24.1
1 week (occ > 1)	0.025	1880.0	19.4	55.8
	0.05	1127.6	18.8	54.0
	0.075	431.6	17.0	48.9
	0.1	152.0	13.4	38.5
1 month (occ > 2)	0.025	3795.6	21.4	**61.5**
	0.05	2473.8	20.8	59.8
	0.075	1010.2	19.4	55.8
	0.1	334.4	17.0	48.9

As for the mutual-information-based method, considering only one day time period to retrieve new PNs seems unsatisfactory. The best compromise between the recall and the number of selected PNs is obtained for the period of one month and a threshold of 0.05 (59.8 % of recall).

4.5 Automatic Speech Recognition Results

For validating the proposed approaches, we performed the automatic transcription of the 5 test documents using an augmented lexicon generated by the three proposed methods.

We generate an augmented vocabulary for each test file, for each time period and for each PN selection method. To generate the pronunciations of added PNs, we use an automatic approach based on CRF (*Conditional Random Fields*). We chose this approach because it has shown very good results compared to the best approaches of the state-of-art [10]. The CRF [11] is a probabilistic model for labeling or segmentation of structured data such as sequences, trees or trellises. The CRF allows to take into account long-term relations, achieve a discriminating training and converge to a global optimum. Using this approach, we obtained a precision and recall of more than 98 % for phonetization of common names in French (*BDLex*) [10]. In the context of this article, we have trained our CRF with 12,000 phonetized proper names.

Table 7 presents the recognition results for five test documents using the local-window-based method for two time periods (one week and one month) and 100 for the window size. Compared to our standard lexicon, the augmented lexicon gives a significant decrease of the word error rate for a week period (confidence interval ± 0.4 %). We recall that the OOV rate of OOV PNs in the test corpus is about 1 % (cf. Sect. 3.1). So, the expected improvement will hardly exceed that rate.

The results for the mutual information method (threshold 0.001) are presented in Table 8. On average, the augmented lexicon reduces slightly the Word Error Rate.

Table 7. Word Error Rate (%) for local-window-based method according to time period (local window size 100).

	Standard lexicon	Augmented lexicon (local-window size 100)	
		1 week	1 month
Doc 1	19.7	17.7	17.6
Doc 2	20.9	19.9	20.1
Doc 3	28.3	28.2	28.7
Doc 4	24.5	23.9	24.5
Doc 5	36.5	36.0	36.6
All	27.1	**26.4**	26.9

Table 8. Word Error Rate (%) for mutual-information-based method according to time period (threshold 0.001)

	Standard lexicon	Augmented lexicon (MI threshold 0.001)	
		1 week	1 month
Doc 1	19.7	18.0	18.4
Doc 2	20.9	19.7	20.0
Doc 3	28.3	28.1	28.2
Doc 4	24.5	24.2	24.2
Doc 5	36.5	36.1	36.0
All	27.1	**26.6**	26.7

The results for the cosine-similarity-based method (threshold 0.025 for a week and 0.05 for a month) are presented in Table 9. For both time periods, the WER is significantly reduced.

For the three methods, performance depends on the test document. For documents 1 and 2, regardless the time period used to create the augmented lexicon, the word error rate improvement is significant. But for document 3, no improvement or degradation is observed. This can be due to the fact that the OOV proper names in the test document are not observed in the corresponding diachronic documents. The detailed results show that the performance in terms of WER depends on the type of documents: for some broadcast programs we do not observe any improvement (for example, a debate on nuclear), for others a strong improvement is reached (news).

Finally, the three proposed methods give about the same performance.

Table 9. Word Error Rate (%) for cosine-similarity-based method according to time period.

	Standard lexicon	Augmented lexicon	
		1 week thr 0.025 occ > 1	1 month thr 0.05 occ > 2
Doc 1	19.7	18.0	18.2
Doc 2	20.9	19.5	19.4
Doc 3	28.3	27.9	28.0
Doc 4	24.5	23.8	23.7
Doc 5	36.5	35.8	35.8
All	27.1	**26.4**	**26.4**

If we consider only the recognition of proper names, using the standard lexicon, the *Proper Name Error Rate* (PNER) is 47.7 %. However, using augmented lexicon obtained by cos method (one month time period), PNER dropped to 37.4 %. Therefore, we observe a huge decrease of PNER, which shows the effectiveness of our proposed methods.

5 Conclusion and Discussion

This article has focused on the problem of out-of-vocabulary proper name retrieval for vocabulary extension using diachronic text documents (which change over time). This work is performed in the framework of automatic speech recognition. We investigated methods that augment the vocabulary with new proper names. We propose to use the lexical and temporal features. The idea is to use in-vocabulary proper names as an anchor to collect new linked proper names from the diachronic corpus. Our context model is based on the co-occurrences, mutual information and cosine similarity.

Experiments have been conducted on broadcast news audio documents (ESTER2 corpus) using AFP and AWP text data as a diachronic corpus. The results validate the hypothesis that exploiting time and the lexical context could help to retrieve the missing proper names without excessive growth of the vocabulary size. The recognition results show a significant reduction of the word error rate using the augmented vocabulary and a huge reduction of the proper name error rate.

An interesting perspective could be to exploit "semantic" information contained in the test document: when a precise date is recognized in a test document, the diachronic document around this date could be used to bring new proper names. Our future work will also focus on investigating the use of several Internet sources (Wiki, texts, videos, etc.).

Acknowledgements. The authors would like to thank the ANR *ContNomina* SIMI-2 of the French National Research Agency (ANR) for funding.

References

1. Allauzen, A., Gauvain, J.-L.: Diachronic vocabulary adaptation for broadcast news transcription. In: Proceedings of Interspeech (2005)
2. Bechet, F., Yvon, F.: Les Noms Propres en Traitement Automatique de la Parole. In: Revue Traitement Automatique des Langues, vol. 41(3), pp. 672–708 (2000)
3. Bertoldi, N., Federico, M.: Lexicon adaptation for broadcast news transcription. In: Adaptation 2001, pp. 187–190 (2001)
4. Bigot, B., Senay, G., Linares, G., Fredouille, C., Dufour, R.: Person name recognition in ASR outputs using continous context models. In: Proceedings of ICASSP (2013)
5. Church, K., Hanks, P.: Word association norms, mutual information, and lexicography. In: Proceedings of the 27th Annual Meeting of the Association for Computational Linguistics (1989)
6. Federico, M., Bertoldi, N.: Broadcast news LM adaptation using contemporary texts. In: Proceedings of Interspeech, pp. 239–242 (2001)
7. Friburger, N., Maurel, D.: Textual similarity based on proper names. In: Proceedings of the Workshop Mathematical/Formal Methods in Information Retrieval, pp. 155–167 (2002)
8. Galliano, S., Geoffrois, E., Mostefa, D., Choukri, K., Bonastre, J.-F., Gravier, G.: The ESTER Phase II evaluation campaign for the rich transcription of french broadcast news. In: Proceedings of Interspeech (2005)
9. Illina I., Fohr, D., Mella, O., Cerisara, C.: The automatic news transcription system: ANTS, some real time experiments. In: Proceedings of ICSLP (2004)
10. Illina I., Fohr D., Jouvet, D.: Grapheme-to-Phoneme conversion using conditional random fields. In: Proceedings of Interspeech (2011)
11. Lafferty, J., McCallum, A., Pereira, F.: Conditional random fields: probabilistic models for segmenting and labeling sequence data. In: Proceedings of International Conference on Machine Learning, pp. 282–289 (2001)
12. Lee, A., Kawahara, T.: Recent development of open-source speech recognition engine Julius. In: Asia-Pacific Signal and Information Processing Association Annual Summit and Conference APSIPA ASC (2009)
13. Oger, S., Linarès, G., Béchet, F.: Local methods for on-demand out-of-vocabulary word retrieval. In: Proceedings of the Language Resources and Evaluation Conference LREC (2008)
14. Parada, C., Dredze, M., Filimonov, F., Jelinek, F.: Contextual information improves OOV Detection in Speech. In: Proceedings of NAACL (2010)
15. Schmid, H.: Probabilistic part-of-speech tagging using decision trees. In: Proceedings of ICNMLP (1994)
16. Singhal, A.: Modern information retrieval: a brief overview. Bull. IEEE Comput. Soc. Tech. Committee Data Eng. 24(4), 35–43 (2001)
17. Stolcke, A.: SRILM - an extensible language modeling toolkit. In: Proceedings of ICSLP (2002)

Advances in the Slovak Judicial Domain Dictation System

Milan Rusko[1], Jozef Juhár[2], Marian Trnka[1], Ján Staš[2], Sakhia Darjaa[1], Daniel Hládek[2], Róbert Sabo[1], Matúš Pleva[2(✉)], Marian Ritomský[1], and Stanislav Ondáš[2]

[1] Institute of Informatics, Slovak Academy of Sciences,
Dúbravská cesta 9, 845 07 Bratislava, Slovakia
{milan.rusko,marian.trnka,utrrsach,robert.sabo,
marian.ritomsky}@savba.sk

[2] Faculty of Electrical Engineering and Informatics, Department of Electronics and Multimedia Communications, Technical University of Košice, Park Komenského 13, 042 00 Košice, Slovakia
{jozef.juhar,jan.stas,daniel.hladek,matus.pleva,
stanislav.ondas}@tuke.sk
http://ui.sav.sk/speech/, http://kemt.fei.tuke.sk/en/

Abstract. This paper describes evaluation and recent advances in application of speech dictation system for the judicial domain. The dictation system incorporates Slovak speech recognition and uses a plugin for widely used office suite. It was introduced recently after preliminary user evaluation in the Slovak courts. The system was improved significantly using new acoustic databases for evaluation and acoustic modeling when compared to the previous version. The speaker adaptation procedure and gender dependent models significantly improve the overall accuracy below 5 % WER for domain specific test set. The language resources were extended and the language modeling techniques were improved as it is described in the paper. An end-user questionnaire about the user interface was evaluated and new functionalities were introduced. According to the available feedback, it can be concluded that the dictation system is able to speed up the court proceedings significantly for each user willing to cooperate with new technologies.

Keywords: Continuous speech recognition · Slovak language · Judicial domain · Language modeling · User interface

1 Introduction

Dictation systems for major languages are available on the market and also the huge corporations provide a free dictation applications using application interface from branded solutions for free [1]. The only disadvantage of these systems is that the applications need stable high speed internet connection, all audio data are transferred to the server based recognizer controlled by the corporation and the user cannot control the language or acoustic model – so no acoustic adaptation or domain specific tasks are possible.

Also, the low resource languages suffer from the lack of speech and language databases, and these are the primary reasons for the absence of a dictation system to date.

© Springer International Publishing Switzerland 2016
Z. Vetulani et al. (Eds.): LTC 2013, LNAI 9561, pp. 55–67, 2016.
DOI: 10.1007/978-3-319-43808-5_5

In this paper the design, development, evaluation and recent advances in the dictation system for the judicial domain named APD ("Automatický Prepis Diktátu" – Automatic Transcription of Dictation) are described. This domain was selected because of market demand, and it presents a very complex problem to solve, because the court proceedings and the courtroom acoustic environment are one of the most challenging from the research point of view [2].

Also during the implementation phase the feedback from end-users provides researchers a very important practical point of view and new research ideas for future work described below.

The paper is organized as follows: Sect. 2 introduces the used source data, Sect. 3 describes the building of the APD system and new features introduced recently, Sect. 4 presents the evaluation of the dictation system, Sect. 5 describes the user opinion summarized from collected questionnaires, Sect. 6 presents the future work and Sect. 7 closes the paper with the discussion.

2   Source Data

2.1   Speech Audio Databases

Several speech audio databases were used for training of acoustic models and evaluation the speech recognition performance during the development of the APD system:

- **The APD database** is gender-balanced and contains 250 h of recordings (mostly read speech) from 250 speakers. It consists of two parts: APD1 and APD2 databases. APD1 contains 120 h of real judicial readings from the court with personal data changed, recorded in sound studio conditions. APD2 contains 130 h of read phonetically rich sentences, newspaper articles and spelled items. This database was recorded in offices and conference rooms [3]. A part (5.8 h, 3,426 speech utterances: 1,476 female and 1,949 male) of the APD2 database was excluded from training process for testing and evaluation purposes of the final reference testing setup of the APD system;
- **The extended Parliament database** (PARext) contains 136 h of recordings ("PAR" – 96 h, "PAR3" – 40 h) realized in the main conference hall of the National Council of the Slovak Republic using conference "goose neck" microphones [4]. In accordance with the gender structure of the Slovak Parliament it has 90 % male speakers;
- **The mixture of BN** (broadcast news) **databases** consist of the part of the Slovak Cost278 BN Database [5], TUKE-BNews-SK database [6, 7] with 265 h of material and 186 h of clean transcribed speech (the rest are fillers or music) and BA BN part with 36 h of broadcast news TV and radio shows.

The acoustic databases were manually annotated by our team of trained annotators using the Transcriber annotation tool [8], slightly adapted to our needs and all recordings were converted to 16 kHz and 16 bit PCM mono format.

2.2 Text Corpora

The Slovak language is morphologically rich and uses a very large vocabulary. The amount of text, required to create a proper training corpus for a statistical modeling of the Slovak language is significantly larger than for English. The second problem is that there are only a small amount of language resources is commercially available in the form of corpus, ready for the statistical modeling. The existing research corpora are maintained by the Slovak National Corpus [9], but the corpora are publicly available only in the form of statistics of n-grams. However, these text data are not sufficient for regular statistical modeling. As a consequence, a web-based text data have to be gathered and processed to obtain suitable text corpora. A custom web-crawling, gathering and processing agent for collecting a large amount of text data have been created [10]. Web-crawling agent explores the Slovak web-sites and content of each web-page is analyzed and stored in a relational database. The text corpora, systematically collected during the last six years, consist of:

- **Web-based corpus** – was collected by crawling whole web-pages from various of Slovak web-sites;
- **Corpus of daily news** – is a collection of articles gathered from the most popular Slovak news web-sites;
- **Corpus of legal texts** – was obtained from the Ministry of Justice of the Slovak Republic;
- **Corpus of contemporary blogs** – consists of web-extracted blog texts from the main news web-sites;
- **Corpus of the Slovak parliament proceedings** – was obtained from the Joint Czech and Slovak Digital Parliamentary Library and consists of a collection of stenographic reports from the meetings in the main conference hall of the National Council of the Slovak Republic and official press releases realized between 2010 and 2013 years;
- **Speech transcripts** – a special portion of the text data obtained from annotations of speech audio databases.

The next step in the text processing includes word tokenization, sentence boundary detection, automatic text correction, orthographic transcription and morphological

Table 1. Statistics on text corpora

Text corpus	# sentences	# tokens
Web-based corpus	50,694,708	748,854,697
Corpus of daily news	36,326,920	554,593,113
Corpus of legal texts	18,524,094	565,140,401
Corpus of fiction texts	8,039,739	101,234,475
Corpus of contemporary blogs	4,071,165	55,711,674
Corpus of the Slovak parliament proceedings	878,955	20,837,816
Speech transcripts	485,800	4,434,217
Development data set	1,782,333	55,163,941
Together	**120,803,714**	**2,105,970,334**

analysis. Several types of tokens were transcribed into the spoken form, such as numerals, abbreviations and punctuation. The resulting training corpus was filtered and the most frequent and erroneous sentences were removed from the training. The prepared training corpus for statistical modeling of the Slovak language [11] is summarized in Table 1.

2.3   Vocabulary

The vocabulary was created from the most frequent words occurring in the collected text corpora. For selection of more specific words from judicial domain, the maximum likelihood approach [11, 12] has been used. The vocabulary was later extended with the classes of the most common proper nouns and geographical names in the Slovak Republic. We have also proposed an automatic tool for generation of inflected word forms for names, surnames and geographical named entities. The final vocabulary contains 384k unique word forms, 97k proper nouns and geographical names included in 22 grammatically dependent classes and 5 noise events which appear in dictionary as transparent words. All words were manually checked and corrected. The dictionary after phonetic transcription contains 543k pronunciation variants together.

3   Building the APD System

3.1   Acoustic Modeling

We have used a triphone mapped HMM system described in detail in [13]. The process of building a triphone mapped HMM system was developed using typical REFREC [14] and MASPER procedure [15], where HMM states tying algorithm was replaced by triphone mapping procedure. We considered these adaptation methods and their combinations for speaker adaptation: MLLR, semi-tied covariance matrices, HLDA, and CMLLR. Finally we have chosen MLLR as the most suitable adaptation method for implementation [16, 17]. In APD LVCSR system, the supervised MLLR adaptation was implemented while using the predetermined regression classes [18].

3.2   Language Modeling

The trigram language models were created using the SRI Language Modeling Toolkit [19], restricted by the vocabulary described in the previous section and smoothed by the Witten-Bell back-off algorithm. All trigram models have been trained on the preprocessed and classified text corpora of more than 2.1 billion of tokens contained in 120 million of Slovak sentences (see Sect. 2.2). The latent Dirichlet allocation [20] has been used for dividing whole text corpus into 5 semantically similar subsets, ready for the training LMs.

Resulting LM was composed from 7 independent LMs generated from the classified text corpora (5 subsets), speech transcripts and statistics of n-grams obtained from Slovak National Corpus. Trigram models were combined to the final model using linear interpolation, performed just between two LMs, continuing until all models were combined. LMs were adapted to the judicial domain by computing interpolation weights based on minimization of language model perplexity on the development data using our proposed algorithm [21, 22]. Perplexity (PPL) is a standard intrinsic measure for evaluating quality of language model which is defined as the reciprocal value of the geometric probability assigned by the LM to each word in the evaluated (development) data and is related to cross-entropy.

Finally, the resulting trigram models were pruned using the relative entropy-based algorithm [23] in order to use it in the real-time application of the Slovak LVCSR. In this article we have compared six language models. The differences between these models are summarized in the Table 2.

Table 2. The differences in statistical modeling of the Slovak language

	12/2011	07/2012	12/2012	04/2013	05/2013	10/2014
# pronunciation variants	475,156	475,357	474,456	474,453	474,453	543,086
# unique word forms	326,299	326,295	325,555	325,555	325,555	384,108
# words under classes	97,471	97,680	97,678	97,678	97,678	97,678
# classes of words	20	22	22	22	22	22
# transparent words	4	5	5	5	5	5
vocabulary extension	×	×	×	×	–	×
classes extension	×	×	–	–	–	–
adding new text data	×	–	–	×	–	×
additional text processing	×	–	×	×	×	×
filled pause modeling	–	×	×	×	×	×
new text categorization	×	–	–	–	×	×

3.3 User Interface

The text output of the recognizer is sent to text post-processing. Some of the post-processing functions are configurable in the user interface. The user interface is that of a classical dictation system. After launching the program, the models are loaded and the text editor (Microsoft Word) is opened. The dictation program is represented by a tiny window with the start/stop and menu buttons as you can see on the Fig. 1. There is also a sound level meter placed in line with the buttons with included button for start/stop recording of input speech.

Main Menu. The main menu contains user profiles, recording options, transcription options, audio setup, program settings, user dictionary, speed setup, help, and "about the program" submenus. The user profiles submenu gives an opportunity to create a new user profile (in addition to the general "female" and "male" profiles that are available with the installation). The procedure of creating a new profile consists of an automatic microphone sensitivity setup procedure and reading of 91 sentences for the acoustic model adaptation. The new profile keeps information about the new user program and audio settings, user dictionary, acoustic model, etc.

Fig. 1. Slovak graphical user interface of recent APD v1.0 system

The second item in the menu enables to set recording capability. APD system enables to record incoming speech during the dictation and to store the recording for the next usage. The following important function enables to transcribe previously made recordings to the text form (offline transcription as you can see on the Fig. 2). The system enables to "rewrite" audio files in several formats (WAV, MP3, etc.) and enables to set output format (text files, word documents, or html files).

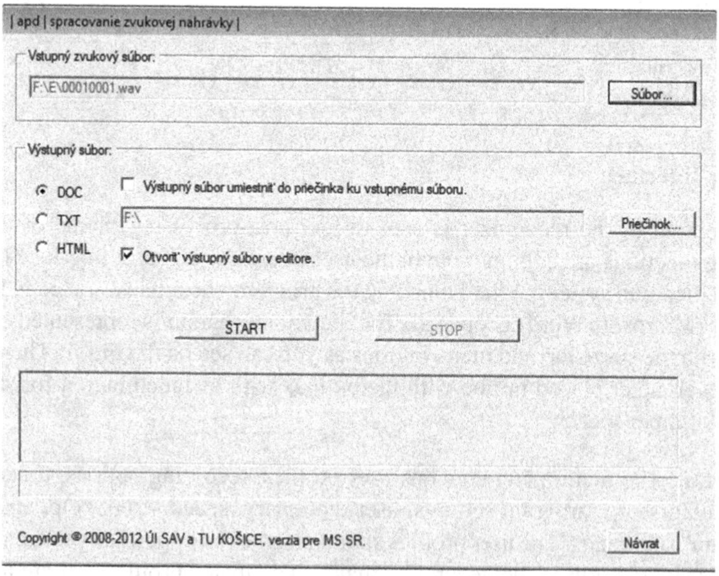

Fig. 2. Offline transcription menu of the APD v1.0 system

The audio setup submenu opens the audio devices settings from the control panel. The program settings submenu makes it possible to:

- create user defined corrections/substitutions (abbreviations, symbols, foreign words, named entities with capital letters, etc.);
- define voice commands;
- insert user MS Word files using voice command.

The user dictionary submenu allows the user to add and remove items in the dictionary. The words are inserted in the orthographic form and the pronunciation is generated automatically.

The speed setup submenu allows the user to choose the best compromise between the speed of recognition and its accuracy. The help submenu shows the list of basic commands and some miscellaneous functions of the program.

Spelling Mode. The dictation program has a special mode for spelling. The characters are entered using the Slovak spelling alphabet. The numerals, roman numerals and punctuation symbols can be inserted in this mode as well. This mode uses its own acoustic and language models. Large amount (approx. 60k words) of Slovak proper nouns is covered by the general language model, but the user can also switch to a special mode for proper names, that have a special, enriched "name vocabulary" (approx. 140k words) and a special language model.

Click-and-Play. Despite APD's high accuracy, the automatic transcripts contain multiple problems. These could either result from mistakes in transcription but also from unclear segments of the original recording.

There is a strong motivation of the court to have transcripts reflecting the original audio as closely as possible. Specifically, the experience with the APD system in courts shows that judge assistants are often responsible for checking the transcriptions and correcting the errors. This task would be greatly simplified if the user could have a direct access to the audio recording around a particular point in the transcribed text.

To facilitate further this type of post-processing of the transcripts, we designed a new Click-and-Play feature in the last APD development system version. This feature provides a virtual connection between the transcribed text of the document and the original audio recording, on which the automatic speech recognition was performed.

To implement this feature, several potentially problematic situations have to be considered. Firstly, before this final post-processing, the transcripts might have been modified multiple times. For example, the judge, or any other authorized person, can enter text not present in the audio. Because APD uses MS Word, some automatic text corrections might be applied.

Secondly, the resulting document might correspond to two separate audio files, or conversely, one audio file might appear in two separate documents; for example when the judge works on parallel document in MS Word during one recording session. These problematic situations results in tracking difficulties, because APD system does not have total control over the dictation process and also cannot use MS Word for tracking all modifications. In these situations, the current text does not correspond to the original transcription and the index of timestamps is not usable.

To solve this complex problem and enable the target functionality, a sophisticated searching mechanism was implemented and tested. The algorithm first searches for the exact match of the text in the vicinity of the clicked position with the original speech recognition output. If this procedure does not yield a match, the algorithm looks for text in the original transcript that is most similar to the target text. This similarity is operationalized from two parameters. Firstly, Levenshtein distance iteration algorithm iteratively increases the "distance" parameter between the two texts until some user-defined limit. Secondly, the requested number of matched words might also be iteratively modified. These two parameters are then manipulated in each subsequent cycle of the search until the closest possible match is found.

Once the search is finished, the user is informed with three modes: the exact match is played; a partial match is played with highlighting the matched (parts of) words in the text; and an unsuccessful search is signaled with a dedicated sound beep.

This algorithmic solution provides a new important functionality that facilitates and speeds up the editing of automatically transcribed documents related to the judge's tasks and responsibilities.

4   Evaluation

The evaluation consists of testing the overall performance of the APD dictation system in the judicial domain on different combinations of language and acoustic models used in the system reference offline test setup based on Julius [24].

The testing set of 5.75 h (3,426 sentences, (1,476 female and 1,950 male speaker utterances, and 41,868 words together), consisted of selected speech utterances taken from APD2 database. It was not included in the training set. Table 3 shows the results for APD2 test set and Table 4 for gender adapted acoustic models on APD2 test set and gender filtered test subsets from APD2 test set (only the same gender speaker utterances where used for tests).

Table 3. Evaluation of APD dictation system [% WER]

PPL	LM	APD1 + APD2 (table microphones) sp. adapt.: no test set: all	APD1 + APD2 (close-talk microphones) sp. adapt.: no test set: all	APD1 + APD2 + PAR sp. adapt.: no test set: all	APD1 + APD2 + PAR + BN sp. adapt.: no test set: all	APD1 + APD2 + PARext sp. adapt.: no test set: all
44.93	12/2011	8.11	6.56	5.79	6.10	6.32
38.97	07/2012	7.67	6.22	5.54	5.70	6.00
40.25	12/2012	7.53	6.14	5.35	5.62	5.89
44.33	04/2013	7.65	6.24	5.47	5.70	5.90
35.94	05/2013	7.54	6.03	5.28	5.63	5.75
34.82	10/2014	7.57	5.98	**5.26**	5.53	5.71

Table 4. Evaluation of gender-dependent AMs in APD dictation system [% WER]

PPL	LM	APD1 + APD2 + PAR sp. adapt.: female test set: all	APD1 + APD2 + PAR sp. adapt.: male test set: all	APD1 + APD2 + PAR sp. adapt.: female test set: female	APD1 + APD2 + PAR sp. adapt.: male test set: male
44.93	12/2011	9.66	7.32	4.23	6.07
38.97	07/2012	8.77	6.82	4.15	5.79
40.25	12/2012	8.72	6.78	4.07	5.70
44.33	04/2013	8.74	6.75	4.08	5.79
35.94	05/2013	8.74	6.76	4.03	5.63
34.82	10/2014	8.55	6.65	**3.93**	**5.58**

The results showed that adding new language databases using similar recording environment improved the recognition accuracy. As expected, the BN databases and table microphone database degraded the results, because the recording environment is different comparing the APD2 test set (close talk headset microphone). As we can see, also a gender dependent AM models improved the accuracy, and if the user creates adapted AM model (using GUI) the subjective accuracy increased significantly. In the future we want to build a new test set containing different acoustic environments to compare the APD system efficiency for mixed end user environments. Currently the use of preferred headset microphones is strongly recommended to end users of the dictation system.

At this time the APD system has been installed and used by more than 3,000 persons (judges, court clerks, assistants and technicians) at different institutions belonging to the Ministry of Justice of the Slovak Republic.

5   End-Users Opinion on the System

Half a year after the system was distributed to all the courts in Slovakia a questionnaire was prepared for collecting the data on the use of APD using experiences from [25]. It was distributed to the 180 judges who activated their license of the dictation system. Currently around 23 responses were obtained. They were carefully evaluated, the probable causes of the problems were identified and solutions were proposed for the future development of the system.

These recommendations could be concluded from the results: the training of the end-users, hardware upgrade and recommended headset microphone usage is necessary; compatibility with new versions of operating system and Word should be solved; the adapted versions for criminal/civil/commercial justice should be released in the near future; the "adding of proper names for next document dictation" function should be implemented; automatic inflection of new added words should be released; more templates for court proceedings should be elaborated; central intranet profile and upgrade management should be realized.

6   Future Work

Our dictation system for the judicial domain has been finished for more than 2 years now and it is used by many judges. Still there are some things that should be improved.

The original plan of introducing the speech recognition technology in the everyday practice of the Ministry of Justice had three phases:

1. Introducing the dictation system for personal use;
2. Use of dictation system at the court hearings (only parts of the speech communication are on-line transcribed: the dictation of the judge (adjudication) and possibly the dictation of prosecutor (indictment);
3. Automatic transcription of the whole speech communication of the court hearings recordings.

The first task has been finished successfully. The dictation system is now available for every employee of the Ministry of Justice of the Slovak Republic. However, only a small part of all judges has been using the system so far. The greatest problem was the obsolete computer equipment. Fortunately the Ministry of Justice bought 1,800 up-to-date PCs in 2012 and all of them have the dictation system installed. In 2013 they bought another 2,200 PCs and the system is being installed on these too.

The use of the personal dictation system is not obligatory and it is therefore used mainly by the younger, dynamic judges and by the judges who often need to include larger amounts of texts in the adjudication. Concerning the second and third phase: Some of the judges (mainly from the civil law) have already been experimenting with using the dictation system at their court hearings.

In general the courts are not equipped with microphones and recording systems yet (except for personal dictation tape-recorders). Some legislative changes still need to be done in order to allow the full size recording of the courtroom hearings.

The whole system of the Slovak justice is based on the paper documents at the moment. The digitalization – creation of the unified information system with digital case files is to be started this year, therefore it will take some time until we can integrate our technology in the "court workflow and/or information system".

Recording devices was bought for all 511 courtrooms in Slovakia in 2013. Unfortunately due to the limited volume of funding they are intended only for documentation purposes. The signal quality is expected to be in general too low for automatic speech recognition.

The third phase a long-term goal the spontaneous speech recognition of people which are often speaking under stress or fear, with emotions, with local dialect, or they are uneducated and not used to speak aloud in front of such an audience. This is really a great challenge. Some of the biggest problems in all the three phases are:

- Need for higher interest and cooperation of the authorities at the Ministry and Courts and they should recognize the advantages of the technology and its contribution of the transparency of justice;
- Many of the judges are conservative, used to the traditional convenient way of using dictation to the assistant and are not willing to try new approaches;

- The thinking of the users must change – they must see the benefits for their own work;
- The electronic databases of the electronic case files have to be created at the courts (they do not exist up till now);
- The methodology of the use of the speech recognition in the legal practice should be anchored in the legislation;
- The methodology of the use must be worked through by the Ministry and incorporated in the internal regulations for judges;
- The supervision of the process of introduction of the technology in the practice and monitoring of its use is needed as well as collecting feedback and ideas from the users;
- The system of periodic training courses should be released and recommended for all courts;
- The system of collection, post-processing, archiving, indexing and re-use of the recordings has to be elaborated;
- And of course more funding is needed.

Even more user-friendly user interface has to be developed, better specialized to different types of legislation areas, such as civil, criminal, commercial, etc. law. This includes development of a new generation of language models. The "manual adding of proper names for next document dictation" function should be implemented; automatic inflection of the newly added words should be developed; central intranet profile and upgrade management should be solved.

7 Conclusion

It can be concluded that the first phase of the project was successfully finished. The dictation system works very well and has a lot of satisfied users who use it on a daily basis. Still the authors are working in cooperation with the Ministry on further intensification of the use of the dictation system. Currently eight one-day courses for the users were realized at different courts starting from October 2013 till end of 2014. The authors get very important and valuable feedback from the users at these courses which serve as an inspiration for further development of the system.

There are more than 80 courts in Slovakia, but some of the training courses were organized for mixed groups of judges coming from several district courts falling under the authority of the same regional court. This approach ensured that (as far as possible) at least some judges from each court will undergo the training of the end-user of the APD dictation system for judicial domain.

Currently a specialized system adapted for public prosecutors is in development and should be released in 2015.

Acknowledgements. The research of *Technical university of Kosice* team presented in this paper was partially supported by the Ministry of Education, Science, Research and Sport of the Slovak Republic under project VEGA 1/0075/15 (50 %) and partially by the Research and Development Operational Programme funded by the ERDF project implementation: University Science Park TECHNICOM for Innovation Applications Supported by Knowledge Technology, ITMS project

26220220182 (50 %). The research of *Slovak Academy of Sciences* team presented in this paper was supported by the Ministry of Education, Science, Research and Sport of the Slovak Republic under research project VEGA 2/0197/15 (100 %).

References

1. Google Speech API Demo. http://www.google.com/intl/en/chrome/demos/speech.html. Accessed 17 September 2015
2. Lööf, J., Falavigna, D., Schlüter, R., Giuliani, D., Gretter, R., Ney H.: Evaluation of automatic transcription systems for the judicial domain. In: Proceedings of the IEEE Spoken Language Technology Workshop, SLT 2010, Berkeley, CA, USA, pp. 194–199 (2010)
3. Rusko, M., Juhár, J., Trnka, M., Staš, J., Darjaa, S., Hládek, D., Cerňák, M., Papco, M., Sabo, R., Pleva, M., Ritomský, M., Lojka, M.: Slovak automatic transcription and dictation system for the judicial domain. In: Proceedings of the 5th Language and Technology Conference: Human Language Technologies as a Challenge for Computer Science and Linguistics, LTC 2011, Poznań, Poland, pp. 365–369 (2011)
4. Darjaa, S., Cerňak, M., Beňuš, Š., Rusko, M., Sabo, R., Trnka, M.: Rule-based triphone mapping for acoustic modeling in automatic speech recognition. In: Habernal, I., Matoušek, V. (eds.) TSD 2011. LNCS(LNAI), vol. 6836, pp. 268–275. Springer, Heidelberg (2011)
5. Vandecatseye, A., et al.: The COST278 Pan-European broadcast news database. In: Proceedings of the 6th Language Resources and Evaluation Conference, LREC 2004, Lisbon, Portugal, pp. 873–876 (2004)
6. Pleva, M., Juhár, J.: TUKE-BNews-SK: Slovak broadcast news corpus construction and evaluation. In: Proceedings of LREC 2014: Ninth International Conference on Language Resources and Evaluation, ELRA, Reykjavik, Iceland, pp. 1709–1713, 26–31 May 2014
7. Pleva, M., Juhár, J.: Building of broadcast news database for evaluation of the automated subtitling service. Commun. (Komunikacie) **15**(2A), 124–128 (2013)
8. Barras, C., Geoffrois, E., Wu, Z., Liberman, M.: Transcriber: development and use of a tool for assisting speech corpora production. Speech Commun. Spec. Issue Speech Annotation Corpus Tools **33**(1–2), 5–22 (2000)
9. Slovak National Corpus, Ľ. Štúr Institute of Linguistics, Slovak Academy of Sciences. http://korpus.juls.savba.sk/prim(2d)6(2e)1.html. Accessed 17 September 2015
10. Hládek, D., Staš, J.: Text mining and processing for corpora creation in Slovak language. J. Comput. Sci. Control Syst. **3**(1), 65–68 (2010)
11. Staš, J., Hládek, D., Juhár, J.: Recent advances in the statistical modeling of the Slovak language. In: Proceedings of the 54th International Symposium ELMAR 2014, Zadar, Croatia, pp. 39–42 (2014)
12. Venkataraman, A., Wang, W.: Techniques for effective vocabulary selection. In: Proceedings of EUROSPEECH 2003, Geneva, Switzerland, pp. 245–248 (2003)
13. Darjaa, S., Cerňak, M., Trnka, M., Rusko, M., Sabo, R.: Effective triphone mapping for acoustic modeling in speech recognition. In: Proceedings of INTERSPEECH 2011, Florence, Italy, pp. 1717–1720 (2011)
14. Lindberg, B., Johansen, F.T., Warakagoda, N., Lehtinen, G., Kacic, Z., Zgank, A., Elenius, K., Salvi, G.: A noise robust multilingual reference recognizer based on SpeechDat (II). In: Proceedings of INTERSPEECH 2000, Beijing, China, pp. 370–373 (2000)
15. Žgank, A., et al.: The COST 278 MASPER initiative - crosslingual speech recognition with large telephone databases. In: Proceedings of the 6th Language Resources and Evaluation Conference, LREC 2004, Lisbon, Portugal, pp. 2107–2110 (2004)

16. Leggetter, C.J., Woodland, P.C.: Maximum likelihood linear regression for speaker adaptation of continuous density hidden Markov models. Comput. Speech Lang. **9**(2), 171–186 (1995)

17. Jokisch, O., Wagner, A., Sabo, R., Jackel, R., Cylwik, N., Rusko, M., Ronzhin, A., Hoffman, R.: Multilingual speech data collection for the assessment of pronunciation and prosody in a language learning system. In: Karpov, A. (ed.) Proceedings of the 13th International Conference Speech and Computer, SPECOM 2009, St. Petersburg, Russia, pp. 515–520 (2009)

18. Papco, M., Juhár, J.: Comparison of acoustic model adaptation methods and adaptation database selection approaches. J. Electr. Electron. Eng. **3**(1), 147–150 (2010)

19. Stolcke, A.: SRILM – An extensible language modeling toolkit. In: Proceedings of ICSLP 2002, Denver, Colorado, USA, pp. 901–904 (2002)

20. Zlacký, D., Staš, J., Juhár, J., Čižmár, A.: Text categorization with latent Dirichlet allocation. J. Electr. Electron. Eng. **7**(1), 161–164 (2014)

21. Staš, J., Hládek, D., Juhár, J.: Language model adaptation for Slovak LVCSR. In: Proceedings of International Conference on Applied Electrical Engineering and Informatics, AEI 2010, Venice, Italy, pp. 101–106 (2010)

22. Staš, J., Juhár, J., Hládek, D.: Classification of heterogeneous text data for robust domain-specific language modeling. EURASIP J. Audio Speech Music Process. **2014**(14), 12 (2014)

23. Chelba, C., Brants, T., Neveitt, W., Xu, P.: Study on interaction between entropy pruning and Kneser-Ney smoothing. In: Proceedings of INTERSPEECH 2010, Makuhari, Japan, pp. 2422–2425 (2010)

24. Lee, A., Kawahara, T.: Recent development of open-source speech recognition engine Julius. In: Proceedings of the Asia-Pacific Signal and Information Processing Association, Annual Summit and Conference, APSIPA ASC 2009, Sapporo, Japan, pp. 131–137 (2009)

25. Alapetite, A., Andersen, H.B., Hertzum, M.: Acceptance of speech recognition by physicians: A survey of expectations, experiences, and social influence. Int. J. Hum Comput Stud. **67**(1), 36–49 (2009)

A Revised Comparison of Polish Taggers in the Application for Automatic Speech Recognition

Aleksander Smywiński-Pohl[1,2,3]([✉]) and Bartosz Ziółko[2,3]

[1] Faculty of Management and Social Communication,
Jagiellonian University, Kraków, Poland
apohllo@o2.pl
[2] Faculty of Computer Science, Electronics and Telecommunication,
AGH University of Science and Technology, Kraków, Poland
[3] Techmo, Kraków, Poland
http://www.techmo.pl

Abstract. In this paper (This is a revised and extended version of the article *A Comparison of Polish Taggers in the Application for Automatic Speech Recognition* that appeared in the *Proceedings of Language and Tools Conference*, Poznan, 2013.) we investigate the performance of Polish taggers in the context of automatic speech recognition (ASR). We use a morphosyntactic language model to improve speech recognition in an ASR system and seek the best Polish tagger for our needs. Polish is an inflectional language and an n-gram model using morphosyntactic features, which reduces data sparsity seems to be a good choice. We investigate the difference between the morphosyntactic taggers in that context. We compare the results of tagging with respect to the reduction of word error rate as well as speed of tagging. As it turns out at present the taggers using conditional random fields (CRF) models perform the best in the context of ASR. A broader audience might be also interested in the other discussed features of the taggers such as easiness of installation and usage, which are usually not covered in the papers describing such systems.

Keywords: Morphosyntactic tagger · Polish · Automatic speech recognition · Language model

1 Introduction

Unlike English, which is a positional language, Polish has a rich morphology, with many morphosyntactic features. This boils down to the observation that many syntactic features that in English are encoded in the relative position of words, in Polish are encoded in the suffix of the word. For instance the expressions *dom Adama* and *Adama dom* (*Adam's house*) although not equally probable, express the same relation between these words. What is more the number of tokens in Polish and other inflectional languages is larger than in English, since words have

© Springer International Publishing Switzerland 2016
Z. Vetulani et al. (Eds.): LTC 2013, LNAI 9561, pp. 68–81, 2016.
DOI: 10.1007/978-3-319-43808-5_6

many forms (e.g. *Adam, Adama, Adamowi, Adamem, Adamie, Adamowie,...* are all forms of *Adam*).

These two facts have important implications when building a language model for an ASR system for Polish [29]. The first one makes the generally accepted methods improving language models, namely class-based n-grams [4] less useful, since they are based only on the positions of words. The second means that when building word-based language model for Polish, the size of the corpus has to be substantially larger than for English, in order to overcome the data-sparseness problem.

In this research we investigate the differences in the performance of taggers in the application for ASR. We want to find out which of the available taggers is the best in terms of tagging quality and speed. Since there are many taggers designed specifically for Polish we are not going to develop our own solution. As a result we asses the primary features of the taggers such as accuracy and speed, but we have also an opportunity to compare their secondary features, such as the easiness of installation and their licenses.

Even though there are results showing which of the implemented taggers performs the best on the reference corpus (Concraft) [24], we want to find out if the differences in accuracy are preserved in a setting which is substantially different from the original one. This is caused by the large number of ungrammatical sentences that are present in the output of an acoustic module as well as restriction on the number of employed grammatical categories (part-of-speech[1] (POS), number, gender and case).

2   Taggers

The comparison of the taggers is restricted to the following systems: WMBT [17], Pantera [1], WCRFT [18] and Concraft [24]. These are the most up-to-date, publicly available systems enlisted on the "Computational Linguistics in Poland"[2] web-page (in the section "Language Tools and Resources for Polish") which were developed specifically for Polish. We do not include in the comparison TaKIPI [12] as well as TnT [2] for which there is a Polish model available. Regarding TaKIPI the reason is that it was bound to a specific tagset which is no longer supported, especially in the primary Polish corpus, that is National Corpus of Polish (NCP) [15]. As a result it is no longer developed and its performance is reported [1,17,18,24] to be inferior to all the presented taggers. The reason for TnT is that it uses second-order Markov models, which are also reported to be inferior to all the presented techniques (with respect to tagging of Polish).

The comparison has the following structure. First we present a short description of the technique used by the tagger, together with the information about its license. Second we describe the issues (if any) connected with the installation

---

[1] We use the terms *part-of-speech* and *grammatical class* interchangeably in this document, due to the way they are used in the literature regarding Polish tagsets and taggers.

[2] http://clip.ipipan.waw.pl/LRT.

and usage of the tagger. Then we present the general overview of the technique implemented in the tagger. We conclude the presentation with a more detailed description of the adaptations employed to solve specific Polish tagging issues.

2.1   WMBT

WMBT[3] (Wrocław Memory-Based Tagger) [17] is a tagger that utilizes the Memory Based Learning (MBL) technique and is distributed under a Lesser General Public License (LGPL). It uses the TiMBL library [5], which is a set of Natural Language Processing (NLP) tools employing MBL methods for various language-related problems. Although TiMBL comes with a specific tool designed for tagging, WMBT only uses its general MBL capabilities.

The installation of WMBT is not straightforward and requires manual installation of several other libraries: Maca [17], Corpus2, Morfeusz [26], WCCL [19] and TiMBL. The first library is used for splitting the analyzed text into paragraphs and segments. It also works as a proxy to the morphological analyzer. Corpus2 provides an efficient access to corpora (NCP in particular). Morfeusz is a quite popular library for morphological analysis of Polish words and is used in all the other taggers. WCCL provides a formalism for expressing and transforming various lexical and morphosyntactic features, such as case agreement. It is also used by WCRFT. TiMBL is the already mentioned library providing MBL tools and algorithms.

The installation requires manual downloading of some of the tools, since not all of them are provided as packages for popular operating systems (e.g. Ubuntu). They also have many dependencies so the overall process is pretty tiresome. The most problematic is the requirement for the TiMBL Python wrapper, which is no longer supported by the developers of that library. Compilation and installation errors are not uncommon. What is more, running WMBL on a plain text requires a separate call to Maca, for the input preprocessing. As a final note we should observe, that the tagger is no longer developed by the team, since it was replaced by WCRFT.

The general idea behind MBL-based tagging [6] is as follows: during the training phase, the word occurrences are transformed into feature-vectors which are, together with the correct value of the morphsyntactic label, stored in the *memory* of the tagger, i.e. they are simply recorded. During the disambiguation phase words are also transformed into feature-vectors, the tagger consults its memory and finds the vectors which are the most similar (w.r.t to a selected metric) to the vector in question and selects the best label using voting among the k-most similar examples.

WMBL uses MBL together with tiered tagging [22]. This is due to the fact, that Polish morphosyntactic labels are positional, i.e. the values of various morphosyntactic categories applicable for a given grammatical class are concatenated and form a complex label. As such the number of possible and also the empirically observed distinct labels is large (more than 4 thousand and 1 thousand

---

[3] http://nlp.pwr.wroc.pl/redmine/projects/wmbt.

respectively). To overcome the data-sparseness problem WMBT disambiguates the input using a sequence of tiers, each using a separate model capturing the features of only one grammatical category (e.g. case) or the grammatical class. It should be noted that due to the sequential nature of the tiers, the error made by a preceding tier cannot be corrected by the following one and in such cases the tagger selects one arbitrary label.

WMBL uses the following features to convert a word occurrence into a feature-vector: values of the grammatical class, number, gender and case of the surrounding words; lowercased orthographical forms of the surrounding words, if they were popular enough (among 500 most popular words in the training corpus) and binary features indicating if there is a possible agreement in number, gender or case between the word in question and the surrounding words. All these features are used on all tiers.

During the disambiguation the labels that are compatible with the word in question are supplied by the morphological analyzer. Then at each tier a separate memory is used to retrieve the most similar vectors. The winning grammatical category value (e.g. nominative case) is selected and all the labels provided by the previous tier that are not compatible with the selected value are removed. If that step would yield the label set empty, no action is taken, with assumption that the remaining ambiguity might be removed by the subsequent tiers. If the ambiguity remains until the end of the procedure, one of the remaining labels is arbitrarily selected.

2.2   Pantera

Pantera[4] ("Polskiej Akademii Nauk Tager Ekstrahujący Reguły Automatycznie", which means in English "Automatic Rule Extraction Based Tagger of the Polish Academy of Sciences") [1] is distributed under General Public License (GPL) and is based on the idea of Brill tagger [3]. In the past (2013) the installation procedure was straightforward, since the tagger was available as a package for many Linux distributions (Ubuntu, Fedora and OpenSuse). But these packages are no longer available for the most up-to-date distributions, so it has to be complied by the user. Fortunately it also does not require any external resources, so the procedure is rather straight-forward. We should also note, that the code of the tagger is available at `code.google.com` – a service that is no longer in operation. Thus we might conclude that the system is no longer developed.

The mode of operation of the tagger is similar to the idea used in the Brill tagger, i.e. during the learning phase the tagger processes the learning material using its current knowledge and then, by comparing the results with the reference corpus it induces rules that are used to fix the observed errors. At each iteration the rule that has the largest *good* to *bad* modifications margin is selected, the text is tagged once again and the procedure is repeated. A unigram label statistic is used as an initial model.

---

[4] http://code.google.com/p/pantera-tagger/.

The modifications implemented in Pantera mainly account for the characteristic features of inflectional languages. The original Brill tagger had very small set of templates used as transformations. The set was extended in Pantera and in particular the transformation rules were split into a test (LHS) and an action (RHS) part, allowing for more flexible rule construction. The morphosyntactic labels were disambiguated in several passes covering only one selected grammatical category. The LHS of the rules might cover lexical features, such as prefix and suffix of the word. And the last but not the least, the implementation was simplified and parallelized.

The generalization of the transformation rules was introduced firstly in order to capture complex conditions that could be useful in Polish (e.g. for capturing case or gender agreement, which can not be expressed by the rules devised in Brill tagger), and secondly in order to allow for assigning the whole morphosyntactic label at once as well as only a part of the label e.g. a value of particular grammatical category or the grammatical class.

The multipass tagging works as follows during the learning phase the tagset is converted to a set of tagsets, each covering smaller number of grammatical categories. The training is started with the most simplified tagset and the rules are recorded. Then a more feature-rich tagset is used and new set of rules is discovered. The procedure is repeated until it reaches the original tagset. Then during the tagging the rules recorded at each step are applied separately and the values of already determined grammatical categories are not changed.

The last interesting extension covered the lexical features. The LHS of the rules may check if the word contains particular letter, starts or ends with particular letter sequence and so on. The authors of the tagger reported that the lexical rules improved the tagging accuracy by 1.5 % point.

2.3   WCRFT

WCRFT[5] (Wrocław Conditional Random Field Tagger) [18] can be treated as a development of the WMBT tagger, since they share the tiered approach. The primary difference is the classifier used to select the labels on each tire in WCRFT the decision is made using Conditional Random Field (CRF) [9,21] linear-chain classifier.

The tagger is distributed under the LGPL license. The installation procedure is similar to WMBL, i.e. it uses similar external libraries (Maca, Corpus2, Morfeusz, etc.) and in many cases this requires manual installation of second-order dependencies. On the other hand the tagging process was simplified, e.g. Maca does not have to be called as a separate step.

Conditional Random Fields is a mathematical model used to estimate the conditional probability of a hidden states assuming given set or sequence of observations. In general they are similar to Hidden Markov Models (HMM) [16], with the primary difference being the fact that CRF is a conditional model while HMM is a generative model. In the context of NLP CRF is gaining popularity,

---

[5] http://nlp.pwr.wroc.pl/redmine/projects/wcrft/.

since unlike HMM it allows to directly represent distant and forward relations, which are quite common in languages as well it works well with dependencies between the input features, which are also very common.

The design of a CRF for NLP tasks boils down to a selection of a number of characteristic functions which indicate if a given feature holds for the observation in question. The values of these functions with respect to the individual tokens are linearly combined using a fixed set of weights. The weights are determined during the training of the model.

Although the model requires that the features are binary, it is usually easier to model at least some of the features as having multiple values. Since this is a very popular scenario, CRF introduces the notion of function-templates which can be formulated using multi-valued features but are transformed into functions with a binary counter-domain. As a side effect a large number of functions might be generated. Since the training time is quadratic with respect to the number of possible labels (more than one thousand in Polish), the straightforward application of CRF to the problem of Polish morphosyntactic tagging fails due to practical time and memory constraints.

This is the reason why WCRFT uses tiered approach towards tagging: by following the same label selection scheme as WMBT, the set of available label values within each tier is significantly reduced and the CRF model may be practically employed. In fact the primary difference between WMBT and WCRFT lays in the label selection method (k-nearest neighbors in the case of WMBT and highest conditional probability in the case of WCRFT) and the fact that in WMBT the classifiers works token by token, while in WCRFT all labels are provided for the whole sentence at once (with respect to the processed tire).

Regarding the features that were used as the input for the model, WCRFT uses: word form of the token, possible values of gender, number and case, agreement between the token and the next token, agreement between three subsequent tokens and capitalization of the word. These primary features are used to define secondary features, which are dependent on the index relative to the analyzed token and in some cases are used to test two or three subsequent tokens.

2.4   Concraft

Concraft[6] (Constrained Conditional Random Fields Tagger) [24] is another tagger utilizing the model of Conditional Random Fields. It is distributed under the BSD two-clause license. The tagger is written in Haskell and comes as a module, that can be downloaded and installed via the Cabal package management tool. Assuming that the Haskell system (including the Cabal manager) is properly installed and configured the installation procedure is very simple and amounts to issuing one command. The tagger is supplemented with a model trained over the NCP corpus which has to be separately downloaded.

On the other hand the documentation of the system is rather minimalistic and amounts to a Readme file. It does not cover any command line options and

---

[6] http://hackage.haskell.org/package/concraft.

since the default output of Concraft is a plain text (using very simple tabulation scheme) we have to assume that this system is unable to produce XML as an output. In order to work properly Concraft also requires Maca and Corpus2 tools to perform the segmentation of the input text.

Concraft uses *Constraint Conditional Random Fields* in order to achieve two goals: the primary, i.e. the disambiguation of morphosyntactic labels and the secondary, i.e. the inference of most probable labels for the unknown words (which are used in constraining the search space during the disambiguation).

It employs second-order linear chain CRF to model the interdependence between the words, their morphosyntactic labels and the previous labels. Since the set of distinct labels contains more than 1000 entries, the model is further simplified by introducing layers: each layer may contain different grammatical categories. As a result the number of distinct labels is reduced. It should be noted however that the layers are not tiers, i.e. they are used in parallel, which allows to model their interdependence. In the development of the model for Polish two layers were used: part-of-speech, case and person in the first layer, and other categories in the second layer.

In order to provide probable labels for the unknown words (i.e. reducing more than 1000 possible labels to a number which is closer to the average 4 labels for the known words) a first-order CRF is used. The feature set covers: lowercase prefixes and suffixes of length 1 and 2, a boolean value indicating if the word is known and a packed shape of the word capturing lower/upper case letters, digits and other symbols. These features together with the label of the previous word are used to estimate the probabilities of the labels, then a fixed number of the most probable labels (10) is provided to the disambiguation phase.

Regarding the features that are used during disambiguation Concraft is very minimalistic. It contains only the lowercase forms of the previous, the current and the next token. In the case of unknown words it also contains lowercase prefixes and suffixes of the word of lengths 1, 2 and 3 and packed shape of the word, together with the information of the first letter case.

3   Evaluation

In order to evaluate the taggers' performance in the context of ASR we have implemented two evaluation scenarios. In both cases the morphosyntactic LM was incorporated into the results of speech recognition according to the following equation:

$$P(h_i) = P(h_i)_{wLM}^{\alpha} * P(h_i)_{mLM}^{\beta} * P(h_i)_{AM}^{1-\alpha-\beta} , \qquad (1)$$

where:

- $P(h_i)$ – probability of the i-th recognition hypothesis,
- wLM – word LM,
- mLM – morphosyntactic LM,
- AM – acoustic model (AM),
- α, β – weights of the respective LMs.

Thus the probabilities of a given hypothesis according to the different models were combined using a set of weights optimized on a *tuning* corpus.

The primary difference between the scenarios was the fact, that the first scenario lacked the word LM (i.e. the α parameter was set to 0). The other differences regarded different systems used to build the AM and different corpora used to evaluate the results.

In both cases in the first step a morphosyntactic n-gram model of Polish was built with the help of SRI LM package [20]. One-million subcorpus of NCP [15] was used to compute the counts of the specific tags combinations. The probability of a given set of morphosyntactic tags, given the set of previous morphosyntactic tags was estimated as:

$$P(h_i)_{mLM} = \prod_{w_j \in h_i} P(V(w_j)|V(w_{j-N+1})...V(w_{j-1})), \qquad (2)$$

where:

- $V(w_j)$ – the set of morphosyntactic tags attached to word w_j,
- N – n-gram order,
- $w_{j-N+1}...w_{j-1}$ – N–1 words preceding the word w_j.

To reduce the data sparsity the set of morphosyntactic tags attached to each word was filtered only to include grammatical class and values of gender, number and case (if applicable for a given class). Then the model was refined using Witten-Bell (WB) discounting [25]. We have used WB discounting, although the Kneser-Ney [8] method is reported to perform the best in the case of language modeling for ASR. The reason for that was the relatively small number of distinct labels, namely 734, which excluded the application of Kneser-Ney discounting.

3.1   HTK + mLM

The following steps depended on the evaluation scenario. In the first scenario the n-best list of speech recognition acoustic hypotheses was produced by HTK [27]. Each of the compared taggers was then used to convert the sequence of words into sequence of tags. These tags were filtered in order to keep only the tags present in the mLM. Then SRI LM was used to assign the probabilities to each sequence of tags according to the mLM (we have used 3-order LM in this scenario). Then the tuning corpus was used to compute the β weight implementing a grid search strategy. That parameter was defined independently for each of the taggers. In the last step the recognition hypotheses of each speech signal in the testing set were re-scored according the Eq. 1. The procedure is depicted on Fig. 1.

To evaluate the impact of the taggers on ASR we used several speech corpora. The first one (C1), which was used as a *tuning* set, included 108 sentences spoken by one male voice, without any added noise, but spoken in an office with working computers. It covered political speeches and spoken fragments of song lyrics. The second corpus (C2) consists of 31 samples of one young female professional speaker. These were recordings without noise, made for a film

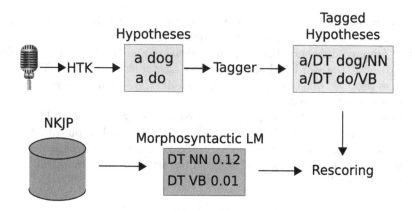

Fig. 1. Rescoring of the hypotheses according to the morphosyntactic LM.

about speech technologies from prepared and checked sentences. The third corpus
(C3) consisted of 281 short sentences and commands recorded during various
tests of speech and speaker recognition systems at AGH University of Science
and Technology with addition of recordings from meetings of the Department
Council. This corpus was collected to combine many various voices (one speaker
say no more than 6 sentences, often just one or two) and recording devices,
often with a natural random noise due to bad acoustic conditions (reverberation
of room, voices of other people in a corridor, cars from outside etc.) We used
also recordings of LUNA corpus [10] which is a corpus of telephone conversations
from a call center of Warsaw public transport information. 192 samples of various
female voices (C4) and 228 of male voices (C5) were used. These are informal
sentences with many questions. The corpus is full of grammar mistakes, very
common in natural conversations. The testing corpus consisted of the C2, C3,
C4 and C5 corpora.

3.2   Kaldi + mLM + wLM

In the second scenario we have used a more recent automatic speech recognition
system called Kaldi [14]. The AM was a triphone HMM Gaussian mixture model
[7]. It was trained on a large dataset of recordings collected by AGH [28] and
Techmo and selection of recordings from the Global Phone acoustic database [23].
The processing pipeline also included a word-level trigram LM (wLM), trained
on a subset (containing approx. 600 million tokens) of NCP. That model was
directly combined with the AM, since both models were expressed as weighted
finite state transducers [11]. The weight of the wLM was determined in separate
set of experiments. As a result the output of the system was similar to that
of HTK, with the exception, that also the wLM was taken into account in the
probability assigned to the hypotheses.

The evaluation was performed solely on the Global Phone corpus, and
included a subset of speakers (4 women and 4 men). The tuning set included

(randomly selected) 10 % of all recording, totaling in 249 entries, while the testing set included 2240 entries. In each case the recordings of the speaker that was tested were excluded from the training set, thus the system was tested in a speaker-independent fashion.

The mLM was used to rescore the hypotheses in the same manner as in the previous scenario, with the exception, that the α parameter was not 0 and the order of the LM was 5. Yet the β parameter was optimized after the α parameter was determined, thus it followed the same grid-search strategy. Moreover the probability of hypotheses produced by Kaldi already included the wLM component. The reason for that was the implemented beam-search strategy, that takes into account both AM and wLM during the search in the hypotheses space.

3.3 Tagging Speed

We also evaluated the speed of the taggers, since this feature is quite important in the case of on-line ASR. We measured separately the start-up time and the processing time. The start-up time was measured as the time required to tag one sentence "Ala.", while the processing time was measured for a set of acoustic hypotheses including 900 entries. The loading time was averaged over 5 runs, while the processing time over 10 runs. In the following reports the loading time is subtracted from the processing time.

In all cases the tests were carried out in hot-boot setting, i.e. the linguistic models employed in the tagging were used on the same computer in previous experiments. As a result all files read by a tagger were cached in the operational memory. The computer used to perform the tests had an Intel i7-3537U CPU clocked at 2.0 GHz with 2 cores and 4 hardware threads, 8 GB of RAM and a 256GB SSD drive. The operating system was 64-bit Ubuntu 14.04 LTS.

4 Results

Table 1 includes the comparison of the taggers in terms of performance in the first scenario. The best performing tagger is Concraft, reaching 25.2 % points (pp.) WERR on average, while the worst is WMBT with 23.2 pp. WERR. The difference between the best and the worst results is not large, but statistically significant. Performing a paired Student t-test with $p < 0.05$ shows that the Concraft tagger is better from both the Pantera and WMBT taggers, but not from the WCRFT tagger. It should be observed that the best performing taggers (Concraft and WCRFT) use the same technique (CRF) and the same training corpus, however their results are slightly different.

Table 2 includes the results of the comparison when both the word-level and morphosyntactic LMs were applied. Here both the absolute results and their differences are much smaller (2 orders of magnitude in case of WERR)[7]. Moreover we have not observed any statistically significant differences between the

---

[7] We have not included the results for WMBT since it was impossible to obtain its results when these tests were performed. Moreover its behaviour was the worst in all the other tests, so we have not expected to see any improvement.

78   A. Smywiński-Pohl and B. Ziółko

Table 1. Comparison of the performance of the taggers in terms of Word Error Rate Reduction [WERR] when only morphosyntactic LM was employed.

Corpus	Weight	WMBT	Pantera	WCRFT	Concraft
C2	0.04	24.7	**28.6**	28.4	26.8
C3	0.39	27.7	28.9	30.7	**31.0**
C4	0.28	25.2	25.4	26.4	**29.0**
C5	0.29	**14.5**	12.5	13.6	13.7
Avg.		23.1	23.1	24.4	**25.2**

taggers. The probable reason for that result is the fact, that the wLM already included important interdependencies between the grammatical classes and categories between the words and the observed improvement was so small. The other explanation could be based on the fact, that the α parameter was optimized independently of the β parameter, thus we have reached a local maximum. Yet a scenario when both parameters are optimized at once is much more implementationally demanding and was out of scope of this paper.

Table 2. Comparison of the performance of the taggers in terms of WERR when both word and morphosyntactic LMs were employed

Tagger	WERR
Pantera	0.28
WCRFT	**0.36**
Concraft	0.31

Table 3 includes the comparison of the speed of the taggers. The WCRFT tagger has the best loading time – below one fifth of a second, while WMBT has the worst loading time exceeding 10 s. It should be stressed that all taggers were trained on the same corpus (1-million subcorpus of NCP), so these differences are caused only by the internal representation of the knowledge used by the taggers and the implementation of the loading procedure. When it comes to the tagging time Pantera is definitely the winner, with the tagging time (around 3.5 s) 2 times shorter than the next fastest tagger namely WCRFT. Here WMBT is the worst once again with the tagging time exceeding 200 s. It is apparent that the speed of the taggers varies significantly and should be strongly considered when choosing the optimal solution for a given settings.

The table also includes the information of the version of taggers. Only in one case (Concraft), the version was given explicitly. In the other cases we provided the Git or SVN revisions of the particular versions that were used in the test. When comparing with our previous test [13] we might observe that only two taggers are actively developed (WCRFT and Concraft). Both of them made

Table 3. Comparison of the speed of the taggers.

Tagger	Version	Load [ms]	Tagging [ms]
WMBT	0d67980	10560	186650
Pantera	r156	2778	**3564**
WCRFT	5fba260	**194**	8202
Concraft	0.7.4	9207	10793

significant improvements in the tagging time (in case of WCRFT it was 4-fold). We should also note, that the loading time of Concraft can be reduced to 0, since the system implements a client-server architecture and the model might be preloaded before the tagging is performed.

5   Conclusion

The general results of the taggers comparison are as follows: both of the actively maintained taggers, i.e. WCRFT and Concraft offer similar results both in terms of accuracy of the tagging and the tagging speed. Concraft installation is simple, assuming you have Haskell and Cabal installed. WCRFT installation is more demanding, since it requires more dependencies to be installed by the user. Pantera offers the highest speed of tagging, but WCRFT is caching up (2 times longer tagging time at present). WMBL does not offer any improvement neither in tagging accuracy nor in speed – this is probably the primary reason it is no longer developed.

Regarding the application of morphosyntactic LMs in ASR: a sole mLM offers significant recognition improvement, compared to the output produced by HTK. Yet if a word-level LM is involved, the improvement is negligible and probably is not worth the extended recognition time.

Acknowledgement. This work was supported by LIDER/37/69/L-3/11/NCBR/2012 grant.

References

1. Acedański, S.: A morphosyntactic brill tagger for inflectional languages. In: Loftsson, H., Rögnvaldsson, E., Helgadóttir, S. (eds.) IceTAL 2010. LNCS, vol. 6233, pp. 3–14. Springer, Heidelberg (2010)
2. Brants, T.: TnT: a statistical part-of-speech tagger. In: Proceedings of the Sixth Conference on Applied Natural Language Processing, pp. 224–231. Association for Computational Linguistics (2000)
3. Brill, E.: A simple rule-based part of speech tagger. In: Proceedings of the Workshop on Speech and Natural Language, pp. 112–116. Association for Computational Linguistics (1992)

4. Brown, P.F., Desouza, P.V., Mercer, R.L., Pietra, V.J.D., Lai, J.C.: Class-based n-gram models of natural language. Comput. Linguist. **18**(4), 467–479 (1992)
5. Daelemans, W., Zavrel, J., van der Sloot, K., van den Bosch, A.: TiMBL: Tilburg Memory-Based Learner (2010)
6. Daelemans, W., Van den Bosch, A.: Memory-Based Language Processing. Cambridge University Press, New York (2005)
7. Gauvain, J.L., Lee, C.H.: Maximum a posteriori estimation for multivariate Gaussian mixture observations of Markov chains. IEEE Trans. Speech Audio Process. **2**(2), 291–298 (1994)
8. Kneser, R., Ney, H.: Improved backing-off for m-gram language modeling. In: International Conference on Acoustics, Speech, and Signal Processing, vol. 1, pp. 181–184. IEEE (1995)
9. Lafferty, J., McCallum, A., Pereira, F.C.: Conditional random fields: probabilistic models for segmenting and labeling sequence data (2001)
10. Marciniak, M.: Anotowany korpus dialogów telefonicznych. Akademicka Oficyna Wydawnicza EXIT, Warszawa (2011)
11. Mohri, M., Pereira, F., Riley, M.: Weighted finite-state transducers in speech recognition. Comput. Speech Lang. **16**(1), 69–88 (2002)
12. Piasecki, M.: Polish tagger TaKIPI: Rule based construction and optimisation. Task Q. **11**(1–2), 151–167 (2007)
13. Pohl, A., Ziółko, B.: A comparison of polish taggers in the application for automatic speech recognition. In: Proceedings of the 6th Language & Technology Conference, pp. 294–298 (2013)
14. Povey, D., Ghoshal, A., Boulianne, G., Burget, L., Glembek, O., Goel, N., Hannemann, M., Motlíček, P., Qian, Y., Schwarz, P., et al.: The kaldi speech recognition toolkit. In: Proceedings of Automatic Speech Recognition and Understanding (2011)
15. Przepiórkowski, A., Bańko, M., Górski, R.L., Lewandowska-Tomaszczyk, B.: Narodowy Korpus Języka Polskiego. Wydawnictwo Naukowe PWN, Warsaw (2012)
16. Rabiner, L.R.: A tutorial on hidden Markov models and selected applications in speech recognition. Proc. IEEE **77**(2), 257–286 (1989)
17. Radziszewski, A., Śniatowski, T.: A memory-based tagger for Polish. In: Proceedings of the 5th Language & Technology Conference, Poznań, pp. 29–36 (2011)
18. Radziszewski, A.: A tiered CRF tagger for Polish. In: Bembenik, R., Skonieczny, Ł., Rybiński, H., Kryszkiewicz, M., Niezgódka, M. (eds.) Intelligent Tools for Building a Scientific Information Platform. SCI, vol. 467, pp. 215–230. Springer, Heidelberg (2013)
19. Radziszewski, A., Wardyński, A., Śniatowski, T.: WCCL: a morpho-syntactic feature toolkit. In: Habernal, I., Matoušek, V. (eds.) TSD 2011. LNCS, vol. 6836, pp. 434–441. Springer, Heidelberg (2011)
20. Stolcke, A.: SRILM-an extensible language modeling toolkit. In: Proceedings of the International Conference on Spoken Language Processing, vol. 2, pp. 901–904 (2002)
21. Sutton, C., McCallum, A.: An introduction to conditional random fields for relational learning. In: Introduction to Statistical Relational Learning, pp. 93–128 (2006)
22. Tufis, D.: Tiered tagging and combined language models classifiers. In: Matoušek, V., Mautner, P., Ocelíková, J., Sojka, P. (eds.) TSD 1999. LNCS (LNAI), vol. 1692, pp. 28–33. Springer, Heidelberg (1999)

23. Vu, N.T., Kraus, F., Schultz, T.: Multilingual a-stabil: a new confidence score for multilingual unsupervised training. In: 2010 IEEE Spoken Language Technology Workshop (SLT), pp. 183–188. IEEE (2010)
24. Waszczuk, J.: Harnessing the CRF complexity with domain-specific constraints. The case of morphosyntactic tagging of a highly inflected language. In: Kay, M., Boitet, C. (eds.) Proceedings of COLING, pp. 2789–2804 (2012)
25. Witten, I., Bell, T.: The zero-frequency problem: estimating the probabilities of novel events in adaptive text compression. IEEE Trans. Inf. Theory **37**(4), 1085–1094 (1991)
26. Woliński, M.: Morfeusz—a practical tool for the morphological analysis of Polish. In: Kłopotek, M.A., Wierzchoń, S.T., Trojanowski, K. (eds.) Intelligent Information Processing and Web Mining. Advances in Soft Computing, vol. 35, pp. 511–520. Springer, Heidelberg (2003)
27. Young, S., Evermann, G., Gales, M., Hain, T., Kershaw, D., Moore, G., Odell, J., Ollason, D., Povey, D., Valtchev, V., Woodland, P.: HTK Book. Cambridge University Engineering Department, UK (2005)
28. Żelasko, P., Ziółko, B., Jadczyk, T., Skurzok, D.: AGH corpus of Polish speech. In: Language Resources and Evaluation, pp. 1–17 (2015)
29. Ziółko, B., Ziółko, M.: Przetwarzanie mowy. Wydawnictwo AGH, Kraków (2011)

Morphology

Automatic Morpheme Slot Identification Using Genetic Algorithm

Wondwossen Mulugeta[1(✉)], Michael Gasser[2], and Baye Yimam[1]

[1] Addis Ababa University, Addis Ababa, Ethiopia
{wondisho,baye.yemam}@aau.edu.et
[2] Indiana University, Bloomington, USA
gasser@cs.indiana.edu

Abstract. We introduce an approach to the grouping of morphemes into suffix slots in morphologically complex languages using genetic algorithm. The method is applied to verbs in Amharic, an under-resourced morphologically rich Semitic language, with a number of non-concatenative prefix and suffix morphemes. We start with a limited set of segmented verbs and the set of suffixes themselves, extracted on the basis of our previous work. Each member of the population for the genetic algorithm is an assignment of the morphemes to one of the possible slots. The fitness function combines scores for exact slot position and correct ordering of morphemes. We use mutation but no crossover operator with various combinations of population size, mutation rate, and number of generations, and models evolve to yield promising morpheme classification results with 90.02 % accuracy level. We evaluate the fittest individuals on the basis of the known morpheme classes for Amharic.

Keywords: Amharic · Morpheme slots · Genetic algorithm · Morphological analysis · Machine learning

1 Introduction

Amharic is a Semitic language with complex morphology, spoken by around 27 million people in Ethiopia. Although Amharic has official status in Ethiopia and many Amharic documents are available online, there are few computational applications in place to manipulate text fragments produced in Amharic. One of the fundamental computational tasks for a language such as Amharic is analysis of its morphology, where the goal is to derive the root and grammatical properties of a word based on its internal structure. Morphological analysis, especially for complex languages like Amharic, is vital for the development of many practical natural language processing systems such as machine-readable dictionaries, machine translation, information retrieval, spell-checkers, and speech recognition. To date, only few hand-coded and machine learning approaches have been attempted for Amharic morphology.

In our previous work, we applied a weakly supervised machine learning approach to the learning of morphological rules [15]. We were able to learn various

© Springer International Publishing Switzerland 2016
Z. Vetulani et al. (Eds.): LTC 2013, LNAI 9561, pp. 85–97, 2016.
DOI: 10.1007/978-3-319-43808-5_7

affixes attached to the stem and analyse the internal stem structure of the verb, which is one of the crucial tasks in Semitic morphology. We were also able to learn stem-boundary orthographic alternation rules in Amharic. While our system is able to analyse a word into a segmented list of morphemes [14], it has not learned the valid positioning of the morphemes in their appropriate slots. The system is not able to distinguish if there are other possible morphemes that could come before, after or in-between the morphemes in the example.

This paper presents the continuation of our previous efforts. Using the already identified morphemes and a set of analysed examples, we show how genetic algorithm can arrive at a relatively accurate morpheme slot model without any initial knowledge of morpheme grouping into slots.

2   Computational Morphology

2.1   Amharic Morphology

For Amharic, like most other languages, verbs have the most complex morphology. In addition to the affixation, reduplication, and compounding common to other languages, in Amharic, as in other Semitic languages, verb stems consist of a merger of root and vowel sequence based on a specific template [2,18]. For example, the verb *seber* /break/ consists of the consonantal root *sbr*. The root combines with vowel sequence *ee* and a particular consonant-vowel template (CVCVC) to yield the verb stem: *sbr* + *ee* + CVCVC → *seber*.[1]

The vowel sequence intercalation with the root by means of a template can be seen as a stem-internal morpheme. This non-concatenative process makes morphological analysis more complex than in languages whose morphology is characterized by simple affixation. The affixes themselves also contribute to the complexity. Verbs can take up to six prefixes and up to six suffixes, and these morphemes have an intricate set of co-occurrence rules. The stem-internal vowel/template combinations as well as the affixes are all associated with grammatical features. In some cases, a grammatical feature is realized as a combination of affixes and/or stem-internal morphemes. Furthermore, some grammatical features realized as different morphemes may be incompatible and prevented from co-occurring in a given word. Thus, there are complex interrelationships and co-occurrence restrictions among the morphemes.

2.2   Morphological Analysis

Morphological analysis takes a surface word form and segments it into its constituent morphemes; it may in addition extract the relevant grammatical features associated with the morphemes. For example, the Amharic verb *alqeberkulxm* /I didn't bury for you (feminine)/ would be segmented into

---

[1] Amharic is written in the Geez script (see http://en.wikipedia.org/wiki/Ge'ez_script). In this paper we write Amharic words using a convention SERA romanization scheme.

al-qbr+ee+CVCVC-ku-l-x-m̩, with one possible grammatical analysis being as follows. root: *qbr*, aspect: *perfective*, polarity: *negative*, subject: *first person singular neuter*, object/dative/benefactive: *second person singular feminine*.

Morphology is simpler than syntax because most combinations can be defined in terms of a set of slots within the word, with particular classes of morphemes appearing in particular slots. In the example above, we see five of these slots, including one for the stem *qeber*, which has its own internal complexity (*qeber → qbr + ee* with CVCVC template). In most of these positions, other morphemes are also possible, with different lexical or grammatical implications and co-occurrence constraints. For example, the morpheme *ku* could be replaced with *u*, changing the subject of the verb from first person singular to third person plural: *alqeberulxm* /they didn't bury for you/.

3   Machine Learning of Morphology

3.1   Previous Work

Early work on computational morphology focused on efficient means of representing and processing hand-coded rules [1,7,8,10]. Unsupervised systems have the advantage of being trained on unprocessed word forms but may not be powerful enough to handle the alternation rules, non-concatenative processes, and complex morpheme interactions of a language such as Amharic. On the other hand, supervised approaches have important advantages of their own where they are less dependent on large corpora, requires less human effort, relatively fast which makes it scalable to other languages and that all rules in the language need not be enumerated.

More recently, attention has turned to the machine learning of morphology, which remains an extremely challenging task [17]. In machine learning, the approaches may be unsupervised [3–5] or supervised [9,16].

Among supervised approaches, the level of supervision is another point of variation. A weakly supervised approach may use pairs of word forms and stems as input [11,13,19]. More strongly supervised systems may require complete segmentation of input words or an analysis in the form of a stem or root and a set of grammatical morphemes.

3.2   Our Definition of the Task

Our long-term goal is an approach that can learn relatively complete knowledge of the morphology of an arbitrarily complex language without any prior knowledge of that language. For a complex language, we can only count on data for a very small proportion of the possible word forms. For example, in the case of Amharic, a single verb root may appear in thousands of distinct word forms.

We assume a weak form of supervision. Specifically, we have access to a single, relatively sophisticated native speaker of the language (the "Teacher") who can provide analyses of a small set of words, say, fewer than 1000, and who can sequence the data presented to the system on the basis of its complexity.

For Amharic verbs, this means that our learning system will work with data consisting of surface verb forms, together with the stem, root, and grammatical features provided by the Teacher. For example, the system is told that the word *seberkulh* can be analyzed as the stem being *seber*, containing the root *sbr*, and the list of grammatical features encoded as *"[1,1,1,2]"*, in which each position represents a grammatical feature such as subject person, number, gender, etc. Note that the information provided does not include the explicit segmentation of the word into its constituent morphemes or the vowel and the root that are combined using the template to produce the stem.

Accordingly, we divide the entire learning task into three stages:

1. Segmentation of the examples into component morphemes, resulting in an inventory of morphemes and initial knowledge about how morphemes combine to form words.
2. Identification of morpheme slots and classification of the morphemes in the inventory into classes corresponding to slots.
3. Discovery of co-occurrence constraints among morphemes.

Following Stage 1, the system is capable of analysing words that match one or more of the examples in the particular combination of morphemes that occur, other than the root, which we essentially treat as a variable [15]. However, because of the complex relationships among the morphemes, the system at this point is not necessarily capable of analysing arbitrary words. To enable this capacity, we need knowledge of the morphological relationships themselves. This is the purpose of Stage 2 and 3.

We briefly review this work in the next section. The rest of the paper discusses our approach to Stage 2. Stage 3 represents future work.

4   Stage 1: Segmentation

We have approached the general learning problem using Inductive Logic Programming (ILP), implemented in CLOG[2] a Prolog-based ILP system developed by [11]. CLOG learns first order decision lists (rules) on the basis of positive examples only. There have been several attempts to apply ILP to morphology [9,11,19]. Although these dealt with languages that are considerably simpler than Amharic, we were encouraged by their results. Inductive Logic Programming (ILP) identifies patterns and perform classification based on the knowledge acquired during training. ILP works through hypothesis generation and testing and is found to be flexibly applicable for language processing applications design [12].

As discussed in Subsect. 2.1, the morphology of Semitic languages features more or less separate processes of root-template combination and affixation; and we treat these as separate subtasks in Stage 1. Our experiments applying ILP to

---

[2] CLOG is a freely available ILP system at http://www-users.cs.york.ac.uk/suresh/CLOG.html.

these subtasks yield a set of rules that correctly analyzes most words with the same morphological structure as one or more of the training examples [15].

Along with the rule extraction, our system in Stage 1 is able to achieve 0.94 precision and 0.97 recall with respect to the identification and segmentation of morphemes in words by implementing incremental morpheme segmentation method [14].

However, we discovered that the order of presentation can potentially confuse the system. Specifically, when examples with affix sequences containing more morphemes are presented before those with fewer morphemes, the system may learn to treat a sequence of morphemes as a single affix.

Now, we are faced with the problem of generalizing from the presentation of particular morpheme combinations to any possible morpheme combination. To achieve this, we start with the fundamental assumption that most of natural language morphology is organized around sequences of morpheme slots, some obligatory, some optional, each filled by at most one morpheme from a particular class. Stage 2 concerns the learning of these slots and classification of the morphemes into classes.

5 Stage 2: Morpheme Classification and Slot Identification

An initial step in going beyond our previous results is to learn one key aspect of morphological knowledge that has, to our knowledge, not been studied in previous work on machine learning of morphology. Morphemes fall into classes, each of which defines a particular slot within the structure of a word. At most one morpheme from each class may appear in a given word. More to this, slots may be obligatory or optional, and they may interact in complex ways with one another.

Thus, our goal in this paper is to learn classes of morphemes and their order, given segmented words such as those output by our system following Stage 1. We assume that each morpheme is associated with a particular slot.[3]

5.1 Data Preparation

The basic data for automatically learning slots and morpheme classification are a simple list of morphemes extracted during the incremental affix segmentation process of our system and a list of segmented examples. The morpheme data is represented as a Prolog fact: *morph(Morpheme,Slot).*, where *Morpheme* is one of the morpheme for Amharic verbs and *Slot* is its corresponding position within a sequence of slots.

The data used to train the system are extracted from the training examples for Stage 1. We assume that Stage 1 has resulted in the capacity to correctly

---

[3] In this paper we do not address the problem of morpheme ambiguity (appearing in multiple slots), which arises in many languages, including Amharic. We leave this for future work.

segment these words on the basis of the learned rules. For the purposes of this paper, we focus on the suffixes of the example words.[4] An example datum is the following: *[[k],[b],[a,t]]*. That is, the word from which these data were extracted contains three suffix morphemes in the specified order. Note that the examples provide no information about which morphemes could be dropped from the given words and which other morphemes could be inserted before, between, or after them. This is the knowledge that we hope to learn on the basis of a number of such positive examples.

5.2 Model Representation

The basic information required to create the model is to identify which morpheme belongs to which slot. This can easily be represented by associating the known morphemes to a location in the slot. By a "model", we mean a possible solution to the slot identification and suffix morpheme classification task. While the experiment populates the model with other intermediate attributes, the most important elements of the model are the list of categorized morphemes, fitness score and relative fitness score of each model. The typical template of a model is:

Model Template: *modelfitness(Model, Score, RelativeScore).*

$$modelfitness(\{([k], [u], [n], [k, u]), ([h], [l, e]), ([b], [t]), ([n, a])\}, 78.52, 0.025).$$

Fig. 1. Slot model representation example

As shown in Fig. 1, the first argument is the sequence of suffix classes, the second argument is the fitness score of the model based on the applied fitness function in covering the examples, and the last is the relative score of the model against all other models generated in the respective population of models.

5.3 Genetic Algorithm

A genetic algorithm (GA) [6] is a search technique modelled based on biological evolution. Unlike heuristic search algorithms, GAs require no domain knowledge and are therefore appropriate for our task.

A GA starts with a randomly generated initial solution sets and iteratively changes the genome of the fittest individual solutions to create better solutions for the next generation. GA performs the task by generating many possible solutions and search through the solutions to identify best optimized model.

---

[4] A similar approach would apply to the prefixes, which are in any cases simpler in Amharic.

Applying a GA to a particular problem includes two crucial steps: determining an encoding scheme that represents each solution as a string of boolean or integers and defining the fitness function that governs which individuals are selected to produce the next generation. In our case, we represent each solution as a sequence of integers; each position in the genome represents a morpheme, and the integer in that position represents the morpheme's class as presented in Fig. 2. We explored various fitness functions, discussed in the next section.

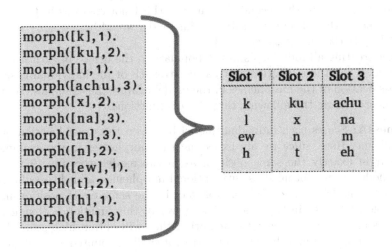

Fig. 2. Sample model encoding (left) and visualization (right)

A GA makes use of three operators to create a new generation, which are *selection*, *mutation* and *crossover*. In our case, mutation is concerned with adding or subtracting 1 to the integer in a particular genome position, that results in moving a morpheme to an adjacent slot position. For model selection we have used fitness proportionate (Roulette Wheel) selection method, which gives proportional selection probability for models based on their relative score. We use no crossover in generating new models. For morphemes found at the boundary of the affix sequence, the operation is either adding 1 on the first slot or subtracting 1 from the last slot number.

5.4 Experiments

For this experiment, we considered 30 suffix morphemes, generating 86 examples containing various grammatical combinations of these morphemes. Although we generated these examples by hand for the purpose of training and testing the system in isolation, we assume they could easily have resulted after Stage 1 of our learning system.

As stated in the previous section, the first step in genetic algorithm is the creation of the individuals with fixed population size. The population size can be adjusted as needed to yield more chance of generating fit individuals. In our case we have used population size of 1000. Accordingly, to initialize the GA, all the 30 suffix morphemes are assigned to random slots for each of the individual models in the population. A sample initial assignment of six morphemes would look as follows:

$morph([k,u],2).$; $morph([h],1).$; $morph([a,t],2).$;
$morph([l,e],2).$; $morph([t],3).$; $morph([k],1).$

In this initial random model, two morphemes belong to the first slot, three morphemes belong to the second slot and the third slot contains just one morpheme. The list-based representation of this model would be:

$\{([h],[k]),([k,u],[a,t],[l,e]),([t])\}.$

After creating all individuals in the population, the fitness of each has been computed. The fitness function assigns the strength of the individual based on the classification of the morphemes in the model against the examples. We have experimented using the following three fitness functions.

– **FitnessA:** Scores each individual model based on the exact location of the morpheme. Here, since we are expecting the morphemes in the example to appear in exactly the same position as in the model, this function penalizes models representing slots with optional morphemes. This fitness function promotes models that contain morphemes in the same exact position in the example as well as in the model. The power of this function is that if morphemes are always adjacent to each other they will obtain high score. If the exact location of a morpheme is not correct it shall be counted as a fail and the next morpheme in the example shall be checked for the subsequent position in the model. That means, all the first morphemes in the example are expected to be found in the first slot of the model, all the second morphemes in the example are expected to be found in the second slot of the model, and so on. The total number of successes against the total number of morphemes in the example will be tracked to compute the overall fitness of the model using the following formula where m_{ij} is the ith morpheme of the jth example.

$$\textbf{FitnessA} = \frac{\sum_{i=1}^{n} \sum_{j=1}^{m} Success(m_{ij})}{Count(m_{ij})} * 100 \tag{1}$$

– **FitnessB:** Scores each individual model based on the correct ordering of morphemes ignoring the actual distance between their slots. The computation for FitnessB is similar to FitnessA except that a morpheme which is not found in a current slot is checked in subsequent slots until it is found. And if this succeeds the function moves to the next morpheme in the example and continues from the next slot in the model without any penalty. If it fails to find the morpheme, ultimately since it will slide to the last slot of the model in an attempt to find the morpheme, all the remaining morphemes of that example are considered as failures, which will penalize the model by that much.
– **FitnessC:** is a hybrid fitness function that combines the exact slot position and correct ordering of morphemes approach. This hybrid fitness function

combines FitnessA and FitnessB to benefit from both exactness and correct ordering of morpheme with some ratio of contribution.

$$\mathbf{FitnessC} = \frac{FitnessA}{P_A} + \frac{FitnessB}{P_B} \tag{2}$$

Where P_A and P_B are the proportionate parameters used to control the contribution of FitnessA and FitnessB to the overall fitness score, and $P_B = 100 - P_A$.

Fitness-proportionate selection without crossover creates a new generation by copying individuals from the current population non-deterministically on the basis of their relative fitness within the population. After computing the fitness values of each individual, the process of computing the relative accuracy of each model should be computed to perform the selection.

As stated above, selection methods should give greater chance of being picked for reproduction in the next generation for fittest individuals. While there are many selection approaches, one of the prominent method is the Roulette Wheel. In Roulette Wheel, the wheel is proportionally divided for all individuals of the population based on the relative fitness value, where an area in the wheel will be reserved for each individual. Based on the number of individuals in the population, the wheel will be consulted with respect to a random number generated and the individual, whose area covers that random number, will be picked for creating the next generation. It is evident that best fit individuals will have a greater chance of being selected more than once since they cover relatively larger area in the wheel than weak individuals.

The next vital step is, creating the next generation from the list of the best individuals selected from the previous step. There are various approaches of creating new generation that includes but not limited to mutation, crossover and elitism [6]. The first two methods are non-deterministic approaches where in the process of creating the new generation, an individual may fail to improve or even degrade. The last method is a deterministic method where some of the best individuals are passed to the next generation without any change to maintain the performance of the new generation. In our experiment, we prefer to implement a non-deterministic method where mutation is preferred as it will not extremely affect the model under evaluation. Mutation changes only a small/few genome from the target individual. Thus, before a new generation is finalized, mutation is applied to the new population. In our experiment, as stated above, mutation is as simple as changing the slot position of a morpheme to the neighbouring slot. Here, the mutation probability is generally kept low so as not to disrupt the whole morpheme grouping to maintain the gradual improvement of individual models. This way, a good number of morphemes will remain in their original slot position.

Before a new generation is finalized, mutation is applied to the selected individuals. Mutation, in our case, is shifting a morpheme one slot to the right or left based on its current position. The morphemes/genomes which will be subjected for mutation are probabilistically selected. An attempt was also made to determine whether a model should be mutated or not in a non-deterministic fashion.

Here we illustrate mutation with a single individual (model) in both the Prolog and list representations.

– Before mutation:
      $morph([k,u],2)$.
      $morph([h],1)$.
      $morph([a,t],2)$.
      $morph([l,e],2)$.
      $morph([t],3)$.
      $morph([k],1)$.
      The Model Would be: $(\{[h],[k]\},\{[k,u],[a,t],[l,e]\},\{[t]\})$

– After mutation:
      $morph([k,u],3)$.
      $morph([h],1)$.
      $morph([a,t],2)$.
      $morph([l,e],1)$.
      $morph([t],3)$.
      $morph([k],1)$.
      The Model Would be: $(\{[h],[l,e],[k]\},\{[a,t]\},\{[l,e],[t]\})$.

In the above example, only the first and the fourth morphemes/genomes are randomly (using small probability) chosen for mutation. This new model will again go through the whole process of begin evaluated for fitness, selection, and mutation in the next generation.

After each members of the new generation are subjected for mutation based on the randomization, the whole process of fitness evaluation, selection based on roulette wheel method and mutation happens as many as the number of maximum generation. To evaluate the GA's performance, we track the average fitness of the population and the fitness of the best individual model from each population. We have also used a review by a linguist as the basic measure of accuracy to verify how many morphemes are placed in their appropriate slot.

5.5   Results and Discussion

We conducted experiments using various mutation rates, population sizes, and maximum number of generations. Overall, our results show that a non-deterministic genetic algorithm can generate a morpheme clustering model from a randomly generated initial model population. Relatively, small mutation rates (around 5 %) with large population size (greater than 500) tend to find better model faster.

The average fitness score ranges between 52.0 % and 65.4 % in different setups. Table 2 shows the best individual models and average population fitness with various parameter values for the proportion of order and exact location of morphemes and mutation rate for models and morphemes. But these fitness scores are not the appropriate measure of accuracy for the model. The validation of the models generated at the end may be done with the count of morphemes that are put in their correct slot with the help of linguistic knowledge of Amharic. Using this criterion, we were able to find a model with 90.2 % individual fitness score to be more accurate in putting the morphemes in their appropriate slot (presented in Table 1). The table shows that a model generated with 2 % morpheme mutation rate and all individual models subjected to mutation exhibits the best result.

Table 1. Model generated with 90.2 % accuracy

Slot-1	Slot-2	Slot-3	Slot-4	Slot-5
$[E]$	$[l]$	$[a, t]$	$[m]$	$[n, a]$
$[k]$	$[b]$	$[a]$	$[a]$	
$[k, u]$		$[h]$		
$[a, c, h, u]$		$[a, c, e, w]$		
$[u]$		$[t]$		

The experiments also shows (see Fig. 3) that the overall population fitness rapidly increases in the early stages of the evolution and gradually attains a certain average fitness value. Moreover, favouring models with the correct order of morphemes rather than exact slot position is found to be closer to the ultimate solution. This result is achieved by generating the model with different ratio for order and exact location where the fitness score is found to be higher for a model with 70/30 ratio (refer the first two columns of Table 2).

In comparing the performance of the three fitness functions, the hybrid fitness function (FitnessC) was found to outperform the rest with the highest possible accuracy, covering 90.2 % of the examples.

6   Conclusion and Future Work

Our experiment shows that genetic algorithms can generate nearly optimal morphological slot models for a complex language. Our method examines the entire search space of possible models and uses a simple list of morphemes and validation examples to measure the accuracy of models. For the moment, our system does not deal with ambiguous morphemes that may appear in multiple slots simultaneously, representing different grammatical features. One way to address this deficiency is to assume two or more possible positions and classes for each morpheme (with its own probability). We also plan to explore other fitness functions. Finally, we will be tackling Stage 3 of our project, the discovery of morpheme interactions.

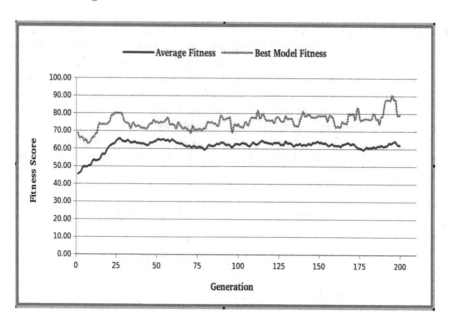

Fig. 3. Average population fitness over generation

Table 2. Fitness after 200 generations with 500 population *Slot Order: proportion of correct order* **Exact Slot:** *proportion of morpheme position accuracy.* **Model MR:** *probability of picking an individual model for mutation.* **Morph MR:** *probability of picking a morpheme in a model for mutation.* **Best Fitness:** *fitness score of best individual model in last generation.* **Avg Fitness:** *average fitness of individuals in last generation.*

Slot order	Exact slot	Model MR	Morph MR	Best fitness	Avg fitness
50 %	50 %	5 %	2 %	60.5 %	58.2 %
50 %	50 %	15 %	2 %	59.9 %	56.9 %
50 %	50 %	100 %	2 %	66.4 %	55.7 %
70 %	30 %	5 %	2 %	90.2 %	65.4 %
70 %	30 %	15 %	2 %	64.7 %	61.4 %
70 %	30 %	100 %	2 %	68.9 %	60.5 %
30 %	70 %	5 %	2 %	63.9 %	61.9 %
30 %	70 %	15 %	2 %	58.4 %	54.8 %
30 %	70 %	100 %	2 %	62.4 %	52.0 %

References

1. Beesley, K.R., Karttunen, L.: Finite State Morphology, CSLI Studies in Computational Linguistics, vol. 3. CSLI Publications, Stanford (2003)
2. Bender, M.L.: Amharic verb morphology: a generative approach. Ph.D. thesis, Graduate School of Texas (1968)

3. De Pauw, G., Wagacha, P.W.: Bootstrapping morphological analysis of gikuyu using unsupervised maximum entropy learning. In: Proceedings of the Eighth INTERSPEECH Conference, Antwerp, Belgium (2007)
4. Goldsmith, J.: The unsupervised learning of natural language morphology. Comput. Linguist. **27**, 153–198 (2001)
5. Hammarström, H., Borin, L.: Unsupervised learning of morphology. Comput. Linguist. **37**(2), 309–350 (2011)
6. Holland, J.H.: Adapt. Nat. Artif. Syst. MIT Press, Cambridge (1992)
7. Kaplan, R.M., Kay, M.: Regular models of phonological rule systems. Comput. Linguist. **20**(3), 331–378 (1994)
8. Karttunen, L., Kaplan, R.M., Zaenen, A.: Two level morphology with composition. In: Proceedings of the International Conference on Computational Linguistics, vol. 14, no. 1, pp. 141–148 (1992)
9. Kazakov, D.: Achievements and prospects of learning word morphology with inductive logic programming. In: Cussens, J., Džeroski, S. (eds.) LLL 1999. LNCS (LNAI), vol. 1925, pp. 89–109. Springer, Heidelberg (2000)
10. Koskenniemi, K.: Two level morphology: a general computational model for word-form recognition and production. In: Proceedings of the 10th International Conference on Computational Linguistics-COLING 1984. Association for Computational Linguistics, pp. 178–181 (1984)
11. Manandhar, S., Džeroski, S., Erjavec, T.: Learning multilingual morphology with CLOG. In: Page, David L. (ed.) ILP 1998. LNCS, vol. 1446, pp. 135–144. Springer, Heidelberg (1998)
12. Mooney, R.J.: Inductive logic programming. In: Mitkov, R. (ed.) Oxford Handbook of Computational Linguistics, pp. 376–394. Oxford University Press, Oxford (1997)
13. Mooney, R.J.: Machine learning. In: Mitkov, R. (ed.) Oxford Handbook of Computational Linguistics, pp. 376–394. Oxford University Press, Oxford (2003)
14. Wondwossen, M., Gasser, M., Baye, Y.: Incremental learning of affix segmentation. In: Proceedings of the 24th International Conference on Computational Linguistics-COLING 2012, pp. 1901–1914. Association for Computational Linguistics (ACL), Mumbai, India (2012)
15. Wondwossen, M., Gasser, M.: Learning morphological rules for Amharic verbs using inductive logic programming. In: Proceedings of SALTMIL-AfLaT Workshop on Language Technology for Normalisation of Less-Resourced Languages, Istanbul, Turkey, pp. 7–12 (2012)
16. Oflazer, K., Nirenburg, S., McShane, M.: Bootstrapping morphological analyzers by combining human elicitation and machine learning. Comput. Linguist. **27**(1), 59–85 (2001)
17. Spiegler, S.R.: Machine learning for the analysis of morphologically complex languages. Ph.D. thesis. University of Bristol (2011)
18. Baye, Y.: Yamarigna Sewasiw (Amharic Grammar). EMPDA Publications, Addis Ababa (1995)
19. Ivanovska, A., Zdravkova, K., Džeroski, S., Erjavec, T.: Learning rules for morphological analysis and synthesis of Macedonian nouns. In: Proceedings of SiKDD-2005 Conference on Data Mining and Data Warehouses, Ljubljana, Sloveniapp, pp. 195–198 (2005)

From Morphology to Lexical Hierarchies and Back

Krešimir Šojat$^{(\boxtimes)}$ and Matea Srebačić

Faculty of Humanities and Social Sciences, University of Zagreb, Zagreb, Croatia
ksojat@ffzg.hr, msrebaci@unizg.hr
http://croderiv.ffzg.hr/

Abstract. This paper deals with language resources for Croatian and discusses the possibilities of their combining in order to improve their coverage and density of structure. Two resources in focus are Croatian WordNet (CroWN) and CroDeriV - a large database of Croatian verbs with morphological and derivational data. The data from CroDeriV is used for enlargement of CroWN and the enrichment of its lexical hierarchies. It is argued that the derivational relatedness of Croatian verbs plays a crucial role in establishing morphosemantic relations and an important role in detecting semantic relations.

Keywords: Derivational morphology · Morphosemantic relations · Semantic relations · Croatian WordNet · CroDeriV

1 Introduction

This paper[1] deals with language resources for Croatian and discusses the possibilities of their inter-connection. The main goal of the paper is to present how a new language resource can enrich an existing one. We are linking Croatian WordNet - a semantic net for Croatian - and CroDeriV - a large morphological database of Croatian verbs. We discuss how data from CroDeriV can enrich Croatian WordNet in terms of its quantity and quality. In this paper we deal exclusively with verbs and the different types of relations that exist among them. The relations among the verbs discussed here are primarily morphosemantic relations. Morphosemantic relations refer to semantic relations between morphologically related verbs, i.e., between verbs from the same derivational family. The paper is structured as follows: in Sect. 2 we describe the most important language resources for Croatian and we focus on CroWN and CroDeriV. In Sect. 3 we describe the experiment we conducted, in Sects. 4 and 5 the obtained results are discussed, and in the conclusion we provide an outline of further work.

---

[1] This is an extended version of the paper "From Morphology to Lexical Hierarchies" [11] presented at the 6th Language Technology Conference in Poznań in December 2013 and published in the Proceedings of the Conference.

© Springer International Publishing Switzerland 2016
Z. Vetulani et al. (Eds.): LTC 2013, LNAI 9561, pp. 98–111, 2016.
DOI: 10.1007/978-3-319-43808-5_8

2 Language Resources for Croatian

Freely available language resources (further *LRs*) for Croatian, an inflectional language with very rich derivational processes and relatively free word order, comprise two big monolingual corpora, the Croatian National Corpus[2] (CNC; ca 234 Mw) and the Croatian Web Corpus[3] (hrWaC; ca 1.2 Bw), several parallel corpora, as well as the Croatian Dependency Treebank [17]), the Croatian Valency Lexicon [5], the Croatian Morphological Lexicon[4] [15] and Croatian WordNet [8].[5] The Treebank and the Valency Lexicon closely follow the theoretical model applied in the building of the Prague Dependency Treebank [1] on the analytical level and Vallex [19] on the tectogrammatical level. The Croatian Morphological Lexicon contains complete inflectional data for ca 125,000 lemmas. At the same time, the Croatian Morphological Lexicon serves as a basis for a lemmatizer and a word-form generator [16]. There are also three stemmers designed to be used in information extraction tasks ([3,7,9]). In order to detect morphological stems, these stemmers remove inflectional endings, as well as a limited number of derivational suffixes, such as suffixes denoting gender pairs or gerunds. A freely available parser for the analysis of Croatian words in terms of morpheme structure does not exist. Unfortunately, the stemmers mentioned above cannot be used as a reliable basis for its construction, since their output is frequently either a stem or a root, and sometimes even a string, which cannot be defined in strict linguistic terms. Furthermore, these stemmers cannot cope with derivational processes and phenomena beyond suffixations - e.g., (multiple) prefixation and compounding. Therefore, for the more accurate performance of existing NLP tools for morphological analysis as well as for the development of new ones, the rich derivational processes that occur in Croatian must be taken into account. As will be shown, the rich derivational morphology of Croatian must not be neglected in the development of other LRs for Croatian, as well. In the following sections, we focus on the role that derivational processes between verbs have in the building of Croatian WordNet and CroDeriV. In the following subsections we present the structure and design of these two LRs and briefly present the problems encountered in coping with derivation in Croatian.

2.1 Croatian WordNet

Croatian WordNet (*CroWN*) is a lexical database built through the so-called expand model [18]. The building of CroWN can be divided into two major phases. The first phase consisted of the translation and adaptation of the basic concept sets from the multilingual projects EuroWordNet (*EWN*) and BalkaNet (*BN*),

---

[2] [14], www.hnk.ffzg.hr.

[3] [2], www.nljubesic.net/resources/corpora/hrwac.

[4] www.hml.ffzg.hr.

[5] All these LRs for Croatian are accessible also through the META-SHARE platform: www.meta-share.eu/, a part of META-NET Network of Excellence (www.meta-net. eu).

originally taken from Princeton WordNet. In its present form, CroWN contains just above 10,000 synsets. 8,500 of these are from the basic concept sets of EWN and BN. Each synset was manually translated and provided with meaning definitions and usage examples. Synsets contain lexical units of the same part of speech. In more detail, CroWN contains 7,391 noun synsets, 2,318 verb synsets, and 310 adjective synsets. As the numbers indicate, nouns make up almost 75 % of the whole lexicon. The strong predominance of noun synsets was a motivation to make CroWN a more balanced and representative resource for Croatian. Therefore, the second phase of the project is primarily focused on enlarging the number of verbal synsets. However, this task proved to be more complicated than was assumed. The main challenge in this phase of the project is determining how to fulfill these two goals and at the same time how to account for the rich derivational processes and relations that hold between Croatian verbs. In order to address these issues, we decided to consult data from CroDeriV, a newly developed LR for Croatian.

2.2   CroDeriV

CroDeriV is a computational lexicon that contains data on the morphological structure of approximately 14,300 Croatian verbs collected from machine readable mono-lingual dictionaries and corpora. The primary motivation for building this resource is to obtain a complete morphological analysis of the Croatian vocabulary. The results of this analysis are to be used in the development of other resources and NLP tools. At its current stage of development, CroDeriV contains only verbal lemmas - i.e., verbs in infinitive form - whereas other POS will be added and analyzed for morphemes and various derivational processes in upcoming phases. The analysis of lexemes in terms of morpheme structure is both a theoretically and methodologically highly challenging task. Full morphological analysis in accordance with linguistic principles requires an elaborate set of linguistic rules for automatic processing. Although the rules for automatic segmentation were carefully designed, the obtained results were in many cases unsatisfactory. The final objective of the designed rules was to detect the basic stock of roots - i.e., lexical morphemes in Croatian. This set will be used as a basis for organizing derivationally related words of other POS to be included.

Verbs in Croatian are derived from other verbs by prefixation and suffixation, with prefixation being far more productive. In the vast majority of cases, base forms - i.e., verbs that serve as a starting point for derivation - take one prefix, but this process can be recursive, and derivatives can further be prefixed. In terms of morphological structure, one verbal root as part of a base form can co-occur in some rare cases with as many as four prefixes. As far as suffixes are concerned, one root usually has two derivational and one inflectional suffix, but this structure can be extended with an additional suffix denoting a diminutive or pejorative action. On top of that, verbs in Croatian can also be formed by compounding - i.e., they can consist of two roots. Thus, the determined maximal morphological structure of Croatian verbs, based on the analysis of a large dataset, is as follows:

(P4) + (P3) + (P2) + (P1) + (R) + (I) + R + (S3) + S2 + S1 + ti, where P = prefix, R = root, I = interfix, S = suffix, ti = infinitive ending, and ( ) = non-obligatory.

The two main problems in the automated processing of Croatian derivation are (1) homography that results in the overlapping of prefixes and suffixes with roots, and (2) numerous phonological changes at the morpheme boundaries resulting in several allomorphs per each base morpheme. For example, the correct surface morphological analysis[6] of the verb *snježiti* 'to snow' is separated as *snjež* + *i* + *ti* (allomorph base *snjež*, from the noun *snijeg* 'snow'), but the output of the automated analysis was *s* + *nijež* + *i* + *ti*, since there is a prefix *s-* in Croatian. Similar problems occur on root-suffix boundaries. Both homography and allomorphy make the complete and exhaustive automatic analysis of words literally impossible. Therefore, all results of automatic segmentation were manually checked, and at the same time, all allomorphs, both affixal and lexical, were connected to one representative morpheme in CroDeriV. This kind of processing enabled (1) the recognition of all allomorphs of a particular morpheme and (2) the detection of all affixes that co-occur with particular roots. This procedure further enabled the detection of complete derivational families of verbs in Croatian. In other words, for the first time, the detection of full derivational spans of particular verbal roots based on large-scale data became possible. Data structured in this way can be used in the enlargement and enrichment of CroWN, which will be shown in Sect. 3.

2.3 Derivationally Motivated Relations

Apart from pure morphological analysis, this kind of structure provides a basis for the investigation of morphosemantic relations - i.e., relations between verbs sharing the same root. As mentioned, verbs in Croatian are derived from other verbs by prefixation and suffixation. Both processes can cause a change in aspect and the addition of a new semantic component to the base form. The semantic impact of affixes on the meaning of base verbs can be either compositional or non-compositional. For example, the verb *lupati* 'to beat, to batter$_{ipf}$' has a true aspectual pair *lupiti* 'to beat, to batter$_{pf}$', but there are other prefixed perfectives of this base verb as well: 1. *iz+lupati* 'to beat one by one$_{pf}$', 2. *pro+lupati* 'to become crazy$_{pf}$', 3. *za+lupati* 'to start to beat$_{pf}$', 4. *na+lupati* 'to beat vigorously$_{pf}$', 5. *po+lupati* 'to break down$_{pf}$', 6. *raz+lupati* 'to break to pieces$_{pf}$', 7. *s+lupati* 'to demolish$_{pf}$', 8. *u+lupati* 'to squander$_{pf}$'. All these prefixes can also be used with other base forms. The base form *lupati* 'to beat, to batter$_{ipf}$' can also be suffixed, e.g. 1. *lup-k-ati* 'to beat$_{ipf}$, diminutive', 2. *lup-nu-ti* 'to hit once$_{pf}$, low intensity', 3. *lup-et-ati* 'to blather$_{ipf}$, pejorative'. Suffixes with diminutive and pejorative meanings can also combine with other base forms. Semantic components such as repetitiveness, distributiveness, beginning or termination of an action, various degrees or quantities, etc. are usually referred to

---

[6] Deep morphological structure should include zero-morphs, but the simplified structure is adequate enough for the present analysis.

as Aktionsart and are typical of Slavic languages. These semantic components are part of the lexical meaning of verbal lemmas in Croatian. As can be seen from the underlined parts in the translations above, these semantic components are expressed with additional lexical units in English. In other words, they are not lexicalized as single lemmas. Due to the expand model used in the building of CroWN, most of the derivatives denoting temporal or spatial components, for example, are not included in its present form. The semantic component of distributivity is generally not a part of the lexical meaning of English verbs, whereas it is a common and frequent feature of verbal meanings in Croatian, provided that the semantics of the base form allows the action to be iteratively performed by multiple subjects and/or on multiple objects. Such derivationally motivated relations, which we refer to as morphosemantic relations, are significantly under-represented in CroWN, resulting in a shallow lexical and semantic structure of the verbal part of the lexicon. In order to overcome this deficiency, we explored the possibility of introducing the data from CroDeriV to CroWN. Our primary aim is to enrich derivational families of verbs from CroWN according to derivationally motivated semantic relatedness of Croatian verbs. The secondary goal is to speed up the building of this resource and to enlarge its structure. For these reasons we have conducted the following experiment.

3   Experiment Setup

The main goal of the experiment is to detect full derivational spans of verbs from CroWN by matching them with verbs from CroDeriV. As far as the relations between the base verb and the discussed derivatives are concerned, very frequently they cannot be captured by the semantic relations used between verbal synsets in CroWN.[7] The secondary goal of the experiment is to determine which type of relations - morphosemantic vs. semantic - prevails in the detected derivational families. The experiment was conducted in several steps. The first step was the extraction of all verbal synsets and all verbs from verbal synsets in CroWN. All metadata from synsets - e.g., definitions, usage examples etc. - was removed. In further processing, all infinitive forms from CroWN were treated as morphological tokens and reduced to a list of morphological types. In other words, all verb-sense pairs from CroWN were reduced to a list of unique verbal forms. In the next step we compared and matched lists of verbs from CroWN and CroDeriV in order to determine the set of verbs present in both resources. The results of the coverage measure are shown in Table 1.

The table indicates that CroDeriV covers almost all verbs treated as morphological types from CroWN (only 297 verbs from CroWN are not listed in CroDeriV, which contains 14,320 verbs). However, more than 2/3 of all verbs in

---

[7] We use the same semantic relations between verbal synsets as in EWN and BN: synonymy, hyponymy / hypernymy, antonymy, cause, and subevent. The most elaborate account of derivationally motivated relations, i.e. morphosemantic relations, between verbs used in a wordnet for a Slavic language is given in [4]. Morphosemantic and semantic relations of Croatian verbs are discussed in [12,13].

Table 1. Coverage

cov(CroDeriV/WN)	**0,9856**
cov(WN/CroDeriV)	**0,3266**

CroDeriV are not included in verbal synsets in CroWN. The subset of matched verbs was used in the further steps. The second part of the experiment was to determine word families in CroDeriV that contain at least one verb from CroWN. The derivational families were extracted from CroDeriV via mutual lexical morphemes and the verbs from CroWN were labeled respectively. Table 2 lists the most- and least-covered verb families.

Table 2. 10 most- and least-covered verb families in CroWN (families with > 6 members)

Highest ratio		Lowest ratio	
dužiti 'to extend'	1,0000	mlatiti 'to thrash'	0,0455
kupiti 'to pick'	1,0000	blistati 'to shine'	0,0476
tražiti 'to seek'	1,0000	cikati 'to squeak'	0,0667
množiti 'to multiply'	1,0000	vojevati 'to wage war'	0,0667
povećati 'to enlarge'	1,0000	drapati 'to tear'	0,0714
gladiti 'to smooth'	1,0000	pasati 'to grid'	0,0714
spomenuti 'to mention'	1,0000	jebati 'to fuck'	0,0769
tratiti 'to waste'	1,0000	šarafiti 'to screw'	0,0833
isključiti 'to exclude'	0,9473	pregnuti 'to exert'	0,0909
držati 'to hold'	0,9444	crnjeti 'to black'	0,1

The final goal of the experiment was to determine how mutual morphological structure of verbs from both resources can enable the expansion of CroWN and how to account for relations that exist among the detected derivational families in CroDeriV. In the next section, we present the results of the experiment.

4   Results

We will present the results we obtained by matching data from both resources with examples from the derivational families of the verbs *pjevati* 'to sing', *pisati* 'to write' and *letjeti* 'to fly'. These derivational families were analyzed in order to determine the type of relations (semantic or morphosemantic) between base verbs and their derivatives. We also wanted to determine whether the type of relations enables or blocks the inclusion of particular members of selected derivational families into CroWN due to the adopted expand model (cf. Sect. 2.1.).

The verb family *pjevati* 'to sing' consists of 28 verbs, but only 3 of them are included in CroWN: base verb *pjevati* 'to sing', and the diminutive verbs *pjevuckati* and *pjevuiti*. All derivatives that could be related to the base verb by morphosemantic relations - derivatives denoting, for example, beginning and termination point (*zapjevati* 'to start singing', *otpjevati* 'to finish singing') or intensity of an action (*ispjevati se* 'to sing one's heart out') - are not included in CroWN.

Derivatives that can be related to the base verb *pjevati* via different morphosemantic relations cannot be translated by a single verb in English. This base form also has derivative forms with non-compositional meaning (e.g., *opjevati* 'to praise (in song)', *spjevati* 'compose a poem') and even metaphorical meaning (e.g., propjevati 'to squeal (on someone)'). Such non-compositional combinations are not members of same lexical hierarchies as their base verb, and they can therefore be related to other synsets via already used semantic relations. However, this is not the case with other members of this derivational family.

The distinction in semantic vs. morphosemantic relations is more obvious within the derivational family of the verb *letjeti* 'to fly'. This family consists of 38 verbs, only 10 of which are included in CroWN. Only the base verb *letjeti* 'to fly' and its derivative *preletjeti* 'to fly over, to finish flying' are present in CroWN in their primary meaning. Eight other derivatives are also present in CroWN - not in their primary meaning ('to start flying', 'to fly by', 'to fly into something', respectively), but in their metaphorical meanings denoting actions such as rushing, hurrying, etc. The same holds for other derivatives from this derivational family. Although the primary meanings of the verbs *doletjeti*, *odletjeti*, and *izletjeti* are respectively 'to fly to', 'to leave by flying', and 'to fly from', they are listed in CroWN only in their metaphorical senses ('to waft', 'to burst', etc.) Finally, the verb *naletjeti* is listed in CroWN only in the senses 'to run into' and 'to come about', although its primary meaning is 'to hit into something when flying'. Croatian prefixed motion verbs retain the meaning of the base verb with further specification of spatial components (e.g., direction) or temporal components (e.g., inchoativity). The semantics of all Croatian motion verbs is in this respect the same. Their primary meaning is always locative, and their polysemous structure is the result of metonymical and metaphorical shifts. However, the inherited structure from PWN does not reveal their primary meaning in Croatian since it is not lexicalized in English verbs (cf. Sect. 2.2.). In other words, spatial components are expressed in constructions such as verb + preposition or verb + adverb in English (e.g., 'to fly from'), but they are lexicalized via prefixes in Croatian verbs (*izletjeti*[8]). To sum up, when affixes modify the lexical meaning of base verbs in terms of locative, quantitative or time components - i.e., when the meaning of the derivative verb is more or less compositional - we are dealing with morphosemantic relations. As a rule, these kinds of semantic modifications are captured neither by PWN synsets nor by the relational structure between them. On the other hand, derivatives with metaphorical shifts in

---

[8] Note that Croatian prefixes are developed from prepositions: the prefix *iz-*, for example, is developed from the preposition *iz*, both meaning 'from'.

their lexical meaning and derivatives with completely idiosyncratic meanings denote independent concepts and have their own counterparts in PWN synsets. This is the reason why Croatian verbs like *poletjeti* 'to start to fly', *proletjeti* 'to fly through' and *odletjeti* 'to fly away' should be related to their base form via morphosemantic relations in the future development of CroWN.

Finally, the verb family *pisati* consists of 36 verbs, among which only 16 are also found in CroWN. This family also contains verbs with multiple prefixes - e.g., *ispotpisati* 'to sign one by one' or *nadopisati* 'to add by writing'. These prefixal combinations further modify or narrow the meaning of the base verb, regarding the categories of distributiveness and intensity of an action. Verbs with multiple prefixes in Croatian denote concepts that cannot be captured by single word units in English. Consequently, the possible synsets to which such morphologically complex verbs could be attached do not exist in PWN. On the other hand, derivatives denoting concepts which are expressed by single units or phrasal verbs in English are included in CroWN, although the relation between them does not reveal their derivational relation. For example, the verb *pisati* 'to write' has the derivative *opisati* 'to describe' present in CroWN, but the derivational relation between them cannot be captured, since it does not exist in English, nor consequently in PWN and CroWN.

All analyzed verb families clearly show the under-representation of derivatives in CroWN, due to the typological differences between Croatian and English, which were further reinforced by using the expand model in the development of CroWN. However, without including derivational data, CroWN cannot be considered as a valid lexico-semantic net for Croatian, because: (1) it does not contain a significant part of Croatian lexicon and (2) it does not reveal semantic relations between verbs based on their derivational properties. Their morphological and semantic relatedness could be captured by introducing morphosemantic relations. A similar situation can be detected in other Slavic languages, so this kind of analysis and language resources enrichment can be conducted for wordnets in all Slavic languages.

5   Discussion

As mentioned above, without including derivational data, CroWN cannot be considered as a valid lexico-semantic net for Croatian, since a significant part of the Croatian lexicon is not included. Furthermore, a significant part of the lexicon cannot be included, since relations between derivationally connected verbs are neither indicated nor provided. We have pointed out that these deficiencies could be overcome by introducing morphosemantic relations used as complementary or parallel to existing semantic relations. Therefore, in this section we focus on the following questions: (1) How can a set of morphosemantic relations as discussed here be identified and determined? and (2) What are the main differences between the morphosemantic relations and semantic relations already used? With regard to the first issue, there are two possible approaches: (a) bottom-up and (b) top-down. Both approaches are based on a previously detected set of derivational affixes and base forms and an analysis of affixes and derivatives in various derivational families.

In a bottom-up approach, an established set of morphosemantic relations would result from the analysis of semantically diverse derivational families and affixal meanings recorded in combinations with different base forms. Although time-consuming and challenging, such an analysis would provide exact information about the frequency and relevance of particular morphosemantic relations. The main precondition for such an effort, however, is a lexicon with an elaborate division of verbal lexemes into word senses. Unfortunately, neither of the lexicons in focus here - CroDeriV and Croatian WordNet - satisfies this precondition. In its present shape, CroDeriV contains verbs in infinitive form and provides information about their morphological structure. On the other hand, verbs in CroWN are divided into lexical units (i.e., word senses) but the lexical hierarchies and senses inherited from PWN are in many cases substantially different from the lexical meaning, number of senses, and sense relations in their Croatian counterparts. For example, the verb *dati* 'to give$_{ipf}$' appears in 28 synsets in CroWN i.e., it is marked for 28 senses. Such a particularization of meaning is a consequence of the adopted expand model, and does not reflect its true semantic structure. Although *dati* is a highly polysemous verb, we found only 12 different senses of this verb in various monolingual dictionaries. Even semantically less complex verbs are divided into senses that do not correspond to their common divisions in Croatian. For example, the verb *jesti* 'to eat$_{ipf}$' has two senses in CroWN, one of them defined as 'to take in solid food', the other one very similarly as 'to eat a meal'.

For these reasons, we determined the initial set of morphosemantic relations between verbs by means of a top-down approach. Generally, a set of morphosemantic relations established in this way results from the analysis of affixal meanings in combination with selected base forms. The precondition for this approach is the analysis of affixal meanings. In [12] and [10] morphosemantic relations are discussed in more detail. The proposed set of morphosemantic relations between verbs is established through the analysis of prefixes and suffixes used in the derivation of verbs from other verbs. In [12], a more detailed theoretical account of morphosemantic relations is given, whereas [10] explore the possibilities of their full integration into CroWN.

As mentioned in Sect. 2.2, apart from the change in aspect prefixes and suffixes generally create a shift in the meaning of base forms. The semantic impact of suffixes is rather limited, and they are predominately used for the formation of verbs denoting diminutive actions or pejorative attitudes. On the other hand, the semantic impact of prefixes is much wider and less predictable and in various combinations they can modify the meaning of base forms differently. In terms of their meaning, combinations of prefixes and base forms can vary from more or less compositional to completely idiosyncratic. Although the majority of verbal prefixes in Croatian developed from prepositions and the original locative component pervades in their meaning, their semantic structure is much more complex and diverse. A good example of this is the verbal prefix *za-*:

1. pure aspectual meaning: *zaklati* 'to slaughter$_{pf}$'
2. locative meanings:
   - to put something behind something: *zabaciti* 'to throw behind$_{pf}$'
   - to put something onto something: *zakačiti* 'to attach$_{pf}$'
   - to change position: *zaleći* 'to lie down$_{pf}$'
   - to move around: *zakrenuti* 'to go in a curve or around the corner$_{pf}$'
3. inchoativity: *zapjevati* 'to start singing$_{pf}$'
4. more or less intensified action: *zamisliti se* 'to ponder$_{pf}$', *zagorjeti* 'to scorch$_{pf}$'
5. change of property: *zacrvenjeti se* 'to become red$_{pf}$'

Other prefixes can have even more complex structures. For example, the verbal prefix *na-* can have at least eight different meanings (divided further into several sub-groups) in combinations with various base forms:

1. pure aspectual meaning: *pisati* 'to write$_{ipf}$' - *napisati* 'to write$_{pf}$'
2. locative meanings:
   - top-down: *baciti* 'to throw$_{pf}$' - *nabaciti* 'to throw onto$_{pf}$'
   - proximity: *letjeti* 'to fly$_{ipf}$' - *naletjeti* 'to bump into$_{pf}$'
   - putting something on something: *slagati* 'to pile$_{ipf}$' - *naslagati* 'to pile one onto another$_{pf}$'
3. inchoativity: *trunuti* 'to rot$_{ipf}$' - *natrunuti* 'to begin to rot$_{pf}$'
4. distributivity: *bacati* 'to throw$_{ipf}$' - *nabacati* 'to throw one by one$_{pf}$'
5. sufficiency: *jesti* 'to eat$_{ipf}$' - *najesti se* 'to eat one's fill$_{pf}$'
6. excessiveness: *piti* 'to drink$_{ipf}$' - *napiti se* 'to get drunk$_{pf}$'
7. addition: *gomilati* 'to accumulate$_{ipf}$' - *nagomilati* 'to accumulate a lot of X$_{pf}$'
8. intensity:
   - low intensity: *gristi* 'to bite$_{ipf}$' - *nagristi* 'to bite a bit$_{pf}$'
   - high intensity: *pisati* 'to write$_{ipf}$' - *napisati se* 'to tire oneself with writing$_{pf}$'

All 19 verbal prefixes recorded in CroDeriV were analyzed in the same manner. This analysis enabled the recognition of the same or similar semantic components shared by different affixes. The established set of morphosemantic relations is based on overlapping components of affixal meanings in combinations with various base forms. Such an analysis enabled the classification of affixal meanings into four broad semantic groups for prefixes and one for suffixes. Four major groups for prefixes - location, time, quantity, and manner - were further divided into subgroups (28 in total). There is only one group for the suffixes provided - diminutive.

The morphosemantic relations and a variety of subrelations based upon this classification are listed below:

1. **Prefixes**
   - location group: bottom-up, top-down, proximity, through, apart, to/towards, over, into, around, under, re-location, behind, across, from
   - time group: inchoativity, finitiveness, distributivity, preceding

- quantity group: sufficiency $(+/-)$, excessiveness, intensity $(+/-)$, exceeding, deprivation, addition
- manner group: inter-connection, change of property
2. **Suffixes**
   - diminutive group: diminutive, pejorative

As far as the semantic impact of prefixes is concerned, relations in the location group mainly hold between verbs of movement, but also between other base verbs and derivatives with spatial relations pervading their lexical meaning (e.g., *ubaciti* 'to throw into', *urezati* 'to carve'). Derivatives in the time group refer to different phases of actions denoted by the base verbs (e.g., its beginning or termination). The morphosemantic relation of distributivity contains meaning components that can be assigned both to the time and quantity groups, since the derivatives denote repetitive actions performed by one or more agents on one or more objects. Since distributive actions are performed iteratively, the relation of distributivity is listed in the time group. Relations from the quantity group hold when derivatives denote various degrees of an action (e.g., *naraditi se* 'to tire oneself out (with work)', *najesti se* 'to eat one's fill'). The smallest group - manner - contains only two relations denoting changes of properties (e.g., *uprljati se* 'to become dirty') and actions performed in a specific manner (e.g., *sufinancirati* 'to co-finance'). As indicated above, the semantic impact of suffixes is significantly narrower and is limited to diminutive and pejorative meaning expressed by derivatives (e.g., *jeduckati* 'to nibble'). The aim of the classification presented above was to establish the set of morphosemantic relations and use them within derivational families of verbs in CroWN.

The goal of the experiment presented in Sect. 3 was to detect full derivational spans of verbs from CroWN by matching them with verbs from CroDeriV. As far as the relations between the base verb and the discussed derivatives are concerned, it was pointed out that in numerous cases they cannot be captured by the semantic relations used between verbal synsets in CroWN. The main reason lies in the fact that the semantic relations used in CroWN basically are not designed to cover specific meanings resulting from the interaction between derivational affixes and base verbs - e.g., movement into or away from something, beginning of the movement, etc. The semantic relations between the verbal synsets used in CroWN, as well as in EWN and BN, are hyponymy/hyperonymy, subevent, cause, and antonymy.

Sometimes base verbs and derivatives are connected via one of the semantic relations that holds between synsets. In these cases, base verbs and derivatives are members of different synsets. However, in the majority of cases, morphosemantic and semantic relations do not overlap, and morphosemantic relations cannot be subsumed by semantic relations. The relation of hyponymy/hyperonymy is crucial for the overall structure of lexical hierarchies. It can be roughly described as 'to do X in a particular manner', where X is a hyperonym. However, this relation cannot be applied to derivatives like *uplivati* 'to swim into', and *otplivati* 'to swim away', *zaplivati* 'to start to swim', or *utrčati* 'to run into', *otrčati* 'to run away' and *potrčati* 'to start to run'. As a consequence, lexical hierarchies in CroWN do not contain derivationally related verbs that express these and similar meaning components. Due to the adopted expand model, these derivatives are not listed in CroWN at all, since there are no adequate English counterparts. One possible solution to this problem would be to significantly loosen up and expand the definition of hyponymy. In this way, the relation of hyponymy would also have to encompass the morphosemantic relations discussed above. We are convinced that the other possible solution to this problem - to introduce a set of morphosemantic relations and to keep them apart from the semantic ones - is more justified for Croatian and other Slavic wordnets. Whereas hyponymy/hyperonymy is used for the structuring of lexical hierarchies, relations such as subevent or cause are non-hierarchical. Subevent denotes the relation between two synsets referring to two simultaneous actions or to an action which is a part of an action denoted by another synset. For example, the PWN synset containing the verb to eat has subevents to chew and to swallow. But this relation does not refer to derivationally related literals, e.g. *plivati* 'to swim' and *zaplivati* 'to start to swim', nor does it reflect particular parts of events, in this case its beginning point. Therefore, we believe that the morphosemantic relations of inchoativity or finitiveness are more suitable for indicating the relation that exists between such base forms and derivatives. The semantic relation cause holds between synsets and denotes the relation between two actions, the first denoting the cause and the second denoting the result or the consequence of the action denoted by the first verb (e.g., *hraniti* 'to feed' - *jesti* 'to eat'). Although this relation partially overlaps with the morphosemantic relation change of property, cause can only encompass pairs such as *topiti* 'to melt$_{ipf}$' - *otopiti* 'to melt$_{pf}$', but not their reflexive counterparts referring to non-agentive action, e.g., *topiti se* 'to become melted$_{ipf}$' - *otopiti se* 'to become melted$_{pf}$'.

The proposed set of morphosemantic relations results from combinations of single verbal affixes and base forms. These relations were divided into four major groups and further into several subgroups for prefixes and one major group for suffixes. The investigation of combinations consisting of multiple prefixes with the same base form is planned for future work.

6 Conclusion and Further Work

In this paper we have shown that LRs containing data on derivationally related words are necessary for the further morphological processing of Croatian. We have also presented a new LR - CroDeriV - containing morphological and derivational data for Croatian. At present it contains only verbs, but its design enables the introduction of other POS in the near future. Further on, we have demonstrated how the data from this new resource can be used in the development of other LRs for Croatian, such as CroWN. After matching lists of verbs from two resources, we have detected full derivational families of verbs present in CroWN. The results of the experiment reveal that derivational families in CroWN are much poorer than the ones in CroDeriV. This is, at least partially, a consequence of the adopted expand model, but also of the typological differences between English and Croatian. In order to overcome the under-representation of Croatian verbs in CroWN, as well as to make this resource more representative, we have shown that data from CroDeriV should be introduced into CroWN via morphosemantic relations that are more applicable to verbs in Croatian, as they are in other Slavic languages, cf. [4,6]. The detection of full derivational families in Croatian enabled by CroDeriV and the relations between their members, both semantic and morphosemantic, can significantly improve the lexical hierarchies in CroWN, resulting in a more dense structure of this lexicon. Finally, the lexicon with derivational data as CroDeriV is valuable in different NLP tools and tasks such as knowledge extraction, word-sense disambiguation, or machine translation.

Acknowledgment. The research was partially supported by MZOS RH projects 130-1300646-0645, 130-1300646-1002 and XLike project (FP7, Grant 288342).

References

1. Hajič, J., Böhmová, A., Hajičová, E., Vidová Hladká, B.: The Prague dependency treebank: a three-level annotation scenario. In: Abeillé, A. (ed.) Treebanks: Building and Using Parsed Corpora, pp. 103–127. Kluwer, Amsterdam (2000)
2. Ljubešić, N., Erjavec, T.: hrWaC and slWac: compiling web corpora for Croatian and Slovene. In: Habernal, I., Matoušek, V. (eds.) TSD 2011. LNCS, vol. 6836, pp. 395–402. Springer, Heidelberg (2011)
3. Ljubešić, N., Boras, D., Kubelka, O.: Retrieving information in Croatian: building a simple and efficient rule-based stemmer. In: Seljan, S., Stančić, H. (eds.) INFuture2007: Digital Information and Heritage, pp. 313–320. Odsjek za informacijske znanosti Filozofskoga fakulteta, Zagreb (2007)
4. Maziarz, M., Piasecki, M., Szpakowicz, S., Rabiega-Wiśniewska, J., Hojka, B.: Semantic relations between verbs in Polish WordNet 2.0. Cogn. Stud. **11**, 183–200 (2011)
5. Mikelić Preradović, N., Boras, D., Kišiček, S.: CROVALLEX: Croatian verb valence lexicon. In: Proceedings of the 31st International Conference on Information Technology Interfaces, pp. 533–538 (2009)
6. Pala, K., Hlaváčková, D.: Derivational relations in Czech WordNet. In: Proceedings of the Workshop on Balto-Slavonic Languages, pp. 75–81 (2007)
7. Pandžić, I.: Oblikovanje korjenovatelja za hrvatski jezik u svrhu pretraživanja informacija. MA thesis. University of Zagreb, Faculty of Humanities and Social Sciences (2012)
8. Raffaelli, I., Tadić, M., Bekavac, B., Agić, Ž.: Building Croatian WordNet. In: Proceedings of the Fourth Global WordNet Conference, Szeged, pp. 349–359 (2008)
9. Šnajder, J., Dalbelo Bašić, B., Tadić, M.: Automatic acquisition of inflectional lexica for morphological normalisation. Inf. Process. Manage. **44**(5), 1720–1731 (2008)
10. Šojat, K., Srebačić, M.: Morphosemantic relations between verbs in Croatian WordNet. In: Orav, H., Fellbaum, C., Vossen, P. (eds.) Proceedings of the Seventh Global WordNet Conference, pp. 262–267. GWA, Tartu (2014)
11. Šojat, K., Srebačić, M., Pavelić, T., Tadić, M.: From morphology to lexical hierarchies. In: Vetulani, Z. (ed.) Human Language Technologies as a Challenge for Computer Science and Linguistics (LTC 2013 Proceedings), pp. 474–478 (2013)

12. Šojat, K., Srebačić, M., Tadić, M.: Derivational and semantic relations of Croatian verbs. J. Lang. Model. (1), 111–142 (2012)
13. Šojat, K., Srebačić, M., Štefanec, V.: CroDeriV and the morphological analysis of Croatian verb. Suvremena lingvistika **39**(75), 75–96 (2013)
14. Tadić, M.: Building the Croatian national corpus. In: Gavrilidou, M., Carayannis, G., Markantonatou, S., Piperidis, S. (eds.) Proceedings of Second International Conference on Language Resources and Evaluation LREC 2000, pp. 523–530. ELRA, Paris-Athens (2002)
15. Tadić, M., Fulgosi, S.: Building the Croatian morphological lexicon. In: Proceedings of the EACL 2003 Workshop on Morphological Processing of Slavic Languages (Budapest 2003), ACL, pp. 41–46 (2003)
16. Tadić, M.: The Croatian lemmatization server. South. J. Linguist. **29**(1–2), 206–217 (2005)
17. Tadić, M.: Building the Croatian dependency treebank: the initial stages. Suvremena lingvistika **63**, 85–92 (2007)
18. Vossen, P. (ed.): EuroWordNet. A Multilingual Database with Lexical Semantic Networks. Kluwer Academic Publishers, Dordrecht (1998)
19. Žabokrtský, Z.: Valency Lexicon of Czech Verbs. Ph.D. thesis. Charles University, Prague (2005)

Parsing Related Issues

System for Generating Questions Automatically from Given Punjabi Text

Vishal Goyal[(✉)], Shikha Garg, and Umrinderpal Singh

Department of Computer Science, Punjabi University, Patiala, India
Vishal.pup@gmail.com

Abstract. This paper introduces a system for generating questions automatically for Punjabi. The System transforms a declarative sentence into its interrogative counterpart. It accepts sentences as an input and produces possible set of questions for the given input. Not much work has been done in the field of Question Generation for Indian Languages. The current paper represents the Question Generation System for Punjabi language to generate questions for the given input in Gurmukhi script. For Punjabi, adequate annotated corpora, POS taggers and other NLP tools are not yet available in the required measure. Thus, this system relies on the Named Entity Recognition tool. Also, various Punjabi Language dependent rules have been developed to generate output based on the named entity found in the given input sentence.

Keywords: Natural Language Processing (NLP) · Named Entity Recognition (NER) · Question Generation (QG)

1 Introduction

Questions are used to express informational needs. When we do not know something, the natural thing which we will do is to ask about it. As computer systems are becoming more advanced and self-directed, their informational needs are growing day by day and such computer systems which has ability to ask questions can have many obvious advantages. State-of-the-art spoken dialogue systems can be considered as a good example. They have the ability to ask questions like about the user's goals ("Where would you like to go?") or about their understanding about user's expressions ("Did you say 'Delhi'?").

The purpose of asking questions is not limited to such tasks but it may serve much more than this. In a classroom, a teacher asks questions to her students. She does not ask questions because she doesn't know the answers but she asks questions because she wants to know whether her students know the answer or not. By asking questions she may also provide a good hint to the students which may help them to solve the problems which they are dealing with. Generating such questions automatically is a central task for intelligent tutoring systems. Exam questions are another example.

In the context of automated assessment, generating questions automatically from educational resources is a great challenge, with, potentially, tremendous impact. Computer systems can be used to generate questions automatically by writing algorithms for it.

© Springer International Publishing Switzerland 2016
Z. Vetulani et al. (Eds.): LTC 2013, LNAI 9561, pp. 115–125, 2016.
DOI: 10.1007/978-3-319-43808-5_9

Thus, a Question Generation system can be designed to take input from the resources and generate a set of possible questions from the given input.

Question Generation is a sub problem or application of Natural Language Processing (NLP). The various applications of Question Generation System include intelligent tutoring systems, Closed-domain Question Answering (QA) systems, and Natural language summarization/ generation systems (for instance, Frequently Asked Questions). Also, automated Question Generation can be helpful:

- To learners by generating good questions that the learners might ask while reading documents and other media.
- In medicine by generating suggested questions for patients and caretakers.
- To human and computer tutors by generating questions that they might ask to promote and evaluate deeper learning.
- To generate suggested questions that might be asked in security contexts by interrogators or in legal contexts by petitioners.
- In many other facilities such as Frequently Asked Question (FAQ) by generating questions automatically from information repositories as candidate questions.

The task of Question Generation can be viewed as a three-step process: content selection, selection of question type and question construction. The first step, Content selection is about deciding what the question should be about i.e. selection of target to ask about. The next step, Selection of Question type is about deciding the most appropriate type of the question (who, why, where etc.) for the selected content from first step. Given the content and question type, the last step, Question construction focuses on the construction of actual question.

For English, a lot of work has already been done in the field of Question Generation. But the research on Question Generation for Punjabi language is still in a preliminary stage, including methodology examination, evaluation criteria selection and dataset preparation, etc. Generating questions in Punjabi implies many challenges that are not present in English. Some of these challenges are:

- In case of Indian languages there is no concept of capitalization. Most Named Entities are represented by writing first letter capital in English (e.g. 'Delhi'). But there are no such rules of capitalization in Punjabi Language and other Indian Languages.
- Ambiguity of Named Entities is always possible. For example: *Khanna* can be a person's name or location name.
- As Punjabi is a free word order language. So, one sentence can be written in multiple ways.
- For Punjabi Language, there is non-availability of large gazetteer. The available gazetteer does not cover all the Named Entities.

Questions can be classified into different categories according to the purpose of the usage. For instance, in terms of target complexity, QG can be divided into deep QG and shallow QG. The questions that focus more on facts (such as who, what, when, where, which, how many/much and yes/no questions) are generated by shallow QG whereas deep questions that involves more logical thinking (such as why, why not, what-if, what-if-not and how questions) are generated by Deep QG. Our Question Generation system focuses on the generation of shallow questions.

2 Description of Question Generation System

In this section, we detail the question generation system. The input is a Punjabi text. The output consists of possible questions which were generated by the system for the input sentence.

The question generation system proceeds by transforming declarative sentences into set of possible questions. As for Punjabi Language, annotated corpora, name dictionaries, good morphological analyzers; POS taggers and other NLP tools are not yet available in the required measure. So, our System relies on Named Entity Recognition (NER) tool for the transformations. The various tags of NER for which the system tries to generate questions include Person Name, Location, Designation, Number, Date/Time, Abbreviations, Title Person, and Measure. Based on these NER tags, some Punjabi language dependent rules have been developed to generate questions. By following these rules, for the given answer phrases, the system mainly tries to generate shallow questions with question words: ਕੀ (What), ਕਦੋਂ (When), ਕਿੱਥੇ (Where), ਕਿਸ (Who/Whom), ਕਿੰਨੇ (How much/How many) etc. The system could be extended to detect and transform other types of phrases to produce other types of questions like ਕਿਉਂ, ਕਿਵੇਂ (Why, How) etc.

2.1 Architecture

The basic architecture of the system is shown in Fig. 1. The system's architecture can be divided into following four phases:

Tokenization Process: In first phase system tokenize input sentence on two levels, sentence and word level. In Punjabi, sentence boundaries marked with "|" char. System divide all the input text into different sentences to generate question based on different predefined rules.

I. Mark phrases that cannot be answer phrases: In this step, the phrases which cannot be the target for answer phrases of the generated questions are detected, which is done by comparing the phrases of input text with the values of different lists of named entities. If they do not match with any of the value in the lists, they are considered as Unmovable, which means that the phrases which are considered as Unmovable are not the named entities and can be other words present in the sentence. In the subsequent steps of answer phrase selection, these phrases are skipped so that the system does not generate questions for them.

II. Select an answer phrase and generate a set of question phrases for it: After marking unmovable phrases, the system iterates over the possible answer phrases, generating possible questions for each one.

To generate the question phrases, the system compares the possible answer phrases with the values in the lists of various Named Entities (Names, Locations, Months, Weeks and others). We have used various named entity rules to mark proper noun words. To identify named entities, system depends on proper noun database. We had collected person names, location named and developed various rules to identify Punjabi person and location names. Rules and collection details as following:

Table 1. Proper noun collection and rules

Collection name	Total
Person First Name	30123
Person Last Name	4231
Person Middle Name	421
Location Name	2394
Person Identification Rules	23
Location Identification Rules	14

We have used various person name identification rules to mark unknown and to resolve ambiguous names in input text. These rules are based on last name, middle name and various postpositions in text. To identify person names in Punjabi text is difficult as compared to European languages, because in Punjabi there is no concept of capital letters.

PN Rule1: If marked person name is last name, it has chances that previous word is first name.

Punjabi: ਰਾਮ ਕੁਮਾਰ ਦਿੱਲੀ ਗਿਆ|

Transliteration: (Rāma kumāra dilī gi'ā)
English: Ram Kumar went to Delhi.

Word ਕੁਮਾਰ (Kumar) is last named which helped us to identify first name ਰਾਮ (Ram) is Ram is output of proper noun list.

PN Rule2: If word is middle name, check for previous and next word for Persons first name and last named.

Punjabi: ਮੈਂ ਰਾਮ ਪਾਲ ਸਿੰਘ ਨੂੰ ਜਾਂਦਾ ਹਾ|

Transliteration: Maiṁ rāma pāla sigha nū jāndā hā
English: I know Ram pal Singh.

Here word 'pal' is middle name and can help us to identify first named if Ram is not part of person name list.

Punjabi is morphological rich language, which help us to identify location named based on suffixes of word. In Punjab and in other state of India location name shared a comma suffix patter. Based on these patterns we can identify unknown location names which are not part of our location collections.

LN Rule1: if word ends with "ਾਬਾਦ" (abad) mark it as location name.

Punjabi : ਉਹ ਹੈਦਰਾਬਾਦ ਤੋਂ ਹੈ।

Transliteration: Uha haidarābāda tōm hai.

English: He is from Hyderabad.

LN Rule2: if word ends with "ਪੁਰ" "pur" mark it as location name.

Punjabi: ਉਹ ਰਾਮਪੁਰ ਗਿਆ।

Transliteration: Uha rāmapura gi'ā.

English: He went to Rampur.

LN Rule3: if word ends with "ਪੁਰਾ" "pur" mark it as location name.

Punjabi: ਰਾਮ ਕਿਸ਼ਨਪੁਰਾ ਵਿਚ ਰਹਿੰਦਾ ਹੈ।

Transliteration: Rāma kiśanapurā vica rahidā hai.

English: Ram lived in Kishanpura.

LN Rule4: if word ends with "ਗੜ੍ਹ" "ghar" mark it as location name.

Punjabi: ਰਾਮਗੜ੍ਹ ਇਕ ਕਾਸਬੇ ਦਾ ਨਾਮ ਹੈ।

Transliteration: Rāmagaṛha ika kāsabē dā nāma hai.

English: Ramghar is a name of town.

If the current phrase is in a particular list, the corresponding feature is set to True otherwise set to False. Depending on the particular list in which current phrase is found, various Punjabi Language dependent rules are applied on the phrase to generate the possible set of questions for the current phrase.

III. Remove the answer phrase and insert the question phrases in the main clause: After generating set of possible question phrases, the next step is to remove the answer phrase from the input sentence. The system removes the selected answer phrase corresponding to which a question has been generated in step 2, and for each possible question phrase generated from the answer phrase, it inserts that question phrase into a separate copy to produce a new question.

Rules. Some of the Punjabi Language dependent rules developed for the Question Generation system are:

1. If the answer phrase's head word is in the list of Location or Organization and the words may or may not be followed by ਵਿਖੇ, ਵਿੱਚ, 'ਚ (vikhē, vicc, 'c), then the answer phrase is target to the question type ਕਿੱਥੇ (Where). For example: ਪੈਰਿਸ (Paris), ਇੰਗਲੈਂਡ ਵਿਖੇ (in England), ਏਸ਼ੀਆ (Asia) (Table 2).

Table 2. "Where" question type catagories.

Examples	Target Question Type
Punjabi: ਉਹ ਪੈਰਿਸ ਗਏ। Transliteration: Uha pairisa ga'ē English:They Went to Paris.	ਕਿੱਥੇ Kithē *Where*
Punjabi: ਇੰਗਲੈਂਡ ਵਿਖੇ ਵਿਸਾਖੀ ਮਨਾਈ। Transliteration: Igalaiṇḍa vikhē visākhī manā'ī. English: Vesakhi Celebrated in England.	ਕਿੱਥੇ Kithē *Where*
Punjabi: ਉਹ ਏਸ਼ੀਆ ਦੀ ਯਾਤਰਾ ਤੇ ਹੈ। Transliteration: Uha ēśī'ā dī yātarā tē hai. English: He is on the Asia's tour.	ਕਿੱਥੇ Kithō *Where*

2. If the answer phrase's head word is of any format of the form dd/mm/yyyy, dd-mm-yyyy or dd.mm.yyyy or the answer phrase's head word is in the list of week or month and if the word is in the list of month, the preceding word can of the type dd (1<=dd<=31) and/or the following word can be of the type yyyy, then the answer phrase is target to the question type ਕਦੋਂ (*When*). Also the word can be followed by the word 'ਈ./ ਈਸਵੀ' (*ī./ īsvī*). For example: 1888 ਈ. (1888 ī.), 18 ਜਨਵਰੀ (18 January), ਸੋਮਵਾਰ (Monday), 27 ਸਿਤੰਬਰ 2013 (27 September 2013) (Table 3).

Table 3. "When" question type catagories.

Examples	Target Question Type
Punjabi: ਉਹ 1888 ਈ. ਨੂੰ ਪੈਦਾ ਹੋਇਆ। Transliteration: Uha 1888 ī. Paidā hō'i'ā. English: He Born on 1888.	ਕਦੋਂ Kadōṁ *When*
Punjabi: ਸੋਮਵਾਰ ਨੂੰ ਵਿਸਾਖੀ ਮਨਾਈ। Transliteration: Sōmavāra nū visākhī manā'ī. English: Vesakhi Celebrated in England.	ਕਦੋਂ Kadōṁ *When*
Punjabi: ਉਹ 27 ਸਿਤੰਬਰ 2013 ਨੂੰ ਚਲਾ ਗਿਆ। Transliteration: Uha 27 sitabara 2013 nū calā gi'ā. English: He went on 27 September 2013	ਕਦੋਂ Kithō *When*

3. If the answer phrase's head word can be parsed into integer or the word is in the list of numbers and the word is not preceded and followed by the word which is in the list of month then the answer phrase is target to the question type ਕਿੰਨੇ (*How much/How many*). For example: 200 ਸਾਲ (*200 years*), 10 ਕਿਤਾਬਾਂ (*10 books*), 8 ਮੁੰਡੇ (*8 boys*), ਦੋ ਵਿਅਕਤੀ(*two persons*) (Table 4).

Table 4. "How Many/How Much" question type catagories.

Examples	Target Question Type
Punjabi: ਇਹ ਕਿਤਾਬ 200 ਸਾਲ ਪੁਰਾਨੀ ਹੈ। Transliteration: Iha kitāba 200 sāla purānī hai. English: This book is 200 years old.	ਕਿੰਨੇ Kinē *How much*
Punjabi: ਉਸ ਦੇ ਕੋਲ 10 ਕਿਤਾਬਾਂ ਹਨ। Transliteration: Usa dē kōla 10 kitābaṁ hana. English: He is 10 books.	ਕਿੰਨੇ Kinē *How many*
Punjabi: ਉਸ ਟੀਮ ਵਿਚ 8 ਮੁੰਡੇ ਹਨ।	ਕਿੰਨੇ
Transliteration: Usa ṭīma vica 8 muḍē hana. English: That team has 10 boys.	Kinē *How many*

4. If the answer phrase's head word is in the list of Names (the preceding word may or may not be in the Prefix List or Designation List and the following word may be in list of Middle Name or Last Name) and whose preposition is like ਦਾ (dā), ਦੇ (dē), (dē), ਨੂੰ (nūṁ), ਨਾਲ (nāl) etc. then ਕਿਸ (*Who/Whom*) type of question can be generated from the answer phrase. For example: ਯੁਵਰਾਜ ਸਿੰਘ ਨਾਲ (*with Yuvraj Singh*), ਮਨਮੋਹਨ ਸਿੰਘ ਦਾ (Manmohan Singh's). Also, if the answer phrase's head word is in the designation list and the word is followed by the prepositions like ਦਾ (dā), ਦੇ (dē), ਨੂੰ (nūṁ), ਨਾਲ (nāl) etc., then the answer phrase can be considered as the target to question type ਕਿਸ (*Who/Whom*). For example: ਪ੍ਰਧਾਨ ਮੰਤਰੀ ਦਾ (Prime Minister's) (Table 5).

5. If the answer phrase's head word is in the list of abbreviation, then ਕੀ (*What*) question type is generated. For example: if the word ਬੀ.ਬੀ.ਸੀ. (*B.B.C.*) is found in the answer phrase, then ਬੀ.ਬੀ.ਸੀ. ਦਾ ਵਿਸਤ੍ਰਿਤ ਰੂਪ ਕੀ ਹੈ (*What is the full form of B.B. C.*) question type is generated.

IV. Post-processing to ensure proper formatting: In the fourth and final step, we do post-processing of the output sentences generated by the step 3. Post-processing of the result generated after step 3 is necessary to ensure the proper formatting of the final output. Thus, the output is de-tokenized to remove the extra whitespace symbols. Also,

Table 5. "Who\Whom" question type catagories.

Examples	Target Question Type
Punjabi: ਮਨਮੋਹਨ ਸਿੰਘ ਦਾ ਸਾਰੇ ਜਾਣਦੇ ਹਨ। Transliteration: Manamōhana sigha dā sārē jāṇadē hana. English: Everyone knows Manmohan Singh's Name.	ਕਿਸਦਾ Kisadā Who
Punjabi: ਮੈਂ ਯੁਵਰਾਜ ਸਿੰਘ ਨਾਲ ਗੱਲ ਕਰ ਰਿਹਾ ਹਾਂ। Transliteration: Yuvarāja sigha nāla gala kara rihā hāṁ. English: I am talking with Yuvraj Singh	ਕਿਸ Kinē Who
Punjabi: ਇਹ ਪ੍ਰਧਾਨ ਮੰਤਰੀ ਦਾ ਜਹਾਜ ਹੈ। Transliteration: Iha pradhāna matarī dā jahāja hai. English: This is president's plane.	ਕਿਸ Kinē *Who*

if a question has been generated, then the final punctuation mark ਡੰਡੀ (dandi) '।' in the output sentence is changed to question mark '?'.

Input Sentence:

ਮੌਲਾਨਾ ਆਜ਼ਾਦ ਦਾ ਜਨਮ ਸੰਨ 1888 ਈ: ਵਿੱਚ ਮੱਕਾ ਵਿਖੇ ਹੋਇਆ। | maulānā āzād dā janam sann 1888 ī: vicc makkā vikhē hōiā.

Output of Question Generation System:

ਕਿਸ ਦਾ ਜਨਮ ਸੰਨ 1888 ਈ: ਵਿੱਚ ਮੱਕਾ ਵਿਖੇ ਹੋਇਆ? kis dā janam sann 1888 ī: vicc makkā vikhē hōiā?

ਮੌਲਾਨਾ ਆਜ਼ਾਦ ਦਾ ਜਨਮ ਕਦੋਂ ਮੱਕਾ ਵਿਖੇ ਹੋਇਆ? maulānā āzād dā janam kadōṁ makkā vikhē hōiā?

ਮੌਲਾਨਾ ਆਜ਼ਾਦ ਦਾ ਜਨਮ ਸੰਨ 1888 ਈ: ਵਿੱਚ ਕਿੱਥੇ ਹੋਇਆ? maulānā āzād dā janam sann 1888 ī: vicc kitthē hōiā?

3   Evaluation

The analysis of output generated by NER based QG system has been done manually. We have collected test data from various Punjabi websites and Punjabi text books. To evaluate the performance of our question generation system, we have used three standard mertics namely Precision, Recall and F-measure. We have evaluated the F-scores through the following formula.

$$Recall = \frac{Q_g \cap Q_a}{Q_a} \qquad (1)$$

$$Precision = \frac{Q_g \cap Q_r}{Q_g} \qquad (2)$$

$$F - Measure = \frac{2 * Recall * Precision}{Recall + Precision} \qquad (3)$$

Where, Qg is the number of questions generated by our QG system, Qa is the number of actual questions generated manually and Qr is the number of related questions generated by the system excluding questions with grammatical error.

We have tested the system for 500 text lines which were taken from various Punjabi websites and Punjabi text books. For 400 text lines, the system was able to generate output. However, for the remaining sentences, the system failed to generate any question because the remaining sentences did not contain any named entity. So we got recall of 0.00 % for those sentences. Thus, our system is able to generate questions

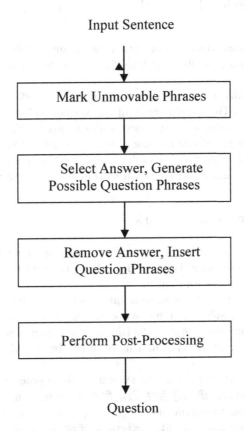

Fig. 1. Architecture of question generation system for Punjabi language

Table 6. Results of question generation system

Question Type	Re-call (%)	Precision (%)	F-measure (%)
ਕਿੱਥੇ (Where)	56.6	74.5	64.32
ਕਿਸ (Whom)	50.0	62.1	55.39
ਕੀ (What)	16.21	41.6	23.32
ਕਦੋਂ (When)	48.23	73.17	58.13
ਕਿੰਨੇ (How many/ How much)	52.33	51.7	52.01

only for those sentences which include any named entity. Table 1 shows the Recall, Precision and F-measure of 400 text lines for which system has generated output (Table 6).

The sentences which do not contain any named entity affect the overall performance of the system. The overall recall of the system including all the sentences (sentences with named entities and sentences without named entity) is calculated to be 35.72 % which has been reduced because of sentences without named entities whose recall is 0.00 %. The overall precision of the system is 63 %. The reason for that is not considering the grammatically wrong constructed questions as the valid questions.

4   Conclusion and Future Work

We have reported our work on the system for generating questions automatically from given Punjabi text. A number of language dependent rules have been formed to extract language dependent features for Punjabi.

The system shows good results for some question types but for other question types the system shows low results. So, future work includes forming new rules to improve the existing rules. Many first names in Punjabi are also common nouns, this limitation lowers the performance of the system. This issue can be considered to improve the system.

From the possible Answer Phrase, the system is able to generate shallow questions with the question words ਕੀ, ਕਦੋਂ, ਕਿੱਥੇ, ਕਿਸ, ਕਿੰਨੇ. In future, the system could be extended to detect and transform other types of phrases to produce other shallow questions and also deep questions like ਕਿਉਂ (Why), ਕਿਵੇਂ (How) etc.

Also, in case of multiple sentences in the input text, the system does not consider any relationship between the different sentences. By taking into consideration the relationships between sentences, the system can give better results for the multiple sentences text.

System is not using POS tagger or POS tagged data. So system always has to do larger number of comparisons to find out entities in a given text. It is difficult to make any decision for the system based on rules because system compares only words but not their part of speech. POS tagged data and stemmer is very essential for QG system and we have not used any POS tagger for our QG. So, in future POS tagger can be used to improve the performance of the system.

To develop the QG system for Punjabi Language we have insufficient resources as we discussed earlier. In future other essential tools for QG for Punjabi Language can be developed.

References

1. Art Graesser. Question Generation, The University of Memphis. http://www.intellimedia. ncsu.edu/.../Graesser-question-generation-061110...
2. Bernhard, D., de Viron, L., Moriceau, V., Tannier, X.: Question generation for french: collating parsers and paraphrasing questions. Dialogue and Discourse 3(2), 43–74 (2012)
3. Ali, H., Chali, Y., Hasan, S.A.: Automatic question generation from sentences. In: TALN 2010, Montreal, 19–23 July 2010
4. http://questiongeneration.org/. Accessed 23 March 2013
5. Kaur, K., Gupta, V.: Topic tracking for Punjabi language. Comput. Sci. Eng. Int. J. (CSEIJ) 1(3), 37–49 (2011)
6. Heilman, M.: Automatic Factual Question Generation from Text, Ph.D. thesis, Carnegie Mellon University (2011)
7. Singh, U., Goyal, V., Lehal, G.S.: Named entity recognition system for Urdu. In: Proceedings of COLING 2012: Technical Papers, COLING 2012, Mumbai, pp. 2507–2518, December 2012
8. Rus, V., Graesser, A.C. (eds.) The Question Generation Shared Task and Evaluation Challenge, Workshop Report, Sponsored by the National Science Foundation, The University of Memphis (2009)
9. Gupta, V., Lehal, G.S.: Named entity recognition for Punjabi language text summarization. Int. J. Comput. Appl. (0975 – 8887) 33(3), 28–32 (2011)
10. Yao, X.: Question Generation with Minimal Recursion Semantics, Master Thesis, University of Groningen & Saarland University (2010)

Hierarchical Amharic Base Phrase Chunking Using HMM with Error Pruning

Abeba Ibrahim and Yaregal Assabie[✉]

Department of Computer Science, Addis Ababa University, Addis Ababa, Ethiopia
abeba.ibrahim@gmail.com, yaregal.assabie@aau.edu.et

Abstract. Segmentation of a text into non-overlapping syntactic units (chunks) has become an essential component of many applications of natural language processing. This paper presents Amharic base phrase chunker that groups syntactically correlated words at different levels using HMM. Rules are used to correct chunk phrases incorrectly chunked by the HMM. For the identification of the boundary of the phrases IOB2 chunk specification is selected and used in this work. To test the performance of the system, corpus was collected from Amharic news outlets and books. The training and testing datasets were prepared using the 10-fold cross validation technique. Test results on the corpus showed an average accuracy of 85.31 % before applying the rule for error correction and an average accuracy of 93.75 % after applying rules.

Keywords: Amharic language processing · Base phrase chunking · Partial parsing

1 Introduction

Chunking is a natural language processing (NLP) task that focuses on dividing a text into syntactically correlated non-overlapping and non-exhaustive groups of words, i.e., a word can only be a member of one chunk and not all words are in chunks (Tjong *et al.* 2000). Chunking is widely used as an intermediate step to parsing with the purpose of improving the performance of the parser. It also helps to identify non-overlapping phrases from a stream of data, which are further used for the development of different NLP applications such as information retrieval, information extraction, named entity recognition, question answering, text mining, text summarization, etc. These NLP tasks consist of recognizing some type of structure which represents linguistic elements of the analysis and their relations. In text chunking the main problem is to divide text into syntactically related non-overlapping groups of words (chunks).

The main goal of chunking is to divide a text into segments which correspond to certain syntactic units such as noun phrases, verb phrases, prepositional phrases, etc. Abney (1991) introduced the concept of chunk as an intermediate step providing input to further full parsing stages. Thus, chunking can be seen as the basic task in full parsing. Although the detailed information from a full parse is lost, chunking is a valuable process in its own right when the entire grammatical structure produced by a full parse is not required. For example, various studies indicate that the information obtained by

© Springer International Publishing Switzerland 2016
Z. Vetulani et al. (Eds.): LTC 2013, LNAI 9561, pp. 126–135, 2016.
DOI: 10.1007/978-3-319-43808-5_10

chunking or partial parsing is sufficient for information retrieval systems rather than full parsing (Yangarber and Grishman 1998). Alongside, partial syntactical information can help to solve many NLP tasks, such as text summarization, machine translation and spoken language understanding (Molina and Pla 2002). For example, Kutlu (2010) stated that finding noun phrases and verb phrases is enough for information retrieval systems. Phrases that give us information about agents, times, places, objects, etc. are more significant than the complete configurational syntactic analyses of a sentence for question-answering, information extraction, text mining and automatic summarization.

Chunkers do not necessarily assign every word in the sentence like full parses to a higher-level constituent. They identify simple phrases but do not require that the sentence be represented by a single structure. By contrast full parsers attempt to discover a single structure which incorporates every word in the sentence. Abney (1995) proposed to divide sentences into labeled, non-overlapping sequences of words based on superficial analysis and local information. In general, many of NLP applications often require syntactic analysis at various NLP levels including full parsing and chunking. The chunking level identifies all possible phrases and the full parsing analyzes the phrase structure of a sentence. The choice of which syntactic analysis level should be used depends on the specific speed or accuracy of an application. The chunking level is efficient and fast in terms of processing than full parsing (Thao et al. 2009). Chunkers can identify syntactic chunks at different levels of the parser, so a group of chunkers can build a complete parser (Abney 1995). Most of the parsers developed for languages like English and German use chunkers as components. Brants (1999) used a cascade of Markov model chunkers for obtaining parsing results for the German NEGRA corpus. Today, there are a lot of chunking systems developed for various languages such as Turkish (Kutlu 2010), Vietnamese (Thao et al. 2009), Chinese (Xu et al. 2006), Urdu (Ali and Hussain 2010), etc.

Although Amharic is the working language of Ethiopia with a population of about 90 million at present, it is still one of less-resourced languages with few linguistic tools available for Amharic text processing. This work is aimed at developing Amharic base phrase chunker that generates base phrases. The remaining part of this paper is organized as follows. Section 2 presents Amharic language with emphasis to its phrase structure. Amharic base phrase chunking along with error pruning is discussed in Sect. 3. In Sect. 4, we present experimental results. Conclusion and future works are highlighted in Sect. 5. References are provided at the end.

2 Linguistic Structures of Amharic

2.1 Amharic Language

Amharic is the working language of Ethiopia. Although many languages are spoken in Ethiopia, Amharic is the lingua franca of the country and it is the most commonly learned second language throughout the country (Lewis *et al.* 2013). It is also the second most spoken Semitic language in the world next to Arabic. Amharic is written using Ethiopic script which has 33 consonants (basic characters) out of which six other characters representing combinations of vowels and consonants are derived for each character.

The base characters have the vowel ኧ(*ä*) and other derived characters have vowels in the order of ኡ(*u*), ኢ(*i*), ኣ(*a*), ኤ(*e*), እ(*ĭ*), and ኦ(*o*). For example, for the base character ከ(*kä*), the following six characters are derived from the base character: ኩ(*ku*), ኪ(*ki*), ካ(*ka*), ኬ(*ke*), ክ(*kĭ*), and ኮ(*ko*).

2.2 Phrasal Categories

Phrases are syntactic structures that consist of one or more words but lack the subject-predicate organization of a clause. These phrases are composed of either only head word or other words or phrases with the head combination. The other words or phrases that are combined with the head in phrase construction can be specifiers, modifiers and complements. Yimam (2000) classified Amharic word classes into five types, i.e. nouns, verbs, adverbs, adjectives and prepositions. In line with this classification, Yimam (2000) and Amare (2010) classified phrase structures of the Amharic language as: noun phrases, verb phrases, adjectival phrases, adverbial phrases and prepositional phrases.

Noun Phrase. An Amharic noun phrase (NP) is a phrase that has a noun as its head. In this phrase construction, the head of the phrase is always found at the end of the phrase. This type of phrase can be made from a single noun or combination of noun with either other word classes including noun word class. Examples are: ቀለበት (*qäläbät*/ring), የአልማዝ ቀለበት (*yä'almaz qäläbät*/diamond ring), ትልቅ የአልማዝ ቀለበት (*tĭlĭq yä'almaz qäläbät*/big diamond ring), ያ ትልቅ የአልማዝ ቀለበት (*ya tĭlĭq yä'almaz qäläbät*/that big diamond ring), etc.

Verb Phrase. Amharic verb phrase (VP) is constructed with a verb as a head, which is found at the end of the phrase, and other constituents such as complements, modifiers and specifiers. But not all the verbs take the same category of complement. Based on this, verbs can be dividing into two. These are transitive and intransitive. Transitive verbs take transitive noun phrases as their complement and intransitive verbs do not. Examples are: ላኮላታል (*lĭkolatal*/[he] sent [her] [something]), ገንዘብ ላኮላታል (*gänzäb lĭkolatal*/[he] sent [her] money), ለሜሪ ገንዘብ ላኮላታል (*lämeri gänzäb lĭkolatal*/[he] sent money to Mary), በባንክ ለሜሪ ገንዘብ ላኮላታል (*bäbank lämeri gänzäb lĭkolatal*/[he] sent money to Mary via bank), etc.

Adjectival Phrase. An Amharic Adjectival phrase (AdjP) is constructed with an adjective as a head word and other constituents such as complements, modifiers and specifiers. The head word is placed at the end. Examples are: ጎበዝ (*gobäz*/clever), በጣም ጎበዝ (*bäṭam gobäz*/very clever), እንደ ወንድሙ በጣም ጎበዝ (*ĭndä wändĭmu bäṭam gobäz*/very clever like his brother), etc.

Prepositional Phrase. Amharic prepositional phrase (PP) is made up of a preposition head and other constituents such as nouns, noun phrases, prepositional phrases, etc. Unlike other phrase constructions, prepositions cannot be taken as a phrase, instead they should be combined with other constituents and the constituents may come either previous to or subsequent to the preposition. If the complements are nouns or NPs, the position of prepositions is in front of the complements whereas if the complements are

PPs, the position will shift to the end of the phrase. Examples are: እንደ ልጅ (*ǐndä lǐj*/like a child), ከወንዙ አጠገብ (*käwänzu aṭägäb*/close to the river), etc.

Adverbial Phrases. Amharic adverbial phrases (AdvP) are made up of one adverb as head word and one or more other lexical categories including adverbs themselves as modifiers. The head of the AdvP is placed at the end. Unlike other phrases, AdvPs do not take complements. Most of the time, the modifiers of AdvPs are PPs that come always before adverbs. Examples are: ከፋኝ (*kǐfuña*/severely), በጣም ከፋኝ (*bäṭam kǐfuña*/ very severely), እንደ ወንድሙ በጣም ከፋኝ (*ǐndä wändǐmu bäṭam kǐfuña*/very severely like his brother), etc.

2.3 Sentence Formation

Amharic language follows subject-object-verb grammatical pattern unlike, for example, English language which has subject-verb-object sequence of words (Yimam 2000; Amare 2010). For instance, the Amharic equivalent of the sentence "John killed the lion" is written as "ጆን (*jon*/John) አንበሳውን (*anbäsawn*/the lion) ገደለው (*gädäläw*/killed)". Amharic sentences can be constructed from simple or complex NP and simple or complex VP. Simple sentences are constructed from simple NP followed by simple VP which contains only a single verb. The following examples show the various structures of simple sentences.

- ጆን መኪና ገዛ።
  jon mäkina gäza።
  John bought a car.
- ማን መኪና ገዛልህ?
  man mäkina gäzalh?
  Who did buy a car for you?
- ጆን መጣ?
  jon mäṭa?
  Did John come?
- ዳቦ ጋግሪ!
  dabo gagri!
  Bake {feminine} bread!
- ሁለት ትልልቅ ልጆች በመኪና ወደ ጎጃም ሄዱ።
  hulät tǐlǐlǐq lǐjoc bämäkina wäda gojam hedu።
  Two big children went to Gojjam by car.

Complex sentences are sentences that contain at least one complex NP or complex VP or both complex NP and complex VP. Complex NPs are phrases that contain at least one embedded sentence in the phrase construction. The embedded sentence can be complements. The following examples show the various structures of complex Amharic sentences.

- [ጆን የገባበት የሳር ቤት] በጣም ትልቅ ነው፡፡
  [jon yägäbabät yäsar bet] bäṭam tïlïq näw፡፡
  [The thatched house that John entered in] is so big.
- ሜሪ [ጆን መኪና እንደገዛ] ሰማች፡፡
  meri [jon mäkina ïndägäza] sämač፡፡
  Mary heard [that John has bought a car].
- ጆን [ከጎጃም እንደመጣ] [ሜሪ ወደ ናዝሬት እንደ ሄደች] ሰማ፡፡
  jon [kägojam ïndämäṭa] [meri wädä nazret ïndä hedäč] säma.
  [When John came from Gojjam] he heard [that Mary went to Nazareth].
- [ከጎጃም የመጣችው ልጅ] [ጆን እንደወደዳት] አወቀች፡፡
  [kägojam yämäṭačïw lïj] [jon ïndäwädädat] awäqäč.
  [The girl who came from Gojjam] knew [that John loved her].

3   Base Phrase Chunking

3.1   Chunk Representation

The tag of chunks can be noun phrases, verb phrases, adjectival phrases, etc. in line with the language construction rules. There are many decisions to be made about where the boundaries of a group should lie and, as a consequence, there are many different 'styles' of chunking. There are also different types of chunk tags and chunk boundary identifications. Nevertheless, in order to identify the boundaries of each chunk in sentences, the following boundary types are used (Ramshaw and Marcus 1995): IOB1, IOB2, IOE1, IOE2, IO, "[", and "]". The first four formats are complete chunk representations which can identify the beginning and ending of phrases while the last three are partial chunk representations. All boundary types use "I" tag for words that are inside a phrase and an "O" tag for words that are outside a phrase. They differ in their treatment of chunk-initial and chunk-final words.

IOB1:   the first word inside a phrase immediately following another phrase receives a **B** tag.
IOB2:   all phrase- initial words receive a **B** tag.
IOE1:   the final word inside a phrase immediately preceding another same phrase receives an **E** tag.
IOE2:   all phrase- final words receive an **E** tag.
IO: words inside a phrase receive an **I** tag, others receive an **O** tag.
"[":   all phrase-initial words receive "[" tag, other words receive "." Tag.
"]":   all phrase-final words receive "]" tag and other words receive "." Tag.

An example of chunk representation for the sentence ሁለቱ ልጆች በትልቅ መኪና ወደ ጎጃም ሄዱ (hulätu lïjoc bätïlïq mäkina wäda gojam hedu / The two children went to Gojjam by a big car) is shown Table 1.

Table 1. Chunk representation for the sentence "ሁሉቱ ልጆች በትልቅ መኪና ወደ ጎጃም ሄዱ".

Chunk	ሁሉቱ	ልጆች	በትልቅ	መኪና	ወደ	ጎጃም	ሄዱ
IOB1	I-NP	I-NP	B-NP	I-NP	I-PP	I-PP	O
IOB2	B-NP	I-NP	B-NP	I-NP	B-PP	I-PP	O
IOE1	I-NP	E-NP	I-NP	I-NP	I-PP	I-PP	O
IOE2	I-NP	E-NP	I-NP	E-NP	I-PP	E-PP	O
IO	I-NP	I-NP	I-NP	I-NP	I-PP	I-PP	O
[	I-NP	.	[	.	[	.	.
]	.	]	.	]	.	]	.

In this work, we considered six different kinds of chunks, namely noun phrase (NP), verb phrase (VP), Adjective phrase (AdjP), Adverb phrase (AdvP), prepositional phrase (PP) and sentence (S). To identify the chunks, it is necessary to find the positions where a chunk can end and a new chunk can begin. The part-of-speech (POS) tag assigned to every token is used to discover these positions. We used the IOB2 tag set to identify the boundaries of each chunk in sentences extracted from chunk tagged text. Using the IOB2 tag set along with the chunk types considered, a total of 13 phrase tags were used in this work. These are: B-NP, I-NP, B-VP, I-VP, B-PP, I-PP, B-ADJP, I-ADJP, B-ADVP, I-ADVP, B-S, I-S and O. The followings are examples of chunk tagged sentences.

- ሁሉቱ NUMCR O ትልልቅ ADJ B-NP ልጆች N I-NP በመኪና NPREP O ወደ Prep B-PP ጎጃም N I-NP ሄዱ V O
- የኢትዮጵያ ADJ B-NP ጠላቶች N B-NP ሀገሪቱ N O በድርጅቱ NPREP B-PP ውስጥ Prep I-PP የተሰባትን V O በታ N O ተቃወሙ V O
- ንጉሱ N O ፋሺስቶች N B-S የተርቢደባዱበትን V I-S ጀግና ADJ B-NP ሰው N I-NP ሰቀሉ V O
- ኢትዮጵያ N O ፈንግጣ N B-S የተወገደበትን V I-S እለት N O ትላንት ADV B-VP አከበረች V I-VP

3.2 Architecture of the Chunker

To implement the chunker component, we used hidden Markov model (HHM) enhanced by a set of rules to prune errors. The HMM part has two phases: the training phase and the testing phase. In the training phase, the system first accepts words with POS tags and chunk tags. Then, the HMM is trained with this training set. Likewise in the test phase, the system accepts words with POS tags and outputs appropriate chunk tag sequences against each POS tag using HMM model. Figure 1 illustrates the workflow of the chunking process.

In this work, chunking is treated as a tagging problem. We use POS tagged sentence as input from which we observe sequences of POS tags represented as T. However, we also hypothesize that the corresponding sequences of chunk tags form hidden Markovian properties. Thus, we used a hidden Markov model (HMM) with POS tags serving as

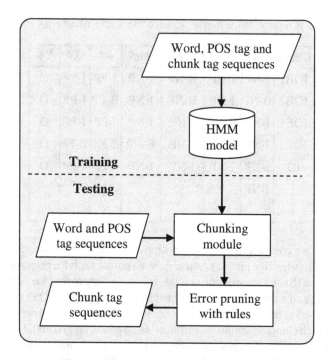

Fig. 1. Workflow of the chunking process.

states. The HMM model is trained with sequences of POS tags and chunk tags extracted from the training corpus. The HMM model is then used to predict the sequence of chunk tags C for a given sequence of POS tag T. This problem corresponds to finding C that maximizes the probability $P(C|T)$, which is formulated as:

$$C' = \arg\max_{C} P(C|T) \tag{1}$$

where C' is the optimal chunk sequence. By applying Baye's rule can derive, Eq. (1) yields:

$$C' = \arg\max_{C} P(T|C) * P(C) \tag{2}$$

which is in fact a decoding problem that is solved by making use of the Viterbi algorithm. The output of the decoder is the sequence of chunk tags which groups words based on syntactical correlations. The output chunk sequence is then analyzed to improve the result by applying linguistic rules derived from the grammar of Amharic. For a given Amharic word w, linguistic rules (from which sample rules are shown in Algorithm 1) were used to correct wrongly chunked words ("$w-1$" and "$w+1$" are used to mean the previous and next word, respectively).

```
1. If POS(w)=ADJ and POS(w+1)=NPREP, NUMCR, then chunk
   tag for w is O.
2. If POS(w)=ADJ and POS(w-1)!= ADJ and POS(w+1)=
   AUX,V, then chunk tag for w is B-VP.
3. If POS(w)=NPREP and POS(w+1)=N ,then chunk tag for w
   is B-NP.
4. If POS(w)=NUMCR and POS(w+1)=NPREP, then chunk tag
   for w is O.
5. If POS(w)=N and POS(w+1)=VPREP and POS(w-1) =N, ADJ,
   PRON, NPREP, then chunk tag for w is    B-VP.
6. If POS(w)=ADJ and POS(w+1)=ADJ, then chunk tag for w
   is B-ADJP.
```

Algorithm 1. Sample rules used to prune chunk errors.

4 Experiment

4.1 The Corpus

The major source of the dataset we used for training and testing the system was Walta Information Center (WIC) news corpus which is at present widely used for research on Amharic natural language processing. The corpus contains 8067 sentences where words are annotated with POS tags. Furthermore, we also collected additional text from an Amharic grammar book authored by Yimam (2000). The sentences in the corpus are classified as training data set and testing data set using 10 fold cross validation technique.

4.2 Test Results

In 10-fold cross-validation, the original sample is randomly partitioned into 10 equal size subsamples. Of the 10 subsamples, a single subsample is used as the validation data for testing the model, and the remaining 9 subsamples are used as training data. The cross-validation process is then repeated 10 times, with each of the 10 subsamples used exactly once as the validation data. Accordingly, we obtain 10 results from the folds which can be averaged to produce a single estimation of the model's predictive potential. By taking the average of all the ten results the overall chunking accuracy of the system is presented in Table 2.

Table 2. Test result for Amharic base phrase chunker.

Chunking model	Accuracy
HMM	85.31 %
HMM pruned with rules	93.75 %

5   Conclusion and Future Works

Amharic is one of the most morphologically complex and less-resourced languages. This complexity poses difficulty in the development of natural language processing applications for the language. Despite the efforts being undertaken to develop various Amharic NLP applications, only few usable tools are publicly available at present. One of the main reasons frequently cited by researchers is the morphological complexity of the language. Amharic text parsing also suffers from this problem. However, not all Amharic natural language processing applications require full parsing. In this work, we tried to overcome this problem by employing chunker. It appears that chunking is more manageable problem than parsing because the chunker does not require deeper analysis of texts which will be less affected by the morphological complexity of the language. Thus, future work is recommended to be directed at improving the chunker and use this component to develop Amharic natural language processing applications that do not rely on deeper analysis of linguistic structures.

References

Abney, S.: Parsing by chunks. In: Berwick, R., Abney, S., Tenny, C. (eds.) Principle-Based Parsing. Kluwer Academic Publishers, Dordrecht (1991)

Abney, S.: Chunks and dependencies: bringing processing evidence to bear on syntax. In: Computational Linguistics and the Foundations of Linguistic Theory. CSLI (1995)

Ali, W., Hussain, S.: A hybrid approach to Urdu verb phrase chunking. In: Proceedings of the 8th Workshop on Asian Language Resources (ALR-8), COLING-2010, Beijing, China (2010)

Amare, G.: ዘመናዊ የአማርኛ ሰዋስው በቀላል አቀራረብ (Modern Amharic Grammar in a Simple Approach). Addis Ababa, Ethiopia (2010)

Brants, T.: Cascaded markov models. In: Proceedings of the Ninth Conference on European Chapter of the Association for Computational Linguistics, EACL 1999, Bergen, Norway (1999)

Kutlu, M.: Noun phrase chunker for Turkish using dependency parser. Doctoral dissertation, Bilkent University (2010)

Lewis, P., Simons, F., Fennig, D.: Ethnologue: Languages of the World, 17th edn. SIL International, Dallas (2013)

Molina, A., Pla, F.: Shallow parsing using specialized HMMs. J. Mach. Learn. Res. **2**, 595–613 (2002)

Ramshaw, A., Marcus, P.: Text chunking using transformation-based learning. In: Proceedings of the Third ACL Workshop on Very Large Corpora, pp. 82–94 (1995)

Thao, H., Thai, P., Minh N., Thuy, Q.: Vietnamese noun phrase chunking based on conditional random fields. In: International Conference on Knowledge and Systems Engineering (KSE 2009), pp. 172–178 (2009)

Tjong, E.F., Sang, K., Buchholz, S.: Introduction to the CoNLL-2000 shared task: chunking. In: Proceedings of the 2nd Workshop on Learning Language in Logic and the 4th Conference on Computational Natural Language Learning, vol. 7, pp. 127–132 (2000)

Xu, F., Zong, C., Zhao, J.: A hybrid approach to Chinese base noun phrase chunking. In: Proceedings of the Fifth SIGHAN Workshop on Chinese Language Processing, Sydney (2006)

Yangarber, R., Grishman, R.: NYU: description of the Proteus/PET system as used for MUC-7. In: Proceedings of the Seventh Message Understanding Conference, MUC-7, Washington, DC (1998)

Yimam, B.: የአማርኛ ሰዋስው (Amharic Grammar). Addis Ababa, Ethiopia (2000)

A Hybrid Approach to Parsing Natural Languages

Sardar Jaf[✉] and Allan Ramsay

School of Computer Science, The University of Manchester, Manchester, UK
{sardar.jaf,allan.ramsay}@manchester.ac.uk

Abstract. Ambiguities in natural languages make processing (parsing) them a difficult task. Parsing is even more difficult when dealing with a structurally complex natural language such as Arabic. In this paper, we briefly highlight some of the complex structure of Arabic, and we identify different parsing approaches and briefly discuss their limitations. Our goal is to produce a hybrid parser, by combining different parsing approaches, which retains the advantages of data-driven approaches but is guided by a set of grammatical rules to produce more accurate results. We describe a novel technique for directly combining different parsing approaches. Results for our initial experiments that we have conducted in this work, and our plans for future work are also presented.

Keywords: Parsing · Hybrid parsing · Natural language processing · Dependency parsing

1 Introduction

Establishing the syntactic relations between natural language words is called parsing [1]. Parsing is one of the core components of many natural language processing applications [2], such as: Machine Translation, Speech recognition, and dialogue based Systems. However, parsing is a challenging task due to language ambiguities [3], which is caused by multiple interpretations of words, word order freedom, and missing items. Hence, adequate parsers are often unavailable, particularly for languages with complex structures such as Arabic [4, p. 82]. It is desirable that parsers have three main features: (i) efficiency (consuming as little time as possible), (ii) robustness (successfully parsing a large proportion of input strings), and (iii) accuracy (produce correct results). It has been argued that it is not possible to achieve all three features at once [5]. Our goal is to optimise speed and accuracy while maintaining a reasonable level of robustness by combining features of data-driven and grammar-driven approaches. We test our parser on Arabic because Arabic is structurally complex, which makes it hard to parse and it will act as a rigorous test-bed for our approach.

2 Natural Language Parsing Approaches

There are two approaches to parsing natural languages: (i) grammar-driven, and (ii) data-drives. Each approach has some limitations. A parser is considered

© Springer International Publishing Switzerland 2016
Z. Vetulani et al. (Eds.): LTC 2013, LNAI 9561, pp. 136–145, 2016.
DOI: 10.1007/978-3-319-43808-5_11

robust if it can analyse a large proportion of a set of natural language sentences. Grammar-driven approaches normally lack robustness for two reasons: sufficient grammatical rules are not available for a natural language in order for parsers to be able to produce analyses for a given input string, and because a given input string may not be part of the natural language, e.g., when a word is spelled or pronounced incorrectly, or if material is omitted in a sentence. Some researchers argue that robustness problem in grammar-driven approaches can be solved by relaxing grammar constraints in parsers. However, relaxing grammar rules may result in parsers producing several analyses for a given input string, which means that parsers will consume more time and computing resources for exploring these analyses which may consequently affect efficiency. Moreover, having several candidate analyses for a given input string may increase the risk of parsers selecting an incorrect analysis as the final result, which could aggravate the problem of accuracy.

Data-driven parsers on the other hand, use an inductive mechanism for mapping input strings to output analyses. According to [5], in most existing data-driven parsers any input strings are assigned at least one analysis, which means that data-driven parsers are highly robust. However, the extreme robustness of data-driven parsers means that they will assign analyses that are grammatically incorrect, hence data-driven parsers may not produce highly accurate parse results compared with its counterpart grammar-driven parsers.

Furthermore, the problem of disambiguation can be severe in data-driven parsers because the improved robustness is achieved through the extreme constraint relaxation. But, this is compensated by the fact that the inductive inference scheme, which is obtained by using machine learning algorithms in data-driven parsers, provides a mechanism for disambiguation by associating a score with each analysis intended to reflect some optimality criterion, or by implicitly maximising this criterion in a deterministic selection. Regarding the problem of efficiency, it is argued that data-driven approaches is superior to grammar-driven approaches [6], but it is often at the expense of less accurate output [7].

3   Arabic

Natural language ambiguities; which affect Parsers' efficiency, robustness, and accuracy, are considered a major problem when processing natural language sentences [3, 8].

Arabic morphology is highly inflected, which makes its syntactic structure complex [9]. There are a number of complexities in Arabic: (i) the canonical order of Arabic sentences is VSO. But, due to the syntactic flexibility of words in the language [9], a range of other word orders such as VOS, SVO and OVS are also possible [10,11]. Reordering words in Arabic sentences makes it hard to distinguish between nominative and accusative cases, for example in the sentence "Ahmad yahatarm Ali" "Ahmed respects Ali" it is clear that "Ahmed" is the subject in the sentence and "Ali" is the object. But, reordering the words as "yahtarm Ahmad Ali" "respects Ahmed Ali" means that the subject could

be either "Ahmed" or "Ali" which lead to structural ambiguity. (ii) Arabic clitics often alter words formation, such as from nouns to verbs, or verb types
from transitive to intransitive [12]. For instance, the sentence "wlyahum AlyuN
fy AlmasAla" "Ali is the leader in their situation" where "wlyahum" "their
leader", which is a noun, is ambiguous because the letters "w" and "l" could
be clitics attached to the word "yahum" "take charge" and can modify these
words into verbs, as in the sentence "wlyahum AlyuN fy AlmasAla" "and Ali
to take charge of the situation", where the word is a verb. (iii) The subject of
an Arabic sentence could be omitted because Arabic verb's agreement features
are rich enough to recover subject's by conjugating themselves to indicate gender, number and person of the omitted pronoun subject [10]. In the sentence
"Akalat Al dajAjT" "ate the chicken", the verb "Akalat" "ate" indicates that
the missing subject is a singular, feminine, and third person pronoun. When a
pronoun subject is dropped, Arabic verbs can be transitive and intransitive, so
it is not clear that the Noun Phrase (NP) "Al dajAjT" "the chicken" following
the verb "Akalat" "ate" is the subject. If the NP is the subject then the verb is
intransitive, but if the NP is the object of the verb and the subject is an omitted
pronoun (as "she") then the verb is transitive.

4   Related Work

There is an increasing trend in combining grammar-driven and data-driven
parsers. Some of the previous works on hybrid parsing involved combining state-
of-art dependency data-driven parsers such as MaltParser [13] and MSTParser
[14] with grammar-driven parsers, where the output of one type of parser is used
as input to another type of parser. For example, the Output of a Lexical Functional Grammar (LFG) parser is used as input to the MaltParser by [15]. The
LFG parser outputs phrase structured trees containing grammatical features.
They have converted the output of the LFG parser to dependency trees in order
to have two parallel versions of their original data: a gold standard Treebank, and
a dependency Treebank, by converting the LFG parser output which contains
additional grammatical features. They have extended the gold standard Treebank with additional information from the corresponding LFG parser's analyses.
They have then trained MaltPaser on the enhanced gold standard Treebank and
their results showed a small improvement in accuracy when they have applied
their technique on English and German.

An alternative approach to hybrid parsing is conducted by [16]. They have
used the output of a data-driven parser to constraint a Head-driven Phrase Structure Grammar (HPSG) parser. HPSG parsers use a small number of schemas
for explaining general construction rules, and a large number of lexical entries
for expressing word-specific syntactic and semantic constraints. During HPSG
parsing process, the lexical head of each partial parse tree is stored and in each
schema application the head child is determined. Having such information about
the head child and the lexical head, the dependency produced by the schema
application is identified and whether the schema application violates the dependencies in the dependency Treebank, which is obtained from a data-driven parser,

is checked. The HPSG parser is forced to produce parse trees that are consistent with the dependency trees. This approach is tested on English and some improvements in accuracy were achieved.

[17] have used lexical and inflectional morphological features to improve a dependencies data-driven parser for Arabic. They have added lexical and morphological features to dependency treebanks (PATB, Columbia, and Prague treebanks) and then trained and tested MaltParser on the extended treebank data. Their testing showed an improvement in parse accuracy when the parse Arabic sentences.

5   Parser Hybridisation

In this section, we describe the steps for implementing a hybrid parser. We have implemented a data-driven dependency parser and we have integrated a scoring technique into it in order to easily convert it to a hybrid parser. We have trained our parser, using a machine learning algorithm, on the Penn Arabic Treebank (PATB) [18] and we have extracted a set of dependency relations from the PATB for restricting the parser in order to produce analyses that obeyed the dependency relation rules. We have used the dependency relation rules to verify that our approach to hybrid parsing is viable. Although the extracted rules are generalized, at this stage, but we believe they are sufficient for conducting our initial experiments.

The first stage of our work was to obtain a dependency format treebank because we are implementing a data-driven dependency parser. We have then experimented with a number of machine learning algorithms in order to identify an algorithm that can classify our data accurately so that we extract question:answer pairs from the selected machine learning's output, we have then used such pairs as a set of parse rules for guiding the parser.

Finally, we have used the dependency relation rules for restricting the parser in order to produce correct analyses.

5.1   From Phrase Structure to Dependency Structure

The Penn Arabic Treebank (PATB) [18] is a large collection of annotated modern standard Arabic text containing linguistic information, such as part of speech tags, which is appropriate for parsing Arabic texts. However, the main challenge in using PATB is that it is based on phrase structure trees but the parser we are developing is a dependency based parser. We opt for dependency parsing because it is proven to be robust, efficient and fairly accurate [5,19]. In order to make the PATB data appropriate for dependency parsers, we have converted it to dependency structures. The principle of the conversion from phrase structures to dependency structures is described clearly by [20] as: (i) use the head percolation table for marking the head child of each node in a constituency format, and (ii) make the head of each non-head child depend on the head of the head-child in the dependency structure.

5.2   Dependency Relations Extraction from PATB

Once we have obtained the dependency format of the PATB, we have extracted
a set of dependency relations rules from it. The technique that we have used
for extracting dependency relations from a bracketed dependency tree is simple,
which we describe below:

1. Get the head of the tree, which is the first item on the dependency tree.
2. Get the daughter(s) of the head, which is the next list of items in the dependency tree that follows the head.
3. If there is more than one daughter for the head, then process each daughter in turn by repeating from step 1 to 2. Otherwise, the daughter is not the head of anything and we proceed to step 4.
4. Establishes dependency relationship between the head and the head of the daughter(s) and record the dependency relationship.

[(V, ate), [(N, man), [(DET, the)]], [(N, apple), [(DET, an)]]]

Fig. 1. A bracketed dependency tree

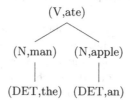

Fig. 2. A dependency tree

[[(V, ate)]>[(N, man)], [(V, ate)>(N, apple)], [(N, man)>(DET, the)], [(N, apple)>(DET, an)]]

Fig. 3. A dependency relation set

For example, we can extract the dependency relations from the bracketed
tree in Fig. 1 using the technique we have described above. We first get the head
of the tree, i.e., the first item in the list, which is "(V, ate)". Second, we get
the daughters of "(V, ate)", which is the lists ([(N, man), [(DET, the)]] and
[(N, apple), [(DET, an)]]). We then establish dependency relations between "(V,
ate)" and its daughters, as "(V, ate)" as the head of "(N, man)" and "(V, ate)"
as the head of "(N, apple)", where "(V, man)" and "(N, apple)" are the head of
the daughters of "(V, ate)", i.e., "(N, man)" and "(N, apple)" are the first items
in the lists [(N, man), [(DET, the)]] and [(N, apple), [(DET, an)]]. Thirdly, we
store the relations in a set of relations as in Fig. 3. Since the head "(V, ate)"

has more than one daughter, we process each of its daughter starting from the first daughter which is [(N, man), [(DET, the)]]. Starting from step 1 above, we choose "(N, man)" as the head and establish relations between "(N, man)" and its daughter(s) which is "(DET, the)". Since the daughter of "(N, man)" does not have any daughter of its own, we process the remaining daughters of "(V, ate)" until all of the daughters of "(V, ate)" and its subdaughters are processed (Fig. 2).

5.3   Developing a Dependency Data-Driven Parser

We have developed a parser based on shift-reduce algorithm [1] with dynamic programming. The parser process an agenda, where an agenda contains a list of parse states. A parse state consists of data structures, a set of dependency relations, a score for each state, and a parse action. States on the agenda are sorted by their scores in descending order. The parser proceeds by processing the first state on the agenda. Processing each state will produce new states which are added to the agenda. The data structures consist of a queue of input strings, and a stack of tokens (which may include processed strings). Input strings contain various features such as: part-of-speech tags, words' forms, words' start position in the sentence, words' end position in the sentence, and parse actions that may have been applied to them.

The parser performs three operations on the queues and the stacks: (i) shift, (ii) left-reduce, and (iii) right reduce, where each of these operations produce new parse state. Shift operation moves the first item from the queue to the top of the stack. Left-reduce operation makes the item from the stack a dependency parent of the item at the beginning of the queue. Right-reduce operation makes the first item on the queue a dependency parent of an item on the stack. The parser processes each state until it reaches a final parse state. If the parser reaches a state where there is an empty queue and a stack with one item, where the item's start and end position on the stack covers the entire sentence length in question, then the parser successfully parsed the given sentence. Otherwise, the parse is unsuccessful.

In order to convert this parser to a hybrid parser where we use the set of dependency relation rules as grammatical rules for restricting the parser, we have implemented a scoring algorithm into the parser which assigns scores to parse states. We can briefly describe our scoring technique below:

(a) WML is 1 if the parser follows machine learning suggestion, otherwise it is 0.

(b) WG is 1 if the machine learning suggestion leads to a grammatical analysis, i.e., the suggested dependency relations by the machine learning algorithm conform to the relations in the set of dependency relations we have extracted from the PATB. Otherwise it is −1.

(c) A is the sum of (ML * WML) + (G * WG), where ML and G are weights that are used to determine the parser type. Given 0 weight to G then the parser follows machine learning suggestions and ignores dependency relation rules, which makes it a data-driven parser. Given 0 weight to ML then the parser follows grammatical rules and ignores the machine learning suggestions, which makes it a grammar-driven parser. Given more or less equal weights to ML and G then the parser pays follows suggestions made by the machine learning algorithm and the rules, which makes it a hybrid parser.

Once we have obtained scores for each parse states, we then sort all states in the agenda in descending order (because states with the highest score indicate that they are suggested by the machine learning algorithm and they also leads to correct analyses).

We have used a software toolkit, Weka [21], which contains a large number of machine learning algorithms in order to experiment with a number of machine learning algorithms for parser training by supplying it with data containing different parse states. Our aim was to train the parser to perform appropriate parse actions in different situations. We have integrated the J48 machine learning algorithm in the parser due to its high classification accuracy rate (91 %) compared with some other machine learning algorithms, such as Support Vector Machine (SVM). We have used the output of the J48 machine learning algorithm for extracting state:action pairs for guiding the parser to perform shift action or reduce action deterministically. Finally, we have conducted some initial experiments on the parser by running it as pure data-driven, grammar-driven, and hybrid parser. We have also tested the parser to check how we can trade off between speed and accuracy by using it as a hybrid parser, These experiments are discussed in the following section.

6   Preliminary Results

We have conducted some experiments on the hybrid parser that is driven by a machine learning algorithm but is constraint by dependency relation rules; we have improved the parser accuracy significantly. Table 1 shows the differences between running the parser as purely data-driven, grammar-driven, and hybrid. We have trained the parser on 100000 words, and tested it with 10000 words. The parser, by construction, is efficient and robust, because we provide it with shift, left-reduce or right-reduce action at each parse step, which deterministically lead to some analyses. However, the efficiency and robustness of the parser comes at the expense of its accuracy because the parser is guided by the machine learning algorithm where it will always leads to some analyses, however, suggestions made by the machine learning algorithm are not always leading to correct

Table 1. Parsing with different approaches

Parsing method	Machine learning weight	Grammar weight	Accuracy (%)	Time taken (seconds)
Data-driven	1	0	63	235
Grammar-driven	0	1	90	878
Hybrid	1	1	88	459

Table 2. Hybrid parsing

Machine learning weight	Grammar weight	Accuracy (%)	Time taken (seconds)
1	0.25	73.64	218
1	0.5	78.57	404
1	0.75	86.45	438
1	1	88.01	461
1	1.25	87.78	453
1	1.5	87.87	451
1	1.75	87.87	453
1	2	87.87	453
1	2.25	87.87	453
1	2.5	87.87	453
1	2.75	87.87	453

analyses, hence the accuracy is affected. However, parsing time and accuracy varies as we constraint the parser by to produce results that conforms to the set of dependency relation rules.

Table 2 show that the more weight we give to dependency relation rules, the more accurate the parse analyses are, but the accuracy is achieved at the expense of the parse speed.

7   Future Work

We would like to find out how the hybrid parser performs when it is evaluated using rules that contain more linguistic features and more restricted. We have conducted these preliminary tests using dependency relations extracted from the PATB which behave as a set of rules for restricting the parser to analyses that obey a set dependency relations. We anticipate that having a more restricted set of rules may have an interesting impact on the hybrid parser, which we are planning to investigate it in the near future. In order to prepare grammatical rules for testing our hybrid parser, we are planning to produce a large number of rules using linguistic data available from the PATB and Parasite [22] which is an in-house grammar driven.

8   Conclusion

Problems associated with using grammar-driven approaches and data-driven approaches are discussed in this paper. The main structural complexities of Arabic are identified and briefly described. We have very briefly highlighted the techniques that we have used for converting the Penn Arabic Treebank form phrase structure to dependency structures, and we also briefly highlighted a technique for extracting a set of dependency relation rules from a dependency tree. The first stage of our approach to hybrid parsing is explained, we also described our technique for developing a hybrid parser that directly combines features from data-driven approaches and grammar-driven approaches. We have extracted a set of relations from the PATB to test that we can constraint the data-driven parser with a set of dependency rules. Our rules are overly generalized but they are sufficient for checking the viability of our approach to hybrid parsing. We have presented our preliminary results for the parser, the results are encouraging. We are going to enrich the dependency rules further in the future. The parser is tested on Arabic because it is a complex language, compared to some other languages, hence it provides a rigorous test-bed. Finally, various related works in hybrid parsing approaches for natural language processing is identified and briefly described.

Acknowledgments. Sardar Jaf's contribution to this work was supported by the Qatar National Research Fund (grant NPRP 09-046-6-001). Allan Ramsay's contribution was partially supported from the same grant.

References

1. Aho, A.V., Ullman, J.D.: The Theory of Parsing, Translation, and Compiling, vol. 1. Prentice-Hall, Englewood Cliffs (1972)
2. Farghaly, A., Shaalan, K.: Arabic natural language processing: challenges and solutions. ACM Comput. Surveys **8**(4), 1–22 (2009)
3. Collins, M.: Head-driven statistical models for natural language parsing. Comput. Linguist. **29**(4), 589–637 (2003). http://dx.doi.org/10.1162/089120103322753356
4. Lee, C., Day, M., Sung, C., Lee, Y., Jiang, T., Wu, C., Shih, C., Chen, Y., Hsu, W.: Boosting Chinese question answering with two lightweight methods: ABSPs and SCO-QAT. ACM Trans. Asian Lang. Inf. Process. (TALIP) **7**(4), 12:1–12:29 (2008)
5. Nivre, J., Hall, J., Nilsson, J., Eryigit, G., Svetoslav, M.: Labeled pseudo-projective dependency parsing with support vector machines, pp. 221–225. Association for Computational Linguistics (2006)
6. Nivre, J.: Inductive Dependency Parsing. Text, Speech and Language Technology. Springer, Netherlands (2006)
7. Kaplan, R.M., Riezler, S., King, T.H., Maxwell Iii, J.T., Vasserman, E., Crouch, R.: Speed and accuracy in shallow and deep stochastic parsing. In: Proceedings of Human Langauge Technology and the Conference of the North American Chapter of the Association for Computational Linguistics, HLT-NAACL, pp. 97–104 (2004)
8. Baptista, M.: On the nature of pro-drop in capeverdean creole. Harv. Working Pap. Linguist. **5**, 3–17 (1995)
9. Daimi, K.: Identifying syntactic ambiguities in single-parse Arabic sentence. Comput. Humanit. **35**(3), 333–349 (2001)
10. Attia, A.M.: Handling Arabic morphological and syntactic ambiguities within the LFG framework with a view to machine translation. Ph.D. Thesis, School of Languages, Linguistics and Cultures, Manchester University (2008)
11. Ramsay, A., Mansour, H.: Local constraints on Arabic word order. In: Salakoski, T., Ginter, F., Pyysalo, S., Pahikkala, T. (eds.) FinTAL 2006. LNCS (LNAI), vol. 4139, pp. 447–457. Springer, Heidelberg (2006)

12. Nelken, R., Shieber, S.M.: Arabic diacritization using weighted finite-state transducers. In: Proceedings of the Association for Computational Linguistics Workshop on Computational Approaches to Semitic Languages. Semitic 2005, pp. 79–86. Association for Computational Linguistics, Stroudsburg (2005)

13. Nivre, J., Hall, J., Nilsson, J.: MaltParser: A Data-Driven Parser-Generator for Dependency Parsing. Springer, Netherland (2006)

14. MacDonald, R.: Discriminative learning and spanning tree algorithms for dependency parsing. Ph.D. Thesis, Computer and Information Science, the University of Pennsylvania (2006). http://www.cis.upenn.edu/grad/documents/mcdonald.pdf

15. Øvrelid, L., Kuhn, J., Spreyer, K.: Improving data-driven dependency parsing using large-scale LFG grammars. In: Proceedings of the Association for Computational Linguistics-International Joint Conference on Natural Language Processing 2009 Conference Short Papers, pp. 37–40. Association for Computational Linguistics, Stroudsburg (2009). http://dl.acm.org/citation.cfm?id=1667583.1667597

16. Sagae, K., Miyao, Y.: HPSG parsing with shallow dependency constraints. In: Proceedings of ACL 2007 (2007)

17. Marton, Y., Habash, N., Rambow, O.: Improving Arabic dependency parsing with form-based and functional morphological features. In: Proceedings of the 49th Annual Meeting of the Association for Computational Linguistics: Human Language Technologies, pp. 1586–1596. Association for Computational Linguistics, Portland (2011). http://www.aclweb.org/anthology/P11-1159

18. Maamouri, M., Bies, A.: Developing an Arabic treebank: methods, guidelines, procedures, and tools. In: Proceedings of the Workshop on Computational Approaches to Arabic Script-based Languages, Geneva, pp. 2–9 (2004)

19. McDonald, R., Lerman, K., Pereira, F.: Multilingual dependency parsing with a two-stage discriminative parser. In: Tenth Conference on Computational Natural Language Learning (CoNLL-X), New York (2006)

20. Xia, F., Palmer, M.: Converting dependency structures to phrase structures. In: Proceedings of the 1st Human Language Technology Conference (HLT-2001), San Diego, pp. 1–5 (2001)

21. Witten, I.H., Frank, E.: Data Mining: Practical Machine Learning Tools and Techniques. Morgan Kaufmann Series in Data Management Systems, 2nd edn. Morgan Kaufmann, San Francisco (2005). http://www.amazon.ca/exec/obidos/redirect?tag=citeulike09-20&path=ASIN/0120884070

22. Ramsay, A.M.: Direct parsing with discontinuous phrases. Nat. Lang. Eng. 5(3), 271–300 (1999)

Experiments in PCFG-like Disambiguation of Constituency Parse Forests for Polish

Marcin Woliński[✉] and Dominika Rogozińska

Institute of Computer Science, Polish Academy of Sciences, Warszawa, Poland
wolinski@ipipan.waw.pl

Abstract. The work presented here is the first attempt at creating a probabilistic constituency parser for Polish. The described algorithm disambiguates parse forests obtained from the Świgra parser in a manner close to Probabilistic Context Free Grammars. The experiment was carried out and evaluated on the Składnica treebank. The idea behind the experiment was to check what can be achieved with this well known method. Results are promising, the approach presented achieves up to 94.1 % PARSEVAL F-measure and 92.1 % ULAS. The PCFG-like algorithm can be evaluated against existing Polish dependency parser which achieves 92.2 % ULAS.

1 Motivation and Context

The main incentive for the present work is the availability of the Składnica treebank of Polish (Woliński et al. 2011; Świdziński and Woliński 2010)[1], which for the first time provides the means to attempt probabilistic parsing of Polish. Składnica is a constituency treebank based on parse forests generated by the Świgra parser and subsequently disambiguated by annotators.

The parser generates parse forests representing all possible parse trees for a given sentence. Then the correct tree is marked in the forest by annotators.

Including a probabilistic module in the parsing process of Świgra would require tight integration and deep insight into its workings. Therefore, for the present experiments we have taken an approach that is technically simpler. We generate complete forests with unchanged Świgra and then the probabilistic algorithm has to select one of the generated trees. This way the algorithm solves exactly the same problem as annotators of the training corpus.

In this paper we present a series of experiments based on Probabilistic Context Free Grammars as a method for assigning probabilities to parse trees.

2 Scoring the Results

For evaluating disambiguated parses we use the PARSEVAL precision and recall measures (Abney et al. 1991), which count correctly recognised phrases in the

---

[1] http://zil.ipipan.waw.pl/Składnica.

© Springer International Publishing Switzerland 2016
Z. Vetulani et al. (Eds.): LTC 2013, LNAI 9561, pp. 146–158, 2016.
DOI: 10.1007/978-3-319-43808-5_12

algorithm output. A phrase, represented in the constituency tree by an internal node, is correct iff it has the right non-terminal and spans the correct fragment of the input text (it has the correct yield).

Precision and recall is computed across the whole set of sentences being processed:

$$\text{Precision} = \frac{\text{number of correct nodes}}{\text{number of nodes selected by the algorithm}}$$

$$\text{Recall} = \frac{\text{number of correct nodes}}{\text{number of nodes in training trees}}$$

In all experiments described below the values of precision and recall are close to each other (within 1 % point). This is not very surprising: the trees selected by the algorithms are close in the number of nodes to the training trees. So usually when a node is selected that should not be (spoiling precision), some of the nodes that should be selected is not (spoiling recall). For that reason we present the results in the aggregated form of F-measure (harmonic mean of precision and recall).

Non-terminals in Składnica are complex terms. The label of a nonterminal unit (e.g., *nominal phrase* fno) is accompanied by several attributes (10 in the case of fno: morphological features such as case, gender, number, and person, as well as a few attributes specific to the grammar in use). We provide two variants of F-measures: taking into account only whether the labels of non-terminal units match – reported as F_L or requiring a match on all attributes – F_A.

We count the measures against internal nodes of the trees only, that is non-terminals. The terminals, carrying morphological interpretations of words, are unambiguous in the manually annotated corpus.

Składnica contains information about heads of phrases, which makes it easy to convert constituency trees to (unlabelled) dependency trees. We perform such a conversion to count *unlabelled attachment score* (ULAS, the ratio of correctly assigned dependency edges) for resulting trees. This allows us to compare our results with those of Wróblewska and Woliński (2012). We do not use Wróblewska's procedure for converting the trees to labelled dependency trees since it contains some heuristic elements that could influence the results.

In all the reported experiments ten-fold cross validation was used. Składnica contains trees for about 8000 sentences. This set was randomly divided into ten parts. In each of ten iterations nine parts were used for building the model and the remaining one to evaluate it.

3   Monkey Dendrologist – The Baseline

For the baseline of our experiments we have selected the following model. The task at hand mimics the work of annotators (called dendrologists by the authors of Składnica), so for the baseline we want to mimic a dendrologist who performs disambiguation by taking random decisions at each step.

In a shared parse forest typically only some nodes are ambiguous. These nodes have more than one decomposition into smaller phrases in the tree. This situation corresponds to the possibility of using more than one grammar rule to obtain the given node. Disambiguation can be seen as deciding for each ambiguous node which rule to take.

In the tree in Fig. 1 ambiguous nodes are marked with rows of tiny rectangles with arrows (which allow to select various realisations in the search tool of Składnica). Each rectangle represents one realisation of the given node. In this tree 5 of 35 internal nodes are ambiguous.

A "monkey dendrologist" considers the ambiguous nodes starting from the root of the tree and for each of them selects with equal probabilities one of possible realisations. Note that these decisions are not independent: selecting a realisation for a node determines the set of ambiguous nodes that have to be considered in its descendant nodes. Ambiguous nodes that lay outside of these selected subtrees will not even be considered.

A variant of monkey dendrologist is a "mean monkey dendrologist". This one when considering a node first checks in the reference treebank which variant is correct and then selects randomly from the other variants.

The following table presents disambiguation quality of monkey dendrologists:

	F_L	F_A	ULAS
Mean monkey	0.859	0.696	0.808
Monkey	0.877	0.759	0.832

For some sentences Świgra generates very many parses, giving the impression that every structure is possible. Nonetheless, the above numbers show that the rules of the grammar limit possible trees quite strongly. The F_A score for the dendrologist that deliberately chooses wrong shows that about 70 % of the nodes are unambiguous.

4   PCFG-like Disambiguation

The idea of Probabilistic Context Free Grammars is to associate probabilities with rules of a context free grammar. Applications of rules are considered independent, and so the probability of a given parse tree is computed as a product of probabilities of all rules used.

Probabilities of rules in PCFG are estimated probabilities of a given non-terminal being rewritten into a given sequence of non-terminals (that is probability of a given sequence of non-terminals to become the children of a given non-terminal). This is counted on a treebank by dividing the number of times a given rule was applied by the number of times all rules with the same left hand side were applied.

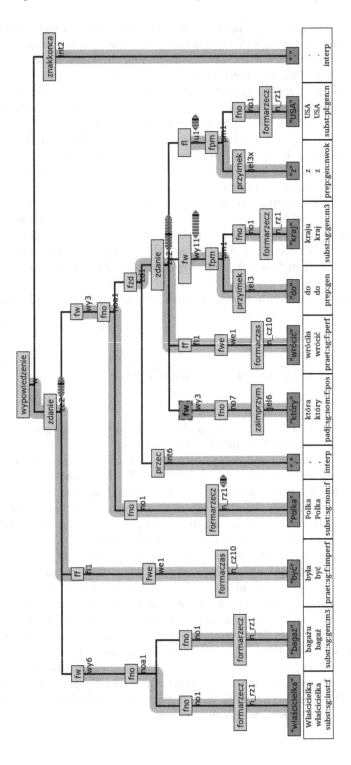

Fig. 1. A Składnica tree for the sentence

Właścicielką	bagażu	była	Polka,	,	która	wróciła	do	kraju	z	USA.
owner	luggage	was	Pole		which	returned	to	country	from	U.S.

'The owner of the luggage was a Pole who returned to the country from the U.S.'

The grammar of Świgra is a Definite Clause Grammar (Pereira and Warren 1980) with an extension allowing its CFG-like rules to include optional and repeatable elements in their right hand sides. This means a single rule can generate nodes of various arities in the trees, which makes assigning probabilities to rules doubtful. Nonetheless this idea can be applied to Składnica trees by assigning probabilities to couples ⟨parent, list of children⟩. In other words, we try to estimate the probability of a given node having a given sequence of nodes as its children.

The algorithm operates on packed (shared) parse forests (Billot and Lang 1989), whose nodes are polynomial in number, even if they represent an exponential number of trees. The key point in effective processing is to construct scores over the trees without constructing all separate trees.

The disambiguation algorithm computes probabilities using a dynamic procedure. The goal is to find the most probable parse tree. As we are maximizing a product, in each ambiguous node (constituent) we can choose the realization with the highest PCFG probability. We perform the computation in a bottom-up manner, which allows us to avoid producing and processing all possible parse trees.

When this idea is used in a straightforward manner we get the following results:

	F_L	F_A	ULAS
simple "PCFG"	0.923	0.833	0.878

This approach corrects 38 % of errors made by monkey dendrologist when counted only on labels and 31 % counted on all attributes.

The PCFG model is rather simplistic as it takes into the account only labels of non-terminals and not complete sets of attributes. In the following we tried to enrich the information taken into the account by adding selected attributes.

The most obvious problem concerns arguments of verbs. The Świgra grammar analyses the sentence (zdanie) as a finite verbal phrase (ff) and a sequence of required phrases (arguments, fw) and free phrases (adjuncts, fl). For example, in Fig. 1 there are two zdanie nodes. The upper one consists of a required phrase realised by a nominal phrase in instrumental, a finite phrase and a required phrase representing the subject (nominal in nominative). The second zdanie comprises a subject (realised by a pronoun), finite phrase, required phrase realised by a prepositional-nominal complement and a free phrase representing prepositional-nominal adjunct. The required phrases (in particular subjects and complements) are indistinguishable for the pure PCFG algorithm.

In the first experiment the labels for required phrases were augmented with types of these phrases, e.g., subj, np(inst), infp (infinitival phrase), prepnp('z',gen), and so on. Note that these symbols include in particular the value of case for required nominal and prepositional-nominal phrases.

We have also added several morphological features: gender, number and person (denoted GNP below). Note that since these attributes of nodes copy the features of the centre of the phrase, this provides the algorithm with data similar to that used with what is called "lexicalisation" in the context of PCFG (Collins 1997).

	F_L	F_A	ULAS
"PCFG"+fw-type	0.941	0.875	0.921
"PCFG"+GNP	0.936	0.876	0.915
"PCFG"+fw-type+GNP	0.932	0.873	0.914

Adding type of required phrases improves the results. This variant of the algorithm is able to avoid 46 % of errors made by a monkey dendrologist. Adding of gender-number-person improves results as well. A bit of surprise is that adding both elements results in slightly worse results than adding types alone. Probably in that case the training data gets too sparse. Note that with the added information various combinations of attributes are treated as completely independent non-terminals.

When the algorithm encounters a combination of children that was not seen in the training data, it uses a small smoothing value as a probability. We have counted the number of such unseen combinations in some variants of the experiment:

	Types	Occurences
simple "PCFG"	3,434	171,130
"PCFG"+fw-type	15,472	248,946
"PCFG"+fw-type+GNP	61,281	416,605

The growth of combinations with attributes added turns out to be very rapid, which unfortunately means that some kind of feature selection would be needed to train a manageable model. The vast majority of these combinations appear in realisations of the nominal phrase fno (where various kinds of attachments can happen at various levels) and in the sentence zdanie (where various combinations of complements and adjuncts are possible).

5   Experiments with Extended Version of Składnica treebank

Since the time the above experiments were conducted, the Składnica treebank has been extended by 2000 new annotated sentences. As the above research showed that the treebank holds too sparse data, experiments on 25 % bigger data set could be expected to give better results.

Baseline results, compared to these for the previous version of Składnica, are significantly worse:

	F_L	F_A
Mean monkey	0.806	0.676
Monkey	0.842	0.735

The ambiguity level of nodes, measured as the number of possible grammar productions that can be used to generate a given node, has grown by 10 %. For comparison, we show a histogram (Fig. 2) presenting the percentage of nodes with a given number of possible productions (please note these are grouped in non-equal buckets). The value of 1 corresponds to unambiguous nodes and the

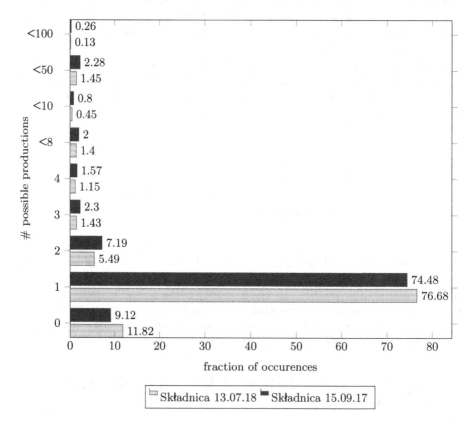

Fig. 2. Changes in the ambiguity level of nodes in two versions of Składnica

value of 0 corresponds to tree leaves. As can be seen in Fig. 1, the extended treebank has more nodes in each group of ambiguous nodes and less in unambiguous ones.

The following table lists results of experiments from the previous section repeated on the larger treebank. We do not provide the ULAS measure, since we do not have (yet) the dependency version of the present Składnica.

	F_L	F_A
simple "PCFG"	0.935	0.857
"simple"+fw-type	0.934	0.864
"PCFG"+GNP	0.930	0.866
"PCFG"+fw-type+GNP	0.927	0.864

The simple PCFG model shows an improvement. This approach now corrects 59 % of errors made by a monkey dendrologist on labels (46 % on all attributes). Even without taking into account that the baseline has been lowered, the overall accuracy of the model raised. This is a promising result which shows that we are able to obtain better results with the growth of the treebank.

Unfortunately, the richer models show slightly worse performance than for the older treebank. As in the prior experiments, it leads us to the conclusion of training data being too sparse. It is worth noting that the new treebank contains new types of constructions (in particular clauses with missing verbs), which we expect to be harder to learn.

6   Complements and Adjuncts

One of the hard problems in describing the syntactic structure of sentences is connected with the distinction between complements and adjuncts. The distinction is much argued about by linguists. It is well established in the tradition, but lacks a set of clear tests that would be agreed upon by a majority of researchers. Some researchers argue for dropping this distinction completely (Vater 1978; Przepiórkowski 1999).

Figure 3 shows some of the alternative variants of the inner sentence in Fig. 1, which differ in the pattern of complements and adjuncts. It is worth noting that all these structures are consistent with the valency frame for 'to return', which allows for the subject and an adjectival phrase (which gets realised here by a prepositional-nominal phrase).

After a discussion, annotators of the treebank decided that for the verb 'to return' the 'to the country' dependent is a complement but 'from the U.S.' is an adjunct. This decision seems to some extent arbitrary or at least based on deep semantics of the verb. The left tree of Fig. 3 shows that the parser can as well generate an interpretation where these two elements are interpreted the other way around. The right example shows a variant with only one complement being

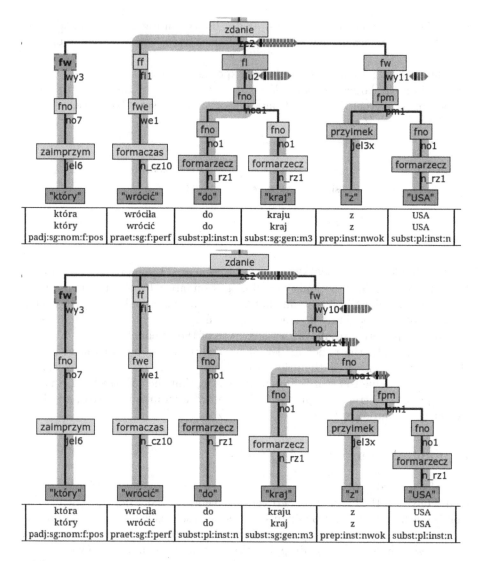

Fig. 3. Two of the other possible subtrees for the inner zdanie node from Fig. 1

a combined prepositional-nominal phrase which contains a sub-phrase 'country from the U.S.' which syntactically is perfectly acceptable ('electronics from the U.S.'). If complements and adjuncts were not marked, the left tree of Fig. 3 would become identical to the tree in Fig. 1, leaving ambiguity only in real structural differences exemplified by the right tree.

The next of our experiments checks to what extent dropping the complement/adjunct distinction could help in disambiguating parse trees.

For that experiment we have modified the structure of Składnica by removing all nodes representing required and free phrases (fw and fl). These nodes have just one child in the tree, so after the change the child takes the place previously occupied by the required or free phrase (compare Figs. 1 and 4).

The following table shows results of experiments repeated on such data:

	F_L	F_A	ULAS
Monkey	0.935	0.890	0.831
simple 'PCFG'	0.960	0.922	0.890
'PCFG'+GNPC	0.943	0.925	0.859

First of all it should be noted that the random baseline changes under such conditions. Strikingly, it gets better than simple PCFG-like algorithm on unchanged trees. ULAS does not change, but that is expected since the complement/adjunct distinction does not influence the shape of dependency trees (it would influence their labels).

The mostly visible change is in F_A for the simple PCFG-like algorithm. It gets better by almost 9 % points when the complements/adjuncts distinction is ignored.

The third row of the table describes an experiment with labels augmented with gender, number, person, and case (which was included here because the case information from fw-type is no longer present). The addition of attributes improves a bit F_A but spoils F_L and ULAS, again probably due to sparseness of data.

These results suggest that indeed it may be reasonable to ignore the complement/adjunct dichotomy at the purely syntactic level. Perhaps the distinction could be reintroduced while considering semantics including semantic features of particular verbs.

We have also taken a closer look at decisions made by the algorithm at the level of zdanie (sentence). In the table below we show percentages of cases when the algoritm selects too few or too many constituents for zdanie compared to the gold standard.

	Too few	Too many
	Constituents	
'PCFG'+fw-type	4.2 %	15.0 %
simple 'PCFG' no fw/fl	2.1 %	26.3 %

The data shows that the PCFG-like algorithm tends to choose productions that split sentences in a too granular way. Unfortunately the effect gets more pronounced when complement/adjunct distinction is ignored.

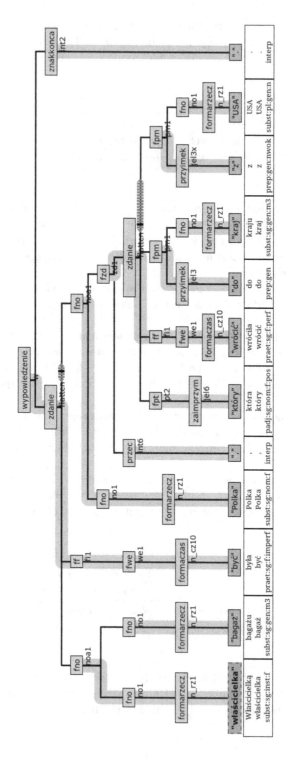

Fig. 4. The tree from Fig. 1 with all fw and fl nodes removed.

7   Summary and Outlook

In this paper we have explored a classical model of PCFG applied to the Polish data. The results are probably biased by the fact we use manually disambiguated morphological descriptions. They would probably be worse if a tagger was used. Nonetheless, we find the results better than we would expect from such a simple model.

In particular, the results are comparable to those of Wróblewska and Woliński (2012), who report 0.922 as ULAS of the best dependency parser trained on Składnica. It is worth noting that our algorithm selects among trees accepted by the non-probabilistic parser, so we have a guarantee that the selected structure is complete and in some way sound. This is hard to achieve in the case of probabilistic dependency parsers, which sometimes generate, e.g., a sentence with two subjects. On the other hand the present algorithm needs a parse forest as its input data, so it can produce trees only for sentences accepted by Świgra. The probabilistic dependency parsers on the other hand produce some result for any sentence.

While the data presented here is already interesting, we have the feeling that we have only scratched the surface. In future experiments we intend to study the errors made by the algorithm. We will try to use extensions to PCFG that were proposed in the literature. But to incorporate selected attributes of nodes without causing the data to become too sparse it may be better to change the method to some form of regression based modelling.

References

Abney, S., Flickenger, S., Gdaniec, C., Grishman, C., Harrison, P., Hindle, D., Ingria, R., Jelinek, F., Klavans, J., Liberman, M., Marcus, M., Roukos, S., Santorini, B., Strzalkowski, T.: Procedure for quantitatively comparing the syntactic coverage of english grammars. In: Black, E. (ed.) Proceedings of the Workshop on Speech and Natural Language, HLT 1991. Association for Computational Linguistics, Stroudsburg (1991)

Billot, S., Lang, B.: The structure of shared forests in ambiguous parsing. In: Meeting of the Association for Computational Linguistics (1989)

Collins, M.: Three generative, lexicalised models for statistical parsing. In: Proceedings of the 35th Annual Meeting of the Association for Computational Linguistics and Eighth Conference of the European Chapter of the Association for Computational Linguistics, ACL 1998. Association for Computational Linguistics, Stroudsburg (1997)

Pereira, F., Warren, D.H.D.: Definite clause grammars for language analysis-a survey of the formalism and a comparison with augmented transition networks. Artif. Intell. **13**, 231–278 (1980)

Przepiórkowski, A.: On complements and adjuncts in Polish. In: Borsley, R.D., Przepiórkowski, A. (eds.) Slavic in HPSG, pp. 183–210. CSLI Publications, Stanford (1999)

Świdziński, M., Woliński, M.: Towards a bank of constituent parse trees for Polish. In: Sojka, P., Horák, A., Kopeček, I., Pala, K. (eds.) TSD 2010. LNCS, vol. 6231, pp. 197–204. Springer, Heidelberg (2010)

Vater, H.: On the possibility of distinguishing between complements and adjuncts. In: Abraham, W. (ed.) Valence, Semantic Case and Grammatical Relations. Studies in Language Companion Series (SLCS), vol. 1, pp. 21–45. John Benjamins, Amsterdam (1978)

Woliński, M., Głowińska, K., Świdziński, M.: A preliminary version of Składnica–a treebank of Polish. In: Vetulani, Z. (ed.) Proceedings of the 5th Language & Technology Conference, Poznań (2011)

Wróblewska, A., Woliński, M.: Preliminary experiments in Polish dependency parsing. In: Bouvry, P., Kłopotek, M.A., Leprévost, F., Marciniak, M., Mykowiecka, A., Rybiński, H. (eds.) SIIS 2011. LNCS, vol. 7053, pp. 279–292. Springer, Heidelberg (2012)

Computational Semantics

A Method for Measuring Similarity of Books: A Step Towards an Objective Recommender System for Readers

Adam Wojciechowski[(✉)] and Krzysztof Gorzynski

Institute of Computing Science, Poznan University of Technology,
Piotrowo 2, 60-965 Poznań, Poland
Adam.Wojciechowski@put.poznan.pl, 0Krzysztof.Gorzynski@gmail.com

Abstract. In the paper we propose a method for book comparison based on graphical radar chart intersection area method. The method was designed as a universal tool and its most important parameter is document feature vector (DFV), which defines a set of text descriptors used to measure particular properties of analyzed text. Numerical values of the DFV that define book characteristic are stretched on radar chart and intersection area drawn for two books is interpreted as a measure of bilateral similarity in sense of defined DFV. Experiment conducted on relatively simple definition of the DFV gave promising results in recognition of books' similarity (in sense of author and literature domain). Such an approach may be used for building a recommender system for readers willing to select a book matching their preferences recognized by objective properties of a reference book.

Keywords: Book content comparison · Text descriptors · Radar chart intersection area method · Recommender system

1 Introduction

The rationale behind our research in text comparison and especially in measuring similarity of books is rooted in three main needs:

- possibility for numerical reader-independent multi-criteria estimation of similarity of books,
- discovering plagiarism,
- building a recommender system which is able to automatically classify books into categories on one hand and recommend a new book to a reader who likes (or dislikes) particular authors or books.

In general, both concepts: the classification problem and recommender systems are not new, however, it is a common practice that book recommender advices are either affected by readers' impressions or by merchant's (vendor's) will to sell particular books. A concise review of recommender systems with their strong and weak features is presented in (Shaffer et al. 1999). Even if we skip marketing goals for a moment, both the practices are prone to human mood, interpretation, and feelings about a particular product. For instance, in case of bundle sell: pairs or groups of products to be sold at

© Springer International Publishing Switzerland 2016
Z. Vetulani et al. (Eds.): LTC 2013, LNAI 9561, pp. 161–174, 2016.
DOI: 10.1007/978-3-319-43808-5_13

eye-catching, bargain price are defined by the seller. Although there is nothing wrong if one tries to read other's opinions on products to be purchased, the weakness of such an opinion system may be especially visible if the number of opinions on particular products is low, and some of the positive opinions seem to be written by a producer or seller. A study of importance of negative opinions is presented in (Lee et al. 2008): A simple negative recommendation (that is, a low-quality online consumer review) can influence the attitude of consumers under high-involvement condition as well as under low involvement condition. Proposals how to avoid the misuse of recommender and price comparison systems are discussed in the literature, where there are approaches based on users' trust (Li et al. 2013) and social network as a guard of information quality (Wojciechowski 2007) Instead of proposing a technique how to protect a recommender system against polite and sweet positive opinions we try to define a system for reader-independent books comparison.

In order to allow objective book comparison we define a set of text descriptors which form a *document feature vector* (DFV), than define some measures of documents similarity in terms of particular sense (particular criteria) and finally we propose a graphical method based on drawing radar figures that combine individual metrics for particular comparison criteria and assess similarity of objects by comparison of intersected fields on radar chart. The use of the method is illustrated by an example experiment where several romance, fantasy and scientific books were used to evaluate the quality of classification.

The aim of our experiments presented in the paper was to verify whether proposed graphical method for book comparison is effective enough to distinguish different types of texts and giving similar results for closely related documents. Thus in the experimental part of our research we focused rather on radar method effectiveness than on very deep study of descriptors which should be included in the *document feature vector*. This may be considered as a limitation of our approach. However, selection of metrics used in DFV and their influence on produced results is subject of further study on the proposed method.

Structure of the paper is as follows: in Sect. 2 we introduce and define some numerical text descriptors and methods of text/document comparison and quantitative classification. Then, in Sect. 3 we present a radar chart approach built on 10 text characteristics applied to books comparison. The method and its use are illustrated by experimental software system designed to support comparing books according to the proposed methodology. The paper ends with some conclusions and references.

2   Metrics Selected for Text Document Feature Description

In order to propose a method for books comparison, we decided to use several metrics that give numerical values that define the *document feature vector*. An exception from the rule of single value metric is *length of words* which is available in our software in form of histogram. We used this feature for books comparison at early stage of our experiments but word length histogram is not included in DFV in radar chart intersection area comparison method in its current development stage.

Metrics selected and defined in Sect. 2 should be considered as examples used to verify the book comparison method. Problem of partial flattening the scale in proposed converting negative to positive attribute values may occur. Optimization of descriptors' definition is a subject of parallel research.

2.1 Length of Words

Measuring length of word (given in number of characters) may be used as a partial descriptor of text. In our experiments we analyzed histograms of word length and it allowed us to distinguish between more and less formal language used in the documents. Higher ratio of shorter words classified analyzed documents to less formal texts using more casual and sometimes spoken language.

2.2 Frequency of Special Characters

Occurrence of digits, exclamations, question marks, commas, semicolons, etc. barely counted or related to the measure of text complexity (e.g. number of sentences or number of words) is another partial text descriptor. Conclusions from our experiments with this metric were predictable (according to the common sense intuition). High probability of exclamation and question mark occurrence in a sentence is a sign of expressive narration. The higher the ratio of commas occurrence per sentence the more complex sentences are present in the text document. Frequent occurrence of digits is typical to science and research documents. High ratio of questions marks is typical to stories and novels with dialogs.

In DFV we included three values based on special characters count: number of exclamations, number of question marks and number of digits.

2.3 Emotional Bias

Among all the words existing in dictionary, some of them have emotional bias. Words like home, happiness, friendship and love carry positive emotions, while war, hate, death, bark, rise negative emotions. Emotional bias intuitively seems to be an important text descriptor in human perception of text.

We felt that this emotional bias attribute was an important descriptor of books, especially novels. In order to confirm our intuition we conducted a small poll among a group of students (22 participants). One of the questions in the poll we asked participants was 'Which of specified text descriptors would you use for a blind recommendation of novel books?' In our survey students selected emotional bias as a primary objective feature of text document which could be considered by humans for blind recommendation of novels. Over 73 % (16 out of 22) of participants selected emotional bias as the most informative, for recommendation purpose, numerical characteristic (among metrics presented in Sect. 2) of novel books.

In order to include book's *emotional bias* metric within DFV in our book comparison algorithm we defined emotional bias according to formula (1):

$$EmotionalBias = \begin{cases} P - N & for\ P \geq N \\ \dfrac{1}{N - P} & for\ P < N \end{cases} \qquad (1)$$

where

P is positive emotions word count
N is negative emotions word count

Emotional bias is a non-negative, non-linear function which value quickly rises with growing advantage of positive over negative emotion words. Using such a definition of emotional bias was based on our intuition and there we did not conduct a wider study whether majority of people share our feeling of this very subjective (attributed to personal acceptance) text feature.

2.4 Readability Level

Readability level is an experimentally derived text descriptor formula used to assess difficulty of understanding documents. One of its implementations is the Flesch-Kincaid readability formula (Kincaid et al. 1975) that was first used by US Army to assess difficulty of language in technical manuals in 1978 and soon it became a US Department of Defense standard.

Currently Flesch-Kincaid Grade Level (FKGL) formula is commonly used in education to estimate how many years of education is required for understanding given text, which directly translates into possibility of statistical assessment whether given text documents are appropriate for particular class level at school.

$$FKGL = 0.39\left(\frac{total\ words}{total\ sentences}\right) + 11.8\left(\frac{total\ syllabes}{total\ words}\right) - 15.59 \qquad (2)$$

Theoretically the lowest readability grade level value may drop to -3.4, however in real book, journal, manual and novel text the formula presented above gives non-negative values corresponding to number of years of education required for smooth reading and understanding.

For automatic text analysis, in our software we used readability level formula based on modified readability formula adjusted for foreign languages given in (Hamilton-Locke 2002, p. 55) where estimation of syllables is based on counting vowels:

$$Readability = 0.39\left(\frac{total\ words}{total\ sentences}\right) + \frac{total\ vowels}{total\ words} - 15.59 \qquad (3)$$

$$ReadabilityLevel = \begin{cases} Readability & for\ Readability \geq 0 \\ \dfrac{-1}{Readability} & for\ Readability < 0 \end{cases} \qquad (4)$$

Low (negative) value of *Readability* factor describes texts relatively easy to read and understand, at least for adult, educated readers. Thus we flatten the scale by reversing negative values of *Readability* (the negative sign is to keep all metrics non-negative) which escalates high values in *ReadabilityLevel*.

2.5 Unique Words Ratio

Another, easy to calculate and interesting text feature is number of unique words that occur once in the entire text document. It is commonly used to assess richness of vocabulary in speeches and documents. We calculated it according to formula given below (Hamilton-Locke 2002, p. 54), however especially in larger text files, unique words ratio could be calculated including words appearing no more than n (n- small natural number) times in compared text.

$$UniqueWordsRatio = \frac{total\ single\ occurence\ words}{total\ words} \tag{5}$$

2.6 Entropy

Entropy is a function of state which defines degree of disorder in a system. This function is used in relation to nature in physics and chemistry but also was defined for text sources. In our approach we calculated entropy by formula provided by (Hamilton-Locke 2002, p. 54):

$$H = \sum_{i=1}^{words} p_i \log p_i \tag{6}$$

words – number of words in text document
p_i – probability of appearance of the i-th word

$$p_i = \frac{(number\ of\ occurences\ of\ the\ ith\ word)}{total\ words} \tag{7}$$

2.7 Yule's Characteristic - K

Characteristic K, also known as *Yule's characteristic*, proposed by Yule (1944) is used to measure lexical repetition rate based on the assumption that the occurrence of a given word is based on chance and can be regarded as a Poisson distribution (Hamilton-Locke 2002). An important attribute of measure K (lexical richness) is its independence from the length of text. Different approaches to compute K and the need for standardization are discussed in (Miranda-Garcia and Calle-Martin 2006). In our experiments we used K formula defined as follows:

$$K = 10^4 \left(\frac{S_1}{S_2^2} - \frac{1}{S_1^2} \right) \tag{8}$$

Where

$$S_1 = \sum_{i=1}^{words} x_i f_x \qquad S_2 = \sum_{i=1}^{words} x_i^2 f_x$$

x_i–number of occurrences of i-th word

f_x–number of words that occur x times

2.8 Stop Words

A stop word may be identified as a word that has the same likehood of occurring in those documents not relevant to a query as in those documents relevant to the query (Wilbur and Sirotkin 1992). These words carry almost no information, but are used in language structures. In case of English these could be for instance: the, and, that, of, to, in.

In our experiments we used attribute non-contextual calculated as a ratio of frequently occurring stop words to rarely occurring stop words.

2.9 Rare/Common Words Ratio

Having counted occurrence of all the words in analyzed text, one can count ratio of rarely used words to frequently appearing words. Two sets: *rare* and *common* words are defined on quantitative criteria. Each of the sets is populated with 0.1 % of total number of words in given document. This attribute provides numerical characteristic of repeatability of information. In other words, using this metric one can distinguish between strongly monothematic documents and rich vocabulary ones.

3 Radar Chart Intersection Area Method for Multiple Criteria Comparison

3.1 RCIA Explained

Comparing object in multidimensional space may be a hard job. Difficulty of the process may be rooted in at least two areas: first – nature of attributes (e.g. descriptive, non-numerical, non-comparable) and character of compensation (lacks or low values in one dimension can be compensated by higher values in another dimension). Being aware of mentioned problems humans often prefer to aggregate assessment on several attributes and calculate one value per object e.g. in form of a utility function. This approach allows to build a linear rank of alternatives, which are comparable in one dimension.

Although it is more difficult to compare objects in multidimensional space than analyzing a linear rank, there are situations where humans like to see and analyze similarity of objects having the possibility to visually or analytically perceive resemblance and difference and draw conclusions from them. *Radar Chart Intersection Area* method (RCIA) is a simple approach which allows to see similarity of objects in multidimensional environment as well as calculate similarity function for each two representatives of the same domain.

Objects being compared are assessed (described) on several numerical attributes. We assume that attributes positive (>0) and growing preference (the higher value the better), which is not a touch constraint because in case of a normalized attribute A with decreasing preference it can be replaced with another attribute A' such that:

$$A' = 1 - A$$

To illustrate the RCIA method let's consider an example. In order to compare alternatives we stretch values of their five attributes $A_1, A_2, \ldots, A_5$ on five centrally anchored axes, as presented on Fig. 1. In this way decision maker may visually compare whether two (or more) compared objects have similar values on selected attributes, may notice in which dimensions they are significantly different and where the differences are negligible. Moreover one can calculate similarity measure defined as intersection area of two figures stretched on axes. In example shown on Fig. 1 the common part of two compared objects is shape of figure delimited by points $<b_1, i_1, a_2, i_2, b_3, i_3, a_4, b_5, i_5>$.

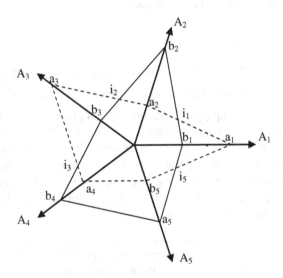

Fig. 1. Radar chart intersection area, example.

RCIA allows for easy to perform visual comparison of alternatives at first sight. It may be good in cases where number of compared objects is low and visual assessment is good enough to notice similarities or differences. Another advantage of this method is the fact that it is relatively easy to build an environment in spreadsheet program to visually compare objects. Students at Poznan University of Technology in Poznan (Poland) liked this exercise for two reasons: first it was a challenging task to build the RCIA infrastructure in MS Excel but secondly it was quite easy and mind opening to compare various sets of objects (mobile phones, football players, animals, etc.) described by several attributes. Even defining a new task and selecting attributes to describe alternatives was an enjoyable task for students. Our academic experiment performed in 2015 with Computer Science students gave very positive impressions and was an occasion for discussion about boundaries of the RCIA method application.

Visual comparison may be not effective if number of alternatives is very high or differences between objects are slight. Even if one plans to compare objects in numerical sense it is useful to define an algebraic function of similarity. RCIA similarity function is based on comparison of areas of figures delimited by values of attributes for particular object and shape of intersection with compared (reference) object. For two objects A and B, their similarity degree is calculated separately 'Similarity A to B', and 'Similarity B to A'. Such a definition goes well with common sense understanding when one say that a child is very similar to her/his parent, while reverse relation is not necessarily true.

$$Similarity(A, B) = \frac{Area\, A \cap B}{Area\, B} \qquad (9)$$

Value calculated in formula (9) may be expressed in percent if it is multiplied by 100 %. Object B in formula (9) is the reference object.

3.2   RCIA Computations

RCIA method is intuitive by its graphical interpretation. Computational procedures are derived from graphical representation. Angle between axes is $\alpha = \frac{2\pi}{n}$, where n is the number of attributes. To simplify calculations we can place each neighboring pair or axes in the beginning of Cartesian coordinates. Let's consider a part of computational procedure in which one calculates sector areas occupied by figures delimited by objects' attributes values of alternatives Q and R on axes representing attributes A_1 and A_2. The procedure need to be repeated for every sector delimited by neighboring attribute axes. One needs to consider two cases shown on Figs. 2 and 3 and proceed with computational procedure on all sectors delimited by attribute axes.

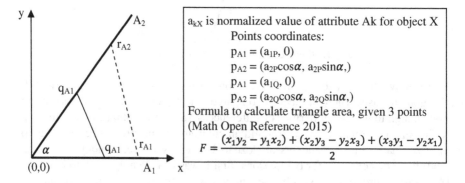

Fig. 2. Partial computations when one object Q is outperformed on two neighboring attributes A1 and A2 by values of object R.

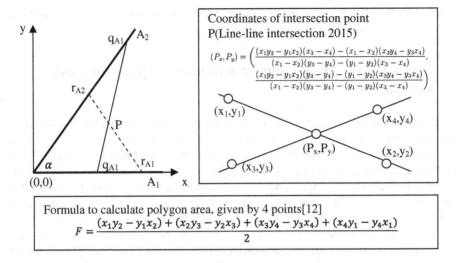

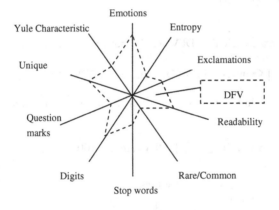

Fig. 3. Partial computations when one object Q is outperformed on two neighboring attributes A1 by values of object R and object R is outperformed by Q on attribute A2.

Fig. 4. DFV *area* of a book stretched on a radar chart.

3.3 Limitations of RCIA

It is important to notice that values of similarity function depend on the order of attributes deployed on the axes. For whole comparison experiment the order of attributes must be kept identical. Influence of different ordering of attributes and selecting the best one for achieving the most stable results in comparison is subject of a separate study.

For practical reasons number of attributes that describe alternatives for comparison using RCIA method cannot be smaller than three. This is the minimal number of attributes which allows for visual and computational comparison of objects. Although there is no upper bound on number of attributes, we observed that for practical use with visual comparison the chart becomes hard to interpret if number of attributes is higher than 12. However the assessment was very subjective.

4   Radar Chart Intersection Area Method Applied for Book Comparison

Attributes defined in Sect. 2 can be calculated independently for each text document (in our case these are books). Those attributes collected in *document feature vector* provide multidimensional partial description of text nature. For ease of human eye analysis and understanding we propose to present the values on a radar chart (see Fig. 1). This is possible because on the stage of attribute definition we paid attention to keep all the values non-negative. Thus we can present each value as a distance on an axis. Set of attributes collected in the DFV are marked on centrally anchored ray axes.

In order to assess similarity of books in sense of graphical representation of the *DFV* values drawn on a radar chart we propose calculating intersection of two *DFV areas* for two compared books. Visual interpretation of the method is shown on Fig. 2.

Method for assessment of book similarity is based on pair comparison. A given book x is individually compared to each of books yi that belong to set of books $Y = \{y_1, y_2, ..., y_n\}$ (Fig. 5).

Algorithm:
Step 1. DFVxArea ← calculate DFV area for book x
Step 2. for i = 1 to n
Similarity_XY[i] ← intersection of DFVxArea and DFVy$_i$Area

This 2-step algorithm provides results which can easily be interpreted in percent scale:

$$Similarity\_XY[i]/DFVxArea * 100\% \tag{10}$$

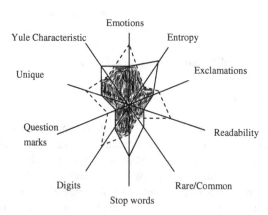

Fig. 5. DFV *area* intersection defines a similarity measure for two compared books.

Book x is 100 % similar to itself while any other comparison with book y_i may only provide similarity measure in scale 0–100 %. This feature gives an easy to understand, intuitive measure for comparison. Formulas used to calculate intersection area (based on triangle area) are derived and presented in (Gorzynski 2013).

5   Experimental Use of Radar Chart Intersection Area Method for Book Comparison

In software designed to conduct experiments with book comparison we implemented functions computing variety of text descriptors. Among the others, we computed all the characteristics defined in Sect. 2 and used in radar chart method described in Sect. 3. We also selected books for comparison. The books were grouped into comparison sets upon selected criteria, e.g. author or literature domain.

5.1   Experiment 1. Distinguishing Authors

We want to assess whether radar chart intersection area method can classify books written by the same or other authors to separate sets. Similarity measure between reference book and comparison set is to be presented on a chart.

Reference Book

    x = *Doctor Who – The Daughter* by Becky Miller

Comparison set Y:

    y_1 = *Doctor Who – Mirror, mirror* by Becky Miller
    y_2 = *Breakdown* by Becky Miller
    y_3 = *Diversion* by Becky Miller
    y_4 = *Amber Moon* by C.L. Bevill
    y_5 = *Silver Moon* by C.L. Bevill
    y_6 = *Black Moon* by C.L. Bevill
    y_7 = *Blood Feathers* by Lou Morgan
    y_8 = *Feathered* by Tamara Boyens
    y_9 = *Arched Wings* by Tamara Boyens

Results of experiment 1 based on radar chart intersection area method where book x was compared to 9 other books (3 from the same author and 6 written by other authors) all from domain of fantasy novels is presented on Fig. 6. Comparison of books written by the same author gave similarity measure from 75 to 90 % while reference book compared with novels written by other authors gave similarity measure from 20 to 35 %.

Similar results were collected when we took other books written by Becky Miller as a reference one. They appeared strongly similar to other books by the same author and they differed in the sense of measured similarity from the books by the other authors used in the experiments.

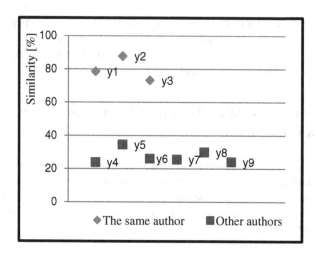

Fig. 6. Results of experiment 1. Similarity of book *Doctor Who – The Daughter* compared to other books written by the same or other authors.

For comparison purpose we confronted collected results with similarity measure collected by other algorithms. When we used algorithm based on similarity derived from occurrence of the same phrases in compared books, similarity measure between books written by the same author were higher by about 10 percent-points than similarity of books written by other authors. The difference was visible on the chart but not as clear as on Fig. 6.

Comparison based on algorithm calculating occurrence frequency of pairs of words and synonyms did not give clear distinguishing in sense of similarity between books written by the same or others authors.

5.2   Experiment 2. Distinguishing Literature Forms

In second experiment we tested sensitivity of radar chart intersection area method for comparing a reference book with other publications from the same or other literature domains. A reference book was a romance novel

x = Bride's Baby by Liz Fielding

Comparison set Y was composed out of 18 books: 6 romance novels, 6 fantasy novels and 6 science (chemistry) books and reports (see details in Gorzynski 2013).

Results of experiment 2 are collected on Fig. 7. Similarity of the reference romance book varied from 50 to 85 % among other romance novels. Similarity to fantasy books and technical chemistry books and reports varied from 5 to 40 %. The difference is easy to catch on a chart even at a glance.

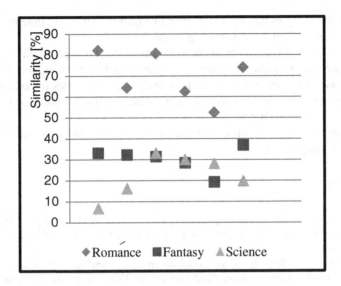

Fig. 7. Results of experiment 2. Similarity of romance book *Bride's Baby* compared to 6 romance novels, 6 fantasy books and 6 science (chemistry) books and reports.

6 Conclusions

The aim of proposed graphical method and conducted experiments was to verify whether the approach based on radar chart area intersection can be used to measure similarity of books. One should notice that selection of attributes has crucial influence on quality of comparison based on values collected in the DFV. It is also important to understand that the order of axes (attributes) on radar chart has an influence on the area embraced by segments connecting points on neighboring axes. Thus to use proposed method for book comparison purpose for each experiment books should have defined and computed identical DFV and radar chart should be drawn in identical order, i.e. in the order defined by position of attributes in the DFV. One should also notice that in proposed method we consider entire book as a single set of words (or phrases). Such an approach may be less effective in discovering plagiarism when confronted with methods that take into account topological information about analyzed text (see Susmaga et al. 2011).

Proposed method based on radar chart intersection area was designed to compare similarity of text documents including books. In spite of several weak points of proposed method, mentioned above, and not too deep study of text attributes selection and their order in the DFV our experiments gave promising results in selecting similar books in assumed sense. In experiments described in the paper we examined similarity of a reference book with other books written by the same or other authors and similarity measure for books belonging to three different domains: romance, fantasy and science. Our initial experiments gave promising results in good recognition of books written by the same author and books belonging to the same literature domain. This is a good prognosis for using this approach for supporting readers with an objective recommendation on books to read. Further study in this field is needed to adjust the DFV and tune the attributes (descriptors) for particular comparison purpose.

An important positive feature of the graphical method is a possibility to present a decision maker (a reader) the set of alternatives and their bilateral similarity in graphical form. The ease of presentation and intuitive understanding relates to both: measuring similarity by radar chart intersection area method and similarity comparison of selected book against other candidate books.

Wider report on experiments conducted with radar chart intersection area method is available in (Gorzynski 2013).

References

Gorzynski, K.: System for analyzing publications to estimate similarity degree. Master thesis under supervision of Adam Wojciechowski. Poznan University of Technology, Poland (in Polish) (2013)

Hamilton-Locke, Inc.: Methods for contextual discovery and analysis (2002). Retrieved http://www.hamilton-locke.com/support_files/Methods_for_Contextual_Discovery_and_Analysis.pdf. Accessed Nov 2013

Kincaid, J.P., Fishburne, R.P., Rogers, R.L., Chissom, B.S.: Derivation of New Readability Formulas (Automated Readability Index, Fog Count, and Flesch Reading Ease formula) for Navy Enlisted Personnel. Research Branch Report 8–75. Chief of Naval Technical Training: Naval Air Station Memphis (1975)

Lee, J., Park, D.-H., Han, I.I.: The effect of negative online consumer reviews on product attitude: an information processing view. Electron. Commer. Res. Appl. **7**(1), 341–352 (2008). Elsevier

Li, Y.-M., Wu, C.-T., Lai, C.-Y.: A social recommender mechanism for e-commerce: combining similarity, trust, and relationship. Decis. Support Syst. **55**(3), 740–752 (2013). Elsevier

Miranda-Garcia, A., Calle-Martin, J.: Yule's Characteristic K Revisited. Lang. Resour. Eval. **39**(4), 287–294 (2006). Springer

Schafer, J.B., Konstan, J.A., Riedl, J.: Recommender systems in e-commerce. In: Proceedings of the First ACM Conference on Electronic Commerce (EC-1999), pp. 158–166. ACM, Denver (1999)

Susmaga, R., Maslowska, I., Budzynska, L.: The concept of topological information in text representation. Found. Comput. Decis. Sci. **36**(1), 57–78 (2011). Poznan University of Technology, Poland

Wilbur, W.J., Sirotkin, K.: The automatic identification of stop words. J. Inf. Sci. **18**(1), 45–55 (1992)

Wojciechowski, A.: Supporting social networks by event-driven mobile notification services. In: Meersman, R., Tari, Z. (eds.) OTM-WS 2007, Part I. LNCS, vol. 4805, pp. 398–406. Springer, Heidelberg (2007)

Yule, G.U.: The Statistical Study of Literary Vocabulary. Cambridge University Press, Cambridge (1944)

Math Open Reference, Area of Polygon (coordinate geometry). http://www.mathopenref.com/coordpolygonarea.html. Accessed Sept 2015

Line-line intersection. https://en.wikipedia.org/wiki/Line–line_intersection. Accessed Sept 2015

Digital Language Resources

MCBF: Multimodal Corpora Building Framework

Maria Chiara Caschera, Arianna D'Ulizia, Fernando Ferri[✉], and Patrizia Grifoni

National Research Council – IRPPS, Via Palestro, 32, 00185 Rome, Italy
{mc.caschera,Arianna.dulizia,fernando.ferri,
patrizia.grifoni}@irpps.cnr.it

Abstract. Designing an effective human-machine multimodal interaction environment requires addressing crucial issues such as the correct interpretation of complex user's input from different modal channels. In this context the use of corpora of multimodal sentences is very important because they allow integrating properties and linguistic knowledge which are not formalised in the grammar. This paper provides framework for dynamic multimodal corpora building that semi-automates the extraction of syntactic and semantic information from multimodal dialogues using both grammar inference and interpretation methodologies based on HMM. This method is based on a Multimodal Attribute Grammar and on an HMM-based approach to syntactically and semantically annotate new multimodal sentences. It allows for improving human-computer dialogue because the multimodal corpus evolves by adapting itself to the dynamic change of the human-computer interaction.

Keywords: Language corpus · Multimodal language · Multimodal corpus

1 Introduction

Multimodal interaction allows flexible interaction between users and systems; in fact users have the freedom to use modalities of interaction that they prefer (e.g. speech, handwriting, gestures, gaze, etc.) according to the different situations, devices and interaction goals. However, a multimodal system is complex and its design and implementation require a strong effort to have a comprehensive representation of the user's message, and for providing a correct interpretation of the user's input.

A multimodal corpus allows capturing not only information from syntax and semantics of a language but the communication features by different modalities, which are frequently expression of contextual and cultural information. Indeed, multimodal corpora provide holistic information about cultural and linguistic processes by giving access to more relevant data. This fact makes multimodal corpora as the basis to fine-tune and to improve computer-based applications. When building a multimodal corpus it is necessary to define which data should be recorded and included in the corpus, and how those data should be recorded, annotated and transcribed [1]. Annotation is a crucial task because it allows corpora to be navigated using software. A multimodal input can be annotated: (1) at level of single term, by adding information about typographic, syntactic or phonetic information, (2) at discourse level, by adding grammatical, semantic, prosodic or pragmatic codes. The annotation of multimodal corpora is a heavy

© Springer International Publishing Switzerland 2016
Z. Vetulani et al. (Eds.): LTC 2013, LNAI 9561, pp. 177–190, 2016.
DOI: 10.1007/978-3-319-43808-5_14

and time-consuming task. To overcome the time-consuming nature of the annotation process, in this paper we propose a building method that semi-automatically extracts syntactic and semantic information from multimodal dialogues using both a grammar inference and an interpretation approach. Specifically, a small set of human-computer interaction dialogues is collected, manually annotated and used to generate a set of grammatical rules of a multimodal attribute grammar [2], which contains syntactic and temporal information about the acquired sentences (Training step: Fig. 1). Afterwards, the generated grammatical rules and reference semantic resources are used by the interpreter to extract the syntactic and semantic of sentences. Finally, all the extracted information (syntactic, temporal, conceptual, and semantic) are used by the trained annotator for annotating the corpus (Annotation step: Fig. 1).

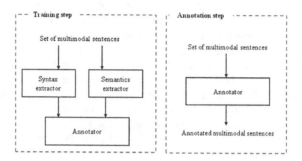

Fig. 1. Process for training and semi-automatic annotation of multimodal corpora

The strengths of this approach relies in the fact that when a new multimodal sentence is acquired, it is not necessary manual annotation, and grammatical rules are applied for extracting the associated syntactic and semantic information. If the new sentence is not interpretable with the available rules, the interpretation process supports the grammar generation by providing the syntactic information. In this way, we obtain a semi-automatic annotation of multimodal corpora that considerably sped up this process. The proposed method uses modules of the multimodal software modules defined in [2–4], and opportunely adapted.

The remainder of this paper is structured as follows. Section 2 provides an overview of related works on multimodal interaction by focussing on grammars, interpretation methods and multimodal corpora. Section 3 introduces the multimodal interaction environment, the main features of the multimodal corpus and the method defined for its generation. Finally, Sect. 4 concludes the paper and discusses future works.

2   Related Works

Generally, in a multimodal system, different multimodal inputs have to be recognised, fused in a multimodal sentence [2], and interpreted by a parser also considering different features, such as available interaction modalities, context of interaction, the user's model, etc. Figure 2 shows an example of multimodal sentence.

Fig. 2. Example of multimodal sentence

In the example the user says by speech "Every man sees the boy with this" (in Italian "Ogni uomo vede il ragazzo con questo"), and s/he indicates binoculars by gesture.

When building a multimodal corpus, a set of multimodal sentences has to be acquired and annotated with several information, such as typographic, syntactic, and phonetic information (at level of terms of the language), as well as grammatical, semantic, prosodic and pragmatic information (at discourse level). The next subsection provides the main concepts on multimodal corpora and a focus on how the existing multimodal corpora acquire and annotate multimodal sentences.

2.1 Multimodal Corpora

Multimodal corpora were first developed to fulfil the need to represent not only data related with NL, but also non-verbal/visual issues of dialogue (e.g. gesture, facial expressions, etc.). A "multimodal corpus" is defined as "a digitized collection of language and communication-related material, drawing on more than one modality" [23]. Generally, linguistic research on multimodal corpora have two different purposes: (a) to analyse multimodal and multimedia studies of discourse in order to address social science issues on human beings [24]; (b) to assemble and use corpora as datasets used to evaluate and improve approaches on human-computer interaction [25]. In this paper, the second purpose is discussed and addressed. The features of multimodal corpora (i.e. their contents, the ways in which they are recorded, their size, etc.) depend on the aims and objectives that they are intended to fulfil [26]. Most of multimodal corpora collect audio- and video-recorded instances of human-human communication connected with annotations or transcriptions of the talk and/or gestures in the recordings. Specifically, they contain audio recordings of the speech and video recordings of the participants' body movements in the interaction. In addition, they contain the annotations which give a kind of descriptive running commentary on what occurs in the recording. Finally, they collect the transcriptions, which are a kind of visual symbolic representation of the speech (and more rarely of the gestures) during the recordings. Several multimodal corpora have been developed in the literature. The QUAKE corpus [29] and the SCARE corpus [30] are based on interactions captured in a 3-D virtual world where two participants collaboratively carry out a treasure hunting task. The REX corpus [31] collects multimodal expressions used in collaborative problem solving dialogues where two participants collaboratively solve geometric puzzles. Further examples come from the health domain. For instance, a multimodal corpus for better understanding conversations during psychotherapy is provided in [44] by coding gesture modality, particularly hand movements, and head movements. A further corpus for health purpose is provided in [45] by annotating modalities, such as presence and audio and human postural transition, for developing an Health Smart Home environment. In the context of Ambient Assisted Living, a multimodal corpus has been built and described in [46] by annotating data captured by cameras, microphones and activity tracking systems. The SmartKom corpus [34] was built analyzing acoustic, visual and tactile modalities: 96 different users were recorded across 172 sessions of 4.5 min each. The TALK corpus [35] contains human-machine dialogues in the tourist information domain, and collects dialogues of users that were asked to perform tasks using an interactive map. Both in SmartKom and TALK, the data were collected using Wizard-of-Oz experiments. RECOLA multimodal corpus is composed of spontaneous collaborative and affective interactions in French [42] and it has been built to develop real-time automatic emotion recognizers. In [32], Rehm et al. provide a corpus of cultural specific interaction patterns that represent data for developing interfaces tailored to German and Japanese cultures. Another example of multimodal annotated corpora is provided in [33]. In this work, different parameters of the corpus, which are involved in a natural interaction process, are annotated considering phonetics, prosody, syntax, humour, backchannels, narrative units, conversational turns. All the above described corpora were developed using manual annotation of the multimodal sentences and are mainly for English, and in minor part for French, German and other languages. For the Italian language, various linguistic (spoken) corpora have been developed. A list of the most important corpora of spoken Italian collected and published since 1965 is provided by BADIP (Banca Dati dell'Italiano Parlato – Database of Spoken Italian) [47] that contains the link to approximately thirty developed Italian linguistic corpora. However, there is a lack of multimodal corpora for the Italian language. The only multilingual and multimodal corpus that also addresses the Italian language is NESPOLE! [46]. In this paper we aim at providing an approach that semi-automates the multimodal annotation process using both a grammar inference and semantic interpretation approach according to Fig. 1. In the following sub-sections we provide the existing grammatical frameworks defined in literature for integrating multimodal input, and the existing interpretation methods for correctly associating semantics and syntax to the multimodal input.

2.2 Multimodal Grammars

Multimodal interaction requires that several alternative or simultaneous inputs, coming from various modalities, are opportunely integrated and combined into a sentence, i.e. a multimodal fusion process has to occur. In the literature, various approaches to the fusion process have been proposed [6]. One of the most promising approaches for integrating the different unimodal inputs in a multimodal sentence is the grammar-based fusion strategy. This approach, is more coherent with the human-human communication paradigm in which the dialogue is seen as a unique and multimodal communication act [7], activating the cognitive dynamics that generally reduces the cognitive load and, thus, increases attention on content. The first reported grammatical framework for multimodal languages is the Multi-Modal Definite Clause Grammar (MM-DCG) [8], which is an extension of Definite Clause Grammar (DCG) [9]. DCGs are an evolution of context-free grammars (CFG), which have proven their usefulness for describing natural languages. MM-DCGs extend DCG by permitting to define chronological constraints among categories and to associate each terminal symbol with the consuming stream name (i.e. the modality). The Finite-state Multimodal Grammar (FMG) has been proposed in [10] to support parsing and interpretation of multimodal sentences. This grammar relies on a finite-state device that allows representing the inputs from n possible modalities and their combined semantic. The Multimodal Functional Unification Grammar (MUG) is defined in [11]. MUG introduces the possibility to support several coordinated modes and to unify one grammar rule for each mode. The Multimodal Combinatory Categorial Grammar (MCCG) [12] is a lexicalised grammar, based on a set of syntactic rules, whose application is conditioned on the syntactic type of their inputs. Finally, the Multimodal Attribute Grammar (MAG) has been defined in [2] on the base of the context-free paradigm and explicit constructs (i.e. attributes). In this paper, we apply the MAG notation since it allows to manage whatever modalities and provides a good compromise between the context-free paradigm and the necessity to represent semantic and temporal features of multimodal input into the grammar rules.

2.3   Interpretation Methods

During the interaction process, an important aspect to address is the correct interpretation that can be achieved by simultaneously considering semantic, temporal and contextual constraints [5, 13]. An overview about methods for correctly interpreted multimodal input is presented in [14]. It is interesting to note that researches are moving towards the development of methods that shift the cognitive load from the user to the system by the definition of probabilistic approaches that can learn the main features of the user's interaction behaviours. As in [15], where authors use graph-matching algorithm that satisfies semantic, temporal and contextual constraints to maximize the matching probability between the history graph and each graph generated by information coming from multiple input modalities and information about the context. Similarly, a probabilistic model is used to define interdependences among components of the language and a set of input features [16], where the sense tag has been assigned to each component (i.e., each word in NL sentences) according to the highest estimated probability in the given context (i.e., the application domain). In [17] the integration of speech and gesture modalities has been probabilistically addressed by assigning a weight to each input combination according to temporal and semantic features. Among methods to interpret user's input, Avola et al. [18] show that (in the example for sketch interaction) Hidden Markov Models (HMMs) are frequently preferred among methods for modeling stochastic processes and sequences of elements to be recognized. This is also confirmed by the large use of HMMs in several different research fields, such as computational molecular biology [19], speech recognition [20], handwriting recognition [21], gaming environments [50], NL modelling [22], etc. In multimodal interaction field, HMMs provide efficient learning and recognition methods that are able to segment an input sequence into its constituent elements.A hybrid approach combining a rule-based with HMMs method has been applied to model a correct interpretation of dialogue between users and a multimodal system in a gaming environment in [50]. In this paper, we use an interpretation approach that is based on HMMs in order to provide a response to the need to deal with complexity involved in multimodal interaction.

3   Dynamic Building a Multimodal Corpus

The semi-automatic method for generating a multimodal corpus relies on a framework that is based on a "grammar inference" method used for generating a Multimodal Attribute Grammar (MAG), proposed in [2], and the method for interpretation and disambiguation based on Hidden Markov Models (HMMs) described in [4]. The architecture of that framework in proposed in the Fig. 3.

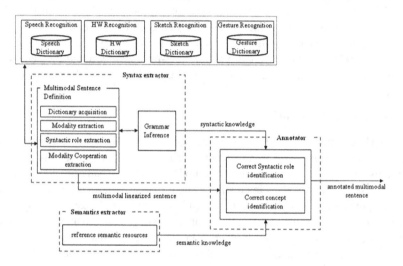

Fig. 3. Architecture of the multimodal corpus building framework

The framework acquires the multimodal sentences during the interaction process between of a set of users and a system. After that, the syntactic knowledge is applied to generate the grammatical rules for parsing the acquired sentences. The multimodal annotator applies the grammar rules and uses the semantic knowledge given by a reference semantic resources in order to annotate the acquired multimodal sentence by the correct interpretation and the correct syntactic roles of the element of the sentence. The modules that compose the framework are described in detail in the following sub-sections.

3.1   Semantics and Syntax Extractor

To build a multimodal corpus, the multimodal annotator needs knowledge given by the Semantics extractor and Syntax extractor modules. The semantics extractor is based on the ItalWordNet [41], and it extracts the semantic of multimodal sentences, returning it to the annotator module. While, the syntax extractor is composed of the *Multimodal Sentence Definition* (MSD) and the Grammar Inference modules.

The MSD module uses the *MSD interface* as Multimodal User Interface (MUI) that is responsible of the interaction between the user and the *MSD* module. This interface allows the acquisition of the data to be used for defining the corpus, i.e. the examples of sentences and the concepts used for expressing these sentences. The *MSD* is responsible for the setting of the sentence and the linearization process. In particular, it takes the elements of the unimodal sentences and their properties (i.e., actual value, syntactic role, modality, and kinds of cooperation between modalities) and combines them opportunely, generating a linear sequence of elements, i.e. the multimodal linearized sentence, which is given in input to the grammar inference and the multimodal annotator. Finally, the Interface with Modal Recognizers provides the bridge between the MSD and the recognizers of the defined modalities, which matches inputs to recognized concepts. Figure 4 shows the architecture of the MSD. The acquisition of multimodal sentences requires the involvement of a set of participants that have to be recorded during the interaction with the system. The total number of participants in this phase was twelve. The trial consisted in interacting with a PC workstation using speech, handwriting and gesture modalities, for formulating the set of nine multimodal sentences, which are shown in the first column of Table 1, with syntactic roles and kinds of cooperation shown in second and third columns of Table 1. The trial included the following phases (in temporal order):

- a training phase, in which an explanation of the task and a short tutorial on how to formulate the multimodal sentences are given. The expected duration of this phase is one hour;
- a familiarization phase, in which the participants were asked to use the system in order to become familiar with their functionalities. The expected duration of this phase is two hours. For this familiarization, a set of sample sentences has been used, different from the sentences of the trial;
- an acquisition phase that is the core of the trial. Once the participants felt comfortable with the system, they were asked to formulate the set of thirty multimodal sentences, like those shown in Table 1.

Table 1. The multimodal sentences for the trial

Multimodal sentences	Syntactic roles	Kinds of cooperation
(S1) speech: "Chiama questa persona" handwriting: the name of the person on the touch- screen display	Chiama → verb John → noun Questa → deictic Persona → noun	Complementarity(Questa, John) Complementarity(persona, John)
(S2) speech: "L'e-mail di questa azienda è" gesture: pointing the icon of the company on the touch-screen display	L' → determiner Azienda → noun E-mail → noun Atos → noun Di → preposition è → verb Questa → deictic	Complementarity(Questa, Atos) Complementarity(Azienda, Atos)

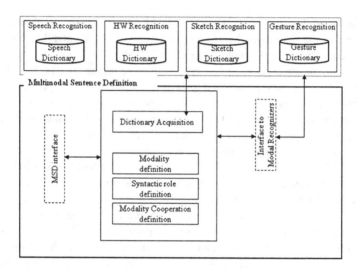

Fig. 4. Architecture of the MSD

The set of acquired multimodal sentences is inputted to the grammar inference algorithm, defined in [3]. The algorithm generates the production rules, expressed in MAG notation, along with the associated semantic functions to parse those examples.

For each element provided by the user's input during the multimodal interaction, annotations can code information as defined in [36], which provide the features characterizing the environment. For instance, the annotation of the multimodal sentence, introduced in Fig. 2, is shown in Fig. 5. However, in this paper we have defined a process for interactively define a multimodal corpus for Italian language by human-computer dialogue according to the generated multimodal grammar and that is usable to train the model for correctly interpret user's input.

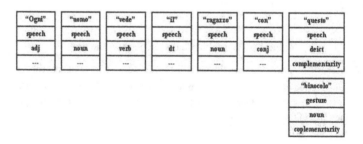

Fig. 5. Example of annotation of the multimodal sentence

It is an interactive and dynamic process of creation of the multimodal corpus for Italian language, that relies on the grammar inference algorithm used for generating a Multimodal Attribute Grammar (MAG) [2]. The MAG contains information about: (1) the modality used to create the element, (2) the representation of the element in the specific modality, (3) the temporal interval connected with the element, (4) the syntactic role that the element plays in the multimodal sentence provided by the user's input, (5) the concept name referred to the conceptual structure of the context, (6) the user's cultural background. As an example, the MAG generated from the set of sentences provided in Table 1 is shown in Table 2.

Table 2. The Multimodal Attribute Grammar for The Trial

P1) S → NP VERB
 R1.1) S.val←NP.val+VERB.val
 R1.2) S.mod←NP.mod+VERB.mod

P2) S →VP NP
 R2.1) S.val← VP.val+NP.val
 R2.2) S.mod←VP.mod+NP.mod

P3) VP → VERBT
 R3.1) VP.val← VERBT.val
 R3.2) VP.mod←VERBT.mod

P4) NP→ NP IN NP
 R4.1) NP.val← NP.val+IN.val+
   NP.val
 R4.2) NP.mod←NP.mod+ IN.mod+
   NP.mod

P5) NP →DT NOUN
 R5.1) NP.val← DT.val+NOUN.val
 R5.2) P.mod←DT.mod+NOUN.mod

P6) NP →DT NOUN NNS
 R6.1) NP.val← NNS.val
 R6.2) P.mod←DT.mod+NOUN.mod
   +NNS.mod

P7) NP →DT NOUN NNP1
 R7.1) NP.val← NNP1.val
 R7.2) P.mod←DT.mod+NOUN.mod
   +NNP1.mod

P8) VERBT → Chiama
 R8.1) VERBT.val ← chiama
 R8.2) VERBT.mod ← speech
 R8.3) VERBT.synrole ← verb

P9) VERB → è
 R9.1) VERB.val ← è
 R9.2) VERB.mod ← speech
 R9.3) VERB.synrole ← verb

P10) DT → Questa
 R10.1) DT.val ← questa
 R10.2) DT.mod ← speech
 R10.3) DT.synrole ← deictic
 R10.4) DT.coop ←
   complementary

P11) DT → L'
 R11.1) DT.val ← l'
 R11.2) DT.mod ← speech
 R11.3) DT.synrole ←
   determiner

P12) NOUN → Azienda
 R12.1) NOUN.val ← azienda
 R12.2) NOUN.mod ← speech
 R12.3) NOUN.synrole ← noun
 R12.4) NOUN.coop ←
   Complementary

P13) NOUN → Persona
 R13.1) NOUN.val ← persona
 R13.2) NOUN.mod ← speech
 R13.3) NOUN.synrole ← noun
 R13.4) NOUN.coop ←
   Complementary

P14) NOUN→ E-mail
 R14.1) NOUN.val ← e-mail
 R14.2) NOUN.mod ← speech
 R14.3) NOUN.synrole ← noun

P15) IN → di
 R15.1) IN.val ← di
 R15.2) IN.mod ← speech
 R15.3) IN.synrole ← preposition

P16) NNS → Atos
 R16.1) NNS.val ← Atos
 R16.2) NNS.mod ← gesture
 R16.3) NNS.synrole ← noun
 R16.4) NNS.coop ←
   complementary

P17) NNP1 → John
 R17.1) NNP1.val ← John
 R17.2) NNP1.mod ←
   handwriting
 R17.3) NNP1.synrole ← noun
 R17.4) NNP1.coop ←
   Complementary

3.2   Annotator

The Annotator (Fig. 6) takes as input the multimodal linearized sentence provided by the Multimodal Sentence Definition (MSD) module, the grammar rules provided by the Grammar Inference module and the semantic knowledge given by the ItalWordNet [41] as reference semantic resource (see Fig. 1).

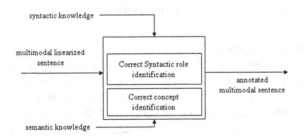

syntactic knowledge

multimodal linearized
sentence

Correct Syntactic role
identification

Correct concept
identification

annotated
multimodal sentence

semantic knowledge

Fig. 6. Architecture of the annotator

Since the Annotator module is HMM-based, it needs to be trained before to be applied.

3.2.1 Training of the Annotator Module

During the training phase, the model acquires:

- the correct associations between the elements of the multimodal sentence and the syntactic roles given by the grammar rules given by the Grammar Inference module, and
- correct associations between the elements of the multimodal sentence and the correct meaning given by is given by the knowledge on the conceptual structure of the context, as described in [48, 49].

This training process allowed to capture the key parameters (i.e., the syntactic role, the concept, etc.) in order to correctly associate multimodal sentences with syntactic roles and concepts. In detail, the syntactic role of each element of the multimodal sentence is given by the production rules, which are produced by the Grammar Inference module; the process follows guidelines for Italian treebanks [40] in order to provide syntactic information for each element. While, the meaning of the multimodal sentence, according to the conceptual structure of the context, is given by the Semantics extractor that uses the ItalWordNet [41] as the reference semantic resource. The Annotator considers the dynamics of the syntactic structure, and of the semantics of multimodal sentences, and it combines the complex information conveyed by different modalities in a holistic perspective. For some of the multimodal sentences, the syntactic structure and semantics may not be defined. In that case, the multimodal sentence is ambiguous. The ambiguity issue has been used to face the problem of the multimodal ambiguities (see their classification provided in [27]) by training the HMMs-based model for solving them provided in [4]. The Multimodal ambiguities solver is supported by the Multimodal ambiguities classifier [28] that recognizes if the ambiguities appears at syntactic or semantic levels. In order to address the correct interpretation of multimodal sentence, the Annotator uses LHMMs [37], that consist of several HHMMs [38] and HMMs [39] that run parallel at different levels from the terminal elements, which are the building units of the multimodal language, to the level of multimodal sentences. In detail, the HHMMs are used in this work to give a multilevel syntactic representation of a multi-modal sentence and to resolve syntactic ambiguities.

3.2.2 Multimodal Corpus Building

Once the grammar rules have been generated for different environments (movies in Italian Language, lessons by teachers of mathematics,...), and the Annotator module is trained to extract the correct syntactic and semantic information from new multimodal sentences, the syntactic and semantic annotation of the multimodal corpus can be performed. The system will provide the user interested in generating the corpus with a framework which is able to provide, for each multimodal sentence, candidate segmentation, alignment, syntax and semantics. The process of building the corpus consists of actions such as:

- Segmentation in elements: user's input is segmented into multimodal elements in order to provide for each element information about the modality used and the representation;

- Alignment: each multimodal element is localized in the list of multimodal elements in order to provide for each element information about the temporal interval;
- Syntax: the syntactic role of each element of the multimodal sentence that is given by the Annotator trained according to the grammar rules produced by the Grammar Inference module; the syntactic knowledge follows guidelines for Italian treebanks [40];
- Semantics: the semantic information are extracted from multimodal linearized sentences by using the Annotator module trained according to the context; the Annotator uses the ItalWordNet [41] as the reference semantic resource. The semantic annotation has the purpose to extract the semantic interpretation of multimodal sentences and to annotate the multimodal corpus.

The output of the multimodal corpus building are XML files containing all information about multimodal sentences (i.e. modality used to create the element, the representation of the element in the specific modality, the temporal interval, syntax, semantics). This approach makes the input independent from the different input devices and from the architecture of the system.

4 Conclusion

This paper presented a dynamic multimodal corpus building method that semi-automates the extraction of syntactic and semantic information from multimodal dialogues using both grammar generation and interpretation approaches. We have shown how the proposed method allows generating a set of grammatical rules starting from a small set of human-computer dialogues and how these rules, combined with a reference semantic resource, are applied to train the interpreter component in order to annotate new multimodal sentences by using the acquired syntactic and semantic knowledge. The syntactic knowledge provided by the interpreter component allows improving grammar knowledge by new sentences that are not interpretable with the available rules. The main contribution of this approach relies in the semi-automatic process of annotation of multimodal corpora that allows sped up the time-consuming process of manual annotation performed by most of the multimodal corpora in the literature. As a future work, we will develop multimodal corpora for Italian language for specific environments and evaluate them in various phases of the interaction process.

References

1. Allwood, J.: Multimodal corpora. In: Lüdeling, A., Kytö, M. (eds.) Corpus Linguistics. An International Handbook, pp. 207–225. Mouton de Gruyter, Berlin (2008)
2. D'Ulizia, A., Ferri, F., Grifoni, P.: Generating multimodal grammars for multimodal dialogue processing. IEEE Trans. Syst. Man Cybern. Part A Syst. Hum. **40**(6), 1130–1145 (2010)
3. D'Ulizia, A., Ferri, F., Grifoni, P.: A Learning Algorithm for Multimodal Grammar Inference. IEEE Trans. Syst. Man Cybern. Part B Cybern. **41**(6), 1495–1510 (2011)
4. Caschera, M.C., Ferri, F., Grifoni, P.: InteSe: an integrated model for resolving ambiguities· in multimodal sentences. IEEE Trans. Syst. Man Cybern. Syst. **43**(4), 911–931 (2013)

5. Caschera, M.C., Ferri, F., Grifoni, P.: Multimodal interaction systems: information and time features. Int. J. Web Grid Serv. (IJWGS) **3**(1), 82–99 (2007)
6. D'Ulizia, A.: Exploring multimodal input fusion strategies. In: The Handbook of Research on Multimodal Human Computer Interaction and Pervasive Services: Evolutionary Techniques for Improving Accessibility, pp. 34–57. IGI Publishing (2009)
7. Manchón, P., Pérez, G., Amores, G.: Multimodal fusion: a new hybrid strategy for dialogue systems. Proceedings of Eighth International Conference on Multimodal Interfaces (ICMI 2006), Banff, Alberta, Canada, pp. 357–363. ACM, New York (2006)
8. Shimazu, H., Takashima, Y.: Multimodal definite clause grammar. Syst. Comput. Japan **26**(3), 93–102 (1995)
9. Pereira, F., Warren, D.H.D.: Definite clause grammars for language analysis - a survey of the formalism and a comparison with augmented transition networks. Artif. Intell. **13**(3), 231–278 (1980)
10. Johnston, M., Bangalore, S.: Finite-state multimodal integration and understanding. Nat. Lang. Eng. **11**(2), 159–187 (2005)
11. Reitter, D., Panttaja, E.M., Cummins, F.: UI on the fly: Generating a multimodal user interface. In: Proceedings of Human Language Technology conference - North American chapter of the Association for Computational Linguistics (HLT-NAACL-2004), Boston, Massachusetts, USA (2004)
12. Baldridge, J., Kruijff, G.J.M.: Multimodal combinatory categorial grammar. In: Proceedings of the 10th Conference of the European Chapter of the Association for Computational Linguistics, Budapest, Hungary, pp. 211–218 (2003)
13. Caschera, M.C., Ferri, F., Grifoni, P.: An approach for managing ambiguities in multimodal interaction. In: Meersman, R., Tari, Z. (eds.) OTM-WS 2007, Part I. LNCS, vol. 4805, pp. 387–397. Springer, Heidelberg (2007)
14. Caschera M.C.: Interpretation methods and ambiguity management in multimodal systems. In: Grifoni, P. (ed.) Handbook of Research on Multimodal Human Computer Interaction and Pervasive Services: Evolutionary Techniques for Improving Accessibility, pp. 87–102. IGI Global, USA (2009)
15. Chai, J., Hong, P., Zhou, M.X.: A probabilistic approach to reference resolution in multimodal user interface. In: Proceedings of the 9th International Conference on Intelligent User Interfaces, Madeira, Portugal, pp. 70–77 (2004)
16. O'Hara, T., Wiebe, J., Bruce, R.F.: Selecting decomposable models for word-sense disambiguation: the Grling-Sdm system. Comput. Human. **34**(1/2), 159–164 (2000)
17. Johnston, M., Cohen, P.R., McGee, D., Oviatt, S.L., Pittman, J.A., Smith, I.: Unification-based multimodal integration. In: Proceedings of the 35th Annual Meeting of the Association for Computational Linguistics and the 8th Conference of the European Chapter of the Association for Computational Linguistics, pp. 281–288 (1997)
18. Avola, D., Caschera, M.C., Ferri, F., Grifoni, P.: Classifying and resolving ambiguities in sketch-based interaction. Int. J. Virt. Technol. Multimedia **1**(2), 104–139 (2010)
19. Krogh, A., Mian, S.I., Haussler, D.: A hidden Markov model that finds genes, E.coli DNA. NAR. 22(22), 4768–4778 (1994)
20. Rabiner, L.R.: A tutorial on hidden Markov models and selected applications in speech recognition. Proc. IEEE **77**(2), 257–285 (1989)
21. Makhoul, J., Starner, T., Schwartz, R., Chou, G.: On-line cursive handwriting recognition using hidden Markov models and statistical grammars. In: Proceedings of the Workshop Hum. Lang. Technol., Plainsboro, NJ, pp. 432–436 (1994)
22. Jelinek, F.: Robust part-of-speech tagging using a hiddenMarkov model. Comput. Speech Lang. **6**(3), 225–242 (1992)

23. Allwood, J.: Multimodal corpora. In: Lüdeling, A., Kytö, M. (eds.) Corpus Linguistics. An International Handbook, pp. 207–225. Mouton de Gruyter. Berlin (2008)

24. Gu, Y.: Multimodal text analysis: A corpus linguistic approach to situated discourse. Text Talk **26**(2), 127–167 (2006)

25. Knight, D., Carter, R., Adolphs, S., Pridmore, T., Mills, S., Crabtree, A., Bayoumi, S.: Beyond the text: construction and analysis of multi-modal linguistic corpora. In: The 2nd International Conference on e-Social Science, June 28–30, University of Manchester, NCeSS (2006)

26. Knight, D.: The future of multimodal corpora. Braz. J. Appl. Linguist. **11**(2), 391–416 (2011)

27. Karypidis, A., Lalis, S.: Automated context aggregation and file annotation for PAN-based computing. Pers. Ubiquit. Comput. **11**(1), 33–44 (2007)

28. Caschera, M.C., Ferri, F., Grifoni, P.: From modal to multimodal ambiguities: a classification approach. JNIT **4**(5), 87–109 (2013)

29. Byron, D.K., Fosler-Lussier, E.: The OSU Quake 2004 corpus of two-party situated problem-solving dialogs. In: Proceedings of the 15th Language Resources and Evaluation Conference (LREC 2006) (2006)

30. Stoia, L., Shockley, D.M., Byron, D.K., Fosler-Lussier, E.: SCARE: A situated cor- pus with annotated referring expressions. In: Proceedings of the Sixth International Conference on Language Resources and Evaluation (LREC 2008), pp. 28–30 (2008)

31. Tokunaga, T., Iida, R., Terai, A., Kuriyama, N.: The REX corpora: a collection of multimodal corpora of referring expressions in collaborative problem solving dialogues, In: Proceedings of the International Conference on Language Re- sources and Evaluation (LREC 2012), pp. 422–429 (2012)

32. Rehm, M., Gruneberg, F., Nakano, Y., Lipi, A.A., Yamaoka, Y., Huang, H.: Creating a standardized corpus of multimodal interactions for enculturating conversational interfaces. In: Workshop on Enculturating Conversational Interfaces by Socio-cultural Aspects of Communication, 2008 International Conference on Intelligent User Interfaces (IUI2008), Canary Islands, Spain, January 2008

33. Blache, P., Bertrand, R., Ferré, G.: Creating and Exploiting Multimodal Annotated Corpora: The ToMA Project. Multimodal Corpora, pp. 38–53 (2009)

34. Schiel, F., Steininger, S., Türk, U.: The SmartKom multimodal corpus at BAS. In: Proceedings of the International Language Resources and Evaluation Conference (LREC) (2002)

35. TALK (2007) project website: http://www.talk-project.org. Accessed 2 May 2011

36. Caschera, M.C., D'Ulizia, A., Ferri, F., Grifoni, P.: Multiculturality and multimodal languages. Multiple sensorial media advances and applications: new developments in MulSeMedia. A book edited by Dr. G. Ghinea (Brunel University), Dr. F. Andres (CVCE/NII), and Dr. S. Gulliver (University of Reading), pp. 99–114. IGI Global Publishing (2012)

37. Oliver, N., Garg, A., Horvitz, E.: Layered representations for learning and inferring office activity from multiple sensory channels. Comput. Vis. Image Underst. **96**(2), 163–180 (2004). [Ch6]

38. Fine, S., Singer, Y., Tishby, N.: The hierarchical hidden Markov model: analysis and applications. Mach. Learn. **32**(1), 41–62 (1998). [Ch7]

39. Rabiner, L.R.: A tutorial on hidden Markov models and selected applications in speech recognition. Proc. IEEE **77**(2), 257–285 (1989). [Ch8]

40. Monachini M.: ELM-IT: EAGLES Specification for Italian morphosintax Lexicon Specification and Classification Guidelines. EAGLES Document EAG CLWG ELM IT/F (1996)

41. Roventini, A., Alonge, A., Calzolari, N., Magnini, B., Bertagna, F.: ItalWordNet: a large semantic database for Italian. Proceedings of the 2nd International Conference on Language Resources and Evaluation (LREC 2000), Athens, Greece, 31 May – 2 June 2000, vol. II, pp. 783–790. The European Language Resources Association (ELRA), Paris (2000)

42. Ringeval, F., Sonderegger, A., Sauer, J., Lalanne, D.: Introducing the RECOLA multimodal corpus of remote collaborative and affective interactions. In: 2nd International Workshop EmoSPACE (2013)

43. Inoue, M., Hanada, R., Furuyama, N., Irino, T., Ichinomiya, T., Massaki, H.: Multimodal corpus for psychotherapeutic situations. In: International Workshop Series on Multimodal Corpora, Tools and Resources, pp. 18–21 (2012)

44. Fleury, A., Vacher, M., Portet, F., Chahuara, P., Noury, N.: A multimodal corpus recorded in a health smart home. In: Proceedings of the LREC 2010, pp. 99–105 (2010)

45. Vacher, M., Lecouteux, B., Chahuara, P., Portet, F., Meillon, B., Bonnefond, N.: The Sweet-Home speech and multimodal corpus for home automation interaction. In: LREC 2014, pp. 1–8 (2014)

46. Costantini, E., Burger, S., Pianesi, F.: NESPOLE!'s multilingual and multimodal corpus. In: LREC (2002)

47. http://badip.uni-graz.at/it/lista-di-corpora

48. Caschera, M.C., D'Ulizia, A., Ferri, F., Grifoni, P.: An Italian Multimodal Corpus: the Building Process. In: Meersman, R., et al. (eds.) OTM 2014 Workshops. LNCS, vol. 8842, pp. 557–566. Springer, Heidelberg (2013)

49. Caschera, M.C., D'Ulizia, A., Ferri, F., Grifoni, P.: Methods for dynamic building of multimodal corpora. In: LTC 2013, pp 499–503 (2013)

50. Caschera, M.C., D'Ulizia, A., Ferri, F., Grifoni, P.: Multimodal interaction in gaming. In: Demey, Y.T., Panetto, H. (eds.) OTM 2013 Workshops 2013. LNCS, vol. 8186, pp. 694–703. Springer, Heidelberg (2013)

Syntactic Enrichment of LMF Normalized Dictionaries Based on the Context-Field Corpus

Imen Elleuch[1(✉)], Bilel Gargouri[1(✉)],
and Abdelmajid Ben Hamadou[2(✉)]

[1] MIRACL Laboratory, FSEGS, B.P. 1088, 3018 Sfax, Tunisia
{imen.elleuch,bilel.gargouri}@fsegs.rnu.tn
[2] ISIMS, B.P. 242, 3021 Sakiet-Ezzit Sfax, Tunisia
abdelmajid.benhamadou@isimsf.rnu.tn

Abstract. In this paper, we deal with the representation of syntactic knowledge, particularly the syntactic behavior of verbs. In this context, we propose an approach to identify syntactic behaviors from a corpus based on the LMF Context-Field in order to enrich the syntactic extension of LMF normalized dictionary. Our approach consists of the following steps: (i) Identification of syntactic patterns, (ii) Construction of a grammar suitable for each syntactic pattern, (iii) Construction of a corpus from the LMF normalized dictionary, (iv) Application of grammars to the corpus and (v) Enrichment of the LMF dictionary. To validate this approach, we carried out an experiment that focuses on the syntactic behavior of Arabic verbs. We used the NooJ linguistic platform and an available LMF Arabic dictionary that contains 37,000 entries and 10,800 verbs. The obtained results concerning more than 7,800 treated verbs show 85 % of precision and 87 % of recall.

Keywords: Syntactic behavior · Enrichment · LMF dictionary · Grammar · Nooj platform · Arabic dictionary

1 Introduction

A syntactic lexicon is a core component for learning and acquiring a language. In NLP (Natural Language Processing), a syntactic lexicon is the cornerstone of several applications. Among these applications, we can mention: the Human–Machine dialogue, machine translation, automatic summarization, etc. The relevance of such a lexicon is due to the kinds of knowledge that it contains. In fact, in a syntactic lexicon, we describe the different manners of using each lemma, which can be the predicate in a sentence. For each use, the lexicon defines the frame of sub-categorization specifying the number, the type of arguments and other complementary information.

Many syntactic lexicons have emerged. For English, we can mention VerbNet [1], which is a verb lexicon. It gathers verbs into classes sharing the same syntactic and semantic behavior, ComLex Syntax [2], which defines a moderately broad coverage English lexicon. It contains detailed information about the syntactic characteristics of each lexical item and is particularly detailed in its treatment of subcategorization.

© Springer International Publishing Switzerland 2016
Z. Vetulani et al. (Eds.): LTC 2013, LNAI 9561, pp. 191–204, 2016.
DOI: 10.1007/978-3-319-43808-5_15

AcquiLex [3] is another lexicon for English language which allows the representation of multilingual syntactic and semantic information extracted from Machine Readable Dictionaries (MRDs).

Regarding the French language, we find the Lefff lexicon (Lexicon of French inflected forms) [4], which is a large-scale morphological and syntactic lexicon representing the intensional and extensional knowledge representation of lexical items. Also, for the French language, we note the existence of the DICOVALENCE [5], which is a type of syntactic dictionary of verbs based on the "pronominal approach" in syntax [6]. Finally, we can cite the Lexicon-Grammar [7], which provides a systematic description of the syntactic properties of French linguistic categories such as verbs, nouns, adjectives and adverbs. It is organized into groups of tables; each table contains elements of lexicon having comparable functions (typical construction, distribution of arguments, etc.).

Concerning the Arabic language, only a few syntactic lexicons have been proposed. We can cite Arabic VerbNet [8] which is an Arabic version of English VerbNet, where Arabic verbs are classified into classes sharing the same syntactic and semantic proprieties. We can mention the Arabic Syntactic Lexicon [9] which describes a syntactic resource for Arabic verbs represented with the LMF (Lexical Markup Language) ISO standard. Finally we can indicate ElixirFM [10], which is an example of a morphological lexicon enriched with the syntactic and semantic valence of verbs according to the morphological classification.

In general, syntactic lexicons suffer from several deficiencies affecting their structures and contents. Regarding structure, these lexicons do not meet generic models. Each one proposes an appropriate structure to the expected applications, which limits their re-use, compatibility and fusion with other resources. As a result of the used models, the content of such lexicons is incomplete regarding syntactic knowledge. We note that the enrichment of syntactic lexicons requires significant effort due to the scarcity of such knowledge, whether in paper or digitized dictionaries.

Recently, the development of electronic lexical resources has benefited from the publication of the LMF (Lexical Markup Framework) ISO 24613 standard [11]. This standard allows a flexible modeling of all levels of linguistic knowledge within fine models. In this context, several lexicons compliant to this standard have been constructed. We can mention for example the conversion of Lexicon-Grammar tables to LMF [12], the ElMadar Arabic LMF dictionary [13] and WordNet-LMF [14]. However, these resources are still poor concerning syntactic knowledge because such lexical information is not always freely available. However, in LMF dictionaries the Context textual content represents a semantic guided content that illustrates the use of the lexical entry by means of sentence.

In this paper, we propose an approach to identify the syntactic behavior of verbs using corpus - constructed from Context field of LMF dictionary - in order to enrich the syntactic extension of LMF normalized dictionary. An experiment of the proposed approach has been carried out using the Arabic normalized dictionary available in our laboratory.

The next part of this paper is organized as follows: We will start with a presentation of the LMF standard and the syntactic extension of the LMF model. Then, we will detail the proposed approach for the enrichment of dictionary with the syntactic behaviors of verbs using a corpus. After that, we will describe the experiment carried out on the ElMadar LMF Arabic dictionary and discuss some of the results obtained. Finally, we will compare our study with related works on Arabic syntactic lexicons.

2 Syntactic Extension of LMF Model

2.1 The LMF Standard

The LMF (Lexical Markup Framework) [11] is a standard for structuring and representing the lexical knowledge of the majority of natural languages.

The LMF provides a meta-model based on a core and a range of extensions related to the various levels of linguistic analysis (i.e., morphological, syntactic and semantic). In order to obtain a lexicon according to the LMF standard, it is sufficient to have the core package, then, optionally select packages of extensions to the representation of the most wanted lexicon. Then, the resulting model will be decorated with the Data Categories Registry (DCR)[1] needed to represent the specificities of the modelized language.

2.2 Syntactic Extension of the LMF Model

The LMF standard reserves a syntactic extension for the description of the syntactic features of lexical entries. The purpose of this extension is to describe the specific syntactic properties of a lexeme when combined with other lexemes in a sentence. Six classes characterize this extension: Syntactic Behavior, Subcategorization Frame, Lexeme Property, Syntactic Argument, Subcategorizatin Frame Set and SynArgMap classes. Syntactic Behavior represents one of the possible behaviors of a lexeme. As shown in Fig. 1 below, the Syntactic Behavior instance is attached to the Lexical Entry instance and optionally to the Sense instance. The attachment of the Syntactic Behavior instance to the Lexical Entry instance means that this lexeme can have this behavior in the language of the lexicon. Also, the presence of Syntcatic Behavior in the Lexicon reinforces the existence of this behavior in this Lexicon. The detailed description of the syntactic behavior of a lexical entry is defined by the Subcategorization Frame instance that represents one syntactic construction. A Subcategorization Frame instance is shared by all Lexical Entry instances that have the same syntactic behavior in the same language. The Subcategorization Frame class has a reflexive link allowing the inheriting of relationships and attributes between one Subcategorization Frame and another more generic one. The Lexeme Property is another class of the LMF syntactic extension. This class is linked only to the Subcategorization Frame because it refers to the current Lexical Entry instance. A Lexeme Property instance connected to a Subcategorization Frame instance is shared by all the lexemes that have the same syntactic behavior. As a syntactic behavior describes the syntactic features of a lexeme when it is

---

[1] www.isocat.org.

combined with other lexemes in a sentence, it is necessary to detail each argument composing this behavior. For that purpose, the LMF standard reserves the Syntactic Argument class to describe each argument of Subcategorization Frame. Regarding the Subcategorizatin Frame Set class, it is a class that describes a set of syntactic constructions and the relationship that can appear between these constructions. The reflexive link existing in the Subcategorization Frame Set fosters the inheritance of attributes and relationships between a Subcategorization Frame Set and another more generic one. Finally, the SynArgMap class is reserved to represent the relationship that can map various Syntactic Argument instances of the same Subcategorization Frame Set instance.

For all the previously-cited classes, DCs will be selected in accordance with the requirement of the modeled language from the DCR in order to decorate each class.

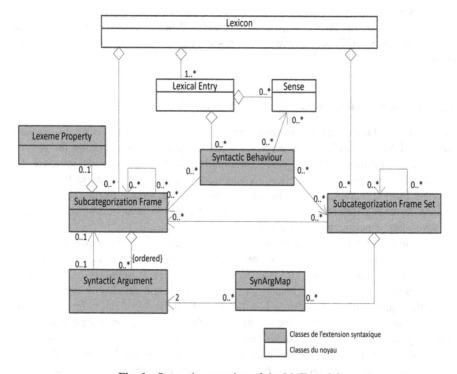

Fig. 1. Syntactic extension of the LMF model

3 The Proposed Approach

In this section we will present the proposed approach and we will detail each step composing it.

3.1   General Presentation

The proposed approach is composed of five steps as shown in Fig. 2. The first step, "Identification of syntactic patterns", is performed by a linguist and results in a list of Syntactic Patterns related to the processed language. The second step, "Construction of a Grammar for each syntactic pattern", is realized by using linguistic tools. It consists in the development of a Grammar for each syntactic pattern identified in the previous step. The third step, "Construction of a corpus from dictionary", intends to create a corpus by selecting all Context-fields from the LMF normalized dictionary. This creation requires linguistic tools in order to be accomplished. The fourth step, "Application of the Grammars to the corpus" aims to apply the constructed Grammars to the created corpuses in order to recognize for each verb found in the corpus its corresponding syntactic behaviors. So the result of this step is a list of verbs-Syntactic behaviors. The last step of the proposed approach, "Enrichment of the LMF dictionary", aims to enrich LMF normalized dictionary with the recognized syntactic behaviors of verbs.

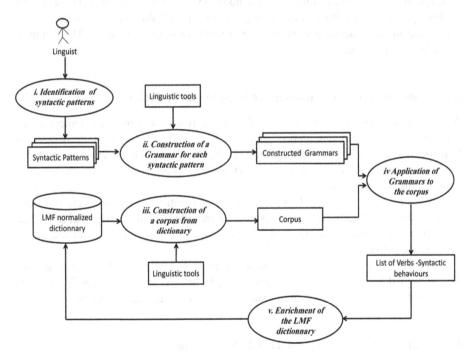

Fig. 2. Proposed approach

3.2   Identification of Syntactic Patterns

The syntactic pattern of a lexeme for a given language is used to encode the number, the type, the used preposition and the arrangement of its arguments (subject and complements). In English or French, a verbal clause begins with the Subject. For example, for the sentence "The girl ate an apple", the corresponding syntactic pattern is [S V C] where "S" is the Subject, "V" is the Verb and "C" is the Complement. So the first argument of the latter sentence is "the girl" compiling the Subject function; the second argument is "ate", related to the Verb; and the third syntactic argument is "an apple", which is the Complement. For the French sentence "Cette bague appartenait à ma grand-mère/This ring belonged to my grandmother", the suitable related syntactic pattern is [S V to C]. This pattern is composed of a Subject "This ring" followed by the Verb "belongs" followed by the preposition "to" and at last by the Complement "grandmother". On the other hand, in the Arabic language, the verb is always the beginning of a verbal sentence (أكلت الفتاة تفاحة/aAkalat alfatAtu tufaAhatan[2] [15]/The girl ate an apple): "أكلت" is the Verb "الفتاة" is the Subject and "تفاحة" is the Complement. Thus the syntactic pattern of the last Arabic sentence is [V S C]. So, each language has its appropriate syntactic patterns.

As we aim to identify automatically syntactic behaviors of lexemes, our proposed approach defines the first step in the "Identification of Syntactic Patterns". This step aims to discover all the specific syntactic patterns of the processed language. To accomplish this goal, we can use different books in linguistics and examples of the use of verb phrases from some dictionaries. At the end of this step, we obtain a list containing all the syntactic patters characterizing the processed language. This list must be validated by a linguist.

3.3   Construction of a Grammar for Each Syntactic Pattern

A syntactic behavior consists of a set of syntactic rules about the arrangement of the syntactic arguments in a sentence governed by a verb. Those rules determine the function and the position of each argument in the sentence. To represent these patterns, we decided to use grammars that allow taking into account two axes: the syntagmatic axis and the paradigmatic one.

The syntagmatic axis involves the analysis of functions – like subject, verb, and object – while the paradigmatic axis operates on the selection of grammatical forms like noun, preposition, verb, adjective, etc. And this is what is needed in the representation of syntactic patterns.

For this construction we need to use linguistic tools like NooJ[3], Gate[4], etc. in order to represent the characteristics of each syntactic pattern. So the output of this step consists of all the constructed Grammars related to each syntactic pattern.

3.4   Construction of a Corpus from LMF Dictionary

The knowledge about syntactic behavior is not frequently found in dictionaries, but such knowledge must be calculated and recognized from a corpus. This knowledge is

---

[2] The Arabic transliteration which has been used is Habash, Soudi and Buckwalter [15].

[3] www.nooj4nlp.net/pages/nooj.html.

[4] https://gate.ac.uk/.

not directly used and is not so explicit, so a specific treatment should be performed on the corpus. The objective of this step is the construction of the corpus to be used. We propose to construct it from the LMF normalized dictionary by collecting all Context textual content related to lexical entries. The Context is an LMF class that represents a text string providing authentic context for the use of the word form managed by the Lemma of Lexical Entry. It is important to mention that this Context can use an inflected form of the Lemma. Contrary to the Definition class, which consists of a narrative description of a sense that can be expressed in a different language and/or script than the one of the Lexical Entry instance and that is displayed for human users to facilitate their understanding of the meaning of a Lexical Entry, the Context class is meant to be processed by computer programs. For this reason we decided to construct our needed corpus by selecting all the Contexts of Lexical Entries from an LMF dictionary. One can ask why we did not treat the original Contexts related to each Lexical Entry in order to identify its syntactic behaviors. The answer is that a treated verb can appear also in the other Contexts of other lexical entries in the LMF dictionary.

3.5 Application of the Grammars to the Corpus

The fourth step of the proposed approach aims to apply the constructed Grammars related to each syntactic pattern to the obtained corpus in order to recognize the corresponding syntactic behaviors of verbs. To do this, we project all the grammars previously defined in the second step on the corpus. This projection is used to extract all the verbs in the corpus respecting the peculiarities of the grammar which is applied. This way, the recognition of the syntactic behavior of a verb is performed and a list containing verbs and their syntactic behaviors is constructed. Indeed, the application each time of a grammar corresponding to a certain syntactic behavior helps to identify all the verbs respecting this behavior. When this step is over, a list of verbs and their related syntactic behaviors is obtained.

3.6 Enrichment of the LMF Dictionary

The objective of this step is the enrichment of the LMF normalized dictionary with the syntactic behaviors of verbs. Firstly, all the syntactic patterns identified in the first step will be attached directly to the Lexicon class. Secondly, for each given verb from the obtained list in the previous step, an instance of it in the LMF dictionary will be searched for. After that, all the corresponding recognized syntactic behaviors presented in the list will be added in the suitable place in the LMF Lexical Entry while respecting the peculiarities of the model.

At the end of this step, we obtain a normalized LMF dictionary enriched with the syntactic behaviors of verbs.

4 Experimentation and Results

To test our approach on a practical level, we conducted an experiment using an available LMF normalized Arabic dictionary named ElMadar[5].

4.1 Choice and Peculiarities of the Arabic Language

We chose to experiment our proposed approach on the Arabic language for two reasons. Firstly, the LMF standard can be applied to different languages including the Arabic language, and an LMF normalized Arabic dictionary is available. Secondly, studies that treat the syntactic knowledge of Arabic lexemes are rare and few in number. Nevertheless, this language has some peculiarities that distinguish it from other languages. Indeed, the Arabic language is a Semitic language that possesses some peculiar and unique characteristics like: (a) It is written from right to left. (b) The absence of vowels with the consonant letters in an Arabic text causes ambiguities in its comprehension. (c) Agglutination is also another striking feature of the Arabic language; in fact, an Arabic word can sometimes correspond to a sentence. For example, the word "أتتذكروننا/Aatata.akaruwnanaA" corresponds in English to the sentence: "Do you remember us?"

4.2 Identification of Arabic Syntactic Patterns

Two types of phrases mark the syntactic knowledge of Arabic language: verbal and noun clauses. "مات الرجل/maAta alrajulu/the man is died" is a verbal clause because the predicate of this sentence is the verb "مات/maAta/to die" while, "صافيةالسماء/alsamaA' SaAfiyah/the clear sky" is a noun clause because the predicate of this sentence is the noun "السماء/alsamaA'/sky". In this paper we are interested in the treatment of only verbal clauses.

For the verbal clause, the Arabic language may have several syntactic behaviors. For example, the pattern [V S] characterizes an intransitive verb that requires only a subject; (مات الرجل/maAta alrajulu/the man died). The pattern [V S C1 pre C2] represents a transitive verb requiring: a Subject followed by a first complement, followed by a preposition, followed by a second complement like in the sentence (أمرهبالخروج/Aamarahu bilxuruwji/he ordered him to go out), while the pattern [V pre C S] corresponds to a verb followed by a preposition, a complement and finally a subject like in the sentence (خطرت له فكرة) (xatarat lahu fikrahun/an idea came to his mind).

To identify all the syntactic patterns of Arabic verbs, we used the following books in linguistics: "Grammaire de l'Arabe Classique" [16] and "Moajam quaeid allogha al-arabiya fi lawhat w souar" [17]. In addition to using these books, we have taken some examples of the use of verb clauses from some Arabic dictionaries, like (الغني) Al-Ghani and (الوسيط) Alwassit, in order to identify the syntactic patterns of these verbs. These patterns were validated by a linguist. This step allowed us to detect 155 different

---

[5] http://elmadar.miracl-apps.com/.

syntactic patterns for Arabic verbs taking into account the variation of prepositions. The following table shows an extract of some syntactic patterns identified in this step (Table 1).

Table 1. Examples of Arabic syntactic patterns

Syntactic Pattern	Description	
[V S]	Verb Subject	Active voice
[V A]	Verb ProAgent	Passive voice
[V S عَنْ C]	Verb Subject Prep «عَنْ» Complement	Active voice
[V بِ C S]	Verb Prep «بِ» Complement Subject	Active voice
[V A C1 C2]	Verb ProAgent FirstComplement Second Complement	Passive voice
[V S C1 C2 C3]	Verb Subject FirstComplement Second Complement ThirdComplement	Active voice

4.3   Construction of Grammars with the NooJ Platform

To represent the rules of each syntactic pattern, we need linguistic tools. The tool that we have chosen is the NooJ linguistic platform. This platform is a development environment used to build different descriptions of natural languages (23 languages, including Arabic) and applied to large corpora in real time. Descriptions of natural languages are formalized by electronic dictionaries and grammars into organized graphs. NooJ can provide tools to describe the inflectional and derivational morphology, terminology variations, spelling, vocabulary (single words, multi-words and idiom units), semi-frozen phenomena (local grammars), syntax (for complete sentences) and semantics (named entity recognition, transformational analysis) of natural languages. Thus, we constructed the NooJ grammars corresponding to the 155 syntactic patterns identified in the previous step. Figure 3 represents a grammar built with the NooJ platform representing the [V S C] syntactic pattern.

This NooJ grammar is composed of two participants, the Subject and the Complement mentioned between brackets. If the Subject is simple (مفرد/muf.rad) the content of the corresponding node is mentioned between "<" and ">" and it describes the grammatical category (noun, pronoun, Adjective,...) of the participant. Otherwise, if the Subject is composite (مركب/murakab such as: مركب إضافي/annexed composite, مركب نعتي/descriptive composite) the related node is another constructed grammar detailing also the grammatical specificities of the type of the processed composite. The same process described for the Subject is detailed for the Complement.

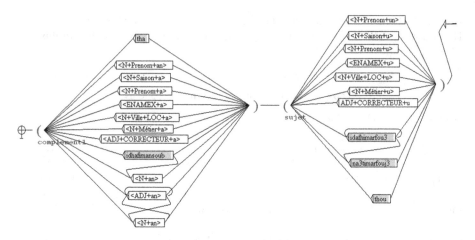

Fig. 3. Example of a NooJ grammar related to the [V S C] syntactic pattern

4.4   The LMF Normalized Arabic Dictionary

An LMF normalized model of Arabic dictionary [13] named El-Madar has been developed. This model takes into account the specificities of the Arabic language and covers the morphologic, syntactic, semantic and syntactico-semantic levels. The current version of this dictionary contains about 37,000 lexical entries: 10,800 verbs, 3,800 roots and 22,400 nouns. These lexical entries include morphological knowledge such as the part-of-speech, some inflected forms, some derived forms etc. It includes also semantic features like the synonymy relationships that can relate one sense with other senses of different lexical entries. Concerning semantic features, the El-Madar dictionary is expanded by semantic classes assigned to the Senses of substantives entries [18]. Each Sense can have one or many Definitions and also one or several Contexts. These Definitions and Contexts contain vowelled words that minimize syntactic ambiguities.

4.5   The Constructed Corpus

Having developed all the grammars constructed earlier, we were then ready to apply these grammars on an Arabic corpus in order to identify the syntactic behaviors of verbs. As mentioned in the proposed approach, the corpus we used was constructed by collecting all Contexts fields from the ElMadar LMF normalized Arabic dictionary. This dictionary contains about 62,157 senses and 71,442 contexts. So, the constructed corpus is composed of 71,442 sentences including 221,998 words. The resulting corpus represents a good sample for the use of the Arabic sentence since they are extracted from the Contexts of the ElMadar LMF normalized Arabic dictionary.

4.6 Results

The experimentation that we carried out on the constructed Arabic corpus from the ElMadar dictionary allowed us to treat 7,800 verbs, 2,000 of them relating to the syntactic behavior [V S], 3,000 having the behavior [V S C], 500 corresponding to the pattern [V S prep C], 7 with the syntactic behavior [V S C1 C2 C3] and about 2,300 complying with the remaining syntactic patterns.

We selected 20 verbs from the ElMadar dictionary as a sample in order to validate the syntactic behaviors assigned to them. For these 20 verbs, 42 assignments of syntactic behaviors were detected. Concerning these 42 syntactic behaviors the linguist acknowledged that 5 syntactic behaviors are missed and 6 syntactic behaviors are false. So, the resulting rates of Recall, Precision and F-measure are given in the following table, Table 2.

Table 2. Results

Recall	Precision	F-Measure
0.87	0.85	0.84

We can point out that the missed syntactic behaviors detected by the linguist are due to the Context of the ElMadar dictionary. On the other hand, the erroneous assignments of syntactic behaviors are caused by syntactic ambiguities related to our constructed grammars which must consider more complex linguistic phenomena.

5   Related Works

As we have tested the proposed approach on the Arabic language, we present in this section three studies interested in the representation of Arabic syntactic knowledge. Among these works, we can mention the lexicon Arabic Syntactic Lexicon [9], the ElixirFM lexicon [10] and the Arabic VerbNet [8]. We will present in the following section the main features characterizing these works; after that, a comparison with the lexicon we obtained will be detailed.

5.1   The Arabic Syntactic Lexicon

The Arabic Syntactic Lexicon [9] is a lexical resource interested in the representation of syntactic knowledge of Arabic verbs. The model of this resource is based on the LMF ISO standard. A semi-automatic process is used to build the sub-categorizations of Arabic verbs. This process is composed of three steps: first, the manual identification of the sub-categorization frames of Arabic verbs; second, the enrichment step using the Lexus editor and third, the edition of Arabic verb lemmas with its corresponding sub-categorization. The resulting lexicon contains about 2,500 verb lemmas with an average of 2, 7 sub-categorizations per verb.

This lexicon takes into account only 17 sub-categorizations of Arabic verbs. In fact, it is a small lexicon to represent syntactic knowledge for Arabic verbs.

5.2   The ElixirFM Lexicon

ElixirFM [10] is a morphological lexicon enriched by the valency frames for selected verbal lexemes. This lexicon is based on the Functional Generative Description (FGD) theoretical approach. To extract the valency frames, this study uses the Prague Arabic Dependency Treebank (PADT) and an annotated corpus of Arabic texts containing three layers of annotations: functional morphology, surface analytical syntax and tectogrammatics. Also, CLARA, Arabic Gigaword and three printed dictionaries are exploited. The valence of a verb is represented as a form of dependency trees. The lexicon contains about 3,500 frames of verb valence: 2,000 frames representing the transitive verbs were created automatically and 1,500 frames were created manually. Both optional and obligatory complements are included in the representation of the frames on the valences of verbs in the ElixirFM lexicon. In fact, this lexicon does not take into consideration the valency of auxiliary, modal, impersonal and defective verbs.

5.3   The Arabic VerbNet

The Arabic VerbNet [8] is a lexicon of Arabic verbs that operates with Levin's classification [19]. This lexicon is based on the procedure used in the development of the English VerbNet [1]. In this lexicon, the verbs are grouped into classes that share syntactic and semantic properties. It contains 173 verb classes and 498 verbs represented by 4,392 frames. These frames include information such as the root of the verb, the derived forms such as the present participle and the past participle, the thematic roles of arguments, the sub-categorization, and the syntactic and semantic description of each verb.

Some Arabic verbs are grouped into subclasses thanks to restrictions based on the thematic role of the participants of a sentence or by semantic predicates that separate their initial classes. An evaluation by experts in linguistics shows that some frames of this lexicon do not respect the features of Arabic verbs. For example, "كَتَبَ" (to write) is a transitive Arabic verb, but the Arabic VerbNet gives the frame [V NP] indicating the intransitivity of this verb.

5.4   Synthesis

All the approaches presented in the above studies suggest some interesting ideas, but each one of them includes some gaps. Indeed, the Arabic Syntactic Lexicon [9] is a very small lexicon representing only the syntactic aspects of traditional Arabic verbs. The ElixirFM does not present the explicit syntactic structure of verbs and neglects the syntactic functions of complements while the Arabic VerbNet does not represent the native characteristics and features of Arabic verbs because it's a simple translation of the classes used in the English VerbNet with some adaptations to the Arabic language (Table 3).

In the following table we make a comparison between those three works and our lexicon according to different criteria:

Table 3. Comparison between existing lexicons

	Arabic Syntactic Lexicon	ElixirFM Lexicon	Arabic Verbnet	Our Lexicon
Normalized format	+	–	–	+
Linguistic levels covered	Syntactic	Morphology Semantic Syntactic	Semantic Syntactic	Morphology Semantic Syntactic
Number of verbs	2,500 Transitive verbs	3,500	4,000	7,800
Corpora used				
Annotated	–	+	–	–
Raw	+	–	–	+
Number of words	781	1,000		221,998
Classification	Transitivity Intransitivity	FGD	Levin's class	Transitivity Intransitivity
Syntactic knowledge	17 sub-categorizations	3,500 valency frames	498 frames	155 syntactic behaviors

6 Conclusion and Future Works

We have proposed in this paper an approach to enrich LMF normalized dictionary with the syntactic behavior of verbs. This approach is characterized by its extensibility because it is based on the LMF standard and takes into account the peculiarities and specificities of the processed language. We have tested the proposed approach on an available LMF Arabic dictionary and we have developed Grammars of syntactic behaviors using the NooJ linguistic platform.

In the future, we hope, first to test our approach on Arabic nouns because an Arabic noun, and a verb as well, can be the predicate in a sentence. Second, we intend to attach the syntactic behavior to the meanings of verbs. Also, we aim to ameliorate the constructed grammars by considering more complex syntactic phenomena. Moreover, we will focus on the syntactico-semantic links between lexical entries in LMF normalized dictionary.

References

1. Kipper, K., Dang, T.H., Plamer, M.: Class-bases construction of a verb lexicon. In: AAAI-2000 Seventeeth National Conference on Artifical Intelligence, Austin (2000)
2. Grishman, R., Macleod, C., Meyers, A.: Comlex syntax: building a computational lexicon. In: Proceedings of COLING 1994, pp. 268–272 (1994)

204   I. Elleuch et al.

3. Sanfilippo, A.: Lkb encoding of lexical knowledge. In: Default Inheritance in Unification-Based Approaches to the Lexiocn. CUP, Cambridge (1993)
4. Sagot, B.: The lefff, a freely available and large-coverage morphological and syntactic lexicon for french. In: 7th Language Resource and Evaluation Conference LREC 2010, La Valette, Malte (2010)
5. Van den Eynde, K., Mertens, P.: Le dictionnaire de valence DICOVALENCE: manuel d'utilisation (2006). http://bach.arts.kuleuven.be/dicovalence/manuel_061117.pdf
6. Van den Eynde, K., Blanche-Benveniste, C.: Syntaxe et mécanismes descriptifs: présentation de l'approche pronominale, Cahiers de Lexicologie n 32, pp. 3–27 (1978)
7. Gross, M.: Méthodes en syntaxe: Régimes des constructions complétives. Hermann, Paris (1975)
8. Mousser, J.: A large coverage verb taxonomy for Arabic. In: LREC 2010, Italy, Malte (2010)
9. Loukil, N., Haddar, K., Ben Hamadou, A.: A syntactic lexicon for Arabic verbs. In: International Conference on Language Resources and Evaluation, LREC, pp. 17–23, Valletta, Malta, May 2010
10. Bielický, V., Smrž, O.: Enhancing the ElixirFM lexicon with verbal valency frames. In: Proceedings of the Second International Conference on Arabic Language Resources and Tools (MEDAR 2009), Cairo, Egypt (2009)
11. Francopoulo, G., George, M.: ISO/TC 37/SC 4 Rev.16. Language resource management – Lexical markup framework (LMF) (2008)
12. Laporte, E., Matthieu-Constant, E.: Conversion of lexicon-grammar tables to LMF: application to French. In: LMF: Lexical Markup Framework, pp. 157–187. Wiley Editions, March 2013. ISBN: 9781848214309
13. Khemakhem, A., Gargouri, B., Haddar, K., Ben Hamadou, A.: LMF for Arabic. In: LMF: Lexical Markup Framework, pp. 83–96. Wiley Editions, March 2013. ISBN: 9781848214309
14. Soria, C., Monachini, M., Vossen, P.: Wordnet-LMF: fleshing out a standardized format for wordnet interoperability. In: International Worksop on Intercultural Collaboration, IWIC 2009, pp. 139–146 (2009)
15. Habash, N., Soudi, A., Buckwalter, T.: Arabic Computational Morphology: Knowledge-Based and Empirical Methods. Springer, Netherlands (2007). ISBN: 978-1-4020-6045-8
16. Blachère, R., Gaudefroy-Demombunes, M.: Grammaire de l'Arabe classique (Morphologie et syntaxe). Troisième édition revue et remaniée. G-P. MAISONNEUE & LAROSE, Editeurs, Paris (1952)
17. Addahdeh, A.: معجم قواعد اللغة العربية في جداول و لوحات Librairie Libanon Nachirun (1996)
18. Elleuch, I., Gargouri, B., Ben-Hamadou, A.: Towards automatic enrichment of standardized electronic dictionaries by semantic classes. In: Proceeding of the 26th International Conference on Computational Linguistics and Speech Processing (ROCLING), Zhongli, Taiwan, 25–26 September 2014, pp. 96-109 (2014)
19. Levin, B.: English Verb Classes and Alternations. A Preliminary Investigation. The University of Chicago Press, Chicago and London (1993)

An Example of a Compatible NLP Toolkit

Krzysztof Jassem[✉] and Roman Grundkiewicz[✉]

Adam Mickiewicz University, ul. Wieniawskiego 1, 61-712 Poznań, Poland
{jassem,romang}@amu.edu.pl

Abstract. The paper describes an open-source set of linguistic tools, whose distinctive features are its customisability and compatibility with other NLP toolkits: texts in various natural languages and character encodings may be read from a number of popular data formats; all annotation tools may be run with several options to differentiate the format of input and output; rule lists used by individual tools may be supplemented or replaced by the user; external tools (including NLP tools designed in independent research centres) may be incorporated into the toolkit's environment.

Keywords: PSI-Toolkit · NLP tools · Polish language · Software architecture · Open source

1 Introduction

PSI-Toolkit is a set of NLP tools designed in the years 2011–2013 within a grant of Polish Ministry of Science and Higher Education. The primary goal of the project is to ensure public and free access to the set of NLP tools designed in the Laboratory of Information Systems (PSI is the abbreviation for the Polish name of the laboratory) at Adam Mickiewicz University in Poznań, Poland. The secondary goal is to enable incorporation of tools developed at other NLP centres. For these reasons, the architecture of the toolkit is designed to allow for customisability and compatibility with other NLP toolkits.

The data structure used in PSI-Toolkit is that of a lattice, where the edges span over the characters of the processed texts. Each annotator (i.e. each NLP tool) of the processing pipeline adds new edges to the existing structure (see [6] for more details).

PSI-Toolkit may be personalised according to users' needs. Users may customise PSI-Toolkit in three ways: by selecting particular annotators to be used in the processing pipeline, by specifying run options for each annotator or by substituting annotation rules. Furthermore, users can easily combine tools of PSI-Toolkit with external applications in one processing pipeline using Unix shell.

The functionality of PSI-Toolkit attempts to combine selected features of well-known NLP toolkits. We follow the Stanford Natural Language Processing Group[1] in letting a user run PSI-Toolkit from a command line. Just like

---

[1] http://nlp.stanford.edu.

© Springer International Publishing Switzerland 2016
Z. Vetulani et al. (Eds.): LTC 2013, LNAI 9561, pp. 205–214, 2016.
DOI: 10.1007/978-3-319-43808-5_16

in the NLTK toolkit [2] and UIMA[2] [14] we want programmers to be capable of building programs that call PSI-Toolkit annotators. We would like users to apply annotator pipelines, as e.g. in GATE[3]. Finally, we aim at encouraging pure linguists to use PSI-Toolkit, by delivering a friendly web-service — this is motivated by Apertium[4] [3].

The full range of PSI-Toolkit functionality is offered in the command-line mode, but the majority of functions are also available in the web-service (that can also be run locally). Figure 1 shows the main window of the service.

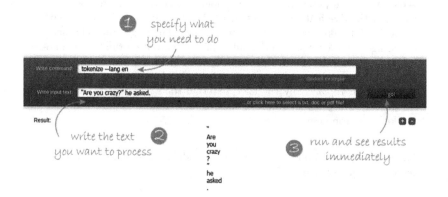

Fig. 1. PSI-Toolkit web-service available at http://psi-toolkit.amu.edu.pl.

A standard PSI-Toolkit command is formed as a pipeline of annotators[5], e.g. reader | segmenter | tokenizer | lemmatizer | writer. In Sects. 2, 3 and 4 we report on customizing various annotators: readers, processors and writers respectively. Then, we describe the different ways of using PSI-Toolkit in Sect. 5, and finally we draw conclusions in Sect. 6.

2   Reading Various Input Data

Readers are PSI-Toolkit annotators that extract texts from input files, split them into characters and build initial edges of the PSI-lattice that span over each character and extracted text fragments. A user may customise the process in two ways: by running one of several types of readers delivered by PSI-Toolkit or by selecting desired options of the chosen reader.

The following readers are delivered by PSI-Toolkit:

– **txt-reader** — reads plain text from a file or standard input,

---

[2] http://uima.apache.org.
[3] http://gate.ac.uk/.
[4] http://www.apertium.org.
[5] The complete list of annotators can be found at http://psi-toolkit.amu.edu.pl/help/documentation.html.

- `apertium-reader` — reads text from various markup formats,
- `pdf-reader` — reads PDF files,
- `nkjp-reader` — reads text from the Polish National Corpus XML files in TEI format [12],
- `utt-reader` — reads files in the UTT (UAM Text Tools) format[6],
- `psi-reader` — reads files in the PSI-Toolkit format[7].

A user may decide not to define the reader, leaving the task to the PSI-Toolkit. In that case, a special processor called `guessing-reader` guesses the input format. It works for most supported textual and binary formats.

Readers may be run with various options depending on the type of the reader: `txt-reader` processes text as the whole (the `--whole-text` option), which is recommended for short texts, or `--line-by-line`, recommended for long texts. The options of `apertium-reader` allow for the processing of RTF, HTML, Open Office or Microsoft Office files, including compressed XML-based file formats, such as PPTX or XLSX. It is also possible to write custom rules for parsing a user's own XML-based format.

Currently PSI-Toolkit supports reading of two annotation formats designed externally: `nkjp-reader` processes the TEI encoding format [1] that contains linguistically annotated sentences of the NKJP corpus [11], and `utt-reader` reads a specialised format that results from annotating text with the UTT tools [10]. The readers convert external annotations into the edges of the PSI-Toolkit lattice. This feature enables co-operation of tools designed independently, e.g. a text tokenised within the NKJP corpus may be parsed syntactically by a PSI-Toolkit parser; a sentence parsed by an UTT dependency parser may be displayed by means of the PSI-Toolkit graphical writer; a corpus parsed by the UTT parser may serve for the training of the syntax-based PSI-Toolkit statistical translator.

2.1 Processing the Language of the Text

PSI-Toolkit puts no constraints on the language of the text. It recognises the input encoded in one of the 40 most popular character encoding standards and can automatically convert the text to UTF-8. If no language is specified, a special processor, called `lang-guesser`, tries to recognise the language based on bigram models.

Lang-guesser may be used for the extraction of foreign fragments from a text, as shown in Fig. 2. There, `lang-guesser` creates an edge tagged with the language code `!en`[8], spanning over the English fragment of the text. The option `--tag !en` of `simple-writer` limits the display of the text to fragments labeled with the `!en` tag.

Users may customise the PSI-Toolkit annotators to process the text according to rules specific for a language. For example, setting the `--lang` option to `en` makes the `segmenter` use the sentence-splitting rules specific for the English language.

---

[6] http://utt.amu.edu.pl/files/utt.html.

[7] http://psi-toolkit.wmi.amu.edu.pl/help/psi-format.html.

[8] Tags that begin with an exclamation mark are so-called plane tags [6].

```
Command
lang-guesser | simple-writer --tag !en
```

Input
Die Familie Grimm war in Hanau beheimatet.
Jacob Ludwig Carl Grimm, born on 4 January 1785, was 13 months older than
his brother Wilhelm Carl Grimm.
Obaj bracia byli członkami Akademii Nauk w Berlinie i uczonymi
(językoznawcami), o znacznym dorobku.

Output
Jacob Ludwig Carl Grimm, born on 4 January 1785, was 13 months older than
his brother Wilhelm Carl Grimm.

Fig. 2. Extraction of a fragment written in a specified language.

3 Customizing PSI-Toolkit Processors

This section reports on customising processors, i.e. annotators that add edges to
the PSI-Toolkit lattice. These include spell-checkers, segmenters, taggers, parsers
and translators.

3.1 Spell-Checking

Spell-checking is customised by choosing the language of the input text. Currently, PSI-Toolkit uses the GNU Aspell spell checker[9] and applies its lexicons
that support over 80 languages. Each `aspell` suggestion for an unrecognised
token is converted into a PSI-lattice edge spanning over the token. A user of
the local version of the toolkit may personalise spell-checking by adding new
lexicons either for supported or unsupported languages. Figure 3 shows a PSI-
Toolkit use-case for a spell-checker.

```
Command
tokenize | aspell --lang en
```

Input
I enjoy travleling

Output
I
enjoy
travleling—travelling—traveling—travailing—travellings—ravelling

Fig. 3. A use-case for a spell-checker.

---

[9] http://aspell.net/.

3.2   Tokenization

`Tokenizer` splits texts into tokens according to rules defined in an SRX (Segmentation Rules eXchange[10]) file. PSI-Toolkit supports segmentation for 9 languages (and one default language). Tokenization may be customised by choosing the language and/or the maximum length of the token. A user of the local version may deliver a personalised SRX file (this is done via the `--rules` option of `tokenizer`) either for supported or unsupported languages.

3.3   Sentence-Splitting

`Segmenter` splits texts into segments (i.e. sentences) according to rules defined in an SRX file. PSI-Toolkit supports segmentation for 9 natural languages: Polish, English, German, Italian, French, Spanish, Finnish, Turkish and Russian. For unsupported languages a "default" is assumed. This triggers the most general segmentation rules that work satisfactory for most Indo-European languages. Sentence-splitting may be customised by choosing the language and/or the maximum length of the sentence.

A user of the local version may deliver a personalised SRX file (this is done via the `--rules` option of `segmenter`) either for supported or unsupported languages.

3.4   Lemmatization

PSI-Toolkit supports lemmatisers for 6 languages: Polish, English, German, Italian, French and Spanish. A user of the local version may create and use a personalised lemmatiser. It suffies to deliver the lemmatization rules in the form of three files:

1. the lexicon (in the binary or plain text format),
2. the text file containing part-of-speech information,
3. the text file containing morphological information.

3.5   Tag-Set Conversion

PSI-Toolkit puts no constraints on the format of the information returned by the lemmatiser. It is allowed for different tools called in the same pipeline to operate on different tag-sets. For example, the Polish lemmatiser supported by PSI-Toolkit is based on the `morfologik`[11] tag-set, whereas the deep parser operates on a different tagset developed for Tree-generating Binary Grammar [5]. Still, the two tools may be called in one pipeline using a tag-set converter that maps the tag-sets. The following pipeline draws a resulting syntactic tree for an input sentence:

---

[10] http://www.gala-global.org/oscarStandards/srx/srx20.html.

[11] http://sourceforge.net/projects/morfologik.

```
morfologik | tagset-converter --lang pl | parse | draw
```

The two translation engines supported by PSI-Toolkit 3.7 use different tag-sets. The syntax-based statistical translator [7] may be trained on the tag-set delivered by the default PSI-Toolkit lemmatiser and then needs no tag-set conversion. The rule-based translator, however, works on its own tag-set. `Tagset-converter` substitutes the tags delivered by the PSI-Toolkit lemmatiser with the tags used by the translator.

Users of the local version may specify their own tag-set converter by delivering a personalised set of tag-conversion rules. The *rules* option is used to specify the path to the tag-conversion text file.

The idea that stands behind tag-set conversion is to ensure that any type of annotator might be used within a PSI-pipeline. The annotations returned by an external tool are represented as PSI-lattice edges and the tag-set converter makes them applicable for other annotators.

3.6   Parsing

Parsing in PSI-Toolkit can be customised in two ways: various types of parsers are admissible in the annotating process, and the format of parsing annotation is customisable to various needs.

The first postulate is satisfied thanks to the PSI-lattice data structure. Thanks to the tag-converters a parser in a PSI-pipeline may work on an arbitrary set of tags. Currently PSI-Toolkit supports three different syntactic parsers, the first of them being the adaptation of an external tool:

- *link grammar* parser for English [13],
- shallow parser for Polish and French [9],
- deep parser for Polish [4].

An exemplary output of the link parser displayed in a tree form is shown in Fig. 4. The deep parser returns the whole sentence structure.

Users may customise parsing by choosing the output format. Graphical output formats serve for educational purposes. Various textual formats facilitate further processing. See Sect. 4 for details.

3.7   Translation Tools

PSI-Toolkit provides two machine translation engines: rule-based (named *Transferer*) and syntax-based statistical (named *Bonsai*). The rule-based PSI-Toolkit engine currently carries out translation from Polish into English and Spanish. Users of the local version may specify personal rules to execute rule-based translation between other languages, provided that the rules comply with the PSI-Toolkit format.

The statistical translator is trained on the European Parliament Proceedings Parallel Corpus [8] and performs translation from Polish into English, French,

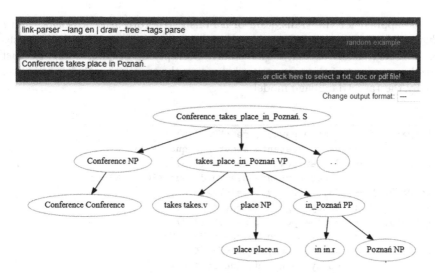

Fig. 4. Link grammar adapted in PSI-Toolkit.

Spanish or Italian. Users of the local version may customise the translator by providing their own translation model in a format of textual translation rules (see Fig. 6).

The **bonsai** translator is a good example of applying several PSI-Toolkit annotators in one task. Figure 5 shows an exemplary translation of a Polish sentence, whose English translation is: *I am sure that the European Union will solve their problems*, into Spanish. Although the final command is simple (**bonsai --lang pl --trg-lang es**), the translation process engages several PSI-Toolkit annotators.

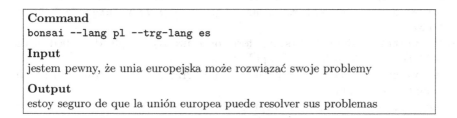

Fig. 5. Bonsai — syntax-based statistical translator.

First, the translation model is trained on texts syntactically annotated by the PSI-Toolkit deep parser. Then, during run time, a source text is segmented, tokenised, lemmatised, tag-converted, and parsed syntactically. For each sentence in turn its parse trees are matched against the right-hand sides of translation rules in the translation model. Figure 6 shows a subset of rules that potentially may be applied for the translation of a Polish structure *Jestem pewny, że VP (English: I am sure that VP)* (rule probabilities are omitted). The final translation of a sentence is obtained by recursive multiplying of translations for each parsed component of the sentence and choosing the translation that is estimated best by the target language model.

```
<VP>(0,8) --> Jestem pewny , że <VP>(4,8)
           :: estoy bastante seguro de que <VP>(4,8)
<VP>(0,8) --> Jestem pewny , że <VP>(4,8)
           :: estoy bastante seguro de que <FC>(4,8) en
<VP>(0,8) --> Jestem pewny , że <VP>(4,8)
           :: estoy seguro de que <VP>(4,8)
<VP>(0,8) --> Jestem pewny , że <VP>(4,8)
           :: estoy seguro de que <VP>(4,8) de
<VP>(0,8) --> Jestem pewny , że <VP>(4,8)
           :: estoy seguro de que la <VP>(4,8)
```

Fig. 6. A subset of translation rules for bonsai.

4 Output Formatting

The results of processing may be returned in various ways according to users' needs. For educational purposes graphical output seems most suitable. For engineering purposes more convenient formats are XML or JSON. Here is the list of the PSI-Toolkit writers:

- `bracketing-writer` tags input text with square brackets (e.g. `(NP[AP[very large] house])`, or with XML tags (e.g. `<np><ap>very large</ap> house </np>`),
- `dot-writer` presents results in a form of a directed graph, described in the DOT language used by the GraphViz software,
- `gv-writer` presents the results in a simple graphical form (directed graph) using GraphViz library,
- `json-writer` returns JSON output,
- `perl-simple-writer` creates a Perl array (used in Perl bindings),
- `psi-writer` displays the content in the PSI format, used for representing the whole PSI-lattice,
- `simple-writer` prints the content of the lattice in a simple, human-readable way.

5   PSI-Toolkit Usage

PSI-Toolkit is distributed in packages for the most popular Linux distributions. Two applications are delivered in each distribution: `psi-pipe` and `psi-service`.

The former serves for using annotators locally as a shell command. The user may easily supplement the PSI-Toolkit pipeline by Unix text utils.

The latter allows users to design their own PSI-Toolkit web services. A service owner may set the PSI-Toolkit to their liking: XML reader may use custom parsing rules, tokenisers and segmenters may operate on SRX rule sets different from original ones, lemmatisers and POS-taggers may use their own lexicons and tagsets, translators may operate on translation rules delivered or supplemented by the owner.

Moreover, PSI-Toolkit processors can be embedded in Perl or Python applications. This is an example that shows how to run the tokeniser inside a Python application:

```
import PSIToolkit
text = 'A short text to lemmatize'
command = 'tokenize --lang en | lemmatize'
psi = PSIToolkit.PipeRunner(command)
result = psi.run(text)
```

6   Conclusions

The paper reports on the rationale standing behind PSI-Toolkit, a customisable and compatible set of linguistic tools. The toolkit provides access to a set of NLP tools that deal mostly with Polish, but also (with lesser extent) with English, French, German, Spanish and Russian.

The main idea of the solution is its extensible architecture that allows for compatibility with other NLP toolkits. The toolkit can process texts in a number of natural languages and character encodings. Input data can be read from various data formats, including formats generated by other toolkits. The tools may be run with several options in order to differentiate the format of input and output. The rules used by individual tools may be supplemented or replaced by the user. Annotators using different tag-sets may co-operate in harmony. Finally, external tools may be incorporated into the PSI-Toolkit environment, and the PSI-Toolkit itself may be a part of Perl or Python application.

The PSI-Toolkit package contains the `psi-service` application, which allows for free-license setting of a new web service. This feature will hopefully give rise to new instances of PSI-Toolkit web services.

Wikipedia lists 43 most popular NLP toolkits[12]. One may expect the number to grow up in near future. Is it possible for a new NLP toolkit to be compatible with existing ones? The paper shows a positive example.

---

[12] https://en.wikipedia.org/wiki/Outline_of_natural_language_processing,   access: 8 August, 2015.

References

1. Bański, P., Przepiórkowski, A.: The TEI and the NCP: the model and its application. In: LREC2010 Workshop on Language Resources: From Storyboard to Sustainability and LR Lifecycle Management. ELRA, Valletta (2010)
2. Bird, S., Klein, E., Loper, E.: Natural Language Processing with Python, 1st edn. O'Reilly Media Inc., Sebastopol (2009)
3. Forcada, M.L., Ginestí-Rosell, M., Nordfalk, J., O'Regan, J., Ortiz-Rojas, S., Pérez-Ortiz, J.A., Sánchez-Martínez, F., Ramírez-Sánchez, G., Tyers, F.M.: Apertium: a free/open-source platform for rule-based machine translation. Mach. Transl. **25**(2), 127–144 (2011)
4. Graliński, F.: Some methods of describing discontinuity in Polish and their cost-effectiveness. In: Sojka, P., Kopeček, I., Pala, K. (eds.) TSD 2006. LNCS (LNAI), vol. 4188, pp. 69–77. Springer, Heidelberg (2006)
5. Graliński, F.: Formalizacja nieciągłości zdań przy zastosowaniu rozszerzonej gramatyki bezkontekstowej. Ph.D. thesis, Adam Mickiewicz University in Poznań, The Faculty of Mathematics and Computer Science, Poznań, supervisor: Zygmunt Vetulani (2007)
6. Graliński, F., Jassem, K., Junczys-Dowmunt, M.: PSI-Toolkit: Natural language processing pipeline. Comput. Linguist. Appl. **458**, 27–39 (2012)
7. Junczys-Dowmunt, M.: It's all about the trees – towards a hybrid syntax-based MT system. In: 4th International Multiconference on Computer Science and Information Technology, Mrgowo, Poland, pp. 219–226 (2009)
8. Koehn, P.: Europarl: a parallel corpus for statistical machine translation. In: Conference Proceedings: The Tenth Machine Translation Summit, vol. 5, pp. 79–86 (2005)
9. Manicki, L.: Płytki parser języka polskiego (eng: A shallow parser for Polish) (2009). supervisor: Krzysztof Jassem
10. Obrębski, T., Stolarski, M.: UAM text tools – a text processing toolkit for Polish. In: Proceedings of 2nd Language and Technology Conference, pp. 301–304 (2005)
11. Przepiórkowski, A., Bańko, M., Górski, R., Barbara, L.T. (eds.): Narodowy Korpus Języka Polskiego. Wydawnictwo Naukowe PWN, Warsaw (2012)
12. Przepiórkowski, A., Bański, P.: XML text interchange format in the national corpus of Polish. In: Proceedings of Practical Applications in Language and Computers PALC, pp. 55–65 (2009)
13. Sleator, D.D., Temperley, D.: Parsing English with a link grammar. Technical report, Carnegie Mellon University Computer Science Technical report CMU-CS-91-196 (1995)
14. Verspoor, K., Baumgartner Jr., W., Roeder, C., Hunter, L.: Abstracting the types away from a UIMA type system. In: From Form to Meaning: Processing Texts Automatically, pp. 249–256 (2009)

Polish Coreference Corpus

Maciej Ogrodniczuk[1]([⊠]), Katarzyna Głowińska[2], Mateusz Kopeć[1],
Agata Savary[3], and Magdalena Zawisławska[4]

[1] Institute of Computer Science, Polish Academy of Sciences, Warsaw, Poland
maciej.ogrodniczuk@gmail.com
[2] Lingventa, Warsaw, Poland
[3] Laboratoire d'informatique, François Rabelais University Tours, Blois, France
[4] Institute of Polish Language, Warsaw University, Warsaw, Poland

Abstract. The Polish Coreference Corpus (PCC) is a large corpus of Polish general nominal coreference built upon the National Corpus of Polish. With its 1900 documents from 14 text genres, containing about 540,000 tokens, 180,000 mentions and 128,000 coreference clusters, the PCC is among the largest coreference corpora in the international community. It has some novel features, such as the annotation of the quasi-identity relation, inspired by Recasens' near-identity, as well as the mark-up of semantic heads and dominant expressions. It shows a good inter-annotator agreement and is distributed in three formats under an open license. Its by-products include freely available annotation tools with custom features such as file distribution management and annotation adjudication.

Keywords: Corpus · Coreference · Mention detection · Anaphora

1 Introduction

One of the main challenges in linguistics is to understand how entities of the language refer to those of the discourse world. Modelling and studying this phenomenon – as many others – is frequently based on corpus annotation. Since discourse world referents are hard to represent, instead of representing reference phenomena directly, one usually builds coreference chains between linguistic entities and considers those chains (or clusters) abstract representatives of referents. Additionally, other coreference-related (non-transitive) relations, such as bridging anaphora, near-identity or quasi-identity (introduced here), find other specific representations in coreference annotation schemas.

Coreference-annotated corpora of considerable size have an increasingly rich bibliography and concern about a dozen languages from several language families (cf. [12, Chap. 3]). In this paper we present one of these resources, the Polish Coreference Corpus (PCC) [12], a large manually annotated corpus of general

The work reported here was carried out within the *Computer-based methods for coreference resolution in Polish texts (CORE)* project financed by the Polish National Science Centre (contract number 6505/B/T02/2011/40).

© Springer International Publishing Switzerland 2016
Z. Vetulani et al. (Eds.): LTC 2013, LNAI 9561, pp. 215–226, 2016.
DOI: 10.1007/978-3-319-43808-5_17

Polish coreference, encoded in an extended format of the National Corpus of Polish – NKJP [20]. Its size is comparable to the anaphora annotation layer of the Polish KPWr corpus [2] but its scope is broader (e.g. coreference links are not restricted to named entities and markables are not limited to heads) and its development methodology includes revision of annotations. With a total number of approx. 540,000 tokens, the PCC is among the largest coreference corpora in the international community, together with Tüba/DZ [5] for German, NAIST Text [6] for Japanese, OntoNotes 2.0 [18] for English, Arabic and Chinese, the Prague Dependency Treebank [10] for Czech and ANCOR [9] for French.

We describe the composition of this (largely balanced) corpus, its annotation process and results, as well as its availability and future work.

2   Text Base of the Corpus

The PCC consists of two subcorpora:

- 1773 "short" texts, i.e. containing 250–350 segments in length, constituting fragments of longer documents (but always full consecutive paragraphs)
- 21 "long" texts – complete documents.

We believe that this composition allows for testing the correlation between length and completeness of Polish text and the nature of its coreferential links.

2.1   Short Texts

"Short texts" are plain text fragments of randomly selected documents (of certain types, to create a balanced representation) from NKJP. For each document, paragraph sequences were also extracted randomly.

Short text types in PCC correspond to NKJP text types and text type representation is similarly balanced, matching the 1-million-word manually annotated subcorpus of NKJP. The number of texts, their size and the distribution of text genres is shown in Table 1.

The subcorpus contains 1773 short texts, 31,136 sentences and 503,981 segments, i.e. approx. 284 segments/text and 18 sentences/text. The average sentence length is 16 segments.

2.2   Long Texts

"Long texts" are complete texts from the so-called Rzeczpospolita Corpus (RC) [19] – press articles retrieved in HTML from the online edition of Rzeczpospolita, one of the most prominent daily newspapers in Poland. The length of the selected texts varies from 1000 to 4000 segments. Collection of data, ultimately converted to plain text, has been performed semi-randomly (with interviews or documents combining a series of short press notes removed from the selection). Based on the metadata present in the original HTML (DZIAL attribute) 7 most common

Table 1. Short text types in PCC

Type of text	Texts	Segments	%
Dailies	459	127,840	25.36
Magazines	406	117,694	23.35
Fiction literature (prose, poetry, drama)	288	80,263	15.92
Non-fiction literature	96	27,743	5.50
Instructive writing and textbooks	100	27,728	5.50
Spoken-conversational	83	25,336	5.02
Internet non-interactive (static pages, Wikipedia)	63	17,734	3.51
Internet interactive (blogs, forums, usenet)	63	17,694	3.51
Misc. written (legal, ads, manuals, letters)	55	15,190	3.01
Spoken from the media	44	12,806	2.54
Quasi-spoken (parliamentary transcripts)	43	12,783	2.53
Academic writing and textbooks	35	10,255	2.03
Journalistic books	19	5492	1.08
Unclassified written	19	5423	1.07
Any	1773	503,981	100.00

text domains in RC were determined and 3 texts representing each domain have been included into PCC. Number of texts and their size in segments are shown in Table 2.

The subcorpus contains 21 texts, 1996 sentences, 36,234 segments, which makes approx. 1725 segments/text and 95 sentences/text. The average sentence length is 18 segments.

Table 2. Long text types in PCC

Domain	Texts	Segments	%
Journalism	3	7078	19.53
Law	3	5915	16.32
Economics	3	5843	16.13
Domestic news	3	5172	14.27
Sport	3	4324	11.93
Culture	3	4113	11.35
Science and technology	3	3789	10.46
Any	21	36,234	100.00

3   Annotation

3.1   Annotation Levels

Extracted texts were automatically annotated with Morfeusz, a morphosyntactic analyser [25], Pantera, a sentence- and token-level segmenter and morphosyntactic tagger [1] and prepared for manual annotation (by means of automatic pre-annotation) with Ruler – a mention and coreference cluster detector [14]. Segmentation and tagging errors were manually corrected only when errors introduced by the automatic tools would make coreference annotation impossible.

3.2   Annotation Procedure

Pre-annotated texts have been evaluated by human annotators. Wherever the automatic annotation was wrong or unavailable, their task was to:

- mark mention borders
- indicate mention heads
- mark quasi-identity relations
- cluster coreferential mentions
- indicate dominant expressions in each cluster (see Sect. 3.3 for details).

For the large majority of the corpus the annotation methodology followed the so-called *series approach* in which each document was first reviewed by one human annotator, and his/her results were further corrected and validated by an adjudicator. This approach is non-standard for the NKJP corpus, where each previously performed annotation task followed a *parallel approach* with two independent annotators reviewing each document and an adjudicator comparing their decisions and solving discrepancies. We performed an annotation experiment [12, Chap. 6.2], which showed that, with equivalent human resources (two annotators and one adjudicator), the series annotation mode yields better results than the parallel annotation mode, as far as mention detection and coreference cluster markup is concerned. Conversely, the annotation of dominant expressions and of quasi-identity links was of a higher quality in the parallel mode. Since the two latter annotation aspects are of lower importance than the two former ones, we believe that the series mode is more appropriate for coreference annotation (but due to budgetary constraints, only one annotator instead of two, and one adjudicator, worked on each text). The final annotation statistics are shown in Table 3 (please see also [13] for a detailed analysis of various linguistic constructs in PCC).

3.3   Annotation Guidelines

The PCC annotation schema and strategies conform with [11]. The scope of annotation covers all nominal groups (NGs) including pronouns, since we consider the difference between an NG and a mention too controversial to be reliably decided in a general case. As far as introducing coreference links is

Table 3. Annotation statistics

Type of text	# mentions	# quasi-identity links	# singleton clusters	# non-singleton clusters
Short	167,679	4699	102,160	17,636
Long	12,562	407	7167	1259
Any	180,241	5106	109,327	18,895

considered, we limit ourselves to those semantic relations which cannot be deduced directly from syntax. Firstly, nominal predicates (*Helena jest dyrektorką.* 'Helena is the principal.') are never linked with their subjects (although, as all other NGs, they are considered mentions). Secondly, unlike in [3,10], an apposition is not viewed as a sequence of coreferent mentions but as one mention only (*Oskarżony, mąż ofiary, ojciec trojga dzieci został dowieziony do sądu.* 'The accused, husband of the victim, father of three children was brought into court.'). Thirdly, like [5,10,22], we mark split NGs as unitary mentions (*To był delikatny, że tak powiem, temat.* 'It was a touchy, so to speak, subject.'). Finally, like [6,16,18,22], we take special care in annotating zero subjects, pervasive in Polish.

We take two coreferential relations into account: the identity (leading to splitting the set of mentions into clusters, i.e. equivalence classes) and – experimentally – the quasi-identity inspired by the concept of near-identity proposed in [21]. The four specific types of quasi-identity relation are: (i) a relation between a pair of mentions of which the second one distorts properties of the object, so that both of them begin to refer to the meta-object, e.g.: *Nie widziała "Przeminęło z wiatrem", ale czytała je.* 'She hasn't seen "Gone with the wind", but she has read it.'; (ii) a relation between a pair of mentions of which the second one is created by distinguishing a given property of the object called by the first reference, e.g.: *Warszawa jest pięknym miastem, ale przedwojenna Warszawa była jeszcze piękniejsza.* 'Warsaw is a beautiful city, but pre-war Warsaw was even more beautiful.; (these expressions refer to the same city, but from different periods); (iii) a relation between the name of the substance and the container in which the substance remains, e.g.: *Zdjął z półki wino i włożył je do koszyka.* 'He put the wine down from the shelf and put it into the basket.'; (iv) a relation between the set (described by pluralia tantum, collectiva, nouns in plural with numerals) and its distinguished element, e.g.: *Rodzice przyszli na zebranie. Jeden z nich poruszył problem agresji wśród dzieci.* 'Parents came to the meeting. One of them touched upon the problem of aggression among children'. However, the annotators were instructed to mark with this notion other close-to-identity relations, which are not characterised by identity or non-identity.

The definition of quasi-identity is interesting in that it allows us to see coreference in terms of a degree of identity rather than as a binary relation. Nevertheless the frequency of quasi-identity links introduced by our annotators, and the inter-annotator agreement are too low in our corpus to consider this relation as reliably annotated. Due to the novel (wrt. Polish) character of our project, all relations different from identity and quasi-identity are outside the scope of annotation: indirect (bridging or associative) anaphora and discourse deixis [5,7,10,17], ellipses (with the exception of zero anaphora), predicative and bound relations [4], split antecedent [5], identity of sense [6], etc.

Besides annotating quasi-identity, other original aspects of our annotation schema are: indicating the dominant expressions in each cluster and marking semantic (rather than syntactic) mention heads.

Dominant expression is the expression that carries the richest semantics or describes the referent the most precisely. The best candidates for dominant expressions are proper names, descriptions of unequivocal reference, or expressions with richest semantics (hyponyms), most likely originally present in annotated texts, but often in inflected form (cluster: *Prezesa PKP* '(of the) CEO of PKP'; *go* 'him'; dominant expression: *Prezes PKP* 'CEO of PKP').

Semantic heads (i.e. the most important word from the point of view of mention's sense) were identified because of the prevalence of semantic information over the mention's structure (cf. *jedna$_{synh}$ z dziewcząt* 'one$_{synh}$ of the girls$_{semh}$').

3.4   Annotation Tools

For the purpose of manual text annotation, two tools were used. The first one was DistSys – an application for managing the distribution process of texts among annotators and adjudicators inspired by the design of a similar tool created for the NKJP annotation [24]. It is a general purpose tool, not focused on any specific type of annotation. It may serve any project if only the annotation task involves distributing text fragments from a central server among a number of annotators, annotating them locally (using some other application) and uploading them back to the central repository.

The second tool used is MMAX4CORE, a heavily modified version of MMAX2 [8], which was used for the annotation task of a single text (when it was acquired by the annotator via DistSys). For the sake of simplicity and annotation speed, many options were removed from the original version of the application while some new features were added, as requested by the annotators (for example the possibility of undoing the last change).

The modifications included a superannotation plugin, which allowed to see the annotation differences between two versions of the same text and easily merge them into one final version. Differences at each level are shown separately: an example of superannotating mention boundaries is depicted in Fig. 1. Each row represents one difference between annotators A and B: the first column describes which mention is relevant to the difference, the second column shows the decision of annotator A, and the third column shows the decision of annotator B. In the second row, we can see that annotator A marked the mention *gorzką czekoladę* 'dark chocolate' (plus) while annotator B didn't (minus) since he decided to mark the complete (discontinued) mention *gorzką czekoladę, ... której połykam od 2–10 kostek dziennie* 'dark chocolate ... 2–10 squares of which I gulp down every day'. With such information, adjudicator needed to double-click the plus or minus depending on the version he agrees with to resolve to difference (B's decision in this case, according to the broad understanding of mention borders as clarified in the annotation guidelines).

Figure 2 presents a similar interface for adjudicating cluster contents. Mentions from each cluster are assigned the same cluster number and colour. For example, two occurrences of mention *gorzką czekoladę* 'dark chocolate' are in the same cluster according to annotation A, and are singletons according to annotation B. A single click on any of these decisions displays their textual context in the main application window while a double click selects the clicked version as the adjudicated one and updates the remaining clustering to match it.

Both DistSys and MMAX4CORE are available for free download at the http://zil.ipipan.waw.pl/PolishCoreferenceTools web page.

Attributes

Mention	A_mentions.xml	B_mentions.xml
[gorzką czekoladę][, której połykam od 2 - 10 kostek dziennie]	-	+
[gorzką czekoladę]	+	-
[pianki i][żelki anyżkowe]	-	+

Refresh	Accept visible version

Fig. 1. MMAX4CORE superannotation window — mention adjudication

Attributes

Mention	A_mentions.xml	B_mentions.xml
[gorzką czekoladę]	cluster 1 (2 occ.)	singleton
[tą 99 %]	singleton	cluster 19 (2 occ.)
[jakieś super słodkie ciasteczka , pianki i] [żelki anyżkowe]	cluster 4 (4 occ.)	cluster 20 (2 occ.)
[nadają]	cluster 4 (4 occ.)	cluster 21 (2 occ.)
[gorzką czekoladę]	cluster 1 (2 occ.)	singleton
[tą 99 %]	singleton	cluster 19 (2 occ.)
[jakieś super słodkie ciasteczka , pianki i] [żelki anyżkowe]	cluster 4 (4 occ.)	cluster 20 (2 occ.)
[nadają]	cluster 4 (4 occ.)	singleton
[nadają się]	singleton	cluster 21 (2 occ.)

Refresh	Accept visible version

Fig. 2. MMAX4CORE superannotation window — cluster adjudication

4 Corpus Availability

Polish Coreference Corpus is freely available for download under the Creative Commons Attribution 3.0 Unported License at: http://zil.ipipan.waw.pl/ PolishCoreferenceCorpus. There are 3 download formats, described briefly below. PCC is also available for browsing online (see Fig. 3) in a modified version of the Brat annotation tool (visualization tweaks were needed for the readability of long coreference chains). For a detailed description, visit the web page.

4.1 Brat

Brat [23] is an online collaborative annotation environment which uses a simple standoff annotation format described at http://brat.nlplab.org/standoff.html. Each text in this format is represented by two files: one containing raw text, the other one with information about mentions (marked as spans of characters in the former file) and relations between them (both coreference and quasi-identity).

4.2 MMAX

The MMAX format is described in the MMAX2 manual (see http://mmax2. net). In this format, each text is stored in 3 files:

- a file with the .mmax extension, storing the text source (named with the original NKJP text identifier) and text type

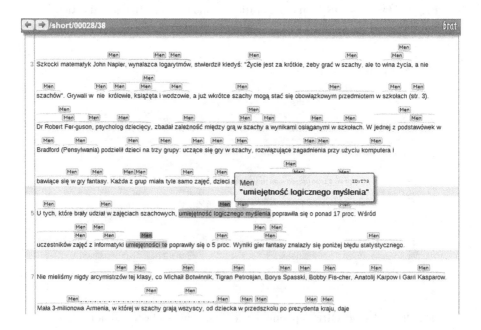

Fig. 3. Online corpus visualisation

```
<!-- umiejętność logicznego myślenia -->
<seg xml:id="mention_8">
  <fs type="mention">
    <f name="semh" fVal="ann_morphosyntax.xml#morph_1.1.23-seg"/>
  </fs>
  <ptr target="ann_morphosyntax.xml#morph_1.1.23-seg"/>
  <ptr target="ann_morphosyntax.xml#morph_1.1.24-seg"/>
  <ptr target="ann_morphosyntax.xml#morph_1.1.25-seg"/>
</seg>
```

Fig. 4. Mention encoding in `ann_mentions.xml`

- a file with the `_words.xml` ending, containing the text segmented into words, enriched with morphological annotation
- a file with the `_mentions.xml` ending with information about mentions (represented as spans of words from the previous file), together with identity and quasi-identity relations between them.

4.3 TEI

The PCC TEI format is an extension of the TEI format of the National Corpus of Polish. In addition to standard files: `text_structure.xml`, `ann_segmentation.xml`, `ann_morphosyntax.xml` and `header.xml` each text in the corpus also has two additional files: `ann_mentions.xml` and `ann_coreference.xml`.

```
<!-- umiejętność logicznego myślenia; umiejętności te -->
<seg xml:id="coreference_0">
  <fs type="coreference">
    <f name="type" fVal="ident"/>
    <f name="dominant" fVal="umiejętność logicznego myślenia"/>
  </fs>
  <ptr target="ann_mentions.xml#mention_8"/>
  <ptr target="ann_mentions.xml#mention_14"/>
</seg>
...
<!-- filharmonia; nowa filharmonia -->
<seg xml:id="coreference_2">
  <fs type="coreference">
    <f name="type" fVal="quasi-ident"/>
  </fs>
  <ptr target="ann_mentions.xml#mention_5"/>
  <ptr type="source" target="ann_mentions.xml#mention_30"/>
</seg>
```

Fig. 5. Identity and quasi-identity encoding in `ann_coreference.xml`

The first file contains all the mentions, annotated as sets of segments from the `ann_morphosyntax.xml` file (similar to the named entity annotation in NKJP). In Fig. 4 we can see mention *umiejętność logicznego myślenia* 'logical thinking ability' marked as a list of 3 pointers to segments in `ann_morphosyntax.xml`, out of which one is the head of the mention (as marked by the feature `<f name="semh">` in the feature structure `<fs name="mention">`).

The second file provides the coreference and quasi-identity cluster information as groups of mentions from the former file. Figure 5 presents the encoding of two relations: coreference identity cluster (containing `mention_8` and `mention_14`) and quasi-identity relation (between `mention_30` and `mention_5`). In the case of identity, the encoding also contains the information about the dominant expression (`<f>` element with "dominant" name attribute).

5   Conclusions and Perspectives

The Polish Coreference Corpus is a large, manually validated resource intended to boost linguistic studies on coreference phenomena, as well as the development of advanced text analysis tools for Polish, most prominently, computer coreference resolvers. By referring to concepts of quasi-identity, dominant expressions and semantic approach to identity-of-reference it may contribute to a high-quality methodology for constructing similar corpora, particularly for other richly inflected languages. Our ongoing work based on corpus data and tools includes experiments with improvement of extractive summarization algorithms by incorporating coreference information into sentence selection procedure and using mention detectors and coreference resolvers in a linguistic chaining environment (see [15]).

Since our current efforts were limited to direct nominal coreference, an obvious direction for further improvements of the corpus is its extension with other types of anaphoric and coreferential relations, such as identity-of-sense, bridging or bound anaphora as well as different types of clustered mentions (e.g. verbal or adverbial constructs, references to relative clauses etc.). Another underexplored topic seems the notion of a dominant expression. We believe that dominant expressions could facilitate cross-document annotation, as well as facilitate the creation of a semantic framework covering different expressions/descriptions of the same object.

As far as coreference-related tools and resources are concerned, their results are much dependent on further development of lower-level tools for Polish such as morphosyntactic analysers (still skipping certain abbreviations, diminutives, slang words etc.), or taggers, directly influencing further processing. New data extraction sources for interpretation of periphrastic (e.g. *Kraj Wschodzącego Słońca = Japonia* 'Land of the Rising Sun = Japan') or knowledge-based expressions (e.g. *mąż Celiny Szymanowskiej = Adam Mickiewicz* 'the husband of Celina Szymanowska = Adam Mickiewicz') seem also urgently needed.

References

1. Acedański, S.: A morphosyntactic brill tagger for inflectional languages. In: Loftsson, H., Rögnvaldsson, E., Helgadóttir, S. (eds.) IceTAL 2010. LNCS, vol. 6233, pp. 3–14. Springer, Heidelberg (2010)
2. Broda, B., Marcińczuk, M., Maziarz, M., Radziszewski, A., Wardyński, A.: KPWr: Towards a Free Corpus of Polish. In: Calzolari, N., Choukri, K., Declerck, T., Dogan, M.U., Maegaard, B., Mariani, J., Odijk, J., Piperidis, S. (eds.) Proceedings of the Eighth International Conference on Language Resources and Evaluation, LREC 2012, pp. 3218–3222. ELRA, Istanbul (2012)
3. Linguistic Data Consortium: ACE (Automatic Content Extraction) Spanish Annotation Guidelines for Entities (2006). https://www.ldc.upenn.edu/sites/www.ldc. upenn.edu/files/spanish-entities-guidelines-v1.6.pdf. Accessed on 28 Aug 2015
4. Hendrickx, I., Bouma, G., Daelemans, W., Hoste, V., Kloosterman, G., Mineur, A.M., Van Der Vloet, J., Verschelde, J.L.: A coreference corpus and resolution system for Dutch. In: Proceedings of the Sixth International Conference on Language Resources and Evaluation (LREC 2008), pp. 144–149. European Language Resources Association (ELRA), Marrakech (2008)
5. Hinrichs, E.W., Kübler, S., Naumann, K.: A unified representation for morphological, syntactic, semantic, and referential annotations. In: Proceedings of the ACL Workshop on Frontiers in Corpus Annotation II: Pie in the Sky, Ann Arbor, Michigan, USA, pp. 13–20 (2005)
6. Iida, R., Komachi, M., Inui, K., Matsumoto, Y.: Annotating a Japanese text corpus with predicate-argument and coreference relations. In: Proceedings of the Linguistic Annotation Workshop (LAW 2007), pp. 132–139. Association for Computational Linguistics, Stroudsburg (2007)
7. Korzen, I., Buch-Kromann, M.: Anaphoric relations in the Copenhagen Dependency Treebanks. In: Proceedings of DGfS Workshop, Göttingen, Germany, pp. 83–98 (2011)
8. Müller, C., Strube, M.: Multi-level annotation of linguistic data with MMAX2. In: Braun, S., Kohn, K., Mukherjee, J. (eds.) Corpus Technology and Language Pedagogy: New Resources, New Tools, New Methods, pp. 197–214. Peter Lang, Frankfurt a.M. (2006)
9. Muzerelle, J., Lefeuvre, A., Antoine, J.Y., Schang, E., Maurel, D., Villaneau, J., Eshkol, I.: ANCOR, premier corpus de français parlé d'envergure annoté en coréférence et distribué librement. In: Proceedings of the 20th Conference Traitement Automatique des Langues Naturelles (TALN 2013), Les Sables d'Olonne, France, pp. 555–563 (2013)
10. Nedoluzhko, A., Mírovský, J., Ocelák, R., Pergler, J.: Extended coreferential relations and bridging anaphora in the Prague Dependency Treebank. In: Proceedings of the 7th Discourse Anaphora and Anaphor Resolution Colloquium (DAARC 2009), pp. 1–16. AU-KBC Research Centre, Anna University, Chennai (2009)
11. Ogrodniczuk, M., Głowińska, K., Kopeć, M., Savary, A., Zawisławska, M.: Interesting linguistic features in coreference annotation of an inflectional language. In: Sun, M., Zhang, M., Lin, D., Wang, H. (eds.) CCL and NLP-NABD 2013. LNCS, vol. 8202, pp. 97–108. Springer, Heidelberg (2013)
12. Ogrodniczuk, M., Głowińska, K., Kopeć, M., Savary, A., Zawisławska, M.: Coreference in Polish: Annotation, Resolution and Evaluation. Walter De Gruyter, Berlin (2015). http://www.degruyter.com/view/product/428667. Accessed on 28 Aug 2015

13. Ogrodniczuk, M., Kopeć, M., Savary, A.: Polish coreference corpus in numbers. In: Calzolari, N., Choukri, K., Declerck, T., Loftsson, H., Maegaard, B., Mariani, J., Moreno, A., Odijk, J., Piperidis, S. (eds.) Proceedings of the 9th International Conference on Language Resources and Evaluation (LREC 2014), pp. 3234–3238. European Language Resources Association, Reykjavík (2014). http://www.lrec-conf.org/proceedings/lrec2014/pdf/1088_Paper.pdf. Accessed on 28 Aug 2015
14. Ogrodniczuk, M., Kopeć, M.: End-to-end coreference resolution baseline system for Polish. In: Vetulani, Z. (ed.) Proceedings of the 5th Language & Technology Conference: Human Language Technologies as a Challenge for Computer Science and Linguistics, Poznań, Poland, pp. 167–171 (2011)
15. Ogrodniczuk, M., Lenart, M.: Web Service integration platform for Polish linguistic resources. In: Proceedings of the Eighth International Conference on Language Resources and Evaluation, LREC 2012, pp. 1164–1168. ELRA, Istanbul (2012)
16. Osenova, P., Simov, K.: BTB-TR05: BulTreeBank Stylebook. BulTreeBank Version 1.0. Tech. Rep. BTB-TR05, Linguistic Modelling Laboratory, Bulgarian Academy of Sciences, Sofia, Bulgaria (2004)
17. Poesio, M., Artstein, R.: Anaphoric annotation in the ARRAU Corpus. In: Proceedings of the Sixth International Conference on Language Resources and Evaluation (LREC 2008). ELRA, European Language Resources Association, Marrakech (2008)
18. Pradhan, S.S., Ramshaw, L., Weischedel, R., MacBride, J., Micciulla, L.: Unrestricted coreference: identifying entities and events in ontonotes. In: Proceedings of the First IEEE International Conference on Semantic Computing (ICSC 2007), pp. 446–453. IEEE Computer Society, Washington, DC (2007)
19. Presspublica: Rzeczpospolita corpus (2013). http://www.cs.put.poznan.pl/dweiss/rzeczpospolita. Accessed on 28 Aug 2015
20. Przepiórkowski, A., Bańko, M., Górski, R.L., Lewandowska-Tomaszczyk, B. (eds.): Narodowy Korpus Języka Polskiego [Eng.: National Corpus of Polish]. Wydawnictwo Naukowe PWN, Warsaw (2012). http://nkjp.pl/settings/papers/NKJP_ksiazka.pdf. Accessed on 28 Aug 2015
21. Recasens, M., Hovy, E., Martí, M.A.: Identity, non-identity, and near-identity: Addressing the complexity of coreference. Lingua 121(6), 1138–1152 (2011)
22. Recasens, M., Martí, M.A.: AnCora-CO: Coreferentially annotated corpora for Spanish and Catalan. Lang. Resour. Eval. 44(4), 315–345 (2010)
23. Stenetorp, P., Pyysalo, S., Topić, G., Ohta, T., Ananiadou, S., Tsujii, J.: BRAT: a web-based tool for NLP-assisted text annotation. In: Proceedings of the Demonstrations at the 13th Conference of the European Chapter of the Association for Computational Linguistics, EACL 2012, pp. 102–107. Association for Computational Linguistics, Stroudsburg (2012)
24. Waszczuk, J., Głowińska, K., Savary, A., Przepiórkowski, A., Lenart, M.: Annotation tools for syntax and named entities in the National Corpus of Polish. Int. J. Data Min. Model. Manag. 5(2), 103–122 (2013)
25. Woliński, M.: Morfeusz - a practical tool for the morphological analysis of Polish. In: Kłopotek, M.A., Wierzchoń, S.T., Trojanowski, K. (eds.) Proceedings of the International Intelligent Information Systems: Intelligent Information Processing and Web Mining 2006 Conference, Wisła, Poland, pp. 511–520, June 2006

Ontologies and Wordnets

GeoDomainWordNet: Linking the Geonames Ontology to WordNet

Francesca Frontini[(✉)], Riccardo Del Gratta, and Monica Monachini

Istituto di Linguistica Computazionale 'A. Zampolli',
Consiglio Nazionale Delle Ricerche (CNR), Pisa, Italy
{francesca.frontini,riccardo.delgratta,monica.monachini}@ilc.cnr.it

Abstract. This paper illustrates the transformation of GeoNames' ontology concepts, with their English labels and glosses, into a Geo-Domain WordNet-like resource in English, its translation into Italian, and its linking to the existing generic WordNets of both languages. The paper describes the criteria used for the linking of domain synsets to each other and to the generic ones and presents the published resource in RDF according to the w3c and *lemon* schema.

Keywords: GeoNames · WordNet · Language resources · Lexicons · Linguistic linked data · *lemon* · RDF

1 Introduction

GeoNames[1] is a well-known and widely used geographical database containing over 10 million geographical names and over 8.3 million unique toponyms, organized in a complex data structure. The GeoNames Ontology[2] contains two kinds of relations: topographic relations, such as "parentCountry", linking for instance a city such as Embrun to the country France, and taxonomic relations, e.g. describing the relation between Embrun and a feature code such as "#P.PPL", which corresponds to the concept of populated place. More specifically all features in GeoNames are categorized into one of nine feature classes and further subcategorized into one of over 600 feature codes. The nine features correspond grossly to administrative subdivisions, hydrological features, areas, populated places, roads, buildings, mountains, underwater landscape features, vegetation.[3]

GeoNames is available as a database dump, and also as Linked Open Data in RDF, meaning that each of the toponyms is identified by a public Uniform Resource Identifier (URI). So information about the town of Embrun will be found at:

http://sws.geonames.org/3020251/about.rdf

---

[1] http://www.geonames.org. [All links and URIs in this paper were last accessed on 08/09/2015].

[2] http://www.geonames.org/ontology/documentation.html.

[3] For more information see also http://www.geonames.org/export/codes.html.

© Springer International Publishing Switzerland 2016
Z. Vetulani et al. (Eds.): LTC 2013, LNAI 9561, pp. 229–242, 2016.
DOI: 10.1007/978-3-319-43808-5_18

Also the categories or feature codes are defined in an OWL ontology[4] and can be referred to by a URI. These URIs can be used to add geographical information to other resources in the semantic web.

GeoNames - although not a lexical resource *per se* - is very important for language technologies as it is often used as a look-up database for many Natural Language Processing (NLP) tasks involving the recognition of geographic named entities. It was used to this purpose in the KYOTO project[5] and later in the GloSS project.[6]

In the framework of GloSS, which addressed issues of data mining for documents containing information related to environmental emergencies for civic protection agencies, it was considered important to build a bridge between terminological resources used (such as WordNets and other domain specific terminologies) and the geographical resource GeoNames. This was meant to facilitate queries for toponyms belonging to a certain category in a specific area, such as "All rivers in Tuscany". In order to do this, it was decided to build the core of a geographic domain WordNet in Italian and English starting from 657 GeoNames categories, or feature codes, and to link it to the generic WordNets in both languages.

In this paper we first present the GeoNames ontology and show how it was transformed into a WordNet-like resource, then we describe how the linking to the generic resources ItalWordNet (IWN) [14] and WordNet (PWN) 3.0 [7] were achieved; subsequently the Resource Description Framework (RDF) formalization of the resource is described and finally the resource is placed within the framework of the Italian and English (Linguistic) Linked Open Data ((L)LOD) cloud. Some possible uses are also presented.

2   Deriving a GeoDomain Terminological Resource from the GeoNames Ontology

2.1   Previous Experiences and Concept

A previous attempt at mapping GeoNames to (Multi)WordNet was carried out as part of the GeoWordNet project [9]. The resulting resource is currently available in RDF.[7] GeoWordNet enriches WordNet using information from GeoNames. A mapping between synsets and feature codes was also performed, and all GeoNames instances of each mapped concept were imported as instance hyponyms in the WordNet structure. So, for instance, the concept "dependent political entity" from GeoNames is mapped onto "synset-dependent_political_entity-noun-1", and all instances of this concept in GeoNames (e.g. Nouvelle-Caledonie, Bouvet Island, . . .) become synsets of this enriched version of WordNet.

---

[4] See current version at http://www.geonames.org/ontology/ontology_v3.1.rdf.

[5] FP7 ICT-211423 funded under the FP7 http://www.kyoto-project.eu - [16].

[6] GloSS is an Italian project, developed to continue the KYOTO Project in a national perspective [8]; its main goal was the semantic annotation and mining of documents in the public security domain.

[7] datahub.io/dataset/geowordnet.

This solution is not entirely convincing for two reasons:

1. ideally one would want to access the complete version of GeoNames from a lexical resource, with all its information (and periodical updates), rather than its reduced version as incorporated into WordNet;
2. the resulting GeoWordNet is a large resource and does not exploit the potential of linked open data, in that it incorporates information rather than linking it.

In addition to this, we wanted to provide an alignment with ItalWordNet, which is not available in GeoWordnet.

Another possible approach, which is more in line with LOD practices, is the automatic mapping of resources - in this case of WordNet and GeoNames, as in [1]; despite the high precision and recall that can be obtained, a manually checked mapping is more appropriate given the size of the ontology and the fact that it does not vary in time.

2.2   GeoDomainWN, the GeoDomain WordNet

Our solution was thus to produce a minimal mapping, namely a mapping between GeoNames concepts (feature codes) and WordNet synsets, thus making the entire structure of the GeoNames accessible via its ontology from the synsets using the linked data paradigm. From the lexicographic point of view named entities, such as localities, should not be included in WordNets unless they have a specific lexical relevance. The mapping to knowledge bases, at the concept level, should connect the concept of, say, "populated place" to lists of populated places outside WordNets (WNs).

In order to preserve the independence and integrity of both resources, the geographic concepts derived from the GeoNames feature codes have been implemented in two independent GeoDomain WordNets, GeoDomainWN, English and Italian, that are linked to WN3.0/IWN respectively on the one side and to GeoNames on the other.

The English resource was created by using the GeoNames ontology, transforming each concept and its gloss into a domain synset and each English label into a lexical entry.

Subsequently the English labels and glosses have been translated into Italian to produce an equivalent Italian resource. The final outcome was two resources with 657 geographic synsets per language. Each synset is constituted of one word only, but the same lexical item can participate in more than one synset. For instance underwater geographic categories often have the same name as above-water ones (for instance "valley"). Therefore these ambiguous lexical entries must be managed according to the WN philosophy that is to say by adding a sense number.

Obviously each domain synset is automatically provided with an external mapping to its corresponding GeoNames category via the feature code. In addition to this a mapping between both the English and the Italian geographical concepts and the respective English and Italian WordNet synsets (from PWN 3.0 and IWN) was manually carried out.

The mapping between existing generic synsets and the newly established geographic synsets produced three different possible outcomes:

1. A perfect mapping, as for instance with "lake, a large inland body of standing water": the GeoNames code "#H.LK" is mapped to the WN3.0 synset 109328904 "a body of (usually fresh) water surrounded by land". In this case a dmgEquivalent ("dmg" stands for Domain Generic Mapping) relationship was created;
2. The domain concept is more specific than the generic synset found as in "mangrove swamp, a tropical tidal mud flat characterized by mangrove vegetation": the GeoNames code, "#H.MGV", with respect to synset 109452395 "low land that is seasonally flooded; has more woody plants than a marsh and better drainage than a bog". In this case a dmgHyponym relation was set;
3. No mappable generic synset was found, as in the case of "section of lake", code "#H.LKX".

In the latter case internal relations are manually inserted in order to ensure that these domain synsets are not isolated nodes, but that they are at least indirectly linked to the generic resource. In the example, "section of lake" is linked to the domain synset of "lake" via a meronymic relation, and thanks to this relation, also indirectly connected to the generic synset of "lake". All non mappable domain synsets are linked indirectly by connecting them other domain synsets. Meronymy relations are manually inserted between features and sections of/parts of features (such as is the case for the domain synset containing "canal bend", that is now a part meronym of the domain synset containing "canal bend"); in other cases hyponymy relations are more appropriate (as is the case for "navigation canal" and "canal").

To improve the consistency of the resource, internal relations were not only added when domain synsets are not mappable directly onto the generic resource, but also systematically in all appropriate cases. On the one hand all domain synsets derived from features containing the strings "section of/part of" were treated as part meronyms of the relevant main feature, and all features containing a modifier were set to be hyponyms of the unmodified feature (the domain synset containing "concession area" is also defined as a hyponym of the domain synset containing "area" although it is also mapped onto a generic synset). On the other hand a manual inspection was carried out to identify other eligible cases (so for instance the domain synset containing "estuary" becomes a part meronym of the domain synset containing "river", but it is obviously also mapped onto the appropriate generic synset).

Overall 306 (see Table 2) internal relations were added for both English and Italian alike, whereas the mapping produced 609 DGM links for English, and 416 for Italian. The resulting resource contains therefore a much more structured set of synsets with respect to the original GeoNames ontology, that grouped features in only nine macro categories and contained no horizontal relations.

Taking domain and generic WordNets together, we can generate a graph that is much richer and better connected. This is an important feature for a resource that is intended to be used in semantic applications, considering that many natural language processing algorithms use graph based approaches, especially in word sense disambiguation [13].

The possible relations within *geosynsets*[8] follow the WN naming conventions. So far three have been implemented, namely:

- partMeronymOf
- hyperonymOf
- hyponymOf

From the theoretical point of view it is important to underline how, in this solution, domain and generic synsets remain independent even when an equivalent relation is set. This is to signify that the former express domain specific concepts, with a precise definition. These synsets may have an almost perfect correspondence to a generic synset but cannot be completely identified with it. At the same time they are also independent from the GeoNames ontology concepts, to which they are also mapped. Such concepts are not language specific, but they are represented by codes (such as "#H.LKX") for which the domain synsets represent a language specific label.

This tripartite model was first introduced in the lexical and conceptual organization of the KYOTO project. Indeed the present work extends a mapping already in place in the KYOTO Named Entity disambiguation functionalities[9] between Geonames categories and PWN synsets. Here the mapping is done systematically for two languages and resulting domain synsets are organized hierarchically, thus adding a structure that is absent from the current GeoNames ontology.

3   Geodomain Resources in RDF

Although still quantitatively a minority within the linked data cloud, the linguistic linked data cloud (L)LOD,[10] [4,5], is growing [11] and becoming a central modality for publishing linguistic data and especially lexical data. Lexicographic data may not always be big in terms of triples, but it is significant in specific weight - especially the resources manually developed/checked, as they contain complex semantic information that has been encoded by humans. The advantage of rendering GeoDomainWN in RDF is its immediate connection to both RDF versions of the English and the Italian WordNets.

---

[8] *geosynset* is, clearly, the synset of the newly created GeoDomainWN. See Sect. 3.2 for the naming conventions.

[9] http://weblab.iit.cnr.it/kyoto/.

[10] http://linguistic-lod.org/llod-cloud.

The RDF version of PWN is an important hub for the English (L)LOD cloud, therefore, thanks to its link to PWN (in its WN3.0 version[11]), the English GeoDomainWN can be indirectly accessible to many other language resources. As for Italian, the already existing RDF version of IWN is the natural target for the domain-generic mapping [2].[12]

In addition, English and Italian GeoDomainWN are parallel resources (see Sect. 2) and WN3.0 and IWN have been already connected, again see [2]. These double connections, together with the connection to the OWL GeoNames in its RDF format, enforce the role that GeoDomainWN resources can play in the (L)LOD cloud.

3.1   Strategy

In this section we describe the strategy used to create a domain WordNet from an human made list of domain lexical entries. Even if the resource is strictly connected to a specific domain, in principle we have to take into consideration the fact that the same lexical entry can belong to different concepts, such as for example the lexical entry "hill" which can be both an underwater and an above ground feature.

Ambiguous lexical entries are managed according to the WN philosophy: by adding a sense. The strategy used to represent the GeoDomainWNs in RDF was as follows:

i Senses and sense numbers are created for ambiguous lexical entries;
ii A name for the synset is defined. According to W3C wn20 schema (described in http://www.w3.org/TR/wordnet-rdf, and followed also in the publications of WordNet3.0 and ItalWordNet), synsets are identified by combining a lexical entry (among those in the synset) with its part of speech and sense[13] cf. Sect. 3.2;
iii Internal relations among domain synsets are then declared, also in accordance with the wn20 schema for both the Italian and the English resource;
iv The domain synsets previously created in (ii) are connected to the corresponding concepts in the GeoNames ontology through the *owl:sameAs* property;
v Domain synsets are finally connected to their corresponding WN3.0 / IWN generic synsets using a specifically defined set of relations called "Domain Generic Mapping", see Sect. 2.2

---

[11] http://purl.org/vocabularies/princeton/wn30/. The 3.1 WN version is now also available in RDF and can be consulted at http://wordnet-rdf.princeton.edu/. Thanks to the mapping between both resources, links to 3.1 could also be derived.
[12] http://datahub.io/dataset/iwn.
[13] See the WordNet documentation at http://wordnet.princeton.edu/wordnet/documentation/.

3.2   GeoDomainWN Naming Convention

To sum up, the unique identifiers for a domain *Synset, WordSense* and *Word*
follow the syntactic pattern defined by the wn20 schema; a prefix `geo` was added
to each identifier to avoid confusion:

`geosynset-[lexicalentry]-[pos]-[sensenr]`

`geowordsense-[lexicalentry]-[pos]-[sensenr]`

`geoword-[lexicalentry]`

For example:

- `geoword-lago` identifies the domain lexical entry "lago" (lake);
- `geowordsense-lago-N-1` identifies the first sense of the domain lexical entry
  lago ("lake");
- `geosynset-lago-N-1` identifies the synset whose list of members contains the
  sense 1 of the lexical entry "lago" (lake).

Therefore, the URIs of the resources corresponding to the main classes are
obtained by combining the basic namespace (hereafter, `BASE`):

`www.languagelibrary.eu/owl/geodomainWN/`

with the language identifier (`ita` or `eng`), the keyword `instances` and the corresponding class identifiers. For example:

`BASE/ita/instances/geosynset-lago-n-1`

is the URI where the geosynset (identified by geosynset-lago-N-1) is accessible
and

`BASE/eng/instances/geosynset-lake-N-1`

is the URI where its English equivalent is accessible.

3.3   GeoDomainWN Dataset Description

Table 1 provides the number of effective *subject-predicate-object* triples.

Since the GeoDomainWN synsets are 1 : 1 mapped onto the GeoNames
ontology, the final resource also contains 657 relations connecting the concepts
using the `owl:sameAs` property. As for the other relations the total counts are
given in Table 2, where the internal relations are WN-like relations defined among
the synsets in the GeoDomainWN resources and the external relations are the
domain-generic links (DGM).

Table 1. Files, units and triples

File	Original units	Triples
synset	657	1,971
wordsenseandwords	657 (wordsenses)	4,781
	632 (words)	

Table 2. Internal and External relations

Resource	Internal relations		External relations	
ItaGDWN	meronymOf	52	DGM	416
	hyperonymOf	254		
	hyponymOf	254		
	Total	560		416
EngGDWN	meronymOf	52	DGM	609
	hyperonymOf	254		
	hyponymOf	254		
	Total	560		609

3.4   GeoDomainWN Synset Example

To sum up and clarify, Listing 1.1 is an example of a complete synset, corresponding to the English domain concept of *lake*. We have used the turtle[14] notation and reported the main prefixes only. The concept of *lake* in GeoDomainWN is mapped on both Princeton WordNet version 3.0 and 3.1.

Listing 1.1. The entry of *lake* and its mapping to WordNet

```
@prefix gn: <http://www.geonames.org/ontology/ontology_v3.1.rdf#> .
@prefix geoenginstances: <http://www.languagelibrary.eu/owl/geodomainWN/eng/
    instances/> .
@prefix wn20schema: <http://www.w3.org/2006/03/wn/wn20/schema/> .
@prefix gdwn: <http://www.languagelibrary.eu/owl/geodomainWN/schema/> .
@prefix wn31: <http://wordnet-rdf.princeton.edu/wn31/> .
@prefix wn30: <http://purl.org/vocabularies/princeton/wn30/> .

geoenginstances:geosynset-lake-N-1
    gdwn:dgmEquivalent wn31:109351810-n, wn30:synset-lake-noun-1 ;
    a wn20schema:NounSynset ;
    rdfs:label"lake"@us-us ;
    owl:sameAs gn:H.LK ;
    wn20schema:containsWordSense geoenginstances:geowordsense-lake-N-1 ;
    wn20schema:gloss"(Hydrographic Feature: a large inland body of standing
        water)"@us-us ;
    wn20schema:hyperonymOf geoenginstances:asphalt_lake-N-1,
    geoenginstances:crater_lake-N-1, geoenginstances:crater_lakes-N-1,
    geoenginstances:intermittent_lake-N-1,
    geoenginstances:intermittent_lakes-N-1,  geoenginstances:
        intermittent_salt_lake-N-1,
    geoenginstances:intermittent_salt_lakes-N-1,
    geoenginstances:lake_bed-N-1, geoenginstances:reservoir-N-1,
    geoenginstances:salt_lake-N-1, geoenginstances:salt_lakes-N-1,
    geoenginstances:underground_lake-N-1 ;
    wn20schema:synsetId"73"@us-us .
```

As you can see from this example, each domain synset is linked to its equivalent in the Geonames ontology by the `owl:sameAs` link. Each synset also points to its sense, and from it, to the lexical entry, following the wn20schema. Moreover, the internal links between domain synsets are made explicit (here for

---

[14] http://www.w3.org/TR/turtle/.

instance the `geosynset-lake-N-1` is described as a hyperonym of more specific `geosynset-crater_lake-N-1`, among others)

Finally and most crucially, the geoDomainWN synset is linked to its generic equivalent synset in PWN version version 3.0 and 3.1 through the relation `dmgEquivalent`. In cases when the domain concept is more specific than its corresponding entry in PWN, the relation `dmgHyponym` is used, as in Listing 1.2.

Listing 1.2. The entry of *mangrove swamp* and its mapping to WordNet

```
@prefix gn: <http://www.geonames.org/ontology/ontology_v3.1.rdf#> .
@prefix geoenginstances: <http://www.languagelibrary.eu/owl/geodomainWN/eng/
    instances/> .
@prefix wn20schema: <http://www.w3.org/2006/03/wn/wn20/schema/> .
@prefix gdwn: <http://www.languagelibrary.eu/owl/geodomainWN/schema/> .
@prefix wn31: <http://wordnet-rdf.princeton.edu/wn31/> .
@prefix wn30: <http://purl.org/vocabularies/princeton/wn30/> .

geoenginstances:geosynset-mangrove_swamp-N-1
    gdwn:dmgHyponym wn31:109475525-n, wn30:synset-swamp-noun-1 ;
    a wn20schema:NounSynset ;
    rdfs:label"mangrove swamp"@us-us ;
    owl:sameAs gn:H.MVG ;
    .....
```

In other cases, as described above, no direct mapping to the generic PWN is possible, not even a hyponymic one; in that case only the links to GeoNames and to other domain concepts are present, as in the following example, where the domain concept of *part of lake* is linked to the domain concept of *lake*, which (see Listing 1.1) is in turn linked to Princeton WordNet, see Listing 1.3.

Listing 1.3. The entry of *section of lake* and its mapping to geosynset *lake*

```
@prefix gn: <http://www.geonames.org/ontology/ontology_v3.1.rdf#> .
@prefix geoenginstances: <http://www.languagelibrary.eu/owl/geodomainWN/eng/
    instances/> .
@prefix wn20schema: <http://www.w3.org/2006/03/wn/wn20/schema/> .
@prefix gdwn: <http://www.languagelibrary.eu/owl/geodomainWN/schema/> .

geoenginstances:geosynset-section_of_lake-N-1
    a wn20schema:NounSynset ;
    rdfs:label"section of lake"@us-us ;
    owl:sameAs gn:H.LKX ;
    wn20schema:containsWordSense geoenginstances:geowordsense-section_of_lake
        -N-1 ;
    wn20schema:gloss"(Hydrographic Feature:)"@us-us ;
    wn20schema:partMeronymOf geoenginstances:lake-N-1 ;
    wn20schema:synsetId"86"@us-us .
```

3.5   GeoDomainWN in *lemon*

lemon (LExicon Model for ONtologies)[15] [12] is a descriptive model that supports the linking up of a computational lexical resource with the semantic information stored in one or more ontologies, as well as enabling the publishing of such lexical resources on the web according to the (L)LOD paradigm. Following the work carried out as part of the Monnet project[16] to create a WordNet

---

[15] http://www.lemon-model.net/.

[16] http://www.monnet-project.eu.

in *lemon* we decided to represent the GeoDomainWN lexical entries also using *lemon*.

The resulting resource (632 units and 6,373 triples) is a collection of *lemon* lexical entries linked to the aforementioned geosynsets. In *lemon* lexical entries are formally equivalent to the *word* in WordNet but contain more details such as the part of speech and the explicit "narrower/broader" relations among *lemon* senses, that mirror the corresponding hypernimic/hyponymic relations between the synsets that constitute their referents.

Moreover it is also possible to add the relation between a specific (*lemon*) sense of the lexical entry and the corresponding synset in PrincetonWordNet, using the same dmgEquivalent/Hyponym relations of the previous examples. Listing 1.4 reports the *lemon* entry for "lake".

Listing 1.4. The *lemon* entry of *lake*

```
@prefix geoenginstances: <http://www.languagelibrary.eu/owl/geodomainWN/eng/
    instances/> .
@prefix lemon: <http://www.monnet-project.eu/lemon#> .
@prefix gdwn: <http://www.languagelibrary.eu/owl/geodomainWN/schema/> .
@prefix wn30: <http://purl.org/vocabularies/princeton/wn30/> .
@prefix wn31: <http://wordnet-rdf.princeton.edu/wn31/> .

<http://www.languagelibrary.eu/owl/geodomainWN/eng/lemon/9/97d/lake>
    lexinfo:partOfSpeech lexinfo:noun ;
    lemon:canonicalForm [
        lemon:writtenRep "lake"@en ;
        a lemon:Form
    ] ;
    lemon:sense <http://www.languagelibrary.eu/owl/geodomainWN/eng/lemon/9/97
        d/lake#lake_1> ;
    a lemon:LexicalEntry .

<http://www.languagelibrary.eu/owl/geodomainWN/eng/lemon/9/97d/lake#lake_1>
    gdwn:dmgEquivalent wn30:synset-lake-noun-1.rdf,wn31:109351810-n.rdf ;
    lemon:broader http://www.languagelibrary.eu/owl/geodomainWN/eng/lemon
        /0/040/lake_bed#lake_bed_1>, <http://www.languagelibrary.eu/owl/
        geodomainWN/eng/lemon/1/1ac/underground_lake#underground_lake_1>,
        ..........
    lemon:reference geoenginstances:geosynset-lake-N-1 ;
    a lemon:LexicalSense .
```

4   Data Distribution

The lexical resources described in this paper are freely available from:

http://www.languagelibrary.eu/owl/geodomainWN

as well as from the *datahub* portal[17]. More specifically, those interested can directly access/download the resources from the following sites:

http://datahub.io/dataset/iwn

---

[17] http://www.datahub.io/.

for ItalWordNet

http://datahub.io/dataset/geodomainwn

for the two GeodomainWNs.

5   GeoDomainWNs Within the Framework of Other LOD Resources

In this section we briefly present the linked data cloud of Italian lexical resources currently made available, and illustrate how the addition of the GeoDomainWN in Italian can enrich the system. For a broader discussion see also [3].

Figure 1 sums up the connections between the Italian (L)LOD cloud. IWN is linked to PWN by the Interlingual Index (ILI) mapping. More specifically, a manual ILI mapping is available between IWN and PWN 1.5 and a semi-automatic mapping is derived between IWN and Princeton WordNet version 3.0 and 3.1.

IWN is also mapped to PAROLE SIMPLE CLIPS (PSC) Italian lexicon [6,10,15], thanks to which IWN synsets are enriched with complex semantic information coming from PSC [2]. In particular the depth of information provided by PSC surpasses that available through IWN, and can be accessed both from Italian and from English, thanks to existing IWN - PWN mapping. The mapping between GeoDomainWN and IWN guarantees that words contained in the former resource can inherit information from the latter.

Although a direct linking between SIMPLE senses (known as *Usems*) in different languages is not currently available, it is imaginable that it might be automatically attempted by combining an automatic translation of the corresponding lexical form and the disambiguation that is provided by the common ontological concepts.

Finally, the newly established linking to GeoNames connects the other Italian resources to the rest of the linked data cloud, e.g. the word "lago" (lake) is connected to the GeoNames ontology concept "#H.LK", and via the concept, to all instances of "lake" listed in GeoNames. Most specifically the linking to GeoNames offers possible applications for Named Entity Recognition and data mining: for example in order to solve the (Italian) (unambiguous) query such as "Trova tutti i laghi in Italia" (Select all lakes in Italy), the system can:

i access from the lemma to the generic synset for "lago" (lake);
ii access via the latter to the domain synset for "lago" (lake);
iii retrieve the equivalent GeoNames code - "#H.LK";
iv query GeoNames for all instances having that code that are found in the relevant area, namely all lakes that are located within the administrative boundaries of Italy.

Besides the specific case of question answering, this model can be used to improve on the kind of information can be annotated and disambiguated on a

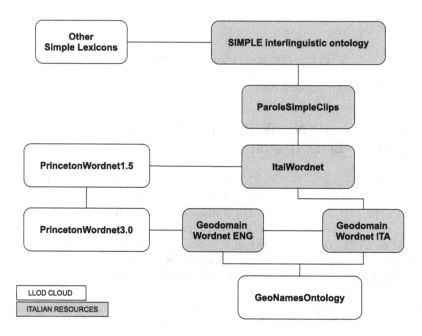

Fig. 1. The linguistic linked data network for Italian

text. Imagine for instance a NLP pipeline with WSD and Named Entity Recognition (NER) modules, assigning synsets to content words and disambiguating named entities with links to Geonames. If no mapping is present a mention of "Italia" would receive both a Geonames reference and a synset, since that word is also an entry in IWN. On the contrary the small Italian hamlet of "Navacchio" would point to no synset, but only be annotated with its Geonames code. Of course Geonames would categorize this as "populated place", but such information woud be totally disconnected from the net of linguistic concepts of WordNet.

Consider that many WSD algorithms [13] use a graph based approach to disambiguate, analyzing the paths between potential synsets in each context. The mention of "Navacchio" would produce no useful information for WSD. In our scenario instead, each mention of an entity can be connected via its feature code to a synset; this means that GeoNames and WordNet can be browsed as one connected graph, and graph based approaches can be successfully applied both for word sense and named entity disambiguation.

6 Conclusion and Future Work

In this paper we have presented GeoDomainWN, a resource in English and Italian containing important links to the available linguistic linked data and connecting them to the rest of the linked data network. In particular for Italian they provide an enrichment to the already existing Italian (Linguistic) Linked

Open Data cloud, and this has particular relevance for those who wish to build applications for information extraction and reasoning.

These two resources have been built by adhering to the principles of linked open data, that is linking together existing resources when available, thus guaranteeing that the linked concepts are always updated. The resource is light and easily accessible via URIs.

ILC-CNR will continue to maintain the resource, in particular checking for mappings to new versions of PWN and IWN, as well as importing new Geonames features as they are added in the new releases of the Geonames ontology. Future work will make the two resources, now available as a RDF dump, also searchable from a SPARQL endpoint, together with the rest of the Italian (L)LOD resources powered by ILC-CNR.

Acknowledgements. The work described in this paper was partly funded by GloSS, a Regione Toscana funded project (Bando Unico R&S anno 2008 - linea A).

References

1. Ballatore, A., Bertolotto, M., Wilson, D.C.: Linking geographic vocabularies through wordnet. Ann. GIS **20**(2), 73–84 (2014)
2. Bartolini, R., Del Gratta, R., Frontini, F.: Towards the establishment of a linguistic linked data network for Italian. In: Proceedings of the Workshop on Linked Data in Linguistics (LDL 2013) (2013)
3. Bartolini, R., Del Gratta, R., Frontini, F.: Towards the establishment of a linguistic linked data network for Italian. In: Proceedings of the 2nd Workshop on Linked Data in Linguistics, pp. 76–81 (2013)
4. Chiarcos, C.: Linked Data in Linguistics. Springer, Heidelberg (2012)
5. Chiarcos, C., Hellmann, S., Nordhoff, S.: Towards a linguistic linked open data cloud: the Open Linguistics Working Group. TAL **52**(3), 245–275 (2011)
6. Del Gratta, R., Frontini, F., Khan, F., Monachini, M.: Converting the PAROLE SIMPLE CLIPS Lexicon into RDF with lemon. Semant. Web J. **6**(4), 387–392 (2015)
7. Fellbaum, C.: WordNet. In: Poli, R., Healy, M., Kameas, A. (eds.) Theory and Applications of Ontology: Computer Applications, pp. 231–243. Springer, Netherlands (2010)
8. Frontini, F., Aliprandi, C., Bacciu, C., Bartolini, R., Marchetti, A., Parenti, E., Piccinonno, F., Soru, T.: GloSS, an infrastructure for the semantic annotation and mining of documents in the public security domain. In: Proceedings of EEOP 2012: Exploring and Exploiting Official Publications Workshop Programme, pp. 21–25 (2012)
9. Giunchiglia, F., Maltese, V., Farazi, F., Dutta, B.: GeoWordNet: a resource for geo-spatial applications. In: Aroyo, L., Antoniou, G., Hyvönen, E., ten Teije, A., Stuckenschmidt, H., Cabral, L., Tudorache, T. (eds.) ESWC 2010, Part I. LNCS, vol. 6088, pp. 121–136. Springer, Heidelberg (2010)
10. Lenci, A., Bel, N., Busa, F., Calzolari, N., Gola, E., Monachini, M., Ogonowski, A., Peters, I., Peters, W., Ruimy, N., Villegas, M., Zampolli, A.: SIMPLE: a general framework for the development of multilingual lexicons. Int. J. Lexicography **13**(4), 249–263 (2000)

11. Lezcano, L., Sanchez, S., Roa-Valverde, A.J.: A survey on the exchange of linguistic resources: publishing linguistic linked open data on the Web. Program: Electron. Libr. Inf. Syst. **47**(3), 263–281 (2013)
12. McCrae, J., Spohr, D., Cimiano, P.: Linking lexical resources and ontologies on the semantic web with lemon. In: Antoniou, G., Grobelnik, M., Simperl, E., Parsia, B., Plexousakis, D., De Leenheer, P., Pan, J. (eds.) ESWC 2011, Part I. LNCS, vol. 6643, pp. 245–259. Springer, Heidelberg (2011)
13. Navigli, R., Lapata, M.: An experimental study of graph connectivity for unsupervised word sense disambiguation. IEEE Trans. Pattern Anal. Mach. Intell. **32**(4), 678–692 (2010)
14. Roventini, A., Alonge, A., Bertagna, F., Calzolari, N., Girardi, C., Magnini, B., Marinelli, R., Zampolli, A.: ItalWordNet: building a large semantic database for the automatic treatment of Italian. In: Computational Linguistics in Pisa, Special Issue, XVIII-XIX, Pisa-Roma, IEPI 2, pp. 745–791 (2003)
15. Ruimy, N., Corazzari, O., Gola, E., Spanu, A., Calzolari, N., Zampolli, A.: The European LE-Parole project: the Italian syntactic Lexicon. In: Proceedings of the First International Conference on Language resources and Evaluation, pp. 241–248 (1998)
16. Vossen, P., Bosma, W., Agirre, E., Rigau, G., Soroa, A.: A full knowledge cycle for semantic interoperability. In: Fang, A., Ide, N., Webster, J. (eds.) Proceedings of the 5th Joint ISO-ACL/SIGSEM Workshop on Interoperable Semantic Annotation, in conjunction with the Second International Conference on Global Interoperability for Language Resources (ICGL 2010), Hong Kong, 15–17 January 2010

Building Wordnet Based Ontologies
with Expert Knowledge

Jacek Marciniak[✉]

Faculty of Mathematics and Computer Science, Adam Mickiewicz University,
ul. Umultowska 87, 61-614 Poznań, Poland
jacekmar@amu.edu.pl

Abstract. The article presents the principles of creating wordnet based ontologies which represent general knowledge about the world as well as specialist expert knowledge. Ontologies of this type are a new method of organizing lexical resources. They possess a wordnet structure expanded by domain relations and synsets ascribed to hierarchical structures representing general domain and local-context conceptualizations. Ontologies of this type are handy tools for indexers and searchers working on massive content resources such as internet services, repositories of digital images or e-learning repositories.

Keywords: Wordnet based ontologies · Indexing and searching resources

1 Introduction

Contemporary IT systems, which collect and share knowledge resources such as internet services, repositories of digital images or repositories of e-learning content, require effective tools to support indexing and resource searching. One such method, particularly popular in Web 2.0 (blogs, wiki, etc.), is tagging with lexis and expressions arbitrarily selected by the indexer [16]. In an attempt to make indexing and searching more precise so-called enhanced tagging systems introduced mechanisms to display words similar and related to keywords typed by users in search engine's input field [13]. Thus, while indexing the resource users can select keywords more adequate than originally planned. Similarly, it is possible to surf a repository with reference to semantic fields for keywords typed.

If a system is aimed at wider audiences it faces additional challenge of the necessity to support users who are not experts in a subject. This means that indexing and searching tools created for experts such as e.g. controlled vocabularies may prove inadequate. This is due to the fact that a user, not being an expert in an area, while searching a repository will formulate queries unaware of conceptualizations already made and shared by experts. The user will refer to conceptualization which stems from his/her general knowledge. This does not mean, however, that expert knowledge should be disregarded. It should be integrated into used tools so that users can easily share and make use of it when necessary.

For all these objectives to be achieved it is necessary to equip an information system with vocabulary interconnected in relations to enable suggesting similar and related

© Springer International Publishing Switzerland 2016
Z. Vetulani et al. (Eds.): LTC 2013, LNAI 9561, pp. 243–254, 2016.
DOI: 10.1007/978-3-319-43808-5_19

words and expressions. This article presents an approach in which such vocabulary creates lexical ontology, expanded with expert knowledge. A central point in this solution is wordnet-like lexical database (or wordnet). Thus, the ontology contains conceptualization of the world co-shared by language users. Expert knowledge is expressed through additionally introduced domain relations between synsets and by synset mapping in domain categories that are used to create hierarchical structures of concepts replicated from thesauri or local-context hierarchies built by domain experts to satisfy the needs of a given repository.

The presented method was developed and verified while building two wordnet based ontologies, i.e. Old Polish History and Culture ontology and Protection and management of archaeological heritage ontology. The algorithm for creation of ontologies of this type is based on a bottom-up approach, i.e. it allows to integrate into the ontological structure concepts indispensable for indexation of given resources, and not merely concepts that are available for example in an existing thesaurus. The processed concepts are described under proper names but also they are highly specialized terms resulting from specialization of resources being indexed.

2   Other Approaches for Indexing and Searching Resources

Methods to support resource indexation and searching include classification and thesaurus use [1]. These methods are representative of indexing languages serving as a tool to describe documents in terms of subject content. Indexing languages are glossaries, dictionaries, subject headings systems, bibliographic classifications, taxonomies, classification schemes, semantic networks or ontologies [5, 15].

A universally used method of classification is this using symbols (combination of numbers and letters), in which classification is done by assigning a symbol to a resource being classified. Such systems are e.g. Universal Decimal Classification (UDC), a bibliographic and library classification or IconClass, a classification system popular in museums designed for art and iconography [7]. Classification systems always reflect an expert's point of view.

Thesauri are tools designed to be used in situations when it is possible to impose controlled vocabulary on users. They are particularly useful in indexing resources by experts and in situations when vocabulary contained in a thesaurus fully covers a given area of knowledge. This last condition is difficult to meet. The essence of thesauri is that they describe an area of knowledge from a standpoint of a group of experts [14].

3   Domain Conceptualizations

3.1   Conceptualization in Thesauri and Lexical Databases

An important feature of contemporary thesauri is that terms contained within are connected by means of relationships [1]. The latest specification for creation of thesauri – ISO 25964 – lists three types of relationships: equivalence (synonymy and near-synonymy), hierarchical (broader and narrower concepts), and associative (to show that concepts are closely related). These relationships allow the user to gain access to similar terms while indexing and searching. Figure 1 shows a typical hierarchy expressed as a genus/species relationship in thesaurus Getty AAT [4][1].

Visual Works (Hierarchy name)
[G] visual works, visual work
  [G] <visual works by subject type>
   [G] portraits, portrait
    [G] chinzo
    [G] clipei
    [G] companion portraits, companion portrait
    [G] composite portraits, composite portrait
    ....
    [G] self-portraits, self-portrait

Fig. 1. Hierarchy for portrait in Getty AAT Thesaurus

Conceptualization is realized in Getty AAT by means of three different components: concepts (terms), facets and nodes in hierarchy. The terms are interconnected or are connected to facets (see: <visual works by subject type>) by means of a relationship genus/species [G]. Facets are a major subdivision of AAT hierarchical structure. In the tree also hierarchy names (nodes) are marked off (see: Visual Works or portraits).

Concepts create hierarchies also in wordnet-like lexical databases and in some dictionaries. Figure 2 shows a hierarchy for the concept portrait in WordNet 2.0c, and Fig. 3 in WordNet 3.1. Figure 4 shows a hierarchy in the Universal Polish Dictionary (Uniwersalny słownik języka polskiego). In the examples relationship H is a relationship hyperonym/hyponym. The examples show that hierarchies and conceptualizations can be very different, e.g. in Wordnet 3.1 the concept portrait has a different definition and is linked to a totally different hierarchy than in Wordnet 2.0c. The conceptualization in the Universal Polish Dictionary seems to combine approaches to conceptualization as presented in examples for WordNets. In this case the word portrait is linked to two hyperonyms: dzieło sztuki (work of art) and wyobrażenie (image/likeness).

[H] art:1
 [H] graphic art:1
  [H] painting:1
   [H] portrait:1 ("a painting of a persons's face")
    [H] self-portrait:1 ("a portrait of yourself created by yourself")

Fig. 2. Hierarchy for portrait in WordNet 2.0c

---

[1] Getty AAT is a structured vocabulary (ca. 51 000 concepts) providing terminology from art, architecture, and material culture.

[H] picture:1
 [H] likeness:2
  [H] portrait:2 ("any likeness of a person, in any medium")
   [H] self-portrait:1 ("a portrait of yourself created by yourself")
   [H] half-length:1

Fig. 3. Hierarchy for portrait in WordNet 3.1

[H] dzieło sztuki (work of art)
 [H] wyobrażenie (image/likeness)
  [H] portret (portrait)
   [H] autoportret (self-portrait)
   [H] karykatura (caricature)
   [H] portret pamięciowy (sketch)

Fig. 4. Hierarchy for portrait in Universal Polish Dictionary

The demonstrated differences in conceptualization of identical concepts are a result of differences in the level of specificity adopted by the authors, of subject competence (or its lack) of the lexicographer developing a given fragment of hierarchy, or simply of error. The differences may also arise from varying approaches to conceptualization of an individual domain among different experts, cultural or social differences, etc. [6, 8, 14].

3.2 Need of Local-Context Conceptualization

Approaches to conceptualization presented above show that a method of conceptualization is related to competence of experts. Hierarchies may be created on several levels with reference to various components (hierarchy nodes, concepts, facets, synsets). Thus a question arises whether in a situation when selecting vocabulary for indexing a definite resource (collection of texts, e-learning contents, collection of digital images, etc.) reference should be made only to a conceptualization of a field developed by one group of experts and contained in a shareable thesaurus or other indexing language? Or should the expert or experts working with a given resource be provided with an indexing tool which will take into account 'local' conceptualization of an area of knowledge? What should the structure be of such resource?

These questions are particularly important in a situation in which an expert is supposed to index resources of a specialist repository with the help of a thesaurus or other indexing language which has already been created, but which does not fully meet the requirements, that is does not possess the required vocabulary. Deficient terminology leads to a major problem: the indexer, faced with the absence of a right entry will either choose a concept more generalized to the detriment of indexing quality, or will use a right one but from beyond the thesaurus. This problem applies in general to the usage of controlled vocabularies for indexing due to the fact that indexers always tends to use it in arbitrary ways [6, 10]. Some researchers point out that for this reason there is no guarantee that the usage of an existing indexing language will allow to describe subject of resources in the different repositories in a uniform manner [6, 9].

Another problem appears when an expert has a set of vocabulary (e.g. a set of tags used in indexing) and wishes to arrange it in a hierarchical structure. It may then turn out that any attempt at mapping such vocabulary into existing hierarchical conceptualizations may prove difficult due to absence of nodes in the existing hierarchy (e.g. absence of adequate facets in thesaurus), which will correctly – in the expert's opinion – conceptualize the area of knowledge. To solve the problem of arranging available vocabulary to tackle local-context needs and to preserve at the same time the external domain conceptualizations replicated from thesauri or other indexing languages our suggestion is to create multiple domain conceptualizations within wordnet based ontologies with the use of domain categories.

4 Structure of Wordnet Based Ontology with Expert Knowledge

Structure of a wordnet based ontology extends the structure of wordnet by a possibility to express domain and expert knowledge [13]. It contains the following types of relationships:

- Synsets and lexical relations between synsets taken from wordnet-like lexical databases
- Linking synsets with Top Concept Ontology
- Linking synsets with hierarchical conceptualizations replicated from thesauri or built by domain experts to satisfy the local-context needs
- Domain relations between synsets.

Synset is a set of words with the same-part-of-speech which can be used interchangeably in a certain context [2]. Lexical relations between synsets are relations such as hyponymy, antonymy, holonymy, near synonymy, etc. but also relations connecting individual entities (instances) and classes – belongs to class relation [17]. This last relation is particularly important because in ontologies based on tags, proper names occur quite frequently (family names, geographical names, names of towns and villages, etc.). Top Concept Ontology is a hierarchy of language-independent concepts, reflecting important semantic distinctions, e.g. Object and Substance, Location, Dynamic and Static [17]. Connecting synsets to top concepts allows determining the character of a concrete synset in isolation from its specific field conditions [3]. Ontologies such as CYC, SUMO, DOLCE, etc. may be used as Top Concepts Ontology.

In wordnets synsets can be also attributed to semantic domains. For example in WordNet all verbs can be subdivided into 14 semantic domains, in EuroWordnet synsets can attributed to domain labels which are intended to group meanings by taking into consideration the needs of field [2, 17]. It was pointed out in EuroWordnet that domain labels may be hierarchized, however the principles of hierarchy making were not analyzed.

In the presented approach domain conceptualizations (domain ontologies) are created with so-called domain categories (DC). Expert knowledge may express general and/or local domain conceptualizations. Thus two kinds of domain conceptualizations may be distinguished:

- General domain conceptualization, or general hierarchy borrowed from already existing thesaurus or other hierarchical conceptualization,
- Local-context conceptualization, or hierarchy created by an expert who is indexing resources in order to arrange vocabulary in his/her possession.

When hierarchy from an existing thesaurus is used components from the thesaurus hierarchy such as hierarchy node, facets and certain concepts will become nodes in domain categories hierarchy. In the case of local context ontology nodes will be built by experts from scratch to encompass local needs. Synsets are linked to domain categories via an introduced relation domain_category/domain_representant. Figure 5 shows a conceptualization of the concept portrait in the Old Polish History and Culture ontology. In the example a word portrait is mapped into two hierarchies. One is of linguistic origin and was built with a relation hyperonymy/hyponymy (has_hyperonym relation). The other was developed by domain experts and built with the use of domain categories. This local-context conceptualization possesses a level of specificity matching the resources it refers to. The example shows that for works of art hierarchy (sztuki plastyczne/visual arts node) is flatter (deprived of at least one level) than presented above general domain conceptualizations. This results from the fact that local-context conceptualization arrange in a hierarchy vocabulary not just from one field of art (other areas may be customs or military); therefore simplifications are tolerated or even expected by domain experts.

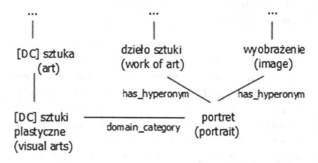

Fig. 5. Hierarchy for portrait in Old Polish History and Culture ontology

Domain relations between synsets are relations absent from wordnets. This absence results from the assumption that wordnet contains no relations that indicate the word's shared membership in a given topic of discourse [2]. This means that wordnet does not have direct relations linking words which in a certain context are naturally connected (e.g. king and crown). This limitation is known as the tennis problem (there is a lack of relations linking the racquet, ball, net and court game) [2]. Such limitation is too powerful in systems in which similar or related words are requested [13]. Relations between words of this type contain a great deal of useful information on possible directions in resource searching.

Domain relations between synsets may be defined in many different ways, depending on the character of a created ontology. As in the presented approach a certain part of relations is separated as wordnet relations between synsets, it is assumed that domain relations will have an associative character, similarly to norm ISO 25964 determining thesaurus structure. Synsets will be linked via relations of the type is_related_to. Individual subtypes of relations may be marked as the need arises. For example in Old Polish History and Culture Ontology two subtypes of relations are listed: attribute and link. Each of them denotes a different level of similarity between concepts (see below). Whether the relations will be marked off and how numerous they will be in a given ontology depends on the needs, e.g. how individual relations are related to similarities between synsets.

5   Algorithm

The algorithm for creating a wordnet based ontology with expert knowledge assumes the bottom-up approach. This means that ontology is built for the existing set of words which were used to tag resources, or that such a list was made based on frequency dictionary built for words and expressions collected from a set of digital resources (corpus) considered as representative for a given domain.

The steps for creation of an ontology are presented below. It is assumed that prior to building ontology, a local-context conceptualizations and general domain conceptualizations are built with the appropriate set of domain categories. Using an existing wordnet-like lexical database is also allowed. If such a resource is not available, its corresponding fragments will be built during the construction process. It is also indispensable to have a monolingual dictionary (further called reference dictionary).

For the next word from the list of words:

1. Map the word to synset in wordnet:
   a. Find all synsets for the word in wordnet
   b. If synsets are found, choose the most adequate. To do that, for each synset:
      i. analyze gloss
      ii. analyze hyperonyms and hyponyms for synset
      iii. analyze other relations for synset
   c. If no synset is found:
      i. go to reference dictionary and find word that is closest in meaning, create a synset
      ii. link the created synset in a hyponymy/hyperonymy relation to other synsets in the ontology
      iii. link the created synset by means of other lexical relations according to expected wordnet structure
      iv. if in the ontology there is no synset which is to be hyponym/hyperonym follow step 1c (doing step 1.c omit step 1.c.iv).
2. Add domain relations to synset:
   a. check that ontology contains synsets that you want to link to a given synset by means of domain relations; if not, do step 1.c

    b. add relation is_related_to between synsets
    c. if domain relation type is available add it to relation is_related_to.
3. Add synset to local-context conceptualization:
    a. find all domain categories to which this synset should be linked
    b. connect synset to appropriate domain category by means of relation domain_category.
4. Add synset to general domain conceptualization:
    a. check if the word can be found as a term in the thesaurus used to create general domain conceptualization
    b. if the word is in plural form in the thesaurus add the plural form to synset
    c. connect synset by means of relation domain_category to a domain category created as an equivalent either to the term being a node in the thesaurus hierarchy, or the facet to which the term corresponding to the word is connected with; if the term corresponding to the word is a node in the thesaurus hierarchy connect synset with a domain category created as an equivalent to this term
    d. if the term corresponding to the word is connected in the thesaurus with other terms by means of associative relations, do steps 2.

This algorithm is bottom-up and develops horizontally. The former means that the algorithm aims to include all the available words into ontology. It does not aim to incorporate into ontology all the terms from thesaurus in use because they will not be used in the analyzed context. The algorithm develops horizontally because it expands ontology in those fragments in which a new synset is included in ontology (see step 1.c.ii). In this way candidates for similar terms are introduced.

The algorithm refers to the algorithm for creating wordnets introduced by Vetulani et al. [18] because it is designed for creating ontologies manually and not quasi-automatically. This approach is designed for experts, therefore ontology is meant to express knowledge obtained from them. In the presented algorithm step 1.c can be fully replaced by algorithm presented by Vetulani et al. [18].

The algorithm in the presented form can be used to link any thesaurus to a wordnet based ontology and to domain conceptualizations contained within (Fig. 6). Thus a domain expert can supplement the ontology with the required vocabulary, simultaneously preserving thesaurus hierarchy as one of domain conceptualizations built with the use of domain categories.

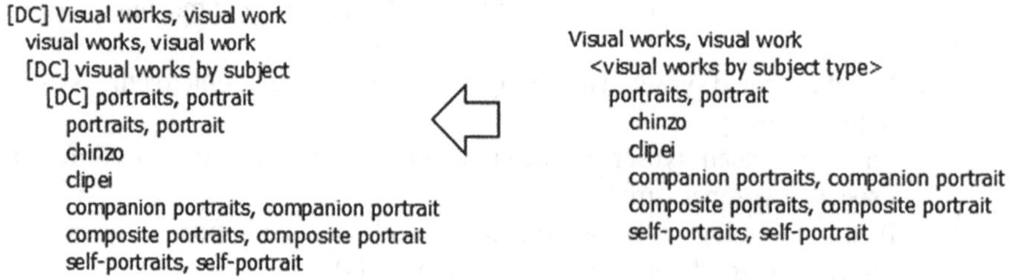

Fig. 6. Mapping thesaurus on wordnet based ontology

6 Verification of the Mehod

The method of creating wordnet based ontologies with expert knowledge was verified in the process of building two ontologies. In both cases ontologies were built on the bases of sets of tags used by experts for tagging specialist resources. The created ontologies were then used to create enhanced tagging systems.

6.1 Old Polish History and Culture Ontology

The Old Polish History and Culture is an ontology built on the base of 5434 words and expressions which were used on the Wilanów Palace Museum vortal to tag resources (around 3000 articles from the field of Polish history and culture). The tagging was designed in a way which allowed assigning a desired number of tags to each article. Among the words and expressions there were proper names, family names, geographical names and dates.

In the process of creating the ontology following the algorithm presented above the initial set of tags was widened by around 1300 new words and expressions. Newly introduced words expanded the ontology in accordance with the bottom-up approach, i.e. to the primary set of tags new ones were added with a broader/narrowed meaning. Furthermore, words were added as a result of application of domain relations. The ontology was not created on the base of any wordnet, therefore wordnet relations were introduced into the ontology in accordance with the algorithm. The reference dictionary in this ontology was the Universal Dictionary of the Polish Language. In the ontology two types of relations of associative type are distinguished [13]:

- Attribute
- Link.

The relation of the attribute shows a strong relationship between two words or expressions within the framework of the same field. In the ontology this relation was used to describe the connection between events (e.g. battles), their dates, venues and connected persons. Similarly for places (e.g. Wilanów), their relation with people was presented (e.g. Jan III Sobieski). Figure 7 shows a fragment of ontology for the event Vienna battle.

Domain experts connected all the synsets making up the ontology to 378 domain categories by means of a relation of the type domain_category. Domain categories were connected hierarchically and created a local-context conceptualization, reflecting the needs of the museum to conceptualize the vocabulary possessed, and, indirectly, the content collected on the museum vortal. Since an earlier solution on the museum vortal presented tags grouped in five different (flat) indexes, the new ontology retained this approach. Therefore, highest in the local-context hierarchy were five domain categories which acted as five indexes: subject, people, important places, geographical and chronological (Fig. 8).

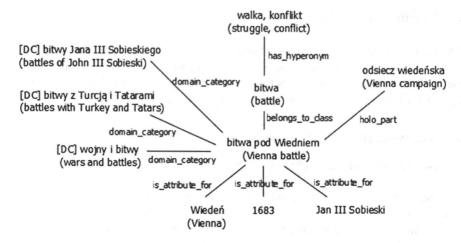

Fig. 7. Relations for Vienna battle

[Index] rzeczowy (subject)
  [DC] sztuka (art)
    [DC] sztuki plastyczne (visual art)
      fresk, al fresco (fresco)
      portret (portrait)
      ...
  [DC] wojskowość (army)
    [DC] wojny i bitwy (wars and battles)
      bitwa pod Wiedniem (Vienna battle)
      ...
[Index] ważne miejsca (important places)
  [DC] rezydencje, pałace (residences, palaces)
  [DC] pola bitewne (battle fields)
    [DC] bitwy Jana III Sobieskiego (battles of John III Sobieski]
      bitwa pod Wiedniem (Vienna battle)

Fig. 8. Local-context conceptualization hierarchy in Old Polish History and Culture ontology

6.2 Protection and Management of Archaeological Heritage Ontology

Protection and management of archaeological heritage ontology (PMAH ontology) was built to satisfy the requirements of tagging e-learning content in the repository of e-learning content in the field of protection and management of archaeological heritage [11]. This ontology is built of approximately 1500 tags and 150 categories. Wordnet relations were built based on PWN relations. Among domain relations only relation of the link type was considered. Local-domain conceptualization was built in accordance with conceptualization developed by a group of experts who were tagging e-learning content (env 1000 learning objects) in the field of protection and management of archaeological heritage. A fragment of the ontology is presented in Fig. 9.

> [DC] Fields of archaeology
>> anthropology
>> archaeology
>
> ...
>
> [DC] Archaeological heritage
>> [DC] Archaeological heritage management
>> [DC] Developement
>> [DC] Ethics
>> [DC] General public
>> [DC] Legislation
>
> ....

Fig. 9. Local-context conceptualization hierarchy in PMAH ontology

7   Conclusions

Wordnet based ontologies with expert knowledge presented in this paper were developed to build enhanced tagging systems. Incorporation of this type of ontology enables prompting similar and related words automatically generated by the system. However, in general, wordnet based ontologies have a much wider application. This approach can be successfully applied in any system in which it is necessary to combine general with expert knowledge. The fact that entire solution is based on wordnet-like lexical database provides organized knowledge about the world all at once. An example of such approach is the use of wordnet based ontology (PMAH ontology) in the intelligent tutoring system that operate on dynamically growing e-learning content repository [12]. In this system wordnet based ontology is used for content indexing and it is a basic component of domain model applied in the process of searching a repository, and making decisions in the course of conducting teaching strategies.

The method presented in the article enables construction of ontological systems which contain general knowledge about the world referring to linguistic conceptualization, which then may be expanded by domain relations as need arises. This approach requires an algorithm to be used which in the form presented refers to competence of domain expert. The presented method may become an interesting alternative to solutions in which expert knowledge is presented independently of general knowledge about the world.

References

1. Dextre Clarke, S.G., Lei Zeng, M.: From ISO 2788 to ISO 25964: the evolution of thesaurus standards towards interoperability and data modeling. ISO Inf. Stand. Q. Winter **24** (2012)
2. Fellbaum, C. (ed.): WordNet: An Electronic Lexical Database. MIT Press, Cambridge (1998)

3. Gangemi, A., Guarino, N., Masolo, C., Oltramari, A.: Sweetening WordNet with Dolce. AI Mag. **24**(3), 13–24 (2003)
4. Getty AAT: About the AAT. http://www.getty.edu/research/tools/vocabularies/. Accessed December 2015
5. Hodge, G.: Systems of knowledge organization for digital libraries. Beyond traditional authority files, Council on Library and Information Resources (2000). http://www.clir.org/pubs/reports/pub91/contents.html. Accessed December 2015
6. Hjørland, B.: Is classification necessary after Google? J. Documentation **68**(3), 299–317 (2012)
7. Iconclass RKD, web site of IconClass. www.iconclass.nl. Accessed December 2015
8. Lakoff, G.: Women, fire, and dangerous things: what categories reveal about the mind. University of Chicago Press (1987)
9. Lancaster, F.W.: Indexing and Abstracting in Theory and Practice. 3rd edn. University of Illinois, Graduate School of Library and Information Science, Champaign (2003)
10. Maniez, J.: Database merging and the compatibility of indexing languages. Knowl. Organ. **24**(4), 213–224 (1997)
11. Marciniak, J.: Building e-learning content repositories to support content reusability. Int. J. Emerg. Technol. Learn. (iJET) **9**(3), 45–52 (2014)
12. Marciniak, J.: Building intelligent tutoring systems immersed in repositories of e-learning content. Procedia Comput. Sci. **35**, 541–550 (2014)
13. Marciniak, J.: Enhancing tagging systems by Wordnet based ontologies. In: Vetulani, Z., Mariani, J. (eds.) LTC 2011. LNCS, vol. 8387, pp. 367–378. Springer, Heidelberg (2014)
14. Seidel-Grzesińska, A., Stanicka-Brzezicka, K.: Wielojęzyczne słowniki hierarchiczne w dokumentacji muzealnej w Polsce. Muzealnictwo **55**, 116–126 (2014)
15. Slavic, A.: A definition of thesauri and classification as indexing tools. Metadata Dublin Core (2000). http://dublincore.org/documents/2000/11/28/thesauri-definition/. Accessed December 2015
16. Smith, G.: Tagging: People-Powered Metadata for the Social Web. New Riders, Berkeley (2008)
17. Vossen, P. (ed.): Euro WordNet General Document. Version 3. University of Amsterdam (2002)
18. Vetulani, Z., Walkowska, J., Obrębski, T., Marciniak, J., Konieczka, P., Rzepecki, P.: An algorithm for building lexical semantic network and its application to PolNet - Polish WordNet Project. In: Vetulani, Z., Uszkoreit, H. (eds.) LTC 2007. LNCS, vol. 5603, pp. 369–381. Springer, Heidelberg (2009)

Diagnostic Tools in plWordNet Development Process

Maciej Piasecki[✉], Łukasz Burdka, Marek Maziarz, and Michał Kaliński

G4.19 Research Group, Computational Intelligence Department,
Wrocław University of Technology, Wrocław, Poland
{maciej.piasecki,marek.maziarz}@pwr.wroc.pl, luk.burdka@gmail.com
http://nlp.pwr.edu.pl

Abstract. With the growing size of a wordnet, it is becoming more and more difficult to avoid, identify and eliminate errors in it, especially when a group of editors work in parallel. That is the case of *plWordNet*. Thus we need elaborated tools for both error prevention during editing, and diagnostic tools for error detection after the work was completed. In this paper, first, we present error prevention mechanisms built-in the *plWord-Net* editor application and the system for group-working of a linguistic team. Next, we discuss diagnostic tests and diagnostic tools dedicated to *plWordNet* – the Polish wordnet. *plWordNet* has been in steady development for almost ten years and has reached the size of 193 k synsets and 255 k lexical meanings. We propose a typology of the diagnostic levels: describe formal, structural and semantic rules for seeking errors within *plWordNet*, as well as, a new method of automated induction of the diagnostic rules. Finally, we discuss results and benefits of the approach.

1 Introduction

The size of a wordnet matters, and a wordnet is never too big. However, the larger the network is, the more difficult is to maintain its consistency and to minimise the number of errors in it. What is worse, many editing decisions depend on the editor's language competence. Wordnet relations are a kind of generalisation across the continuum[1] of the lexico-semantic associations [10] and thus we cannot expect perfect agreement among linguists.

A wordnet is meant to provide description of the lexico-semantic system. As for most languages there is no other resource to compare a given wordnet with[2], a wordnet can be only *manually verified* by lexicographers or evaluated by applying it in some language processing task. The first method is laborious and cannot be applied for a large scale. Moreover, we can hardly expect strict consistency even among proper decisions of linguists editing a wordnet. The application-based evaluation provides only indirect hints about the wordnet quality and is

---

[1] According to semanticists lexical relations form a continuum [5, p. 143].

[2] The vast majority of dictionaries is significantly different than wordnets, so the comparison is difficult.

© Springer International Publishing Switzerland 2016
Z. Vetulani et al. (Eds.): LTC 2013, LNAI 9561, pp. 255–273, 2016.
DOI: 10.1007/978-3-319-43808-5_20

most insightful if we compare two wordnets for the same task. Summing up, automated evaluation of a wordnet is hardly possible and the manual evaluation cannot be applied for the whole large wordnet.

Many errors are caused by minor mistakes or even typos in the encoding of the wordnet files, imperfect knowledge about specification details of some editors, e.g. the direction of a relation, inconsistencies in applying work procedures, lack of information about similar decisions taken by other team members, etc. Many such errors can be prevented, if editors are supported by enough elaborated wordnet editing system.

Taking in account the problems with the consistency and error prevention during wordnet editing, as well as wordnet evaluation, our goal is to develop a system supporting editor team in avoiding errors during wordnet editing and completed with an automated diagnostic method for a wordnet, i.e. a set of tools that identify and signal potential faults in the wordnet. The diagnostic method is intended to provide support for wordnet editors but it is not expected to make the final decisions about the errors. The precision of the method does not need to be perfect, but its recall should be close to 100 %, i.e. the method may signal some percentage of false errors, but it should not omit any real error. The method should point to different elements of a wordnet as potentially erroneous.

The problem is not new, a couple of wordnet editing systems and several diagnostic tools have been proposed in the literature. However, as we will show in Sect. 3, most approaches focus on selected error types and do not offer overall solutions. The wordnet is a complex structure of a double interlinked graphs: of synsets and also lexical units. Graph links represent different lexico-semantic relations, and the graph node can be described by several attributes, e.g. lemma, part of speech, semantic domain etc. Thus we aim at automated identification of as many error types as possible and systematic analysis of the wordnet structure on different levels.

2   Related Works

When the quality of a wordnet is a concern, developers need to possess a way of testing the integrity of their structure, as well as, finding typical errors that happen during the development. A few tools exist that can aid this process. *Hydra* [16] allows a user to formulate his own custom validation queries. This way the user can get a list of all objects that satisfy a query written in a modal logic language. However this is only a tool that may be used to find some anomalies in the wordnet. It requires the user's intuition in defining potential types of anomalies. Kubis [7] has developed a WQuery which is another language for formulating diagnostic queries to WordNet-like databases. It is however dependant on the internal structure of the database and is suitable for wordnets that match the assumed structure. Some error types cited in literature cannot occur in *plWordNet*, because it has been developed with the help of the wordnet editing system called *WordnetLoom* from the very beginning [14]. WordnetLoom, based on the Graphical User Interface (GUI), provides visual editing of the wordnet structure and supports distributed work of a linguistic team on the central database. Linguists are separated from the internal encoding of the wordnet, so encoding errors are excluded. WordnetLoom implements several constraints that protect against several types of errors in the relation structure, e.g. in the case of symmetric relations like hypo/hypernymy the reverse relations is always added automatically. However, those constraints are not described declaratively, they are implemented directly in the the Java code, and as we could notice they do not encompass all types of errors that could be detected, cf. Sect. 6.1.

Most existing advanced languages for querying the wordnet structure, like WQuery or Hydra, assume a specific format of the wordnet representation that limits their wider applicability to other wordnets.

After some potential errors have been found by a diagnostic tool, a lexicographer needs a way to verify them. Authors of [8] emphasise the importance of the visual analysis of the wordnet graph structure as a diagnostic procedure. Direct visual browsing and editing of the structure of wordnet relations is also emphasised as an important feature in WordnetLoom.

The problem of defining a comprehensive set of diagnostic rules receives much less attention in literature. There is no complete overview of all potential sources of errors and the extent to which they can be discovered. Different works concentrate on selected aspects of wordnet integrity, e.g. [18].

WordnetLoom also implements several constraints on the relation structure, but as we discovered the system is not complete and lacks more complicated rules.

For those reasons a set of robust diagnostic tests have been developed for *plWordNet* that can be used in other wordnets with a similar structure or serve as an inspiration for every developer of a custom wordnet editing tool while implementing an error prevention system.

3 Diagnostic Levels

A wordnet is a complex graph structure with two types of nodes and many types of relations. Nodes and relation links (in some wordnets) can be described with attributes. Graph nodes represent lexical meanings and each link contributes to their description. A manually edited graph can include errors that cannot be automatically blocked by an editing tool.

All non-trivial errors are related to the graph semantics and cannot be blocked by an editing tool, as this could limit proper decisions of the linguists. For instance, introducing a new LU requires two-stage process: first a new word-sense pair must be created, then it must be described using some defining relations (see Sect. 6). Neither the order can be reversed, nor it is possible to introduce and define the LU simultaneously. Thus, we aim at detecting problematic elements and sub-structures in some kind of post-process error detection.

Three basic error types of the possible errors in the wordnet can be distinguished:

- *formal* errors made in the wordnet source files,
- *structural* errors, i.e. flaws in the wordnet structure that can be identified on the basis of the relation definitions and the link structure without more advanced analysis of the semantics of the elements linked,
- *semantic* errors that result from linking wordnet elements that do not match semantically the link type – including improper grouping of LUs into synsets.

Errors of the first two types can be prevented to a very large extent by a wordnet editing system. In the next section, we will present error prevention mechanisms in the WordnetLoom [14] – a wordnet editing system with a Graphical User Interface (GUI), together with a set of web-based applications supporting linguistic team cooperation and supervision of the team.

Contrary to the first two types, semantic errors are flaws that can be recognised only by analysing the meanings of LUs from synsets and the wordnet relations linking them. Contrary to the structural errors it is not enough to know the link types, e.g. many semantic errors are associated with the wrong placement of a lemma in a synset:

- an LU as intended by the linguist exists but its meaning (sense) does not fit the given synset and its relation links (i.e. the meaning description)[3],
- or the synset can describe a non-existing sense.

Two synsets can be also erroneously linked by a relation. In order to discover errors in synsets and links we need to refer to lexicons or knowledge extracted from large corpora. However, in the case of selected particular semantic domains or even hypernymy branches, it is possible to define specific semantic constraints that should be preserved to a very large extent if not completely. We will come back to this point in Sect. 6

Typos in synset lemmas or words in the glosses should be also classified as semantic errors. In the case of a large wordnet developed on the basis of a huge corpus, we cannot expect the full coverage of a morphological analyser. Words, unknown to the analyser, but frequent, can be met and should be added to the wordnet. Thus, each unrecognised token can be a unknown word of an unknown meaning and cannot be simply corrected or deleted for sure. The relation between the unknown lexical meaning and the rest of the synset or a gloss is not determined.

4   Error Prevention During Wordnet Development

WordnetLoom [14] is a wordnet editor in which all operations are done by linguists via GUI. It is based on a distributed network architecture with a central database. WordnetLoom 1.0 [14] was based on a thick client model, in which a lot of database operations were carried out on the client side. In a new version 2.0 (https://clarin-pl.eu/dspace/handle/11321/226), the responsibility of the client

---

[3] In the *plWordNet* model two LUs are synonymous if they share all *constitutive* relations to other LUs, for details, please, look at [10].

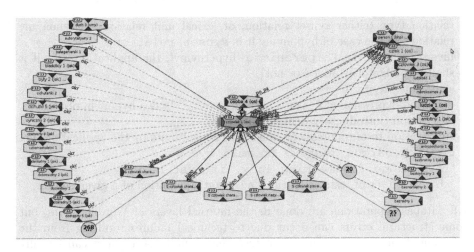

Fig. 1. WordnetLoom graph-based editor: neighbourhood of the lexical unit *czowiek*₁ 'human being'.

application was reduced and the central fully fledged database server has been introduced. WordnetLoom was implemented in Java and can be run on almost any computer platform. It has been tested in a rich variety of configurations (including different versions of the Windows, Linux and MacOS).

[14] offers several different *perspectives* (i.e. different types of *views*) on the wordnet database: a form-based view focused on lexical-units, a form-based view focused on LUs, and graph-based view presenting the structure of the wordnet network with synsets as the nodes. The last type of view have gained great popularity among linguists. An example of the use of the graph-based perspective is presented in Fig. 1. This perspective allows for editing wordnet by direct operations on the structure of wordnet relations that is presented visually on the screen. Every relation link can be added directly on the presented graph by pointing to the selected synsets and linking them with the mouse. In a similar way links can be modified or deleted. The formal representation of the wordnet structure in the XML native format, as well as in other export formats (e.g. LMF-based export *plWordNet* format) is completely hidden from the wordnet editors. We have not faced any case in which the XML representation had to be directly modified during the last couple of years. Thus the proper syntax of the relation graph encoding is guaranteed by the wordnet editor, and structural errors caused by human editor do not happen. For instance, there is no chance for the use of erroneous labels for relations, as relations of the given wordnet are defined before editing and only symbols included in the specification of the relations are presented in the user interface for selection.

All relations (both synset relations and relations of LUs) have to be defined prior to their use. A definition of a relation specifies:

- relation name (i.e., hiponimia 'hyponymy'),
- list of Parts of Speech for which the relation is defined,

- relation type (either synset relation, or lexical unit relation, or synonymy relation[4], in the case of hyponymy it is synset relation,
- inverse relation (i.e., hiperonimia 'hypernymy', the application asks if it shall be obligatorily added or not),
- short-cut ("hypo"),
- displayed expression ("x jest hiponimem y" 'x is a hyponym of y'),
- description (introductory definitions),
- substitution tests (expressions filled with lexical units by the application, i.e. Jeśli ktoś/coś jest x, to musi być y.
  'If someone / something is x, it must be y.'
  – the whole set of tests constitutes a semantic definition of a given sense).

All database operations are done in the internal layers of WordnetLoom, but some structural errors can occur due to technical failures resulting from the distributed and parallel work of linguists, e.g. content of a synset can be fully deleted, but an empty synset remains existing due to the imperfect synchronisation between threads in a Java library. However, such errors are easy to be eliminated with simple automated cleaning procedures.

The relation definition allow for constraining relation links that editors are going to add, i.e. Parts of Speech of the source and target LU, direction of the relation, relation subtypes and automated adding the inverse relation link.

However, some operation sequences cannot be fully automated and still require human decisions. For instance LUs that are not included in any synset[5] can be found in the wordnet database, as a synset for a LU must be selected by an editor, that is possible in WordnetLoom only after the LU was created.

Links without the obligatory inverse counterpart for symmetric relations can occur. This can happen in WordnetLoom when a relation definition is mistakenly changed for some period. However, this could be classified as an intentional decision of the wordnet editor. That is why creation and modification of the relation definitions is restricted only to the coordinators. The constraining mechanism can be further extended to controlling the interaction between relations and the constitutive attributes, i.e. lexical register, verb and adjective classes, and verb aspect.

Cycles in relations (e.g. hypernymy or meronymy) are sometimes introduced by editors and can be automatically recognised without analysing the content of the linked synsets. Unfortunately, the recognition of cycles is a very computationally expensive operation and cannot be done in real time in parallel to the work of editors (i.e. after every change added). This operation can be only performed off-line, as a part of the wordnet diagnostics.

All operations performed on the *plWordNet* database have been recorded in time-stamped way in the additional database tables almost since the begging of *plWordNet*. That allows us for monitoring:

---

[4] The application gives special position to the synonymy relation.

[5] Linguists sometimes create several LUs in advance and later forget to add them to synsets.

- changes done in the wordnet database,
- editors' operations on the database.

The first is a base for the reverse functionality that enables going back to the previous versions and tracing back changes to the previous states, e.g. previous versions of a synset.

The second kind of the monitoring has become a basis for the development of a web-based system for monitoring *plWordNet* development and group working, called *plWordNet Monitor*[6]. plWordNet Monitor is a set of tools useful in supervising linguist work. It consists of the three main parts:

- monitor of lexical units, with
    - the history of changes (adding/modification/deleting LUs),
    - and a list of lexical units which do not belong to any synset.
- monitor of synsets, with
    - the history of changes (creating/modification/deleting synsets, as well as, adding and deleting LUs to/from synsets),
    - a list of synsets without any hypernymic synset,
    - a list of synset pairs linked with either hyponymy, or hypernymy instance without an inverse relation instance,
    - synset browser in which one may search for synsets using an identifier or a lemma.
- Inspection, consisting of
    - summary of all changes concerning LUs, synsets and relations,
    - summary of *plWordNet* editor activities,
    - the history of changes concerning mapping relations from *plWordNet* onto the Princeton WordNet.

The variety of possibilities given by the monitor is huge, although there are three tools that are used most often:

1. the LU change history,
2. list of LUs which do not have any synset,
3. and the summary of *plWordNet* editor activities.

The last one is used by team coordinators to monitor activities of individual *plWordNet* editors (see Fig. 2). The data could be filtered through date. In this perspective one may control time and work efforts and analyse *plWordNet* growth rate.

The first two tools are directly utilised in the quality control process. The LU change history helps to monitor changes to LU attributes:

a lemma – the Part of Speech – a wordnet domain[7] – register label – definition – usage examples – sentiment annotation.

This perspective may be filtered according to following criteria: time ("Zakres"), editor ("Edytor"), part of speech ("POS") and lemma ("Lemat";

---

[6] It is called unofficially 'plWordNet Big Brother'.

[7] *plWordNet* domains follows those of Princeton WordNet that originated from the names of the lexicographer files.

Śledzenie zmian w bazie Słowosieci

Podsumowanie aktywności edytorów (po 15 kwietnia)

Zakres: 2010-04-15 - 2012-09-02   [Wyświetl]

Użytkownik	lexicalunit			lexicalrelation			synset			synsetrelation			unitandsynset		Łącznie
	dodane	usunięte	zmienione	dodane	usunięte	zmienione	dodane	usunięte	zmienione	dodane	usunięte	zmienione	dodane	usunięte	
	31552	72	603876	93922	12	158	21571	15	1856	2	1	1762	32155	219	3
	15116	1050	5380	15107	4232		11989	1491	58570	42866	12433	24	30770	16693	215721
	18			2			15	1	42	44			23	5	150
	21580	1002	6968	15069	2526		18453	809	55256	57517	7851	12	31811	11326	230090
	3290	36	1224	3519	451		3298	598	10528	4083	312		5723	2471	35527
										8	10				18
	698	70	722	1341	1101		566	451	6166	8260	7375	16	5019	4407	36192
										133	2				135
	40		2				39	3	94	4763	788		46	7	5782
												6			6
	278	21	38	32	2		166	26	884	455	71	4	1576	1341	4874
	2781	57	860	1520	109	16	2197	121	7360	6989	940	4	4818	2093	29865
	17	1	46	94	87		9	10	154	17	27	30	53	37	584
	10442	1313	20750	22235	12065	18	9325	1835	61088	65149	36736	92	48583	39412	329063
	30	1	12	3	2		21	1	94	349	82		45	16	656
	4580	298	4798	597	375	2	3315	338	19150	29195	13462	40	13055	4786	97989
	21	4	26	12	2		17	3	126	65	24		234	218	752
	5341	567	2060	2996	1302	4	4448	597	18960	20458	7611	4	10538	5785	81277
	1	1		1			1		2				1		7
	430	23	264	185	11		381	5	1218	2641	715		589	182	6648
	7187	287	244	846	89	8	5221	107	16050	12531	1628	38	10653	3975	58864
	21231	785	6312	15065	2449	8	14987	1308	63760	38963	9871	44	50250	29891	255524
										44	2	2	230	230	508
	206976	3	4	92235			117659	2	4510	285348		4	207371	396	914510
										2					2
										46716					46716
										4					4
	3317	71	382	484	46	2	2706	77	7878	6227	803	26	4568	1380	27927
	2			1			1		12				7	5	28
	1	2		2			1		6				1	2	15
Łącznie	334941	5656	654568	265848	24861	216	216386	7822	380512	586069	100744	2106	458121	128857	3166707

Fig. 2. The plWordNet monitor: summary of linguist activities. Names of *plWord-Net* editors were blurred in the column "Użytkownik" 'user' (selected glosses: *dodane* 'added', *zmienione* 'modified', *usunięte* 'deleted', *Łącznie* 'Total', *Zakres* 'period, time from-to').

see Fig. 3). By manual inspection a coordinator may analyse history of any LU that is or was a part of the Polish wordnet (for instance, LUs containing lemma *krążownik* 'cruiser, warship').

Since LUs and synsets are independently defined in our database it is important to monitor whether there are LUs that do not belong to any synset. Such list is displayed by the plWordNet Monitor, and helps a coordinator to find the lost LUs (cf. Fig. 4).

plWordNet editors work in several small teams of 4–5 persons with a coordinator supervising their work. At the top of the hierarchy there is a main coordinator who is responsible for the team coordination, providing explanations for specific problematic cases to coordinators, as well as individual editors, and amending editor guidelines during the development process. Every editor is first specially trained for the task that are assigned to him. An editor is provided dedicated guidelines[8], as well as, many tools and resources that improve work quality:

---

[8] There are four guidelines created for the need of the four Parts of Speech covered by *plWordNet* and several more written for specific tasks: register label applying, multi-word LU recognition, differentiating gerunds from other deverbal nouns, describing adjectives derived from proper nouns etc.

Śledzenie zmian w bazie Słowosieci

Historia zmian jednostek leksykalnych

Kryteria filtrowania
Zakres: 2010-01-01 - 2015-08-02
Edytor: Maciej Piasecki
POS: rzeczowniki
Lemat: krążownik
filtruj

#	Data	Kto	Akcja	Klucz	Atrybuty									
					lemma	domain	pos	tagcount	source	status	comment	variant	project	owner
#42008	2010-05-13 10:35:27	Maciej Piasecki	dodanie	#37631 krążownik liniowy	krążownik liniowy	wytw	2	0	1	0		1	2	Maciej Piasecki
#41972	2010-05-13 10:32:25	Maciej Piasecki	dodanie	#37628 krążownik minowy	krążownik minowy	wytw	2	0	1	0		1	2	Maciej Piasecki
#41955	2010-05-13 10:29:53	Maciej Piasecki	dodanie	#37625 krążownik pancernopokładowy	krążownik pancernopokładowy	wytw	2	0	1	0		1	2	Maciej Piasecki
#41546	2010-05-13 10:27:54	Maciej Piasecki	dodanie	#37624 lekki krążownik	lekki krążownik	wytw	2	0	1	0		1	2	Maciej Piasecki
#41938	2010-05-13 10:26:22	Maciej Piasecki	dodanie	#37623 krążownik traktatowy	krążownik traktatowy	wytw	2	0	1	0		1	2	Maciej Piasecki
#41933	2010-05-13 10:25:27	Maciej Piasecki	dodanie	#37622 ciężki krążownik	ciężki krążownik	wytw	2	0	1	0		1	2	Maciej Piasecki

Fig. 3. The plWordNet Monitor: The lexical unit change history (selected glosses: *rzeczowniki* 'nouns', *krążownik* 'cruiser', *Akcja* 'activity', *dodanie* 'adding', *Atrybuty* 'Attributes').

Śledzenie zmian w bazie Słowosieci

Jednostki nie przypisane do synsetu

Kryteria filtrowania
Zakres: 2010-01-01 - 2015-09-02
Edytor:
filtruj

ID	lemma	domain	pos	tagcount	source	status	comment	variant	project	owner	kiedy
640128	phenethylline 1	24	6	0	1	0		1	1	Marta Błaszczak	
678768	Refreshment Sunday 1	25	6	0	1	0		1	1	Marta Błaszczak	2012-03-12 14:48:49
678769	Mid-Lent Sunday 1	25	6	0	1	0		1	1	Marta Błaszczak	2012-03-12 14:48:49
684572	balsa 3	3	6	0	1	0		3	1	Kacper Paszke	2012-03-12 14:49:13

Fig. 4. The plWordNet Monitor: The list of lexical units (LUs) which do not belong to any synset. Here we can see LUs added to enWordNet. For instance, the LU *phenethylline*1 'a prodrug, chemical linkage of amphetamine and theophylline' was introduced and then not linked to any synset at that moment, during the process of extending the Princeton WordNet.

- corpus browsers,
- lists of usage examples automatically clustered into groups that mostly represent one individual word sense induced from the corpus [4],
- lists of words that are semantically similar on the basis of the Measure of Semantic Relatedness extracted from a large corpus [15],
- a sophisticated tool called WordnetWeaver cf. [3] that suggests for a given new lemma positions of its potential LUs in the wordnet[9],
- as well, as existing electronic dictionaries, lexicons, and encyclopaedias.

An editor equipped in such a way is well prepared for expanding the wordnet and less prone for making errors. Moreover, the use of the same supporting tools among the editor team according to the same ranking list improves the consistency among the editor decisions.

The work of individual editors is systematically monitored by the coordinators from the point of view of their productivity and quality. A coordinator periodically draws small samples of editors' work, and analyses them. If mistakes are found, the coordinator contact the supervised person (via email or Skype, or in urgent cases on phone) and tries to re-explain guidelines and asks the evaluated editor to repair the spotted errors, as well as potential other similar

---

[9] Suggestions are not obligatory for the editors and who can choose a different place for the LUS of the given lemma.

errors in the work done by the given editor. In more difficult cases a coordinators contact the main coordinator or even a discussion is initiated on the level of the whole team. From time to time coordinators have a meeting to discuss the recent problems. Editors are requested to closely cooperate with their coordinators, and the coordinators are invited to closely cooperate with the chief coordinator.

A fair help both for the management of the work and keeping quality is a group working web-tool called *Pilotka* ('~woman-pilot') that has been implemented on the basis of the *Redmine*[10] system. At this site coordinators announce assignment of new tasks for editors, i.e. packages of lemmas to be added, share information, answer questions, and announce guidelines or modifications to the guidelines. *Pilotka* is also used for reporting potential errors noticed by the editors, asking questions to editors responsible for the suspicious decisions and discussing about them. As everything published on this site is kept accessible, the whole site is a rich knowledge source that complements the basic guidelines. The problems described on the site and the recorded discussion are often a starting point for the modification of the guidelines (Fig. 5).

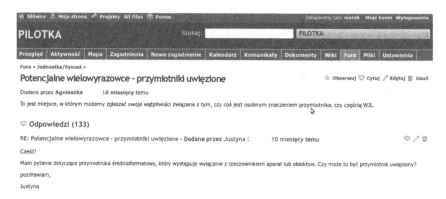

Fig. 5. The *Pilotka* system that supports group working of the editor teams, and is based on the *Redmine* system. The presented web page includes posts on recognition of multi-word lexical unit candidates containing bounded adjectives. The guidelines for this task state that if a part of a combination of words is severely or exclusively restricted to this combination we consider it to be lexicalised. The editor Justyna presents her doubts: "Hi! I have question concerning the adjective *średnioformatowy* '(adj.) medium format' which occurs exclusively with nouns *aparat* 'camera' and *obiektyw* 'lens'. May it be a bound adjective? Best, Justyna."

5   Formal and Structural Analysis

WordnetLoom takes care about the wordnet data encoding, but we found one minor formal error that could be also corrected by the tool. WordnetLoom does

---

[10] http://www.redmine.org/.

not prevent adding extra white spaces at the beginning or end of a lemma. They can next disturb database searching, if not removed. So, a procedure for automated removing extra spaces in wordnet lemmas and reducing each space sequence inside a lemma to one single space was implemented[11]. As it was said in the previous section, typos could be fully automatically eliminated with the help of a morphological analyser, but they can represent semantic errors, as well.

Simple structural rules are meant to discover problems caused by the distributed thick client model of WordnetLoom and inconsistencies introduced by coordinators who edited the different versions of relation definitions:

Str1. *Lexical Unit without a Synset* – LUs that do not belong to any synset are discovered.

Str2. *Lacking Element in a Relation Link* – recognition of the links with lacking elements among synset relations and lexical relations (mostly a result of the non-completed relation link deletion).

Str3. *Symmetric Relation With No Counterpart* – identification of symmetrical relations links that lacks the obligatory link of the reverse relation.

WordnetLoom 1.0 is a client application which works via network on a central database. Distributed work of the editors can sometimes cause errors due to connection or application faults. The above rules discover errors that cause serious inconsistencies in the database. LUs without synsets or with broken relation links[12] can be automatically removed, but each corresponds to some intended editing action, and should be analysed by editors before being deleted.

Relation definitions are stored in the *plWordNet* database and each relation can be described as obligatory reverse and associated with the reverse relation, e.g. *hypernymy – hyponymy* or *type – instance*. For such relations, WordnetLoom adds automatically the reverse links, unless the connection with the database fails[13].

The next group of the structural rules refers to selected semantic properties that can be discovered only on the basis of the link structure analysis:

Str4. *Link Cycle* – discovering the graph cycles formed by links of the same type, e.g. hypernymy or meronymy.

Str5. *Multiple Hypernyms* – identification of synsets with larger numbers of the direct hypernyms

Str6. *Overlapping Relations* – more than one relation link a pair of synsets, or direct and indirect relations link mutually a pair of synsets;

Hyper/hyponymy and holo/meronymy are relations that are most frequently used in wordnet applications in the text processing. Cycles in those relations

---

[11] In WordnetLoom 2.0 this problem has been eliminated on the level of editing.

[12] For instance, There may also occur instances of relations, where at least one of its sides was deleted without proper removal of the relation.

[13] In one case, erroneous modifications in the relation definitions made by a human had the same effect.

result in open recursive searches and cause serious problems during the processing. Cycle elimination can be hardly done during wordnet editing, due to complexity of cycle identification.

When one synset has got many hypernyms it is not necessarily an error, but for the sake of usability of the wordnet as a resource, the multiple hyponymy should be limited to only unavoidable cases. Therefore the *Multiple Hypernyms* rule is used to find synsets with the number of hypernyms exceeding a pre-defined threshold. All discovered synsets are next verified manually.

In the majority of cases two synsets can be linked by only one relation link. Almost all cases of the overlapping relations that are detected by the last rule represent errors.

6 Semantic Analysis

6.1 Structurally Supported Constraints

Wordnet editors – following guidelines[14] and the whole procedure briefly summarised in Sect. 3 – make their decisions. Thus semantics shapes *plWordNet* structure. Definitions of relations could be used in some cases to check correctness of a given relation instance. We developed two types of such rules:

Sem1. *Rules for LU placement*: prerequisites for placing LUs in the net of lexico-semantic relations, e.g., nouns should possess either hyponymy, or meronymy, or inter-register synonymy, or femininity, or markedness (there are 3 such rules, one for each PoS).

Sem2. *Rules for specific noun and adjective relations*: Many semantic constraints concerning verbs and adjectives have been described in [11,12], such rules make use of aspect, verb class (9 rules for verbs), and adjective semantic domains (13 rules for adjectives).

The whole set is used to generate reports on a special website or to files.[15]

Sem1. It is important to define LUs properly. In *plWordNet* the main way of defining LU is to describe them with *constitutive relations*[16] [10]. The set for nouns was briefly described above. The set for adjectives includes:

– hyponymy – i.e., *czerwonopomarańczowy 1* adj. 'red-orange' ⟼ *pomarańczowy 1* adj. 'orange',
– value of the attribute – i.e., *pomarańczowy 1* adj. 'orange' ⟼ *kolor 1* n. 'colour',

---

[14] There are three documents describing the lexico-semantic systems available on the site [2]: for nouns (31 pages), for verbs (66 pages) and for adjectives (32 pages).

[15] *Here will be a link to a full description of the rules.*

[16] Glosses appeared in *plWordNet* since the version 2.2, but they became numerous in the version 2.3, but still they are intended to be more comments for the users than a tool for defining the LU semantics. In a lexico-semantic network it are relations that should be the primary defining means. Constitutive relations are frequent and shared among groups of LUs, cf. [10].

- cross-categorial synonymy (for relational adjectives) – *polski 1* adj. 'Polish' ⟼ *Polska 1* n. 'Poland'[17],
- and inter-register synonymy to a well-defined adjective – see vulgar *zajebisty 1* adj. 'shit-hot' ⟼ *fantastyczny 1* adj. 'fantastic'.

By a *well-defined* LU we understand a LU that possesses either hyponymy, or value (of the attribute), or cross-categorial synonymy (if it is a relational adjective). *Fantastyczny 1* is the case, because it possesses a hypernym (*jakość 2* 'quality') – The rule is described below in the Procedure 1.

Procedure 1. Rules for adjective defining relations. Legend: hypernym(·) – a hypernym of an adjective, value(·) – returns an atrribute for a given adjective denoting its value, D(·) – domain of an adjective (rel - relational adjectives), XPOS-synonymy(·) – cross-categorial synonymy for a given adjective, IR-synonymy(·) – inter-register synonymy for a given adjective.

For every adjective X there exist adjectives A_1, A_2 and nouns N_1, N_2 such that

1. either hypernym$(X) = A_1$,
2. or value$(X) = N_1$,
3. or if D$(X) =$rel, then XPOS-synonymy$(X) = N_1$,
4. or IR-synonymy$(X) = A_1$ and

   - either hypernym$(A_1) = A_2$
   - or value$(A_1) = N_2$,
   - or XPOS-synonymy$(A_1) = N_2$, if only D$(A_1) = $rel.

Sem2. Another set of rules was prepared for adjectival and verbal relations. Rules for verbs take into account the aspect and Vendler-like verb classes. For example, subtype of iterativity (imperfective-imperfective: *jadać* 'to eat from time to time' ⟼ *jeść* 'to eat') gained rule presented in the Procedure 2.

Procedure 2. Rule for iterativity(·) (variant impf-impf). Legend: A(·) – aspect of a verb, impf - imperfective, Class(·) – semantic verb class: ACTIV – activities, EVE – eventives, English labels after [10, p. 791].

For a given pair of verbs V_1, V_2

1. if iterativity$_{impf-impf}$ $(V_1) = V_2$,
2. then

   - A$(V_1) = $ A$(V_2) = $ impf,
   - and Class$(V_1) \epsilon$ {ACTIV, EVE}.

There are even more complex rules, see for instance the rule for secondary aspectuality rule presented in the Procedure 3. Secondary aspectuality links only

---

[17] The cross-categorial synonymy was introduced into *plWordNet* after EuroWord-Net [9].

specific classes of verbs: relation instances between telic verbs are forbidden, see [11, p. 186]. First, the aspect of verbs V_1, V_2 is checked, then semantic classes are introduced.

Procedure 3. Rule for `sec(ondary) aspectuality(·)` (variant pf-impf). Legend: `A(·)` – aspect of a verb, `(im)pf` - (im)perfective aspect, `Class(·)` – semantic verb class: `ACTIO` – actions, `ACTIV` – activities, `ACTS` – acts, `EVE` – eventives, `HAP` – happening, `PROC` – processuals, `ST` – states, `ACC` – accumulatives, `DEL` – delimitatives, `DIS` – distributives, `PER` – perduratives, English labels after [10, p. 791], with "×" we denote a Cartesian product.

For a given pair of verbs V_1, V_2

1. if `sec-aspectuality`$_{pf-impf}$ $(V_1) = V_2$,
2. then

   - `A`(V_1) = pf and `A`(V_2) = impf,
   - and `Class`(V_1) × `Class`(V_2) ∈ {ACTIO$_{pf}$, PROC$_{pf}$, ACTS, HAP, ACC, DEL, DIS, PER} × {ACTIV, EVE, ST} ∪ {ACTS, HAP, ACC, DEL, DIS, PER} × {ACTIO$_{impf}$, PROC$_{impf}$}.

Rules for adjectives are constructed with the usage of adjectival semantic domains. There are four such domains: `rel` - relational adjectives, `grad` - gradable denominal adjectives, `deverb` - deverbal adjectives and `deadj` - deadjectival adjectives. Each of the adjective types (domain) has its own relation set. In the Procedure 4 a rule for the *similarity* relation is presented. The relation links gradable denominal adjectives with their derivational bases [12, pp. 22–23], *esowaty* '*S*-shaped' ⟼ *S* 'letter *S*', that is why relational adjectives are excluded with two parallel constraints (relational adjectives should be linked to nouns with cross-categorial synonymy and should possess the `rel` domain).

Procedure 4. Rule for `similarity(·)`. Legend: `D(·)` – domain of an adjective, `rel` – relational adjective, `XPOS-synonymy(·)` – cross-categorial synonymy.

For a given pair of an adjective A and a noun N

1. if `similarity`$(A) = N$,
2. then

   - `D`$(A) \neq$ `rel`
   - and there does not exist N_2 such that `XPOS-synonymy`$(A) = N_2$.

6.2 Practical Application

Structural and semantic constraints described in Sects. 5 and 6.1 have been implemented in *Constrainer* – a wordnet diagnostic tool. It was first used to prepare the version 2.0 of *plWordNet* and was next applied to clean the extended version 2.1. The applied constrains signalled 760 errors in total, including:

- 31 cases of the wrong Part of Speech in lexical relations,
- 11 cases of the wrong Part of Speech in synset relations,
- 715 cases of multiple relations between a given pair of synsets, and 2 cases of LUs without a synset.

Errors from the first two groups were caused in fact by assigning a wrong relation to a given pair of LUs or synsets.

After the correction performed by editors, we ran *Constrainer* again and only 37 errors were signalled: 1 wrong PoS for a lexical relation and 36 cases of the multiple relations between synsets. As all these cases are not genuine errors, then the precision of the tool is 95.13 %. It definitely does not over-generate.

6.3   Automated Induction of the Diagnostic Rules

Manual construction of the diagnostic rules is not very laborious (less than 2 person-weeks), but can have limited coverage. However, because a wordnet is so large and mostly correct, we assumed that it is possible to derive diagnostic rules directly from the wordnet data. Training instances were LU pairs from the same synsets or linked by a relation. We considered several features: LU Part of Speech, morphological characteristics, wordnet domain, LU high hyperonym, etc. However, taking into account our experience with the manual rules, we limited the feature set to: Parts of Speech and wordnet domains of LUs from the same synset, Parts of Speech and wordnet domains of LUs linked by a certain lexical or synset relation. The set of training instances is extracted from the wordnet taking into account all LUs, synsets and relation links. The *Predictive Apriori* rule induction algorithm implemented in Weka[18] system [19] was used with the number of rules limited to 1000. We assumed 0.9 as a value for the accuracy threshold for positive rules (*rules of correctness*), and 0.05 for the negative ones. The accuracy is measured during the induction of the rules on the basis of the training instances. Rules of correctness correspond to more frequent sets of instances representing general dependencies present in the wordnet. Next, instances that do not match these rules are presented to lexicographers as potential anomalies requiring verification. Very rare sets of instance types are also considered to represent anomalies. All induced rules of correctness and incorrectness are presented for a verification. If some rules are judged as infallible, their results do not need to be validated any more. Some rules can be discarded as inaccurate.

We applied this approach to the data from *plWordNet* 2.0. The extracted rules include very general and obvious rules that we expected to appear, e.g. *LU Parts of Speech has to be consistent inside a synset* or *The Parts of Speech in a hypernymy link has to be same.*

A few mistakes were discovered with those rules. They concerned mostly wrong selection of the PoS for inter-lingual link targets. Some more interesting anomalies have been found when analysing domains of relations, caused mostly by the inconsistent selection of domains in hypernymic chains.

---

[18] http://www.cs.waikato.ac.nz/ml/weka/index.html.

6.4   Content Analysis

The evaluation of the meanings of LUs, synsets and relation links defined in the wordnet is only possible if we have some external definitions to compare with. We extract for each *plWordNet* word *context sets* of connected words from monolingual dictionaries and encyclopaedias used as knowledge sources, e.g. Wikipedia headword and words from the first paragraph of the Wikipedia article. We assume that for a word x words associated with x according to the knowledge sources should be found in the close surrounding of x in the wordnet, i.e. in the synset of x and synsets linked to it. Such a set of associated words we will call a *context set*. In the case of some knowledge sources, e.g. dictionaries, we can even attempt to extract word pairs that represent a particular lexico-semantic relation, e.g. synonymy or hypernymy and use them to enrich context sets. If for a word x and its synset s any member of s or any member of synset linked to s by short relation path is not found in the context set of x, we consider the given placement of x in s as suspicious. With this rule we aim at analysing co-inclusion of LUs into synsets, hypernymic links between synsets and synset glosses.

In order to asses the idea feasibility of this approach we performed an experiment consisting of two tests. During the first, for each LU x we checked if any other LU from this synset is included in the context set of x. During the second we analysed hypernymic links in a similar way. For a LU x in a synset s we tested whether x is included in a context set of at least one LU from a synset which is a hypernym of s. Because some definitions from knowledge sources may use more general terms to define a word, this test was extended to indirect hypernyms up to three hypernymy levels. After both tests had been applied, LUs were divided into four groups depending on the tests matched: from 0 to 2. The groups are presented to editors, but the most important is the 0-match group which signals potential anomalies. LUs from a result group are illustrated by their wordnet context (a synset plus its hypernyms) and their context sets.

Context sets were built on the basis of the five resources: three Polish internet dictionaries: [1,17][19], *Wikisłownik*[20] (Polish Wiktionary), and *Open Thesaurus* [13]. We used also a Measure of Semantic Relatedness (MSR) which was extracted from a large corpus of Polish of about 1.5 billion tokens by a method described in [15]. MSR was applied to produce for each input word a list of the top 5 words that are most semantically related to the input one. The list was used as a context set. Because the coverage of all knowledge sources is limited, we have finally merged them into one joint context set. For instance, an example of the 0-match LU *ekspres 3* 'zip' from the synset {zamek błyskawiczny 1, suwak 1, zamek 6, ekler 2, ekspres 3} 'slide fastener, zip, zipper'

- hypernyms: {zapięcie 2 'fastener'} — {zamknięcie 12 ≈'lock'} — {mechanizm 2 'mechanism'} and {przedmiot 1 'artifact'},

---

[19] http://sjp.pwn.pl/.
[20] https://pl.wiktionary.org/.

- SJP context set: pośpieszny 'fast', przesyłka 'letter/parcel', pocztowy 'postal', goniec 'messenger', expres 'express', posłaniec 'courier',
- MSR context set: pociąg 'train' 0.264775, pociąg osobowy 'slow train' 0.221895, pociąg pospieszny 'fast train' 0.200059, pociąg międzynarodowy 'international train' 0.188448, autobus 'bus' 0.185934.

The word sense *ekspres* 3 'zip' failed the tests, as a little old-fashioned way of saying and infrequent sense. Its placement in the *plWordNet* 2.1 structure is proper, but it should be considered as old fashioned according to its stylistic register and moved to a separated synset linked by inter-register synonymy to the original one.

This method was applied to verify 116 320 synsets from *plWordNet* 2.0: Among those synsets: 6 183 did not pass the test 1 for synset integrity, 15 901 did not pass the test 2 and can be considered as potentially located in a incorrect place, and 2 729 synsets did not pass both tests.

Concerning LUs, 160 041 were tested. Among them, 10 602 did not pass the test 1 of integration with a synset, 21 446 did not pass the test 2 of the placement and 14 244 did not pass both tests. The number of the tested LUs is lower than we could expect on the basis of the number of synsets, as from 106 241 words described in the synsets of *plWordNet* 2.0, we could find 14 244 words in any of the potential knowledge sources.

7   Conclusions

Automated wordnet evaluation is barely possible, if for a given language there is no similar resource which provides description of the lexico-semantic relations. Experiments that we performed on automated comparison of electronic dictionaries with the *plWordNet* structure, see Sect. 6.4, showed that it brings insightful results, but with low precision. Thus, we proposed a systematic overview of the possible diagnostic procedures for the wordnet. They are intended to provide support for wordnet editors by signalling potential errors.

Systematic classification of errors was proposed. For most types, sets of constraints were proposed with special attention given to the level of the semantic structures. A set of structurally supported constraints was developed that verifies semantically wordnet descriptions, but are still formulated in terms of the link types and properties of the synsets and LUs. The constructed complex diagnostic tool was applied in the development process of a very large wordnet. The tool helped to identify a substantial number of errors.

Finally, the long term experience of the *plWordNet* project shows, that is it is better to prevent errors than to correct them. This is especially important for the development of a large lexico-semantic network, in which an error made in one node can influence large number of other nodes. Thus we have developed a linguistic procedures supported by a set of tools. They help to maintain consistency of the editors' decisions by a applying varied means: tests built into the relation definitions, common way of using knowledge sources and tools for coordination and communication inside the linguistic team. Moreover, due to the use of the WordnetLoom editing system, wordnet editors have been separated from the direct encoding of the wordnet source files. Such an wordnet editing system is also a good place to implement possible control procedures. All the tools and systems developed for *plWordNet* are available on open licences.

Acknowledgments. Work financed by the Polish Ministry of Science and Higher Education, a program in support of scientific units involved in the development of a European research infrastructure for the humanities and social sciences in the scope of the consortia CLARIN ERIC and ESS-ERIC, 2015–2016.

References

1. Słownik Języka Polskiego. Wydawnictwo Naukowe PWN (2007)
2. The site of Wroclaw University of Technology Language Technology Group G4.19 (2013). http://www.nlp.pwr.wroc.pl
3. Broda, B., Maziarz, M., Piasecki, M.: Tools for plWordNet development. Presentation and perspectives. In: Calzolari, N., Choukri, K., Declerck, T., Dovgan, M., Maegaard, B., Mariani, J., JanOdijk, Piperidis, S. (eds.) Proceedings of the Eight International Conference on Language Resourcesand Evaluation (LREC 2012), pp. 3647–3652. European Language Resources Association (ELRA), Istanbul, Turkey, May 2012
4. Broda, B., Piasecki, M.: Evaluating LexCSD in a large scale experiment. Cont. Cybern. **40**(2), 419–436 (2011)
5. Cruse, A.: Meaning in Language. An Introduction to Semantics and Pragmatics. Oxford University Press, Oxford (2004)
6. Huang, C.R., Calzolari, N., Gangemi, A., Oltramari, A., Prévot, L. (eds.): Ontology and the Lexicon. A Natural Langue Processing Perspective. Studies in Natural Langue Processing. Cambridge University Press, Cambridge (2010)
7. Kubis, M.: A query language for WordNet-like lexical databases. In: Pan, J.-S., Chen, S.-M., Nguyen, N.T. (eds.) ACIIDS 2012, Part III. LNCS, vol. 7198, pp. 436–445. Springer, Heidelberg (2012)
8. Lohk, A., Vare, K., Võhandu, L.: Visual study of Estonian wordnet using bipartite graphs and minimal crossing algorithm. In: Proceedings of 6th Global Wordnet Conference, Matsue, Japan, January 2012
9. Maziarz, M., Piasecki, M., Rabiega-Wisniewska, J., Szpakowicz, S.: Semantic relations among nouns in Polish wordnet grounded in lexicographic and semantic tradition. Cogn. Stud. **11**, 161–181 (2011). http://www.eecs.uottawa.ca/~szpak/pub/Maziarz_et_al_CS2011a.pdf
10. Maziarz, M., Piasecki, M., Szpakowicz, S.: The chicken-and-egg problem in WordNet design: synonymy, synsets and constitutive relations. Lang. Resour. Eval. **47**(3), 769–796 (2013)
11. Maziarz, M., Piasecki, M., Szpakowicz, S., Rabiega-Wiśniewska, J., Hojka, B.: Semantic relations between verbs in Polish WordNet 2.0. Cogn. Stud. **11**, 183–200 (2011)
12. Maziarz, M., Szpakowicz, S., Piasecki, M.: Semantic relations among adjectives in Polish WordNet 2.0: a new relation set, discussion and evaluation. Cogn. Stud. **12**, 149–179 (2012)
13. Miłkowski, M.: Open thesaurus - polski thesaurus (2007). http://www.synomix.pl/

14. Piasecki, M., Marcińczuk, M., Ramocki, R., Maziarz, M.: WordNetLoom: a Word-Net development system integrating form-based and graph-based perspectives. Int. J. Data Min. Model. Manage. **5**(3), 210–232 (2013)
15. Piasecki, M., Szpakowicz, S., Broda, B.: A WordNet from the Ground Up. University of Technology Press, Wrocław (2009)
16. Rizov, B.: Hydra: a modal logic tool for wordnet development, validation and exploration. In: Calzolari, N., et al. (eds.) Proceedings of the Sixth International Conference on Language Resources and Evaluation (LREC 2008). European Language Resources Association (ELRA), Marrakech, Morocco, May 2008
17. SJP.PL, Z.: Słownik języka polskiego [A dictionary of the Polish language] (2015). http://sjp.pl/
18. Smrž, P.: Quality control and checking for wordnet development: a case study of balkanet. Rom. J. Inf. Sci. Technol. **2004**(1), 173–182 (2004)
19. Witten, I., Frank, E., Hall, M.: Data Mining: Practical Machine Learning Tools and Techniques. Morgan Kaufmann Publishers, San Francisco (2011)

Written Text and Document Processing

Simile or Not Simile?

Automatic Detection of Metonymic Relations in Japanese Literal Comparisons

Pawel Dybala[1(⊠)], Rafal Rzepka[2], Kenji Araki[2],
and Kohichi Sayama[3]

[1] Institute of Middle and Far Eastern Studies, Jagiellonian University, ul.
Gronostajowa 3, Kraków, Poland
paweldybala@res.otaru-uc.ac.jp
[2] Graduate School of Information Science and Technology,
Hokkaido University, Kita-ku, Kita 14 Nishi 9, Sapporo, Japan
{kabura,araki}@media.eng.hokudai.ac.jp
[3] Department of Information and Management Science,
Otaru University of Commerce, Midori 3-5-21, Otaru, Japan
sayama@res.otaru-uc.ac.jp

Abstract. In this paper we propose a method of automatic distinction between two types of formally identical expressions in Japanese: similes and "metonymical comparisosn", i.e. literal comparisons that include metonymic relations between elements. Expression like "*kujira no you na chiisai me*" can be translated into English as "eyes small as whale's", while in Japanese, due to the lack of possessive case, it can be misunderstood as "eyes small as a whale". The reason behind this is the presence of metonymic relation between components of such expressions. In the abovegiven example the word "whale" is a metonymy and represents "whale's eye". This is naturally understandable for humans, although formally difficult to detect by automatic algorithms, as both types of expressions (similes and metonymical comparisons) realize the same template. In this work we present a system able to distinguish between these two types of expressions. The system takes a Japanese expression as input and uses the Internet to check possessive relations between its elements. We propose a method of calculating a score based on co-occurrence of source and target pairs in Google (e.g. "whale's eye"). Evaluation experiment showed that the system distinguishes between similes and metonimical comparisons with the accuracy of 74 %. We discuss the results and give some ideas for the future.

Keywords: NLP · AI · Metaphor processing · Similes · Metonymies

1 Introduction

This paper summarizes our work on automatic distinguishing between similes an what we call "metonymical (or literal) comparisons" in Japanese. This research is a part of our larger project, aimed at constructing a conceptual network for processing Japanese metaphors [1].

© Springer International Publishing Switzerland 2016
Z. Vetulani et al. (Eds.): LTC 2013, LNAI 9561, pp. 277–289, 2016.
DOI: 10.1007/978-3-319-43808-5_21

Figurative speech is persistently present in our daily life. We often use metaphors to explain difficult words, to delicately suggest or emphasize something. Humans usually have no problems with creating and understanding such expressions. However, metaphor processing is in fact a complex cognitive process [2] and constructing its computational model is a very challenging task.

The most popular theories on metaphor understanding are the categorization view [3], the comparison view [4] and three hybrid views – the conventionality view [5], the aptness view [6] and the interpretive diversity view [7].

In our work, however, we use Ortony's conception of salience imbalance, which states that in metaphorical expressions certain highly salient properties of the metaphor source are matched with less salient properties of metaphor target. In other words, certain properties of the target, which are normally perceived as not very salient, become more salient by comparing the common ground between the target and the source [8]. In metaphorical comparison like this: "Billboards are like warts - they are ugly and stick out", very salient properties of "warts", such as "ugliness" or "sticking out", are at the same time not very salient (albeit not completely implausible) properties of "billboards" [8].

Alike other existing research on metaphor processing, such as Masui et al. [9], in our work we focus on the simplest and the most popular metaphorical figure of speech – a simile. A simile differs from a "classical" metaphor in that the latter compares two unlike things by saying that the one thing is the other thing, while simile directly compares two things through connective, usually "like", "as" or by specific verbs like "resembles". This genre is also present in Japanese - see Fig. 1.

Metaphor: *Ringo no you ni akai hoo*
(cheeks red as apple)

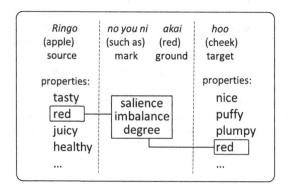

Fig. 1. Salience imbalance theory in Japanese metaphors (similes)

Although it is often argued that similes are not metaphors and should be seen rather as a different type of expressions, in our research we treat them as realisations of the same mechanisms. Whether we say "this man is a wolf" or "this man is like a wolf", we do compare his traits to those of a wolf, and the salience imbalance theory can be applied in both these cases. Thus, in our works we propose to define similes as a particular type of metaphors.

In metaphor most processing research that use the salience imbalance theory, like [9], metaphorical expressions are processed by first generation lists of target and source properties, and then comparing these lists in search of common grounds. An example of such process is shown on Fig. 1.

In our research we use commonly known notions of metaphor elements: source (phrase to which the target is compared), target (phrase compared to the source), ground (common ground between the source and the target) and mark (formal indicator of simile, like "such as" in "A such as B") – see Fig. 1 for example.

One common problem with Japanese similes is that there are two types of formally identical expressions: similes and what we call "metonymical comparisons".

As mentioned above, similes are expressions in which properties of target are explicitly compared to those of source, and no metonymical relations between the components occur. For example, in the expression "*chi no you ni akai kuchibiru*" (lips red as blood) the property of being red (*akai*), possessed by target "lips" (*kuchibiru*) is compared to one of the source "blood" (*chi*).

On the other hand, metonymical comparisons are literal comparisons, in which one entity is directly compared to another, very similar, also in terms of ontology. It is possible to state that "A has eyes like a whale", which does not mean that the properties of A's eyes are compared to those a whale. The "whale" here is a metonymy for "whale's eye". Thus, to human language users it is clear that A's eyes are somewhat similar to eyes of a whale. This comparison is not metaphorical, but clearly literal.

However, what is natural and understandable for humans may cause severe problems in automatic language processing. For a computer algorithm, expression "A has eyes like a whale" is formally a realization of the same pattern as "A has cheeks like apple". This problem is also present in Japanese. For example, the expression "*kujira no you na chiisai me*" (eyes small as whale's) can be translated into English as "eyes small as whale's", while in Japanese, due to the lack of possessive case, it literally sounds as "eyes small as a whale" (no apostrophe). Such expressions use the same pattern as similes, like "*ringo no you ni akai hoo*" ("cheeks red as an apple").

In other words, also in Japanese both similes and metonymical comparisons use the same templates (like "A *no you na* B" – "A such as B"), which makes it impossible to formally distinguish between them. Table 1 depicts this problem on examples.

Table 1. Example of simile and metonymical comparison realising the same template

Template	Source (noun)	*no you ni* (such as)	Ground (adjective)	Target (noun)
Simile	*Ringo* (apple)	*no you ni*	*akai* (red)	*hoo* (cheek)
Metonymical comparison	*Kujira* (whale)	*no you ni*	*chiisai* (small)	*me* (eye)
Non-metonymical comparison	*Kujira* (whale)	*no you ni*	*ookii* (big)	*doubutsu* (animal)

Thus, in metonymical comparisons, what seems to be the source of the metaphor is actually an abbreviation of the whole phrase. "*Kujira*" ("whale") in "*kujira no you na chiisai me*" ("eyes small like whale's") is an abbreviation (metonymy) for "*kujira no me*" ("whale's eyes") – however, due to the fuzzy nature of Japanese possessive particle "*no*" (which can be an indicator of possessive as well as other relations between words), formally it represents the same template as actual metaphorical similes, like "*ringo no you ni akai hoo*" ("cheeks red as apple").

Needless to say, this causes problems in metaphor processing. Many existing works focus on generation of source and target description. However, if a system that performs such processing cannot distinguish between similes and literal comparisons, it can mistakingly generate descriptions and search for common grounds for wrong sources. Examples of such incorrect and correct processing are shown on Fig. 2.

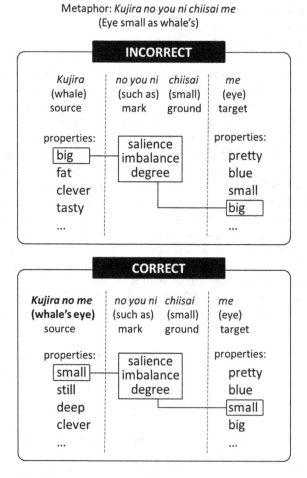

Fig. 2. Example of incorrect metaphor processing caused by not distinguishing between similes and metonymical (literal) comparisons, and its correct version after proper recognition of metonymical relations.

Therefore, not distinguishing between these two formally identical types of expressions may cause numerous problems in research on metaphor processing. However, many existing works in this field tend to treat Japanese literal comparisons as similes (metaphors). This problem is present also in existing Japanese metaphor dictionaries, including those most popular, like Retorika [10] or Nakamura's "Dictionary of metaphorical expressions" [11]. The latter, for instance, includes examples as: "*hirame no you na me*" (eyes like halibut's) or "*kani no you na kanashii kaotsuki*" (face sad as crab's), which, according to the above given explanation, are not metaphors, but literal comparisons which include metonymy.

Also Onai's dictionary [12], which we used to construct our corpus of metaphors (see Sect. 2) does not distinguish between these two types of expressions.

This problem is also present in research works. Tokunaga and Terai [13] claim that expressions like "*hana no you na nioi*" ("scent like flower's") is a metaphor, while it clearly is a literal comparison, in which *hana* (flower) is a metonymy for "*hana no nioi*" (flower's scent). Terai et al. [14] analogically call phrases like "*oni no you na hyoujou*" ("expression like devil's") metaphors, while also in this case it is a literal comparison with metonymical relationship.

That said, there have been some attempts to distinguish between these two types of expressions. Tazoe et al. [15] proposed a system that automatically detects what they call literals (literal comparisons with metonymical relations between components). The system is pattern based and uses noun categorization based rules to calculate whether inputted expression is a simile or a literal. The categorization rules were based on the output of a Japanese parsing tool. The system's accuracy, tested on expressions extracted from newspaper articles, was shown to be on 80 % level, which is slightly better than in our system (74 %). However, the system we proposed does not require any patterns that would be specifically designed for the purpose of metonymy detection (see also discussion in Sect. 6). Also, the authors used notions like "almost literal" to annotate some expressions, which does not seem very useful.

In this paper we present our approach to the topic of metonymy recognition.

2 Data Set

2.1 Japanese Metaphor Corpus

In this project we use a corpus of Japanese metaphors based on Onai's Great Dictionary of Japanese Metaphorical and Synonymic Expressions [12]. The dictionary contains metaphors selected from Japanese modern literature and Japanese translations of foreign works. The dictionary contains approximately 30,000 metaphorical entries. According to the author, it was created to assist in finding interesting and sophisticated expressions that can be used instead of common phrases. The expressions are sorted by topics and used phrases. Below we present an entry example after compilation to fit our corpus (Table 2).

Table 2. Example of an entry from Japanese metaphor corpus based on Onai's Great Dictionary of Japanese Metaphorical and Synonymic Expressions [12].

Topic	Phrase	Metaphor example
唇;くちびる *kuchibiru* lips	あかい唇;あかいくちびる *akai kuchibiru* red lips	チェリーのような唇で笑う *Cherii no you na kuchibiru de warau* Smile with lips red as cherries

From the metaphors included in the corpus we automatically selected expressions (i.e. similes or comparisons) that match the templates described in Sect. 2.2. From this group, for the need of this particular study we selected expressions that realize the pattern: "noun - mark - adjective - noun", as presented in Table 3.

Table 3. Examples of expressions from data set that realize the template: "noun - mark - adjective – noun"

Noun source	Mark	Adjective ground	Noun target	Direct or Metonymical?
1. Koori no you ni tsumetai te (Hand cold as ice)				Simile
koori (ice)	*no you ni* (as)	*tsumetai* (cold)	*te* (hand)	
2. Kujira no you na chiisai me (Eyes small as whale's)				Literal comparison
kujira (whale)	*no you na* (as)	*chiisai* (small)	*me* (eye)	
3. Chi no you ni akai kuchibiru (Lips red as blood)				Simile
chi (blood)	*no you ni* (as)	*akai* (red)	*kuchibiru* (lips)	
4. Maruta mitai na futoi ryouashi (Legs fat as log)				Simile
maruta (log)	*mitai na* (as)	*futoi* (fat)	*ryouashi* (legs)	

To conduct the experiment described in this paper, from this group we randomly selected 100 similes. All were annotated as "simile" or "literal comparison" by two Japanese linguists (see Table 4 for summary).

Table 4. Data set summary

Similes	36
Literal comparisons (with metonymy)	64
Total	100

2.2 Templates Set

To extract expressions that can be similes or literal comparisons from the metaphor corpus (see Sect. 2.1), we manually prepared a set of 81 templates frequently used in

Japanese similes. Every template includes metaphor's source, target, ground and mark. Each template has also POS tags, which means that the same marks are used multiple times, as shown below on the example of mark "*mitai*" ("as", "alike"):

noun - *mitai na* - noun (noun - such as - noun)

verb - *mitai na* - noun (verb - such as - noun)

noun - *mitai ni* - verb (noun - such as - verb)

noun - *mitai ni* - adjective (noun - such as - adjective)

verb - *mitai ni* - verb (verb - such as - verb)

verb - *mitai ni* - adjective (verb - such as adjective).

3 System

The system described in this section uses online and offline resources to distinguish between metaphorical similes and literal comparisons (with metonymy) in Japanese. Its algorithm's outline is shown on Fig. 3.

The system's input is an expression in Japanese (simile or literal comparison). First the system uses templates (see Sect. 2.2) to extract source, target, mark and ground from the inputted expression. Next, it tries to determine whether an "is-a" or "has-a" relationship exists between the target and source. If, for instance, input is "*Zou no you na chiisai me*" ("Eye small as elephant's"), the system will check if "*zou*" ("elephant") can have a "*me*" ("eye"). To do so, we initially intended to perform a co-occurrence check in the Internet or offline corpora and query the phrase "*zou no me*" ("elephant's eye"). However, as mentioned above, Japanese particle "*no*" performs also other functions as possessive, and thus it is problematic to define which meaning of it is used in this particular expression. For example, expression "*gin no kami*" can mean "Silver's hair", but also "silver hair", depending on the context.

Thus, we decided to perform this query in English, which does not cause such problems. To do that, we use E-dict Japanese-English dictionary [16]. After translating source and target to English, the system queries the phrase "source's target" (in the example above – "elephant's eye") in Google (www.google.com).

In some cases in E-dict, English translations of Japanese words have more than one word. For example, word "*hazakura*" is translated as "cherry tree in leaves". Querying such long phrases in Google is pointless and returns none or very few results. Thus, we decided to introduce two additional rules to the algorithm:

(1) if English translation of the source has more than one word, the system uses *Bunrui goi hyou* [17], a Japanese thesaurus dictionary, to check which category the Japanese word (source) belongs to. Next the system translates the category name to English and uses it in Google query, instead of the original phrase. If the translation of the category name is also longer than one word, the system repeats this operation and checks one more category above. Example of this is shown below:

Expression: *Uguisu no you ni kawairashii koe*

(Voice sweet as Japanese bush warbler's)

Source: *uguisu* (Japanese bush warbler)

Number of words in source's translation: 3
Source belongs to category: *chourui* (birds)
Query phrase: "bird's voice"

(2) if English translation of target has more than one word, the system uses Stanford NLP Parser [18] to extract the root of inputted phrase, as in this example:
Expression: *Kodomo no you na shinken na kaotsuki.*
(Facial expression serious as child's)
Target: *kaotsuki* (facial expressions)
Number of words in target's translation: 2
Target phrase's root: expression
Query phrase: "child's expression".

Thus, the system preprocesses the phrases to be queried in Google. The assumption was that if the phrase "source's target" has high hit rate, it is highly likely that the relationship between these two is commonsensically possessive. The phrase "elephant's eye", for example, has over 100, 000 matches, which means that, according to the Internet, elephants tend to have eyes.

However, at this stage we faced a serious noise problem, caused by the fact that Google queries are by default case insensitive. In the above-mentioned example, the results for "elephant's eye" include those actually related to the visual organ that can be possessed by elephants, as well as hits for a famous restaurant "Elephant's Eye". This can significantly hinder the outcome of this process, as in the example where the input is "*koori no you ni tsumetai te*" ("hand cold as ice"), for which the system queries the phrase "ice's hand". The hit rate in this case should be close to zero, as, commonsensically speaking, ice does not have hands. However, with Google's case insensitivity, in this case results also include those for "Ice's hands", where "Ice" is someone's surname or nickname. Therefore, the hit rate for the phrase "ice's hands" (with case insensivity) is about 2,290 (result acquired on September 15th, 2015) – see Fig. 4.

Due to this noise, this expression ("hand cold as ice") can be mistakingly detected as a metonymical comparison (non-metaphor). Therefore, although initially we planed to base only on simple Google hit rates for inputted phrases, in order to deal with this noise we decided to introduce a method of calculating what we call the "metonymy score" (Ms). The score is calculated as follows:

$$Ms = \log HitRate \times \frac{s\_s}{s\_s + s\_b + b\_s + b\_b}$$

"HitRate" is the inputted phrase's hit rate in Google, "s_s" (abbreviation from "small_small") is the occurance of the inputted phrase where both source and target begin with small letters, in first 100 snippets for the particular query (or less, if hit rate < 100). The reason for taking only 100 snippets into consideration is that checking all of them would be time consuming, especially for phrases with very high hit rate; "s_b" ("small_big") is the occurrence of the inputted phrase where source begins with small letter, and target begins with capital; "b_s" ("big_small") is the occurrence of the inputted phrase where source begins with capital, and target begins small letter. Finally,

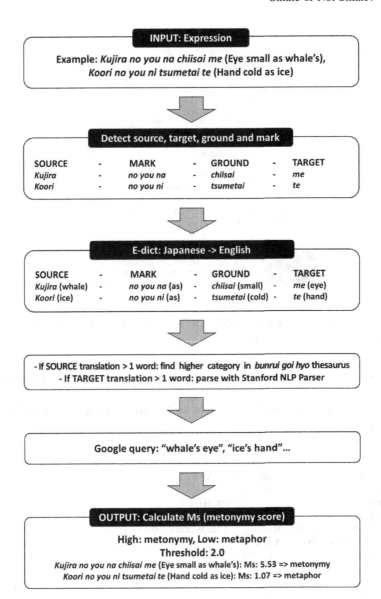

Fig. 3. Metonymy detection system – algorithm outline

"b_b" ("big_big") is the occurrence of the inputted phrase where both source and target begin with capital.

The reason we use logarithm is that the difference in hit rate does not change gradually. The difference between HitRate = 1 and HitRate = 2 is 1, but in fact it doubles, while between HitRate = 10000 and HitRate = 10001 it is still 1, but it is of not so high importance.

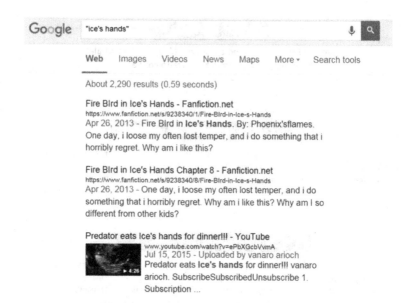

Fig. 4. Query results for the phrase "ice's hands" in Google – example of results bias caused by case insensivity (www.google.com).

The right part of the formula represents what percentage of all phrases found in snippets is s_s.

Below we present the score calculation for the two examples mentioned above:

Example 1:

Input:	*Kujira no you na chiisai me.*
	(Eye small as whale's)
Source:	*kujira* (whale)
Target:	*me* (eye)
Ground:	*chiisai* (small)
Mark:	*no you na* (such as)
Simile or literal comparison?	literal comparison
Query phrase:	"whale's eye"
Hit rate:	11 500
s_s:	39
s_b:	0
b_s:	8
b_b:	19
Ms:	5.53

$$Ms = \log 11500 \times \frac{39}{39 + 0 + 8 + 19}$$

Example 2:

Input:	*Koori no you ni tsumetai te.*
	(Hand cold as ice)
Source:	*koori* (ice)
Target:	*te* (hand)
Ground:	*tsumetai* (cold)
Mark:	*no you ni* (such as)
Simile or literal comparison?	simile
Query phrase: "ice's hand"	
Hit rate:	3380
s_s:	10
s_b:	0
b_s:	63
b_b:	3
Ms:	1.07

$$Ms = \log 3380 \times \frac{10}{10 + 0 + 63 + 3}$$

4 Experiment

To verify our approach, we conducted an experiment in which we calculated Ms (metonymy scores) for 100 phrases from our metaphor corpus that realize the pattern: "noun - mark - adjective - noun" (see Sect. 2.2). The threshold to distinguish between similes and literal metonymical comparisons was experimentally set to 2.0, which means that if Ms was below 2.0, input was recognized as a simile, and if Ms was equal to or higher than 2.0, input was recognized as a literal comparison.

The results were compared to annotations (simile/comparison) made by our experts.

5 Results

The experiment showed that our system can distinguish between similes and comparisons literal with the accuracy of 74 %. Results are shown in Table 5.

Table 5. Experiment results

Expressions recognized correctly		Expressions recognized incorrectly	
74/100 (74 %)		36/100 (36 %)	
Literal comparisons	Similes	Literal comparisons	Similes
31/36 (86.1 %)	43/64 (67.2 %)	5/36 (13.9 %)	21/64 (32.8 %)
Accuracy		74 %	
Precision		59.6 %	
Recall		86.1 %	
F measure		0.704	

6   Discussion

The experiment results show that the proposed system distinguishes between similes and literal comparisons with metonymy with fairly high accuracy of 74 %. This is slightly lower than the above mentioned system by Tazoe et al. [15] (accuracy of 80 %). That system, however, used complex sets of rules based on noun categorization. The set was prepared specifically for that study. In our system we do not use any tools or resources that were developed for the purpose of this research. The algorithm is much more simple and yet it achieved comparable level of accuracy (only 6 % difference).

Worth mentioning is the fact that from 30 inputted expressions for which the Ms (metonymy score) was 0, 29 were actually not comparisons, but similes. Thus, it can be stated that expressions for which Ms = 0 are recognized as metaphors with 96.7 % accuracy.

That said, the overall results could be higher and there is still place for improvement. With Ms threshold set to 2.0, 21 similes were mistakingly recognized as literal comparisons, and 5 comparisons were mistaken for similes. The analysis of results and stages of processing revealed that there are two main reasons of system failures: (1) cultural differences and (2) conceptual differences between languages.

(1) Cultural differences in metaphors occur when the source metaphor (here: Japanese) contains elements that are specific to that particular culture. For example, expression "*Daruma no you na marui me*" ("eye round as Daruma's"), was falsely recognized by our system as a metaphor, as the phrase "Daruma's eye" has low hit rate in Google. Daruma is a traditional Japanese doll with round eyes English speakers may not be familiar with.

(2) Conceptual differences between languages occur when what is commonly called "way of thinking" differs between languages. For example, "*kobato no you na adokenai kao*" ("face innocent as squab's") was mistaken for metaphor, while it is a metonymy. The reason for this is that in English it is not very natural to say that birds have faces, and thus phrase "squab's face" did not score high on Google. In Japanese, however, saying that birds have faces is natural.

To improve the system and avoid such errors in the future, we plan to use ontology check, as we did in one of earlier stages of the system algorithm (see Sect. 3). If the system will be able to check that Daruma is a doll, it could easily alter the query (to "doll's eye") and produce more accurate results.

We are also planning to check all snippets, not only 100, as in this version of the system. This will significantly extend the processing time, but should lead to improvement in system's accuracy.

7   Conclusions and Possible Applications

In this paper we introduced our system that automatically distinguishes between Japanese metaphorical similes and metonymical comparisons. The system works with 74 % accuracy, which is fairly encouraging.

The results of this work can be useful not only in metaphor processing, but also in machine translation. Google translator (www.translate.google.com), for instance, is not able to translate metonymies, as it does not distinguishes between them and actual metaphors. To the authors' best knowledge, neither does any other existing MT system. The use of our algorithm, however, would allow to fix this error and improve such systems' performance.

References

1. Dybala, P., Ptaszynski, M., Rzepka, R., Araki, K., Sayama, K.: Metaphor, humor and emotion processing in human-computer interaction. Int. J. Comput. Linguist. Res. 4(1), 1–13 (2013)
2. Lakoff, G., Johnson, M.: Metaphors We Live By. University of Chicago Press, Chicago (1980)
3. Glucksberg, S.: Understanding Figurative Language: From Metaphors to Idioms. Oxford University Press, New York (2001)
4. Gentner, D.: Structure mapping: a theoretical frame- work for analogy. Cogn. Sci. 7, 55–170 (1983)
5. Bowdle, B., Gentner, D.: The career of metaphor. Psychol. Rev. 111(1), 193–216 (2004)
6. Jones, L., Estes, Z.: Metaphor comprehension as attributive categorization. J. Mem. Lang. 53, 110–124 (2005)
7. Utsumi, A., Kuwabara, Y.: Interpretive diversity as a source of metaphor-simile distinction. In: 27th Annual Meeting of the Cognitive Science Society, Mahwah, NJ, pp. 2230–2235 (2005)
8. Ortony, A.: Beyond literal similarity. Psychol. Rev. 86, 161–180 (1979)
9. Masui, F., Kawamura, Y., Fukumoto, J., Isu, N.: MURASAKI: web-based word sense description system. In: ITC-CSCC 2008, Shimonoseki, Japan, pp. 1285–1288 (2008)
10. Hangai, Y.: Retorika Hiyu hyougen jiten (Rhetorica: Figurative Expressions Dictionary). Hakusuisha (1994)
11. Nakamura, A.: Hiyu hyougen jiten (Metaphorical Expression Dictionary). Kadokawa shoten (1995)
12. Onai, H.: Great Dictionary of 33800 Japanese Metaphors and Synonyms (in Japanese). Kodansha (2005)
13. Tokunaga, T., Terai, A.: Hiyu rikai no tame no gengo shori (Language processing for metaphor understanding – in Japanese). Gekkan Gengo 37(8), 46–53 (2008)
14. Terai, A., Nakagawa, M., Tokunaga, T.: Hiyu rikai katei ni okeru souhatsu tokuchou no shinri jikken ni yoru kenshou (Experimental examination of emerging characteristics in metaphor understanding). In: 23rd Conference Meeting of Japanese Cognitive Science Society, Nagoya, Japan, pp. 388–389 (2006)
15. Tazoe, T., Shiino, T., Masui, F., Kawai, A.: The metaphorical judgement model for "Noun B like Noun A" Expressions (in Japanese). J. Nat. Lang. Process. 10(2), 43–58 (2003)
16. Breen, J.: Building an electronic Japanese- English dictionary. In: Japanese Studies Association of Australia Conference, Brisbane, Australia (1995)
17. National Institute for Japanese Language. Bunrui Goi Hyo: revised and enlarged edition Dainippon Tosho (2004)
18. Socher, R., Bauer, J., Manning, C.D., Ng, A.Y.: Parsing with compositional vector grammars. In: 51st Annual Meeting of the Association for Computational Linguistics, Sofia, Bulgaria, pp. 455–465 (2013)

Spanish Diacritic Error Detection and Restoration—A Survey

Mans Hulden[1] and Jerid Francom[2]([⊠])

[1] University of Colorado, Boulder, CO 80303, USA
mans.hulden@colorado.edu
[2] Wake Forest University, Winston-Salem, NC 27109, USA
francojc@wfu.edu

Abstract. In this paper we address the problem of diacritic error detection and restoration—the task of identifying and correcting missing accents in text. In particular, we evaluate the performance of a simple part-of-speech tagger-based technique comparing it to other established methods for error detection/restoration: unigram frequency, decision lists, discriminative classifiers, a machine-translation based method, and grapheme-based approaches. In languages such as Spanish (the focus here), diacritics play a key role in disambiguation and results show that a straightforward modification to an n-gram tagger can be used to achieve good performance in diacritic error identification without resorting to any specialized machinery. Our method should be applicable to any language where diacritics distribute comparably and perform similar roles of disambiguation.

1 Introduction

Lexical disambiguation is key to developing robust natural language processing applications in a variety of domains such as grammar and spell checking [1] and text-to-speech applications [2], among other direct applications. Effective diacritic restoration, usually a pre-processing task, is also essential to the accuracy and reliability of any subsequent text processing and ever more important as NLP investigations are applied to 'real-world' contexts in which normalized text cannot be assumed.

The primary areas of investigation on lexical disambiguation have focused on syntactic, or part-of-speech (**house/noun** vs. **house/verb**) and semantic, or word sense (**bug/insect** vs. **bug/small microphone**) ambiguities. Less attention has focused on ambiguities that arise from orthographic errors. An important component of the orthography of many of the world's languages, diacritic markings are often stripped or appear inconsistent due to technical errors— OCR errors, 8-bit conversion/stripping, ill-equipped keyboards, etc.—as well as human error like native speaker errors related to the level of formality and/or orthographic knowledge. For example, email communication in Spanish more often than not lacks systematic diacritic markings, most probably for convenience. Also, of all lexical errors for high school and early college students in Spain, orthographic accentuation is the most common [3].

© Springer International Publishing Switzerland 2016
Z. Vetulani et al. (Eds.): LTC 2013, LNAI 9561, pp. 290–303, 2016.
DOI: 10.1007/978-3-319-43808-5_22

Whereas identified diacritic errors can be restored quite trivially in Spanish, because in Spanish all words have maximally one diacritic mark and there rarely are more than two-way ambiguous words in the lexicon, reliable detection of diacritic errors is less straightforward. One the one hand, stripping diacritics from some words produce non-ambiguous non-words such as **según/*segun** (according to), **quizás/*quizas** (perhaps), etc. which can be resolved easily with access to a large lexicon and/ or morphological analysis resources. On the other hand, stripping diacritics from other words produces semantic or syntactic ambiguity, such as pairs for the verb 'hablar' (to speak) **habló [3p/past]/hablo [1p/pres]**, **hablará[3p/fut]/hablara[3p/past/subj]**, noun pairs **secretaría/secretaria** (secretariat vs. secretary) or demonstrative/noun **estas/éstas** (these) or demonstrative/verb **estas/estás** (these/are [2p/pres]) pairs. These are real-world, context-dependent errors which are much more difficult to reliably identify.

In this paper we focus on a novel, potentially informative angle to the problem of diacritic error detection which leverages the observation that the disambiguation a modern HMM part-of-speech tagger performs can be extended to give a judgment on whether a particular word is correctly diacriticized. For our main target language, Spanish, the correction itself is a relatively straightforward task as almost all words have maximally one diacritic mark and because we rarely find more than two-way ambiguous words in the lexicon. Hence, in the following, we shall focus on the identification of incorrectly diacriticized words and assume the availability of auxiliary techniques to perform the correction. Although some of the methods described below actually do perform restoration, we make no distinction between the task of detecting incorrect diacritization and actually providing the correct version of a word.

2 Prior Work

There are several studies that are relevant to the current investigation. First, Yarowsky [4,5] advocates a decision-list approach combining simple word form frequency, morphological regularity and collocational information to restore diacritics.[1] This decision-list implementation is motivated in that each strategy in the decision list show complementary strengths and weaknesses. Results from Yarowsky's study, looking at Spanish in particular, appear to show high levels of accuracy for individual strategies and even higher levels when combining methods. It is worth noting, however, that the impressive results reported in these results may, in part, result from the fact that the training and evaluation data are drawn from the same genre or register and most likely show homogeneity that cannot be expected in all training/evaluation tests. Moreover, the strategies employed require fairly large training sets of orthographically correct(ed) text—a characteristic that potentially limits the application of these methods to

---

[1] The suffix-based approach described by Yarowsky [4,5] is not considered here as morphological form merely serves as a proxy for part-of-speech category, the primary variable of the current POS-tag approach.

diacritic restoration of text for less-resourced languages in which the availability of correctly marked text is lacking.

A second approach to diacritic restoration explored in the literature, partly motivated by the resource-scarcity problem [6], hypothesizes that local graphemic distribution can provide sufficient information to cue effective diacritic restoration, even based on small training sets [7]. An implementation of a memory-based learning (MBL) algorithm, De Pauw et al. [8], reports mixed restoration accuracy rates for a variety of African, Asian and European languages, including the Romance language French, using a grapheme-based learning approach. In the authors' assessment, memory-based restoration effectiveness hinges on LexDiff, a metric of orthographic ambiguity calculated by taking the ratio of the number of unique latinized forms over the total number correctly marked forms. However, it is not clear how robust the technique is, as reported performance varies for languages matched for LexDiff for various training corpus sizes.

A recently proposed method for Hungarian diacritic correction is to train an off-the-shelf statistical machine translation (SMT) system to 'translate' fully undiacriticized sentences to their correctly diacriticized counterparts [9]. We evaluate a similar model using varying quantities of training data. The potential advantage of this approach, unlike the POS-based method, is that any correctly diacriticized raw text can be used during training.

Similar to the SMT approach, a discriminative classifier that is trained to classify undiacriticized words into two classes ('should have diacritic'/'should not have diacritic') has also been proposed [10]. Other similar models that use variants of feature-based classification (e.g. Support Vector Machines) for the same purpose have been used for other languages such as Arabic [11] and Vietnamese [12]. Following this, we implement an averaged perceptron to detect whether words should carry a diacritic or not. The perceptron was chosen because of the relatively small models it yields, its training speed, and the small number of parameters to tune. This approach has the same advantage as the SMT method: plain, roughly correctly diacriticized text is sufficient for training.

Most closely related to the current part-of-speech based work, Simard and Deslauriers [13] present a POS-tagger based approach for the restoration of French diacritics. In essence, the proposed solution is to try different variant 'candidate' diacritizations of an input sentence and use a Hidden Markov Model (HMM) tagger to produce a probability score for each 'candidate' restoration. The combination of diacritics with the highest likelihood, as judged by the POS tagger, is finally chosen as the correct restoration. As in the current approach, POS-tag information is harnessed to provide cues for diacritic error detection. However, this POS-candidate approach requires more machinery and is somewhat more involved than the current POS-tag approach, which—all else being equal—would be preferred, given implementation considerations.

3 Part-of-Speech Based Method

The core idea behind our POS based method is to train an n-gram tagger on a tagged corpus which is augmented with information about diacritic placement. More concretely, given a corpus C, we divide the corpus into two copies C_1 and C_2—one with diacritics stripped, and another with the correct diacritic placement intact. For each word/tag pair in the stripped corpus, we then augment the corresponding tag for each word with information about whether the word is correctly diacriticized (by adding a sequence BAD or OK to the original tag). Naturally, only some words in the stripped corpus will be marked BAD, while the rest will all carry the OK-tag. See Table 1 for an illustration of a hypothetical sentence 'According to them (he/she/you[formal]) (did) not buy anything there' from both corpora.[2] From this new corpus, which is twice the size of the original corpus, we train a Hidden Markov Model tagger in the usual way.

Table 1. Example of generation of diacritic-stripped variant corpus for training, from original sentence (1). Tags are simply augmented with information about whether words are correctly diacriticized.

(1)		(2)	
Según	SPS00-OK	Segun	SPS00-BAD
ellos	PP3MP000-OK	ellos	PP3MP000-OK
no	RN-OK	no	RN-OK
compró	VMIS3S0-OK	compro	VMIS3S0-BAD
nada	RG-OK	nada	RG-OK
allí	RG-OK	alli	RG-BAD
.	Fp-OK	.	Fp-OK

After the tagger is trained on the corpus, we in effect produce a POS tagger that not only is able to tag words where the diacritics are missing, but that also marks each word as having either correct or incorrect accent marks. That is, the output of the tagger would look like the two columns in Table 1.

The motivation behind such an approach is threefold. First, there is the obvious direct connection behind part-of-speech and diacritic-induced ambiguity: some words are ambiguous entirely along these lines (**completo** [N] (complete) / **completó** [V] (completed), **esta** [PRON] (this) / **está** [V] (is), etc.). Secondly, as has been noted in the literature on decision lists, POS sequences themselves are very good indicators of a given correct accent placement, although the ambiguity may not distinguishable by local POS class alone: for example, the sequence **(1) PREP (2) que (3) ... -ara**, is a very strong clue to word **(3)** being in

---

[2] The widely-adopted EAGLES tagset for Spanish is used for part-of-speech annotation (see Freeling: http://nlp.lsi.upc.edu/freeling/doc/tagsets/tagset-es.html [last accessed September 20, 2015]).

the subjunctive mood and thus diacriticized -ara, vs. the future -ará (para que terminara / comprara / empezara/etc.). Contrariwise, the sequence (1) NOUN (2) que (3) ... -ara, is usually indicative of the opposite choice: the future tense (cosa que terminará / acabará / etc.).[3] Thirdly, assuming the tagset is fine-grained enough, distinguishing between person and tense of verbs, for instance, we can evaluate common diacritic placement errors that are distinguishable along those lines: hablo [1p/pres] vs. habló [3p/past] (to speak), toco[1p/pres] vs. tocó[3p/past] (to touch), etc.

It should be noted that such discriminative power can be obtained by first part-of-speech tagging a text (keeping in mind that the tagger needs to be able to handle incorrectly diacriticized input), and then applying a separate decision list trained to identify such sequences as described above. However, by including the information about correct accent placement in the tags themselves, we can produce equally effective results without the decision list.

As the output of the system does not give us the correct form of an incorrectly accented word, further processing is necessary. The augmented POS tag only tells us whether a word is correctly or incorrectly diacriticized. The task of actually restoring the diacritics may require further methods that depend on the language and the types of ambiguity it contains. In the case of Spanish, one can restore diacritics to most words correctly even without access to a dictionary. Since Spanish stress placement is predictable in the absence of diacritics, one can rule out a number of implausible corrections using only knowledge of Spanish stress rules and ambiguity types (such as -ara/-ará and -o/ó mentioned above). Having access to a simple dictionary or morphological analyzer would resolve the restoration problem almost perfectly. This because almost all words in Spanish are maximally two-way-ambiguous in diacritization and only a few exceptions such as esta/está/ésta exist. However, more elaborate treatment would be required for other languages, such as French, where the diacritization behaves differently and is less predictable.

It is worth noting that while a standard trigram tagger would not be expected to yield accuracies over 97 % in a plain POS tagging task, the diacritic restoration task is much simpler and we can expect to exceed POS tagging accuracies by a fair margin.

4   Evaluation

In all the experiments that follow, we consider the possible Spanish diacriticized graphemes to be á,é,í,ó,ú,ü and their uppercase counterparts. We do not consider ñ to be a diacriticized letter.

---

[3] We assume here that the relevant n-gram tagger that is trained has some suffix-based mechanism for guessing parts-of-speech for unknown words as is generally the case with better-performing taggers, such as TnT [14], or HunPos [15].

4.1 Alternative Restoration Methods

To evaluate the performance of the POS-based method, we compare its performance to various methods, each documented in the previous literature and implemented as follows.

A Frequency Baseline. As a baseline model we have chosen the simple approach of simply choosing the most frequent orthographic word form if it is ambiguous. In the case that an input word is already diacriticized, we do not remove accent marks, working on the assumption that anything diacriticized is reliable. This baseline has been shown quite difficult to substantially improve upon for many languages, including Spanish [4] and French [13].

Character-Based Restoration. We have also evaluated the performance of a character-based restoration algorithm, available directly through the *Charlifter* program [16] and based on the description in Wagacha et al. [17].

Decision List. As another alternative, we have implemented the decision list strategy described in Yarowsky [4]. The method involves collecting collocational information for each ambiguous word in a corpus, using pre-specified contexts, and then creating a decision list from the collocation counts. The decision lists are rigged so that the most reliable collocations are applied first. The types of collocations considered in the learning task are the following:

- Word to the left ($-1w$)
- Word to the right ($+1w$)
- The previous two words ($-2w$, $-1w$)
- The following two words ($+1w$, $+2w$)
- Any word in a ± 20 word window ($+-20w$)

Once the collocation counts are collected from a corpus, the decision list is sorted by log-likelihood ratio so that more reliable rules are applied before less reliable ones. In the absence of any applicable rule, a 'default' rule will choose the most frequent accent marking for ambiguous words.

As an example of the types of rules output by the decision list method, one highly-ranked rule from the induced rule set reads as follows:

```
inicio (-1w,se) => inició    4.11087386417331
```

That is, **inicio** should be corrected as **inició**, if preceded by the word **se**.

Averaged Perceptron. We also implemented a discriminative classifier, an averaged perceptron [18], using features similar to the ones in the decision list. For this model, the training data was stripped of diacritics and the classifier was trained to assign de-diacriticized input into one of two classes: **word has diacritic/word does not have diacritic**. In other words, it only distinguishes whether a word should carry a diacritic based on context features. The binary features used were the following:

- Current word (0w)
- Preceding word (−1w)
- Following word (+1w)
- Two preceding words (−1w, −2w)
- Two following words (+1w, +2w)
- All suffixes of current word of length 2–5.
- Current word and preceding word (0w, −1w)
- Preceding word (−1w) and current word suffix of length 3
- The surrounding two words (−1w, +1w)

These features were the result of feature selection on 10 % of the training data set aside for development. The original features before selection contained all the combinations of the final features described here, and also "word-in-window" features, as per [4]. The "word-in-window" features were all discarded as they did not improve performance on the development set.

A Machine Translation Model. A statistical machine translation approach was also included in our survey of diacritic restoration methods. Using methods similar to those for a recent implementation of a machine translation system for diacritic restoration for Hungarian [9], we used the freely available Moses toolkit [19] which provides tools out-of-the-box for both the creation and decoding of translation models. Language models were created using SRILM [20]. The translation models were created using a parallel corpus of lowercased unigram phrases to capture the distribution of diacritized forms and corresponding language models were restricted to 1:5 g phrases in mixed-case form accounting for local word context.

4.2   Training and Evaluation Data Sets

In order to evaluate the performance of these various methods and contrast them with our POS-tag approach, we trained each on the same data set and then evaluated each model produced on three separate evaluation sets constituting varying types of diacritic error detection challenges. Our training data set was the POS-tagged portion of the Gigaword Corpus which consists of AFP newswire text [21], henceforth AFP. In total, it contains over 1.2 million word tokens (1,202,573). The AFP training set includes a somewhat simplified part-of-speech tag set that includes major grammatical category information—key for the POS-tag error detection algorithm.

The evaluation sets include a small subsection of the AFP data not included in the training set (19,720 word tokens) and a subsection of the ACTIV-ES film dialogue corpus [22] based on data drawn from Spanish language films (19,381 word tokens). The film data was selected from the larger film dialogue corpus; given that in the original data acquired on the web, diacritic markings were only partially correct and reflected errors typically made by native speakers. The original film data set was hand-corrected by the authors in order to produce a gold-standard version for evaluation purposes. Finally, diacritic-stripped versions of both the AFP (AFP-stripped) and film evaluation (Film-stripped) data sets were created and the original, partially-correct film (Film-original) data set was retained and included in the evaluation as a measure of the effectiveness of these restoration strategies in a real-world test case.

4.3   POS Tagger Method Details

To apply the method proposed in this paper, we used the freely available HunPos tagger [15]. First, the AFP corpus was augmented with the tags that mark stress placement correctness as described above, after which a trigram tagger was trained using the default options.[4] This tagger was then used to provide information about whether a word in the test set was correctly or incorrectly stressed—i.e. the output of the tagger would simply be a sequence of tags, where each tag also indicates correctness as in Table 1 above.

5   Results

We applied the training models from each of the six detection/restoration methods (baseline, *Charlifter*, decision list, SMT, POS, and Perceptron) to each of the three evaluation data sets (AFP-stripped, Film-stripped and Film-original) and compared the restored versions to normalized versions reporting an overall accuracy as a percentage.

Base scores for the three evaluation sets differ with the original film data which already starts at 95.22 % accuracy—as expected, the stripped film set showing the most diacritic ambiguity at only 86.66 % of all words being correctly stressed, and the AFP evaluation set at 88.79 % accuracy from the outset as seen in Table 2. Applying a simple unigram frequency as a baseline, accuracy rates show relatively high improvement scores for the stripped data sets (AFP: 10.0 %, Film 5.31 %). In fact, the improvement is quite dramatic for the AFP evaluation set, which reaches 98.79 % accuracy with the baseline strategy,

---

[4] The default options train a trigram tagger that also trains a separate suffix tree to help tag previously unseen words. This obviously has great bearing on the ability to generalize to errors in unseen words as many competing diacritizations are found on the suffixes of words, as in the **-ara/-ará** subjunctive vs. future example given above. The HunPos tagger, unlike standard trigram taggers which condition pos-word pairs only on the previous two tags, also conditions its tagging choice on the previous word.

Table 2. Accuracy scores for all restoration methods and evaluation sets trained on 1.2 million word tokens from the AFP section of the Spanish Gigaword corpus and improvement relative pre-restoration base scores.

Model evaluation results			
Method	Evaluation set	Accuracy	Improvement (>base score)
Baseline	AFP-stripped	98.79 %	10.00 %
	Film-stripped	91.97 %	5.31 %
	Film-original	95.27 %	0.05 %
Charlifter	AFP-stripped	98.54 %	9.75 %
	Film-stripped	92.03 %	5.37 %
	Film-original	92.03 %	−3.19 %
Decision List	AFP-stripped	98.92 %	10.13 %
	Film-stripped	93.26 %	6.60 %
	Film-original	**95.88 %**	**0.66 %**
SMT	AFP-stripped	97.34 %	8.55 %
	Film-stripped	91.43 %	4.77 %
	Film-original	95.40 %	0.18 %
POS	AFP-stripped	**99.05 %**	**10.26 %**
	Film-stripped	**93.27 %**	**6.61 %**
	Film-original	95.57 %	0.35 %
Perceptron	AFP-stripped	98.99 %	10.20 %
	Film-stripped	92.79 %	6.13 %
	Film-original	92.79 %	−2.43 %

whereas the partially correct film data improves very minimally (0.05 %) from its starting base score.

Comparing the other five methods to the baseline scores, we see that both decision list and POS approaches match or improve on baseline accuracy whereas *Charlifter* and the SMT approach remain at or below baseline accuracy overall. When evaluated on both stripped AFP and film data sets, *Charlifter* fares somewhat better than the SMT approach, particularly for the AFP evaluation set. However, performance on the original, partially-correct film data is low using the SMT method, yet *Charlifter* actually increases orthographic errors (−3.19 %), suggesting that the language contained in the AFP training set fails to inform the grapheme-based algorithm precisely where residual human-based errors occur.

For the decision list and POS-tag methods, overall accuracy scores are quite similar. Performance differences are negligible for the Film-stripped set at 93.26 % and 93.27 % respectively, whereas for the AFP data set the POS (99.05 %) shows a slight advantage over the decision list (98.92 %), the opposite being true for the original film data, a difference of less than 1 % (.31 %). The perceptron classifier slightly trails the POS approach with this training data.

Also, its inability to classify already diacriticized text—that is, it strips all existing diacritics before classifying—leads to lower accuracies with the film data set.

5.1 Augmenting the Training Data

Two of the methods evaluated on the AFP 1.2 million word training corpus do not require any labeled data—the perceptron classifier and the SMT approach. To explore the extent to which availability of more training data may improve results, these methods were also trained on a larger section of the AFP news corpus consisting of 15 million words (14,825,292 word tokens), thus providing us with a learning curve that may illustrate the tradeoff between using labeled data, as in the POS-approach, and unlabeled data.

Table 3. Accuracy and improvement scores for unlabeled data methods on larger 14.8 million word token corpus from the AFP.

Augmented training data results			
Method	Evaluation set	Accuracy	Improvement (>base score)
Baseline	AFP-stripped	98.03 %	9.24 %
	Film-stripped	91.43 %	4.77 %
	Film-original	94.98 %	−0.24 %
SMT	AFP-stripped	97.61 %	8.82 %
	Film-stripped	92.53 %	5.87 %
	Film-original	95.64 %	0.42 %
Perceptron	AFP-stripped	**99.27 %**	**10.48 %**
	Film-stripped	**95.39 %**	**8.73 %**
	Film-original	95.39 %	0.17 %

By augmenting the training data, performance improves for both the SMT and perceptron classifier, as is expected (Table 3). The SMT performance appears to show modest gains across all three testing sets yet the perceptron classifier benefits more markedly from the increase in training data—most notably in the genre/register-mismatched Film-stripped test set. Worth noting is the slight difficulty in exact comparison; while the SMT system provides an actual restoration, the perceptron only categorizes words to note whether a diacritic is missing or superfluous. The actual restoration, while relatively simple for Spanish, may vary in complexity across languages.

5.2 POS-method Sensitivity to POS-tag Granularity

Findings from these experiments suggest that, minimally, the POS-tag approach achieves similar accuracy levels as the decision list approach on a large training data set with a relatively shallow (AFP) POS tag set. As an exploratory step to assess the extent to which part-of-speech information can be leveraged from training data sets with richer POS tag specifications, the same POS-tag implementation (POS) was trained using the AnCora corpus [23], a part-of-speech tagged corpus of Spanish drawn from newswire text consisting of roughly 100k word tokens and 'manually corrected', and evaluated on the same three sets as in the previous round of experiments. Notably, the annotation of the AnCora corpus is much more fine-grained (including tense and person information missing from AFP) and thus one expects better results in the error detection/correction task. Naturally, this advantage will be somewhat neutralized by the small size of the training data (100k tokens vs. 1.2 million tokens in AFP).

Comparing accuracy and improvement results (Table 4) from the AFP and AnCora trained POS-based restorer, we see that while AFP training/evaluation scores both show very high improvement (10.26 %) and accuracy (99.05 %), the POS-tagger restorer trained on AnCora outperforms the AFP-trained POS-based restorer in accuracy and improvement for the film data sets by 1.29 %. This latter result is informative in that while the lower performance on the AFP test set is to be expected because of a genre mismatch—a restoration strategy trained on a separate part of the same corpus as it is evaluated on will naturally yield better results—the better performance on the 'real-world' film corpus restoration task is directly attributable to the more fine-grained nature of the POS tags in the AnCora corpus.

Table 4. Accuracy and improvement scores for POS-restoration method trained on AFP and AnCora data sets.

POS method results contrasting size and POS-granularity of training data				
Training data	Amount of data	Evaluation set	Accuracy	Improvement (>base score)
AFP	1.2M	AFP-stripped	99.05 %	10.26 %
		Film-stripped	93.27 %	6.61 %
		Film-original	95.57 %	0.35 %
AnCora	100k	AFP-stripped	97.40 %	8.61 %
		Film-stripped	**94.53 %**	**7.87 %**
		Film-original	**96.89 %**	**1.67 %**

6   Discussion and Further Work

As the results show, leveraging a POS tagger to provide a judgment on the correctness of accentuation marks and diacritics is a strategy that appears to be competitive with other approaches to diacritic restoration. One naturally expects the best results whenever targeting a language that has high correlation between different diacritizations and the information provided by a POS tagger. In this scenario, Spanish (and potentially other Romance languages including French, Italian, and Portuguese) appear suited for this approach. The foremost advantage of the method is that it is very simple to apply, given access to a tagged corpus and a POS tagger. Also, the size of the language model induced from training data may be substantially smaller: our POS-tagger model occupied 10 Mb while the decision list induced from the same data set occupied 257 Mb. The adaptability of the method to other languages warrants further testing. Similarly, combinations of decision list, feature-based classifiers, and POS-tagger-based methods may be profitable, if the resources are available.

Additionally, many of the remaining errors in the POS-tagger based method, the decision list method, and the classifier-based one are easily disambiguated by humans using strictly local contextual information. In other words, despite a fairly large training set, many 'obvious' generalizations remain unseen in the training data. This suggests that a hybrid method based on a set of hand-written rules may be profitably combined with the existing methods.

Also, the POS-based method presented here appears to generalize better across genres than either a decision list or a discriminative classifier—although with several times more unlabeled training data, the classifier performs or par with the POS approach. This robustness is seen in the third experiment where training on a very small tagged corpus using a fine-grained tagset outperformed other methods when applied to the film dialogue restoration task. This flexibility is useful in that many of the scenarios where diacritic error detection is desirable involve a genre or sublanguage that is unpredictable and where little genre-specific training data is available.

Most noticeable throughout the experiments is the cost of training and test data genre mismatches, which is substantial. Training solely on newspaper text yield models that fail to significantly improve restoration quality over simple frequency-based baselines if the target language is drawn from a very divergent source, such as colloquial film language.

References

1. Tufiş, D., Ceauşu, A.: DIAC+: a professional diacritics recovering system. In: Proceedings of the Sixth International Language Resources and Evaluation (LREC) (2008)
2. Ungurean, C., Burileanu, D., Popescu, V., Negrescu, C., Dervis, A.: Automatic diacritic restoration for a TTS-based e-mail reader application. Bull. Ser. C **70**, 3–12 (2008)
3. Paredes, F.: La ortografía en las encuestas de disponibilidad léxica. Reale **11**, 75–97 (1999)
4. Yarowsky, D.: Decision lists for lexical ambiguity resolution: application to accent restoration in Spanish and French. In: Proceedings of the 32nd Annual Meeting on Association for Computational Linguistics, pp. 88–95 (1994)
5. Yarowsky, D.: A comparison of corpus-based techniques for restoring accents in Spanish and French text. In: Armstrong, S., Church, K., Isabelle, P., Manzi, S., Tzoukermann, E., Yarowsky, D. (eds.) Natural Language Processing Using Very Large Corpora. Text, Speech and Language Technology, vol. 11, pp. 99–120. Springer, Netherlands (1999)

6. Scannell, K.P.: The Crúbadán project: corpus building for under-resourced languages. In: Building and Exploring Web Corpora: Proceedings of the 3rd Web as Corpus Workshop, Incorporating Cleaneval, p. 5 (2007)
7. Mihalcea, R.F.: Diacritics restoration: learning from letters versus learning from words. In: Gelbukh, A. (ed.) CICLing 2002. LNCS, vol. 2276, pp. 339–348. Springer, Heidelberg (2002)
8. De Pauw, G., Wagacha, P.W., de Schryver, G.-M.: Automatic Diacritic Restoration for Resource-Scarce Languages. In: Matoušek, V., Mautner, P. (eds.) TSD 2007. LNCS (LNAI), vol. 4629, pp. 170–179. Springer, Heidelberg (2007)
9. Novák, A., Siklósi, B.: Automatic Diacritics Restoration for Hungarian. In: EMNLP 2015, pp. 2286–2291 (2015)
10. Hulden, M., Silfverberg, M., Francom, J.: Finite state applications with Javascript. In: Proceedings of the 19th Nordic Conference of Computational Linguistics, pp. 441–446 (2013)
11. Roth, R., Rambow, O., Habash, N., Diab, M., Rudin, C.: Arabic morphological tagging, diacritization, and lemmatization using lexeme models and feature ranking. In Proceedings of the 46th Annual Meeting of the Association for Computational Linguistics on Human Language Technologies: Short Papers, pp. 117–120. Association for Computational Linguistics (2008)
12. Trung, N.M., Nhan, N.Q., Phuong, N.H.: Vietnamese diacritics restoration as sequential tagging. In: 2012 IEEE RIVF International Conference on Computing and Communication Technologies, Research, Innovation, and Vision for the Future (RIVF), pp. 1–6. IEEE (2012)
13. Simard, M., Deslauriers, A.: Real-time automatic insertion of accents in French text. Nat. Lang. Eng. **7**(02), 143–165 (2001)
14. Brants, T.: TnT: a statistical part-of-speech tagger. In: Proceedings of the Sixth Conference on Applied Natural Language Processing, pp. 224–231. Association for Computational Linguistics (2000)
15. Halácsy, P., Kornai, A., Oravecz, C.: HunPos: an open source trigram tagger. In: Proceedings of the 45th Annual Meeting of the ACL on Interactive Poster and Demonstration Sessions, pp. 209–212. Association for Computational Linguistics (2007)
16. Scannell, K.P.: Statistical unicodification of African languages. Lang. Resour. Eval. **45**(3), 375–386 (2011)
17. Wagacha, P., De Pauw, G., Githinji, P.: A grapheme-based approach for accent restoration in Gikuyu. In: Proceedings of the Fifth International Conference on Language Resources and Evaluation, pp. 1937–1940 (2006)
18. Freund, Y., Schapire, R.E.: Large margin classification using the Perceptron algorithm. Mach. Learn. **37**(3), 277–296 (1999)
19. Koehn, P., Hoang, H., Birch, A., Callison-Burch, C., Federico, M., Bertoldi, N., Cowan, B., Shen, W., Moran, C., Zens, R., Dyer, C., Bojar, O., Constantin, A., Herbst, E.: Moses: open source toolkit for statistical machine translation. In: Proceedings of the 45th Annual Meeting of the ACL on Interactive Poster and Demonstration Sessions, pp. 177–180. Association for Computational Linguistics, Prague (2007)
20. Stolcke, A., Zheng, J., Wang, W., Abrash, V.: SRILM at sixteen: update and outlook. In: Proceedings of IEEE Automatic Speech Recognition and Understanding Workshop, p. 5 (2011)

21. Mendonça, Â., Jaquette, D., Graff, D., DiPersio, D.: Spanish Gigaword Third Edition LDC2011T12 (2011). https://catalog.ldc.upenn.edu/LDC2011T12
22. Francom, J., Hulden, M., Ussishkin, A.: ACTIV-ES: a comparable, cross-dialect corpus of "everyday" Spanish from Argentina, Mexico and Spain. In: The Ninth International Conference on Language Resources and Evaluation, pp. 1733–1737 (2014)
23. Taulé, M., Martí, M.A., Recasens, M.: AnCora: multilevel annotated corpora for Catalan and Spanish. In: Proceedings of the Sixth International Conference on Language Resources and Evaluation (LREC-2008) (2008)

Identification of Event and Topic
for Multi-document Summarization

Fumiyo Fukumoto[1]([✉]), Yoshimi Suzuki[1], Atsuhiro Takasu[2],
and Suguru Matsuyoshi[3]

[1] Graduate Faculty of Interdisciplinary Research,
University of Yamanashi, Kofu 400-8510, Japan
{fukumoto,ysuzuki}@yamanashi.ac.jp
[2] National Institue of Informatics, Tokyo, Japan
takasu@nii.ac.jp
[3] Interdisciplinary Graduate School of Medicine and Engineering,
University of Yamanashi, Kofu, Japan
sugurum@yamanashi.ac.jp

Abstract. This paper focuses on continuous news documents and presents a method for extractive multi-document summarization. Our hypothesis about salient, *key* sentences in news documents is that they include words related to the target *event* and *topic* of a document. Here, an event and a topic are the same as Topic Detection and Tracking (TDT) project: an event is something that occurs at a specific place and time along with all necessary preconditions and unavoidable consequences, and a topic is defined to be "a seminal event or activity along with all directly related events and activities." The difficulty for finding topics is that they have various word distributions. In addition to the TF-IDF term weighting method to extract event words, we identified topics by using two models, *i.e.*, Moving Average Convergence Divergence (MACD) for words with high frequencies, and Latent Dirichlet Allocation (LDA) for low frequency words. The method was tested on two datasets, NTCIR-3 Japanese news documents and DUC data, and the results showed the effectiveness of the method.

Keywords: Latent Dirichlet Allocation · Moving Average Convergence/ Divergence · Multi-document summarization

1 Introduction

Multi-document summarization differs from single document summarization in that it is important to identify differences and similarities across documents. This can be interpreted as the question of how to identify an event and a topic in series of documents. Here, an event and a topic are the same as TDT project [1,2], *i.e.*, an event is something that occurs at a specific place and time associated with some specific actions. A topic, on the other hand, refers to a seminal event or activity along with all directly related events and activities. For example, a

Z. Vetulani et al. (Eds.): LTC 2013, LNAI 9561, pp. 304–316, 2016.
DOI: 10.1007/978-3-319-43808-5_23

topic concerning to Hurricane Mitch includes estimates of damage, relief efforts by the Red Cross and other aid organizations, and impact of the hurricane on the economies. Words related to a topic are widely distributed in the target news documents, and sometimes it frequently appears in the target documents, but sometimes not. Consider the following two documents concerning to the Humble, TX, flooding from the TDT corpus.

A Word marked with "{}" in Fig. 1 refer to a word related to an event. We call it an event word. The first document says that seven people were dead in flash floods in southeast, and torrential rains have pounded Conroe, Texas. The second document, on the other hand, states that relief help has been granted by the president. The event of the document is different from the earlier one, *i.e.*, the event has shifted. The notion of a topic, on the other hand is a seminal event. Words marked with the underlined words in Fig. 1 related to a topic. We call it a topic word. We can see that words such as "flood" appear in both documents. In contrast, words such as "Texas", "Conroe", and "Houston-Conroe" which are also associated with a topic, but appeared only once. These observations show that topic words have various word distribution.

1-1. At least {7} {people} are dead and thousands more fled their homes as flood waters buried large sections of southeast Texas - {16} {counties} have been declared {disaster} areas - and more heavy rain is predicted.

1-2. Bernie, good afternoon from Conroe.

1-3. The count of {counties}, {disaster} area {counties}, is now up to 17. {Seven} {dead}, as you say, an estimated 10,000 forced out of their homes as flood waters from two southeast Texas rivers ran out of their banks, raged out of their banks, if you will.
. . .

2-1. We might say that there is good news.

2-2. {Relief} help has been granted by the {president}, so {relief} help is on the way for residents here of this flood.

2-3. {Federal} {officials} will be coming here to the Houston-Conroe area later on today and tomorrow and so far, no damage estimates have been set.
. . .

Fig. 1. Event and topic words from "Humble, TX, flooding"

This paper focuses on extractive summarization, and presents a method for detecting key sentences from continuous newspaper documents where data is collected over an extended period of time. Here, extractive summarization assigns saliency scores to sentences or paragraphs of the documents, and extracts those with highest scores. We assume that a key sentence in multiple documents includes words related to the target topic, and events of each document. An event is something that occurs at a specific place and time associated with some specific actions. It refers to the *theme* of the document itself, *i.e.*, something a writer wishes to express, and it frequently appears in the document. We used the traditional term weighting method TF-IDF to identify event words.

Topic words, on the other hand, are identified by using two models. The first model we used is a model of "topic dynamics". We defined a burst as a time interval of maximal length over which the rate of change is positive acceleration. We used Moving Average Convergence Divergence (MACD) to identify topic. MACD is a technique to analyze stock market trends. It shows the relationship between two moving averages of prices modeling bursts as intervals of topic dynamics, *i.e.*, positive acceleration. It is effective for identifying topics appearing across documents. In contrast, for low frequency word distribution, we used a model, Latent Dirichlet Allocation (LDA). LDA [3] is widely utilized as a statistical generative model. It relates documents and words through latent variables which represent the topics. It is a completely unsupervised algorithm that models each document as a mixture of topics. The model generates automatic summaries of topics in terms of a discrete probability distribution over words for each topic, and further infers per-document discrete distributions over topics. It makes the explicit assumption that each word is generated from one underlying topic [23]. We collected documents that are semantically related to the target documents to be summarized, and applied Latent Dirichlet Allocation (LDA) to these documents to extract topic words.

2   Related Work

Most of the work on extractive summarization has applied statistical techniques based on word distribution to the target documents. Lin *et al.* proposed multi-document summarization by using several features, *e.g.*, sentence position, term frequency, topic signature and term clustering to select important content [16]. Other approaches have investigated the use of machine learning to find patterns which make use of scoring sentences. Marcu presented a machine learning approach to classify RST relationships [17]. Hatzivassiloglou *et al.* introduced a machine-learned similarity measure to find whether two paragraphs contain common information or not [11]. Several authors have attempted to find topic themes in the documents for summarization [7]. Harabagiu investigated five different topic representations and introduced a novel representation of topics based on topic themes [10]. Mimno and Celikyilmaz used hierarchical topic models to retrieve coherent sentences for extractive summarization [6,19]. Mimno *et al.* focused on topic and hierarchical depth to characterize word distribution in every hierarchy model. Celikyilmaz *et al.* presented a method called two-tiered topic model which used word distribution in specific topics, and directly extracts sentences including these high-level topic words as coherent sentences.

In the context of graph-based ranking method, Erkan *et al.* presented a method called LexPageRank for computing sentence importance based on the concept of eigenvector centrality [8]. It constructs a sentence connectivity matrix and computes sentence importance based on an algorithm similar to PageRank [22]. Similarly, Mihalcea proposed a method based on HITS and PageRank to compute sentence importance [18]. Wan *et al.* proposed two models, the Cluster-based conditional Markov Random Walk model and the Cluster-based HITS model, both use the theme clusters in the document set [27]. Our work is similar to those methods in the use of the graph-based ranking technique. The difference is that the sentence scoring by our approach incorporates a model on document arrivals in time that predicts event distribution change over a period of time.

The analysis of concept or topic bursts is an attempt dealing with temporal effects in a series of document streams [9,13,14]. The earliest known approach is the work of [21]. They presented a method to handle concept changes with SVM. They used $\xi\alpha$-estimates to select the window size so that the estimated generalization error on new examples is minimized. The result which was tested on the TREC dataset shows that the algorithm achieves a low error rate and selects appropriate window sizes. Kleinberg's burst algorithm models bursts with an infinite state automaton in which each state represents a message arrival rate [13]. The higher the state, the smaller the expected time gap between messages. Similarly, Zhu *et al.* have developed several burst definitions based on hierarchies of fixed-length time intervals, motivated originally by a problem of modeling bursts of gamma rays [29]. He *et al.* proposed a method to find bursts, periods of elevated occurrence of topics as a dynamic phenomenon instead of focusing on arrival rates [12]. They used a Moving Average Convergence/Divergence (MACD) histogram which was used in technical stock market analysis [20] to detect bursts. They tested their method using MeSH terms and reported that the model works well for tracking bursts, while it is difficult to identify topics with low frequency. Moreover, their method can not extract such burst terms automatically, *i.e.*, it is necessary to give these terms in advance as the input of their model. For the topic words that are frequently appear in the documents to be summarized, we reinforced these words by collecting documents from the corpus, each of which is related to the target documents, and applied LDA to these documents to extract topic words.

3 System Design

3.1 Event Detection

We assume that event words frequently appear in the document but not appear frequently in other documents. We then used the traditional term weighting method TF-IDF to identify event words in the document. The weight of term t in document d is defined to be

$$w(t, d) = \frac{(1 + log_2 tf(t, d)) \times \log_2(N/n_t)}{\| d \|}. \tag{1}$$

$tf(t, d)$ refers to the within-document term frequency and N denotes to the number of documents. n_t shows the number of documents in which t occurs. $\| d \|$ is the 2-norm of d. We extracted words whose TF-IDF value is larger than a certain threshold value, and regarded these as event words.

3.2 Topic Detection

Topic Detection by MACD. He *et al.* have attempted to find bursts, periods of elevated occurrence of events as a dynamic phenomenon instead of focusing on arrival rates [12]. They used a Moving Average Convergence/Divergence (MACD) histogram that was used in technical stock market analysis [20] to detect bursts. The MACD of a variable x_t is defined by the difference of the n_1-day and the n_2-day moving averages:

$$MACD(n_1, n_2) = EMA(n_1) - EMA(n_2). \tag{2}$$

Here, $EMA(n_i)$ in Eq. (2) refers to n_i-day Exponential Moving Average (EMA). For a variable $x = x(t)$ which has a corresponding discrete time series $x = \{x_t \mid t = 0,1,\cdots\}$, the n-day EMA is defined by Eq. (3).

$$EMA(n)[x]_t = \alpha x_t + (1 - \alpha)EMA(n - 1)[x]_{t-1}$$
$$= \sum_{k=0}^{n} \alpha(1 - \alpha)^k x_{t-k}. \tag{3}$$

α refers to a smoothing factor and it is often taken to be $\frac{2}{(n+1)}$. The MACD histogram shows the difference between the MACD and its moving average.

$$hist(n_1, n_2, n_3) = MACD(n_1, n_2) - EMA(n_3)[MACD(n_1, n_2)]. \tag{4}$$

The procedure for topic detection by using MACD is illustrated in Fig. 2. Let A be a set of articles to be summarized. A set of topic words T are detected as follows:

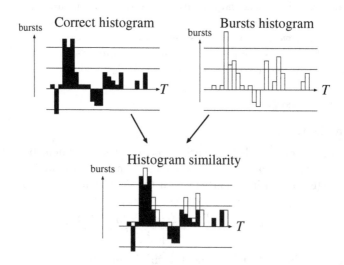

Fig. 2. Similarity between correct and bursts histograms

1. Create document-based MACD histogram, *i.e.*, the number of documents in A originating on dates during T. X-axis in the histogram refers to a period of time length T, and Y-axis denotes the frequency of documents A. Hereafter, referred to as correct histogram.
2. Create term-based MACD histogram where X-axis refers to T, and Y-axis denotes bursts of word w in A. Hereafter, referred to as word histogram.
3. We assume that burst histogram of w is close to the correct histogram if w is a topic word. Because w is a representative word of each document in a set A. We compute similarity between correct and term histograms. We tested Bhattacharyya distance, histogram intersection and KL-distance to obtain similarities. We used Bhattacharyya distance in the experiments as it was the best results among them.

Let p be a correct histogram, and q be a term histogram. Bhattacharyya distance between p and q is defined by $\rho(p,q) = \sum_{i=1}^{T} \sqrt{p_i q_i}$. p_i refers to the frequency of documents that arrive in time i, and q_i indicates bursts of w in time i. If the value of $\rho(p,q)$ is larger than a certain threshold value, w is regarded as a topic word.

In the procedure 2, we assume that burst histogram of the word w is close to the correct histogram if w is a topic word. Because burst histogram obtained by procedure 1 refers to a burst of a topic concerning to a set of documents A. Thus, we can assume that it is similar to the histogram obtained by using a frequency of A concerning to the target topic.

Topic Detection by LDA. We note that topic detection by MACD is a frequency-based technique. However, there are topic words with low frequency in the target documents to be summarized. We reinforced these words by collecting documents from the corpus, and applied LDA technique to these documents. LDA presented by [3] models each document as a mixture of topics, and generates a discrete probability distribution over words for each topic. The generative process for LDA can be described as follows:

1. For each topic $k = 1, \cdots, K$, generate ϕ_k, multinomial distribution of words specific to the topic k from a Dirichlet distribution with parameter β;
2. For each document $d = 1, \cdots, D$, generate θ_d, multinomial distribution of topics specific to the document d from a Dirichlet distribution with parameter α;
3. For each word $n = 1, \cdots, N_d$ in document d;
   (a) Generate a topic z_{dn} of the nth word in the document d from the multinomial distribution θ_d
   (b) Generate a word w_{dn}, the word associated with the nth word in document d from multinomial ϕ_{zdn}

Like much previous work on LDA, we used Gibbs sampling to estimate ϕ and θ. The sampling probability for topic z_i in document d is given by:

$$P(z_i \mid z_{\backslash i}, W) = \frac{(n_{\backslash i,j}^v + \beta)(n_{\backslash i,j}^d + \alpha)}{(n_{\backslash i,j} + W\beta)(n_{\backslash i,\cdot}^d + T\alpha)}. \tag{5}$$

$z_{\backslash i}$ refers to a topic set Z, not including the current assignment z_i. $n_{\backslash i,j}^v$ is the count of word v in topic j that does not include the current assignment z_i, and $n_{\backslash i,j}$ indicates a summation over that dimension. W refers to a set of documents, and T denotes the total number of unique topics. After a sufficient number of sampling iterations, the approximated posterior can be used to estimate ϕ and θ by examining the counts of word assignments to topics and topic occurrences in documents. Detection of topic words based on LDA is as follows:

1. Each target document from the summarization task and documents from the corpus are represented using a vector of frequency weighted words. Compute similarity between them. We used cosine similarity.
2. For each document d_i in the target documents TD to be summarized, extract the topmost X documents from the corpus with the highest similarity value.
3. For each document d_i, we applied LDA to the number of $X+1$ documents, i.e., the extracted documents and documents d_i, and obtain $P(w|t)$ and $P(t|d)$. Compute $P(w|d) = P(w|t) \times P(t|d)$. For each document d_i in TD, extract the topmost l words with the highest $P(w|d)$ value as topic words.

3.3 Sentence Extraction

We recall that our hypothesis about key sentences in multiple documents is that they include topic and event words. Each sentence in documents TD is represented using a vector of frequency weighted words that can be event or topic words. We used Markov Random Walk (MRW) model to compute the rank scores for the sentences, i.e., given a document set TD to be summarized, a graph G consists of a set of vertices V and each vertex v_i in V is a sentence in the document set. For the results of MRW, we applied the maximal Marginal Relevance (MMR) [4] to reduce redundancy.

$$MMR = \arg \max_{s_i \in R \backslash S} (\lambda \cdot Imp(s_i) - (1 - \lambda) \cdot \max_{s_j \in S} sim(s_i, s_j)). \qquad (6)$$

R refers to the ranked list of documents by MRW, and S indicates the subset of documents in R already selected. $R \backslash S$ denotes the set of as yet unselected documents in R. $Imp(s_i)$ refers to the normalized saliency scores obtained by MMR. After the saliency scores of sentences have been obtained by MMR, choose a certain number of sentences according to the rank score into the summary.

4   Experiments

4.1   NTCIR Data

We made an experiment by using the NTCIR-3[1] SUMM to evaluate our approach. NTCIR-3 has two tasks, single, and multi-document summarization. The data is collected from two years (1998–1999) of Mainichi Japanese Newspaper

---

[1] http://research.nii.ac.jp/ntcir/.

documents. We used the multi-document summarization task. There are two types of gold standard data provided to human judges, FBFREE DryRun and FormalRun, each of which consists of 30 tasks. There are two types of correct summary according to the character length, "long" and "short", All documents were tagged by a morphological analysis, MeCab[2]. We used noun words in the experiment.

We randomly chose 16 tasks extracted from the FBFREE DryRun data for tuning parameters, $i.e.$, the number of extracted words W_T according to the TF-IDF value, Bhattacharyya distance $\rho(p,q)$, the number of X documents in LDA, the topmost l words in LDA, and λ in MMR. Eight tasks are used for training and the remains are used for testing to estimate parameters. The size that optimized the average Precision and Coverage across eight tasks was chosen. Here, Precision and Coverage evaluation measures are provided by NTCIR-3. As a result, W_T, $\rho(p,q)$, X, l and λ are set to 100, 0.95, 5,000, $N/100$, and 0.97, respectively. Here, N refers to the number of different words in the target documents. We used FormalRun consisting of 30 tasks as a test data. We also used 1,876,766 documents collected from 20 years Mainichi newspaper documents as a corpus used in LDA. We ran Gibbs samplers for 500 iterations for each configuration throwing out first 5,000 documents as burn-in.

We compared our method with the following six approaches to examine how the results of event and topic detection affect summarization performance.

1. MRW model (**MRW**)
   The method applies the MRW model to the sentences consisting of noun words,
   $i.e.$, the method does not use the results of event and topic detection.
2. MRW and MMR (**MRW & MMR**)
   The method applies the MRW model, and MMR.
3. Event detection (**Event**)
   The method applies the MRW model to the result of event detection.
4. Topic detection by MACD (**MACD**)
   The method applies MRW to the result of topic detection by MACD.
5. Topic Detection by LDA (**LDA**)
   MRW is applied to the result of topic detection by LDA.
6. Event and topic detection (**Without MMR**)
   The method is the same as our method except for MMR.

The results are shown in Table 1. We can see from Table 1 that precision and coverage obtained by our approach, "Event & Topic" outperforms other approaches, regardless of the summary type (long/short). The result obtained by "MRW" was better than "MRW & MMR" when the summary type was short. On the other hand, when the summary was long, the latter was better to the former. This indicates that the MRW model works well, especially for extracting salient sentences with high ranked scores. The results obtained by "Event" was the best compared with "MACD" and "LDA". However, integrating

---

[2] http://mecab.googlecode.com/svn/trunk/mecab/doc/index.html.

Table 1. Sentence Extraction (NTCIR-3 test data)

	Short		Long	
	Prec	Cov	Prec	Cov
MRW	0.369	0.408	0.454	0.482
MRW & MMR	0.305	0.340	0.407	0.428
Event	0.389	0.433	0.449	0.480
MACD	0.367	0.405	0.421	0.440
LDA	0.363	0.410	0.451	0.484
Without MMR	0.390	0.434	0.456	0.482
Event & Topic	0.395	0.440	0.486	0.496

these methods, *i.e.*, "Without MMR" was the best performance among them. Moreover, "Event & Topic" was better than "Without MMR" in both short and long summary. This shows that the method integrating event, topic detection and MMR is effective for key sentence extraction.

4.2 DUC Data

Another data we used is DUC2005, DUC2006 and DUC2007 English data. To estimate parameters, we used DUC2005 consisting of 50 tasks for training, and DUC2006 consisting of 50 tasks for testing. We set W_T, $\rho(p,q)$, X, l, λ to 80, 0.9, 5,000, $N/250$, and 0.9, respectively. 45 tasks from DUC2007 were used to evaluate the performance of the method. All documents were tagged by Tree Tagger [24]. Similar to the Japanese data, we used noun words in the experiments. We used Reuters 1996 data consisting of 809,381 documents as a corpus in LDA. We used ROUGE as an evaluation measure because it is a standard DUC evaluation metric. We report results in ROUGE-1, recall against unigrams. The results are shown in Table 2. We can see from Table 2 that ROUGE-1 obtained by our approach was the best compared to other six approaches. Similar to the NTCIR-3 data, MRW model works well for extracting salient sentences with high ranked scores. The result obtained by "LDA" was the best compared with "Event" and "MACD", while the results obtained by "Event" was the best performance when we used the NTCIR-3 data.

Table 3 illustrates the performance of our method compared to the other research sites. Each site is reported by [6]. The training and test data are the same as our method. "PYTHY" model utilizes human generated summaries to train a sentence ranking system [25]. "HybHSum" is a semi-supervised learning. It builds a hierarchical LDA to score sentences in training dataset [5]. "hPAM" uses two hierarchical topic models to detect high and low-level concepts from documents [15]. "TTM" also combines approaches from the hierarchical topic models [6]. It captures correlated semantic concepts in documents as well as characterizing general and specific words to identify topically coherent sentences

Table 2. Sentence Extraction (DUC2007 test data)

	ROUGE-1
MRW	0.362
MRW & MMR	0.344
Event	0.366
MACD	0.373
LDA	0.396
Without MMR	0.418
Event & Topic	0.425

Table 3. Comparative results (DUC2007 test data)

	ROUGE-1
PYTHY	0.426
HybHSum	**0.456**
hPAM	0.412
TTM	**0.447**
Event & Topic	0.425

in documents. We can see from Table 3 that the top site was "HybHSum" and ROUGE-1 was 0.456, while the method is a semi-supervised technique that needs a tagged training data. "TTM" was unsupervised model and it was better than our approach. The performance by our method is competitive to "PYTHY" and "pPAM" as the result by our method (0.425) is very similar to "PYTHY" (0.426) and "hPAM"(0.412).

5   Conclusions

We presented a method for detecting key sentences from documents for extractive multi-document summarization. We assumed that a key sentence in multiple documents includes words related to the target topic, and events of each document. We used the traditional term weighting method TF-IDF to identify event words. Topic words, on the other hand, are identified by using two models. The first model we used is a model of "topic dynamics". We defined a burst as a time interval of maximal length over which the rate of change is positive acceleration. We used Moving Average Convergence Divergence (MACD) to identify topic. MACD is a technique to analyze stock market trends. It is effective for identifying topics appearing across documents. In contrast, for low frequency word distribution, we used a model, Latent Dirichlet Allocation (LDA). We collected documents that are semantically related to the target documents to be summarized, and applied Latent Dirichlet Allocation (LDA) to these documents to extract topic words. We had an experiments by using two data, NTCIR-3 Japanese data, and DUC English data. We compared our method with the six baseline approaches, and the results showed that MACD and LDA are effective for extractive summarization. We also found that the results using DUC data showed that our approach was competitive to other research sites except for "TTM" and "HybHSum".

There are a number of interesting directions for future research. We used cosine similarity to collect documents. However, there are a number of similarity measures. It is worth trying with our method for further improvement. We used surface information of words in our method. For future work, we will apply WSD technique such as lexical chains to detect semantically similar words for further efficacy gains with event and topic word detection. We used LDA to the documents to extract topic words. There are number of other topic models such as continuous time dynamic topic model [28] and a biterm topic model [26]. It is worth trying to test these methods for further improvement. Finally, for quantitative evaluation, we will apply the method to other data such as TDT4 and TDT5[3] provided by the TDT project.

References

1. Allan, J., Carbonell, J., Doddington, G., Yamron, J., Yang, Y.: Topic detection and tracking pilot study final report. In: Proceedings of the DARPA Broadcast News Transcription and Understanding Workshop (1998)
2. Allan, J.: Topic Detection and Tracking. Kluwer Academic Publishers, USA (2003)
3. Blei, D.M., Ng, A.Y., Jordan, M.I.: Latent Dirichlet allocation. J. Mach. Learn. Res. **3**, 993–1022 (2003)
4. Carbonell, J., Goldstein, J.: The use of MMR, diversity-based reranking for reordering documents and producing summaries. In: Proceedings of the 21st Annual International ACM SIGIR Conference on Research and Development in Information Retrieval, pp. 335–336 (1998)
5. Celikylmaz, A., Hakkani-Tur, D.: A hybird hierarchical model for multi-document summarization. In: Proceedings of the 48th Annual Meeting of the Association for Computational Linguistics, pp. 815–824 (2010)
6. Celikylmaz, A., Hakkani-Tur, D.: Discovery of topically coherent sentences for extractive summarization. In: Proceedings of the 49th Annual Meeting of the Association for Computational Linguistics: Human Language Technologies, pp. 491–499 (2011)
7. Conroy, J.M., Schlesinger, J.D., O'Leary, D.P.: Topic-focused multi-document summarization using an approximate oracle score. In: Proceedings of the 21st International Conference on Computational Linguistics and 44th Annual Meeting of the Association for Computational Linguistics, pp. 152–159 (2006)
8. Erkan, G., Radev, D.: LexPageRank: prestige in multi-document text summarization. In: Proceedings of the 2004 Conference on Empirical Methods in Natural Language Processing, pp. 365–371 (2004)
9. Folino, G., Pizzuti, C., Spezzano, G.: An adaptive distributed ensemble approach to mine concept-drifting data streams. In: Proceedings of the 19th IEEE International Conference on Tools with Artificial Intelligence, pp. 183–188 (2007)

---

[3] https://www.ldc.upenn.edu.

10. Harabagiu, S., Hickl, A., Lacatusu, F.: Satisfying information needs with multi-document summaries. Inf. Process. Manag. **43**(6), 1619–1642 (2007)
11. Hatzivassiloglou, V., Klavans, J.L., Holcombe, M.L., Barzilay, R., Kan, M.-Y., McKeown, K.R.: Simfinder: a flexible clustering tool for summarization. In: Proceedings of the 2nd Meeting of the North American Chapter of the Association for Computational Linguistics Workshop on Text Summarization, pp. 41–49 (2001)
12. He, D., Parker, D.S.: Topic dynamics: an alternative model of bursts in streams of topics. In: Proceedings of the SIGKDD International Conference on Knowledge Discovery and Data Mining, pp. 443–452 (2010)
13. Kleinberg, J.M.: Bursty and hierarchical structure in streams. In: Proceedings of the 8th ACM SIGKDD International Conference on Knowledge Discovery and Data Mining, pp. 91–101 (2002)
14. Lazarescu, M.M., Venkatesh, S., Bui, H.H.: Using multiple windows to track concept drift. Intell. Data Anal. **8**(1), 29–59 (2004)
15. Li, W., McCallum, A.: Pachinko allocation: dag-structure mixture model of topic correlations. In: Proceedings of the 23rd International Conference on Machine Learning, pp. 577–584 (2006)
16. Lin, C.-Y., Hovy, E.H.: From single to multi-document summarization: a prototype system and its evaluation. In: Proceedings of the 40th Annual Meeting of the Association for Computational Linguistics, pp. 457–464 (2002)
17. Marcu, D., Echihabi, A.: An unsupervised approach to recognizing discourse relations. In: Proceedings of the 40th Annual Meeting of the Association for Computational Linguistics, pp. 368–375 (2002)
18. Mihalcea, R., Tarau, P.: Language independent extractive summarization. In: Proceedings of the 43rd Annual Meeting of the Association for Computational Linguistics, pp. 49–52 (2005)
19. Mimno, D., Li, W., McCallum, A.: Mixtures of hierarchical topics with pachinko allocation. In: Proceedings of the 24th International Conference on Machine Learning, pp. 633–640 (2007)
20. Murphy, J.: Technical Analysis of the Financial Markets. Prentice Hall, Upper Saddle River (1999)
21. Klinkenberg, R., Joachims, T.: Detecting concept drift with support vector machines. In: Proceedings of the 17th International Conference on Machine Learning, pp. 487–494 (2000)
22. Page, L., Brin, S., Motwani, R., Winograd, T.: The Pagerank Citation Ranking: Bringing Order to the Web. Technical report, Stanford Digital Libraries (1998)
23. Ramage, D., Hall, D., Nallapati, R., Manning, C.D.: Labeled LDA: a supervised topic model for credit attribution in multi-labeled corpora. In: Proceedings of the 2009 Conference on Empirical Methods in Natural Language Processing, pp. 248–256 (2009)
24. Schmid, H.: Improvements in part-of-speech tagging with an application to German. In: Proceedings of the European Chapter of the Association for Computational Linguistics SIGDAT Workshop, pp. 47–50 (1995)
25. Toutanoval, K., Brockett, C., Gammon, M., Jagarlamudi, J., Suzuki, H., Vanderwende, L.: The phthy summarization system: Microsoft research at DUC. In: Proceedings of Document Understanding Conference (2007)
26. Yan, X., Guo, J., Lan, Y., Cheng, X.: A biterm topic model for short texts. In: Proceedings of the 22nd International Conference on World Wide Web, pp. 1445–1456 (2013)

27. Wan, X., Yang, J.: Multi-document summarization using cluster-based link analysis. In: Proceedings of the SIGIR Conference on Research and Development in Information Retrieval, pp. 299–306 (2008)
28. Wang, C., Blei, D., Heckerman, D.: Continuous time dynamic topic models. In: Proceedings of the 24th Conference on Uncertainty in Artificial Intelligence, pp. 579–586 (2008)
29. Zhu, Y., Shasha, D.: Efficient elastic burst detection in data streams. In: Proceedings of the 9th ACM SIGKDD International Conference on Knowledge Discovery and Data Mining, pp. 336–345 (2003)

Itemsets-Based Amharic Document Categorization Using an Extended *A Priori* Algorithm

Abraham Hailu and Yaregal Assabie[(⊠)]

Department of Computer Science,
Addis Ababa University, Addis Ababa, Ethiopia
abraham.hailu.b@gmail.com,
yaregal.assabie@aau.edu.et

Abstract. Document categorization is gaining importance due to the large volume of electronic information which requires automatic organization and pattern identification. Due to the morphological complexity of the language, automatic categorization of Amharic documents has become a difficult talk to carry out. This paper presents a system that categorizes Amharic documents based on the frequency of itemsets obtained after analyzing the morphology of the language. We selected seven categories into which a given document is to be classified. The task of categorization is achieved by employing an extended version of *a priori* algorithm which had been traditionally used for the purpose of knowledge mining in the form of association rules. The system is tested with a corpus containing Amharic news documents and experimental results are reported.

Keywords: Amharic language processing · Text categorization · Document classification · *A priori* algorithm · Itemsets

1 Introduction

Due to the ongoing expansion of the Internet and electronic technologies, availability of electronic documents is dramatically increasing. The presence of large volume of electronic information requires analysis of documents for the purpose of natural language processing, pattern identification, knowledge organization and information management (Morshed 2006). However, due to the difficulty of organizing very large volume of documents manually, automatic categorization of documents is introduced as a solution. Document categorization is the process of assigning documents to one or more classes or categories, and has many applications. Some of these applications are spam filtering, indexing of electronic documents, automatic online cataloging of web resources, categorizing news stories etc. The applications of automatic categorization also extend to fraud detection and automatic essay grading (Han and Kamber 2006). Documents may be categorized according to their subjects or other attributes such as document type, author, and printing year, etc. (Sebastiani 2002). There are two main types of subject categorization of documents: content based approach and request based

© Springer International Publishing Switzerland 2016
Z. Vetulani et al. (Eds.): LTC 2013, LNAI 9561, pp. 317–326, 2016.
DOI: 10.1007/978-3-319-43808-5_24

approach. Content based categorization is a method in which the weight is given to particular subjects in a document that determines the class to which the document is assigned. Request oriented categorization is a kind of policy based categorization targeted towards a particular audience or user group. The categorization is done according to some ideals that reflect the purpose of doing the categorization.

Depending on how automatic document categorization systems are trained, we can use supervised or unsupervised approach. In supervised approach, some external mechanism (such as human feedback) provides information on the correct categorization of documents. In unsupervised approach, however, the categorization is carried out entirely without reference to external information. Unsupervised categorization is also referred to as document clustering due to the fact that documents are clustered based on their similarity. There is also a semi-supervised document categorization, where parts of the documents are labeled for training by external mechanism. Various techniques have been employed to develop document categorization systems. Some of the most popular techniques include expectation maximization (EM), Naive Bayes categorizer, latent semantic indexing, support vector machines (SVM), artificial neural network, K-nearest neighbor algorithms, decision trees, concept mining, rough set based categorizer, soft set based categorizer, and multiple-instance learning approaches (Goller et al. 2009). A major difference among them is in how categorizers are built. Another difference within the text categorization approach is in the document pre-processing and indexing part, where documents are represented as vectors of term weights. Calculating the term weights can be based on a variety of heuristic principles which is enabling a computer to discover or learn something for itself. Many research works have been conducted on automatic document classification for several languages around the world. However, only few researches have been attempted on Amharic document classification. The techniques employed so far for Amharic document classification are cosine similarity (Tilahun 2001), Naïve Bayes and K-nearest neighbor (Teklu 2003), artificial neural network (Eyassu and Gambäck 2005), and decision tree and support vector machines (Afework 2008). In our approach, we applied an extended *a priori* algorithm (Agrawal et al. 1993) for document categorization based on frequent itemsets. The algorithm had been traditionally used for the purpose of knowledge mining in the form of association rules. However, its convenience for document categorization was explored more recently and found to be an effective method to successfully categorize short documents such as abstracts and summaries in a digital library (Hynek et al. 2000). We have adopted their work to categorize unstructured Amharic texts into one of the following seven categories: *sport, politics, meteorology, tourism, religion, education* and *health*.

This paper presents an automatic categorization of Amharic documents. The remaining part of this paper is organized as follows. Section 2 presents the characteristics of Amharic language with emphasis to its morphological features. The design of the proposed system is discussed in Sect. 3. Experimental results are presented in Sect. 4, and conclusion and future works are highlighted in Sect. 5. References are provided at the end.

2 Amharic Language

Amharic is the working language of Ethiopia having a population of over 90 million. Even though many languages are spoken in Ethiopia, Amharic is dominant and is spoken as a mother tongue by a large segment of the population and it is the most commonly learned second language throughout the country (Lewis et al. 2013). It is also the second most spoken Semitic language in the world next to Arabic. Amharic is written using Ethiopic script which has 33 consonants (basic characters) out of which six other characters representing combinations of vowels and consonants are derived for each character. The base characters have the vowel ኧ(ä) and other derived characters have vowels in the order of ሁ(u), ሂ(i), ሃ(a), ሄ(e), ህ(ï), and ሆ(o). For example, for the base character ረ(rä), the following six characters are derived from the base character: ሩ(ru), ሪ(ri), ራ(ra), ሬ(re), ር(r), and ሮ(ro). This leads to have a total of 33 × 7 (=238) Amharic characters. In addition, there are about two scores of labialized characters such as ሏ(l^wa), ሟ(m^wa) ሯ(r^wa) ሷ(s^wa), etc. used by the language for writing.

As observed in Semitic languages, Amharic is one of the most morphologically complex languages. Amharic nouns and adjectives are marked for any combination of number, definiteness, gender and case. In addition, they are affixed with prepositions. For example, the noun መኪና (mäkina/car) is inflected as መኪናዎች (mäkinawoč/cars), መኪናው (mäkinaw/the car {masculine}/his car), መኪናዬን (mäkinayän/my car {objective case}), መኪናሽ (mäkinaš/your {feminine} car), መኪናህ (mäkinah/your {masculine} car),መኪናህን (mäkinahn/your {masculine} car {objective case}),መኪናዎቻችሁ (mäkinawočačïhu/your cars), ለመኪና (lämäkina/for car), በመኪና (bämäkina/by car), ስለመኪና (sïlämäkina/about car), ከመኪና (kämäkina/from car), etc. Similarly, the adjective ረጅም (räjïm/tall) is inflected as ረጅሞች (räjïmoč/tall {plural}), ረጅሞቹ (räjïmoču/tall {definite} {plural}), ረጅሙ (räjïmu/tall {definite} {masculine} {singular}), ረጅምዋ (räjïm^wa/tall {definite} {feminine} {singular}), etc.

The morphology of Amharic verbs is even more complex than those of nouns and adjectives. Verbs are derived from verbal stems, and stems in turn are derived from verbal roots. For example, from the verbal root ግድል (gdl/to kill), we can derive verbal stems such as *gädl, gädäl, gadl, gädadl, tägädadl*, etc. From each of these verbal stems we can derive many verbs in their surface forms. For example, from the stem *gädäl* the following verbs can be derived: ገደለ (gädälä/he killed), ገደለች (gädäläč/she killed), ገደልኩ (gädälku/I killed), ገደልኩት (algädälkut/I killed [him]), አልገደልኩም (algädälkum/I didn't kill), አልገደለችም (algädäläčïm/she didn't kill), አልገደለም (algädäläm/he didn't kill), አልገደለኝም (algädäläñïm/he didn't kill me), ስላተገደለ (sïlätägädälä/as [he] was killed), etc. Amharic verbs are marked for any combination of person, gender, number, case, tense/aspect, and mood resulting in thousands of words from a single verbal root. As a result, a single word may represent a complete sentence cosutructed with subject, verb and object.

3   The Proposed System

The proposed Amharic document categorizer has the following major process components: *preprocessing, training,* and *prediction.* The preprocessing component prepares text data to generate frequent itemsets. In the training phase, frequent itemsets are used to generate terms linked with categories. The prediction phase uses the corpus and linked terms repository to predict the category of a given document. Process relatioships between these components are shown in Fig. 1.

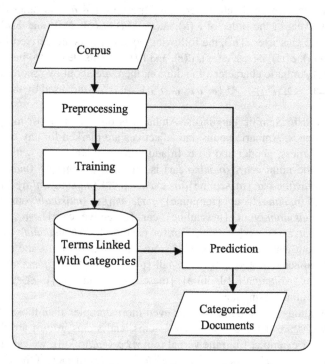

Fig. 1.   Architecture of the proposed system.

3.1   Preprocessing

Preprocessing of the text involves three major tasks: *removal of stopwords, stemming* and *removal of infrequent terms.* Preprocessing starts with the removal of non-letter tokens and stopwords from the text. Stopwords in Amharic may appear as standalone words or they may also be affixed with other words. Examples of stopwords that appear standalone are: ነው (*näw*/is), ናቸው (*načäw*/are), ተባላ (*täbalä*/said), ነበር(*näbär*/was), እና (*ïnna*/and), ምክንያቱም (*mïknyatum*/because), ቢሆንም (*bihonïm*/even if), እንደ (*ïndä*/like), ወደ (*wädä*/to), ስለዚህ (*sïläzih*/therefore), etc. Some of the stopwords (in most cases they are prepositions coming as prefixes) that are affixed with other words are: ከ...(*kä*.../from, if),

ሰላ...(*sĭlä*.../about), በ...(*bä*.../with, using), ቢ...(*bi*.../in case), እስከ...(*ĭski*.../until), ያላ...(*yalä*.../without), የ...(*yä*.../of), ለ...(*lä*.../for, to), etc. While standalone stopwords can be easily removed, it is difficult to identify and remove stopwords that are affixed with other words. For example, the character በ(*bä*) in በቅቤ (*bäqĭbe*/with butter) is used as a preposition affixed with the word ቅቤ (*qĭbe*/butter) where as it is just part of the word in በቅሎ (*bäqlo*/mule). Thus, removal of such stopwords requires analysis of words which we used stemming for this work. Stemming is used not only to remove stopwords (prefixes) that are affixed with other words but also to remove other commonly occurring suffixes introduced as a result of derivations and inflections of words. Most commonly occurring suffixes are: ...ዎች(...*woč*), ...ኦች(...*oč*), ...ና(...*na*), ...ንኘም(...*nĭnĭm*), ...ውን(...*wn*), ...ኣሉ(...*alu*), ...ኣላን(...*alän*), ...ኦችም(...*očĭm*), ...ኣችው(...*ačäw*), ...ዎችም(...*wočĭm*), ...ኦቻችን(...*očačĭn*), ...ዎቻ(...*wočĭna*), ...ውናም(...*wnam*), etc. For nouns and adjectives, the suffixes mark for number, case, definiteness and gender. For verbs, suffixes are introduced to mark for person, gender, number, case, tense/aspect and mood. Thus, removal of prefixes and suffixes retains the stem which would be used in subsequent processes. For example, the stem ገደል (*gädäl*) is taken as the representative term for surface words such as ገደለ (*gädälä*) ገደልኩ (*gädälku*), ገደልኩት (*algädälkutm*), አልገደልኩም (*algädälkum*), ገደላች (*gädäläč*), ኣልገደላችም (*algädäläčĭm*), ስለተገደላ (*sĭlätägädälä*), ኣልገደላም (*algädäläm*), ኣልገደላኝም (*algädäläñĭm*), etc. Then, the frequency of each representative term (stem) is computed where we remove infrequent terms as they only have minimal effect in document categorization. Thus, the preprocessing phase results in a list of frequent terms (decision is based on a threshold value set empirically) in the text.

3.2   Training

Frequent terms obtained in the preprocessing phase are used as inputs for the training process. The frequent terms are further processed to generate document frequency information using inverted index. Document frequency is a representation showing the number of documents that contain a particular term. Terms which are found frequently in at least two or more documents are considered to be non-informative and would be ignored. From a list of the remaining terms, we generate frequent sets of terms using an extended form of *a priori* algorithm as shown in Algorithm 1. The terminologies of *item*, *itemsets* and *transactional database* are used to mean term, sets of items and a set of documents (represented by sets of significant terms), respectively. A *frequent itemset* is defined as an itemset whose frequency exceeds a threshold value employed for the minimum frequency of an itemset. Frequent itemsets are searched using an iterative process beginning with frequent 1-itemsets, which in turn are used to search frequent 2-itemsets. Then, frequent 2-itemsets are used to find frequent 3-itemsets, and so on. The weights of the frequent itemsets are calculated to identify the category.

1. Scan the transactional database to get the frequency of each item.
2. If the frequency of an item is greater than or equal to the minimum frequency, calculate the frequency of the item in each category. Else remove the item from the database.
3. If an item has document frequency greater than a threshold in at least in 2 categories then remove the item from the database.
4. If document frequency of an item is greater than the minimum support threshold (θ), then add to frequent 1-itemset (Π_1).
5. Use Π_{k-1} join Π_{k-1} to generate a set of candidate k-itemsets.
6. Scan the transactional database to get the support of each candidate k-itemsets.
7. If support is greater than or equal to the minimum support, add to k-frequent itemsets.
8. Repeat step 6 until generated set is NULL.
9. Calculate weight for all frequent itemsets.
10. Link a term with a category which has maximum weight.

Algorithm 1. An extended form of *a priori* algorithm used to categorize documents.

To find out which itemsets fall into which categories, itemset Π_j is mapped with category C_i based on the maximum value of $w\Pi_j$. For each frequent itemset Π_j, the weight $w\Pi_j$ is calculated as (Hynek et al. 2000):

$$w\Pi_j = (D\Pi_j \cap DC_i)/nDC_i \tag{1}$$

where nDC_i is the number of terms in document category i ($i = 1,2,3,...,7$ since we used seven categories). $D\Pi_j \cap DC_i$ is to mean the frequency of item Π_j in DC_i. The denominator nDC_i is used for normalizing with the number of documents associated with category DC_i. It takes into account whether an itemset occurs in other categories as well. The significance of terms occurring frequently in documents other than DC_i is thus suppressed.

3.3   Prediction

Based on previous training, the category of a new document is supposed to be predicted correctly. As a result correct category label should be assigned for each new uncategorized document. Since there are frequent 1-itemsets, 2-itemsets, 3-itemsets, etc. a weight factor must be determined for the prediction purpose. This will give the possibility to measure in which category a given document falls. The algorithm we implemented to predict unknown documents is shown in Algorithm 2.

```
1. Scan the transactional database to get each item.
2. Calculate the weight factors for all itemsets.
3. Calculate the sum of weight factors of all itemsets
   for each category.
4. Select the category which has highest weight factor
   and associate (link) the category with the document.
```

Algorithm 2. An algorithm used to predict the category of new documents.

The weight factor *wf* is defined corresponding to the cardinality of itemsets. For example, 1-itemsets are defined by wf_1, 2-itemsets by wf_2, 3-itemsets by wf_3, etc. Suppose S_i be a set of itemsets $\{\prod_1, \prod_2, \prod_3, \cdots \prod_{|S_i|}\}$ representing a particular category C_i where $|S_i|$ refers to the number of itemsets characterizing C_i. Then, the weight $W_{C_i}^D$ corresponding to the accuracy of associating document D with category C_i is computed as:

$$W_{C_i}^D = \sum_{j=1}^{|S_i|} wf_{|\prod_j|} \tag{2}$$

The document D will be associated with category C_i corresponding to the highest weight. However, if two or more categories have got the same maximum weight factor, the document will be associated with all of categories having the maximum weight factor.

4 Experiment

4.1 Corpus Collection

To train and test the system, we collected a total of 985 Amharic documents from ten various news sources dealing with *sport, politics, tourism, meteorology, religion, health* and *education*. The corpus is further divided into training set (65 % of the courpus) and test set (35 % of the corpus). The number of collections in each category is shown in Table 1.

Table 1. Corpus used for experimentation.

No.	Category	No. of documents		
		Training	Test	Total
1	Sport	84	45	129
2	Politics	203	109	312
3	Tourism	63	33	96
4	Meteorology	68	45	113
5	Religion	71	38	109
6	Health	70	37	107
7	Education	78	41	119
Total		637	348	985

4.2   Test Results

Precision, recall and F1 were used to evaluate the performance of our proposed system. Different support threshold (θ) values for document frequency were used to calculate precision, recall and F1 values and the results are shown in Fig. 2. In the figure, it can be observed that the maximum performance achieved in both precision and recall is when the value of θ is close to 6 % which corresponds to a document frequency threshold of 38 (out of the total training documents which is 637). Accordingly, this threshold value was used in the extended *a priori* algorithm implemented in this work. For θ = 6 %, the average performance results obtained were 96 %, 97 % and 96 % for precision, recall and F1, respectively. Details of the the performance of the system (θ = 6 %) with respect to each category is shown below in Table 2.

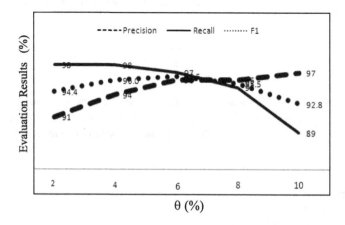

Fig. 2.   Performance results for various values of θ.

Table 2.   Performance of the system when θ = 6 %.

Category	Test documents	Precision (%)	Recall (%)	F1 (%)
Sport	45	94	96	95
Politics	109	94	95	94
Tourism	33	97	100	98
Meteorology	45	100	100	100
Religion	38	100	100	100
Health	37	92	96	94
Education	41	95	90	92

We also conducted an experiment to check the effect of stemming in Amharic document categorization. Experiments showed that processing stemmed documents saves computational time. Training stemmed documents took less time than that of non-stemmed documents. Using the same computer (Dell OptiPlex 780, Core 2 Duo, 2.93 GHz, 4 GB RAM) training stemmed documents took an average of 28 min but to

Table 3. F1 values for both stemmed and non-stemmed documents.

	F1 (%)	
	Stemmed documents	Non-stemmed documents
5	96	81
10	93	79
15	87	74

train non-stemmed documents an average of 41 min was required. Furthermore, we selected three different values of θ and then F1 values were computed for both stemmed and non-stemmed documents. Table 3 shows the summary of the results.

4.3   Comparison with Related Work

The performance obtained in this work was compared with other Amharic document categorization systems designed so far. Table 4 provides a summary of comparisons of such related works where our proposed approach is found to be outperforming others.

Table 4. Comparison of our approach with related works.

No.	Categorization method	No.of categories	Precision (%)
1	Naïve Bayes and K-nearest neighbor (Teklu 2003)	7	89.9
2	Cosine similarity (Tilahun 2001)	3	90.5
3	Decision tree and support vector machines (Afework 2008)	5	95.2
4	Artificial neural network (Eyassu and Gambäck 2005)	–	69.5
5	Our proposed approach	7	96.0

5   Conclusion and Future Works

In this work, itemssets-based Amharic document categorization is presented. An extended *a priori* algorithm was used to implement the proposed system. Test results show that the proposed itemsets-based method has superior performance over other methods tested so far for Amharic text categorization. Although stemming significantly improved the task of categorization, we suggest that a complete morphological analyzer would perform better as every surface word derived from a single root form is represented by a single word in stead of various stems. Thus, future work is directed towards developing and incorporating a more efficient morphological analyzer into the proposed system.

References

Afework, Y.: Automatic amharic text categorization. Master's thesis, Addis Ababa University, Ethiopia (2008)

Agrawal, R., Imielinski, T., Swami, A.: Mining association rules between sets of items in large databases. In: Proceedings of the ACM SIGMOD International Conference on Management of Data, Washington, DC (1993)

Eyassu, S., Gambäck, B.: Classifying amharic news text using self-organizing maps. In: Proceedings of 43rd Annual Meeting of the Association for Computational Linguistics, Michigan, USA (2005)

Goller, C., Löning, J., Will, T., Wolff, W.: Automatic document classification: a thorough evaluation of various methods (2009). doi:10.1.1.90.966

Han, J., Kamber, M.: Data Mining Concepts and Techniques, 2nd edn. Morgan Kaufmann Publishers, USA (2006)

Hynek, J., Jezek, K., Rohlik, O.: Short document categorization - itemsets method. In: The Proceedings of PKDD 2000 Conference, Lyon, France (2000)

Lewis, M.P., Simons, G.F., Fennig, C.D.: Ethnologue: Languages of the World, Seventeenth edn. SIL International, Dallas (2013)

Morshed, A.: Towards the automatic categorization of documents in user-generated categorizations, Technical report No. DIT-06-001, University of Trento, Italy (2006)

Sebastiani, F.: Machine learning in automated text categorization. ACM Comput. Surv. **34**(1), 1–47 (2002)

Teklu, S.: Automatic categorization of Amharic news text: a machine learning approach. Master's thesis, Addis Ababa University, Ethiopia (2003)

Tilahun, S.: Automatic Amharic news categorization. Master's thesis, Addis Ababa University, Ethiopia (2001)

NERosetta for the Named Entity Multi-lingual Space

Cvetana Krstev[1]([✉]), Anđelka Zečević[2], Duško Vitas[2], and Tita Kyriacopoulou[3]

[1] Faculty of Philology, University of Belgrade, Studentski trg 3, Belgrade, Serbia
cvetana@matf.bg.ac.rs
[2] Faculty of Mathematics, University of Belgrade, Studentski trg 16, Belgrade, Serbia
{andjelkaz,vitas}@matf.bg.ac.rs
[3] Laboratoire d'informatique Gaspard-Monge, Université Paris-Est,
Marne-la-Vallé, France
tita@univ.mlv.fr

Abstract. Named Entity Recognition has been a hot topic in Natural Language Processing for more than fifteen years. A number of systems for various languages have been developed using different approaches and based on different named entity schemes and tagging strategies. We present the *NERosetta* web application that can be used for comparison of these various approaches applied to aligned texts (bitexts). In order to illustrate its functionalities, we have used one literary text, its 7 bitexts involving 5 languages and 5 different NER systems. We present some preliminary results and give guidelines for further development.

Keywords: Aligned texts · Named-Entity Recognition · Named-entity scheme · META-NET

1 Motivation

Named Entity Recognition (NER) has been a hot topic in the Natural Language Processing (NLP) community for more than fifteen years. Ever since their introduction at the Sixth Message Understanding Conference [5], named entities have been attracting interest of developers of various NLP applications. A comprehensive overview of NER research literature is presented in [18]. The authors point out that although most of the research in this field is still being done for English, it can be observed that this task draws attention of the research community at large, and not only of those dealing with the languages well-provided with NLP resources and tools, like German, French, Dutch, and Spanish. Moreover, the languages for which some or substantial work in the NER field has been reported belong to various language families.

Another piece of evidence concerning the level of achievement in the NER field can be found in the Language White Papers Series, produced as part of the METANET project [14]. According to this source, at least some information extraction tools and applications (including NER) exist for 28 out of 30 analyzed European languages.

© Springer International Publishing Switzerland 2016
Z. Vetulani et al. (Eds.): LTC 2013, LNAI 9561, pp. 327–340, 2016.
DOI: 10.1007/978-3-319-43808-5_25

According to [11], the term "Named Entity" usually refers to names of persons, locations and organizations, and numeric expressions including time, date, money and percentage. In the last decade, this definition of basic named entities has often been redefined and refined, mostly by adding a few new major types, like "products" and "events", and several marginal types, like "e-mail addresses" and "book titles".

The majority of NER systems are monolingual systems developed for a particular language. Consequently, most of them rely on the language resources of that language and/or language-dependant methods. Recently, a number of authors have reported on multilingual NER applications [17].

The applied methods vary from handcrafted rule-based systems that rely heavily on linguistic knowledge to machine-learning techniques. The usual approaches in machine-learning are supervised learning [18], semi-supervised learning [8] and unsupervised learning [12]. Rule-based systems usually rely on large-scale lexical resources and grammars, often in the form of regular expressions or FSTs [10]. Some authors benefit from combining rule-based and machine-learning approaches when developing their NER systems [1].

In Sect. 2, we will discuss the variations between different NE schemes and tagging techniques that make the comparison between them difficult. In Sect. 3, we will present a new web application, NERosetta that enables a comparison of different NER approaches, while in Sects. 4 and 5, we will give the first results obtained for one text in several languages tagged using several NER systems. Finally, in Sect. 6, we will give some concluding remarks.

2   Variety of Named Entity Schemes and Tagging Strategies

NER systems apply various approaches when defining a named entity structure, ranging from those offering just a few types, like those proposed in the MUC-6 task: ENAMEX, TIMEX, NUMEX, each having just a few attributes for further refinement [3], to those offering a named entity hierarchy which includes as many as two hundred different types [16]. Useful guidelines on how to tag named entities in texts are also given in Chap. 13 of TEI Guidelines P5 [2]. A balanced named entity structure in that respect is defined in the Quaero project [15]. The hierarchy of named entities in the Quaero project consists of eight top-level types: persons, functions, organizations, locations, human products, amounts, temporal expressions, and events. All of these types, except amounts and events, have one or two levels of sub-types.

Various named entity schemes differ not only by the basic set of entities they take into consideration, but also as to whether these entities are refined and to what extent. For instance, the Quaero NE structure has only the type amount that does not have sub-types. However, many NE schemes distinguish various sub-types: money, measurement, percentage, etc. Moreover, two-level sub-types are sometimes distinguished, like the NE scheme presented in [10] in which the amount type has two sub-types – money (called *valeur monétaire*) and measurement (called *valeur physique*) – while the latter has nine sub-subtypes: for duration, temperature, distance, etc.

The same example can be used to illustrate one more difference between the various NE structures. Namely, a sub-type can be present in two NE schemes, but as a sub-type of different types. For instance, duration is a sub-type of measurement, and thus amount both in [10] and Quaero. The NE scheme presented in [6] relies on the international standard for semantic annotation of time and events [13], and therefore, duration is a sub-type of time, along with date, hour and set (sets of time). Similarly, in TEI Guidelines P5 [2], duration is connected to time, but it is not at the same level as date and hour; it is rather their sub-type, since it is introduced as an attribute of the corresponding elements.

Differences in NE schemes naturally reflect the way NEs are tagged in texts. Named entity tagging proposed for the European newspapers project[1] introduces only three entities: person, organization and location, but does not allow nested tagging, e.g. *Canada* is not tagged as a location in the organization name *Library and Archives Canada*. The same strategy is not applied in [6,10,15], where several levels of nesting can actually occur in a text.

The similar applies to the span of a named entity. According to the European newspapers project, titles such as *Dr.* are not part of the person NE, while some other strategies include them [2,6,10,15]. The other aspect of tagging is connectedness of tagged entities: for instance, [10,15] treat the function (a person holds) as separate from a persons name, both of which can be connected by the person entity, but can be tagged separately, as well. One example from the Quaero project illustrates this:

```
<pers.ind>
    <title>
        Son Altesse Royal le
            <func.ind> prince </func.ind>
    </title>
    <name.ind> Rainier </name.ind>
</pers.ind>
```

versus

```
Le <func.ind>roi</func.ind>
<pers.ind>
    <name.first>Mohamed</name.first>
    <qualifier>VI</qualifier>
</pers.ind>
```

In the strategy used by [6] a persons name and function are both mandatory part of the content of the tag person.

In some strategies, named entities can be specified hierarchically, as illustrated by an example from TEI Guidelines [2]:

---

[1] http://www.europeana-newspapers.eu/focus-on-newspaper-refinement-quality-assessment-in-belgrade/.

```
<orgName>
    <orgName>Department of Modern History</orgName>
    <orgName>
        <name type="city">Glasgow</name>
        <name type="role">University</name>
    </orgName>
</orgName>
```

The same approach is taken by the Quaero project and [6]; naturally, such a possibility cannot occur in the strategies that do not allow nesting, as in the European newspaper project.

Finally, NE tagging strategies differ in determining the semantic scope of each NE type and sub-type. It is interesting that both Quaero and the European newspaper projects give *The Beatles* as an example: the former strategy treats it is as a collective person, while the latter treats it as organization.

3 Comparison of Named Entity Schemes and Tagging Strategies

In order to be able to compare various NE structures and tagging strategies primarily qualitatively, we have developed a web application dubbed *NERosetta*[2]. The comparison is performed through a reference NE scheme. At present, our reference scheme relies mostly on the Quaero project, with addition of some sub-types, e.g. for amount. We have chosen this particular scheme for several reasons: (a) it has quite an elaborate and balanced structure with respect to NE types and sub-types; (b) it is well documented; (c) the NER systems that were at our disposal for testing were developed independently from it. This reference NE scheme can be easily replaced by another one.

NERosetta does not perform NE recognition and tagging, rather it works with the documents previously tagged with some NER system. It can accept any document as long as it is a well-formed XML document with NEs tagged with XML tags. It is also presupposed that a document is segmented into paragraphs and sentences (or segments). In order to work with it, it is necessary to define the NE structure used, which is done by defining the mapping to the reference scheme, for instance: **amount.money** → money.exact (*70.000 miliona evra*) and **amount.money** → money.range (*(izmedu) 5,5 i šest miliona dolara*). As a rule, each mapping is followed by an example. It should be noted, however, that this is performed only once for each structure and need not be repeated for each document in the system that uses it.

In general, the established mapping between the newly defined NE scheme and the reference scheme is many-to-many:

1. In some cases, an entity type or a sub-type is mapped to one and only one type or a sub-type in the reference structure. Such is the case with the type

---

[2] http://www.korpus.matf.bg.ac.rs/nerosetta/.

MONEY in the NE scheme Stanford NER 7 [4], which is mapped only to the sub-type AMOUNT.MONEY in the reference NE structure and vice versa.

2. There are cases where an entity type or a sub-type is mapped to more than one type or sub-type in the reference scheme. Such is the case with the type ORGANIZATION in the NE scheme Stanford NER 7, which is mapped to two sub-types in the reference NE structure: ORG.ADM and ORG.ENT.

3. Finally, there are cases where several entity sub-types are mapped to one type or sub-type in the reference scheme. Such is the case with the various measurement sub-types in the NE scheme described in [10]: AMOUNT.PHY.DUR, AMOUNT.PHY.TEMP, AMOUNT.PHY.LEN, etc. that are all mapped to one sub-type in the reference NE scheme: AMOUNT.MEASURE.

NERosetta has three different modes. It can work with: (a) one particular document tagged with one NER system; (b) one document tagged with two different NER systems; (c) one document in two languages (e.g. source and translation language), each tagged with some NER system developed for the corresponding language. For working in mode (c) it is necessary for the two texts to have been previously aligned at the segment level (paragraphs, sentences, or sub-sentence). The format of alignment is described in Section 16.4.2 of the TEI P5 Guidelines [2]. It basically relies on two separate files for each language in which all segments that should be aligned are labeled by unique identifiers. A third file consists of a group that links the corresponding segments. Such a format can be produced, for instance by XAlign[3]. However, it is also possible to import an aligned text in a TMX (translation memory interchange) format and *NERosetta* will split it in three files that are in the requested format.

The search is performed only by the types and sub-types of the reference scheme. Before formulating the search, a user has to decide whether she/he is looking for the exact match, the sub-types of the chosen type, and/or the super-types of the chosen type. These options are necessary in order to overcome different kinds of mappings. If only the exact match were supported, then only case 1 mapping would give the expected results. However, if one NE structure supported only a top level type (e.g. location in Stanford NER 7) and the other supported sub-types of the reference scheme (cases 2 and 3 of the mapping) the exact match would yield no results, but the option "match sub-types" solves the problem. The option "match super-types" is adequate if just some sub-types are to be included in a search. A user can select one or more types and sub-types and they are combined in a conjunction query. All the results obtained are preceded by the chosen search criteria and the corresponding mapping, so that a user can better understand the results. The aligned concordances are presented ten at a time.

A user can work with *NERosetta* at two levels. As an unregistered user, she/he can view all applied NE schemas and search the available textual resources. If a user becomes registered, then she/he can also define new NE schemas, upload new texts and/or new tagging, and delete her/his own texts. The "How to Use *NERosetta*" document is put at the disposal of all users.

---

[3] A tool developed by P. Bonhomme, T. M. H. Nguyen and S. O'Rourke, http://led.loria.fr/outils/ALIGN/align.html.

The application is organized as a classic 3-tier web application: the first, presentation tier, reflects user information needs and performs data visualization; the second, logic tier, is the most complex one as it joins outer tiers - it processes data obtained from the first tier with the help of the third tier and sends back the results; the third, data tier, is where data is stored and retrieved from a data-base system. Due to potentially big XML files that correspond to data and linking instructions, its content is not loaded into memory at once, but a stream-based parser is used. It requires knowledge of file character encoding so a user performing a file upload should provide the system with the appropriate information. As mentioned above, the application is developed with a wide set of users in mind. All the changes, such as a new file upload or addition of a new NER schema description are immediately visible to the public and ready for use.

4 Vernes Novel "Around the World in 80 Days" in *NERosetta*

For the first application of *NERosetta* we have chosen Vernes novel "Around the World in 80 Days" which is available through the META-SHARE repository in 18 languages – the French original and 17 translations[4]. Moreover, the 32 parallel versions aligned 1:1 at the sentence level are also available in the TMX format (4436 segments in all bitexts). The availability of this text in many languages would not have been enough if it had not been suitable for experimenting with named entity tagging, because of the nature of the text itself.

However, we restricted this experiment only to those languages for which some NER system was at our disposal. The languages we covered and the NER systems we used are:

- *French* – we have used the frMaurel system described in [10].[5] This system is based on a cascade of finite-state transducers and e-dictionaries and it is implemented in the Unitex corpus processing tool.[6] It recognizes the following top-level types: amount, event, function, location, organization, person, product, time.
- *English* – we have used Stanford NER 3 and NER 7 classifiers. The classifiers are statistical in nature and based on conditional random fields information extraction systems boosted with the Gibbs sampling technique for incorporating non-local information. The algorithm is described in depth in [4], while the most up-to-date versions can be downloaded from the official website.[7] The first classifier labels persons, locations and organizations, while the second covers a wider set of types: person, location, organization, time, date, money and percent.

---

[4] http://www.meta-share.eu/.

[5] We have used the version of the cascade and e-dictionaries from February 2012.

[6] http://www-igm.univ-mlv.fr/~unitex/.

[7] http://nlp.stanford.edu/software/CRF-NER.shtml.

- *Serbian* – we have used the srKrstev system described in [6]. This system is also based on a cascade of finite-state transducers and e-dictionaries. It recognizes the following top-level types: amount, location, organization, person, time. It can be used not only in the Unitex environment, but also through the *NERanka*[8] web interface. We have applied the NER system developed for Croatian (described in the next item) to Serbian too. The reasons for this were twofold: firstly, Serbian and Croatian belong to the same South-Slavic family and are therefore often regarded as closely related, and secondly, NER systems for Serbian and Croatian were developed on different principles and thus are interesting to compare.

- *Croatian* – we have used the system described in [9] here denoted as hrNER. It is based on the Stanford named entity recognizer and adapted to the specific task of Croatian and Slovenian NER. The hrNER that we downloaded from the official website[9] tags three top-level types: location, organization and person. For the reasons explained above, we have applied the NER system developed for Serbian to Croatian as well.

- *Greek* – we have used the grTita NER system presented in [7]. This system is also based on finite-state transducers and e-dictionaries applied in Unitex. The Greek NER system tags only two top-level types: person and time.

For these five languages and the NER systems described we have produced the pairs listed in Table 1.

Table 1. Language/NER system pairs in *NERosetta*

	Language	NER	Language	NER
A	French	frMaurel	English	Stanford-7
B	French	frMaurel	Serbian	srKrstev
C	English	Stanford-7	Serbian	srKrstev
D	Greek	grTita	English	Stanford-3
E	Croatian	hrNER	Serbian	srKrstev
F	Croatian	hrNER	Serbian	hrNER
G	Serbian	srKrstev	Croatian	srKrstev
H	English	Stanford-7	Croatian	hrNER
I	French	frMaurel	Croatian	hrNER
J	Greek	grTita	French	frMaurel
K	Greek	grTita	Serbian	srKrstev
L	Greek	grTita	Croatian	hrNER

---

[8] http://hlt.rgf.bg.ac.rs/VebRanka/NERanka.aspx.
[9] http://nlp.ffzg.hr/resources/models/ner/.

5   Qualitative and Quantitative Analysis of NER with *NERosetta*

The main purpose of *NERosetta* is to facilitate comparison between various NE schemes, strategies and systems. It can directly provide insight into translation strategies for various types of named entities, as illustrated by the following example of organization recognition (tagged sequences are given in bold):

FR: Rowan, directeur police, administration centrale, Scotland place.

CR: Rowanu, upravitelju redarstva, sredinja uprava, **Scotland yard**.

SR: Rovanu, upravniku policije, centralna uprava, trg Skotland.

EN: Rowan, **Commissioner of Police**, Scotland Yard:

In French and Serbian the organization name is not recognized (due to the lack of upper-case letters), while in English and Croatian different sequences are recognized as organization names: in Croatian a location name is recognized (often used as an alias of the organization in question), while in English a span of the name is not correct.

Additionally, the differences among NE systems can be used as input features to machine learning algorithms and their adaptation to various domains and languages. This is especially important for closely related languages.

NERosetta can be useful for quantitative assessment of different NER systems. One of the criteria can be based on the number of concordance lines in which at least one named entity was recognized, correctly or not, either in the first or in the second language pair. In order to assess the quality of one particular system it is enough to investigate concordance lines obtained for any pair in which a chosen NER system applied to a language appear. For instance, in order to assess srKrstev system applied to Serbian one could look at the concordances for B, C, E, G or K from Table 1 – the results would always be the same. *NERosetta* calculates these values automatically and displays above the result list for each pair.

To illustrate these, we have analyzed the results obtained by various NER systems presented in Sect. 4 using the type PERSON as an example, because of its being the only type presented in all the systems used. *NERosetta* produced from 596 concordance lines (for the pair F) to 1,654 lines (for the pair K). We have restricted our research only to the first 500 segments of each bitext. For pairs I and J the alignment is done not on the whole document level but only for the first 500 segments. Data in Table 2 summarize the obtained results.

NERosetta also supports the traditional assessment of information extraction systems by the precision (as the ratio of all correctly retrieved NEs and all retrieved NEs), the recall (as the ratio of all correctly retrieved NEs and all NEs in a text) and the F1-score which gives an equal importance to the both precision and recall. This is possible due to more sophisticated module for a manual assessment of a result list. For each entity present an evaluator should firstly decide on if it is recognized by the system or not and if it is, she/he should mark it as correct, not correct or partially correct. If both the type and the span of an entity are valid, it is considered as correctly recognized. The entity is partially correct if the type is correct and the span is either underestimated

Table 2. The number of concordance lines for PERSON (with sub-categories) in the first 500 segments of the text – the lowest percent of concordance lines is given in bold

Pair	in 500	in both	in 1st	in 2nd
A	127	24	24+6	24+97
%	14.46	18.90	23.62	95.28
B	156	22	22+9	22+125
%	14.93	14.10	**19.87**	94.23
C	162	121	121+10	121+31
%	13.99	74.69	80.86	100
D	207	123	123+77	123+7
%	12.72	59.42	96.61	**62.80**
E	171	71	71+19	71+81
%	14.45	41.52	52.63	88.89
F	98	29	29+61	29+8
%	16.44	29.59	91.83	**37.76**
G	153	15	15+137	15+1
%	14.40	9.80	99.34	**10.45**
H	147	74	74+57	74+16
%	14.71	50.34	89.11	61.22
I	111	10	10+21	10+80
%	100	9.00	27.93	81.08
J	205	27	27+174	27+4
%	96.69	13.17	98.05	15.12
K	210	142	142+59	142+9
%	12.70	67.61	95.71	**71.90**
L	211	79	79+122	79+10
%	13.10	37.44	**95.26**	42.18

or overestimated. Regardless of the span, if the type of the entity is wrong it is considered as incorrect. For each result's segment of both language pairs, an evaluator can count and note per entity level each of these values. The list with evaluations can be further stored, updated and extended according to user's needs as a user can work not only with whole document but with a specified interval of segments or a randomly generated set of segments.

In order to evaluate the precision and the recall of the systems of interest, we have used the manually generated evaluations for entity types PERSON and LOCATION. As aforementioned, PERSON is the only entity type supported by all systems while LOCATION is not supported only by grTita system and therefore can contribute to the comparison of the systems to a large extent.

The evaluation was done by several evaluators, and one super-evaluator checked their work. When performing the manual evaluation all evaluators followed the same principle. The most important and that caused most dilemmas are two following cases:

- A PERSON or LOCATION name is used for some other NE type – in such cases recognition was treated as correct expecting that NER system recognizing this other NE type would resolve this ambiguity. For instance, the name of a ship *Mongolia* was recognized by en-Stanford7 and srKrstev as a location name, and skipped by hrNER and frMaurel.
- Some systems recognized a title or a function a part of a PERSON, some did not. We treated as correct when it was recognized, but we did not treat it as partially correct when it was not recognized. For instance, both recognitions were treated as correct:
  - EN: At this point, he had learned that **Phileas Fogg**, Esq., was looking for a manservant.
  - SR: U to vreme sazna da **gospodin Fileas Fog** traži slugu.
  We used the same principle for possessive adjectives derived from a NE.
  - HR: Iz **Passepartoutovih** ruku uze torbu... (possessive adjective, recognized → correct)
  - EN: He took the bag from Passepartout... (name, not recognized; miss)
  - SR: On uzme torbu iz ruku Paspartuovih... (possessive adjective, not recognized → correct)

As stated, the evaluation encompassed work with partially correct entities. For instance, for the pair of segments

Table 3. The precision (P) and average precision (P_{avg}) for all Language/NER system pairs in *NERosetta* for PERSON (with sub-categories)

	Lang/NER	P	P_{avg}	Lang/NER	P	P_{avg}
A	fr/frMaurel	96.77	93.94	en/Stanford-7	97.86	97.52
B	fr/frMaurel	96.77	93.94	sr/srKrstev	96.03	91.62
C	en/Stanford-7	94.98	88.61	sr/srKrstev	92.74	85.75
D	gr/grTita	83.87	81.54	en/Stanford-3	98.66	98.66
E	cr/hrNER	89.37	81.03	sr/srKrstev	93.73	86.61
F	cr/hrNER	89.94	81.28	sr/hrNER	90.32	83.78
G	sr/srKrstev	93.54	89.35	cr/srKrstev	77.78	69.23
H	en/Stanford-7	97.15	90.52	cr/hrNER	88.41	80.58
I	fr/frMaurel	96.97	95.59	cr/hrNER	89.36	87.00
J	gr/grTita	83.49	80.93	fr/frMaurel	96.67	93.75
K	gr/grTita	86.99	85.48	sr/srKrstev	94.28	92.43
L	gr/grTita	83.56	81.14	cr/hrNER	90.42	88.78

Table 4. The recall (R) and average recall (R_{avg}) for all Language/NER system pairs in *NERosetta* for PERSON (with sub-categories)

	Lang/NER	R	R_{avg}	Lang/NER	R	R_{avg}
A	fr/frMaurel	20.69	21.09	en/Stanford-7	93.20	92.90
B	fr/frMaurel	16.95	17.32	sr/srKrstev	88.96	85.47
C	en/Stanford-7	79.58	75.99	sr/srKrstev	84.98	79.66
D	gr/grTita	94.30	90.91	en/Stanford-3	76.17	76.16
E	cr/hrNER	36.85	38.17	sr/srKrstev	81.03	76.57
F	cr/hrNER	76.06	71.12	sr/hrNER	25.81	27.07
G	sr/srKrstev	88.17	84.69	cr/srKrstev	4.70	5.88
H	en/Stanford-7	90.52	79.14	cr/hrNER	43.67	44.38
I	fr/frMaurel	25.40	25.59	cr/hrNER	70.00	69.05
J	gr/grTita	93.33	89.67	fr/frMaurel	13.87	14.22
K	gr/grTita	86.29	84.82	sr/srKrstev	69.06	68.47
L	gr/grTita	93.37	89.90	cr/hrNER	41.06	41.23

Table 5. The precision (P) and average precision (P_{avg}) for all Language/NER system pairs in *NERosetta* for LOCATION (with sub-categories)

	Lang/NER	P	P_{avg}	Lang/NER	P	P_{avg}
A	fr/frMaurel	87.5	86.36	en/Stanford-7	93.26	92.78
B	fr/frMaurel	83.52	82.45	sr/srKrstev	100.00	100.00
C	en/Stanford-7	83.59	82.82	sr/srKrstev	86.10	85.55
E	cr/hrNER	85.96	85.65	sr/srKrstev	82.89	82.89
F	cr/hrNER	88.07	87.39	sr/hrNER	78.16	78.16
G	sr/srKrstev	80.53	80.42	cr/srKrstev	75.51	75.51
H	en/Stanford-7	86.66	85.96	cr/hrNER	85.96	85.96
I	fr/frMaurel	84.61	83.51	cr/hrNER	94.00	94.00

- EN: Some people supported **Phileas Fogg**; others - who soon formed a significant majority - came out against.
- SR: Jedni su bili **pristalice Fileasa Foga**, drugi - kojih je bilo veina - izjasnie se protiv njega.

PERSON recognition in the EN part is correct while in the SR part it is partially correct as the span of the entity is overestimated. In order to use these information apart from traditional (strict) precision and recall values, we calculated the average versions which allocate a half weight to partially correct matches.

The results of the evaluation are denoted in Tables 3, 4, 5 and 6 for all pairs of systems at our disposal. The number of segments we investigated is 500.

Table 6. The recall (R) and average recall (R_{avg}) for all Language/NER system pairs in *NERosetta* for LOCATION (with sub-categories)

	Lang/NER	R	R_{avg}	Lang/NER	R	R_{avg}
A	fr/frMaurel	73.68	73.07	en/Stanford-7	80.58	80.29
B	fr/frMaurel	81.72	80.73	sr/srKrstev	64.77	64.77
C	en/Stanford-7	74.82	74.31	sr/srKrstev	78.52	78.12
E	cr/hrNER	37.12	37.17	sr/srKrstev	82.58	82.58
F	cr/hrNER	51.61	51.59	sr/hrNER	36.96	36.96
G	sr/srKrstev	85.42	85.28	cr/srKrstev	44.94	44.94
H	en/Stanford-7	80.95	80.39	cr/hrNER	35.90	35.90
I	fr/frMaurel	86.52	85.33	cr/hrNER	44.76	44.76

Table 7. The precision, the recall and the F1-score for all Language/NER system pairs

	Person			Location		
	Precision	Recall	F1-score	Precision	Recall	F1-score
sr/srKrstev	0.941	0.824	0.878	0.874	0.778	0.823
gr/grTita	0.845	0.918	0.880	-	-	-
en/enNER-7	0.972	0.849	0.906	0.878	0.788	0.831
cr/hrNER	0.895	0.535	0.670	0.885	0.423	0.573
sr/hrNER	0.903	0.258	0.401	0.782	0.370	0.502
fr/frMaurel	0.968	0.192	0.321	0.852	0.806	0.829
cr/srKrstev	0.778	0.047	0.089	0.755	0.449	0.563

For the fixed language and NER system the values of the precision and recall should be constant. However, the slight deviation of values is possible due to different segment alignments for different system pairs and therefore variable number of entity matches. Such an example is en/Stanford-7 combination in A and C pairs. The additional source of noise can be attributed to inter-annotator disagreement as different persons were working on "gold standards" for evaluation. The combination cr/hrNER in E and F pairs can confirm such an exception. The examination of the original files produced by evaluators for the E pair results in 43 partially correct and 17 incorrect matches for the type PERSON, while for the pair F the values are 44 and 16 respectively.

In order to rank all NER systems uniformly a macro-average across entity types is applied. The precision, recall and F1-score are calculated for both PERSON and LOCATION entity types on a system level and then the results are averaged. The results in terms of strict measures are presented in Table 7 and sorted according to the average value of F1-score in Table 8. The systems frMaurel and srKrstev (on the Croatian text) have a low rank because they had

Table 8. The macro-averaged precision, recall and F1-score for all Language/NER system pairs

	Precision	Recall	F1-score
gr/grTita	0.845	0.918	0.880
en/enNER-7	0.925	0.818	0.865
sr/srKrstev	0.9075	0.801	0.850
cr/hrNER	0.890	0.479	0.621
fr/frMaurel	0.91	0.499	0.575
sr/hrNER	0.842	0.314	0.451
cr/srKrstev	0.766	0.248	0.326

problems with the recognition of foreign personal names. The system grTita has a high rank but its recall was estimated on the basis of just one aligned pair. On the other hand, srKrstev applied to the Serbian text has the highest rank and its recall was estimated on the basis of five aligned pairs.

6 Future Work

We have presented the first results of comparison of the performance of several NER systems. These results are far from conclusive – they were presented to point to the usefulness of *NERosetta* for qualitative and quantitative analysis, rather than to provide a detailed analysis of these systems. Our plans for the future are to have more users of *NERosetta*, and to work with more texts, languages and NER systems in order to establish a steady ground for entity studying.

Acknowledgments. This research was conducted through the project 178006 financed by the Serbian Ministry of Education, Science and Technological Development.

References

1. Béchet, F., Sagot, B., Stern, R., et al.: Coopération de méthodes statistiques et symboliques pour l'adaptation non-supervisée d'un système d'étiquetage en entités nommées. In: TALN 2011-Traitement Automatique des Langues Naturelles (2011)
2. Burnard, L., Bauman, S.: TEI P5: Guidelines for Electronic Text Encoding and Interchange (2008)
3. Chinchor, N.: MUC-6 Named Entity Task Definition (Version 2.1) (1995)
4. Finkel, J.R., Grenager, T., Manning, C.: Incorporating non-local information into information extraction systems by Gibbs sampling. In: Proceedings of the 43rd Annual Meeting of the ACL, pp. 363–370 (2005)
5. Grishman, R., Sundheim, B.: Message understanding conference-6: a brief history. COLING, vol. 1, pp. 466–471. Association for Computational Linguistics, Stroudsburg (1996)

6. Krstev, C., Obradović, I., Utvić, M., Vitas, D.: A system for named entity recognition based on local grammars. J. Logic Comput. (2013). doi:10.1093/logcom/exs079

7. Kyriacopoulou, T., Martineau, C., Mavropoulos, T.: Les noms propres de personne en français et en grec: reconnaissance, extraction et enrichissement de dictionnaire. In: Proceedings of the 30th Conference on Lexis and Grammar, LGC 2011, Cyprus (2011)

8. Liu, X., Zhang, S., Wei, F., Zhou, M.: Recognizing named entities in tweets. In: Proceedings of the 49th Annual Meeting of the ACL: Human Language Technologies, vol. 1, pp. 359–367 (2011)

9. Ljubešić, N., Stupar, M., Jurić, T., Agić, Ž.: Combining available datasets for building named entity recognition models of Croatian and Slovene. In: Slovenščina 2.0: Empirical, Applied and Interdisciplinary Research (2013) (in press)

10. Maurel, D., Friburger, N., Antoine, J.-Y., Eshkol, I., Nouvel, D., et al.: Cascades de transducteurs autour de la reconnaissance des entités nommes. Traitement Automatique des Langues **52**(1), 69–96 (2011)

11. Nadeau, D., Sekine, S.: A survey of named entity recognition and classification. In: Sekine, S., Ranchhod, E. (eds.) Named Entities: Recognition, Classification and Use, pp. 3–28. John Benjamins Pub. Co., Amsterdam/Philadelphia (2009)

12. Nadeau, D., Turney, P., Matwin, S.: Unsupervised named-entity recognition: generating gazetteers and resolving ambiguity. In: 19th Canadian Conference on Artificial Intelligence, Québec City, Québec, Canada (2006)

13. Pustejovsky, J., Lee, K., Bunt, H., Romary, L.: ISO-TimeML: an international standard for semantic annotation. In: 7th LREC 2010. ELRA, Valletta (2010)

14. Rehm, G., Uszkoreit, H. (eds.): META-NET White Paper Series. Springer, Heidelberg (2012)

15. Rosset, S., Grouin, C., Zweigenbaum, P.: Entités Nommées Structurées: guide d'annotation Quaero. LIMSI-CNRS, Orsay (2011)

16. Sekine, S., Nobata, C.: Definition, dictionaries and tagger for extended named entity hierarchy. In: LREC, Lisbon, Portugal (2004)

17. Steinberger, R., Bruno, P.: Cross-lingual named entity recognition. In: Sekine, S., Ranchhod, E. (eds.) Named Entities: Recognition, Classification and Use, pp. 137–164. John Benjamins Pub. Co. (2009)

18. Tatar, S., Cicekli, I.: Automatic rule learning exploiting morphological features for named entity recognition in Turkish. J. Inf. Sci. **37**(2), 137–151 (2011)

A Hybrid Approach to Statistical Machine Translation Between Standard and Dialectal Varieties

Friedrich Neubarth[1]([✉]), Barry Haddow[2], Adolfo Hernández Huerta[3], and Harald Trost[4]

[1] Austrian Research Institute for Artificial Intelligence (OFAI), Vienna, Austria
friedrich.neubarth@ofai.at
[2] ILCC, School of Informatics, University of Edinburgh, Edinburgh, Scotland
bhaddow@staffmail.ed.ac.uk
[3] Nuance Communications Aachen, Aachen, Germany
adherhu@gmail.com
[4] Medical University of Vienna, Vienna, Austria
harald.trost@meduniwien.ac.at

Abstract. Using statistical machine translation (SMT) for dialectal varieties usually suffers from data sparsity, but combining word-level and character-level models can yield good results even with small training data by exploiting the relative proximity between the two varieties. In this paper, we describe a specific problem and its solution, arising with the translation between standard Austrian German and Viennese dialect. In general, for a phrase-based approach to SMT, complex lexical transformations and syntactic reordering cannot be dealt with satisfyingly. In a situation with sparse resources it becomes merely impossible. These are typical cases where rule-based preprocessing of the source data is the preferable option, hence the hybrid character of the resulting system. One such case is the transformation between synthetic imperfect verb forms to perfect tense with finite auxiliary and past participle, which involves detection of clause boundaries and identification of clause type. We present an approach that utilizes a full parse of the source sentences and discuss the problems that arise using such an approach. Within the developed SMT system, the models trained on preprocessed data unsurprisingly fare better than those trained on the original data, but also unchanged sentences gain slightly better scores. This shows that introducing a rule-based layer dealing with systematic non-local transformations increases the overall performance of the system, most probably due to a higher accuracy in the alignment.

Keywords: Statistical machine translation · Hybrid approaches to MT · Preprocessing in SMT · Language varieties · Dialects · Syntactic parsing

© Springer International Publishing Switzerland 2016
Z. Vetulani et al. (Eds.): LTC 2013, LNAI 9561, pp. 341–353, 2016.
DOI: 10.1007/978-3-319-43808-5_26

1   Introduction

The standard paradigm of statistical machine translation (SMT) is tailored towards major languages where large bilingual and perhaps even larger mono-lingual text corpora are at hand. Such mandatory prerequisites make it almost impossible to apply the same methods to less resourced languages, not to speak of dialectal varieties that most often lack written resources. On the other hand, less resourced languages and even more so dialects may be closely related enough to a resource-rich language to exploit its resources in a sensible way. This offers new possibilities for the application of language technology methods to languages and varieties that were previously excluded from such a treatment. In the absence of huge corpora for a particular dialectal language variety that offer themselves for machine learning techniques, alternative methods have to be developed to trans-form the input for SMT in such a way that it sufficiently resembles a resource-rich language. There are certain challenges for such an approach.

For example, usually dialects lack an authoritative orthography, which makes it necessary to develop a coherent standard for spelling and moreover, calls for methods to normalize the spelling of existing written texts.[1] Once such a standardized orthography is achieved, it can be taken for granted that parallel (bilingual) resources written in this standard do not exist. However, the relative proximity between a standard language and its varieties can be used to bootstrap a larger corpus from rather little data that has to be translated and encoded in the orthography by hand. Given that character based and word based models trained on small data sets provide useful though not correct output, bilingual data can be obtained by only validating and correcting these translations, which is much less effort than translating from scratch. Then these data can be used to improve the models in an iterative way. This method proved rather successful in our project and it enabled us to establish a SMT system for translating from a standard to a dialectal variety that delivers considerably good results.

In addition, a resourced-rich language can be used as a 'pivot language' for translating a closely related less resourced language or variety into another major language. The SMT models of the pivot language are exploited by transforming the data of the less resourced language in such a way that it resembles the pivot language to a high degree – a strategy that has been successfully applied to language pairs such as Macedonian and Bulgarian, or Bahasa Indonesia and Malayan (see Sect. 2).

Another issue in SMT is that local dependencies can well be represented within phrase tables, but non-local ones usually cannot. Differences in syntac-tic structures that are reflected in different orderings on the level of terminal strings (words) pose specific problems. State-of-the-art MT attempts to resolve such reorderings by identifying the relevant sub-structures from tree-banks, and applying phrase-based SMT to the sub-trees while the tree structures are trans-formed according to the models of source and target language. Thus, syntactic reordering is captured over the tree structures. To some extent, this problem

---

[1] See [1] for details on the orthography developed for this project.

can be neglected with closely related languages or varieties, since the syntax of the two languages is usually similar enough. However, there are still cases where syntactic reordering must be taken into account, even though the syntactic properties of the two varieties are almost identical. These arise when for a certain construction, there are two syntactic configurations available in the source language, but only one of them exists in the target variety.

In this paper, we will present such a case that appears in the context of translating Austrian German (AG), the standard variety, into a dialectal variety spoken in the capital of Austria – Viennese dialect (VD) [2,3]. Most syntactic differences between these varieties can be attributed to morpho-syntactic properties and result in the different use of function words (e.g., relative clauses in VD often employ the indefinite pronoun *wås* 'what' in addition to the relative pronoun: *dea wås* 'D-who what'). Nevertheless, these words generally appear in the same local context and can in principle be easily 'learned' by the phrase table, provided the relevant constructions are found in the training data. The phenomenon in focus is the lack of imperfect verb forms in VD (and most other Bavarian dialects).[2] Imperfect verb forms are synthetic, while the perfect used in VD is analytic, consisting of an auxiliary in the position of the finite verb and a past participle at the very end of the clause.[3]

The solution is apparently simple: one has to make the source look more similar to the target, i.e. imperfect forms are all transformed into perfect (which does not even change acceptability, at least in AG). After this preprocessing step, the phrase tables can be learned based on an input where the alignment is straightforward (auxiliary in finite position, participle at the end of the clause in input and target variety). With such a move, the MT system has hybrid characteristics: data from the source language (AG) is preprocessed in a rule-based approach, incorporating linguistic knowledge about both varieties, and only after that, statistical modeling is applied in standard fashion. Collins et al. [4] propose a similar approach to tackle the problem of non-local dependencies in German being translated into English.

The most prominent reason for such a hybrid strategy lies in the fact that statistical alignment will not be able to identify the (remote) perfect participle as part of the verb group. Hence, only the imperfect verb form and the finite auxiliary end up in the phrase tables, and the lexical information of the verb, conveyed by the participle is lost in translation.

In the following section, we discuss some peculiarities of working with dialectal varieties and give a brief outline of similar methods that have been applied

---

[2] There are two exceptions which indeed have imperfect forms: the auxiliary *sein* 'to be' and the two modals *sollen* 'ought to' and *wollen* 'want'.

[3] A phenomenon with similar consequences for SMT is the lack of genitive case in VD. It is either replaced by dative, or – in possessive constructions – by a prepositional phrase (*s auto fon da schwesda* – *das Auto von der Schwester* 'the car of the sister'). Alternatively, with animate possessors, there is also a construction not existing in Standard German: the possessor in dative case, and a resumptive possessive pronoun (*da schwesda ia auto* – [?]*der Schwester ihr Auto* 'the sister-Dat her car'). These constructions will not be discussed in this paper.

to other closely related language pairs. Section 3 provides information about the bilingual corpus, and in Sect. 4, we discuss in detail the rule-based component of our MT system. Results of combining rule-based preprocessing with common methods of SMT are presented and discussed in Sect. 5.

2   Background

From a linguistic perspective, it has to be noted that dialects are never confined to a well-defined or delineated unique variety, also they are under constant influence of other varieties (most dominantly a standard variety), thus inherently subject to ample variation, synchronic as well as diachronic. Lacking (or resisting) standardization initiatives, reinforcement by education or public media, and predominantly being confined to oral usage, dialects most often form a dynamic continuum between different varieties and speaker groups. Being defined by social group rather than geographical regions, the Viennese variety is a sociolect in the strict sense, where dialects in urban regions are generally associated with lower social classes [5]. Moreover, speakers very often switch (or gradually shift) between their dialect and the standard variety, due to pragmatic reasons determined by the situation of the communication, the content, or to express emphasis. Therefore, the aim is to generate a consistent model of a dialectal variety that conforms to a stereotype of that dialect rather to incorporate all its variability.

Pairs of closely related languages (or language varieties) offer themselves to exploit the linguistic proximity in order to overcome the usual scarcity of parallel data. Nakov and Tiedemann [6] take advantage of the great overlap in vocabulary and the strong syntactic and lexical similarity between Bulgarian and Macedonian. They develop an SMT system for this language pair by employing a combination of character and word-level translation models, outperforming a phrase-based word-level baseline. The character-based SMT approach has been also used to process historical language, Scherrer and Erjavec [7] follows this strategy to modernize historical Slovene words. Nakov and Ng [8] propose a language-independent method to improve phrase-based SMT from a resource-poor language X1 into a language Y by exploiting the similarity of X1 to a related resource-rich language X2, by using bi-texts of the pair X2-Y. The proposed method is a hybrid approach of concatenation and combination of phrase-tables that are built by bi-texts X1-Y and X2-Y. Regarding MT of dialects, Zbib et al. [9] used crowdsourcing to build Levantine-English and Egyptian-English parallel corpora; Sawaf [10] normalizes non-standard, spontaneous and dialect Arabic into Modern Standard Arabic to achieve translations into English.

3   The Corpus

As mentioned before, dialect speakers in Vienna often switch between the dialect and the standard variety, depending on the communicative situation, but also on the content that may invite to use a higher register. Text data with a bias towards the standard by virtue of standard orthography quite often also reflects such switching processes. In order to circumvent such biases, we carefully selected colloquial data of VD that are as authentic to the dialect as possible. The basic material consists of transcripts of TV documentaries and free interview recordings of dialect speakers. The transcripts (TR) were manually translated into both AG and VD in order to ensure that (rarely occurring) switches to the standard variety do not end up in the target model, and to handle repetitions, truncations and uninformative interjections.

(1) TR: kenn ich, jåjå dån, åiso i maan
     VD: ken   i,   jå dån,   åiso i   maan
     AG: kenne ich, ja dann, also ich meine
     EN: know I,   yes then, well I   mean
     'I know (it), yes then, well I mean'

In an early stage, the task was to align these parallel sentences on a word-by-word basis, in order to simultaneously train a character-level translation model that would help to improve the alignment and generate lexical resources comprising morphology and morpho-syntactic features (PoS tags, grammatical features, such as number, person, tense, etc.). Usually the two translations (AG/VD) are syntactically very similar, with little re-ordering and/or n-to-n correspondences. In addition, many corresponding words are 'cognates', meaning that they are lexically (and morphologically) the same in both varieties, with different phonology and spelling (e.g., AG *also* corresponds to VD *åiso* 'thus/well'). The version of the corpus we used for the first, preliminary experiments described in this paper comprises 4909 sentence pairs with 39108 tokens for AG and 40031 tokens for VD. For further details regarding the development of a SMT system based on this corpus see Haddow et al. [11].

In a second stage of the project, we utilized the obtained translation models in order to generate a pool of bilingual sentence candidates obtained from standard German news texts with reference to Vienna that were translated with the preliminary SMT system. These sentences were presented to users that had to validate and to correct the output of SMT. We also experimented with random selection versus selection weighted by a function that takes into account the frequency of words within the corpus and global frequency values taken from DeReWo [12]. The differences between the two approaches were not significant, however, the amount of data for training new models gained more than double its initial size (10796 sentence pairs altogether).

4   Rule Based Preprocessing

In VD, imperfect tense verb forms generally do not exist, but such forms quite often occur in AG. Sentences that express past tense with imperfect in AG have to use the analytic perfect tense in VD. Regarding AG, the choice between imperfect and perfect is more a matter of style than of meaning, perhaps due to the influence of Bavarian dialects spoken in Austria that always use perfect.

Thus, transforming imperfect to perfect in the source language (AG) in order to match with the target (VD) always yields grammatical sentences.

The property that makes this task a real challenge is the verb second property of Germanic languages, which means that the finite verb in main clauses resides in a position next to a sentence initial phrase, whereas in subordinate clauses it resides in its base position at the end of the clause [13]. Crucially, the initial phrase in main clauses can be of any category that makes up a phrasal constituent (noun/prepositional phrase, adverbial, subordinated clause, VPs, but also a phonologically zero operator for yes/no questions, conditionals or discourse topics yielding verb-first order on the surface). In subordinate clause structures, the finite verb marks the end of the clause, phrases appearing to the right of it (but still belonging to the same clause) are regarded as extraposed. Consider the following example:

(2)   Gustav schenkte   ihr eine Blume, als   er sie wieder traf.
      Gustav offered-PAST her a   flower when he her again   met-PAST
      'Gustav offered her a flower when he met her again.'

The main verb *schenkte* in imperfect resides in second position, the first being occupied by the subject (*Gustav*). The subordinate clause is extraposed, and the finite verb form *traf* (again imperfect) appears at its end. Now, if we replace imperfect verb forms with perfect tense, the structures appear quite different:

(3)   Gustav hat   ihr eine Blume geschenkt,   als   er sie wieder
      Gustav has-PRES her a   flower offered-PART when he her again
      getroffen   hat.
      met-PART has-PRES
      'Gustav offered her a flower when he met her again.'

Now the finite auxiliary (*hat*) in the main clause is in second position, while the participle of the main verb appears at the end of the main clause. In the subordinate clause, which comes after the participle of the main clause – hence extraposed, the finite (auxiliary) verb form *hat* is at the end of the clause, the past participle (*getroffen*) surfaces left adjacent to the finite verb. There are two further complications, the first concerning the auxiliary itself: not all verbs take the auxiliary of the base *haben* 'to have', some verbs such as *ankommen* 'to arrive' select an auxiliary form based on *sein* 'to be'. The second complication arises if the finite verb is a modal or the verb *lassen* ('let', 'have sb. + V') with an infinitival complement. Then an infinitive verb form occurs in the place of the past participle of the main (modal) verb. This is called the IPP-effect (*infinitivus pro participio*). In addition, if there are more than two verbs in a subordinate clause, the order of them can be changed in specific ways depending on the particular dialect. In Bavarian dialects, the order main-verb > modal > finite-auxiliary (e.g., *ich ... lesen müssen habe* 'I ... read had-to have') turns out as main-verb > finite-auxiliary > modal (e.g., *i ... lesn håb miassn* 'I ... read have had-to'). The rule-based transformation from imperfect to perfect tense is done in successive steps; to illustrate how the procedure works, consider the list of individual steps:

1. identify finite imperfect verb forms
2. identify the person and number features
3. generate the form of the appropriate auxiliary (*haben* or *sein*) according to these features
4. generate the past participle of the main verb (or, if it is a modal, the infinitive form)
5. decide whether (i) the clause is a main clause (with verb second) or (ii) a subordinate clause
6. replace the finite verb with the correctly inflected auxiliary and
   - if (i) find the right clause boundary and place the participle (or the modal infinitive) there, or
   - if (ii) place the participle before the auxiliary (or the modal infinitive after the auxiliary)

Provided extensive lexical resources for Standard German, some of these tasks are rather simple, in particular 1, 3, 4 and 6(ii). Regarding task 2, person and number features are straightforward for all persons except 1P.SG and 3P.SG, since they use the same endings in imperfect verb forms (e.g., *sagte* 'I or s/he said', *schrieb* 'I or s/he wrote') but have different forms for the auxiliary used to form perfect tense (e.g., *habe* '(I) have', *hat* 's/he has'). This is done by checking the domain of the clause for a 1P.Sg.Nom personal pronoun (*ich* 'I'). If the features are identified, the generation of the appropriate forms (task 3) amounts to just looking them up in the lexicon (we use an FST compressed format for fast generation and lookup of full forms.) What is more difficult is to identify the appropriate base of the auxiliary. Transitive and many intransitive (unergative) verbs use the base *haben*, whereas a certain class of verbs (unaccusative) uses the base *sein*. Quite a few verbs of this class are ambiguous. Some of these ambiguous verbs alternate between a causative (transitive) and an inchoative (intransitive) meaning, reflected also by the choice of auxiliary. Verbs of movement (especially if they have a goal argument, or a modification indicating directionality) generally belong to the class selecting *sein* (see Haider 1985 for an extensive overview [14]), only in contexts where they convey a meaning expressing (physical) activity, they select *haben* in perfect tense. (E.g., *ich bin ins Zimmer getanzt* 'I danced into the room' vs. *ich habe die ganze Nacht getanzt* 'I danced the whole night long'). (See Diedrichsen [15] who provides a detailed analysis of the relevant (semantic) properties of these verbs.) For this 'proof-of-concept', we just collected a list of verbs that select *sein* or go with both auxiliaries depending on directionality/causativity and perform a lookup upon that list, but it would be preferable to retrieve more comprehensive information on auxiliary selection by applying data-driven, corpus-linguistic methods.

While task 4 is straightforward, task 5 and task 6i require sufficiently accurate information about the clause structure, in order to determine the domain of the clause itself and to decide whether that clause has root or subordinate clause structure. For a first study, we used a standard parser for German, BitPar [16], which was trained on data from version 2 of the TIGER corpus [17]. The advantages of this parser - it employs the same set of PoS-tags (STTS) as we use in our lexicon and it is very efficient in terms of runtime as well as space require-ments - are outweighed by the fact that the statistical model of the parser was trained on a news text corpus, whereas our data was collected from speech data. As a consequence, the parser did not deliver an output for all sentences (only for 584 out of 997, that is 58.5 %), and where it did, the structures and labels were often incorrect in many ways. Therefore the rule-based algorithm must yield greater robustness in order to determine the right clause boundary and to decide whether it is a main or subordinate clause structure.

The algorithm proceeds in the following steps: (1) perform a lookup on all terminal nodes, and if one is recognized as a finite imperfect verb form then assign these features regardless of the label coming from the parser. (2) for each finite verb, find the highest structural node that contains the verb but no other finite verb. This delimits the potential clause domain for a given finite verb. (3) determine the clause type using the following criteria: a clause is subordinated if (i) it contains a subordinating complementizer (KOUS), (ii) the functional label of the clause is RC (relative clause), (iii) the verb is at the end of the clause domain, and the number of phrases preceding it is greater than one. Otherwise, the clause is considered a main clause. As one can imagine, the output of this algorithm is highly sensitive towards the parser output. Upon manual inspection, 129 out of 584 (22 %) processed sentences were not grammatical and were therefore excluded from the training data of the first experiment.

In the second set of experiments, we replaced BitPar with the *anna*-parser from MATE-tools [18]. This parser displayed similar problems regarding the correctness of PoS-tags and syntactic structures (the German models were also trained on the same data set), but at least it always provides an output, even in cases where the models do not fit the input well. As before with BitPar, several rule based filters are applied to remedy critical errors in the layer of PoS-tags and morphological features, and the algorithm that attempts to find the relevant information mentioned above from the syntactic parse also had to be amended. Upon all these improvements, the data set, too, has grown to an extent that it became possible to test the effect of preprocessing in a statistically meaningful way.

5   Experiments with SMT

In this section, we report on some experiments using the data set described in Sect. 3 and the set of preprocessed data as outlined in Sect. 4 to build statistical machine translation systems, using Moses [19]. In the first part of this section, we report upon results obtained in experiments that did not use the extended corpus and that still relied on the output of the BitPar parser.

The corpus was split into four sections, TRAIN, DEV, DEVB and TEST, where the first was used for estimation of phrase tables and language models, the second for tuning the MT system parameters and the third for testing during system development. The last was reserved for final testing. The three tuning and test sets contained 600 sentences each, while the rest (4909 sentences) were taken into the TRAIN set.

The SMT system we developed for our purposes has two layers. The first layer is a standard word-level phrase table, the second builds phrase tables on the level of characters (using unigram character strings). While the word-level models are useful to learn 'interesting' translations (i.e. different lexical items or phrases in source and target), it is highly affected by data sparsity, meaning that the number of out-of-vocabulary (OOV) words is considerably high. The character-level may be affected by misalignments or by translations that involve different lexical items, but they can be very useful for the treatment of OOV words.

After observing the performance of word and character-level models in isolation, we decided to combine the two models into a 'backoff' model. It uses the word-level translation wherever possible, but applies the character-level model for OOV words. A similar trait is presented in Nakov and Tiedemann [6], where the combination of a word and a character model gave the best results when translating between closely related languages.

Earlier work on MT for closely-related languages [6,20,21], experiments with character-level translation models that are also built using phrase-based Moses, but allowing it to treat single characters or groups of characters as "tokens". In our backoff model, we use unigram character-level models that are trained on 'cognates' from the training set to avoid training from noisy data. This means that the training data should not contain German-Viennese word-pairs which either represent lexical differences between the two varieties, or which are the result of bad alignments. To filter out cognates from the statistically aligned data (using GIZA++ [22]), we used a function based on the Levenshtein distance between two candidates, log-normalized by length, where the two word candidates are converted into a format similar to the output of the Kölner Phonetik algorithm [23], thus utilizing the phonological similarity reflected in spelling.

Using the word-level model as a baseline and the backoff model as the model relevant for testing, we can observe the following differences between models built on training data that has not been preprocessed and models built on preprocessed data (imperfect to perfect, reordering), tested on data from DEVB.

Table 1. BLEU scores for DEVB sentences

Model	Original	Preprocessed
Word-level (WRD)	63.28	64.01
Backoff (BCK)	68.30	69.10

For both, baseline and backoff model, there is a slight improvement on preprocessed training data. Note that the BLEU scores are relatively high compared to the typical values reported in the MT literature, reflecting the restricted vocabulary of the data set. Now, since the proportion between modified and unchanged sentences is rather unbalanced (only 39 out of 600 sentences affected by preprocessing), it would be worthwhile to have a look on the results for the two different sets of sentences:

Table 2. BLEU scores for modified and unchanged sentences of the DEVB set

Model	Modified		Unchanged	
	Orig.	Preproc.	Orig.	Preproc.
Word-level (WRD)	49.67	56.71	64.26	64.68
Backoff (BCK)	55.75	61.02	69.13	69.84

Examining the performance on the (39) modified versus (561) unchanged sentences shows quite a big jump in BLEU on the modified sentences (as expected), but also a small improvement on the unchanged sentences. This shows that the performance of the SMT system gets better with preprocessed data due to an increased accuracy of the alignment, even though only a subset of sentences with imperfect (455 out of 997) could be successfully transformed in this first experiment.

With the extended corpus comprising 10796 sentence pairs and an improved preprocessing algorithm, we repeated this experiment. This time we reserved 1000 sentences each as test and tuning set, the rest went to the training data. In order to minimize a bias due to a specific random selection, we performed the experiment as a 5-fold cross-validation, where we ensured that each tuning or test set contained exactly 176 sentence pairs that would be modified upon preprocessing, while the others would remain unchanged. This number corresponds to the proportion of sentences that contain imperfect verb forms to be transformed into perfect over the whole corpus.

Within 5 iterations, we calculated BLEU scores and word error rates (WER) for each test set, but also for the subsets of sentences that were modified by preprocessing and those that were left unchanged. The following table only contains mean value and standard deviation (sd) over all iterations.

Table 3. BLEU scores and WER for modified and unchanged sentences of the test set (WRD is the word-level model, BCK is the combined backoff model)

	BLEU- WRD- ALL	BLEU- WRD- MODIF	BLEU- WRD- UNCHG	BLEU- BCK- ALL	BLEU- BCK- MODIF	BLEU- BCK- UNCHG	WER- WRD- ALL	WER- BCK- ALL
Original sentences:								
mean	60.54	50.42	63.61	67.50	56.36	70.75	62.69	53.06
sd	1.16	1.85	0.94	0.71	0.81	0.61	0.82	1.82
Preprocessed sentences:								
mean	62.73	59.21	63.86	70.09	66.05	71.37	59.31	48.02
sd	1.04	1.22	1.18	0.99	2.06	1.13	1.63	2.51
Differences (BLEU/WER) between original and preprocessed data:								
mean	2.20	8.79	0.24	2.59	9.68	0.62	-3.38	-5.04
sd	0.48	1.50	0.51	0.55	2.02	0.54	1.71	0.83

The first section of the table is the baseline where no preprocessing has obtained (original sentences), the second evaluates preprocessing while the third section shows the differences between the baseline and the translation with preprocessing. A first look into the BLEU scores of the baseline setup shows that sentences that would be modified by preprocessing fare much worse compared to the overall performance: WRD-ALL = 60.54, BCK-ALL = 67.5, vs. WRD-MODIF = 50.42, BCK-MODIF = 56.35 – almost 10 points below. Comparing these values with those from the setup with preprocessing immediately shows how high the gain is on the overall performance, but especially on those sentences that have been modified: WRD-ALL = 62.73, BCK-ALL = 70.09, vs. WRD-MODIF = 59.21, BCK-MODIF = 66.05. Considering the differences given in Sect. 3 of the table, it is striking that the preprocessed sentences boost up almost 10 points (WRD-MODIF = 8.79 ± 1.5, BCK-MODIF = 9.68 ± 2.02), still they are not as good as compared to unchanged sentences or the overall test set, the former improve over the baseline just a bit, the differences not being significant: WRD-UNCHG = 0.24 ± 0.51, BCK-UNCHG = 0.62 ± 0.54. Taken over the whole test set, the improvement from baseline to preprocessed data is definitely significant: WRD-ALL = 2.2 ± 0.48, BCK-ALL = 2.59 ± 0.55. This underlines the importance of combining phrase-based statistical MT with rule-based preprocessing for certain linguistic phenomena.

6   Discussion and Outlook

It could be shown that preprocessing is a successful strategy for dealing with constructions that involve complex lexical transformations together with syntactic reordering. The reason why a phrase-based SMT cannot learn such a transformation mainly lies in the non-local nature of the process. Such non-local dependencies can in principle also be learnt by statistical methods of MT, but only if syntactic structures (taken from a tree-bank) and reordering are taken into account in the pipeline of processing. These methods crucially rely on large resources (tree-banks, huge amounts of training data) that are not available for dialectal varieties. A way out is to make the input syntactically resemble the target, on the basis of rule-based transformations. For SMT between Austrian German and Viennese Dialect, the necessary transformation from AG imperfect verb forms to analytic perfect (existing in both, AG and VD) is such a case. The improvement in performance not only affects sentences that have this construction, but also the overall performance yields better results due to an increased accuracy in the alignment. The crucial information for such a rule-based preprocessing step is taken from parsing the input sentences. Using a statistical parser provides output that yields relatively good results with an algorithm that has been developed in order to determine clause type and clause boundaries. This is true even for data that has been collected from free speech, as opposed to news text corpora. While there are other linguistic issues (the lack of genitive noun phrases in VD) that await a similar treatment, it could be shown that tackling the relatively frequent problem of non-existing imperfect with rule-based preprocessing improves the models for SMT significantly.

Acknowledgements. The work presented in this paper was carried out within the project 'Machine Learning Techniques for Modeling of Language Varieties' (MLT4MLV - ICT10-049, 2011–2013) which was funded by the Vienna Science and Technology Fund (WWTF).

References

1. Hildenbrandt, T., Moosmüller, S., Neubarth, F.: Orthographic encoding of the Viennese dialect for machine translation. In: Vetulani, Z., Uszkoreit, H. (eds.) Human Language Technologies as a Challenge for Computer Science and Linguistics, Proceedings of the 6th Language & Technology Conference (LTC 2013), 7–9 December 2013, Poznan, Poland, pp. 399–403 (2013)
2. Schikola, H.: Schriftdeutsch und Wienerisch. Österreichischer Bundesverlag für Unterricht, Wissenschaft and Kunst, Wien (1954)
3. Hornung, M.: Wörterbuch der Wiener Mundart. ÖBV - Pädagogischer Verlag, Wien (1998)
4. Collins, M., Koehn, P., Kučerová, I.: Clause restructuring for statistical machine translation. In: Proceedings of the 43rd Annual Meeting of the Association for Computational Linguistics (ACL), Ann Arbor, June 2005, pp. 531–540 (2005)
5. Labov, W.: Principles of Linguistic Change (II): Social Factors. Blackwell, Massachusetts (2001)
6. Nakov, P., Tiedemann, J.: Combining word-level and character-level models for machine translation between closely-related languages. In: Proceedings of the 50th Annual Meeting of the Association for Computational Linguistics, Jeju, Rep. of Korea, 8–14 July 2012, pp. 301–305 (2012)
7. Scherrer, Y., Erjavec, T.: Modernizing historical Slovene words with character-based SMT. In: Proceedings of the 4th Biennal Workshop on Balto-Slavic Natural Language Processing of the 51th Annual Meeting of the Association for Computational Linguistics (ACL 2013), Sofia, Bulgaria, pp. 58–62 (2013)
8. Nakov, P., Ng, H.T.: Improving statistical machine translation for a resource-poor language using related resource-rich languages. J. Artif. Intell. Res. **44**, 179–222 (2012)
9. Zbib, R., Maldiochi, E., Devlin, J., Stallard, D., Matsoukas, S., Schwartz, R., Makhoul, J., Zaidan, O., Callison-Burch, C.: Machine translation of arabic dialects. In: Proceedings of NAACL: HLT 2012, Montreal, Canada, pp. 49–59 (2012)
10. Sawaf, H.: Arabic dialect handling in hybrid machine translation. In: Proceedings of the 9th Conference of the Association for Machine Translation in the Americas (AMTA), Denver, Colorado (2010)
11. Haddow, B., Hernández Huerta, A., Neubarth, F., Trost, H.: Corpus development for machine translation between standard and dialectal varieties. In: Proceedings of the Workshop Adaptation of Language Resources and Tools for Closely Related Languages and Language Variants of the 9th International Conference on Recent Advances in Natural Language Processing (RANLP 2013), 13 September 2013, Hissar, Bulgaria, pp. 7–14 (2013)
12. Korpusbasierte Wortgrundformenliste DEREWO, v-ww-bll-320000g-2012-12-31-1.0, mit Benutzerdokumentation, Institut für Deutsche Sprache, Programmbereich Korpuslinguistik, Mannheim, Deutschland (2013)

13. den Besten, H.: On the interaction of root transformations and lexical deletive rules. In: Abraham, W. (ed.) On the Formal Syntax of the Westgermania. Papers from the 3rd Groningen Grammar Talks, pp. 47–131. John Benjamins, Amsterdam (1983)
14. Haider, H.: The case of German. In: Toman, J. (ed.) Studies in German Grammar, pp. 65–101. Foris, Dordrecht (1985)
15. Diedrichsen, E.: Zu einer semantischen Klassifikation der intransitiven *haben*- und *sein*- Verben im Deutschen. In: Katz, G., et al. (ed.) Sinn & Bedeutung VI, Proceedings of the 6th Annual Meeting of the Gesellschaft für Semantik, University of Osnabrück (2002)
16. Schmid, H.: Efficient parsing of highly ambiguous context-free grammars with bit vectors. In: Proceedings of the 20th International Conference on Computational Linguistics (COLING 2004), vol. 1, Geneva, Switzerland, pp. 162–168 (2004)
17. Brants, S., Dipper, S., Eisenberg, P., Hansen, S., König, E., Lezius, W., Rohrer, C., Smith, G., Uszkoreit, H.: TIGER: linguistic interpretation of a German corpus. J. Lang. Comput. **2004**(2), 597–620 (2004)
18. Björkelund, A., Bohnet, B., Hafdell, L., Nugues, P.: A high-performance syntactic and semantic dependency parser. In: Coling 2010: Demonstration Volume, Beijing, 23–27 August 2010, pp. 33–36 (2010)
19. Koehn, P., Hoang, H., Birch, A., Callison-Burch, C., Federico, M., Bertoldi, N., Cowan, B., Shen, W., Moran, C., Zens, R., Dyer, C., Bojar, O., Constantin, A., Herbst, E.: Moses: open source toolkit for statistical machine translation. In: Annual Meeting of the Association for Computational Linguistics (ACL), demonstration session, Prague, Czech Republic, 2007, pp. 177–180 (2007)
20. Vilar, D., Peter, J.-T., Ney, H.: Can we translate letters? In: Proceedings of the 2nd Workshop on Statistical Machine Translation, Prague, Czech Republic, ACL, pp. 33–39 (2007)
21. Tiedemann, J.: Character-based PSMT for closely related languages. In: Marqués, L., Somers, H. (eds.) Proceedings of 13th Annual Conference of the European Association for Machine Translation (EAMT 2009), Barcelona, Spain, pp. 12–19 (2009)
22. Och, F.J., Ney, H.: Improved statistical alignment models. In: Proceedings of the 38th Annual Meeting of the Association for Computational Linguistics (ACL00), Hongkong, China, pp. 440–447 (2000)
23. Postel, H.J.: Die Kölner Phonetik. Ein Verfahren zur Identifizierung von Personennamen auf der Grundlage der Gestaltanalyse. In: IBM Nachrichten, 19, pp. 925–931 (1969)

Evaluation of Uryupina's Coreference Resolution Features for Polish

Bartłomiej Nitoń[(✉)]

Institute of Computer Science Polish Academy of Sciences,
Jana Kazimierza 5, 01-248 Warsaw, Poland
bartek.niton@gmail.com

Abstract. Coreference is usually defined as phenomenon consisting in different expressions relating to the same referent. Therefore automatic coreference resolution is an extremely difficult and complex task. It can be approached in two different ways: using rule-based tools or machine learning. This article is dedicated to the second approach and describes an evaluation of a set of surface, syntactic, discourse, salience and anaphoric features proposed by Uryupina and their usefulness for coreference resolution in Polish texts.

Keywords: Uryupina · Machine learning · Coreference resolution · Polish language · Surface features · Syntactic features · Salience · Discourse · Anaphoricity and antecedenthood · BART

1 Introduction

Olga Uryupina's PhD thesis [1] describes over 350 linguistic features which can be used to recognize coreference. Since they are considered language-independent, we intend to verify this statement by checking the impact of a certain subset of features on coreference resolution for Polish. Uryupina's classification of features is based on:

- surface similarity;
- syntactic knowledge;
- semantic compatibility;
- discourse structure and salience;
- anaphoricity and antecedenthood.

This paper concentrates on: surface similarity; syntactic information; discourse structure and salience; as well as anaphoricity- and antecedenthood-related features.

The study was cofounded by the European Union from resources of the European Social Fund. Project PO KL "Information technologies: Research and their inter-disciplinary applications", Agreement UDA-POKL.04.01.01-00-051/10-00 and the *Computer-based methods for coreference resolution in Polish texts* project financed by the Polish National Science Centre (contract number 6505/B/T02/2011/40).

© Springer International Publishing Switzerland 2016
Z. Vetulani et al. (Eds.): LTC 2013, LNAI 9561, pp. 354–367, 2016.
DOI: 10.1007/978-3-319-43808-5_27

2 Features

This section describes features implemented and examined during research. They are grouped in accordance with Uryupina's classification. For example usage of presented configurations and more precise descriptions of them please refer to [1].

2.1 Surface Similarity Features

Co-referring descriptions frequently have similar surface form. Strings can be simplified, partially modified or kept intact. Surface similarity features are therefore based mostly on comparing mentions or their specified fragments.

In our study, we implemented and examined about 88 surface similarity features described in Uryupina's thesis. The thesis decomposes surface similarity problem into three sub-tasks: *normalization*, specific *substring selections* and *matching* proper.

Normalization covers different spellings of same name throughout a text, such as "MCDONALD'S" and "McDonald's", obviously referring to the same name. Uryupina describes three normalization functions: *no_case*, *no_punctuation* and *no_determiner*. The first function ignores case in strings, the second one strips off all punctuation marks and other auxiliary characters (like "-" or "#"), while the last one strips off determiners from text. During our research, the function *no_determiner* was ignored due to inapplicability of its direct definition in Polish (which lacks articles and displays a complex linguistic model of definiteness).

Substring selection covers the fact that some words in a mention are more informative and important than other ones. Therefore, instead of matching whole strings, one can compare only their most valuable, representative fragments. Uryupina describes four key words of a mention string:

- *head*;
- *last* word in mention string;
- *first* word in mention string;
- *rarest* word in mention string[1].

The last sub-task, *matching*, is based on a string comparison function. Uryupina describes five string comparison algorithms:

- *exact match*, comparing whole mention strings;
- *approximate_match*, which is based on the minimum edit distance (MED) measure [3]; because MED does not take into consideration the length of a string, minimum edit distance is normalized by the length of anaphor or antecedent; length normalizations are marked as *length_s* or *length_w*;
- *matched_part*, counts overlap between strings in words or symbols;

---

[1] For the purpose of checking word rarity we used 1-grams extracted from the balanced subcorpus of the National Corpus of Polish [2] to create two word frequency lists of orthographic word forms and their base forms. All features using *rarest* word are implemented for both of those lists.

- *abbreviation*, one of four abbreviation algorithms, in our experiment limited to two: *abbrev1* takes the initial letter of all the words in the mention string, produces an abbreviated word out of them and compares the created string with the head of the second mention; *abbrev2* algorithm works in the same way but ignores words starting with lowercase characters for building an abbreviated word (e.g. *abbrev1* would change the string "Federal Bureau of Investigations" into "FBoI" whereas *abbrev2* would change it into "FBI");
- *rarest(+contain)*, finds the rarest word in a mention string and checks if it occurs in some other mention.

In our experiment, we have implemented all surface features described in Uryupina's PhD thesis excluding ones using *no_determiner* normalization and using more complex abbreviation algorithms (*abbrev3* and *abbrev4*). All of them have been implemented in BART, a modular toolkit for coreference resolution [4], supplemented with a Polish language plugin.

In further experiments, we decided to use Uryupina's original configurations, i.e.:

- *all*: all 88 implemented surface features;
- *baseline1*: exact match for full names only, without use of normalization;
- *baseline2*: *baseline1* features and head exact matching without normalization (triple: *no_normalization, head, exact_match*);
- *MED+head*: *baseline1* and all approximate match features (triple: _, _, *approximate_match*);
- *MED-head*: *baseline1* features and approximate match algorithms without substring selection (triple: _, *no_substring_selection, approximate_match*);
- *MED_w-head*: *baseline1* and minimum edit distance (MED) measured in words features (*MED_w, MED_w_anaph, MED_w_ante* etc., *no_substring_selection*);
- *MED_s-head*: *baseline1* and minimum edit distance (MED) measured in symbols features (*MED_s, MED_s_anaph, MED_s_ante* etc., *no_substring_selection*);
- *MED_bare-head*: *baseline1* and all minimum edit distance without MED length normalizations and substring selection (*MED_s, MED_w* etc., *no_substring_selection*);
- *MED_ante-head*: *baseline1* and all MED features with normalization by antecedent length and without substring selection (*MED_s_ante, MED_w_ante* etc., *no_substring_selection*);
- *MED_anaph-head*: *baseline1* and all MED features with normalization by anaphor length and without substring selection (*MED_s_anaph, MED_w_anaph* etc., *no_substring_selection*);
- *Last*: *baseline1*, exact match for full names (triple: _, *no_substring_selection, exact_match*) and exact match for last word in mentions (triple: _, *last, exact_match*);
- *First*: *baseline1*, exact match for full names (triple: _, *no_substring_selection, exact_match*) and exact match for first word in mentions (triple: _, *first, exact_match*);

- *Rarest*: *baseline1*, exact match for full names (triple: _, *no_substring_selection*, *exact_match*) and *rarest* word-based features (triples: _, *rarest*, *exact_match* and _, *rarest*, *contain*), each *rarest* feature is implemented for base forms of words and orthographic forms;
- *No_MED*: all implemented features without approximate match features;
- *No_abbrev*: all implemented features without *abbrev1* and *abbrev2*-based features;
- *No_rarest*: all features without *rarest* word-based ones;
- *No_rarest_parser*: all features without the *rarest* word-based ones and features using parsing (i.e., all types of matching except for abbreviation and head matching algorithms).

For each of the configurations presented above, different normalization strategies were used. We distinguished five types of possible normalization strategies: *no_normalization*, *no_case*, *no_punctuation*, *full normalization* and *all normalizations together*. *Full normalization* involves only *no_case+no_punctuation* features, while *all normalizations together* involves all specified features with normalization, e.g. all features with *no_case* and *no_punctuation* normalization and also features containing both normalizations (*no_case+no_punctuation*).

2.2 Syntactic Knowledge Features

Though none of the existing approaches rely solely on syntactic information, it is considered to be a valuable part of anaphora resolution algorithms. While Uryupina presents 61 different syntactic features in her thesis, due to time constraints we have taken into account only the 9 core syntactic features for the purpose of our research. Enlisted syntactic features implemented in BART coreference resolution system [4] during research for Polish coreference resolution are provided below:

- *Post-modification* (features: *postmodified(Mi)*, *postmodified(Mj)*): checks whether the markable is a syntactic construction where the head is not the last word.
- *Number* (features: *number(Mi)*, *number(Mj)*): checks the grammatical number of the anaphor or the antecedent.
- *Person* (features: *person(Mi)*, *person(Mj)*): checks the grammatical person of the anaphor or the antecedent.
- *Same number* (features: *same_number(Mi,Mj)*): checks if the anaphor and the antecedent share the same number.
- *Same person* (features: *same_person(Mi,Mj)*): checks if the anaphor and the antecedent share the same person.
- *Syntactic agreement* (features: *synt_agree(Mi,Mj)*): checks if the anaphor and the antecedent share the same number and person.

The last 5 configurations from the above list may also be considered morphological agreement features. By definition, all markables in a coreference chain refer to the same object, thus they should share the number and person categories.

2.3   Discourse Structure and Salience Features

Next layer which can be used for coreference resolution improvement is discourse structure and salience features. Salient entities are those which are likely to be antecedents, they are considered more important than the others and bring new objects to the text. Though "salient entities" seem to be very important for text understanding, their recognition is very difficult to formalize. To approach this problem one must use salience measures that, on the one hand are possible to formalize and then implement, on the other hand are theoretically sound and make predictions appropriate for coreference resolution problem. Uryupina presents 97 discourse and salience-based features; our project implemented about half out of them.

To formalize salience features, Uryupina notices that in a short discourse, the main topics of text should be introduced in its beginning. Locally, each paragraph starts with some of the main entities and then brings new information about them, represented as coreference chains or single markables. These new entities are related to the paragraph's topic and thus are not likely to be mentioned once again later. However, those hypotheses are very simplistic and may not work for long texts. Uryupina described five hypotheses used to define salience and discourse structure features:

- Earlier fragments of document contain fewer anaphors because of introducing new entities.
- Earlier fragments of document contain more antecedents for the same reason like in the previous point.
- Entities at the beginning of document segment (paragraph) can be anaphor or antecedent, whereas markables closer to its end are more likely to be anaphors and not antecedents.
- Short coreference chains are more likely to hold in a single paragraph than span over multiple text segments. Short chains, unlike long ones, correspond to local entities and are fully discussed in a single paragraph.
- *Proximity.* Markables closer to one another are more likely to be coreferent than markables with wider span between them.

First two hypotheses are resolved by implementing paragraph number and sentence number features (*paragraph_number_bin(Mi)*, *paragraph_number_bin(Mj)*, *sentence_number_bin(Mi)*, *sentence_number_bin(Mj)*). Paragraph number features are based on the position of anaphor or antecedent and then normalized by the total number of paragraphs (in this research we resigned from 10 bins discretization). Same algorithm is working for sentence number, but taking into account number of a sentence containing a given markable and the total number of sentences.

Third hypothesis was resolved using paragraph rank and sentence rank features (*paragraph_rank_bin(Mi)*, *paragraph_rank_bin(Mj)*, *sentence_rank_bin(Mi)*, *sentence_rank_bin(Mi)*). Paragraph rank features are counted as the distance measured in markables to the beginning of the paragraph, normalized by the total number of markables in it (in this research we resigned from 10 bins discretization). Same algorithm is working for sentence number, but taking into account number of a sentence containing a given markable and the total number of sentences. In this group we also included features *first_in_sentence(Mi)*, *first_in_sentence(Mj)*, *first_in_paragraph(Mi)* and *first_in_paragraph(Mj)*, describing if markable is first markable in sentence or paragraph.

Fourth hypothesis was omitted during our research.

Fifth hypothesis can be resolved by a set of proximity features. Though text in most cases is devoted to one topic, it talks about it from different angles, introducing new entities and abandoning the ones introduced before. Therefore anaphors and antecedents are usually close to one another. To examine this hypothesis, we used three different types of distance between possible anaphor and antecedent:

- markable distance, measured in markables, implemented as *markable_distance(Mi,Mj)* feature.
- sentence distance, measured in sentences, implemented as *sentence_distance(Mi,Mj)* feature.
- paragraph distance, measured in paragraphs, implemented as *paragraph_distance(Mi,Mj)* feature.

In this group we also included features *same_sentence(Mi,Mj)* and *same_paragraph(Mi,Mj)*, describing if anaphor-antecedent pair is in the same sentence or paragraph.

Another approach for using discourse and salience features for coreference resolution is to represent each feature by a triple *proximity, salience, agreement* where:

- *Proximity* can be measured by the following functions: *same* (*true*, if anaphor and antecedent are in the same sentence), *prev* (*true*, if anaphor and antecedent are in the adjacent sentences), *closest* (*true*, if the antecedent is the closest markable to the anaphor).
- *Salience* can be measured by the following functions: *closest* (*true*, if the antecedent is the closest markable to the anaphor), *sfirst* (*true*, if first markable in a sentence), *pfirst* (*true*, if first markable in the paragraph). *Subject*, *ssubject* and *cb* functions were omitted during this research.
- *Agreement*, encoded by *agree* in features names (*true*, if *synt_agree(Mi,Mj)* returns *true*).

Because proximity factor is described in [1] as very crucial for pronominal anaphora. Uryupina introduced another encoding, *proana* (*true*, if anaphor is pronominal).

Using those predefined encodings we implemented such triples as: *closest_closest_agree(Mi,Mj)*, *closest_prev_agree(Mi,Mj)*, *closest_same_agree(Mi,Mj)*, *sfirst_prev_agree(Mi,Mj)*, *sfirst_same_agree(Mi,Mj)*, *sfirst_closest_agree(Mi,Mj)*, *pfirst_prev_agree(Mi,Mj)*, *pfirst_same_agree(Mi,Mj)*, *pfirst_closest_agree(Mi,Mj)*, *closest_prev(Mi,Mj)*, *closest_same(Mi,Mj)*, *sfirst_prev(Mi,Mj)*, *sfirst_same(Mi,Mj)*,

pfirst_prev(Mi,Mj), *pfirst_same(Mi,Mj)*, *proana_closest_closest_agree(Mi,Mj)*,
proana_closest_prev_agree(Mi, Mj), *proana_closest_same_agree(Mi,Mj)*,
proana_sfirst_prev_agree(Mi,Mj), *proana_sfirst_same_agree(Mi,Mj)*,
proana_sfirst_closest_agree(Mi,Mj), *proana_pfirst_prev_agree(Mi,Mj)*,
proana_pfirst_same_agree(Mi,Mj), *proana_pfirst_closest_agree(Mi,Mj)*,
proana_closest_prev(Mi,Mj), *proana_closest_same(Mi,Mj)*,
proana_sfirst_prev(Mi,Mj), *proana_sfirst_same(Mi,Mj)*,
proana_pfirst_prev(Mi,Mj), *proana_pfirst_same(Mi,Mj)*.

2.4 Anaphoricity and Antecedenthood

Anaphoricity- and antecedenthood-related features are responsible for discovering how likely it is that a given mention is an antecedent of another mention.

Features for discovering anaphoricity have been divided by Uryupina into six groups:

- *surface*;
- *syntactic*;
- *semantic*;
- *salience*;
- *same-head*;
- Karttunen-motivated features (*apposition, copula, negation, modal constructions, determiner, grammatical role* and *semantic class*) [5].

Surface, syntactic and salience features have already been presented in this paper while the evaluation of semantic features and Karttunen-motivated factors has been postponed for the time being. In current research, we have implemented *same-head* features. The *same-head* feature group consists of Uryupina's *same_head_exists(Mi)*, *same_head_exist(Mj)*, *same_head_distance(Mi)*, *same_head_distance(Mj)* features. They represent coreference knowledge on a very basic level. *Same_head_exist* checks if there is a mention with same head as given in the preceding text, *same_head_distance* describes distance between given markable and one with the same head in the preceding text.

3 Evaluation

Following i.a. CONLL-2011 [6], for evaluation we used an average score of MUC [7], B³ [8] and CEAFE [9] metrics which track influence of different coreference dimensions (the B³ measure being based on mentions, MUC on links and CEAFE based on entities); we will also present CEAFM [9] metric for consideration. In order to train coreference decisions, tests were performed with J48, WEKA's [10] implementation of the C4.5 decision tree learning algorithm [11] and weka classifier, which uses WEKA machine learning toolkit for classification. As data for learning, we used a fragment of the Polish coreference corpus built within the

CORE project[2]. As training data, we used 390 texts from the Polish Coreference Corpus[3] [12].

3.1 Surface Similarity Features

Table 1 presents results of coreference resolution for Polish using various definitions of surface feature configurations, with each configuration evaluated using all presented types of normalizations. Table 2 presents a set of coreference scores for different measure methods and *no_case* normalization.

The finding here is that using normalizations for Polish coreference resolution can result in slight, but not very noticeable increase. Best score is obtained for *no_case* normalization. An interesting conclusion results from the worst setting, *no_punctuation* (worse even than the score for no normalization), which can indicate that in Polish punctuation can in some cases help resolve coreferring pairs of markables. But it is apparent that proper normalization does not significantly increase coreference resolution results in Polish.

Table 1. Different surface similarity configurations, the classifier's performance (average F-score for B[3], MUC and CEAFE measures) in 10 fold cross-validation on the 390 files sample from Polish Coreference Corpus.

Configurations	no	no_case	no_ punct.	full	all
all	**0.72**	**0.72**	**0.72**	**0.72**	**0.72**
baseline1	0.69	**0.70**	0.69	**0.70**	**0.70**
baseline2	**0.69**	0.69	**0.69**	0.69	0.69
MED+head	**0.70**	**0.70**	**0.70**	**0.70**	**0.70**
MED-head	**0.71**	**0.71**	**0.71**	0.71	0.71
MED_w-head	0.69	**0.70**	0.69	**0.70**	0.69
MED_s-head	**0.72**	**0.72**	**0.72**	**0.72**	**0.72**
MED_bare-head	0.70	0.70	0.70	0.70	**0.71**
MED_ante-head	**0.72**	**0.72**	**0.72**	**0.72**	**0.72**
MED_anaph-head	**0.72**	**0.72**	0.71	**0.72**	**0.72**
last	0.69	**0.70**	0.69	**0.70**	**0.70**
first	0.69	**0.70**	0.69	**0.70**	**0.70**
rarest	**0.72**	**0.72**	**0.72**	**0.72**	**0.72**
No_MED	**0.71**	**0.71**	**0.71**	0.71	0.70
No_abbrev	**0.72**	**0.72**	**0.72**	0.71	0.71
No_rarest	**0.70**	**0.70**	**0.70**	**0.70**	**0.70**
No_rarest_parser	**0.70**	**0.70**	**0.70**	**0.70**	**0.70**

---

[2] Computer-based methods for coreference resolution in Polish texts, see http://core. ipipan.waw.pl/ (accessed: *18.09.2015*).

[3] http://zil.ipipan.waw.pl/PolishCoreferenceCorpus (accessed: *18.09.2015*).

Table 2. F-scores for different classifiers, different variants of configuration and *no_case* normalization, the *average* column describes average value of B³, MUC and CEAFE metrics, best results and configurations are marked in bold font.

Configuration	CEAFM	CEAFE	MUC	B³	average
all	0.75	0.80	**0.52**	0.83	**0.72**
baseline1	0.77	**0.82**	0.43	**0.86**	0.70
baseline2	0.75	0.80	0.44	0.84	0.69
MED+head	0.74	0.78	0.49	0.83	0.70
MED-head	0.76	0.81	0.48	0.85	0.71
MED_w-head	0.77	**0.82**	0.43	**0.86**	0.70
MED_s-head	0.77	**0.82**	0.49	0.85	**0.72**
MED_bare-head	0.77	**0.82**	0.44	**0.86**	0.70
MED_ante-head	0.77	**0.82**	0.49	**0.86**	**0.72**
MED_anaph-head	**0.78**	**0.82**	0.49	**0.86**	**0.72**
last	0.77	**0.82**	0.43	**0.86**	0.70
first	0.77	0.81	0.43	**0.86**	0.70
rarest	0.76	**0.82**	0.50	0.84	**0.72**
no_MED	0.74	0.80	0.50	0.83	0.71
no_abbrev	0.75	0.80	**0.52**	0.83	**0.72**
no_rarest	0.74	0.78	0.50	0.83	0.70
no_rarest_parser	0.75	0.80	0.48	0.83	0.70

From the configuration point of view, the best score is acquired for *all*, *MED_s-head*, *MED_ante-head*, *MED_anaph-head*, *rarest* and *no_abbrev* configurations. The average F-score approaches 0.72 and this result corresponds to proper normalization for *MED_anaph-head* and *no_abbrev*, while for the rest of configurations it is reached despite of normalization.

All implemented surface features are used by the *all* profile while *no_abbrev* uses most of them — which can point to the reason why they obtain the highest score.

As can be seen, a slight score increase (by 0.03) is obtained when rarest words are used. Most of MED-based features specially with normalization usage (in this case normalization is understood as division by anaphor or antecedent length in signs or words) also work very well so as minimum edit distance based on signs which is better than the one based on words.

What is interesting, configurations using head words obtain slightly lower scores than those not using it. This may be caused by a large number of different orthographic forms in Polish. In further research, it should also be checked how those features would work when they take into consideration base forms of words. Those forms can be received using a morphological analyzer called Morfeusz[4] [13].

---

[4] http://sgjp.pl/morfeusz/ (accessed: *18.09.2015*).

3.2   Syntactic and Same-Head Features

Table 3 presents coreference scores for configurations using syntactic and *same--head* features combined with the surface ones. As can be seen, the only configuration with a score higher than 0.72 (obtained using only surface features) is the

Table 3. F-score for different coreference resolution metrics and best surface features configurations alone or combined with syntactic (*synt*) and *same-head* features. The *average* column describes average value of B^3, MUC and CEAFE metrics. Best results and configurations are marked with bold font, minus and plus signs are marking whether selected configuration is better or worse than the one using surface features only (used normalization is *no_case* normalization).

Configuration (F-score)	CEAFM	CEAFE	MUC	B^3	average
all	0.75	0.80	0.52	0.83	0.72
MED_s-head	0.77	**0.82**	0.49	0.85	0.72
MED_ante-head	0.77	**0.82**	0.49	**0.86**	0.72
MED_anaph-head	**0.78**	**0.82**	0.49	**0.86**	0.72
rarest	0.76	**0.82**	0.50	0.84	0.72
no_abbrev	0.75	0.80	0.52	0.83	0.72
syntactic	0.71	0.77	0.00	0.83	0.53
all + synt	0.75	0.80	**0.53+**	0.84+	0.72
MED_s-head + synt	0.76−	0.80−	0.48−	0.84−	0.71−
MED_ante-head + synt	0.77	**0.82**	0.49	0.85−	0.72
MED_anaph-head + synt	0.77−	0.81−	0.49	0.85−	0.72
rarest + synt	0.77+	**0.82**	0.51+	0.85+	**0.73+**
no_abbrev + synt	0.74−	0.79−	0.52	0.83	0.72
same_head	0.71	0.77	0.00	0.83	0.53
all + same_head	0.61−	0.66−	0.45−	0.72−	0.61−
MED_s-head + same_head	0.71−	0.77−	0.44−	0.81−	0.67−
MED_ante-head + same_head	0.71−	0.76−	0.44−	0.81−	0.67−
MED_anaph-head + same_head	0.73−	0.78−	0.45−	0.82−	0.68−
rarest + same_head	0.76	**0.82**	0.50	0.84	0.72
no_abbrev + same_head	0.61−	0.66−	0.45−	0.72−	0.61−
synt + same_head	0.72	0.78	0.07	0.83	0.56
all + synt + same_head	0.57−	0.62−	0.45−	0.68−	0.58−
MED_s-head + synt + same_head	0.68−	0.74−	0.44−	0.78−	0.65−
MED_ante-head + synt + same_head	0.70−	0.76−	0.45−	0.80−	0.67−
MED_anaph-head + synt + same_head	0.69−	0.75−	0.44−	0.79−	0.66−
rarest + synt + same_head	0.74−	0.80−	0.49−	0.83−	0.71−
no_abbrev + synt + same_head	0.57−	0.61−	0.45−	0.68−	0.58−

one based on the rarest words and syntax (*rarest + synt* configuration). It can be said that the rarest features are very good predictors of coreference in the Polish language (*rarest* configuration gives satisfying score even with *same_head* features) and it cooperates very well with syntactic features. For other configurations, syntactic features do not provide any advantage, or even decrease the coreference resolution score. Configurations using *same_head* affect coreference in a very negative way. Also, using only syntactic information, *same_head* or even both of those feature groups at the same time does not produce satisfying results. The conclusion is that surface similarity features are indispensable in coreference resolution for Polish and no sufficient score is likely to be obtained with higher-level features only.

3.3 Discourse Structure and Salience Features

Table 4 presents coreference scores for best surface features configurations, using *no_case* normalization, combined with discourse and salience features. Discourse and salience features were divided into five groups:

- *Thesis[1,2]*, features representing hypothesis 1 and 2 described in Sect. 2.3;
- *Thesis[3]*, features representing hypothesis 3 described in Sect. 2.3;
- *Thesis[5]*, features representing hypothesis 5 described in Sect. 2.3;
- *Triples*, features representing *proximity, salience, agreement* triples;
- *All*, all implemented discourse and salience features.

Table 4. F-score for best surface features configurations combined with discourse and salience feature groups. Presented scores are average values of B^3, MUC and CEAFE metrics. Best results and configurations are marked with bold font (used normalization is *no_case* normalization).

Configuration	thesis[1,2]	thesis[3]	thesis[5]	triples	all
all	0.70	0.69	0.71	0.71	0.48
MED_s-head	0.70	0.69	0.70	0.71	0.61
MED_ante-head	0.71	**0.72**	**0.72**	**0.72**	0.52
MED_anaph-head	0.70	0.71	0.71	**0.72**	0.53
rarest	0.70	0.70	**0.72**	**0.72**	0.45
no_abbrev	0.69	0.69	0.71	0.71	0.50

Comparing Tables 2 and 4 we can see that despite of used discourse and salience features, none of them provides any advantage for Polish texts. For some configurations they even lower coreference resolution scores. It is especially visible when configuration is using all implemented discourse and salience features. Only using triples, thesis 3 and thesis 5 for couple of surface features configurations, it is possible to keep coreference score on the level provided when only surface features are used.

Summarizing, discourse and salience features do not provide any advantage, or even lower the coreference resolution score when used with surface features only. In the last experiment we tested how best discourse and salience features cooperate with other features groups.

Table 5 presents F-scores for the best combinations of discourse and surface features combined with syntactic and *same_head* ones. As we can see, once again, for configurations using syntactic features a slightly lower score was observed. This decrease, however, is not affecting *MED_ante-head + triples + synt* and *rarest + triples + synt* configurations. For *MED_ante-head + triples + synt* we can see even a slight rise of the MUC score. Also, once again using *same_head* feature is affecting F-score in a very negative way for all configurations using it.

Table 5. F-score for different coreference resolution metrics, best surface features configurations and best salience and discourse features alone or combined with syntactic (*synt*) and *same-head* features. The *average* column describes average value of B^3, MUC and CEAFE metrics. Best results and configurations are marked with bold font, minus and plus signs are marking whether selected configuration is better or worse than the one using best surface and discourse features only (used normalization is *no_case* normalization).

Configuration (F-score)	CEAFM	CEAFE	MUC	B^3	average
MED_anaph-head + triples	**0.78**	**0.82**	0.49	**0.85**	**0.72**
MED_ante-head + thesis[3]	0.77	**0.82**	0.49	**0.85**	**0.72**
MED_ante-head + thesis[5]	0.76	0.81	0.49	**0.85**	**0.72**
MED_ante-head + triples	0.77	**0.82**	0.48	**0.85**	**0.72**
rarest + thesis[5]	0.76	**0.82**	0.49	0.84	**0.72**
rarest + triples	0.76	**0.82**	**0.50**	0.84	**0.72**
MED_anaph-head + triples + synt	0.76−	0.81−	0.49	0.84−	0.71−
MED_ante-head + thesis[3] + synt	0.75−	0.80−	0.47−	0.84−	0.70−
MED_ante-head + thesis[5] + synt	0.75−	0.80−	0.48−	0.84−	0.71−
MED_ante-head + triples + synt	0.77	**0.82**	0.49+	**0.85**	**0.72**
rarest + thesis[5] + synt	0.76	0.81−	**0.50+**	0.84	0.71−
rarest + triples + synt	0.76	**0.82**	**0.50**	0.84	**0.72**
MED_anaph-head + triples + same_head	0.72−	0.78−	0.45−	0.80−	0.68−
MED_ante-head + thesis[3] + same_head	0.66−	0.73−	0.43−	0.77−	0.64−
MED_ante-head + thesis[5] + same_head	0.72−	0.77−	0.47−	0.81−	0.68−
MED_ante-head + triples + same_head	0.75−	0.80−	0.47−	0.83−	0.70−
rarest + thesis[5] + same_head	0.74−	0.80−	0.48−	0.82−	0.70−
rarest + triples + same_head	0.75−	0.81−	0.49−	0.83−	0.71−
MED_anaph-head + triples + synt + same_head	0.65−	0.72−	0.44−	0.75−	0.64−
MED_ante-head + thesis[3] + synt + same_head	0.56−	0.64−	0.42−	0.68−	0.58−
MED_ante-head + thesis[5] + synt + same_head	0.72−	0.77−	0.47−	0.81−	0.68−
MED_ante-head + triples + synt + same_head	0.64−	0.71−	0.44−	0.75−	0.63−
rarest + thesis[5] + synt + same_head	0.74−	0.80−	0.49	0.83	0.71−
rarest + triples + synt + same_head	0.64−	0.72−	0.46−	0.74−	0.64−

4   Conclusions

The next step for checking applicability of Uryupina's features for Polish language would be checking how semantic ones affect coreference resolution scores.

Because all features are implemented and evaluated in BART, coreference resolution toolkit, the endpoint would be resolving the best feature configuration for Polish coreference resolution and, based on that, creating an end-to-end Polish coreference resolution system getting raw Polish text as input.

For now, the best score was obtained for a combination of rarest word-based surface features and a couple of implemented syntactic ones.

Even at this point it can be said that Uryupina's features are mostly language-independent (as she claimed in her PhD thesis) and the ones described in this paper excluding *same_head* and simple discourse ones work quite well also for Polish.

References

1. Uryupina, O.: Knowledge acquisition for coreference resolution. Ph.D. thesis, Saarland University (2007). http://d-nb.info/985573333
2. Przepiórkowski, A., Bańko, M., Górski, R.L., Lewandowska-Tomaszczyk, B. (eds.): Narodowy Korpus Języka Polskiego [Eng.: National Corpus of Polish]. Wydawnictwo Naukowe PWN, Warsaw (2012)
3. Wagner, R.A., Fisher, J.M.: The string-to-string correction problem. J. Assoc. Comput. Mach. **21**(1), 168–173 (1974)
4. Versley, Y., Ponzetto, S.P., Poesio, M., Eidelman, V., Jern, A., Smith, J., Yang, X., Moschitti, A.: BART: a modular toolkit for coreference resolution. In: Association for Computational Linguistics (ACL) Demo Session (2008)
5. Karttunen, L.: Discourse referents. In: McCawley, J.D. (ed.) Syntax and Semantics 7: Notes from the Linguistic Underground, pp. 363–386. Academic Press, New York (1976)
6. Pradhan, S., Ramshaw, L., Marcus, M., Palmer, M., Weischedel, R., Xue, N.: CoNLL-2011 shared task: Modeling unrestricted coreference in ontonotes. In: Proceedings of the Fifteenth Conference on Computational Natural Language Learning: Shared Task. CONLL Shared Task 2011, Stroudsburg, PA, USA, Association for Computational Linguistics, pp. 1–27 (2011)
7. Vilain, M., Burger, J., Aberdeen, J., Connolly, D., Hirschman, L.: A model-theoretic coreference scoring scheme. In: Proceedings of the 6th Message Understanding Conference (MUC-6), pp. 45–52 (1995)
8. Bagga, A., Baldwin, B.: Algorithms for scoring coreference chains. In: The First International Conference on Language Resources and Evaluation Workshop on Linguistics Coreference, pp. 563–566 (1998)
9. Luo, X.: On coreference resolution performance metrics. In: Proceedings of the Conference on Human Language Technology and Empirical Methods in Natural Language Processing, HLT 2005, Vancouver, Canada, Association for Computational Linguistics, pp. 25–32 (2005)
10. Witten, I.H., Frank, E.: Data Mining: Practical Machine Learning Tools and Techniques, 2nd edn. Morgan Kaufmann, San Francisco (2005)

11. Quinlan, J.R.: C4.5: Programs for Machine Learning. Morgan Kaufmann Publishers Inc., San Francisco (1993)
12. Ogrodniczuk, M., Głowińska, K., Kopeć, M., Savary, A., Zawisławska, M.: Interesting linguistic features in coreference annotation of an inflectional language. In: Sun, M., Zhang, M., Lin, D., Wang, H. (eds.) CCL and NLP-NABD 2013. LNCS, vol. 8202, pp. 97–108. Springer, Heidelberg (2013)
13. Woliński, M.: Morfeusz - a practical tool for the morphological analysis of polish. In: Kłopotek, M.A., Wierzchoń, S.T., Trojanowski, K. (eds.) Proceedings of the International Intelligent Information Systems: Intelligent Information Processing and Web Mining'06 Conference, pp. 511–520. Wisła, Poland (June (2006)

Information and Data Extraction

Aspect-Based Restaurant Information Extraction for the Recommendation System

Ekaterina Pronoza[✉], Elena Yagunova, and Svetlana Volskaya

Saint-Petersburg State University,
7/9 Universitetskaya Nab., Saint-Petersburg, Russia
katpronoza@gmail.com, iagounova.elena@gmail.com,
svetlana.volskaya@gmail.com

Abstract. In this paper information extraction task for the restaurant recommendation system is considered. We develop an information extraction system which is intended to gather restaurants aspects from users' reviews and output them to the recommendation module. As many of the restaurant aspects are subjective, our task can also be called sentiment analysis, or opinion mining. Thus, we present an aspect-based approach towards sentiment analysis of reviews about restaurants for e-tourism recommender systems. The analyzed frames are service and food quality, cuisine, price level, noise level, etc. In this paper we focus on service quality, cuisine type and food quality. As part of the preprocessing phase, a method for Russian reviews corpus analysis (as part of information extraction) is proposed. Its importance is shown at the experimental phase, when the application of machine learning techniques to aspects extraction is analyzed. It is shown that the information obtained during corpus analysis improve system performance. We conduct experiments with several feature sets and classifiers and show that the use of resources learnt from the corpus leads to the improvement of the models. Naïve Bayes appears to be the best choice for sentiment classification, while Logistic Regression and SVM are best at deciding on the relevance of a review with respect to the particular aspect.

Keywords: Corpus analysis · Restaurant reviews · Aspect-based information extraction · Recommendation system · Machine learning · E-tourism · Sentiment analysis · Opinion mining

1 Introduction

In this paper information extraction (IE) method for the Russian restaurant recommendation system is proposed. Our main intention is the implementation of aspect values extraction module of the restaurant recommendation system, and our current task is reviews corpus analysis and the application of machine learning techniques to the problem using the information obtained during corpus analysis.

The approach for corpus analysis presented in this paper is based on non-contiguous bigrams and part of speech (POS) distribution analysis. Trigger words dictionaries are learnt using bootstrapping method.

The frames to be extracted include service quality, food quality, cuisine type, price level, noise level, etc. Each frame has its own set of aspects. According to the design of

© Springer International Publishing Switzerland 2016
Z. Vetulani et al. (Eds.): LTC 2013, LNAI 9561, pp. 371–385, 2016.
DOI: 10.1007/978-3-319-43808-5_28

our recommendation system, all the aspects to be extracted from the reviews are predefined by the experts. We do not employ any techniques of automatic aspects identification which inevitably introduce noise into the information extraction model.

We suppose that the most important characteristics of a restaurant are service and food quality and cuisine type and focus on these three frames (and the extraction of their aspects). Our assumption is proved by the distribution of the aspects in the data.

We also suppose that the proposed IE system can be highly effective despite the difficulties imposed by the structure of a typical Russian restaurant review. The fact is that, when such a review is concerned, the key information about restaurant characteristics does not always lie on the surface. However, tuning models with respect to the results gained during corpus analysis can improve IE system performance.

2 Related Work

Information extraction as part of a recommendation system is discussed in [18]. The authors propose a rule-based approach to the extraction of key words from user's email. These keywords are put into a car recommendation system which is using content-based filtering approach with Jaccard Coefficient method.

In [12] a tag extraction algorithm for web pages entering a recommendation system is presented. The algorithm is based on semi-supervised document classification.

An approach to key words extraction for a learning recommendation system is described in [8]. The algorithm employs TF-IDF measure and a combination of collaborative filtering [23, 26] and content-based filtering strategies [21, 23, 27].

Bootstrapping approach has been successfully applied in web page classification [13], text classification [10, 14], named entity classification [5, 16, 19], parsing [29] and information extraction [4, 9, 24, 30].

As some of restaurant aspects are quite subjective and represent users' opinion or sentiment, our task is similar to sentiment classification. In our research we experiment with Naive Bayes, Logistic Regression and Linear Support Vector Machines commonly used in sentiment analysis [1, 3, 7, 11, 17, 20, 25, 28, 32].

When it comes to machine learning with respect to sentiment analysis, it is crucially important to identify relevant features, and we pay special attention to it. The most commonly used features in sentiment analysis are n-grams [1, 7, 20, 31, 32]. Sometimes words in n-grams are substituted with their semantic classes [7]. Valence shifters (intensifiers and diminishers) are included in bigram features in [11].

Part-of-speech (POS) and POS-tagged n-grams are also experimented with [1]. For example, adverb-adjective pairs are used in [2]: classification of adverbs of degree into five categories and a scoring method of adverb-adjective combination are proposed. Adverbs are shown to improve model performance with respect to the identification of sentiment degree. Negation handling techniques (e.g., adding "not_" to a negated word) are described in [1, 6, 7, 17].

In this paper we use contiguous n-grams as our baseline. We further extend it with non-contiguous n-grams and with features obtained from corpus analysis (predicative attributive words and modifiers). The latter ones generalize the adverb-adjective combination idea from [2] and are similar to the notion of valence shifters from [11].

Non-contiguous bigrams also cover negations which can be expressed in different ways in Russian. Following [20], we construct n-gram-occurrence feature vectors instead of n-gram-frequency ones as they are reported to be more effective.

At the corpus analysis stage we conduct bootstrapping for trigger words dictionary learning as part of restaurant information extraction. A simple semi-supervised scheme is applied to the identification of new trigger words from the list of non-contiguous bigrams. At this stage our focus is on the estimation of trigger words and patterns coverage of users' reviews, and at the experimental stage we show the importance of preliminary corpus analysis.

3 Data

The analyzed corpus consists of 32525 users' reviews about restaurants (4.2 millions of words). The data is represented by a collection of Russian colloquial texts, review length varies from 1 to 96 sentences, and average value equals about 10 sentences. A part of the corpus is annotated in a semi-supervised way. It includes 1025 reviews about 206 restaurants located in the centre of Saint-Petersburg.

The list of aspects in our subcorpus is given in Table 1 (aspects related to food quality, cuisine type and service quality frames, are given in bold).

Table 1. Restaurant aspects

Restaurant aspects			
Cuisine type	**Service quality**	Price level	Parking place
Food quality	**Service speed**	Average cheque	VIP room
Noise level	**Staff politeness**	Children	Dancefloor
Cosiness	**Staff amiability**	Children's room	A railway station (nearby)
Romantic atmosphere	Company	Dancefloor	A hotel (nearby)
Crampedness	Audience	Bar	A shopping mall (nearby)

Our task is actually a classification problem. For each aspect the system should either label a review with one of the possible classes or reject it as irrelevant with respect to the given aspect. As most restaurants characteristics are never mentioned in the reviews, we define an empirical threshold frequency value of 10 % and consider aspects mentioned in at least 10 % of reviews frequent. We only train classifiers for the frequent aspects (they are divided into groups in Table 2).

Table 2. Frequent restaurant aspects distribution in the corpus

Occurrence Percentage	List of Aspects
[85 %; 100 %]	Food quality (86 %)
[55 %; 85 %)	Service quality (55 %)
[25 %; 55 %)	Staff politeness & amiability, service speed, price level, cosiness
[10 %; 25 %]	Noise level, crampedness, romantic atmosphere, company

Thus, the task of information extraction related to food and service quality can be reformulated as sentiment analysis with respect to the restaurant aspects in question.

4 Corpus Analysis

4.1 Main Phases of Analysis

Corpus analysis procedure is conducted in our via several phases:

- Corpus preprocessing (tokenization, lemmatization, normalization and sentence splitting). We also include unigrams and bigrams calculation here (4.2);
- Trigger words dictionaries and predicative-attributive dictionaries construction (4.3). The words from the dictionaries are further used in patterns (4.5);
- The estimation of trigger words dictionaries coverage of the reviews corpus (4.4);
- Patterns construction based on POS-distribution of the trigger words context (4.5);
- The estimation of patterns coverage of the reviews corpus (4.6). We focus on NP patterns (which dominate in the corpus according to the statistics obtained in 4.5):
- The estimation of aspect values distribution in the annotated corpus (4.7).

4.2 Corpus Preprocessing

The corpus is tokenized, then lemmatized using pymorphy2[1] tool and split into sentences. Taking into account our data characteristics (Russian colloquial language), we also normalize the corpus by reducing multiplied vowels and consonants which are often used to express author's strong emotions (e.g., in words like "ооочень" / veeeery/or "оччень" /verrry/which refer to "очень" /very/) to single ones.

We adopt a (lexeme, POS) pair as an element of analysis and calculate unigram and bigram frequencies. We consider both contiguous and non-contiguous bigrams, with window size equal to 2. The reason for that is that at the primary stage of information extraction task we intend to look at the context of words for both trigger words dictionaries construction and patterns development.

4.3 Dictionaries Construction

In the primary stage of information extraction, our task is to construct a dictionary of trigger words, which indicate the presence of a certain frame in a review, and to develop patterns for frame aspects extraction.

All trigger words dictionaries described in this paper are constructed using bootstrapping method. The seed for service quality frame consists of a small set of nouns which Russian native speakers presumably use to refer to service (e.g., "персонал" / staff/, "официант" /waiter/, "официантка" /waitress/, "обслуживание" /service/, etc.).

---

[1] http://pymorphy2.readthedocs.org/.

We use bigrams list during bootstrapping iterations to get the context for the trigger words. Context words are restricted to adjectives and participles. During each iteration we check the new words and cut off the irrelevant ones. The words are ranged according to their scores.

Thus, having a seed word "персонал" /staff/with score X and a bigram "гостеп-риимный, П персонал, С" (hospitable, Adjective staff, Noun) with score Y we record "гостеприимный" /hospitable/into our current trigger words list with X*Y score. The initial scores for all the seed words are chosen to be equal to 1. After 5 iterations new trigger words no longer emerged: there were 73 lexemes in the dictionary, and 10 most frequent trigger words constituted 90 % of the total number of words.

Bootstrapping also reveals misprints in the words related to restaurant service. It was actually applied twice: first, to the bigrams based on "raw" reviews, and then to the bigrams based on the edited reviews (with misprints corrected).

A predicative-attributive dictionary for service quality frame is also constructed. It includes 226 lexemes (namely, adjectives and participles) revealed during the boot-strapping procedure as the neighbours of the trigger words.[2]

As food quality and cuisine type reveal the intersection of their entity objects nominations (e.g., "кухня" /cuisine/), they share the same trigger words dictionary. In fact, these two frames do not need separate trigger words as they only differ in the characteristics given to food.[3] The trigger words dictionary for food quality and cuisine type frames is constructed using bootstrapping method as well, and at the moment it contains 455 words for these two frames. We construct two predicative-attributive dictionaries for food quality and cuisine type (112 and 48 lexemes respectively). Bootstrapping procedure actually only constructs one dictionary and then it is manually divided into two. Both trigger words dictionary and predicative-attributive dictionaries are going to be expanded in our further work.

4.4 Dictionary Coverage Estimation

We consider it important to estimate the portion of reviews our dictionary could cover. Estimation results are presented in Table 3. Thus, it turned out that in 66 % of reviews people used at least one of the trigger words to describe service quality.

As far as the two frames with intersecting nominations like "кухня" /cuisine/(food quality and cuisine type) are concerned, their common dictionary covers 96 % of reviews. This is an encouraging result, but we should bear in mind that, firstly, it means that a review presumably contains the information we need but does not indicate the

---

[2] We should also note that after the first iteration top trigger words included "цена" /price/, "место" (place), "атмосфера" /atmosphere/, "блюдо" /dish/, "еда" /food/, "интерьер" /interior/ and "ресторан" /restaurant/. It means that service and food quality, price and noise level and general impression of a restaurant are described with roughly the same adjectives, and therefore the same IE scheme can probably be applied to these restaurant aspects.

[3] For example, "кухня" /cuisine/ is referred to as "восточная" /eastern/ (which describes cuisine type) almost as frequently as "хорошая" /good/ and "вкусная" /tasty/ (which describes food quality) in the reviews corpus.

Table 3. Dictionary Coverage Estimation

Frame	Dictionary coverage (%)
Service quality	66
Food quality	71
Cuisine type	25

way it is expressed, and, secondly, it shows the coverage by the two frames. The latter problem can be solved using predicative-attributive dictionaries described in 4.2.

We estimate food quality and cuisine type coverage separately by calculating the portion of reviews where a corresponding trigger word occurred in the context of a word from the corresponding predicative-attributive dictionary. The reason for such a low value for the cuisine type frame (25 %) is, on the one hand, the limited amount of cuisine type predicative-attributive words and, on the other hand, the vast amount of the cuisine trigger words.

4.5 Patterns Construction

Having estimated trigger words dictionary and justified the use of a standard pattern scheme for the reviews, we proceed to patterns development.

We adopt an approach to pattern development based on POS-distribution of the neighbours of trigger words. We consider 5 most frequent trigger words in the corpus and retrieve POS-distribution of their context from non-contiguous bigrams list. We only include POS-distribution for "обслуживание" /service/neighbours (see Table 4, four leftmost columns) into this paper as for the other four words it is similar.

According to POS-distribution of the neighbours of trigger words, service trigger nouns are mostly used together with nouns both to the left and to the right.[4] Prepositions and conjunctions take the 2nd place, but we are interested in the characteristics of service, and looking further at the 3rd place we have adjectives and, later on, verbs.

POS-distribution for the neighbours of "кухня" /cuisine/as one of the most frequent trigger-word for food quality and cuisine type frames is also shown in Table 4 (see 4 rightmost columns). In fact, POS-distribution shown in Table 4 suggests that trigger words for the frames in question occur mostly as parts of noun phrases (NPs) and then, less frequently, as parts of verbal phrases (VPs).

As part of the research a tool for trigger words context extraction was implemented. We use it to extract NP patterns (related to food and service quality) from the corpus.

---

[4] Phrases like "В этом ресторане обслуживание ..." /In this restaurant the service is.../ or "Обслуживание ресторана..." /The service of the restaurant is.../ are quite common in the Russian language when restaurant reviews are considered.

Table 4. POS-distribution for "обслуживание" /service/and for "кухня" /cuisine/left (see POS Left column) and right (see POS Right column) neighbour words (top-10)

POS Left	%	POS Right	%	POS Left	%	POS Right	%
Noun	21	Noun	19	Adjective	23	Noun	17
Conjunction	20	Preposition	15	Noun	20	Adjective	13
Adjective	12	Adjective	14	Conjunction	11	Conjunction	11
Preposition	11	Adverb	10	Preposition	10	Preposition	11
Verb	8	Conjunction	10	Verb	9	Verb	11
Pronoun	7	Verb	9	Pronoun	7	Pronoun	9
Adverb	5	Particle	6	Adverb	4	Adverb	8
Particle	5	Pronoun	6	Adjective pron.	4	Particle	5
Adjective pron.	4	Adjective (sh.)	4	Infinitive	3	Adjective (sh.)	5
Adjective (sh.)	3	Adjective pron.	3	Particle	3	Adjective pron.	4

4.6 Patterns Coverage Estimation

To estimate the percentage of reviews covered by the patterns constructed as described in 4.5, the same scheme as in the case of trigger word dictionaries is used.

It appears that NP patterns constructed for service quality frame cover 38 % of reviews. For food quality and cuisine type aspects, NP patterns cover 82 % of reviews. Although the result is obtained for the shared trigger words dictionary, we have already shown in 4.4 that in 71 % of reviews a food-related trigger word is mentioned together with an adjective or participle from our predicative-attributive dictionary. And therefore one can be sure that in 71 % of reviews there would be some food quality description matching some NP pattern.

NP patterns coverage results for cuisine type and service and food quality (on the whole corpus and on the annotated subcorpus) are presented in Table 5.

Were we to implement a rule-based (namely, NP-patterns-based) aspect extraction system, such an estimate could be considered an upper bound for the recall score. To compare the performance of such hypothesized system to that of the classifiers, we also estimate NP patterns coverage on the annotated subcorpus (on the reviews where the aspects are not missing) – see the rightmost column in Table 5. It is shown in Sect. 6 that the classifiers performance scores are higher than those presented here.

4.7 Aspect Values Distribution

Having annotated our training subcorpus, we found out that while some of the restaurant aspects were quite often mentioned by users in their reviews (e.g., food quality), others were almost never spoken of (e.g., railway station or hotel). As our annotated subcorpus is limited at the moment, we must ensure that there is enough training data for an aspect to be extracted using machine learning. Our aspects can be

Table 5. NP patterns coverage estimation (on the whole corpus)

Frame	The whole corpus, %	The annotated data, %
Service quality	38	39
Cuisine type & Food quality	81	59[a]

This figure reflects only the coverage for food quality aspect (and not for cuisine type).

Table 6. Aspect values distribution (Aspects with 99 % and more missing values in the annotated corpus (Parking place, VIP room, Hotel, Shopping mall, Railway station) are omitted.)

Aspect	Value	%	Aspect	Value	%	Aspect	Value	%
Service quality	−2	5	**Food quality**	−2	4	Average cheque	non-NaN	8
	−1	8		−1	7		NaN	93
	0	2		0	4	**Price level**	−2	4
	1	19		1	30		−1	10
	2	21		2	42		0	3
	NaN	45		NaN	14		1	17
Staff amiability	−2	2	**Company**	large	7		2	4
	−1	5		small	3		NaN	62
	0	1		NaN	90	**Romantic atmosphere**	yes	9
	1	16	**Cosiness**	yes	32		no	2
	2	11		no	5		NaN	89
	NaN	66		NaN	63	Children	yes	7
Staff politeness	−2	3	**Crampedness**	yes	5		no	1
	−1	2		no	7		NaN	92
	0	0		NaN	88	Children's room	yes	2
	1	13	**Noise level**	−2	1		no	2
	2	9		−1	3		NaN	98
	NaN	73		0	0	Bar	yes	5
Service speed	−2	6		1	9		NaN	95
	−1	6		2	2	Dancefloor	yes	2
	0	1		NaN	86		NaN	98
	1	11						
	2	9						
	NaN	68						

divided into two groups: fequent ones, which are going to be extracted using machine learning, and infrequent ones, for which a list of hand-crafted rules is going to be used.

To classify all the aspects into these two groups, we calculate their values frequencies in the annotated subcorpus. The obtained distribution is given in Table 6.

In Table 6 NaN stands for a missing value and "non-NaN" stands for any value different from NaN. The aspects which, in our opinion, can be extracted using machine learning techniques ("frequent" ones), are given in bold. They are chosen according to their NaN value portion (not exceeding 90 %).

Some aspect values represent sentiment (food quality, staff amiability, staff politeness, etc.) and are subjective, while others refer to a particular restaurant amenity and are quite objective. All sentiment-related aspects are categorized into five classes.

5   Experiments

For the aspects chosen as the most frequent ones, we try the following classifiers: Naive Bayes (NB), Logistic Regression (LogReg) and Support Vector Machines (SVM) as implemented in scikit-learn.[5] As we have already mentioned, in this paper we are taking a closer look at service and food quality and cuisine type aspects, but since the latter suggests a multilabel task, we shall only consider machine learning models with respect to food and service quality at the moment.

Since the annotated corpus includes a large amount of missing values (NaNs), we divide our classification task into two parts: first, a classifier is trained to tell between missing and present values, and then, if the value is present, it is to predict its class. In this paper the second classification task (i.e., categorization for non-NaN values) is considered.

Our baseline feature set consists of unigrams and bigrams (on the lemma-level, only contiguous ones). We also tried trigrams but since they did not improve performance much while making feature space larger, we decided not to include them in the feature set. We experiment with two extended features sets. First, we only add non-contiguous bigrams (with window size equal to 3 as it appeared to perform best). In the second set, we add emoticons and exclamations, predicative-attributive words and key words and expressions instead. All the three feature sets are presented in Table 7. A detailed features description is given in Table 8.

Table 7. Feature sets

Features	Baseline	Extended1	Extended2
Unigrams	+	+	+
Contiguous bigrams	+	+	+
Non-contiguous bigrams		+	
Emoticons & exclamations			+
Predicative-attributive words			+
Key words and expressions			+

---

[5] http://scikit-learn.org .

Table 8. Features description

Feature Name	Feature Value
Unigrams	1, if a unigram occurs in the review, else 0
Contiguous bigrams	1, if a bigram occurs in the review, else 0
Non-contiguous bigrams	1, if a bigram occurs in the review, else 0
Emoticons & exclamations	1, if any emoticon occurs in the review in the same sentence with some trigger word, else 0 1, if an exclamation mark occurs in the review in the same sentence with some trigger word, else 0
Predicative-attributive words	1, if a predicative-attributive word occurs in the review within 4 words to the left from some trigger word, else 0 1, if a predicative-attributive word occurs in the review within 4 words to the left from some trigger word AND a modifier occurs in the review within 4 words to the left this predicative-attributive word, else 0
Key words and expressions	1, if a key word or expression occurs in the review, else 0

In n-gram features use occurrence- (and not count-) vectors as it has been proved to be a better strategy for sentiment analysis [20]. Since the number of features is more than 1.6 million, we conduct feature selection to remove unimportant features. We tried linear SVM and LogReg for penalizing irrelevant features and chose Randomized LogReg as it demonstrated best performance on our data.

6   Evaluation

As stated earlier in this paper, reviews corpus analysis results help us to improve the performance of our models, and it refers not only to the dictionaries learn at the preprocessing stage but also to the idea of using non-contiguous bigrams.

To evaluate the models, we conduct shuffle 10-fold cross-validation. Average weighted F1 scores for food and service quality are given in Table 9. The weights are calculated as relative frequencies of the classes in the annotated subcorpus. We consider F1 the most important measure for our system and therefore choose it as an aggregated score.

According to the results in Table 9, NB appears to be the best among the three classifiers (but its baseline and extended versions show similar scores while SVM and LogReg extended versions improve compared to their baseline ones) for both aspects.

For food quality all the three models both extended versions achieve more or less the same performance score, while the second feature set evidently takes less space than the first one. It means that in fact, having learnt the necessary dictionaries, we can do without having all the non-contiguous bigrams in the feature set and thus reduce

Table 9. Food and service quality F1 scores (best average weighted F1 score in bold)

Aspect	Model	Baseline, %	Extended (1), %	Extended (2), %
Food quality	NB	**69,45**	**70,08**	**70,26**
	LogReg	64,24	68,77	68,64
	SVM	63,99	65,57	66,21
Service quality	NB	**64,37**	**68,77**	**65,33**
	LogReg	56,14	65,05	57,90
	SVM	54,30	63,80	56,27

its size. Therefore dictionaries-based approach seems to be more effective for food quality aspect.

For service quality scores of extended models differ: extended (1) is better than extended (2) while both of them are better than baseline. It means that the best strategy for service quality extraction involves non-contiguous bigrams. In fact, such an assumption conforms to the results of corpus analysis: NP patterns (which are indirectly included in the extended (2) feature set by using predicative-attributive words preceded by modifiers) coverage is quite low for service quality (39 %) on the annotated data, especially when compared to that of food quality (59 %). It is caused by the fact that service quality can be expressed in a review in wide variety of ways which are better captured by non-contiguous bigrams than by patterns and dictionaries.

As extended (2) includes several different features we tested each of them separately to find those which contributed most to the overall performance. It was found out that both SVM and Logistic Regression are most sensitive to emoticons and exclamation marks, less sensitive to predicative-attributive dictionaries and least sensitive to key words and expressions.

7 Discussion

In our further phases of research we also considered other restaurant aspects (apart from food and service quality and cuisine type, described in this paper) and experimented with classifiers other than NB, LogReg and SVM (we also tried Multinomial NB, Decision Trees, Random Forests and Perceptron). We selected optimal combinations of feature and classifier for each frequent (see 4.7) aspect. The details of the selection procedure are described in [22], and the results are presented in Table 10.

In relevance/irrelevance task, LogReg performs best. For crampedness, politeness and service quality LogReg is significantly better than the other classifiers ($p = 0.05$). For most of the other aspects it performs better than NB, MNB and Perceptron. Indeed, LogReg is known to perform well on large training sets, and for the task in question there is more training data than for the task of classifying relevant reviews.

Thus, we suggest that LogReg could be recommended for the classification of informal unstructured Russian texts into those which contain information or opinion about the specific aspect and those which do not.

Table 10. Optimal models and feature sets for „frequent"aspects

Aspect	Model:Feature Set	Accuracy, %	Average F1, %
Class Selection			
amiability	MNB:extended_All	77,30	76,84
cosiness	MNB:extended_Distant	96,00	95,74
crampedness	MNB:baseline	87,86	87,52
price level	MNB:baseline	65,00	61,82
noise	MNB:extended_KWs	82,67	80,40
politeness	NB:extended_All	79,66	79,20
service quality	MNB:extended_Distant_Emoticons	72,71	71,96
food quality	MNB:extended_Distant	75,05	74,05
speed	MNB:extended_KWs_PredAttr_Lex	69,71	68,72
Relevant vs. Irrelevant			
amiability	NB:baseline	82,78	82,76
company	LogReg:baseline	93,24	92,66
cosiness	LogReg:baseline	89,91	89,78
crampedness	*LogReg:baseline*	*92,22*	*91,73*
price level	LogReg:baseline	92,96	92,95
noise	LogReg:baseline	93,89	93,68
politeness	*LogReg:baseline*	*87,59*	*87,52*
service quality	*LogReg:baseline*	*82,87*	*82,79*
romantic	Prcp:baseline	93,98	93,91
speed	LogReg:baseline	88,33	88,30

At sentiment classification task, NB is best for all the aspects. It can be partly explained by the nature of the classifier: NB, having high bias, usually behaves better on the small amount of training data. Therefore it might be suggested that NB is good at classifying sentiment in the informal texts on the small training set.

We should also note that including emoticons and exclamations into the extended_Distant feature set is not a good idea unless the aspect is service quality. For the other aspects it does not improve F1 or even worsens it.

For service frame, dictionaries do improve the results (see Table 10). But food quality, one of the most important aspects, is best extracted using non-contiguous bigrams which cover a wide variety of the expressions of opinion. Thus, a more elaborate lexicon and dictionaries construction could be one of our future work directions.

In this paper we cannot but mention SentiRuEval – a recent Russian contest of aspect-based sentiment analysis systems [15]. It included 5 tracks, from the automatic extraction of the aspects occurrences to the classification of the reviews with respect to the aspects, and provided several labeled datasets, including restaurants dataset. There were 5 predefined aspects: food, interior, price, service and general impression, and 4 classes of sentiment: positive, negative, neutral and both. Thus, we can hardly provide an appropriate comparison of our results with those of SentiRuEval participants, however, we shall try. Our task is most similar to the track where a review is to be classified with respect to each of the aspects, but we have 5 sentiment classes instead of 4. The best result demonstrated at SentiRuEval equals 45.36 % for food aspect, 51.09 % for service aspect and 45.39 % for price aspect. Our current scores (see Table 10) are higher, although 5-classes task is more complex than 4-classes one. But our training set is about 5 times larger than the one in SentiRuEval. Thus, we leave the elaborate comparison for future work, as it demands modifications in both the annotation and the evaluation schema.

8 Conclusion and Future Work

In this paper we have demonstrated our approach towards the extraction of restaurant aspect values from the reviews for the recommendation system.

As part of our research we have conducted a thorough corpus analysis (based on non-contiguous bigrams and POS-distribution of the trigger words context). We have also experimented with several classifiers and have shown that their performance can be improved by the results and ideas derived from corpus analysis thus proving the importance of the latter. In particular, it has been shown that using trigger words and predicative-attributive words dictionaries is an effective approach for food quality extraction while service quality aspect, which is harder to deal with, demands a wider range of features (in our research, non-contiguous bigrams are used).

We should note that our corpus consists of Russian colloquial texts, and Russian is known for its rich morphology and free word order which complicate its automatic processing. Another complicating factor is the fact that the use of recommendation systems is not yet widespread in Russia, and therefore users' reviews are often not what one would expect them to be (e.g., free narratives are quite common). However, according to our results, an information extraction system for Russian can still be successful, especially when based on the ideas obtained from corpus analysis.

References

1. Bakliwal, A., Patil., A., Arora, P., Varma, V.: Towards enhanced opinion classification using NLP techniques. In: Proceedings of the Workshop on Sentiment Analysis where AI Meets Psychology (SAAIP), IJCNLP, pp. 101–107 (2011)
2. Benamara, F., Cesarano, C., Picariello, A., Reforgiato, D., Subrahmanian, V.S.: Sentiment analysis: adjectives and adverbs are better than adjectives alone. In: Proceedings of the International Conference on Weblogs and Social Media (ICWSM)(2007)
3. Bermingham, A., Smeaton, A.: Classifying sentiment in microblogs: is brevity an advantage? In: CIKM 2010, Toronto, Ontario, Canada, 26–29 October 2010
4. Carlson, A., Betteridge, J., Wang, R.C.: Coupled semi-supervised learning for information extraction. In: Third ACM International Conference on Web Search and Data Mining, New York, pp. 101–110 (2010)

5. Collins, M., Singer, Y.: Unsupervised models for named entity classification. In: Empirical Methods in NLP (EMNLP) (1999)
6. Das, S.R., Chen, M.Y.: Yahoo! for Amazon: sentiment parsing from small talk on the web. Manage. Sci. **53**(9), 1375–1388 (2007)
7. Dave, K., Lawrence, S., Pennock, D.M.: Mining the peanut gallery: opinion extraction and semantic classification of product reviews. In: Proceedings of the 12th International Conference on World Wide Web, New York, pp. 519–528 (2003)
8. Emadzadeh, E., Nikfarjam, A., Ghauth, K.I., Why, N.K.: Learning materials recommendation using a hybrid recommender system with automated keyword extraction. World Appl. Sci. J. **9**(11), 1260–1271 (2010)
9. Huang, R., Riloff, E.: Multi-faceted event recognition with bootstrapped dictionaries. In: NAACL-HLT 2013, Atlanta, Georgia, USA, 9–14 June 2013, pp. 41–51 (2013)
10. Joorabchi, A., Mahdi, A.E.: A new method for bootstrapping an automatic text classification system utilizing public library resources. In: 19th Irish Conference on Artificial Intelligence and Cognitive Science (2008)
11. Kennedy, A., Inkpen, D.: Sentiment classification of movie reviews using contextual valence shifters. Comput. Intell. **22**(2), 110–125 (2006)
12. Leksin, V.A., Nikolenko, S.I.: Semi-supervised tag extraction in a web recommender system. In: Brisaboa, N., Pedreira, O., Zezula, P. (eds.) SISAP 2013. LNCS, vol. 8199, pp. 206–212. Springer, Heidelberg (2013)
13. Lim, E.P., Sun, A., Marissa, M.: Conceptual classification of web pages using bootstrapping and co-training strategies. Cyberscape J. **4**(1) (2006). Research Collection School of Information Systems
14. Lin, F., Cohen, W.W.: The MultiRank bootstrap algorithm: semi-supervised political blog classification and ranking using semi-supervised link classification (2007). Retrieved: http://www.cs.cmu.edu/~wcohen/postscript/icwsm-2007-frank-submitted.pdf. Accessed 18 September 2015
15. Loukachevitch, N.V., Blinov, P.D., Kotelnikov, E. V., Rubtsova, Y.V., Ivanov, V.V., Tutubalina, E.: SentiRuEval: testing object oriented sentiment analysis systems in Russian. In: Proceedings of International Conference Dialog, pp. 3–9 (2015)
16. Murphy, T., Curran, J.R.: Experiments in mutual exclusion bootstrapping. In: Australasian Language Technology Workshop 2007, pp. 66–74 (2007)
17. Narayanan, V., Arora, I., Bhatia, A.: Fast and accurate sentiment classification using an enhanced naive bayes model. arXiv:1305.614 (2013)
18. Naw, N., Hlaing, E.E.: Relevant words extraction method for recommendation system. Int. J. Emerg. Technol. Adv. Eng. **3**(1), 680–685 (2013)
19. Niu, C., Li, W., Ding, J., Srihari, R.K.: A bootstrapping approach to named entity classification using successive learners. In: 41st Annual Meeting of the ACL (2003)
20. Pang, B., Lee, L., Vaithyanathan, S.: Thumbs up? Sentiment classification using machine learning techniques. In: Proceedings of the Conference on Empirical Methods in Natural Language Processing (EMNLP), pp. 79–86 (2002)
21. Pazzani, M.J., Billsus, D.: Content-based recommendation systems. In: Brusilovsky, P., Kobsa, A., Nejdl, W. (eds.) Adaptive Web 2007. LNCS, vol. 4321, pp. 325–341. Springer, Heidelberg (2007)
22. Pronoza, E., Yagunova, E., Volskaya, S.: Corpus-based information extraction and opinion mining for the restaurant recommendation system. In: Besacier, L., Dediu, A., Martín-Vide, C. (eds.) SLSP 2014. LNCS, vol. 8791, pp. 272–284. Springer, Heidelberg (2014)
23. Ricci, F., Rikach, L., Shapira, B., Kantor, P.: Recommender Systems Handbook, p. 62. Springer, Heidelberg (2010)

24. Riloff, E., Jones, R.: Learning dictionaries for information extraction by multi-level bootstrapping. In: Sixteenth National Conference on Artificial Intelligence (1999)
25. Saif, H.: Sentiment Analysis of Microblogs. Mining the New World. Technical Report KMI-12-2, March 2012 (2012)
26. Schafer, J.B., Frankowski, D., Herlocker, J., Sen, S.: Collaborative filtering recommender systems. In: Brusilovsky, P., Kobsa, A., Nejdl, W. (eds.) Adaptive Web 2007. LNCS, vol. 4321, pp. 291–324. Springer, Heidelberg (2007)
27. Semeraro, G.: Content-based recommender systems: problems, challenges and research directions. In: 8th Workshop on Intelligent Techniques for Web Personalization & Recommender Systems (2010)
28. Shah, K., Munshi, N., Reddy, P.: Sentiment Analysis and Opinion Mining of Microblogs (2013)
29. Smith, A.D., Eisner, J.: Bootstrapping feature-rich dependency parsers with entropic priors. In: 2007 Joint Conference on Empirical Methods in Natural Language Processing and Computational Natural Language Learning, Prague, June 2007, pp. 667–677 (2007)
30. Thelen, M., Riloff, E.: A bootstrapping method for learning semantic lexicons using extraction pattern contexts. In: Empirical Methods in NLP (EMNLP) (2002)
31. Turney, P.: Thumbs up or thumbs down? Semantic orientation applied to unsupervised classification of reviews. In: Proceedings of the 40th Annual Meeting of the Association for Computational Linguistics (ACL), Philadelphia, July 2002, pp. 417–424 (2002)
32. Wang, S., Manning, Ch.D.: Baselines and bigrams: simple, good sentiment and topic classification. In: Proceedings of the 50th Annual Meeting of the Association for Computational Linguistics, vol. 2, pp. 90–94 (2012)
33. Yangarber, R., Grishman, R., Tapanainen P., Huttunen, S.: Automatic acquisition of domain knowledge for information extraction. In: 18th Conference on Computational Linguistics (COLING 2000), vol. 2, pp. 940–946 (2002)

A Study on Turkish Meronym Extraction Using a Variety of Lexico-Syntactic Patterns

Tuğba Yıldız[1,2(✉)], Savaş Yıldırım[1,2], and Banu Diri[1,2]

[1] Department of Computer Engineering, Istanbul Bilgi University,
Dolapdere, 34440 Istanbul, Turkey
{tdalyan,savasy}@bilgi.edu.tr
[2] Department of Computer Engineering, Yildiz Technical University,
Davutpasa, 34349 Istanbul, Turkey
banu@ce.yildiz.edu.tr

Abstract. In this paper, we applied lexico-syntactic patterns to disclose meronymy relation from a huge Turkish raw text. Once, the system takes a huge raw corpus and extract matched cases for a given pattern, it proposes a list of whole-part pairs depending on their co-occur frequencies. For the purpose, we exploited and compared a list of pattern clusters. The clusters to be examined could fall into three types; general patterns, dictionary-based pattern, and bootstrapped pattern. We evaluated how these patterns improve the system performance especially within corpus-based approach and distributional feature of words. Finally, we discuss all the experiments with a comparison analysis and we showed advantage and disadvantage of the approaches with promising results.

Keywords: Meronym · Lexico-syntactic patterns · Corpus-based approaches

1 Introduction

Meronym has been referred to as a part-whole relation that represents the relationship between a part and its corresponding whole. It is a subject of some disciplines like logic, philosophy, linguistic and cognitive psychology. In many studies, it has been primarily discussed the types of meronym relation, relatedness of meronym relation with other relations and transitivity of meronym relation. One of the most important and well-known study is designed by [1]. They identified part-whole relations as falling into six types: Component-Integral (CI), Member-Collection (MC), Portion-Mass (PM), Stuff-Object (SO), Feature-Activity (FA) and Place-Area (PA).

Recently, there have been many significant studies in automatically extracting meronym relation from a raw text. Some of these methods are based on lexico-syntactic patterns (LSP) that is useful technique especially used in semantic relation extraction. It is the most preferred method due to its simplicity and the success. A set of LSP that indicate hyponymic relations has been applied

© Springer International Publishing Switzerland 2016
Z. Vetulani et al. (Eds.): LTC 2013, LNAI 9561, pp. 386–394, 2016.
DOI: 10.1007/978-3-319-43808-5_29

to unrestricted text by [2]. Although the same technique was applied to extract meronym relations, it was reported that the efforts concluded without great success.

In computational linguistics, pattern-based approaches have been widely used by other researchers for other semantic relations and various attempts have been made to extend the Hearst patterns. In [3], some statistical methods were applied to a very large corpus to find parts using Hearst's methods. At the end, five reliable lexical patterns were retrieved using some initial seeds.

A semi-automatic method was presented in [4] for learning semantic constraints to detect part-whole relations. The method picks up pairs from Word-Net and searches them on text collection: SemCor and LA Times from TREC-9. Sentences containing pairs were extracted and manually inspected to obtain a list of LSP. Training corpus was generated by manually annotated positive and negative examples where the decision tree was applied as learning procedure.

Another attempt is a weakly-supervised algorithm; Espresso [5] used patterns to find several semantic relations besides meronymic relations. The method automatically detected generic patterns to decide correct and incorrect ones and to filter them with the reliability scores of the patterns and the instances.

In Turkish, recent studies to harvest meronym relations and types of meronym relations for Turkish are based on dictionary definition (TDK) and WikiDictionary [6–8]. The other major attempt [9] modeled a semi-automatically extraction of part-whole relations from a Turkish raw text. The model takes a list of manually prepared seeds to induce syntactic patterns and estimates their reliabilities. It then captures the variations of part-whole candidates from the corpus.

In our study, three different clusters of Turkish patterns are analyzed within a huge corpus. First cluster is based on general patterns which are the most widely used in literature. Second one is based on dictionary patterns that are extracted from TDK and WikiDictionary. Third one is based on bootstrapping of the unambiguous seeds.

The rest of the paper is organized as follows: Sect. 2 includes the methodology of the study. Analysis of pattern-based approach is introduced in Sect. 3. Details of challenges and evaluation are explained in Sect. 4.

2   Methodology

The methodology employed here is to apply the lexico-syntactic patterns to acquire part-whole pairs from a corpus. We evaluate three different clusters of patterns; General Patterns, Dictionary-based Patterns, Bootstrapped Patterns. While general patterns are widely used and well known especially within a huge corpus, the dictionary based patterns are suitable and applicable to dictionary-like resources (TDK, WordNet, Wikipedia, etc.). Although the latter is suitable for the dictionary, we discuss that it can have a capacity to disclose semantic relation even from a corpus. The last approach is to bootstrap patterns using a set of part-whole seeds.

2.1 General Patterns

The most precise acquisition methodology earlier applied by [2] relies on LSPs. We start with the same idea of using the widely used patterns, General Patterns, to acquire part-whole relations, which are the widely used and well-known patterns from several studies [1,4,10]. One of these studies is proposed by Winston et al. used frames as "part of", "partly" and "made of" for six different types of meronymic relations. [11] represented that some of patterns always refer to part-whole relation in English text, while most of them are ambiguous. Keet and Artale developed a formal taxonomy, distinguishing transitive mereological (1) part-whole relations from intransitive meronymic (2) ones. All general patterns are listed in Table 1. Although there are also various studies that have used patterns-based approaches, most of them are subsumed by the following patterns.

Table 1. Patterns that are used in three different studies

Winston (1987)	Girju (2006)	Keet (2008)
NPx part of NPy	parts of NPy include NPx	NPx member of NPy (1)
NPx partly NPy	NPy consist of NPx	NPx constituted of NPy (1)
NPy made of NPx	NPy made of NPx	NPx subquantity of NPy (1)
	NPx member of NPy	NPx participates in NPy (1)
	One of NPy constituents NPx	NPx involved in NPy (2)
		NPx located in NPy (2)
		NPx contained in NPy (2)
		NPx structural part of NPy (2)

We adopted the all these patterns to Turkish domain. As expected, those patterns which are not suitable and applicable for Turkish language are eliminated. The remaining patterns are evaluated in terms of the capacity and reliability.

To extract prospective sentences that include part-whole relations by using LSPs from a Turkish corpus of 490M tokens, developed by [12], Turkish equivalents of these patterns are constructed in regular expression forms. General patterns, type of patterns, number of cases matched in corpus, number of wholes that matches the pattern, the most frequent wholes are listed in Table 2.

Adoption of the pattern to Turkish domain is difficult due to free word order language with agglutinating word structures. The noun phrases can easily change their position in a sentence without changing the meaning of the sentence. However this replacement can only affect the emphasis. Besides that other part of speech tags can lie between NPs and hence parts can be found away from whole in a sentence. For example, ultraviyole radyasyon (ultraviolet radiation) - güneş enerjisi(solar energy) is part-whole pair in the following sentence.

"Ultraviyole (UV) radyasyon, dünya yüzeyine erişen güneş enerjisinin doğal bir parşasıdır."

Table 2. A summary for general patterns

GP	Type	#ofCases	#ofWhole	The most frequent wholes
NPx part of NPy	CI, MC, PA	16K	2.4K	Life, Culture, Turkey
NPx member of NPy	MC	23K	2K	Commission, Turkey, Group
NPy constituted of NPx	CI, SO	530	276	System, Program, Project
NPy made of NPx	SO, FA	5K	1K	Questionnaire, Public opinion
NPy consist of NPx	CI	9.2K	2K	Report, Material, Product
NPy has/have NPx	CI, MC, FA, PA	22K	3.7K	Turkey, Person, Job

(Ultraviolet (UV) radiation is a natural part of the solar energy that access to the Earth's surface.)

Determining a window is crucial for the potential parts. If it keeps too smaller, it might not be even enough to catch parts. However a bigger window leads to many irrelevant NPs extracted with large context and it deteriorates the system. We observed that the window size of 15 allows us to capture more reliable parts and the sentences.

In order to evaluate the approach, we picked up the most frequent wholes for each LSPs. Each whole and its potential parts are ranked according to their frequencies.

To distinguish the distinctiveness, we utilized inverse document frequency (idf) that is obtained by dividing the number of times a part occurs with whole by number of times a part retrieved by all the patterns. We selected first 20 candidates ranked by their scores for evaluation. The proposed parts were manually evaluated by looking at their semantic role.

2.2 Dictionary-Based Patterns

The most efficient and reliable way of applying LSP is to extract information from Machine Readable Dictionaries (MRDs). The language of use in dictionary is generally simple, informative, and structured and it highly includes a set of syntactic patterns. Thus, many studies have exploited the dictionary definition recently. For Turkish, the recent studies to harvest meronym relations used dictionary definition (TDK) and WikiDictionary [6–8]. In [7], semantic relations are extracted to build semantic network. Another study [8] presents different automatic methods to extract semantic relationships between concepts using two Turkish dictionaries. They efficiently used regular expressions to extract part-whole relation.

We examined all these findings and provided a summary report for relations, type of patterns, number of cases in corpus, number of wholes that matches the pattern, the most frequent as shown in Table 3.

Member-of, made-of and consist-of can be confused with the ones in the general patterns whereas pattern specifications are different from each other. All patterns are applied to Turkish corpus as same as general patterns and a similar

Table 3. A summary for dictionary-based patterns (#ofC: number of cases, #ofW: number of wholes)

Relations	Type	#ofCases	#ofWhole	Frequent wholes
Group-of (whole|group|set|flock|union)	MC	140	111	Game, Human
Member-of (class|member|team)	MC	207	159	Turkey, Team
Member-of (from the family of Y)	MC	192	56	Legumes, Rosacea
Amount-of (amount|measure|unit)	PM	91	81	Bank, Dollar, Euro
Has/Have	CI, MC, FA, PA	58K	16K	Game, Woman
Consist-of	CI, MC	12.4K	2.7K	Group, Team
Made-of	SO	6K	1.7K	Payment, Import

process is carried out. Even though these patterns are usefulness especially in dictionary, they could return redundant and incorrect results for Turkish.

2.3 Bootstrapped Patterns

Methodology of bootstrapped patterns is different from that of others described above. The bootstrapped pattern-based approach proposed here is implemented in two phases: Pattern identification and part-whole pair detection. For the pattern identification, we begin by manually preparing a set of unambiguous seed pairs that definitely convey a part-whole relation. For instance, the pair (engine, car) would be member of that set. The seed set is further divided into two subsets: an extraction set and an assessment set. Each pair in the extraction set is used as query for retrieving sentences containing that pair. Then we generalize many LSPs by replacing part and whole token with a wildcard or any meta-character.

The second set, the assessment set, is then used to compute the usefulness or reliability scores of all the generalized patterns. Those patterns whose reliability scores, rel(p), are very low are eliminated. The remaining patterns are kept, along with their reliability scores. A classic way to estimate rel(p) of an extraction pattern is to measure how it correctly identifies the parts of a given whole. The success rate is obtained by dividing the number of correctly extracted pairs by the number of all extracted pairs. The outcome of entire phase is a list of reliable LSP along with their reliability scores.

In order to run second phase, the previously generated patterns are applied to an extraction source that is a Turkish raw text. The instantiated instances (part-whole pairs) are assessed and ranked according to their reliability scores. We experiment with three different measures of association (pmi, dice, t-score) to evaluate their performance in scoring function. We also utilized idf to cover more specific parts. The motivation for use of idf is to differentiate distinctive features from common ones. All formulas, results have been already reported in other study [9].

Based on reliability scores, we decided to filter out some generated patterns and finally obtained six different significant patterns. The list of the patterns and their examples can be found in Table 4.

Table 4. Bootstrapped patterns and examples

P1. NPy+gen NPx+pos	door of the house	evin kapısı
P2. NPy+nom NPx+pos	House door	ev kapısı
P3. NPy+Gen (N-ADJ)+ NPx+Pos	back garden gate of the house	Evin arka bahçe kapısı
P4. NPy of one-of NPxs	the door of one of the houses	Evlerden birinin kapısı
P5. NPx whose NPy ﹡	The house whose door is locked	Kapısı kilitli olan ev
P6. NPxs with NPy	the house with garden and pool	bahçeli ve havuzlu ev

All patterns are evaluated according to their usefulness. We roughly order the pattern as P1, P2, P3, P6, P4, and P5 by their normalized average scores. P1, which is the genitive one, is the most reliable pattern with respect to all measures (Table 5).

Table 5. Reliability of bootstrapped patterns

Measures	rel(p1)	rel(p2)	rel(p3)	rel(p4)	rel(p5)	rel(p6)
pmi	1.58	1.53	0.45	0.04	0.07	0.57
dice	0.01	0.003	0.01	0.004	0.001	0.003
tscore	0.11	0.12	0.022	0.0004	0.001	0.03

For the evaluation phase, we manually and randomly selected five whole words: book, computer, ship, gun and building. For a better evaluation, we selected first 10, 20 and 30 candidates ranked by the association measure defined above. However the results based on first 20 candidates will be used to fairly compare performance with other clusters of patterns.

3 Challenges

The very basic problem of natural language processing is sense ambiguity. Almost all studies suffer from the ambiguity problem. For a given whole, proposed parts could be incorrect due to polysemous words. [11] represented that some of patterns always refer to part-whole relation in English text, while most of them are ambiguous. Their listings of unambiguous and ambiguous patterns are given in Table 6. Part-of pattern, genitive construction, the verb "to have", noun compounds and prepositional construction are classified as ambiguous meronymic expressions.

For Turkish domain, we could not easily do such classification and find even one unambiguous pattern to extract part-whole relation. Additional methods are needed to cope with the problem and to find more accurate results from extracted pairs.

Another problem is that the patterns can also encode other semantic relations such as hyponymy, relatedness, cause etc. Although use of genitive case is popular

Table 6. Ambiguous and unambiguous pattern list

Unambiguous	Ambiguous
parts of NPy include Npx	NPx part of NPy
NPy consist of Npx	NPy has NPx
NPy made of Npx	NPy's NPx
NPx member of NPy	NPx of NPy
One of NPy constituents NPx	NPy NPx
	NPy with NPx

for detecting part-whole relations, the characteristic of the genitive is ambiguous. The morphological feature of genitive is a good indicator to disclose a semantic relation between a head and its modifier. In this case, we found that the genitive has a good indicative capacity, although it can encode various semantic interpretations. Taking the example, "Ali's team", and the first interpretation could be that the team belongs to Ali, the second interpretation is that Ali's favorite team or the team he supports. It refers such relations "Ali's pencil/Possession", "Ali's father/Kindship", "Ali's handsomeness/Attribute". Same difficulties are valid for other patterns. To overcome the problem, researchers have done many studies based on statistical evidence.

Even the best patterns could not be safe enough all the time. The sentence "door is a part of car" strongly represents part-whole relation, whereas "he is part of the game" gives only ambiguous relation. The word "part-of" has nine different meanings in Turkish Dictionary. It means that it is nine times more difficult to disclose the relation.

Some expressions can be more informal than written language or grammar. Indeed, in any language, different kinds of expression can be appropriate in many different situations. From the formal to the informal, the written to the spoken, from jargon to slang, all type of expressions are a part of corpus. This variety can cause another bottleneck for applying regular expression or patterns.

4   Evaluation and Analysis

Three clusters of pattern were taken into consideration. The first two patterns, general patterns and dictionary patterns are predefined list that are obtained by literature and other studies. On the other hand, third cluster of patterns, bootstrapped patterns are semi-automatically obtained by giving initial unambiguous part-whole pairs. The main problem of first two clusters is limitedness. We could not execute these patterns for any arbitrary whole. Instead, the most frequent wholes occurred in these patterns were evaluated. Looking at the Tables 2 and 3, each pattern has its own list of potential wholes.

However, thanks to the simplicity, bootstrapped patterns are so broader that for an arbitrary whole, the system can propose a list of parts. Especially genitive case pattern has enormous capacity and it can produce reliable results.

The tendency of the all patterns is to capture mostly semantic relatedness especially when two words or concepts are associated in some way. How could the relation between train and the rail be classified? Thus, both evaluation and error analysis for the system improvement get harder due to that problem.

The clearest observation is that applying dictionary based pattern to a corpus rather than a dictionary is quite limited. For instance, the pattern "amount-of" obtains 91 cases and it consists of 81 different wholes. Each whole has only 1.1 cases matched on average. The "has-a" (II) pattern, one of dictionary-based patterns, is the most productive pattern. It captures over 500K cases. However, it also suffers from the same typical problems mentioned before. The most reliable pattern from the dictionary cluster is consist-of. The case capacity is 12K, average number of cases of each whole is nearly 6 and its average success ratio is 80 %.

However, general patterns are more productive. On average, for each whole, about 10 cases can be matched. For this group of patterns, the most reliable pattern is to have ("vardir"). The size of matched cases is 22K, average number of cases is 7, and overall success score is about 75 %.

Even though the first two clusters have a promising result, they have limited capacity. Any system relying on these patterns can just give limited number of part-whole pairs. On contrary, third cluster of pattern which based on bootstrapping methodologies can produce more than the other. The system with this approach could work for any given whole. When looking at the success rate of the bootstrapped techniques, its general average is 67 %. We conducted another experiment to distinguish distinctive parts from general ones. Excluding general parts from the expected list, we re-evaluated the result of the experiments. When idf is applied, measures are increased by 4.3 % on average as expected.

5 Conclusion

Applying lexico-syntactic patterns to disclose meronymy relation from a huge corpus is very naïve and effective way. We employed the same idea for Turkish language domain. Once, the system takes a huge text and morphologically extracts matched cases for a given pattern, it proposes and ranks a list of parts depending on frequencies and some other statistics. Three different clusters of patterns were taken into consideration to acquire meronymy relations. While first two clusters, general patterns and dictionary based patterns, are pre-defined, the last cluster consists of those patterns that are iteratively bootstrapped with a small set of unambiguous seeds. All these bootstrapped patterns are weighted by a reliability scores which are calculated with a special function.

Although general patterns are more productive and broader than dictionary ones, both share the similar performance in precision when only looking their limited results. Thus, general pattern has better success in terms of recall. The best score among dictionary based methods is one with success rate of 80 %. For the general pattern, the best has the score of 75 % in precision. The problem for these two patterns is their limitedness of production. Third cluster, bootstrapped patterns, is much broader than the others. It can give response for any arbitrary whole thanks to its simplicity and its learning procedure. It also gives successful result when compare to other approaches especially in terms of recall.

The core challenge that we faced during the experiment is ambiguity and polysemous word. Another problem is use of language. Different type of expressions such as formal, informal, written or spoken is the main challenge to apply pattern matching or other string matching-based methodologies. They are among the future study plan to be completed.

References

1. Winston, M.E., Chaffin, R., Herrmann, D.: A taxonomy of part-whole relations. J. Cogn. Sci. **11**(4), 417–444 (1987)
2. Hearst, M.A.: Automatic acquisition of hyponyms from large text corpora. In: The 14th International Conference on Computational Linguistics, COLING 1992, pp. 539–545 (1992)
3. Berland, M., Charniak, E.: Finding parts in very large corpora. In: The 37th Annual Meeting of the Association for Computational Linguistics on Computational Linguistics, pp. 57–64 (1999)
4. Girju, R., Badulescu, A., Moldovan, D.: Learning semantic constraints for the automatic discovery of part-whole relations. In: The Human Language Technology Conference of the North American Chapter of the Association for Computational Linguistics, pp. 1–8 (2003)
5. Pantel, P., Pennacchiotti, M.: Espresso: leveraging generic patterns for automatically harvesting semantic relations. In: The 21st International Conference on Computational Linguistics and 44th Annual Meeting of the Association for Computational Linguistics, pp. 113–120 (2006)
6. Orhan, Z., Pehlivan, I., Uslan, V., Onder, P.: Automated extraction of semantic word relations in Turkish lexicon. J. Math. Comput. Appl. **16**(1), 13–22 (2011)
7. Serbetşi, A., Orhan, Z., Pehlivan, I.: Extraction of semantic word relations in Turkish from dictionary definitions. In: The ACL 2011 Workshop on Relational Models of Semantics, RELMS 2011, pp. 11–18 (2011)
8. Yazıcı, E., Amasyalı, M.F.: Automatic extraction of semantic relationships using Turkish dictionary definitions. EMO Bilimsel Dergi **1**, 1–13 (2011)
9. Yıldız, T., Yıldırım, S., Diri, B.: Extraction of part-whole relations from Turkish corpora. In: Gelbukh, A. (ed.) CICLing 2013, Part I. LNCS, vol. 7816, pp. 126–138. Springer, Heidelberg (2013)
10. Keet, C.M., Artale, A.: Representing and reasoning over a taxonomy of part-whole relations. J. Appl. Ontol. **3**(1–2), 91–110 (2008)
11. Girju, R., Badulescu, A., Moldovan, D.: Automatic discovery of part-whole relations. J. Comput. Linguist. **32**(1), 83–135 (2006)
12. Sak, H., Güngör, T., Saraçlar, M.: Turkish language resources: morphological parser, morphological disambiguator and web corpus. In: Nordström, B., Ranta, A. (eds.) GoTAL 2008. LNCS (LNAI), vol. 5221, pp. 417–427. Springer, Heidelberg (2008)

Less-Resourced Languages

A Phonetization Approach
for the Forced-Alignment Task in SPPAS

Brigitte Bigi[(✉)]

Laboratoire Parole et Langage, CNRS, Aix-Marseille Université,
5, Avenue Pasteur, BP80975, 13604 Aix-en-Provence, France
brigitte.bigi@lpl-aix.fr
http://www.lpl-aix.fr/~bigi

Abstract. The phonetization of text corpora requires a sequence of processing steps and resources in order to convert a normalized text in its constituent phones and then to directly exploit it by a given application. This paper presents a generic approach for text phonetization and concentrates on the aspects of phonetizing unknown words. This serves to develop a phonetizer in the context of forced-alignment application. The proposed approach is dictionary-based, which is as language-independent as possible. It is used on French, English, Spanish, Italian, Catalan, Polish, Mandarin Chinese, Taiwanese, Cantonese and Japanese in SPPAS software, a tool distributed under the terms of the GPL license.

Keywords: Phonetization · Graphemes-phonemes · Unknown words · LRL

1 Introduction

Phonetic transcription of text is an indispensable component of text-to-speech (TTS) systems and is used in acoustic modeling for automatic speech recognition (ASR) and other natural language processing applications. Phonetic transcription can be implemented in many ways, often roughly classified into dictionary-based and rule-based strategies, although many intermediate solutions exist. The "Forced Alignment" (FA) task included both phonetization and alignment tasks: phonetization is the process of representing sounds by phonetic signs; alignment is the process of aligning speech with these sounds. The FA takes as input the orthographic transcription of a speech signal and produces a time-segmentation of the supposed pronunciation.

Clearly, there are different ways to pronounce the same utterance. Different speakers have different accents and tend to speak at different rates. When a speech corpus is transcribed into a written text, the transcriber is immediately confronted with the following question: how to reflect the orality of the corpus? Conventions are then designed to provide rules for writing speech corpora. These conventions establish phenomena to transcribe and also how to annotate them.

There are commonly two types of Speech Corpora. First is related to "Read Speech" which includes book excerpts, broadcast news, lists of words, sequences

© Springer International Publishing Switzerland 2016
Z. Vetulani et al. (Eds.): LTC 2013, LNAI 9561, pp. 397–410, 2016.
DOI: 10.1007/978-3-319-43808-5_30

of numbers. Second is often named as "Spontaneous Speech" which includes dialogs - between two or more people (includes meetings), narratives - a person telling a story, map-tasks - one person explains a route on a map to another, appointment-tasks - two people try to find a common meeting time based on individual schedules. One of the characteristics of Spontaneous Speech is an important gap between a word's phonological form and its phonetic realizations. Specific realization due to elision or reduction processes are frequent in spontaneous data. For example, in Italian, *perchè* is commonly pronounced as /b e k/, in French *parce que* is frequently /p s k/ and in English *because* is /k o z/. Spontaneous speech also presents other types of phenomena such as non-standard elisions, substitutions or addition of phonemes which intervene in the automatic phonetization and alignment tasks.

After the state-of-the-art, we describe our phonetization system that implements a language-independent algorithm to phonetize unknown words. We also briefly describe the automatic aligner. We finally propose evaluations of the phonetization system.

2   State-of-the-Art

Grapheme-to-phoneme conversion is a complex task, for which a number of diverse solutions have been proposed. It is a structure prediction task; both the input and output are structured, consisting of sequences of letters and phonemes, respectively. Phonetic transcription of text is an indispensable component of text-to-speech systems and is used in acoustic modeling for speech recognition and other natural language processing applications. Converting from written text into actual sounds, for any language, cause several problems that have their origins in the relative lack of correspondence between the spelling of the lexical items and their sound contents. While Grapheme-to-phoneme conversion has been heavily studied for Text-To-Speech systems, it has been very little for Automatic Speech Recognition and not at all for forced-alignment. One can suppose that it's because forced-alignment is often considered as an ASR sub-problem.

2.1   Text-To-Speech Synthesis

Grapheme-to-Phoneme conversion is necessary for determining the *canonical* phonemic transcription of a word from its orthography in a Text-To-Speech system. It is commonly implemented in the form of a Letter-To-Sound module which is responsible for the automatic determination of the phonetic transcription of the incoming text. In this context, the Letter-To-Sound module can not simply perform the equivalent of a dictionary look-up. As mentioned in [15], this is for the following reasons:

1. Dictionaries in TTS systems only refer to word roots pronunciation: they do not include morphological variations (i.e. plural, feminine, conjugations).

2. Languages contain heterophonic homographs, i.e. words that are pronounced differently even though they have the same spelling. The appropriate pronunciation could often be determined by using a Part-of-Speech Tagger.
3. "Pronunciation dictionaries merely provide something that is closer to a phonemic transcription than from a phonetic one (i.e. they refer to phonemes rather than to phones)."
4. Words embedded into sentences are not pronounced as if they were isolated.
5. "Not all words can be found in a phonetic dictionary: the pronunciation of new words and of many proper names has to be deduced from the one of already known words."

The Letter-To-Sound modules can be implemented in many ways, often roughly classified into dictionary-based and rule-based strategies, although many intermediate solutions exist. Dictionary based solutions consist in storing a maximum of phonological knowledge in a lexicon and rule based systems consist on rules that are based on inference approaches or proposed by expert linguists. Both dictionary-based and rule-based methods on Grapheme-to-Phoneme conversion have their own advantages and limitations. Looking a word up in a lexicon is relatively cheap computationally, whereas most algorithms for rule-based systems use considerably more processor resource to produce the phoneme sequence. Furthermore, a large sized phonetic dictionary and complex morphophonemic rules are required for the dictionary-based method and the Letter-To-Sound rule-based method itself cannot model the complete morphophonemic constraints.

Initially, dictionary based approach was developed in the MITTALK system [1] where a dictionary of up to 12,000 morphemes covered about 95 % of the input words. In the same way, the AT&T Bell Laboratories TTS system followed the same guideline [26], with an augmented morpheme lexicon of 43,000 morphemes.

At its first stage, [14] proposed a transformation rules system for French. The rules system is based on the application of a partially ordered set of phonological rules: left-hand side of each rule indicates the graphemes involved by the rule, right-hand side of each rule specifies the corresponding phonemes and possibly the preceding and succeeding graphemic context. Exceptional pronunciation rules are first examined in the set and the last examined rules are the more general ones. Since the 1990s, considerable efforts have been made towards designing sets of rules with a very wide coverage (starting from computerized dictionaries and adding rules and exceptions until all words are covered, for various languages. Often rule-based Grapheme-to-Phoneme systems also incorporate a dictionary as an exception list. In [2], a descriptive language permits the integration of rules and lexica into a text-to-phonetics grammar. A minimal grammar, constituting the core of the phonetization process, has been enlarged by systematically exploring a representative lexicon of French. A clearly disadvantageous consequence of such a knowledge-based strategy is that it requires a large amount of hand-crafting of linguistic rules (and data). In contrast to the knowledge-based approach outlined above, the data-driven approach to grapheme-to-phoneme conversion is based on the idea that given enough examples it should be possible to predict the pronunciation of unseen words purely by analogy. Such systems are based on a training stage from aligned data, alignments between letters and phonemes can be discovered reliably with unsupervised generative models. Given such an alignment, Letter-To-Sound conversion can be viewed either as a sequence of classification problems, or as a sequence modeling problem. In the classification approach, like in [11,18], rules are trained from a given set of examples in a language and the Grapheme-to-Phoneme system was automatically produced for that language. To train rules, the training data consists of letter strings paired with phoneme strings, without explicit links connecting individual letter to sound. These systems predict a phoneme for each input letter, using the letter and its context as features. In the sequence modeling approach, various models was proposed. In [30], a supervised Hidden Markov Model is applied, where phonemes are the hidden states and graphemes the observations. Several other approaches have been adopted, such as Kohonen's concept [32] finite state transducers [9], etc. For a review, see [7].

Finally, there are many competing techniques for Letter-To-Sound conversion for TTS systems and the system developer must make a rational selection among them. For comparison and evaluation of different methods, we refer to [12,34] and [22]. In [12], authors report a comparative assessment of the competitor methods of Letter-To-Sound rules (for English only), pronunciation by analogy, feedforward neural networks and a k-nearest neighbor method, with respect to their success at automatic phonemization. [34] reports on a cooperative international evaluation of Grapheme-To-Phoneme conversion for Text-To-Speech in French. The systems involved was all relying on a rule-based approach. The evaluation was performed on the phonemization of 12000 sentences. Overall, the eight systems fared relatively well: they all achieve at least 97 % phonemes correct. Difficulties are due to proper names, heterophonous homographs, pre-processing, schwa and liaison. Recently, [22] proposed a discriminative structure-prediction model and compared performances with six publicly available data sets representing four different languages: English, German and Dutch CELEX, French Brulex, English Nettalk and English CMUDict data sets. The results for the CMUDict range from 57.8 % to 71.99 % accuracy.

2.2   Automatic Speech Recognition

Grapheme-to-phoneme technology is also useful in speech recognition, as a way of generating pronunciations for new words that may be available in grapheme form, or for naive users to add new words more easily. In that case, the system must generate the multiple variations of the word. In recent works, we noticed [28] that created Grapheme-To-Phoneme models for Indo-European languages with word-pronunciation pairs from the GlobalPhone project and from Wiktionary and tested for Czech, English, French, Spanish, Polish, and German ASR. Wiktionary pronunciations have been provided by the Internet community and can be used to quickly and economically create pronunciation dictionaries for new languages and domains. An other solution was proposed in [25], where the Grapheme-To-Phoneme system uses statistical machine translation techniques.

The generated word pronunciations are employed in the dictionary of the ASR system.

2.3   Under-Resourced Languages

There are more than 6000 languages in the world but only a small number possess the resources required for implementation of Human Language Technologies (HLT). Thus, HLT are mostly concerned by languages which have large resources available or which suddenly became of interest because of the economic or political scene. On the contrary, languages from developing countries or minorities were less treated in the past years. Among HLT, phonetization is also concerned about this fact: less-resourced languages are also investigated since the 2000s. It is not possible to make an exhaustive review, but we noticed the followings: for Malay [17], for Thai [29], for Korean [24], for Punjabi [19], for Romanian [23], for Arabic [16], for Greek [10] or for Polish [13]. In all these studies, authors adopted various solutions in which the algorithms mainly depend on the availability of resources and on the structural of the language.

It is also important to mention that in some languages, code-switching is a common practice and the phonetization system can be face on such a phenomena. In that case, some specific strategies can be adopted, as proposed in [31].

3   Phonetization Approach for Forced-Alignment

3.1   Overview

The "Forced Alignment" (FA) task includes both phonetization and alignment sub-tasks. Phonetization is the process of representing text by phonetic signs. Alignment is the process of aligning speech with these sounds; it can also select the relevant pronunciation from a grammar.

To our knowledge, only one public FA system includes a rule-based phonetization step; this system is described in [20]. The grapheme conversion tool is provided by an external TTS system and suggests some pronunciation variants. The optional phonemes are marked as an expert annotator can compare the sequence of phonetic symbols with the audible speech of each utterance and select the most appropriate. This approach is well suited for read speech, but we can expect to manual corrections in case of spontaneous speech. Moreover, this approach implies a new Letter-To-Sound system to be entirely developed to handle any new language.

In many FA systems based on ASR technologies, the phonetization step is limited to a sequence of dictionary look-ups. The dictionary contains words with a set of pronunciations (the canonical one, and optionally some common reductions, etc.). Phonetization is then proposed for the aligner to choose the phoneme string *because the pronunciation generally can be observed in the speech*. The Hidden Markov Toolkit (HTK), for example, is proposing such a command-line tool to perform the FA task [33]. In this approach, it is then assumed that all words of the speech transcription and their phonetic variants are mentioned in the pronunciation dictionary. So, it's relevant for read speech but many entries could miss for spontaneous speech. Actually, the dictionary can not include all possible truncated words or invented words for example. For the variants, a large set of these instances can be extracted from a lexicon of systematic variants even if it will not cover all the possible observed and sometime frequent realizations like /t i l/ for the word *until* in English.

Moreover, with time, computer memory is becoming ever cheaper, then larger and better dictionaries are now available for many languages. Accordingly, it could be argued that the importance of some kind of "back-up" strategy is declining. Although 1/ it is of course true for the couple (computers, major-languages) but this argument can be less important for an under-resourced language and 2/ the more pronunciations are added, the more confusion may occur for the aligner.

The solution we propose aims to combine the advantages of the various approaches and can be applied to a large set of languages. Firstly, we choose a knowledge-based approach, as data-driven approaches requires a large set of data for the training stage and such a data are not always available (particularly for less-resourced languages). We did not introduced specific rules in the system, in order that the system is language-independent (only the given resources are language-specific). Moreover, our approach does not depend on the writing system (it works indifferently on French or Cantonese).

In spontaneous speech, many phonetic variations occur. Some of these phonologically known variants are predictable and can be included in the pronunciation dictionary but many others are still unpredictable (especially invented words, regional words or words borrowed from another language).

3.2   Forced-Alignment in SPPAS

SPPAS is an annotation software that allows to create automatically, visualize and search annotations for audio data. Among others, SPPAS gives to Phoneticians the opportunity to automatically produce annotations which include utterance, word, syllabic and phonetic segmentation from a recorded speech sound and its orthographic transcription. In other words, it can automatize the phonetic transcription task for speech materials, as well as the alignment task of transcription and speech recordings for further acoustic analyses.

The process of transcribing text into sounds starts by pre-processing the text and representing it by lexical items to which the phonetization are applicable. In principle, any system that deals with unrestricted text need the text to be normalized. Texts contain a variety of "non-standard" token types such as digit sequences, words, acronyms and letter sequences in all capitals, mixed case words, abbreviations, roman numerals, URL's and e-mail addresses... Normalizing or rewriting such texts using ordinary words is then an important issue. SPPAS implements the multilingual text normalization approach proposed in [3]. The main steps of such a text normalization are to remove punctuation, lower the text, convert numbers to their written form, replace some symbols by their written form, and the word segmentation (based on a lexicon). After tokenization, the text is phonetized with the approach proposed in this paper. Then, time-alignment is performed for aligning speech with its corresponding transcription at the phone level. The alignment problem consists of a time-matching between a given speech unit along with a phonetic representation of the unit. SPPAS is based on the Julius Speech Recognition Engine [27].

3.3 Phonetization Based on Resources

As in ASR systems, we choose the dictionary based solution, which consist in storing a phonological knowledge in a lexicon. In this sense, this approach is *language-independent* unlike rule-based systems. The dictionary includes phonetic variants that are proposed for the aligner to choose the phoneme string. The hypothesis is that the answer to the phonetization question is in the signal.

An important step is to build the pronunciation dictionary, where each word in the vocabulary is expanded into its constituent phones. For example, the French sentence "je suis" (*I am*) can be:

- /ʒsɥi/ is the standard pronunciation,
- /ʒsɥiz/ is the standard pronunciation plus a liaison,
- /ʒəsɥi/ is the South of France pronunciation,
- /ʒəsɥiz/ is the previous pronunciation plus a liaison,
- /ʃɥi/ is a very frequent specific realization observed in spontaneous speech.

The dictionary entries for both words are presented in Table 1.

Table 1. Entries of the dictionary for the French words *je* and *suis*

je [je] ʒ	suis [suis] sɥi
je(2) [je] ʒə	suis(2) [suis] sɥiz
je(3) [je] ʃ	suis(3) [suis] sui
	suis(4) [suis] ɥi
	suis(5) [suis] ɥiz

Depending on the language, the availability of resources is different. In our data set, for example the dictionary includes a large set of entries (English, French, Italian), an acceptable number of entries (Mandarin Chinese) or a poor number of entries (Taiwan Southern Min). See Table 2 for details about the resources included in SPPAS, version 1.7.2. All dictionaries are UTF-8 encoded and file format is HTK-standard [33]. Such files are distributed under the terms of the GNU Public License.

The English dictionary was downloaded from the CMU and was not modified. The French and the Italian dictionaries were created by merging available TTS

Table 2. Description of the dictionaries included SPPAS, with their names encoded in the international standard ISO639-3 code, the number of entries and the number of pronunciation variants.

Language	ISO639-3	Nb of entries	Nb of variants
French	fra	347,786	304,268
English	eng	121,245	10,173
Italian	ita	389,511	201,194
Spanish	spa	22,917	882
Catalan	cat	94,010	24
Polish	pol	300,670	18
Mandarin Chinese	cmn	88,158	0
Taiwan Southern Min	nan	1,028	0
Hong Kong Cantonese	yue	13,308	0
Japanese	jpn	19,849	0

system dictionaries and ASR system dictionaries. They was also enriched by word pronunciations observed in spontaneous speech corpora. We corrected manually a large set of these both phonetizations. For example, the Italian dictionary contains a set of possible pronunciations of words, including accents as *perchè* pronounced as /b e r k e/, and reduction phenomena as /p e k/ (or /k wa/ for the word *acqua*).

3.4   Phonetization Algorithm

As in TTS systems, a specific algorithm to phonetize unknown entries was also developed. As the data-driven approaches, our grapheme-to-phoneme conversion system is based on the idea that given enough examples it should be possible to predict the pronunciation of unseen words purely by analogy. Unlike these approaches, our system is then applied to missing words during the phonetization process (and not during a training stage), based on knowledge provided by the dictionary.

The algorithm consists in exploring the unknown entry first from left to right then from right to left and in both cases to find the longest strings in the dictionary. Since this algorithm uses the dictionary, the quality of such a phonetization will depend on this resource. The algorithm is described in the following Python code (the right to left is of course identically made):

```python
def phonetize_lr(word):

    if len(word) == 0:
        return ""

    # Find the longest left string that can
```

```
# be phonetized from the dictionary
left = get_longest_part(word)
phonleft = get_in_pronunciationdict(left)
if len(left) == len(word):
    return phonleft

# Find how to phonetize right part
# Get the right un-phonetized subpart
right = subpart(word)
if len(right) == 0:
    return phonleft

phonright = get_in_pronunciationdict(right)
if phonright is None:
    phonright = phonetize(right)

return concatenate(phonleft, phonright)
```

One difficulty by applying this algorithm is due to phonetic variants. Actually, the function get_in_pronunciationdict() applied to any string sequence returns all available pronunciations of this entry. For example, if this algorithm is applied to the string "jesuis", with our French dictionary, the result will contains all variants described previously:

ʒ|ʒə|ʃ sɥi|sɥiz|sui|ɥi|ɥiz where pipes separates variants and the white space separates left/right parts. For a sake of simplicity, the result is stored into a DAG - a Directed acyclic graph (Fig. 1), and left-to-right/right-to-left DAGs are merged into a single DAG.

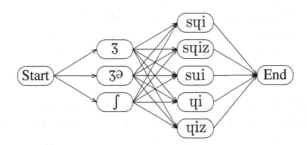

Fig. 1. DAG with phonetic variants

The final pronunciations are extracted by exploring all paths of this DAG. As we can see, the number of variants can significantly increase. That's the reason why, we introduced the possibility to get only a limited number of variants. We choose to select the shortest ones (i.e. the fewest number of nodes), which is a reasonable solution due to a larger number of speech reductions than speech over-production.

4   Results

4.1   Phonetization of Unknown Words

The experiments were carried out on French because all required resources were freely available: the dictionary and the test corpus. The dictionary is available in SPPAS software, as described in Table 2. The Marc-FR corpus was used as test corpus [5]. This corpus is based on parts of three different French corpora and was downloaded from the SLDR - Speech & Language Data Repository, at:

http://www.sldr.fr/sldr000786/fr

About two minutes of 3 different corpora (7 min altogether) were manually segmented and transcribed (see details in Table 3):

– read speech from the AixOx Corpus [21];
– conversational speech from CID - Corpus of Interactional Data [8];
– a political discourse at the French National Assembly, Grenelle II [6].

Table 3. Marc-FR corpus description

	AixOx	Grenelle II	CID
Duration of the extract	137s	134s	143s
Number of speakers	4	1	12
Number of phonemes	1744	1781	1876
Short silent pauses	23	28	10
Filled pauses	0	5	21
Noises (breathes, ...)	8	0	0
Laughter	0	0	4
Truncated words	2	1	6

The phonetization system was launched on the Marc-FR corpus, by using the whole French dictionary (650 k). The results are as follow:

– 1175 tokens are in the dictionary and the manual phonetization is proposed;
– 13 tokens are in the dictionary but the manual phonetization is not proposed (i.e. 1,07 %);
– 32 tokens are not in the dictionary (i.e. 2.62 % of the tokens), this is not including the 9 truncated words.

This result confirms that even with a very large dictionary, a quite significant number of phonetization (or variants) are missing (3.69 %). The list of unknown tokens consists in 3 proper names and 29 reductions or mispronunciations, distributed as:

- 6 in the read speech,
- 2 in the political discourse,
- 21 in the conversational corpus.

As expected, missing entries are mainly coming from spontaneous speech. The proposed algorithm is then used to phonetize these tokens.

If the number of variants is limited to 4, 22 tokens are phonetized properly (i.e. 69 %). While the number of variants is extended to 8, 26 tokens are phonetized properly (i.e. 81 %).

4.2   SPPAS Software

The algorithm and resources described in this paper are integrated in SPPAS [4]. Both program and resources are distributed under the terms of the GNU Public License. Figures 2 and 3 show examples of SPPAS output, including the phonetization of unknown words as proposed in this paper.

Both examples can be automatically tokenized, phonetized and segmented by using the Graphical User Interface (GUI), as shown in Fig. 4 or by using a Command-line User Interface (with a command named `annotation.py`).

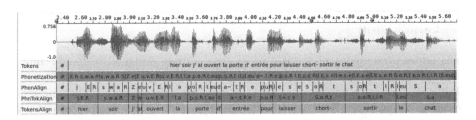

Fig. 2. SPPAS output example from AixOx (read speech). The truncated word "chort-" was missing in the dictionary and automatically rightly phonetized /ʃ o ʁ t/ by the algorithm proposed in Sect. 3.4.

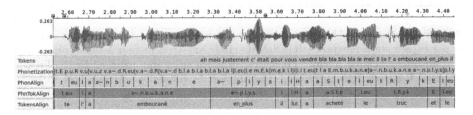

Fig. 3. SPPAS output example from CID (spontaneous speech). The regional word "emboucané" was missing in the dictionary and automatically rightly phonetized /ã b u k a n e/ by the algorithm proposed in Sect. 3.4.

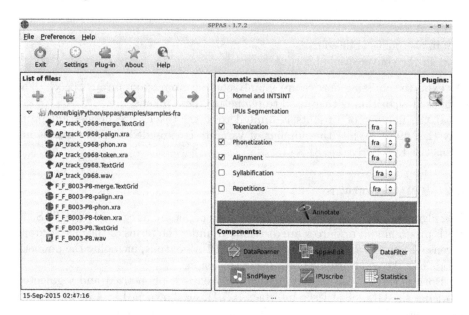

Fig. 4. SPPAS GUI.

5 Conclusion

This paper presented a phonetization system entirely designed to handle multiple languages and/or tasks with the same algorithms and the same tools. Only resources are language-specific, and the approach is based on the simplest resources as possible. Next work will consist to reduce the number of entries in the current dictionaries. Indeed, all tokens that can be phonetized properly by our algorithm could be removed of the dictionary. Hence, we hope this work will be helpful in the future to open to new practices in the methodology and tool developments: thinking problems with a generic multilingual aspect, and distribute tools with a public license.

Acknowledgement. This work has been partly carried out thanks to the support of the French state program ORTOLANG (Ref. Nr. ANR-11-EQPX-0032) funded by the "Investissements d'Avenir" French Government program, managed by the French National Research Agency (ANR). The support is gratefully acknowledged (http://www.ortolang.fr).

References

1. Allen, J., Hunnicutt, M.S., Dennis, H.: From Text to Speech: The MITalk System. Cambridge University Press, New York (1987)
2. Belrhali, R., Aubergé, V., Boë, L.J.: From lexicon to rules: toward a descriptive method of french text-to-phonetics transcription. In: The Second International Conference on Spoken Language Processing (1992)

3. Bigi, B.: A multilingual text normalization approach. In: Vetulani, Z., Mariani, J. (eds.) LTC 2011. LNAI, vol. 8387, pp. 515–526. Springer, Heidelberg (2014)
4. Bigi, B.: SPPAS: a tool for the phonetic segmentations of speech. In: The Eighth International Conference on Language Resources and Evaluation, Istanbul, Turkey, pp. 1748–1755 (2012). ISBN 978-2-9517408-7-7
5. Bigi, B., Péri, P., Bertrand, R.: Orthographic transcription: which enrichment is required for phonetization? In: The Eighth International Conference on Language Resources and Evaluation, Istanbul, Turkey, pp. 1756–1763 (2012). ISBN 978-2-9517408-7-7
6. Bigi, B., Portes, C., Steuckardt, A., Tellier, M.: Multimodal annotations and categorization for political debates. In: ICMI Workshop on Multimodal Corpora for Machine learning, Alicante (Spain) (2011)
7. Bisani, M., Ney, H.: Joint-sequence models for grapheme-to-phoneme conversion. Speech Commun. **50**(5), 434–451 (2008)
8. Blache, P., Bertrand, R., Bigi, B., Bruno, E., Cela, E., Espesser, R., Ferré, G., Guardiola, M., Hirst, D., Magro, E.P., Martin, J.C., Meunier, C., Morel, M.A., Murisasco, E., Nesterenko, I., Nocera, P., Pallaud, B., Prévot, L., Priego-Valverde, B., Seinturier, J., Tan, N., Tellier, M., Rauzy, S.: Multimodal annotation of conversational data. In: The Fourth Linguistic Annotation Workshop, Uppsala, Sueden, pp. 186–191 (2010)
9. Caseiro, D., Trancoso, L., Oliveira, L., Viana, C.: Grapheme-to-phone using finite-state transducers. In: IEEE Workshop on Speech Synthesis, pp. 215–218 (2002)
10. Chalamandaris, A., Raptis, S., Tsiakoulis, P.: Rule-based grapheme-to-phoneme method for the Greek. Trees **18**, 19 (2005)
11. Daelemans, W.M.P., van den Bosch, A.P.J.: Language-independent data-oriented grapheme-to-phoneme conversion. In: van Santen, J.P.H., Olive, J.P., Sproat, R.W., Hirschberg, J. (eds.) Progress in Speech Synthesis, pp. 77–89. Springer, New York (1997)
12. Damper, R., Marchand, Y., Adamson, M., Gustafson, K.: Comparative evaluation of letter-to-sound conversion techniques for english text-to-speech synthesis. In: The Third ESCA/COCOSDA Workshop (ETRW) on Speech Synthesis (1998)
13. Demenko, G., Wypych, M., Baranowska, E.: Implementation of grapheme-to-phoneme rules and extended sampa alphabet in polish text-to-speech synthesis. Speech Lang. Technol. **7**, 79–97 (2003)
14. Divay, M., Guyomard, M.: Grapheme-to-phoneme transcription for French. In: IEEE International Conference on Acoustics, Speech, and Signal Processing, vol. 2, pp. 575–578 (1977)
15. Dutoit, T.: An Introduction to Text-to-Speech Synthesis. Text, Speech and Language Technology, vol. 3. Springer, Dordrecht (1997)
16. El-Imam, Y.: Phonetization of Arabic: rules and algorithms. Comput. Speech Lang. **18**(4), 339–373 (2004)
17. El-Imam, Y., Don, Z.: Text-to-speech conversion of standard Malay. Int. J. Speech Technol. **3**(2), 129–146 (2000)
18. Galescu, L., Allen, J.: Bi-directional conversion between graphemes and phonemes using a joint n-gram model. In: 4th ISCA Tutorial and Research Workshop (ITRW) on Speech Synthesis (2001)
19. Gera, P.: Text to speech synthesis for Punjabi language. M.Tech Thesis, Thapar University (2006)
20. Goldman, J.P.: EasyAlign: a friendly automatic phonetic alignment tool under Praat. In: Interspeech. No. Ses1-S3: 2, Florence, Italy (2011)

21. Herment, S., Loukina, A., Tortel, A., Hirst, D., Bigi, B.: A multi-layered learners corpus: automatic annotation. In: 4th International Conference on Corpus Linguistics Language, Corpora and Applications: Diversity and Change, Jaén (Spain) (2012)
22. Jiampojamarn, S., Cherry, C., Kondrak, G.: Joint processing and discriminative training for letter-to-phoneme conversion. In: ACL, pp. 905–913 (2008)
23. József, D., Ovidiu, B., Gavril, T.: Automated grapheme-to-phoneme conversion system for Romanian. In: 6th Conference on Speech Technology and Human-Computer Dialogue, pp. 1–6 (2011)
24. Kim, B., Lee, G.G., Lee, J.H.: Morpheme-based grapheme to phoneme conversion using phonetic patterns and morphophonemic connectivity information. J. ACM Trans. Asian Lang. Inf. Process. 1(1), 65–82 (2002)
25. Laurent, A., Deléglise, P., Meignier, S.: Grapheme to phoneme conversion using an SMT system. In: Interspeech, pp. 708–711 (2009)
26. Levinson, S., Olive, J., Tschirgi, J.: Speech synthesis in telecommunications. IEEE Commun. Mag. 31(11), 46–53 (1993)
27. Nagoya Institute of Technology: Open-source large vocabulary CSR engine Julius, rev. 4.1.5 (2010)
28. Schlippe, T., Ochs, S., Schultz, T.: Grapheme-to-phoneme model generation for Indo-European languages. In: IEEE International Conference on Acoustics, Speech and Signal Processing, pp. 4801–4804 (2012)
29. Tarsaku, P., Sornlertlamvanich, V., Thongprasirt, R.: Thai grapheme-to-phoneme using probabilistic GLR parser. In: Interspeech, Aalborg, Denmark (2001)
30. Taylor, P.: Hidden Markov models for grapheme to phoneme conversion. In: Interspeech, pp. 1973–1976 (2005)
31. Thangthai, A., Wutiwiwatchai, C., Rugchatjaroen, A., Saychum, S.: A learning method for Thai phonetization of English words. In: Interspeech, pp. 1777–1780 (2007)
32. Torkkola, K.: An efficient way to learn English grapheme-to-phoneme rules automatically. In: IEEE International Conference on Acoustics, Speech, and Signal Processing, vol. 2, pp. 199–202 (1993)
33. Young, S., Young, S.: The HTK hidden Markov model toolkit: design and philosophy, vol. 2, pp. 2–44. Entropic Cambridge Research Laboratory, Ltd. (1994)
34. Yvon, F., de Mareüil, P.B., et al.: Objective evaluation of grapheme to phoneme conversion for text-to-speech synthesis in French. Comput. Speech Lang. 12(4), 393–410 (1998)

POS Tagging and Less Resources Languages Individuated Features in CorpusWiki

Maarten Janssen[✉]

Centro de Lingustica, Universidade de Lisboa, Lisbon, Portugal
maarten.janssen@campus.ul.pt

Abstract. CorpusWiki (http://www.corpuswiki.org) is an online tool for building POS tagged corpora in (almost) any language. The system is primarily aimed at those languages for which no corpus data exist, and for which it would be very difficult to create tagged data by traditional means. This article describes how CorpusWiki uses individuated morphosyntactic features to combine the flexibility required in annotating less-described languages with the requirements of a POS tagger.

Keywords: POS tagging · Less-resourced languages · Morphosyntax

1 Introduction

Part-of-Speech (POS) tags have been a fundamental building block for many Natural Language Processing (NLP) tasks for quite a while. And in that time, POS taggers have been developed for an ever-growing number of languages. With these efforts, the vast majority of texts can now be automatically provided with morphosyntactic labels, since there are POS taggers for all the major languages.

However, when viewed from a different angle, the number of POS taggers is very limited: although it is hard to provide a solid estimate, the number of languages for which there is a working POS tagger is less than a hundred, whereas according to the ISO language codes, there are about 4.000 languages still spoken in the world today, which would mean that less than 2,5 % of the existing languages can be tagged automatically.

CorpusWiki is an initiative to remedy this situation. It is an online environment that allows linguists to develop POS annotated corpora, and automatically train a POS tagger, for almost any language in the world. The system tries to guide the linguists through the process via easy to use graphical interfaces, where the linguist only has to provide linguistic judgement about the language, and the system will automatically take care of the computational management behind the screens.

With the help of CorpusWiki, it becomes easier to develop POS-based resources for languages for which there are no such resources available yet, since it only requires native speakers with sufficient linguistic awareness, and does not require the involvement of computational linguists. This makes it possible to

© Springer International Publishing Switzerland 2016
Z. Vetulani et al. (Eds.): LTC 2013, LNAI 9561, pp. 411–419, 2016.
DOI: 10.1007/978-3-319-43808-5_31

develop resources not only for widely spoken languages with little to no computational resources, such as Runyankore or Mapudungun, but also languages with few speakers, such as Upper Sorbian or Svan, and even dialects that are not considered separate languages, but have sufficiently many distinctive traits to merit a treatment of their own, such as Aranese, a dialect of Occitan spoken in the north of Spain, or Talian, the form of Venetian spoken by the immigrants on the border between Brazil and Argentina.

In order to allow building corpora for as wide a range of languages as possible, CorpusWiki attempts to be as language independent as possible, and the development of a truly language independent framework faces a wide range of problems. Apart from computational challenges, such as getting rid of the need for language-specific computational resources like a tokenization module [5], logistic issues such as the support for right-to-left writing system, and human-computer interface issues such as allowing users to correct structural errors using a pure HTML interface, there is also a more fundamental problem with POS tagging less resourced languages.

The problem that this article deals with is of a more fundamental level: for a significant number of the languages for which no POS tagged resources exist, it is not even that known what the correct morphosyntactic labels are. Part of the motivation for doing corpus-based research in such languages is exactly to find out what the morphosyntax of the language is. And in practical terms, this leads to a vicious circle: before being able to POS tag a corpus, it is first necessary to POS tag a corpus (to find out what the correct labels are).

This article describes the approach used in CorpusWiki which is aimed at overcoming this problem: assigning individuated morphosyntactic labels to words, instead of single morphosyntactic labels. But before turning to the implementation of labelling, the next section will first give a more detailed description of the CorpusWiki project.

2   CorpusWiki

CorpusWiki (http://www.corpuswiki.org) is an online tool for building POS tagged corpora in (almost) any language. The system is primarily aimed at those languages for which no corpus data exist, and for which it would be very difficult to create tagged data by traditional means (although it has been used for large languages like Spanish and English as well). For large but less-resourced languages there are often corpus projects under way, in the case of Georgian there is for instance the corpus project by Paul Meurer [7] as well as corpora without POS tags, such as the dialectal corpus by Beridze and Nadaraia [2]. But for smaller languages such as for instance Ossetian, Urum, or Laz corpus projects of any size are much less likely. Corpora for these languages without POS tags often exist, for these specific languages in the TITUS project (Gippert), but annotating such corpora involves a computational staff that is typically not available for such languages.

CorpusWiki attempts to provide a user-friendly, language-independent interface in which the user only has to make linguistic judgements, and the computational machinery is taken care of automatically behind the screens. The system is designed for the construction of gold-standard style corpora of around 1 millions tokens that are manually verified, although there is no strict upper or lower limit to the corpus size. CorpusWiki intends to make its resources as available as possible, and all corpora, as well as their associated POS tagger, can in principle be downloaded. Corpora are built in a collaborative fashion, in which people from all over the globe can contribute to the various corpora, although the corpus administrator (in principle the user who created the corpus) can determine which users can collaborate on the corpus.

In CorpusWiki, a corpus is not a single object, but a collection of files containing individual texts. Each text is stored in TEI XML format, and each file is individually treated, where the treatment consists of three steps: first, the text is added to the system. Then the text is automatically assigned POS tags using an internal POS tagger, which is trained on all tagged texts already in the system. And finally, the errors made by the automatic tagger have to be corrected manually. Once the verification of the tags is complete, the tagger is retrained automatically. In this fashion, with each new text, the accuracy of the tagger improves and the amount of tagging errors that have to be corrected goes down. The only text that is treated differently in this set-up is the very first text, since for the first text, there are no prior tagged data. The system uses a canonical fable as the first text for each language to make the initial manual tagging of the first text go as smoothly as possible.

The objective of CorpusWiki is to create languages resources that are as available as possible. All corpora and their derived products are available for use online, where the corpora are indexed using the CWB system and can be searched using the CQP query language. Furthermore, from the moment the corpus reaches a minimum critical size, it becomes possible to download the corpus itself, the POS tagger with the parameter files for the language, and other related resources where applicable. Downloading is done via a Java exporter tool that can export the corpora in a number of standardized formats such as TEI and TIGER XML. Each corpus is attributed to the list of its contributors.

The tagging in CorpusWiki is done by the dedicated Neotag tagger, which was designed to be purely data driven: it does not require a language specific tokenization module, but rather tokenization is initially done by simply splitting on white spaces (and punctuation marks), and space-separate unit can be split or merged by the tagger itself. And Neotag does not require an external lexicon, since it uses the lexicon of the training corpus itself as its lexicon. Other than that, it is a relative standard n-gram tagger that uses word-endings for tagging out-of-vocabulary items. With the 1 million token target size of the CorpusWiki corpora, the tagger typically provides a 95–98% accuracy, although the actual accuracy of course depends a lot on both the language itself and the tagset it uses.

2.1   Interlinear Glosses Versus POS Tagging

CorpusWiki is built around a POS tagging system. However, its aim of allowing the creation of (computational) resources for less-resourced languages places it more in the domain the class of tools for linguistic fieldwork, and specifically makes it comparable to tools for Interlinear Glossed Texts (IGT), such as Shoebox [3] or Typecraft [1] This section provides a comparison between IGT systems and CorpusWiki.

For the large, mostly western-European languages there is a long tradition of morphosyntactic description. Assigning POS tags to words in a text in those language is not always easy, as anybody who has ever worked with a POS tagged corpus can vouch for, but the labels themselves are clear: even though it might be difficult to decide exactly when to call a past-participle, like *boiled*, an adjective and when to call it a verb-form, it is clear that those are the two choices, wherever the border is placed exactly. And even though there are several different names for the gender in Dutch and Norwegian that is not the neutral gender, including non-neuter, masculine/feminine, and common gender, it is clear that there is such a gender, independently of what it is called.

But for the majority of languages in the world, there is no such extensive grammatical tradition, and it is difficult to list the morphosyntactic features of the language to start with: native speakers are capable of correctly using the morphosyntax, but often not consciously aware of what the exact role of the morphemes is, which morphosyntactic categories can be used with which word classes, or what the possible values for each morphosyntactic feature are. An important task in the creation of corpora for such languages is often exactly to find out the morphosyntax of the language, which makes it difficult if not impossible to define a tagset at the start of the process.

For less-resourced, and less-described languages, the typical tool of choice is therefore not a POS tagging system, but rather an IGT application. In IGT, each word is provided with a variety of labels, most relevantly for the issues at hand with morphosyntactic labels. Words can either be split into morphemes, where each morpheme is provided with a label, or multiple labels can be assigned to the word itself, separated typically by a dot.

In Shoebox, the choice of which labels to use in the morphosyntactic labelling is up to the user, and tagging a texts consists largely of assigning the morphosyntactic label(s) by hand. This makes it very easy to develop the tagset while creating the corpus: you can decide which morphemes there are the moment they first appear, and if in the process of assigning labels it becomes clear that some of the labels were assigned incorrectly, one just has to search though the text for all occurrences of the incorrectly tagged morpheme (or feature), and change the labels.

Despite the ease of use, complete freedom in the assignment of labels makes it unlikely that the labels in one corpus will end up the same as the labels in another corpus. More interactive IGT tools such as Typecraft therefore ask the user to first define a list of labels, where the labels are selected from a list of predefined morphosyntactic features - in the case of Typecraft following the

GOLD ontology [4]. This method keeps the flexibility of creating the tagset on-the-fly, since it is possible to add new labels the moment they are required, while keeping the tagging of various corpora comparable, since the labels are selected from a centralized list.

Although IGT tools are very flexible, they are difficult to scale: IGT tools are not meant for assigning tags automatically, and in principle, each label has to be assigned manually, although several systems like Typecraft can automatically assign a tag to words that had been tagged before. This makes annotation in IGT time consuming: each new word will have to be labelled by hand, and each ambiguous word, such as *hammer* which can be either a noun or a verb, will have to be disambiguated by hand.

POS taggers, on the other hand, are exactly meant for determining the most likely tag for a word given its context, and based on the training corpus. This means that for new sentences, POS taggers will attempt to imitate the decision you made before in that context. To take the (relatively easy) case of past participles in English: in the currently common setting where a PP within a verb cluster is marked as a verb form, whereas a PP within a nominal cluster is marked as an adjectival form, a POS tagger will automatically suggest that a participle next to (auxiliary) verbs, as in *has boiled*, should be a verb form, whereas a participle next to a noun, as in *boiled egg*, should be adjectival. So POS taggers help to tag similar words in similar ways, since they use the context to disambiguate words. As a result, POS taggers help to keeping a consistent tagging within the corpus. Since many taggers can provide confidence scores, it can even alert you to doubtful cases, guiding you where to pay more attention in the correction process.

However, as mentioned before, the traditional design of building a POS tagger is not really meant for discovering the morphosyntax of a language: a traditional (statistical) POS tagger requires that you first define a tagset, then manually annotate a training corpus with that tagset, and inflect a dictionary using that tagset, and only then do you obtain a parameter set for the tagger that you can then use to tag additional tags. This makes it hard to build up the tagset (that is to say, define the morphosyntactic features of the language) during the construction of the corpus, making them only usable for language for which the morphosyntax is well established, and dictionary resources are available, which is often not the case in less-resourced languages. That is why CorpusWiki does not work with a simple tagset, but rather by individuated morphosyntactic features, as will be explained in the next section.

3   Individuated Features in CorpusWiki

In order to allow flexibility similar to that of IGT systems in a POS tagging environment, CorpusWiki uses a simple idea: rather than working with fixed lists of monolithic tags, CorpusWiki treats each morphosyntactic feature separately as individuated attribute/value pairs. Each attribute is stored as an XML attribute on the XML token element.

Like Typecraft, CorpusWiki uses a pre-defined tagset that defines which morphosyntactic features the language has, and which possible values each feature has. Each morphosyntactic feature is associated with a main POS tag, and when annotating a word, this pre-defined tagset is used to let the user select first which main POS the word has, and then select the correct value for each feature associated with that POS. For instance, when (manually) tagging the word *shoes* in English, the user first indicates that it is a (common) noun, and since nouns in English have a number, which is either singular or plural, the user is then asked to select whether *shoes* is a singular or a plural noun.

Because the features are individually stored, it is easy to modify the tagset when the need arises. Say that after a couple of words or texts, we run into the words *mother's*, which shows that English noun actually also have a case, which can be genitive, or non-genitive, which is called *base* in CorpusWiki, but is also called nominative, default or structural case. Like in Typecraft, we can then modify the tagset and add case as a feature for common nouns, with *genitive* and *base* as possible values. For all subsequent nouns, the system will then also ask for the case of the noun, and we can indicate that *base* is the default value.

Although it is easy to insert a new feature, that does not mean that feature is automatically assigned to all words already tagged. After adding case for nouns, all nouns that were already tagged will have to be (manually) marked for case. CorpusWiki attempts to make this easier by allowing the user to search for all nouns, and mark them for case quickly from a list of all nouns in the corpus. Yet even so, it makes adding new features more and more problematic as the corpus grows. In CorpusWiki, users can therefore only modify the tagset as long as the corpus is small. But since for a larger corpus, the tagset should have been largely established, flexibility is also no longer that needed when the corpus reaches a certain critical mass.

The use of individuated features is that it is less efficient as a storage method than position-based representation. For large corpora, this would provide a problem, but CorpusWiki is meant typically for small to medium-sized corpora of up to a couple of million words. With those kinds of sizes, the corpus files are small enough to not be problematic with the current size of hard disks. For extension beyond that, there is a built-in functionality in CorpusWiki to export the corpus to a position-based system, where they can be used in other tools, including the TEITOK system which is a spin-off from the CorpusWiki project and uses the same file structure and architecture.

As should be obvious from the description above, CorpusWiki associates morphosyntactic features with words, and not with morphemes. This has several consequences. Firstly, it gives a similar treatment to languages like Turkish, where each feature can (almost always) be associated to a morpheme, and languages like Spanish, where it is clear that a form like *corrí* is past, perfective, 1st person, and singular, but there is only one single morpheme expressing all these different features. Secondly, it means that it is crucial to correct distinguish different features that can have the same values, as for instance in the case of (female) gender for possessive pronouns, there are different attributes for the possessor gender (as in the English *her*) and object gender (as in the French *sa*). And morphemes below the stem are never marked: when referring to child seats, the Portuguese word *cadeirinhas* is not marked as a diminutive, but only as a plural of *cadeirinha*.

When training and using the Neotag POS tagger, the individuated features are compressed into a single string, which is not a position-based tag, but a monolithic tag nevertheless. Since the tagger is retrained at regular intervals, adding additional features will simply create larger tag strings for the same words when the tagger gets retrained.

3.1 Searching with Individuated Features

The use of individuated features has an additional advantage: searching becomes more transparent. If we want to search for words with specific features, in a traditional, position-based corpus, it is necessary to search in the right position in the tagset. For instance if we want to use CQP to search for singular nouns in the Multext Slovak corpus, the correct expression would be: [msd="Nc.s.*"]. With individuated features in CorpusWiki, this type of search query become much more transparent and easy to use: [pos="N" & number="singular"]. However, the advantages go beyond merely making searches easier: it allows for searching on agreement in ways that are impossible with position-based or other non-individuated tagsets. In languages with morphological number, the number on the adjective and noun have to agree. If a noun does not have the same number as the adjective following it (or preceding it), that is either a tagging error, or a case in which the noun and adjective do not belong to the same NP. Therefore, it is useful to be able to search for noun that do or do not match the adjacent adjective in number, especially in an environment like CorpusWiki where the corpus is constantly being corrected. In a position based framework, there is no real way to do this, it is only possible to search for specific combinations of tags (using regular expression). With individuated adjectives, on the other hand, it becomes easy to directly compare the number of two adjacent items, and a noun/adjective pair that does not agree in number can be found in the following manner in CQL:

a:[pos="N"|pos="A"] b:[pos="N"|pos="A"] :: a.number != b.number

4   Conclusion

CorpusWiki attempts to combine the flexibility needed for linguistic fieldwork and the creation of linguistic, POS annotated corpora for less-described languages with the advantages in terms of work-load and consistency provided by a POS tagger. It does this by using individual morphosyntactic feature/value pairs as input, rather than a fixed list of POS tags as traditionally used in POS tagger systems. The use of a flexible tagset is only one of many features implemented in CorpusWiki in an attempt to provide as much as possible an easy-to-use system that is fully language independent, and usable for well-described languages and linguistic fieldwork alike.

The framework has proven to be properly language independent and has been used to create corpora for over 50 different languages of very different language families, for many of which no prior POS taggers existed. Although most of these corpora are very restricted in size for the moment, the tagging and lemmatization process is working well for each and every one of them, meaning that CorpusWiki is well under way to significantly increase the number of languages for which POS taggers are available.

As is not unexpected in a setting like CorpusWiki, the first few text are the most labour intensive since the tagset is still unstable, and the accuracy of the tagger is still low, but the work speeds up considerably after the corpus reaches a critical size. A good part of the existing corpora have been built by students as part of a term project, where the creation of a corpus of 5.000 to 10.000 words (after which the tagger starts tagging with a decent accuracy) from scratch is well feasible for students without any computational background.

Despite the fact that the creation of corpora for new languages is incomparably easier using CorpusWiki than it is using traditional POS methods, practice has shown that the initial effort required provides a large stumbling block for users attempting to create a corpus, and too many external users have abandoned the corpus they started much earlier than we would have hoped. From the limited feedback we managed to obtain from people abandoning their efforts, there are two important reasons for this. Firstly, the creation of a corpus consists of two relatively independent parts: the collection of the actual texts, and the annotation of these texts. And users interested in doing the latter often are not at ease doing the former. And secondly, even with the computational help CorpusWiki provides, creating a corpus is still labour intensive, and people do not feel comfortable investing this time in an online system they do not have under their own control.

To address these issues, we added the option to CorpusWiki to keep a corpus private during its creation, which allows editors to only have access to the corpus for themselves during, say, the writing of their thesis. On top of that, two subsequent projects were developed: the Multilingual Folktale Database (MFTD, http://www.mftd.org) and TEITOK [6] (http://teitok.corpuswiki.org).

MFTD is an online system where people can contribute folktales in any language to be accessible online for the language community at large. These can be originals or translations, which hence includes translations into less resourced languages of well known fairytales by Grimm or Andersen, as well as original folktales from all around the globe, and translations of those traditional folktales in less resources languages into "colonial" languages to make them accessible to a larger audience.

TEITOK is a distributable variant of CorpusWiki, which people can install on their own server. The main thing TEITOK does not include is the system of individuated features, rather in exporting a CorpusWiki to TEITOK, the individuated features are mapped onto a traditional position-based tagset, with a structural description of the tagset that allows translating the position based tagset back into individual attribute/value pairs, allowing for efficient storage once the tagset has been stabilized. Given the advantages described in this article, this means that in order to create a locally installed POS annotated corpus for a new language in TEITOK, the easiest way is to first create a corpus in CorpusWiki, and then export it to TEITOK for further development.

Although it is too early to tell, we hope that with these additions, the number of languages available in CorpusWiki will grow even faster than it has thus far.

References

1. Beerman, D., Mihaylov, P.: TypeCraft collaborative databasing and resource sharing for linguists. In: Proceedings of the 9th Extended Semantic Web Conference, Workshop, Interacting with Linked Data, 27th–31st May 2012 (2012)
2. Beridze, M., Nadaraia, D.: The corpus of Georgian dialects. In: Proceedings of the Fifth International Conference, Slovakia (2009)
3. Drude, S.: Advanced glossing: a language documentation format and its implementation with shoebox. In: Paper presented at the International Workshop on Resources and Tools in Field Linguistics, Las Palmas, Spain, 26–27 May 2002 (2002)
4. Farrar, S., Langendoen, D.T.: A linguistic ontology for the semantic web. GLOT Int. **7**, 97–100 (2003)
5. Janssen, M.: Inline contraction decomposition: language independent POS tagging in the CorpusWiki project. In: Paper presented at the 10th Tbilisi Symposium, Gudauri (2013)
6. Janssen, M.: Multi-level manuscript transcription: TEITOK. In: Paper presented at Congresso de Humanidades Digitais em Portugal, Lisboa (2015)
7. Meurer, P.: Constructing an annotated corpus for Georgian. In: Paper presented at the 9th Tbilisi Symposium, Kutaisi (2011)

Author Index

Printed in the United States
By Bookmasters